Professional
Visual Studio® 2005

Professional
Visual Studio® 2005

Andrew Parsons and Nick Randolph

WILEY

Wiley Publishing, Inc.

Professional Visual Studio® 2005

Published by
Wiley Publishing, Inc.
10475 Crosspoint Boulevard
Indianapolis, IN 46256
www.wiley.com

Copyright © 2006 by Wiley Publishing, Inc., Indianapolis, Indiana

Published simultaneously in Canada

ISBN-13: 978-0-7645-9846-3
ISBN-10: 0-7645-9846-5

Manufactured in the United States of America

10 9 8 7 6 5 4 3 2 1

1MA/QT/QY/QW/IN

Library of Congress Cataloging-in-Publication Data

Parsons, Andrew, 1970-
    Visual studio 2005 / Andrew Parsons and Nick Randolph.
        p. cm.
    Includes index.
    ISBN-13: 978-0-7645-9846-3 (paper/website)
    ISBN-10: 0-7645-9846-5 (paper/website)
    1. Microsoft Visual studio. 2. Microsoft .NET Framework. 3. Web site development—Computer programs.
    4. Application software—Development—Computer programs.   I. Randolph, Nick. 1978-   II. Title.
    TK5105.8885.M57P38 2006
    006.7'86—dc22
    2006014685

Credits

Acquisitions Editor
Katie Mohr

Development Editor
Brian Herrmann

Technical Editors
Neil Whitlow and Todd Meister

Production Editor
William A. Barton

Copy Editor
Luann Rouff

Editorial Manager
Mary Beth Wakefield

Production Manager
Tim Tate

Vice President and Executive Group Publisher
Richard Swadley

Vice President and Executive Publisher
Joseph B. Wikert

Graphics and Production Specialists
Carrie A. Foster
Denny Hager
Barbara Moore
Barry Offringa
Lynsey Osborn
Alicia B. South

Quality Control Technicians
John Greenough
Leeann Harney

Project Coordinator
Adrienne Martinez

Media Development Specialists
Angela Denny
Kit Malone
Travis Silvers

Proofreading and Indexing
Techbooks

About the Authors

Andrew Parsons

Andrew Parsons is an accomplished programmer, journalist, and author. He created, launched, and served as chief editor for *Australian Developer* magazine, which was so successful that it expanded globally and is now known as *International Developer*. Subsequent to that success, Parsons launched the local Australian and New Zealand edition of *MSDN* magazine. In addition, he has written a variety of technical books, including topics as diverse as HTML and CSS, Photoshop, and Visual Basic Express. When not writing, Parsons consults on .NET programming implementations for a number of clients, and currently serves as a senior consultant at Readify Pty, Ltd (`www.readify.net`), as well as running his own business, Parsons Designs (`www.parsonsdesigns.com`), and GAMEparents (`www.gameparents.com`), a website dedicated to helping parents understand and enjoy computer and video games.

Nick Randolph

Nick Randolph is an experienced .NET developer and solution architect. During his time with Software Engineering Australia, a not-for-profit industry body, Nick founded the Perth .NET Community of Practice and has been integrally involved in the local .NET community since. When Nick joined AutumnCare (`www.autumncare.com.au`) as Development Manager, he was responsible for their product architecture, which incorporated best practices around building smart client applications using the .NET Framework. Nick is currently a solutions architect with SoftTeq (`http://softteq.com`), which provides consulting, training, and mentoring services. Outside of his consulting role, Nick takes a proactive approach toward technology, ever seeking to learn, use, and present on beta products. As a Microsoft MVP, Nick has been invited to present at IT conferences such as TechEd, MEDC, and Code Camp, and has been a worldwide finalist judge for the Microsoft Imagine Cup for the last two years.

Acknowledgments

Andrew Parsons

First, I want to thank the team at Wrox for putting their trust in me yet again to write a book for their technical series. Without the encouragement of Katie Mohr, Brian Herrmann, and the rest of the team who often remain faceless in these things, I doubt that this book would have made it to completion. Brian, thanks for continuing to kick my butt to "get it done."

Next, I have to say thanks to my co-author. Nick Randolph, who volunteered to jump on board and co-write this book with me, was always available for helpful about how to illustrate the finer points, and most definitely kept his end of the bargain going, flying across the country to work with me at the tail end of the project to make sure we had everything important covered. Nick and I have worked together previously on much smaller projects and it was a delight to discover how focused and organized he is when tackling something as big as this book.

Of course, everyone needs their critics and technical support, and I benefited greatly from advice from Andrew Coates, Frank Arrigo, and Charles Sterling from Microsoft, as well as Mitch Denny, Greg Low, and Darren Neimke, all from Readify (www.readify.net).

On a much more personal note, I most definitely need to thank my family. Even more so than my last book, my beautiful wife, Glenda, put up with my highs and lows over the months it took to write this book, and was without question the biggest supporter I had throughout the process. My kids amazed me with their maturity, letting their dad spend night after night locked away in his office. They seemed to realize how important it was for me to concentrate, and often left me to it when they could (justifiably) have demanded more of my time. I love both of them very much and am looking forward to spending "oodles and oodles" of time with them.

Nick Randolph

Writing this book was one of the more challenging projects that I've embarked on—in particular, the process of getting started and putting the first words onto paper. A massive thank you has to go to my gorgeous partner, Meg, who not only put up with me ranting and raving over the "cool feature" that I was currently writing about, but also encouraged me to think logically and never lose sight of the endgame.

This being my first book, I would especially like to thank everyone at Wiley who has helped me through the learning phase—in particular, Brian Herrmann, who put up with some dreadful writing sins when I was getting started, and Katie Mohr (whose ability to get us back on track was a life-saver), who made the whole process possible.

Acknowledgments

I have to pass on a big thank you to my co-author, Andrew Parsons, who invited me to join him in writing this book. Despite our completely different work hours, Andrew managed to coordinate the whole process. I also have to thank him for ensuring that information flowed between the various stakeholders and that we achieved the key milestones.

Lastly, I would like to thank all of my fellow developer MVPs (Mitch Denny, Greg Low, Bill McCarthy) and the Microsoft staff (Dave Glover, Charles Sterling, Andrew Coates), who were always able to answer any questions along the way.

Contents

Contents

Contents

Contents

Contents

Contents

Contents

Contents

Contents

Contents

Contents

Contents

Contents

Contents

Contents

Contents

Contents

Contents

Introduction

Visual Studio 2005 is an enormous product no matter which way you look at it. Incorporating the latest advances in Microsoft's premier programming languages, Visual Basic and C#, along with a host of improvements and new features in the user interface, it can be intimidating to both newcomers and experienced .NET developers.

Professional Visual Studio 2005 looks at every fundamental aspect of this new developer tool, showing you how to harness each feature and offering advice about how best to utilize the various components effectively. This book shows you the building blocks that make up Visual Studio 2005, breaking the user interface down into manageable chunks for you to understand.

It then expands on each of these components with additional details about exactly how it works both in isolation and in conjunction with other parts of Visual Studio to make your development efforts even more efficient.

Who This Book Is For

Professional Visual Studio 2005 is for all developers new to Visual Studio as well as those programmers who have some experience but want to learn about features they may have previously overlooked.

If you are familiar with the way previous versions of Visual Studio worked, you may want to skip Part I, which deals with the basic constructs that make up the user interface, and move on to the remainder of the book where the new features found in Visual Studio 2005 are discussed in detail.

If you're just starting out, you'll greatly benefit from the first part, where basic concepts are explained and you are introduced to the user interface and how to customize it to suit your own style.

This book does assume that you are familiar with the traditional programming model, and uses both the C# and Visual Basic languages to illustrate features within Visual Studio 2005. In addition, it is assumed that you can understand the code listings without an explanation of basic programming concepts in either language. If you're new to programming and want to learn Visual Basic, please take a look at *Beginning Visual Basic 2005* by Thearon Willis and Bryan Newsome. Similarly, if you are after a great book on C#, track down *Beginning Visual C# 2005,* written collaboratively by a host of authors.

What This Book Covers

Microsoft Visual Studio 2005 is arguably the most advanced integrated development environment (IDE) available for programmers today. It is based on a long history of programming languages and interfaces and has been influenced by many different iterations of the theme of development environments.

The next few pages introduce you to Microsoft Visual Studio 2005, how it came about, and what it can do for you as a developer. If you're already familiar with what Visual Studio is and how it came to be, you may want to skip ahead to the next chapter and dive into the various aspects of the integrated development environment itself.

A Brief History of Visual Studio

Microsoft has worked long and hard on their development tools. Actually, their first software product was a version of BASIC in 1975. Back then, programming languages were mainly interpretive languages in which the computer would process the code to be performed line by line. In the last three decades, programming has seen many advances, one of the biggest by far being development environments aimed at helping developers be efficient at producing applications in their chosen language and platform.

In the 32-bit computing era, Microsoft started releasing comprehensive development tools, commonly called IDEs (short for integrated development environments), that contained not just a compiler but also a host of other features to supplement it, including a context-sensitive editor and rudimentary IntelliSense features that helped programmers determine what they could and couldn't do in a given situation. Along with these features came intuitive visual user interface designers with drag-and-drop functionality and associated tool windows that gave developers access to a variety of properties for the various components on a given window or user control.

Initially, these IDEs were different for each language, with Visual Basic being the most advanced in terms of the graphical designer and ease of use, and Visual C++ having the most power and flexibility. Under the banner of Visual Studio 6, the latest versions of these languages were released in one large development suite along with other "Visual" tools such as FoxPro and InterDev. However, it was obvious that each language still had a distinct environment in which to work, and as a result development solutions had to be in a specific language.

One Comprehensive Environment

When Microsoft first released Visual Studio .NET in 2002, it inherited many features and attributes of the various, disparate development tools the company had previously offered. Visual Basic 6, Visual InterDev, Visual C++, and other tools such as FoxPro all contributed to a development effort that the Microsoft development team mostly created on their own. They had some input from external groups, but Visual Studio .NET 2002 and .NET 1.0 were primarily founded on Microsoft's own principles and goals.

The next version of Visual Studio was labeled Visual Studio .NET 2003 and focused on fixing bugs and the various issues that cropped up due to introducing such a radical new technology as the .NET Framework. The Framework itself was upgraded to 1.1 and the changes made to the IDE were similarly minor.

At this point, end users of Visual Studio and the various Microsoft-owned languages didn't really get to help direct the shape of the programs, but only offer feedback about what was wrong, while Microsoft itself worked on internal issues developers had found with the first version of .NET.

However, at the same time, Microsoft announced that the next version of .NET, then code-named Whidbey, would be the "user's .NET," giving every developer using .NET the ability to submit feature requests and track issues as they progressed through the development cycle. Microsoft also worked closely with a large number of partners ensure that they were shaping .NET, and Visual Studio, of course, to be what the developer—that's you—would most benefit from.

The result was the .NET Framework 2.0 and Visual Studio 2005, a set of development tools, editors, languages, and foundation framework classes that goes far beyond anything Microsoft has worked on previously. The Visual Studio 2005 development environment (see Figure I-1) takes the evolution of Microsoft IDEs a huge step further along the road to a comprehensive set of tools that can be used regardless of your purpose as a developer. A quick glance at Figure I-1 shows the cohesive way in which the various components fit together to provide you with an efficient toolset with everything easily accessible.

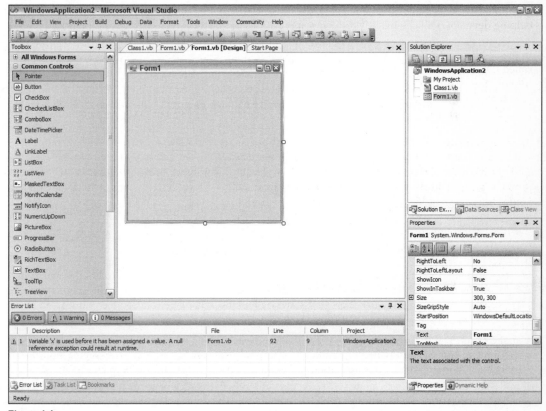

Figure I-1

Visual Studio 2005 comes in two main versions: Visual Studio 2005 Professional and Visual Studio 2005 Team System (to be accurate, there are three distinct flavors of Team System for different roles, but their core Visual Studio functionality remains the same). The majority of this book deals with the Professional Edition of Visual Studio 2005, but some parts utilize features found only in Team System. If you haven't used Team System before, read through Chapter 56 for an introduction to the features it offers over and above the Professional Edition.

How This Book Is Structured

This book's first section is dedicated to familiarizing you with the core aspects of Visual Studio 2005. From the IDE structure and layout to the various options and settings you can change to make the user interface synchronize with your own way of doing things, everything you need is contained in the first six chapters.

From there, the many functions of Visual Studio 2005 are broken down into nine broad categories:

❑ **Project and Solution Design:** In this part, you learn how to take control of your projects, how to organize them in ways that work with your own style, and how to edit application configuration and XML resource files.

❑ **Documentation and Research:** The old adage of "read the manual" applies no less strongly with this latest version of Visual Studio. Microsoft has kept the documentation library completely up-to-date, with the MSDN library available both online and offline. In addition, Microsoft has also strived to help you control your own documentation efforts, and this section walks you through the process of automated XML documentation as well as using the Outline modes to review your code.

❑ **Security and Modeling:** Two extremely important features that are often overlooked or left until the last minute are implementing good security and modeling your solution before commencing development. Rather than follow the trend and leave these two topics to the end of the book, they are placed in a more appropriate order.

❑ **Coding:** While the many graphical components of Visual Studio that make a programmer's job easier have been discussed in many places, you often need help when you're in the process of actually writing code. This section deals with features such as IntelliSense, regionalizing your code, and tagging sections of your program for processing later.

❑ **Automation:** If the functionality found in the previous part isn't enough to help you in your coding efforts, Microsoft has provided many other features related to the concept of automating your programming work. This part starts by looking at code-generation techniques and macros, but also discusses add-ins, extensions, and automation of assembly signing.

❑ **Other Time-Savers:** Think of this part as an informational "Swiss Army knife," with just the right tool for the job always at hand. Controlling your workspace, maximizing your performance in searching, and using both regular expressions and Windows registry hacks are all included in this part, along with coverage about how to harness performance counters, database creation, and diagramming.

❑ **Build and Deployment:** In addition to discussing how to build your solutions effectively and getting applications into the hands of your end users, this part also deals with the upgrade process for Visual Basic 6 projects into the new Visual Basic 2005 format.

❑ **Debugging and Testing:** No matter how good a developer you are, you're bound to need to test your solutions before making them available to users, and this part walks you through the powerful tools at your fingertips for debugging code and even databases.

❑ **Extensions for Visual Studio 2005:** Many third-party add-ins and extensions to Visual Studio 2005 are available, but there are three valuable extensions to the core IDE that Microsoft itself has developed. The last part of this book deals with these—the Team System additions to Visual Studio, the InfoPath 2003 Toolkit for Visual Studio 2005, and Visual Studio Tools for Office for developers who need to work with Microsoft Office.

While this breakdown of the Visual Studio feature set provides the most logical and easily understood set of topics, you may need to look for specific functions that will aid you in a particular activity. To address this need, references to appropriate chapters are provided whenever a feature is covered in more detail elsewhere in the book.

What You Need to Use This Book

To use this book effectively, you'll need only one additional item—Microsoft Visual Studio 2005 Professional Edition. With this software installed and the information found in this book, you'll be able to get a handle on how to use Visual Studio 2005 effectively in a very short period of time.

To get the absolute most out of the book, you can also install the following products, all of which are available from Microsoft:

❑ **Microsoft Visual Studio 2005 Team System:** A more powerful version of Visual Studio, Team System introduces tools for other parts of the development process such as testing and design. Team System is discussed in Chapter 56.

❑ **SQL Server 2005:** The installation of Visual Studio 2005 includes an install of SQL Server 2005 Express, enabling you to build applications that use database files. However, for more comprehensive enterprise solutions, you can use SQL Server 2005 instead. Database connectivity is covered in Chapter 38.

❑ **Visual Studio Tools for Office 2005:** VSTO2005 for short, this add-in integrates new project templates into Visual Studio 2005, enabling you to create managed solutions for Microsoft Word, Excel, and Outlook. Take a look through Chapter 55 for more information.

❑ **InfoPath 2003 Toolkit for Visual Studio 2005:** Another addition to the core Visual Studio 2005 environment, this toolkit integrates managed code solutions with InfoPath forms, doing away with the requirement to use JavaScript for the code behind InfoPath and replacing it with the language of your choice. Discussion on the toolkit can be found in Chapter 54.

❑ **Code Snippet Editor:** This is a third-party tool developed for creating code snippets in Visual Basic. This tool and how to obtain it is covered in Chapter 19.

❑ **Other third-party tools:** Chapter 33 is all about additional third party add-ins and utilities that maximize your effectiveness using Visual Studio 2005. Please review that chapter for more information on each tool and how to obtain it.

Conventions

To help you get the most from the text and keep track of what's happening, we've used a number of conventions throughout the book.

> **Boxes like this one hold important, not-to-be forgotten information that is directly relevant to the surrounding text.**

Tips, hints, tricks, and asides to the current discussion are offset and placed in italics like this.

As for styles in the text:

❑ We *highlight* new terms and important words when we introduce them.

❑ We show keyboard strokes like this: Ctrl+A.

❑ Filenames, URLs, and code appear within the text like so: `persistence.properties`.

❑ We present code in two different ways:

```
In code examples we highlight new and important code with a gray background.
```

```
The gray highlighting is not used for code that's less important in the present
context, or has been shown before.
```

Source Code

As you work through the examples in this book, you may choose either to type in all the code manually or to use the source code files that accompany the book. All of the source code used in this book is available for download at `www.wrox.com`. Once at the site, simply locate the book's title (either by using the Search box or by using one of the title lists) and click the Download Code link on the book's detail page to obtain all the source code for the book.

Because many books have similar titles, you may find it easiest to search by ISBN; this book's ISBN is 0-7645-9846-5 (changing to 978-0-7645-9846-3 as the new industry-wide 13-digit ISBN numbering system is phased in by January 2007).

Once you download the code, just decompress it with your favorite compression tool. Alternately, you can go to the main Wrox code download page at `www.wrox.com/dynamic/books/download.aspx` to see the code available for this book and all other Wrox books.

Errata

We make every effort to ensure that there are no errors in the text or in the code. However, no one is perfect, and mistakes do occur. If you find an error in one of our books, such as a spelling mistake or faulty piece of code, we would be very grateful for your feedback. By sending in errata you may save another reader hours of frustration, and at the same time you will be helping us provide even higher quality information.

To find the errata page for this book, go to `www.wrox.com` and locate the title using the Search box or one of the title lists. Then, on the book details page, click the Book Errata link. On this page you can view all errata that has been submitted for this book and posted by Wrox editors. A complete book list, including links to each book's errata, is also available at `www.wrox.com/misc-pages/booklist.shtml`.

If you don't spot "your" error on the Book Errata page, go to www.wrox.com/contact/ techsupport.shtml and complete the form there to send us the error you have found. We'll check the information and, if appropriate, post a message to the book's errata page and fix the problem in subsequent editions of the book.

p2p.wrox.com

For author and peer discussion, join the P2P forums at http://p2p.wrox.com. The forums are a web-based system for you to post messages relating to Wrox books and related technologies, and to interact with other readers and technology users. The forums offer a subscription feature to e-mail you topics of interest of your choosing when new posts are made to the forums. Wrox authors, editors, other industry experts, and your fellow readers are present on these forums.

At http://p2p.wrox.com you will find a number of different forums that will help you not only as you read this book, but also as you develop your own applications. To join the forums, just follow these steps:

1. Go to http://p2p.wrox.com and click the Register link.

2. Read the terms of use and click Agree.

3. Complete the required information to join as well as any optional information you wish to provide and click Submit.

4. You will receive an e-mail with information describing how to verify your account and complete the joining process.

You can read messages in the forums without joining P2P but in order to post your own messages, you must join.

Once you join, you can post new messages and respond to messages other users post. You can read messages at any time on the Web. If you would like new messages from a particular forum e-mailed to you, click the Subscribe to this Forum icon by the forum name in the forum listing.

For more information about how to use the Wrox P2P, be sure to read the P2P FAQs for answers to questions about how the forum software works as well as many common questions specific to P2P and Wrox books. To read the FAQs, click the FAQ link on any P2P page.

Part I
The Integrated Development Environment

1

A Quick Tour of the IDE

If you haven't used Visual Studio before, you may feel a little overwhelmed at first. There are many different components in the very first encounter with the user interface, from familiar menus and toolbars to a myriad of windows around the sides of the main development interface space, some looking like tabs and others like small forms in their own right.

The next set of pages introduces you to the basic principles of the Visual Studio 2005 Integrated Development Environment (IDE) and shows you how the various menus, toolbars, and windows can be used. This chapter serves as a quick tour of the IDE — it won't show you how to customize its appearance in any great detail, or itemize the various settings you can change. Those topics are covered in the following chapters.

Where to First?

Visual Studio 2005 commences customizing itself to fit into your own work style before you even get to see the development environment. When you first start Visual Studio 2005 it asks you what kind of developer you are (see Figure 1-1). This enables it to customize the appearance of the IDE to most closely suit your way of doing things. Microsoft has researched the way different programmers work; and while you may think Visual Basic programmers work in the same way as C# developers or C++ coders, there are subtle (and sometimes not so subtle) differences.

If you take a moment to review the various options in this list, you'll find that the environment settings that will be affected include the position and visibility of various windows, menus, and toolbars and even keyboard shortcuts. For example, Figure 1-2 describes the changes that will be applied if you select the Visual Basic Development Settings option as your default preference.

Don't worry, though — you can individualize your interface experience to match your own way of doing things exactly, so if the default setup doesn't suit you, you'll be able to change it.

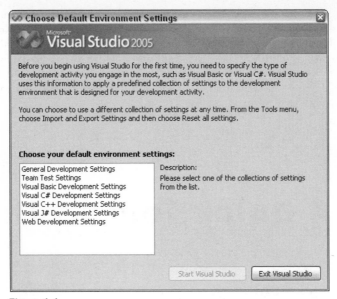

Figure 1-1

After selecting your preferred development settings, click the Start Visual Studio button to have Visual Studio customize the IDE so that windows, toolbars, lists, menus, and a myriad of other options are all appropriate to the generalized developer for that particular language or technology.

Once it has completed this process, Visual Studio will then display the IDE, ready for you to start work. It will remember this setting so you won't have to select from the list again.

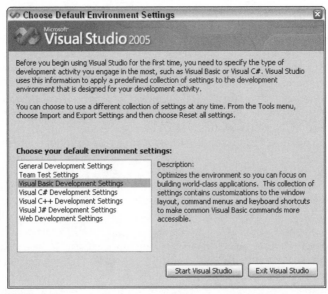

Figure 1-2

The screenshots in Figures 1-3 and 1-4 illustrate how the general interface can appear visually different depending on the settings you choose. The two images/ in Figure 1-3 show the main interface as it appears for the first time to a Visual Basic developer and to a C++ developer, while Figure 1-4 shows how a default Windows Application project is generated for these two different types of programmer. Note how not only do the menus and number and type of windows change, but also the default position of certain essential windows — for example, the Solution Explorer changes depending on what kind of programmer is using Visual Studio.

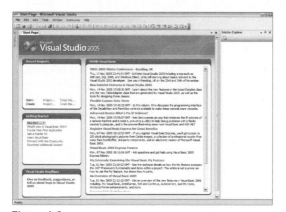

Figure 1-3

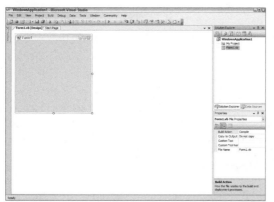

Figure 1-4

IDE Structure

The next step is to understand how the various components fit together to form the comprehensive tool that is the Visual Studio 2005 Integrated Development Environment. The best way to achieve this is by starting Visual Studio 2005 itself, picking a specific development environment, and then examining the individual elements, so in the next few pages you'll do just that. Note that the task list that follows assumes you have already installed Visual Studio 2005 but have not yet started it for the first time.

Getting Familiar with the IDE Structure

1. Start Visual Studio 2005. By default, the shortcut is installed in All Programs⇨Microsoft Visual Studio 2005. After a moment you'll be presented with the Choose Default Environment Settings dialog window. Select Visual Basic Development Settings and click the Start Visual Studio button.

2. When the main user interface is presented, create a dummy project so that the various menus, toolbars, and windows will be populated with usable information. To create a new project (don't worry too much about how this works at the moment; you'll come back to this in Part II of the book), click the New Project command in the File menu. When the New Project dialog appears, leave the default option of Windows Application as is, and click OK to have Visual Studio 2005 automatically create a new Windows application with a default form ready for editing.

3. The last step you need to perform to have the IDE ready for explanation is to pin the Toolbox open. Locate the small buttonlike tab in the top-left area of the IDE labeled Toolbox and hover over it with your mouse. After a moment, it will slide open to reveal a series of components that can be added to your forms, but it would be nice to keep this open to more easily describe it, so locate the button strip at the top of the now visible Toolbox window (see Figure 1-5), and click the middle one, which looks like a horizontal pin.

Figure 1-5

The user interface of Visual Studio 2005 will now appear, as shown in Figure 1-6. Menus and toolbars are positioned along the top of the environment (much like most Windows applications), and a selection of subwindows, or panes, appear on the left and right of the main window area. In the center of the IDE is a graphical representation of the first form in the dummy application you created.

Basic Layout

Starting from the top and moving clockwise around the edges of the Visual Studio 2005 interface, you can see the main components that make up the IDE. The familiar menus and toolbars are in their regular position at the top of the screen. When you first start Visual Studio 2005, the menu bar will have seven entries (the number varies depending on which language you choose), but once you start creating a solution, the menu layout will change to include additional main menu entries.

This is typical behavior in Visual Studio 2005; the whole interface can change based on the context you are in at the time. Therefore, in Figure 1-6 you can see that four additional menus (Project, Build, Debug, and Data) have been added while editing the first form in the project. Various menus are added or removed depending on what you are doing; editing code, changing database structures, and modifying graphical elements all produce different sets of menus.

By default, you'll see the Standard toolbar directly underneath the menu. This toolbar contains the most commonly used commands for your particular language of choice. In the case of Visual Basic, there are save functions along with debug and comment commands, the usual cut, copy, and paste buttons, and shortcuts to common windows such as the Solution Explorer and Properties window, which you'll look at in a moment.

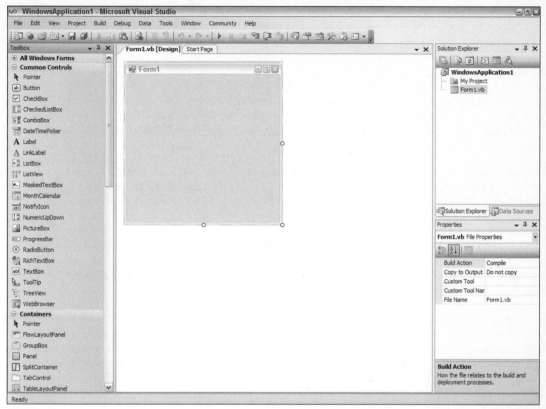

Figure 1-6

Again, as the context changes, the toolbars will change, with more toolbars being shown when you are performing specific functions, and then being removed when you change to a different situation. Edit a database table and additional data-specific toolbars will be automatically added to your interface. Open an XML file and XML-related toolbars are shown. In every instance you can manually add (or remove) toolbars so you have your own preferred layout, just as you can in other applications such as Microsoft Outlook or Word. Visual Studio 2005 will remember your toolbar choices between sessions. Figure 1-7 shows a toolbar area with four additional toolbars in addition to the Standard toolbar.

Figure 1-7

In addition, Visual Studio 2005 maintains two separate layouts: design time and runtime. Menus, tool-bars, and various windows have a default layout for when you are editing a project, whereas a different setup is defined for when a project is being executed and debugged. You can modify each of these lay-outs to suit your own style and Visual Studio 2005 will remember them.

Moving to the right-hand side of the screen shown in Figure 1-6, you can see two smaller windows attached to the side of the main window. These are simply known in Visual Studio 2005 terminology as *windows*, and they are used to house self-contained subsections of the tools found in the IDE. Each of these windows can be resized, moved or removed, and even detached from the main IDE so they float above the form.

By default, the windows shown in this screenshot are attached to the main form. This is known as *dock-ing*. You can undock any window by clicking and dragging its title bar away from the edge to which it is docked. More information on this, as well as customizing your toolbar layout and appearance, can be found in Chapter 5.

In step 3 of the previous task you pinned the Toolbox tab open. You'll see that each of these windows (Solution Explorer, Properties, and so forth) also has the pin button at the top, which enables the win-dow to automatically slide closed when docked to the side of the form. The default setup had the Toolbox automatically hidden, and the other windows pinned open.

Figure 1-8 shows the first of the windows docked to the right-hand side of the IDE. This is the Solution Explorer, where you can manage your current solution, looking at individual projects and their associ-ated files. The Solution Explorer displayed in this example shows a solution containing a single project called IntroProject, which has two files: My Project and Form1.vb. The My Project entry is actually a spe-cial section of the project that contains the various settings and projectwide elements, such as compila-tion and debug parameters.

The projects and files are presented in a hierarchical fashion similar to the folder list in Windows Explorer, with different icons displayed for the various file types, to more easily identify what each entry is.

Figure 1-8

Along the top of the Solution Explorer window is its own toolbar containing six commands. The first is simply a shortcut to the Properties window so you can easily get to the properties for an individual file, rather than the properties for an element on a form. The second is labeled Show All Files. Clicking this for the sample project will reveal many more associated files for this project (see Figure 1-9).

The Show All Files button is a toggle button, so to hide the additional files that you don't need most of the time, simply click the button again to deactivate the functionality. The structure and layout of projects and solutions is discussed at length in Chapter 8.

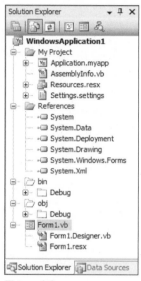

Figure 1-9

The Refresh button sits next to the Show All Files button, and repopulates the Solution Explorer window with the correct file structure. While Visual Studio 2005 will automatically keep the project structure current based on what you do within the IDE, sometimes additional files are created or added to the project via external means. These files may not be automatically shown without either using the Refresh button or closing and re-opening the project — which one do you think is easier?

The remaining three buttons on the toolbar provide quick access to different aspects to an individual file. From left to right, they display the code window, the graphical design of forms and such, and the Class Diagram.

Code view and Design view have been carried over from previous versions of Visual Studio, but the Class Diagram is a new addition to Visual Studio 2005. It offers a visual representation of the form or module and its associated classes, and is discussed in more detail in Chapter 14.

Docked to the right-hand side of the IDE directly underneath the Solution Explorer is the Properties window (see Figure 1-10). The Properties window gives you easy access to individual settings related to a specific form, file, or individual class or control.

Figure 1-10 shows the Properties window displaying properties for the form called Form1 in a project. The properties are currently displayed in alphabetical order. This can be changed to logically group them into properties that deal with the same category; for example, form properties can be grouped into nine discrete groups, including Appearance (for color, fonts, and text-related properties) and Layout (which incorporates such properties as size and location settings). To toggle between alphabetical order and categorized view, use the first two buttons on the Properties window toolbar.

Active settings are highlighted with a colored background (by default orange) and black border. In Figure 1-10, the Properties window is currently sorted alphabetically as evidenced by the black border surrounding the second button.

Figure 1-10

The currently selected property (Text in this case) is highlighted and a small description pane at the bottom explains what the setting is. If you are space constrained and know what you're doing, you can turn this description pane off by right-clicking anywhere in the Properties window and unchecking the Description setting.

There are many different types of properties, but each one can be changed by clicking on the actual value and overtyping the existing information with a new value. Some property types have additional editors to make it even easier to change the values. For instance, properties relating to fonts can display a font chooser dialog window similar to the one you might use in Microsoft Word to change the font settings for a paragraph.

The third and fourth buttons (the icons of a list and lightning bolt) on the toolbar toggle the view between properties and events. The Events view acts in a similar way to the Properties view, giving you access to the various events associated with the currently selected element. Again, like properties, events can be viewed alphabetically or in logical groupings and are only available for elements that have event processing, so if you choose an item that doesn't have events (such as a file) the Events button will be hidden.

The last button on the toolbar displays the property pages associated with the currently selected item. If the item does not have property pages (such as the form in Figure 1-10), this button will be disabled.

Moving over to the left-hand side of the IDE, you can see the Toolbox window, shown in Figure 1-11, that you pinned open (refer back to Figure 1-6 for a full shot of the IDE). This window is used to house all of the various elements you can add to your project. By default, it is populated with the standard windows and .NET components that Microsoft provides with Visual Studio 2005, but you can easily add additional third-party elements to the Toolbox, as well as reposition the existing items, change the view, and sort the lists. A discussion on all of this information can be found in Chapter 3.

Just like the various other components of the Visual Studio 2005 IDE, the Toolbox is contextual, changing its contents based on what you're doing. The three main views of a typical form (Design, Code, and Class Diagram) will produce three completely different sets of items to use.

Figure 1-11 shows the default layout as shown for the sample project you created. There are entries for the commonly used elements such as buttons and `TextBox` controls, as well as Container elements such as Panels and GroupBox components (previously known as the `Frame` control). Other default groups of components include menus and toolbars, data-related elements, and system components.

Figure 1-11

The remainder of the IDE is the actual working space in which you'll design your forms and write your code. The top of the space contains a row of tabs describing the different files that are currently open. Figure 1-12 shows how this area appears after creating the sample project. Form1 is being displayed in Design view, and there is an additional tab for the Start page that is shown when you first start Visual Studio 2005.

The first button on the right-hand side of the tab row (the downward-pointing triangle beside the X in Figure 1-12) provides an alternative method for accessing the various files that are currently open by displaying them in a drop-down list. This is particularly useful when you have a large number of files active and you don't want to navigate through the tab list. The other button closes the currently active file.

As soon as you make a change to a form, file, or class, the tab will be updated with an asterisk (*) after the text to indicate that there are unsaved changes to that particular component. This unsaved marker is also visible in the drop-down list described previously.

The rest of the working space contains the active file. In the case of Figure 1-12, this is the basic form design. Most of this book deals with using this area to maximize your productivity when creating applications, but for a few quick references, see Chapter 6 for basic form design, Chapter 14 for editing class diagrams, and Part V for code-related techniques.

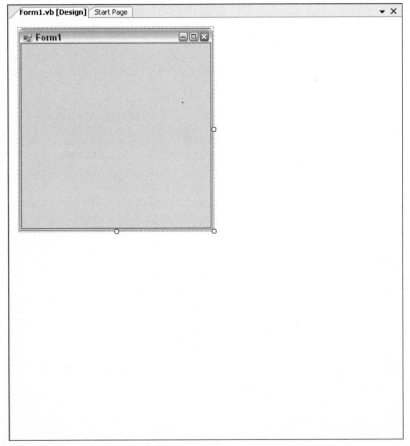

Figure 1-12

Additional Windows

While the default layout for Visual Basic projects only has three windows docked to various parts of the IDE, many additional windows can be shown at either design time or runtime. In fact, just like other parts of the IDE, when you are debugging a solution, additional windows will be shown be default, such as the Immediate window.

In Chapter 5 you'll learn how to customize the appearance of the IDE to include additional windows in the layout. However, two important windows that do not show by default are the Error List window (see Figure 1-13) and the Output window (see Figure 1-14).

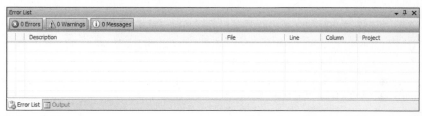

Figure 1-13

The Error List, as you might have surmised, contains a list of issues with your solution. When using Visual Basic as the language, this Error List is continually updated as you create your code, providing instant feedback about what kinds of problems you may be introducing into the application. Other languages may not populate the list until you attempt to build the solution and the code goes through an active compilation process.

You can filter the list by toggling the Errors, Warnings, and Messages buttons at the top of the window and double-clicking a particular error to go directly to that section of code.

By default, the Error List window is placed along the bottom of the main IDE space. This area is shared among many windows, and Figure 1-13 and Figure 1-14 show the tabs along the bottom, indicating that the Error List and Output windows are using the same space.

The Output window contains all the information about the compilation of your application as well as data relating to the debugging of code. Figure 1-14 shows the successful compilation of a simple program. Both the Output and Error List windows can be shown using the View menu.

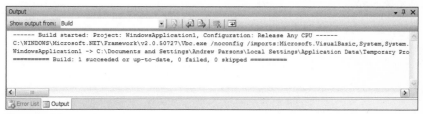

Figure 1-14

Summary

You've now seen how the various components of Visual Studio 2005 form the complete package for creating solutions. Reviewing the default layout for Visual Basic programs, the following list outlines a typical process for creating a solution:

1. Use the File menu to create a solution.

2. Use the Solution Explorer to locate the form that needs editing and click the View Designer button to show it in the main workspace area.

3. Drag the necessary components onto the form from the Toolbox.

4. Select the form and each component in turn and edit the properties in the Properties window.

5. Use the Solution Explorer to locate the form and click the View Code button to access the code behind the form's graphical interface.

6. Use the main workspace area to write code and design the graphical interface, switching between the two via the tabs at the top of the area.

7. Use the toolbars to start the program.

8. If errors occur, review them in the Error List window and Output window.

9. Save the project using either toolbar or menu commands and exit Visual Studio 2005.

While many of these actions can be performed in other ways (for instance, right-click on the design surface of a form and you'll find the View Code command), this simplified process shows how the different sections of the IDE work in conjunction with each other to create a comprehensive application design environment.

In subsequent chapters you'll learn how to customize the IDE to more closely fit your own working style, and how Visual Studio 2005 takes a lot of the guesswork out of form design.

2

Options

Have you ever looked at the Options section of Visual Studio and wondered what you can do to make your life as a Visual Studio developer more efficient? We did too, so we dove right into the depths of the options that Microsoft makes available to programmers and figured out what each one offers you.

Not all of the tips and settings discussed in this chapter may benefit you; all developers are different and prefer to work in their own unique way. The development team at Microsoft understood this, providing options to change the way Visual Studio 2005 works. In this chapter you'll find out what each of the options and settings is for and how to customize them to best suit your own working style.

One with the Lot

By default, the Options screen of Visual Studio 2005 (accessed via Tools➪Options) displays in a simplified mode with only a small subset of the full set of configurable parameters available (see Figure 2-1). This may suit your most general needs, but if you're serious about fine-tuning the system to work as efficiently as possible, you're going to need access to various preference settings that are not available in the basic view.

Fortunately, it's easy to gain access to all the hidden settings. In Figure 2-1, you'll notice a Show All Settings checkbox in the bottom-left corner of the Options dialog window. Simply check the box and immediately Visual Studio 2005 will change the Options interface to accommodate the additional option groups, as shown in Figure 2-2.

In this advanced view of the Options screen, you'll find many more sections and preferences that can be customized to fit in with the way you work. Rather than simply explain what each one does, the rest of this chapter will walk through some of the more relevant options that you may find useful.

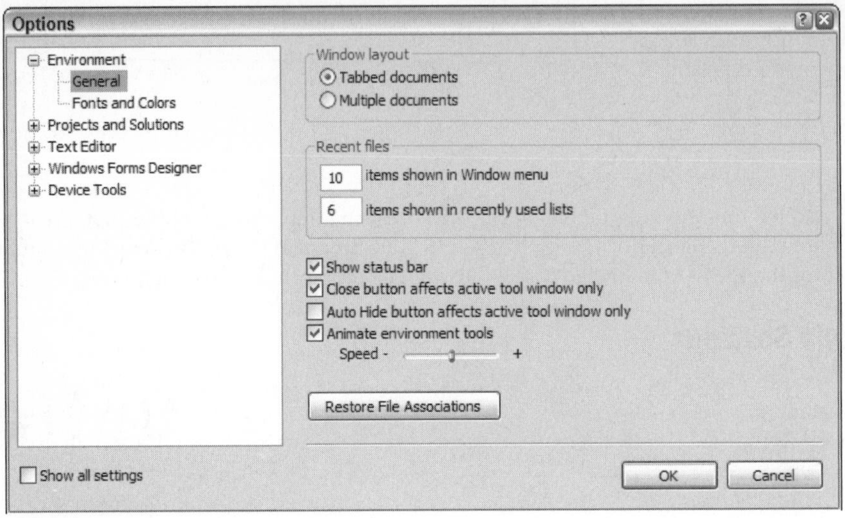

Figure 2-1

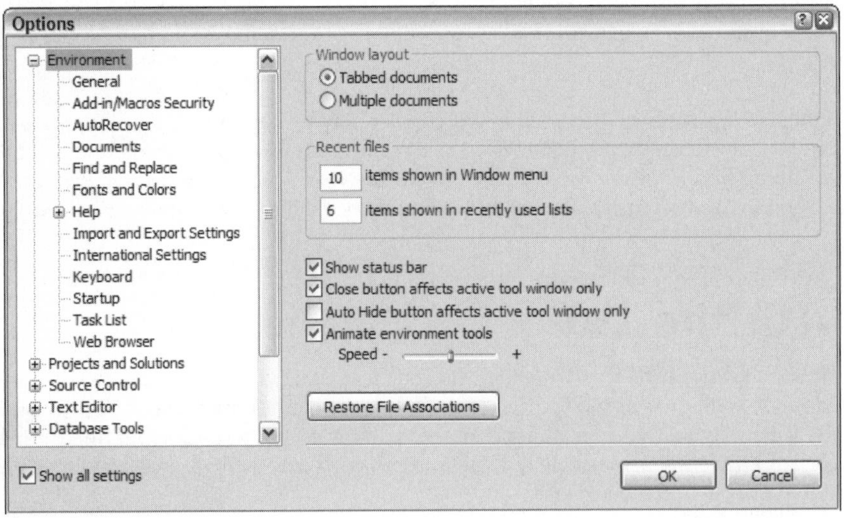

Figure 2-2

Environment Options

The main IDE can be altered to make it more familiar. The first of these alterations is the capability to change the window layout to multiple documents (refer to Figure 2-2). The tabbed interface described in Chapter 1 enables you to quickly navigate between currently active documents via a tab strip along the top of the workspace itself. However, several previous editors, such as Visual Basic 6 (as well as non-Microsoft development environments) utilize a *multiple-document interface* (known as a MDI) whereby individual editor windows can be resized and repositioned independently of each other.

In this mode, the editor windows can be treated much like similar applications that have Cascade and Tile commands available, replacing the subset of commands that deal with the tabbed view. Most important, this mode is especially useful if you're used to easily placing Code and Design views on top of each other, or putting two code listings side-by-side for comparison purposes (note that you can still achieve this in tabbed mode, which you'll see in Chapter 5, but it's a little more difficult to achieve).

Chapter 1 mentioned that Visual Studio 2005 tries to detect when files are added to the solution outside the IDE and let you know that it has happened, but what happens if the files that already exist in the solution are edited externally and then saved? Visual Studio 2005 tries to detect this situation too, and prompts for the file to be reloaded in the IDE if it is a currently active document.

Document Settings

The Documents section of the Environment options (depicted in Figure 2-3) enables you to change the default behavior so that it automatically loads a saved document instead of prompting you for a response. Alternatively, you can switch off the whole detection process if it's too distracting. Just remember if you change either of these settings, as you may be put off by active documents automatically reloading in response to outside changes, or, conversely, you may inadvertently overwrite changes made externally to the IDE.

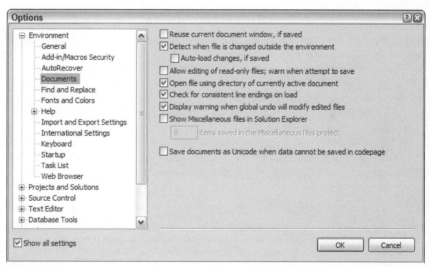

Figure 2-3

As in previous versions of Microsoft development environments, Visual Studio 2005 uses the Courier New font for the code editor windows throughout the IDE. While this font is unarguably available on all machines, plenty of other fonts are available that are almost as universally popular.

Fonts and Colors

The Fonts and Colors section of the Environment options is well worth a visit in your initial setup of the environment, as choosing an appropriate font, and other formatting options, will help you code more efficiently. As shown in Figure 2-4, many different styles can be individually formatted with font, color, and other options such as background color, bold, and so on.

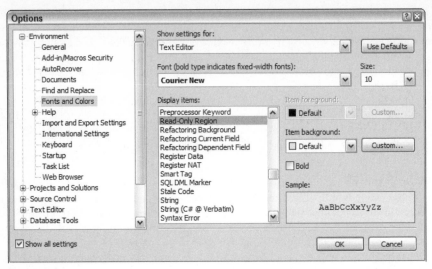

Figure 2-4

In Figure 2-4 you can see the settings displayed for the main Text Editor. However, what many people don't realize is that you can also modify the font style of almost every aspect of the Visual Studio 2005 IDE at this point, including how the tooltips and various windows are displayed. In addition, this is where print settings can be changed so that printouts are output in the way that suits you or your organization.

When choosing a font, remember that proportional fonts are usually not as effective when writing code as nonproportional fonts (also known as fixed-width fonts). As indicated in Figure 2-4, fixed-width fonts are distinguished in the list from the variable-width types so they are easy to locate. One of the problems with Courier New is that it is less readable on the screen than other fixed-width fonts. A viable alternative as a readable screen font is Lucida Console. Figure 2-5 shows a comparison of the default Courier New (top) and the suggested alternative of Lucida Console (bottom).

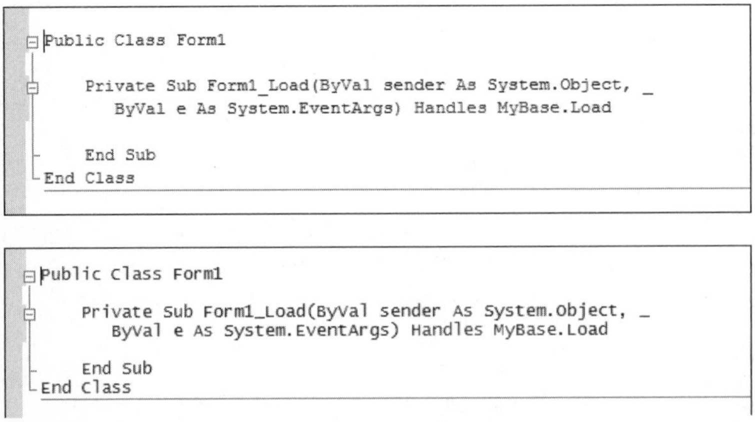

```
Public Class Form1

    Private Sub Form1_Load(ByVal sender As System.Object, _
        ByVal e As System.EventArgs) Handles MyBase.Load

    End Sub
End Class
```

```
Public Class Form1

    Private Sub Form1_Load(ByVal sender As System.Object, _
        ByVal e As System.EventArgs) Handles MyBase.Load

    End Sub
End Class
```

Figure 2-5

Even though proportional fonts may not be as usable when editing code, you may determine that for your own personal interface your eyes can better track variable-width fonts, such as Tahoma, which are used widely on the Internet. For the purposes of consistency, all of the screenshots in this book were taken with fixed-width fonts.

Keyboard Shortcuts

Visual Studio 2005 ships with many ways to perform the same action. Menus, toolbars, and various sub-windows provide direct access to many commands, but despite the huge number available, many more are not accessible through the graphical interface. Instead, these commands are accessed (along with most of those in the menus and toolbars) via keyboard shortcuts.

These shortcuts range from the familiar Ctrl+Shift+S to save changes to the obscure Ctrl+Alt+E to display the Exceptions dialog window. As you might have guessed, you can set your own keyboard shortcuts and even change the existing ones. Even better, you can filter the shortcuts to only operate in certain contexts, meaning you can reuse the same shortcut depending on what you're doing.

Figure 2-6 shows the Keyboard group in the Environment section of Options, with a preset keyboard shortcut displayed for the Build Solution command. Every command in Visual Studio 2005 is available for keyboard shortcut assignations, and you can set multiple shortcuts for the same command. This is especially useful if you want to keep a default shortcut but also add your own personal one. As there are hundreds of commands, you may want to filter them down to a selection by using the Show Commands Containing textbox.

To restrict a shortcut's use to only one contextual area of Visual Studio 2005, select the context from the Use New Shortcut In drop-down list. The Global option indicates that the shortcut should be applied across the entire environment.

Figure 2-6

Depending on which default environment you chose when you first started the IDE, an additional keyboard mapping scheme may be initially chosen for you. For instance, set yourself up as a Visual Basic user and the Visual Basic 6 scheme is added to the default keyboard shortcuts. Note that when there is a conflict between the default keyboard shortcut and one imported by these additional schemes, the default will be used. In the Visual Basic example, this means that the Visual Basic 6 default of F5 running the program without a full compile and Ctrl+F5 forcing a full compilation before execution is ignored in favor of Visual Studio 2005's own shortcuts (which are actually the reverse).

You can change this additional scheme to suit you, so if you regularly use both Visual Basic and Visual C# you can modify your additional set of shortcuts to include Visual C#'s commands.

If a shortcut is already being used by another command, it will appear at the bottom of the dialog window so you don't inadvertently overwrite existing settings.

> *Chapter 26 deals with macros that you can create and maintain to make your coding experience easier. These macros can also be assigned to keyboard shortcuts.*

The Task List

The last section in the Environment options that is useful to look at now is the Task List options. A *token* is a piece of text that is automatically recognized by the IDE as needing to be flagged in the Task List window for later reference. By default, Visual Studio 2005 comes with several preset task list tokens.

You can add your own token, or change the existing ones, by accessing the Task List group in the Environment options. To add a new token, type the text that should be entered in the Name field and click Add. Each token can also be marked with a priority, with high-priority entries sorted to the top of the list so they're more easily located.

Changing an existing token is just as easy. Select its entry in the list, overwrite the name and priority with the new values, and click the Change button. The Task List will be automatically updated as soon as you exit the Options dialog with your changes.

To show how easy it is to set up these automatic Task List entries, follow through this example of adding a new token and then using it to generate a new task:

1. Open the Options dialog by clicking Tools⇨Options. Browse through the list until you locate Task List and select it to display the current Task List tokens and settings.

2. In the Name field, type **WILEY** and change the Priority value to High. To add this new token to the list, click the Add button. Then click OK to apply your changes and close the Options dialog.

3. Open the Task List window by selecting the View⇨Other Windows⇨Task List menu command, or by using the keyboard shortcut Ctrl+Alt+K. By default, the Task List will display User Tasks. Change this to Comments in the drop-down list at the top of the Task List window.

4. To use a token in your code, simply type the text in a commented area and Visual Studio 2005 will automatically add a corresponding entry in the Task List. Open a code window and type the following line to test your new token:

```
' WILEY: This is important!
```

Figure 2-7 shows the Task List with the automatic entry displayed.

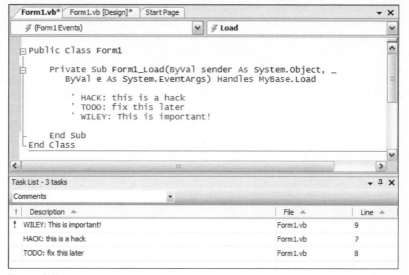

```
Form1.vb*  Form1.vb [Design]*  Start Page                              ▾ ✕
 ⚡ (Form1 Events)                    ▾   ⚡ Load                            ▾

⊟ Public Class Form1

⊟     Private Sub Form1_Load(ByVal sender As System.Object, _
          ByVal e As System.EventArgs) Handles MyBase.Load

          ' HACK: this is a hack
          ' TODO: fix this later
          ' WILEY: This is important!

      End Sub
└ End Class
```

Task List - 3 tasks		▾ 廿 ✕
Comments ▾		
! | Description ▲	File ▲	Line ▲
! | WILEY: This is important!	Form1.vb	9
HACK: this is a hack	Form1.vb	7
TODO: fix this later	Form1.vb	8

Figure 2-7

Projects and Solutions

Several options related to projects and solutions are useful to set to your own preferred values. The first of these is perhaps the most helpful — the default locations of your projects. By default, Visual Studio 2005 uses the standard `Documents and Settings` path common to many applications (see Figure 2-8), but this is usually not where you'll want to keep your development work.

Figure 2-8

Choose a location that is a good base for your various projects. Usually the most common denominator works best, so if you work on multiple projects, then under your C:\Development folder choose that as your default projects folder. From there it's easy to change the folder in any file save dialogs to the specific location for the particular project you're working on.

You can also change the location of template files at this point. If your organization uses a common network location for corporate project templates, you can change the default location in Visual Studio 2005 to point to this remote address, rather than map the network drive.

On the same Options page you will find another useful option that is turned off by default. The Show Output Window When Build Starts setting, when checked, will display the Output window during a build. This is handy when you have a particularly large solution and need to know the state of the build process. It's recommended that you turn it on.

Build and Run

One particularly important section of the Options window is the Build and Run settings page (see Figure 2-9) found in the Projects and Solutions section. This is where Visual Studio 2005 determines how to process any build commands, and you can change its behavior.

The first option to check is the Before Building preference. With the default option of Save All Changes, Visual Studio will apply any changes made to the solution prior to compilation. In the event of a crash during the build process or while you're debugging the compiled code, you can be assured that your code is safe. However, you may want to change this option to Prompt to Save All Changes. This setting will inform you of unsaved modifications made in your solution, enabling you to double-check what changes have been made prior to compilation.

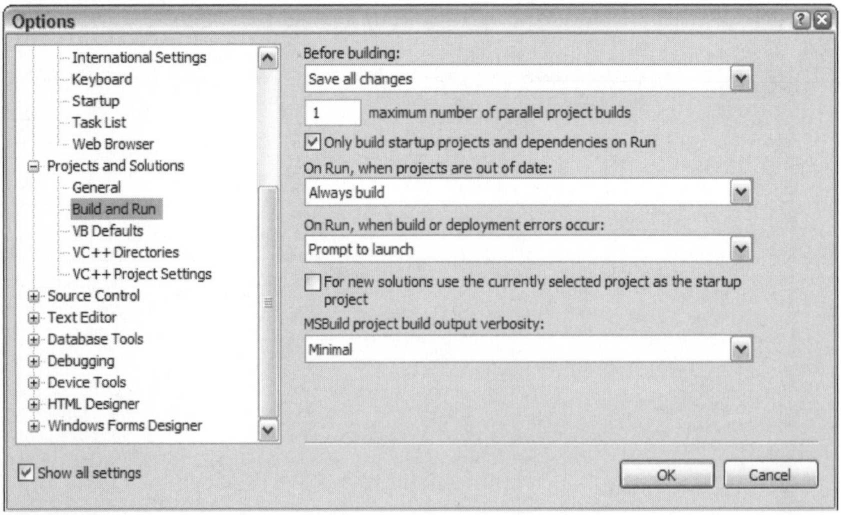

Figure 2-9

Similarly, Visual Studio can prompt you to rebuild out-of-date projects, or automatically rebuild them regardless of their state. In Figure 2-9, the default setting of Always Build is shown, which will force Visual Studio to compile any projects that are deemed out of date. Sometimes you may want to test changes in one project against an older version of another. If you change this option to Prompt to Build, you can control which out-of-date projects will be recompiled prior to the execution of the solution.

Option Strict

One particularly important setting available to Visual Basic programmers is Option Strict, accessible in the VB Defaults page of the Projects and Solutions section. Previous versions of Visual Basic had an Option Explicit, which forced variables to be defined prior to their use in code. When it was introduced, many experts recommended that it be turned on permanently because it avoided many runtime problems in Visual Basic applications due to improper usage of variables.

Option Strict takes the process of enforcing good programming practices one step further by forcing developers to explicitly convert variables to their correct types, rather than let the compiler try to guess the proper conversion method. Again, this results in fewer runtime issues and better performance. We advise strongly that you use Option Strict to ensure that your code is not implicitly converting variables inadvertently.

Text Editor

Visual Studio 2005 comes with many different text editors, with their own formatting styles. This enables you to edit HTML, Visual Basic, C# code, and even resource files, with unique editing options. The File Extension page of the Text Editor section in the Options dialog (see Figure 2-10) enables you to extend the default set of file types with your own file extensions.

To add your own extension mapping, type the extension (for example, VBS) in the textbox provided and choose the editor that should be used from the drop-down list. When you've picked the desired editor, click the Apply button to commit it to the list of processed extensions. If you want to set a default editor for files that don't have any extensions, you can do that from this screen as well.

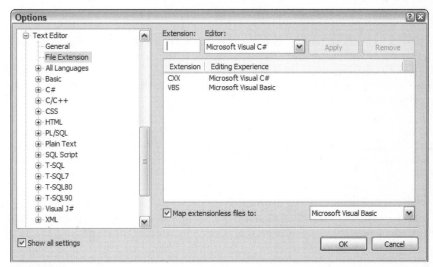

Figure 2-10

All Languages

The Text Editor group of options is extensive, with the many editors all having their own collections of customizable settings. However, several settings can be applied globally across all editors, making it easy to get the environment ready for your way of doing things.

The first commonly used preference is to turn line numbers on. This can be useful for code checking, particularly when reviewing someone else's code for which you need to refer to particular lines in a report. Line numbers can be turned on for all editors in the Display section (select All Languages⇨ General), as shown in Figure 2-11.

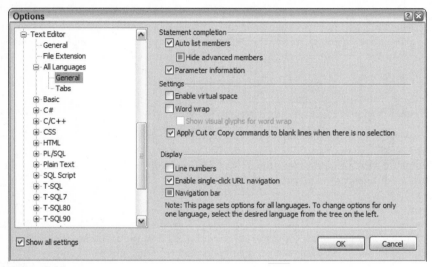

Figure 2-11

While you're in the General section, you may want to also review other global editor options, such as the Auto List Members and Parameter Information options. The first of these options will use IntelliSense to show the members of a particular item when you type the appropriate character (for instance, in Visual Basic, when you type the name of an object immediately followed by a period, the list of properties, events, and methods will be shown).

The latter option uses a formatted tooltip to display the parameters in a method when you commence writing a call to the subroutine. This can be useful if you're unfamiliar with the parameters required for the subroutine. However, it can also occlude your view of other parts of the code, so you can turn it off if you prefer.

Note that all of these options can be overridden for particular languages, so if you prefer to see the parameter information in Visual Basic but not in C#, you can set the environment up by setting a default in the All Languages section and then picking specific options for the languages that differ.

Advanced editing options are available for editing HTML, XML, CSS, and SQL script files.

Debugging

Of course, writing code and designing graphical interfaces is only one part of your programming experience when it comes to an advanced IDE such as Visual Studio 2005. Just as important is the interface you use for debugging your applications. Visual Studio offers options that can be set to enhance the way you interact with your executing programs. In the Debugging➪General options page (see Figure 2-12), you'll find a list of preferences that you can toggle on or off to control the way Visual Studio responds to certain events during the execution of your programs.

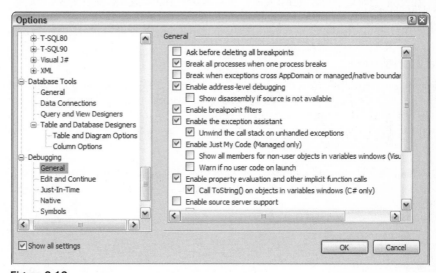

Figure 2-12

The following list contains the options that are most likely to be useful to you in normal debugging situations:

❑ **Break all processes when one process breaks:** Particularly important when multi-threading and running solutions with a number of projects, enabling this option forces the Visual Studio debugger to pause all processes when only one encounters an error. If you choose not to use this option, beware of processes that get out of step during debugged sessions.

❑ **Enable breakpoint filters:** As you'll see in Chapter 49, you can apply filters to breakpoints so that your code will only pause during a debugging session under certain conditions. Disabling this option will cause Visual Studio to ignore any filters applied and always pause execution on a breakpoint.

❑ **Enable Just My Code (Managed code only):** An incredibly useful shortcut option, this setting allows you to ignore all code other than your own. Rather than having to step through low-level system code or external DLLs, the debugging session will step over them and continue to only code in your own projects.

❑ **Enable property evaluation and other implicit function calls:** Without this option active, windows such as the QuickWatch dialog and the variables windows will not be able to evaluate the contents of properties without explicitly converting them. Going along with this is the Call ToString() on Objects in Variable Windows option for C# so that you don't have to call `ToString()` when displaying object contents.

❑ **Require source files to exactly match the original version:** In some cases it's possible to debug source code that does not exactly match the compiled binary containing the debug symbols. This option alters that behavior so that the source file must match the executable, forcing you to find the matching source file prior to debugging.

❑ **Redirect all Output Window text to the Immediate Window:** Sometimes it's handy to have all of your debugging output in one place. This option causes any debug information to be printed to the Immediate window, where you can also interrogate variables and perform simple logic.

Edit and Continue

The most important addition to debugging in Visual Studio 2005, particularly for Visual Basic developers, is the Edit and Continue option. When debugging a problem, the programmer can change the code on-the-fly and let the debug process continue without having to stop and restart the solution. Some programmers don't like this as an option and feel that it can cause bad programming practices because the code can be changed without saving the solution.

In fact, so many developers did not want Edit and Continue reintroduced into Visual Studio that Microsoft has included the option to turn it off, but there's more to it than a simple checkbox, as shown in Figure 2-13.

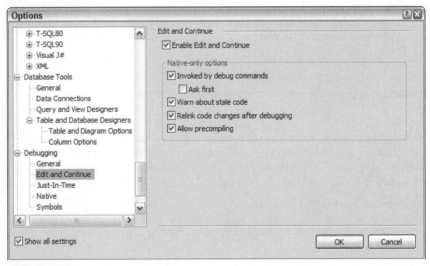

Figure 2-13

When debugging native .NET code, you can also customize how the Edit and Continue process will work. For those who straddle the fence regarding whether to allow Edit and Continue to function, the Ask First checkbox gives you the option to reject the functionality at the time of debugging. This is useful if you occasionally change code during a debug session inadvertently; rather than Visual Studio simply recompiling the code in the background without your knowledge, you will be presented with a prompt to inform you that you are editing currently active code.

Stale code is a new concept. It refers to sections of your program that you have changed previously but that cannot be immediately recompiled for debugging. With this option, code is marked (with a gray background by default) and you cannot further edit it if you encounter it later. When the debugger is able to, it will recompile this code with the changes made; and from that point on you'll be able to re-edit the code. Activating the Warn About Stale Code option will result in the debugger displaying a dialog box whenever a stale code situation arises.

The last option to consider is the Allow Precompiling setting. Precompiling the headers in the background of a debug session allows any code changes applied during an Edit and Continue procedure to be applied more speedily, but it requires a large amount of physical memory to store the precompiled headers. If your machine is RAM constrained, consider deactivating this setting.

Summary

This chapter covered only a core selection of the useful options available to you as you start to shape the Visual Studio interface to suit your own programming style; many other options are available. These numerous options enable you to adjust the way you edit your code, add controls to your forms, and even select the methods to use when debugging code. The settings within the Visual Studio 2005 Options page also allow you to control how and where applications are created, and even customize the keyboard shortcuts you use. Throughout the remainder of this book, you'll see the Options dialog revisited according to specific functionality such as macros, debugging, and compiling.

In the next chapter you'll look at how to further customize a section of the IDE — the Toolbox — and be introduced to the many building blocks Microsoft provides with Visual Studio 2005 to make the creation of your applications easy.

3

The Toolbox

One of the major advantages that Microsoft has offered its developer users over many other so-called integrated development environments (IDEs) is true drag-and-drop placement of many graphical elements for Windows form design. In fact, since early versions of Visual Basic, Microsoft has enabled developers to add nongraphical components such as timers as well. These components are all available in what is known as the *Toolbox*, a special window within the Visual Studio IDE.

This chapter first walks through the details of the Toolbox: how components are organized, how to add additional elements and controls, and how these components can be viewed by the developer. The second part of the chapter describes some of the more commonly used and interesting controls. If you've used previous versions of Visual Studio, you may want to skim this section to look at components that are new to Visual Studio 2005.

Describing the Toolbox

The Toolbox window contains all of the available components for the currently active document being shown in the main workspace. These components can be visual, such as buttons and textboxes, or invisible, service-oriented objects such as Timers and system event logs, or even designer elements such as Class and Interface objects used in the Class Designer view.

Regardless of which set of components are shown, the way they are used in a program is usually the same: Click and drag the desired component onto the design surface of the active document or double-click the component's entry for Visual Studio to automatically add an instance of it to the current file.

With the introduction of Visual Studio .NET (also known as Visual Studio 2002), Microsoft began grouping the components into sections that logically segregated them. Rather than one big mess of components, as presented in Visual Basic 6, Visual Studio 2005 presents the available object types in simple groups.

This default grouping enables you to more easily locate the controls you need; for example, data-related components are in their own Data group.

By default, groups are presented in List view (see Figure 3-1). Each component is represented by its own icon and the name of the component. This differs from the old way of displaying the available objects, where the Toolbox was simply a stacked list of icons that left you guessing as to what some of the more obscure components were.

Each group can be collapsed to hide unnecessary sets of components. You can change the view of each control group individually, so if you know what all the common controls are just by looking at their icon, right-click anywhere within the Common Controls group area and deselect the List View option. The view will switch to the old presentation of icons, all stacked up, with as many sitting horizontally next to each other as can fit in the width of the Toolbox window. In Figure 3-2 you can see that a typical width for the Toolbox results in six icons fitting side by side — certainly a space saver if you know what the icons represent!

Figure 3-1

Figure 3-2

This screenshot also shows you an example of collapsing the groups of components you may not be currently interested in. To expand a group, just click the small plus sign (+) next to its title. On smaller screen resolutions, this technique is essential for quick navigation of your component list.

Arranging Components

Alphabetical order is a good default because it enables you to locate items that are unfamiliar. However, if you're only using a handful of components and are frustrated having to continuously scroll up and down, you can create your own groups of controls and move existing object types around.

Repositioning an individual component is easy. Locate it in the Toolbox and click and drag it to the new location (as shown in Figure 3-3). When you're happy with where it is, release the mouse button and the component will move to the new spot in the list. Moving it to a different group is done in the same way — just keep dragging the component up or down the Toolbox list until you've located the right group. These actions work in both List and Icon views.

If you want to copy the component from one group to another, rather than move it, hold down the Ctrl key as you drag and the process will duplicate the control so that it appears in both groups.

You can't duplicate the control within a group — you can only copy it to another group in which it is not currently present.

Figure 3-3

If you would rather, you can use the Cut, Copy, and Paste commands common to most Windows applications to move or copy your components. The right-click context menu has all three commands at the top of the list, or you can use the familiar keyboard shortcuts of Ctrl+X, Ctrl+C, and Ctrl+V, respectively. If you do attempt to cut a control from a group, Visual Studio 2005 will warn you that you are removing the item to confirm that you really want to perform the action. As long as you immediately paste it to the desired spot, you won't have a problem.

Sometimes it's nice to have your own group or collection of groups to host the controls and components you use the most. Creating a new group in the Toolbox is easy. Right-click anywhere in the Toolbox area and select the Add Tab command. A new blank tab will be added to the bottom of the Toolbox with a prompt for you to name it. Once named, you can then add components to it by following the steps described in this section.

When you first start Visual Studio 2005, the items within each group are arranged alphabetically. However, after moving items around, you may find that they're in a bewildering state and decide that you simply need to start again. All you have to do is right-click anywhere within the group that's become mixed up and choose the Sort Items Alphabetically command. Instantly your control list will be returned to its original order.

If you've become even more confused, with components in unusual groups, and you have lost sight of where everything is, you can choose Reset Toolbox from the same right-click context menu. This will restore all of the groups in the Toolbox to their original state, with components sorted alphabetically and in the groups they started in.

> Note that performing Reset Toolbox will delete any of your own custom-made groups of commands, so be very sure you want to perform this function!

By default, controls are added to the Toolbox using their base name. This means you end up with some names that are hard to understand, particularly if you add COM controls to your Toolbox. Visual Studio 2005 enables you to modify the component's name to something more understandable.

To change the name of a component, right-click the component's entry in the Toolbox and select the Rename Item command (see Figure 3-4). An edit field will appear inline in place of the original caption, enabling you to name it however you like, including the use of special characters.

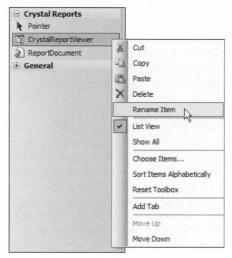

Figure 3-4

Note that if you choose to rename an element in a group that is shown in Icon view, Visual Studio will switch it to List view first, and then place the editor in the place of the caption wherever the component now appears (it will scroll the list if necessary).

Adding Components

Sometimes you'll find that a particular component you need is not present in the lists displayed in the Toolbox. Most of the main .NET components are already present, but some are not. For example, the WebClient class component is not displayed in the Toolbox by default. In addition, many components that are present in the `Microsoft.VisualBasic.Compatibility.VB6` namespace can be useful to Visual Basic programmers who are used to functionality in older versions of VB, such as control arrays.

Finally, .NET solutions can use COM components in their design. Once added to the Toolbox, COM objects can be used in much the same way as regular .NET components, and if coded correctly they can be programmed against in precisely the same way, utilizing the Properties window and referring to their methods, properties, and events in code.

There is an All Windows Forms group of controls at the very top of the Toolbox that is collapsed by default. This group contains all of the components in the other groups, along with several other controls that are not shown anywhere else.

Basically, Microsoft determined that these additional controls were not used very often and relegated them to a secondary location. If you try to add a component and find that it's already selected in the list of items, then it's likely that it has been sitting in this group all along.

To add a component to your Toolbox layout, right-click anywhere within the group of components you wish to add it to and select the Choose Items command. After a moment (this process can take a few seconds on a slower machine, as it needs to interrogate the .NET cache to determine all of the possible components you can choose from), you will be presented with a list of .NET Framework components, as Figure 3-5 shows.

Scroll through the list to locate the item you wish to add to the Toolbox and check the corresponding checkbox. You can add multiple items at the same time by selecting each of them before clicking the OK button to apply your changes. At this time you can also remove items from the Toolbox by deselecting them from the list. Note that this will remove the items from any groups to which they belong, not just the group you are currently editing.

If you're finding it hard to locate the item you need, you can use the Filter box, which will filter the list based on name, namespace, and assembly name. On rare occasions the item may not be listed at all. This can happen with nonstandard components such as the ones you build yourself that are not registered in the global Framework cache. You can still add them by using the Browse button to locate the physical file on the computer.

COM components are added in the same manner. Simply switch over to the COM Components tab in the dialog window to view the list of available, properly registered COM components to add. Again, you can use the Browse button to locate controls that may not appear in the list.

Once you've selected and deselected the items you need, click the OK button to save them to the Toolbox layout.

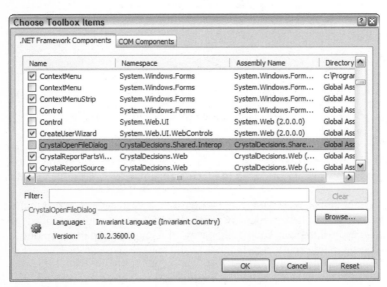

Figure 3-5

Commonly Used Elements

Visual Studio 2005 ships with many components ready for use in your own Windows and web applications. If you're new to creating applications using Microsoft development tools, these next few pages will introduce you to some of the more commonly used controls that appear in the default Toolbox setup.

Figure 3-6 shows a form in Design view packed with controls. All of these controls were simply dragged from the Toolbox onto the design surface of the form and positioned so they were legible. As you can see, most controls come with default settings, such as appropriate size and sample text. All you need to do is customize these settings using the Properties window to fit your particular application's needs and they are ready for use. Chapter 7 walks through the process of form design and discusses not only placing these components onto your forms, but also how the various properties can affect their behavior.

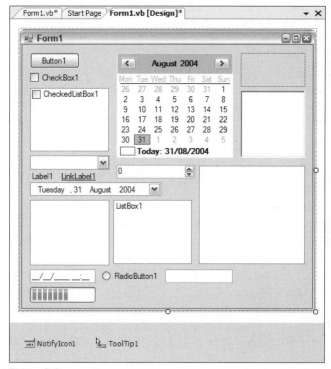

Figure 3-6

The controls shown in Figure 3-6 are described in the following list, starting from the top left and working down and then across:

❑   Button: The Button control is perhaps the most common and simple component you will use on a Windows application form. It adds a single button to your form that the user can click so the application can perform an action or series of actions.

❑   CheckBox: A CheckBox is like a toggle button. Each time the user clicks it, its state changes between unchecked and checked. You can use one of its properties to allow a third state of *indeterminate*, which is commonly used for checkbox controls that have multiple values underneath them in a hierarchy whereby some are active and some are not.

❑ `CheckedListBox`: Using the `CheckedListBox`, you can present users with a list of items from which they can select A property in this control allows you to control whether users can select multiple items simultaneously or if only one list entry can be chosen at a time.

❑ `ComboBox`: Used commonly to present a list of options from which the user can choose only one, the `ComboBox` is a powerful yet simple control to use in your application. You can control the style of each `ComboBox` control in your application to either allow user entries or force users to choose from a preset list.

❑ `Label`: An informational control only, the `Label` doesn't normally allow any user interaction. It is commonly used to inform end users about the various parts of your application's form and state.

❑ `LinkLabel`: Think of a `LinkLabel` as being the Windows application equivalent to a hyperlink on a web page. As hyperlinking has become more prevalent, Microsoft chose to include this extra control to avoid irregular use of the normal `Label` component.

❑ `DateTimePicker`: Let your users select a date or a time using the `DateTimePicker` component. The example shown in Figure 3-6 is using the default format of the date only, but you can change the setting to a time value with a simple property change.

❑ `ListView`: The `ListView` displays a list of items with an optional icon alongside each. The best example of a `ListView` is the right-hand side of Windows Explorer; and just like that interface, you can switch between multiple views, such as large and small icons and Detail view, to give your end users a consistent look and feel, similar to Windows.

❑ `MaskedTextBox`: The `MaskedTextBox` is a type of `TextBox` (see below) that includes additional properties that control how the information can be entered into it. You can choose from several preset masks (the screenshot shows the standard short date and time mask) or you can build your own custom mask that the user must follow in order for the contents to be valid.

❑ `ProgressBar`: The `ProgressBar` control should be immediately familiar as a component that gives feedback to users about the completion state of a long task.

❑ `MonthCalendar`: This control is an alternative to the `DateTimePicker` discussed previously. The `MonthCalendar` component shows a single month at a time by default, but you can customize this using its `CalendarDimensions` property. A number of other properties enable you to add your own special dates in bold and specify how many dates the user can select at one time.

❑ `NumericUpDown`: A common requirement is to enable users to pick a numeric value from a range. The `NumericUpDown` control allows you to do this with more control than a normal textbox, as it restricts the minimum and maximum values allowed and gives the user an easy way of incrementing and decrementing the value. You can change the increment as well as the minimum and maximum values to suit your own application's requirements.

❑ `ListBox`: Similar to the `ListView` mentioned previously, the `ListBox` component will present users with a list of items. It is a lot simpler than the `ListView` and only has one way of displaying entries, but it can be used when all the user needs to do is select items from a list.

❑ `RadioButton`: A `RadioButton` control is normally used in conjunction with at least one other, and represents a single option from a mutually exclusive list of options. When the user selects one `RadioButton`, any others in the same container will be deactivated.

❑ `TextBox`: The `TextBox` forms the basis for all data entry by the end user. There are two main types of `TextBox`: single-line and multi-line. All other text entry controls are inherited from this one, including the `MaskedTextBox`.

- ❏ `PictureBox`: The `PictureBox` is the component you can use to house images in your form. It is useful because it has its own extensive set of events and methods, enabling you to easily create a Paintlike program by capturing mouse clicks and movements.

- ❏ `RichTextBox`: Extending the normal `TextBox`, the `RichTextBox` gives you the ability to host an RTF (Rich Text Format) document in your form. Adding buttons or menu commands to your form, the end user can format selections of text with the normal bold, italic, and color options available to them when editing an RTF file.

- ❏ `TreeView`: When you look at the folder list in Windows Explorer, you're looking at an advanced `TreeView`. Each `TreeView` control can have a hierarchy of nodes with a variety of icons and states.

In addition to those visible controls, you'll notice a small area below the active form's design surface. This tray area is used to contain components that do not have a graphical aspect to them, or that don't display anything on the form itself. The two components listed in this area are the `NotifyIcon`, which is used to place an icon in the Windows notification area in the bottom right of the screen, and the `ToolTip`, which is a special component that adds additional properties to any other controls on the form, giving them the capability to display tooltips when the user hovers the mouse cursor over them during execution.

Besides these commonly used controls, you'll find extensive groups of controls dedicated to database activity, various dialog windows that you can use in your applications, and system components such as timers and event logs. In addition, you'll find a selection of container controls whose only purpose is to house other controls on your form and segregate them in some logical fashion. Chapter 7 goes into detail about how to use container controls in your application form design.

Summary

You should now have your Toolbox customized and ready for development in your own way. Remember that any control or component can be placed into any group, even new groups of your own design. They can be named and positioned in any order, and each group can be viewed in either List or Icon view. The result is your own unique view of the available components, ready for use in your form and class designs.

In the next chapter you'll look at how the Solution Explorer can be customized and used to keep track of your projects and solutions.

4

The Solution Explorer

Developing applications of any kind in Visual Studio 2005 requires first that a solution be created. Most of the time you'll create a solution automatically when you pick the kind of application project you want to design, but you can also create a blank solution for which you can customize every aspect of your development efforts, and even use temporary solutions for a single session of Visual Studio 2005.

Over the next few pages you'll take a look at one of the many windows in the Visual Studio 2005 IDE known as the Solution Explorer, where you can manage the various projects within a particular solution and view and maintain what files belong to each project.

Solution Explorer Structure

When you first start Visual Studio 2005 and create a simple project, the Solution Explorer will look something like what is shown in Figure 4-1. The top toolbar of the Solution Explorer enables you to customize the way the contents of the window appear to you, as well as giving you shortcuts to the different workspace views for individual files.

Figure 4-1

The main space of the tool window contains a hierarchical list of the projects and files found within the currently open solution. When the solution contains only a single project, the Solution file itself does not appear in the tree, as shown in Figure 4-1. However, once multiple projects appear in the solution, the Solution entry is accessible within the tree so that you can easily modify the various properties of the solution (see Figure 4-2).

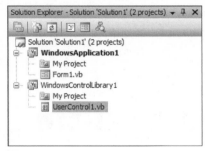

Figure 4-2

In the default view, the Solution is listed at the top of the tree view, with the number of projects that belong to it listed in parentheses. The next level down is the project level; each project has an entry containing its name and an icon representing what type of project it is. The icons in Figure 4-2 indicate that both projects are Visual Basic Windows applications.

The startup project is listed in bold to differentiate it from the other projects in the solution. To change the startup project to another one in the solution, right-click the desired project and choose Set As StartUp Project.

You can set multiple projects to be startup projects. You'll learn how to do this later in this chapter.

Showing Hidden Items

The default view of the Solution Explorer is an excellent representation of your projects because it only displays the files you normally deal with. For instance, Figure 4-2 shows that WindowsApplication1 contains two entries: My Project and Form1.vb. The first entry is to access the various property pages for the project, whereas the second entry provides access to the form that belongs to the project — you can use this entry to access the Design, Code, and Class Diagram views of the form.

However, usually many more files and associations exist in the project than what is shown in this view, and sometimes it's necessary to be able to get at other files within the project. Figure 4-3 shows this same project with the Show All Files toggle button activated and the various entries within the tree view expanded.

The first thing of note is the Form1.Designer.vb entry below Form1.vb. In previous versions of Visual Studio, the designer code for the form layout and contained controls was kept in the same file as your own code. As a result, many developers were tempted to manipulate the form design by editing the code when it was heavily advised not to. Another issue faced with this combined approach was that it was sometimes hard to get to your own code when the designer code kept being regenerated from Design view.

Figure 4-3

Because Visual Studio 2005 is based on the .NET Framework 2.0, it was easy for Microsoft to separate the designer code from the custom code you build into your forms through the use of *partial classes* (which were introduced in this new version of the Framework). This extra entry that is only visible when you show all of the files associated with a project is that same designer code that Visual Studio 2005 generates for you as you create your form layouts (see Chapter 6).

You can still dive into the code and change it manually if you require, but because it's hidden away and separated from your own code the temptation to do so unnecessarily is no longer there.

You can determine that Visual Studio 2005 is using the new partial class functionality by viewing this special "behind the scenes" designer file and looking at the top line. Partial Class *indicates that the definition contained in this file is only part of the total definition of the form's class, with the rest obviously being your own custom code.*

Temporary Solutions

In older development tools such as Microsoft Visual Basic 6, programmers were able to quickly create a temporary solution, write some test code, check the results, and then close the project without leaving vestigial files on the computer. When Visual Studio .NET was first released, this capability disappeared. Every time a developer created a new solution, the IDE would physically create the necessary files; and if the program was executed, even in debug mode, it would create a permanent executable file as well.

To delete these files, you needed to remove them using Windows Explorer after you successfully located them. It was a frustrating experience for many programmers who wanted to be able to create a temporary program, write their arbitrary code, and then be able to leave the IDE without leaving pointless files behind.

Thankfully, Microsoft has introduced the concept of temporary projects and solutions with the release of Visual Studio 2005. Now, when you first create a solution, it is put into a special temporary state until you explicitly save it to a folder location. While in this state, Visual Studio 2005 still creates the files that it needs on the hard drive—including the debug executable in the event that you run the project—but stores them in a temporary folder.

If you leave Visual Studio 2005 or attempt to close the solution before first saving it, the IDE will prompt you to save your changes. If you do not save them at this point, Visual Studio will clean up the temporary files without you needing to do so manually.

Web Solutions

Previously, web applications were created in much the same way as any other project. The New Project dialog box was used to choose from Windows and web applications, as well as for differentiating between Web Services and Windows Controls and Services. Visual Studio 2005 has moved the web development side of things outside the New Project dialog to make the separation between web and Windows development a bit more distinct, but it can be frustrating if you don't realize what happened.

To create a new web site, you use the File⇨New Web Site menu command. This will display the New Web Site dialog from which you can select from half a dozen default project templates as well as custom ones you create yourself (see Chapter 25). Both ASP.NET web sites and web services can be created from this dialog in the language of your choice (see Figure 4-4), along with starter kits that generate a lot of additional code with which you can work.

Creating a web solution also enables you to specify the location where the project should be created. The default is the local file system but you can also now create web solutions based on HTTP and FTP URIs.

The Browse button next to the location displays a customized Find Location dialog window, providing individual windows for locating the correct spot on the file system, local Internet Information Server, or remote FTP or HTTP locations.

Figure 4-4

Once the project has been created, Visual Studio 2005 presents it in a similar way in the Solution Explorer. The main difference is that the Show All Files toggle is no longer available and all associated files are displayed in the tool window.

Remember: If there's only one web site, the Solution level won't be displayed.

Common Project and Solution Tasks

Chapter 7 goes into detail about how to work with projects and solutions, but it's worth looking at the fundamental tasks you often need to perform at this stage. The first task that's often required is to add additional items to a project.

To add a new item to a project within the current solution, right-click on the project's entry and choose Add⇨New Item from the context menu that is displayed. You can add certain default items such as new forms and user controls by selecting their specific entry from the New Item menu (shown in Figure 4-5).

Figure 4-5

Note that selecting the default items from the Add menu will still bring up the New Item dialog, as you must select the filename that is used to set the default name for the item.

The Add New Item dialog is displayed, enabling you to choose from a vast array of default item templates. Figure 4-6 shows the extent of the Add New Item dialog in a default installation of Visual Studio 2005, with entries for new Windows forms, modules, classes, and user controls. All of these items are fairly standard requirements for a typical .NET application, but there are also several templates that shortcut the process of creating certain forms in a typical Windows application.

Some templates (such as the Dialog) simply add a couple of controls to the form using Microsoft's recommended layout, with one or two lines of code to handle the events behind them. Others, including the Explorer form, automatically generate a large amount of code, so you have a huge head start in creating these elements for your application.

Some items are not directly related to code. For instance, the Add New Item dialog also includes the capability to add icons, cursors, and bitmaps to your project, and then edit them with the built-in graphics editor.

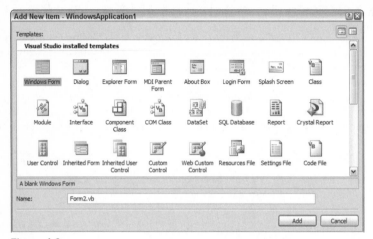

Figure 4-6

Sometimes the file containing the item definition already exists. This might be the case when you have a form shared among projects, or a class or user control definition that you've defined in a previous project and want to use in a new one. In this situation, select Add↪Existing Item from the right-click context menu and Visual Studio 2005 will enable you to browse for the file's location. Remember that an individual project must be developed in a single language, so you can only add existent Visual Basic files to a Visual Basic project, existent C# files to a C# project, and so on.

The default structure of a typical solution is quite flat. It begins with the solution file, which contains a list of project files. These in turn normally contain a list of individual files, such as form and class definitions and two subdirectories for the compiled output of the project (`bin` and `obj`). When you add items to the project, they're added to that project's main folder.

Of course, just because this is the default behavior doesn't mean you need to live with it. The Add submenu from the context menu also has a command to add a new folder. This enables you to create a full folder hierarchy within a project, organizing different parts of the application into different sections. You can add new (or existing) files to these subfolders in the same way you would add to the root folder of the project, or you can simply drag and drop the files already in the project into them.

While there are menu commands that can perform these commonly used tasks, the Solution Explorer provides handy shortcuts in one centralized location.

Adding Windows References

You can add to a project two types of items that are not physical files but instead work more as associations with existing items: *Windows references* and *web references*. Adding references to other items in this fashion enables you to use them in your code by creating objects and consuming public shared methods from within the associated item.

To add a normal Windows reference, locate the project that should take the new reference in the Solution Explorer and right-click its entry. From the context menu displayed, select the Add Reference command and the appropriate dialog will be displayed (see Figure 4-7).

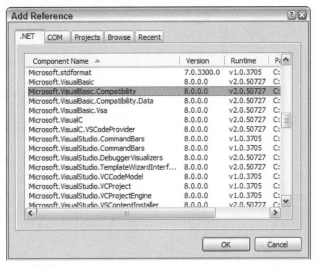

Figure 4-7

Similar to adding items to the Toolbox, .NET and COM references are separated into different lists, as they come from different parts of the Windows system (the COM reference list comes from properly registered COM components found in the Windows registry, while .NET components are sourced from the Global Assembly Cache).

Like other project-based development environments going back as far as the first versions of Visual Basic, you can add references to actual projects, rather than the compiled binary components. The advantage to this model is that it's easier to debug into the referenced component, but it does have a performance impact and you won't want to distribute your final application with a project reference.

If the component you need to reference isn't present in the appropriate list, you can choose the Browse tab, which enables you to locate the file containing the component directly in the file system, while the Recent tab shows a list of references you've added to recent projects so you don't have to find them again (a boon in the often very large COM list!).

Adding Web References

Adding web references is handled in a similar fashion to normal references. It is used to find and connect to web service definitions so that their functions can be consumed from within your application. Choose Add Web Reference from the project's context menu and the associated dialog will appear, as shown in Figure 4-8.

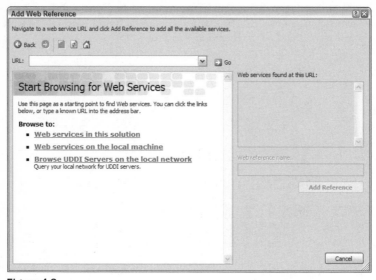

Figure 4-8

At this point you can browse to web services registered on the machine you're working on or those specifically created in the active solution. If the web service is external to both of these locations, enter the URL to the WSDL file associated with the required web service and click the OK button.

After the web service is found (assuming it is), the main window will be populated with a list of functions contained within the web service, and the Web Reference Name field will be enabled. Name the reference something that will make sense in your code, as this is the identifier you need to use when creating items based on the web reference, and click the Add Reference button.

Setting Solution Properties

When there is more than one project within a solution, you can choose to select a single or even multiple startup projects in addition to setting a number of other properties relating to the solution as a whole. Locate the solution's entry in the Solution Explorer, right-click, and choose the Properties command from the context menu.

The Solution Property Pages dialog will be displayed, as shown in Figure 4-9. The first item to choose is how the solution should start up when you begin execution. The default behavior is to set a single startup project, which is usually the first one you added to the solution. To change this to another project, you can choose it from the drop-down menu associated with the Single Startup Project option.

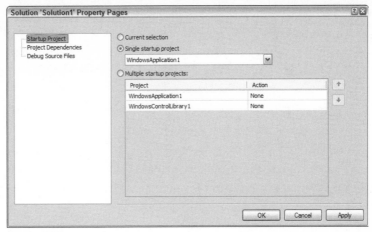

Figure 4-9

Alternatively, if you require multiple projects to start simultaneously, as is sometimes the case when you have a single solution with separate projects that depend on each other (such as a Windows application and a Windows service), select the Multiple Startup Projects option. Each project can be started with or without debugging symbols, depending on how you want to perform the testing.

This dialog also enables you to specify otherwise implicit project dependencies. For example, if you had a solution with a Windows application and a Windows service but didn't have an explicit reference to the service and needed to consume it, you could specify here that the service is a dependency in the application, forcing it to build even if it normally wouldn't need to.

Summary

The Solution Explorer is a powerful tool window that gives you direct access to the structure of the currently active solution, showing you the files that belong to each project and giving you the ability to add or remove items to available projects, and even add whole projects to the solution. In Chapter 7 you'll learn a lot more details about how to manage your projects and solutions by examining the properties that belong to solutions, looking at project configurations, and detailing the solution file structure. The next chapter deals with how to customize the IDE of Visual Studio 2005, including how to fine-tune the Solution Explorer window's position and size.

5

Customizing the IDE

Now that you're familiar with the general layout of Visual Studio 2005 and what all the various components of the IDE mean, it's time to shake them up and have some fun — some fun aimed at making the graphical layout more suited to your own way of doing things.

In this chapter you'll learn several ways to change the environment — from moving the various tool windows and lists around and opening multiple files in separate areas of the workspace so you can view them simultaneously to backing up your settings for retrieval on another machine.

Tool Window Customization

Tool windows are the core of how Visual Studio 2005 can make your working life more efficient, particularly if you're more comfortable working in an environment that uses the mouse extensively. Each tool window focuses on one particular task or aspect of development. You've seen several windows in action already — the Solution Explorer, which enables you to browse through the projects and files that make up the current solution, and the Properties window, which gives you direct access to the properties of the currently selected item in the Design pane, are both tool windows. Similarly, the Toolbox is another window that has a specialized function — to provide the capability to design forms graphically without needing to resort to code to define the various objects that make up a form's layout.

The preconfigured Visual Studio 2005 environment comes with a small number of these tool windows positioned in logical and useful locations, but these windows are only a small subset of what's available to you.

Working with Tool Windows

Before you can do anything with a specific tool window, you need to be able to make it visible. Some are shown by default, such as the Properties and Toolbox windows, whereas others, such as the Immediate window, are shown in certain contexts (the Immediate window is shown while you're debugging but not at design time in all default configurations).

The selection of windows you can choose to display are all found in the View menu. The most commonly used windows, such as the aforementioned Properties window and the Solution Explorer and Server Explorer, are accessible directly from the View menu, as well as their keyboard shortcuts. However, hidden away in the View⇨Other Windows submenu is an even larger selection of windows to add to your IDE configuration.

Each of these menu items acts as a show command only — to close a particular window, you need to use the Close button on the window itself. If you select the menu item corresponding to a window that is hidden, it will be popped open as if you had hovered the mouse cursor over it.

> *Every window has a default location in which it is shown. For example, the Bookmarks window will appear docked to the bottom of the IDE, while the Macro Explorer window shares the same space as the Solution Explorer. However, you can position them however you like, as you'll see in the next section of this chapter.*

The following table lists the available tool windows, their associated access shortcut, and what feature of Visual Studio 2005 they handle:

Window	Menu	Keyboard Shortcut	Function
Server Explorer	View	Ctrl+Alt+S	Provides access to Windows Server components such as SQL Server databases, event logs, and message queues
Solution Explorer	View	Ctrl+Alt+L	Displayed by default, the Solution Explorer enables you to view and modify your solution structure. For more information, refer to Chapter 4.
Properties Window	View	F4	Rather than set properties in code, you can change many aspects of a control, form, or component through this window. Chapter 6 discusses how the Properties window can be used.
Toolbox	View	Ctrl+Alt+X	Provides direct access to the components currently available for use in your form design. Chapter 6 also discusses the Toolbox.
Class View	View⇨Other Windows	Ctrl+Shift+C	Enables you to view your application in a hierarchy of classes, rather than the normal file structure view
Error List	View	Ctrl+W, Ctrl+E	All errors can be viewed in this list, with each entry providing a shortcut link to the problematic code.

Window	Menu	Keyboard Shortcut	Function
Bookmark	View⇨Other Windows	Ctrl+W, K	All bookmarks in your code can be viewed in this summary list. This window enables you to name each bookmark so you can more easily find it.
Code Definition	View⇨Other Windows	Ctrl+\, Ctrl+D	Used for both C# and C++ application projects, this window is useful for viewing the file associated with a selected symbol or definition.
Command	View⇨Other Windows	Ctrl+Alt+A	You can execute commands and command aliases directly from within the Command window.
Document Outline	View⇨Other Windows	Ctrl+Alt+T	Document Outline is a special window that shows you graphically how the current document or file is structured. Chapter 13 deals with the Document Outline window in detail.
Object Test Bench	View⇨Other Windows	None	This is the main window for the object test bench — a tool for testing the various characteristics of your classes.
Output	View⇨Other Windows Debug⇨ Windows	Ctrl+Alt+O	This is the main window for run time and debug generated output. See Chapter 48 for information about how the Output window can be used.
Breakpoints	Debug⇨ Windows	Ctrl+Alt+B	Presents a list of breakpoints currently inserted into the active project. Chapter 49 explains how to use breakpoints when debugging your application code.
Resource View	View⇨Other Windows	Ctrl+Shift+E	Provides an alternative way of viewing the resource files associated with your solution.
Task List	View⇨Other Windows	Ctrl+Alt+K	This window contains a list of both automatically generated and manually created tasks that you can use to track your development progress.

Table continued on following page

Window	Menu	Keyboard Shortcut	Function
Macro Explorer	View⇨Other Windows	Alt+F8	Macros, a way of automating series of functions you use often, are dealt with in Chapter 26. The Macro Explorer enables you to select, run, and edit the macros available to you in the current solution.
Call Browser	View⇨Other Windows	None	Only accessible from within C++ projects, this window enables you to search for function calls.
Immediate	Debug⇨ Windows	Ctrl+G	The Immediate window can be used to debug and execute commands directly, enabling you to modify contents of variables at runtime, as well as examine objects and the effects of various commands even during design time.

Some of the shortcuts listed use what's known as a shortcut chord. This is a sequence of keyboard combinations, rather than just a single combination. For example, the Error List is shown as Ctrl+W, Ctrl+E. This means you should first press Ctrl+W. Visual Studio 2005 will detect that this is the start of a chord and wait for the second keyboard combination before performing the action. In this case, Ctrl+E will then tell it to open the Error List.

Moving Tool Windows

Moving tool windows has always been a challenge in Visual Studio and its precursors. As the window was dragged around you could never tell where it was going to end up — would it appear on top of another window, floating over the IDE, docked to the side of the IDE or another window, or some other configuration? Even Visual Studio 2003 had problems — in fact, it was even worse in some respects because windows could be tabbed but you were still never sure of how it would turn out when a window was moved.

As a result, many developers left the IDE set up with the default layout and didn't experiment to find a more suitable design for their work practices. Fortunately, Microsoft's development team worked hard at introducing a new system for organizing the many windows in the IDE, resulting in an extremely intuitive system for positioning windows accurately.

Figure 5-1 shows the Server Explorer window being dragged across the user interface of Visual Studio. As it is being moved, small icons appear in different parts of the screen. If the window is moved on top of one of these icons, Visual Studio will move the window to the appropriate place. Otherwise, the window will be set to float.

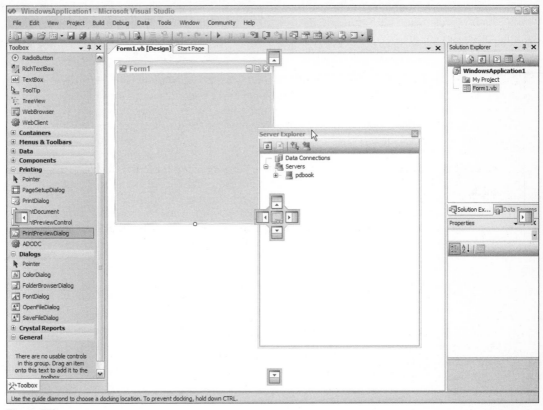

Figure 5-1

The easiest way to understand how this positioning paradigm works is to zoom in on the main graphical indicators. Figure 5-2 shows a close-up of the central set of icons. As you drag the mouse cursor over each of these buttons, Visual Studio will shade a section of the IDE to show you where the window will be placed if you choose it.

Figure 5-2

The idea is that once you're happy with the positional preview of the window, you simply let go of the mouse button and Visual Studio moves the window to the indicated location. In Figure 5-2 there are five such positional indicators — the one in the center means that the window will share space with the window that is underneath the buttons, in a tabbed format similar to the Start Page and Form1 Design view shared space in Figure 5-1.

The four buttons surrounding this tabbed indicator will dock the window to the corresponding side of the window underneath the buttons. In the example shown in Figure 5-1, choosing the bottom button in this central configuration would dock the Server Explorer to the bottom of the main workspace, but between the Toolbox and Properties windows.

The separate buttons on the four sides of the IDE indicate that the window being positioned will actually be docked to the very edge of the IDE, rather than the current area underneath the mouse cursor. In the example discussed, dropping the Server Explorer on the button near the bottom edge of the IDE would result in the window being docked not only below the main workspace area, but also below the Toolbox and Properties windows.

As you drag the window around the IDE's interface, these indicator buttons will change according to the context in which the window will be placed. Figure 5-3 shows the Server Explorer being positioned over the Solution Explorer. Now, the central icons actually represent the Solution Explorer, not the main workspace area, enabling you to dock the Server Explorer window to any of the four sides of the Solution Explorer or to share the space in a tabbed fashion (which is actually the default behavior for the Server Explorer). The four IDE-edge icons remain, as they are independent of which window the mouse pointer is over.

> *To float the window above the main IDE environment, simply let the mouse button go when the cursor is not positioned over any of the indicators.*

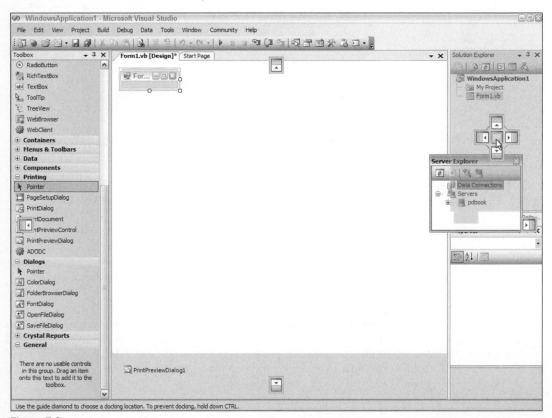

Figure 5-3

Once the windows appear in the layout you want, you can then adjust their height or width by clicking and dragging the pertinent edge of the window, and set each window's auto-hide property with the pin button. Note that unpinning one tool window in a tabbed set will automatically hide the others.

Importing and Exporting IDE Settings

Once you have the IDE in exactly the configuration you want, with the various tool windows placed and sized appropriately and any menu and toolbar customizations done, you may want to back up the settings for future use. This is done by exporting the IDE settings to a file, which can then be used to restore the settings or even transfer the settings to a series of Visual Studio 2005 installations so that they all share the same IDE setup.

To export the current configuration, select Tools⇨Import and Export Settings to start the Import and Export Settings Wizard, shown in Figure 5-4. The first step in the wizard is to select the Export option and which settings are to be backed up during the export procedure.

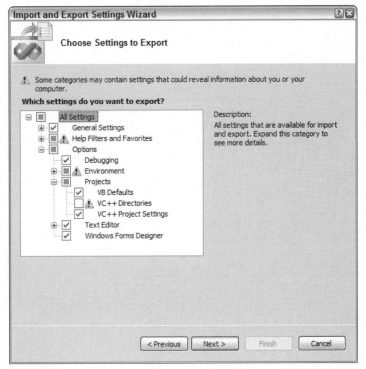

Figure 5-4

As displayed in Figure 5-4, a variety of grouped options can be exported. The screenshot shows the Options section expanded, revealing that the Debugging and Projects settings will be backed up along with the Text Editor and Windows Forms Designer configurations. As the small exclamation icons indicate, some settings are not included in the export by default, because they contain information that may infringe on your privacy. You will need to select these sections manually if you wish them to be included in the backup.

The General Settings section, shown in Figure 5-4 in collapsed state, contains a large array of different settings that can be included or excluded from the backup process. You can choose to back up your settings for individual windows and lists, the Toolbox, and even more esoteric options such as file extension mappings.

After you select the settings you require to be exported, click the Next button to specify where the settings should be saved. Visual Studio 2005 will generate a default filename and location, but you can override either if necessary. Depending on the selection of options, the backup process can take up to a couple of minutes to collect the necessary information.

Importing a settings file is just as easy. The same wizard is used but you select the Import option on the first screen. Rather than simply overwrite the current configuration, the wizard allows you to back up the current setup first (see Figure 5-5).

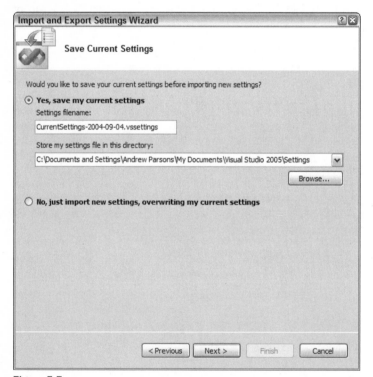

Figure 5-5

You can then select from a list of preset configuration files — the same set of files from which you can choose when you first start Visual Studio 2005 — or browse to a file that you created previously. Once the settings file has been chosen, you can then choose to only import certain sections of the configuration.

The wizard excludes some sections by default, such as the list of External Tools or Command Aliases, so that you don't inadvertently overwrite customized settings. Make sure you select these sections if you want to do a full restore.

If you just want to restore the configuration of Visual Studio 2005 to one of the default presets, you can choose the Reset All Settings option in the opening screen of the wizard, rather than go through the import process.

Splitting Up the Workspace

When using the default Tabbed Windows layout, you normally only see one file at a time in the main workspace. This can be frustrating if you're constantly switching back and forth between two files. For example, when you're working with a form, sometimes you need to work with both Design and Code views simultaneously, and the constant switching between the tabs can be awkward.

As mentioned previously in Chapter 2, you could switch to Multiple Documents view and tile the various windows like previous development environments have done in the past. However, Visual Studio 2005 provides an alternative solution — splitting the workspace either horizontally or vertically.

To split the workspace, choose Window⇨New Horizontal Tab Group or Window⇨New Vertical Tab Group depending on the orientation of the split you need. Figure 5-6 shows the workspace with a single vertical split. Alternatively, you can click and drag the tab off the tab list. Visual Studio will present a small context menu that enables you to choose which type of split you want to perform (or a Cancel button if you didn't intend to split the workspace at all).

You can split the workspace into more than two groups too, with the only limit being that you can't have empty tab groups, and you can't have the one file view in multiple tab groups (the Design view of a form can only be shown in one tab group at a time).

Files can be moved between tab groups by right-clicking their tab and choosing Move to Previous Tab Group or Move to Next Tab Group. These commands are also available in the Window menu once multiple tab groups are visible.

You can split the workspace either horizontally or vertically at any one time, but not both.

If you do need to view the same file in two parts, which is often the case when you're writing code in one section of a class or module that refers to another section of the same code module, you can choose the Window⇨Split command to add a horizontal bar for the code window (this command is only available for code windows, as it doesn't make sense to perform a similar split in Design view).

An alternative method to splitting the code window is to click and drag the small bar above the vertical scrollbar in the code window itself.

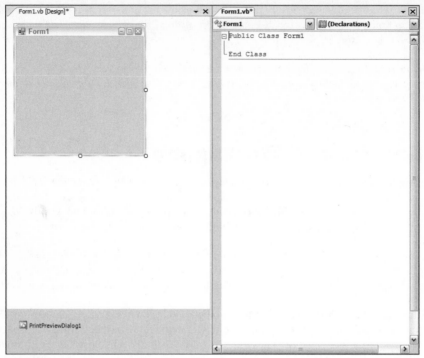

Figure 5-6

Summary

By now you've configured your environment to suit your own working style. The Toolbox contains the elements you need, the Solution Explorer shows the items within your projects in a logical manner, and the various windows of most use to you are positioned in a logical fashion for the way you work. You can also back up all these settings so you don't need to set them again. In the next chapter you'll capitalize on all this work by seeing Visual Studio 2005 in action when designing forms, revealing how the tool windows work with you to efficiently design window layouts.

6

Form Design

Now that you have the Visual Studio 2005 IDE set up in a way that suits you, it's time to take a look at the ways it can help you design your forms and windows. From simple drag-and-drop procedures to place graphical controls onto the form, through the handling of nonvisual elements, to advanced placement and alignment controls, the form editor built in to Visual Studio 2005 provides you with immense power without having to dive into code.

This chapter walks you through these processes, bringing you up to speed with the latest additions to the toolset so that you can maximize your efficiency when creating Windows applications.

The Form Itself

When you create a Windows application project, Visual Studio 2005 will automatically create a single blank form ready for your user interface design (see Figure 6-1). Before you commence placing elements on the form, you might want to set a few properties on it to match your application requirements.

The first action you're likely to take is to set the physical size of the form. To do this you have two options available. The first is to grab any of the three size grippers on the bottom and right edges of the form in Design view and drag it to the size you require.

However, this method can be inexact, as you don't get any feedback on precisely how big the form is. The second option you can choose to set the size is to do it via properties. At the bottom-right corner of Figure 6-1 is the Properties window (you'll see this in detail in a moment), which contains many attributes for the form when it is selected as the active component. The Size property is a compound property made up of Height and Width. You can set the dimensions of the form with pixel values by entering either individual values into the Height and Width properties, or a compound Size value in the form width, height.

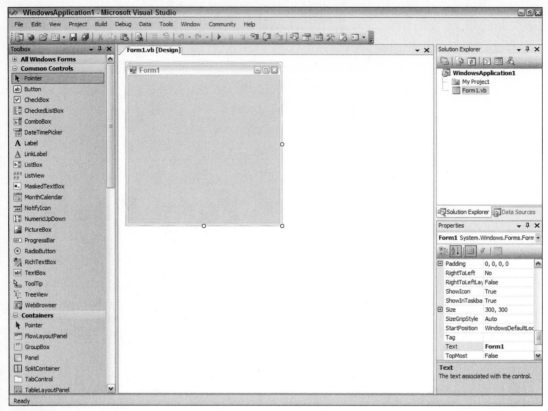

Figure 6-1

The default form created for your application is defined with the most commonly used properties, such as icon; minimize, maximize, and close buttons, and a resizable border. Changing any of these settings is just as simple as changing the `Size` property.

The Properties window shown in Figure 6-2 displays a subset of the available properties for customizing the form's appearance and behavior. As mentioned in Chapter 1, you can arrange the properties either alphabetically or into categories, such as those shown in Figure 6-2. To change most properties, it's just a matter of selecting it from the list and overwriting the existing value with the new data. For example, to change the form's caption bar text from `Form1` to something more appropriate for your application, you would locate the `Text` property and overtype `Form1` with your new caption text.

Some properties have only a small set of options from which to choose. These will be presented in a `ComboBox` from which you select the correct option. For consistency, the Properties window uses this method for simple true or false properties as well.

Figure 6-2

To change the other components that appear in the caption bar of your form, you can use the following properties:

Property	Effect
ShowIcon	This toggle option enables you to hide the form's icon in the top-left corner.
MinimizeButton	The MinimizeButton option enables you to indicate that the minimize button is not required. If the maximize button is displayed, rather than hide the minimize button, setting this value to False will simply disable the button from being used at runtime.
MaximizeButton	Similar to the MinimizeButton option, this property controls whether the maximize button (or restore button depending on the current state of the form) is required. If both the MinimizeButton and MaximizeButton options are set to False, then both buttons will be removed from the caption bar of the form.

Table continued on following page

Property	Effect
HelpButton	Inactive by default, if you want to supply help to your application in the form of the quick help icon, set this property to True. Note that this property setting is ignored if the minimize and maximize buttons are displayed.
ControlBox	Rather than set individual controls for each of the icons and buttons on the caption bar, you can use this property to remove them all at once.

If the form's purpose differs from the normal behavior, you may need a fixed-size window or a special border, as seen in tool windows. The FormBorderStyle property controls how this aspect of your form's appearance is handled. The following table describes the different values and what effect they have on the display of your form:

FormBorderStyle	Effect
FixedSingle	A single-pixel border is drawn around the form but the form itself is fixed in size. Note that if you use this with the MaximizeButton property set to True, your users will still be able to switch the form's state between maximized and the regular, fixed size, which may be undesirable.
Fixed3D	Similar to FixedSingle, Fixed3D draws the form with a sunken look. This style of window is not used actively in modern applications but it may be useful to create a different feel for your application's form.
FixedDialog	FixedDialog is the style of border used for dialog boxes such as color and font selection and confirmation dialogs. It also uses a single-pixel border. The main difference between this and FixedSingle is that the icon is not displayed by default using this style of border.
Sizable	This is the default setting for this property. It draws a slightly wider border suitable for gripping and resizing.
FixedToolWindow	Tool windows are those small windows that are simply headed with a caption bar of text and the close button. This style restricts the size to whatever you specify.
SizableToolWindow	The same as FixedToolWindow except that the end user can resize the window. This is the style Visual Studio 2005 uses for its own tool windows, such as the Properties window.

You can use these properties in conjunction to easily create any of the standard window designs you see in the Windows system, from fixed dialog options screens to sizable forms such as those you see in Notepad.

Form Design Preferences

Before you start placing components on the form, there are some IDE settings you can change to simplify your user interface design phase. In the Options dialog (shown in Figure 6-3) of Visual Studio 2005 there are two pages of preferences that deal with the Windows Forms Designer.

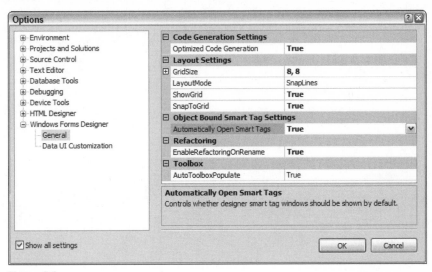

Figure 6-3

The main settings that affect your design are the layout settings. By default, Visual Studio 2005 uses a new layout mode called SnapLines. Rather than position visible components on the form via an invisible grid, SnapLines helps you position them based on the context of surrounding controls and the form's own borders. You'll see how to use this new mode in a moment, but if you prefer the older style of form design that originated in Visual Basic 6 and was used in the first two versions of Visual Studio .NET, you can change the `LayoutMode` property to `SnapToGrid`.

Once the `LayoutMode` property has been changed the other Layout Settings preferences become available. The first is `GridSize`, which is used when positioning and sizing controls on the form. As you move them around the form, they will snap to specific points based on the values you enter here. Most of the time, you'll find a grid of 8 × 8 (the default) too large for fine-tuning, so changing this to something such as 4 × 4 might be more appropriate.

`ShowGrid` will display a network of dots on your form's design surface when you're in `SnapToGrid` mode so you can more easily see where the controls will be positioned when you move them. Finally, setting the `SnapToGrid` property to `False` will deactivate all layout aids and result in pure free-form form design.

While you're looking at this page of options, you may want to change the `Automatically Open Smart Tags` value to `False`. The default setting of `True` will pop open the smart tag task list associated with any control you add to the form, which can be distracting during your initial form design phase.

The other page of preferences that you can customize for the Windows Forms Designer is the Data UI Customization section (see Figure 6-4). This is used to automatically bind various controls to data types when connecting to a database.

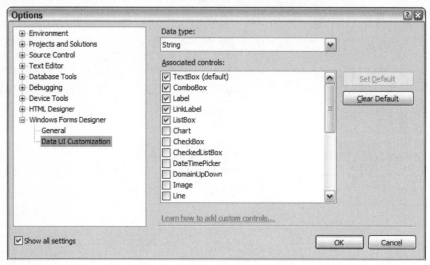

Figure 6-4

As you can see in the screenshot, the `String` data type is associated with five commonly used controls, with the `TextBox` control set as the default. Whenever a database field that is defined as a `String` data type is added to your form, Visual Studio 2005 will automatically generate a `TextBox` control to contain the value.

The other controls marked as associated with the data type (`ComboBox`, `Label`, `LinkLabel`, and `ListBox`) can be optionally used when editing the data source and style, as described in Part VII of this book.

> *It's worth reviewing the default controls associated with each data type at this time and making sure you're happy with the types chosen. For instance, all* `DateTime` *data type variables will automatically be represented with a* `DateTimePicker` *control, but you may want it to be bound to a* `MonthCalendar`.

Adding Controls to Your Form

You can add two types of components to your Windows forms: graphical elements that actually reside on the form itself, and service components that do not have a specific visual interface displaying on the form. The service components will be discussed in a moment, but for now you'll learn how to add the visual controls to your form and customize them.

Adding graphical controls to your form is done in one of two ways. The first method is to locate the control you want to add in the Toolbox and double-click its entry. Visual Studio 2005 will place it in a default location on the form — the first control will be placed adjacent to the top and left borders of the form, with subsequent controls tiled down and to the right.

The second method is to click and drag the entry on the list onto the form. As you drag over available space on the form, the mouse cursor will change to show you where the control will be positioned. This enables you to directly position the control where you want it, rather than first add it to the form and then move it to the desired location. Either way, once the control is on the form, you can move it as many times as you like, so it doesn't really matter how you get the control onto the form's design surface.

When you design your form layouts in SnapLines mode (see previous section), a variety of guidelines will be displayed as you move controls around in the form layout. These guidelines are recommended "best practice" positioning and sizing markers so you can easily position controls in context to each other and the edge of the form.

Figure 6-5 shows a `Button` control being moved toward the top-left corner of the form. As it gets near the recommended position, the control will snap to the exact recommended distance from the top and left borders, and small blue guidelines will be displayed.

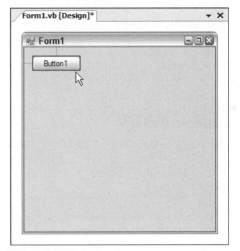

Figure 6-5

Guidelines for Controls

These guidelines work for both positioning and sizing a control, enabling you to snap to any of the four borders of the form — but they're just the tip of the SnapLines iceberg. When additional components are present on the form, many more guidelines will begin to appear as you move a control around.

In Figure 6-6, you can see the `Button2` control being moved. The guideline on the left is the same as previously discussed, indicating the ideal distance from the left border of the form. However, now three additional guidelines are displayed. Two blue vertical lines appear on either side of the control, confirming that the control is aligned with both the left and right sides of the other button control already on the form (this is expected because the buttons are the same width). The other vertical line indicates the ideal gap between two buttons.

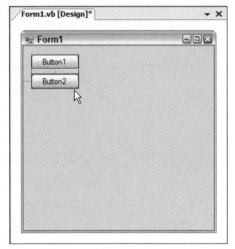

Figure 6-6

Vertically Aligning Text Controls

One problem with alignment of controls that has persisted since the very early versions of Visual Basic is the vertical alignment of text within a control, such as a `TextBox` compared to a `Label`. The problem was that the text within each control was at a different vertical distance from the top border of the control, resulting in the text itself not aligning.

Many programmers went through the pain of calculating the appropriate number of pixels that one control or the other had to be shifted in order to have the text portions line up with each other (and more often than not it was a smaller number of pixels than the grid size, resulting in manual positioning via the Properties window or in code).

As shown in Figure 6-7, an additional guideline is now available when lining up controls that have text aspects to them. In this example, the Cell Phone label is being lined up with the textbox containing the actual Cell Phone value. A line, colored magenta by default, appears and snaps the control in place. You can still align the label to the top or bottom borders of the textbox by shifting it slightly and snapping it to their guidelines, but this new guideline takes the often painful guesswork out of lining up text.

Note that the other guidelines show how the label is horizontally aligned with the `Label` controls above it, and it is positioned the recommended distance from the textbox.

Figure 6-7

Automatic Formatting of Multiple Controls

Visual Studio 2005 gives you additional tools to automatically format the appearance of your controls once they are positioned approximately where you want them. The Format menu is normally only accessible when you're in the Design view of a form (see Figure 6-8). From here you can have the IDE automatically align, resize, and position groups of controls, as well as set the order of the controls in the event that they overlap each other.

The form displayed in Figure 6-8 contains several TextBox controls, all with differing widths. This looks messy and should be cleaned up by setting them all to the same width as the widest control. The old way of doing this would be to adjust the width of each one in turn to match the widest control — the Email field. However, as shown in the screenshot, the Format menu provides you with the capability to automatically resize the controls to the same width.

The commands in the Make Same Size menu use the first control selected as the template for the dimensions, so in this case you would first select the Email field, and then add to the selection by holding the Ctrl key down and clicking each of the other TextBox controls. Once they're all selected, choose the Make Same Size⇨Width command.

Automatic alignment of multiple controls can be performed in the same way. First, select the item whose border should be used as a base, and then select all of the other elements that should be aligned with it. Next, select Format⇨Align and choose which alignment should be performed. In this example, the Label controls have all been positioned with their right edges aligned. This could have been done using the guidelines, but sometimes it's easier to use this mass alignment option.

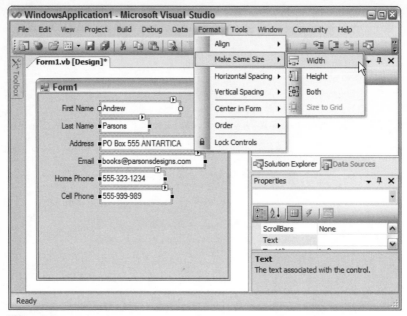

Figure 6-8

Two handy functions are the horizontal and vertical spacing commands. These will automatically adjust the spacing between a set of controls according to the particular option you have selected. The best way to illustrate how effective these commands are is to follow through an example task:

1. Start a new WindowsApplication project and add six `Label` controls and six `TextBox` controls to the form that is generated by Visual Studio. Change the text on the labels to match Figure 6-8: `First Name`, `Last Name`, `Address`, `Email`, `Home Phone`, and `Cell Phone`.

2. Use the SnapLines mode to align the controls to the top edge of the form, and then to the ideal spacing between each `Label` and `TextBox` both vertically and horizontally. Remember to use the text guideline to align the text in the two different types of controls.

3. Once the controls are all positioned in context to each other, you'll notice a large gap below the lowermost controls. This is what you'll use to try out vertical spacing. Move the Cell Phone label and its associated textbox down so they are positioned an ideal distance from the bottom border of the form.

4. Select all of the `TextBox` controls and run the Format➪Vertical Spacing➪Make Equal command as shown in Figure 6-9. Visual Studio will reposition the `TextBox` controls so they span from the topmost control (the First Name textbox) to the bottom Cell Phone textbox with even spacing between each. Repeat the process for the `Label` controls.

   The right side of Figure 6-9 shows the result of the commands with the `Label` and `TextBox` controls repositioned.

An alternative method to change the spacing between the controls to extend them to the bottom of the form is to use the Increase option. This will adjust the spacing in small increments of a few pixels at a time.

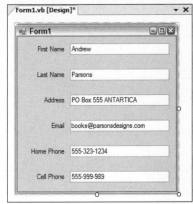
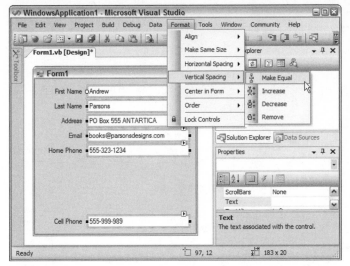

Figure 6-9

Reducing the spacing between the controls can be performed with the Decrease spacing command to perform the process in increments, or the Remove command, to remove all spacing completely.

Locking Control Design

Once you're happy with your form design you will want to start applying changes to the various controls and their properties. However, in the process of selecting controls on the form, you may inadvertently move a control from its desired position, particularly if you're not using either of the snap layout methods or if you have many controls that are being aligned with each other.

Fortunately, Visual Studio 2005 provides a solution in the form of the Lock Controls command, available in the Format menu. When controls are locked, you can select them to set their properties but cannot move them from their position, nor can you change the size of the form itself.

Small padlock icons are displayed on controls that are selected while the Lock Controls feature is active (see Figure 6-10).

Setting Control Properties

Setting the properties on controls is achieved using the Properties window, just as you would for a form's settings. Whereas previously most properties were simple text values, Visual Studio 2005 has increased the number of property editor types, which aids you in setting the values efficiently by restricting them to a particular subset appropriate to the type of property.

Many advanced properties have a set of subordinate properties that can be individually accessed by expanding the entry in the Properties window. Figure 6-11 displays the Properties window for a button, with the Font property expanded to show the individual properties available.

Figure 6-10

Figure 6-11

In addition, many properties provide extended editors, as is the case for Font properties. In Figure 6-11, the extended editor button in the Font property has been selected, causing the Choose Font dialog to appear.

Some of these extended editors invoke full-blown wizards, such as the Data Connection property on some data-bound components, while others have custom-built inline property editors. An example of this is the `Dock` property, for which you can choose a visual representation of how you want the property docked to the containing component or form.

Service-Based Components

As mentioned earlier in this chapter, two kinds of components can be added to your Windows forms — those with visual aspects to them and those without. Service-based components such as timers and dialogs or extender controls such as tooltip and error provider components can all be used to enhance the application; and they work in a similar way to visual controls, with a few exceptions.

Rather than place these components on the form, when you double-click one in the Toolbox, or drag and drop it on to the design surface, Visual Studio 2005 will create a tray area below the Design view of the form and put the new instance of the component type there (see Figure 6-12).

Figure 6-12

To edit the properties of one of these controls, locate its entry in the tray area and open the Properties window.

Smart Tag Tasks

Smart tag technology was introduced in Microsoft Office. It provides inline shortcuts to a small selection of actions you can perform on a particular element. In Microsoft Word, this might be a word or phrase, while in Microsoft Excel it could be a spreadsheet cell. Visual Studio 2005 introduces the concept of design-time smart tags for a number of the controls available to you as a developer.

Whenever a selected control has a smart tag available, a small right-pointing arrow will be displayed on the top-right corner of the control itself. Clicking this smart tag indicator will open up a Tasks menu associated with that particular control.

Figure 6-13 shows the tasks for a `DataGridView` control. The various actions that can be taken usually mirror properties available to you in the Properties window (such as the `Multiline` option for a `TextBox` control), but sometimes they provide quick access to more advanced settings for the component.

In this example, the Edit Columns and Add Column commands are not directly accessible in the list, while the Data Source and Enable settings directly correlate to individual properties (for example, Enable Adding is equivalent to the `AllowUserToAddRows` property).

> *While the Edit Columns and Add Column commands are not represented by individual properties, you'll see in the next discussion that they are still accessible from the Properties window.*

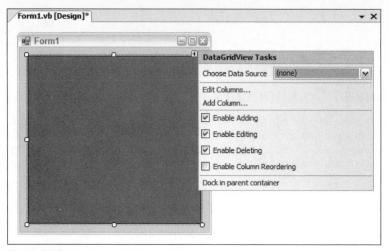

Figure 6-13

Additional Commands

Some components have extra design-time actions that can be performed beyond the simple setting of control properties. These functions are accessible in the Properties window via the Commands section, which sits between the Properties window and the description of the selected property.

The Commands area of the Properties window can be hidden to give you more space when working with the regular properties. Right-click anywhere in the Properties window and select the Commands item from the context menu to toggle it off. To redisplay it, repeat this process and the Commands window will be shown again.

The Commands list is not visible if the selected component does not have functions that can be performed.

Figure 6-14 shows the Properties window view for a ListView control. As you can see in the middle pane, three advanced commands can be executed against this type of component: Edit Items, Edit Columns, and Edit Groups. Each of these hyperlinked labels will fire off a different collection editor dialog so you can easily customize the appearance of the ListView.

The Commands list is where the Edit Columns and Add Column functions (mentioned in the preceding discussion on smart tag tasks) will appear when designing a DataGridView.

Some controls, such as the MenuStrip component, will have commands that can automatically populate them with default values or add a suitable containing component and move the selected control into that container to meet best practices design.

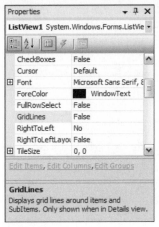

Figure 6-14

Container Controls

Several controls, known as *container controls,* are designed specifically to help you with your form's layout and appearance. Rather than have their own appearance, they hold other controls within their bounds. Once a container houses a set of controls, you no longer need to move the child controls individually, but instead just move the container. Using a combination of Dock and Anchor values, you can have whole sections of your form's layout automatically redesign themselves at runtime in response to the resizing of the form and the container controls that hold them.

Panel and SplitContainer

The `Panel` control is used to group components that are associated with each other. When placed on a form, it can be sized and positioned anywhere within the form's design surface. Because it's a container control, clicking within its boundaries will select anything inside it, so in order to move it, Visual Studio 2005 places a move icon at the top-left corner of the control. Clicking and dragging this icon enables you to reposition the `Panel`.

The `SplitContainer` control (shown in Figure 6-15) automatically creates two `Panel` controls when added to a form (or another container control). It divides the space into two sections, each of which you can control individually. At runtime, users can resize the two spaces by dragging the splitter bar that divides them. `SplitContainers` can be either vertical (as in Figure 6-15) or horizontal, and they can be contained with other `SplitContainer` controls to form a complex layout that can then be easily customized by the end user without you needing to write any code.

> *Sometimes it's hard to select the actual container control when it contains other components, such as in the case of the `SplitContainer` housing the two `Panel` controls. To gain direct access to the `Split Container` control itself, you can either locate it in the drop-down list in the Properties window, or*

right-click on one of the Panel *controls and choose the appropriate* Select *command that corresponds to the* SplitContainer. *This context menu will contain a* Select *command for every container control in the hierarchy of containers, right up to the* Form *itself.*

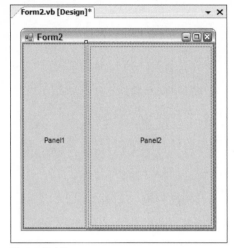

Figure 6-15

FlowLayoutPanel

The FlowLayoutPanel control enables you to create form designs with a behavior similar to web browsers. Rather than explicitly position each control within this particular container control, Visual Studio will simply set each component you add to the next available space. By default, the controls will flow left to right, and then top to bottom, but you can use the FlowDirection property to reverse this order in any configuration depending on the requirements of your application.

Figure 6-16 displays the same form with six button controls housed within a FlowLayoutPanel container. The FlowLayoutPanel was set to fill the entire form's design surface, so as the form is resized, the container is also automatically sized. As the form gets wider and there is available space, the controls begin to be realigned to flow left to right before descending down the form.

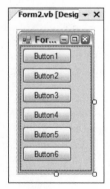 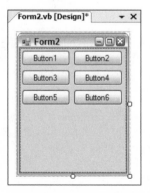 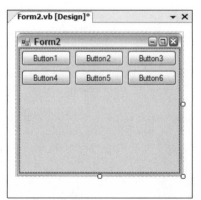

Figure 6-16

TableLayoutPanel

An alternative to the previously discussed container controls is the `TableLayoutPanel` container. This control works much like a table in Microsoft Word or in a typical web browser, with each cell acting as an individual container for a single control.

> *Note that you cannot add multiple controls within a single cell directly. You can, however, place another container control such as a* `Panel` *within the cell, and then place the required components within that child container.*

Placing a control directly into a cell will automatically position the control to the top-left corner of the table cell. You can use the `Dock` property to override this behavior and position it as required.

The `TableLayoutPanel` container enables you to easily create a structured, formal layout in your form with advanced features, such as the capability to automatically grow by adding more rows as additional child controls are added.

Figure 6-17 shows a form with a `TableLayoutPanel` added to the design surface. The smart tag tasks were then opened and the Edit Rows and Columns command executed. As a result, the Column and Row Styles dialog is displayed so you can adjust the individual formatting options for each column and row. The dialog displays several tips for designing table layouts in your forms, including spanning multiple rows and columns and how to align controls within a cell. You can change the way the cells are sized here as well as add or remove additional columns and rows.

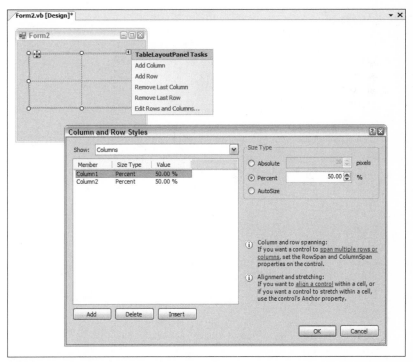

Figure 6-17

Summary

In this chapter you received a good grounding in how to design Windows forms. The various controls and their properties enable you to very quickly and easily create complex layouts that can respond to user interaction in a large variety of ways.

This discussion serves to complete your introduction to the world of Visual Studio 2005. The next section goes into detail about handling solutions and their projects.

Part II

Project and Solution Design

7

Projects and Solutions

Other than the simplest applications, such as Hello World, most applications require more than one source file. This raises a number of issues, such as how the files will be named, where they will be located, and whether they can be reused. Within Visual Studio 2005, the concept of a *solution*, containing a series of *projects*, is used to enable developers to track, manage, and work with their source files. The IDE has a number of built-in features that aim to simplify this process, while still allowing developers to get the most out of their applications. This chapter examines the structure of solutions and projects, looking at available project types and how they can be configured.

Solution Structure

Whenever you're working within Visual Studio, you will have a solution open. When you're editing an ad hoc file, this will be a temporary solution that you can elect to discard when you have completed your work. However, the solution enables you to manage the files that you're currently working with, so in most cases saving the solution means that you can return to what you were doing at a later date without having to locate and reopen the files on which you were working.

The most common way to structure applications written within Visual Studio is to have a single solution containing a number of projects. Each project can then be made up of a series of both code files and folders. Figure 7-1 illustrates a typical multi-project solution.

Folders are used to aid source code navigation and have no application meaning associated with them (with the exception of web applications, which have specially named folders that have specific meaning in this context). Some developers use folder names that correspond to the namespace to which the classes belong. For example, if class `Person` is found within a folder called `DataClasses` in a project called `FirstProject`, the fully qualified name of the class could be `FirstProject.DataClasses.Person`.

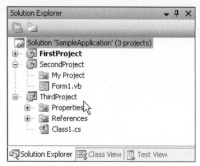

Figure 7-1

There is often a misconception that projects necessarily correspond to .NET assemblies. While this is mostly true, it is possible for multiple .dll files to represent a single .NET assembly. However, this case is not supported by Visual Studio 2005, so this book assumes that a project will correspond to an assembly.

The main window in which you work with solutions and projects is the Solution Explorer, as shown previously in Figure 7-1. By default, new solutions will only show project information about the first project. However, when additional projects are added, the solution node appears. This is configurable via the Tools⇨Options menu. Under the Projects and Solutions tree node is an option Always Show Solution that controls whether the solution node is visible for single-project solutions. Regardless of this setting, a solution file is always generated to maintain information about the application being built.

In Visual Studio 2005, the format for solution and project files has significantly changed. In fact, the whole mechanism used to build applications has changed. MSBuild is the new engine for compiling, linking, and assembling applications. As an external tool, similar to the VB and C# compilers, it can be executed from the command line. Also like other build tools, such as Nant, MSBuild uses a build file, which specifies targets to be built and other information pertaining to the order and build mechanism to use. The new project file format is in fact a build file and can be consumed by MSBuild to build a project.

MSBuild was put together to enable developers to tailor the way their applications are built. This is particularly relevant for large applications where the build process may need to be done in multiple stages and has dependencies that need to be built in a specific order. As MSBuild can be run from the command line, it is easy to schedule the build process and integrate it with source control for continuous builds based on source change notifications. More information about the structure of a build file can be found at C:\WINDOWS\Microsoft.NET\Framework\v2.0.50727\MSBuild.

In addition to tracking which files are contained within an application, solution and project files can record other information, such as how a particular file should be compiled, project settings, resources, and much more. Visual Studio 2005 introduces a new non-modal dialog for editing project properties, while solution properties still open in a separate window. As you might expect, the project properties are those properties pertaining only to the project in question, such as assembly information and references, whereas solution properties determine the overall build configurations for the application.

Solution File Format

Visual Studio 2005 actually creates two files for a solution, with extensions .suo and .sln (solution file). The first of these is a rather uninteresting binary file, and hence difficult to edit. It contains user-specific information—for example, which files were open when the solution was last closed and the location of breakpoints. This file is marked as hidden, so it doesn't appear in the solution folder using Windows Explorer.

The solution file contains information about the solution, such as the list of projects, build configurations, and other nonproject-related settings. Unlike many files used by Visual Studio 2005, the solution file is not an XML document. The format is VB in nature, as it stores information in blocks, as shown in the following example Solution file:

```
Microsoft Visual Studio Solution File, Format Version 9.00
# Visual Studio 2005
Project("{F184B08F-C81C-45F6-A57F-5ABD9991F28F}") = "FirstProject",
    "FirstProject\FirstProject.vbproj", "{FD041258-F0D6-4A69-9426-1A40B52126D4}"
EndProject
Global
    GlobalSection(SolutionConfigurationPlatforms) = preSolution
        Debug|Any CPU = Debug|Any CPU
    EndGlobalSection
    GlobalSection(ProjectConfigurationPlatforms) = postSolution
    {FD041258-F0D6-4A69-9426-1A40B52126D4}.Debug|Any CPU.ActiveCfg = Debug|Any CPU
    {FD041258-F0D6-4A69-9426-1A40B52126D4}.Debug|Any CPU.Build.0 = Debug|Any CPU
    EndGlobalSection
    GlobalSection(SolutionProperties) = preSolution
        HideSolutionNode = FALSE
    EndGlobalSection
EndGlobal
```

In this example, the solution consists of a single project, FirstProject, and a Global section outlining settings that apply to the solution. For instance, the solution will be hidden because the HideSolutionNode setting is FALSE.

Solution Properties

The solution Properties dialog can be reached by right-clicking on the Solution node in the Solution Explorer and selecting Properties. This dialog contains two nodes to partition Common and Configuration properties, as shown in Figure 7-2.

If your dialog is missing the Configuration Properties node, you need to check the Show Advanced Build configurations property in the Projects and Solutions node of the Options window, accessible from the Tools menu. Unfortunately, this property is not checked for some of the setting profiles—for example, the Visual Basic Developer profile. Checking this option not only displays this node, but also displays the configuration selection drop-down in the Project Settings window, discussed later in this chapter.

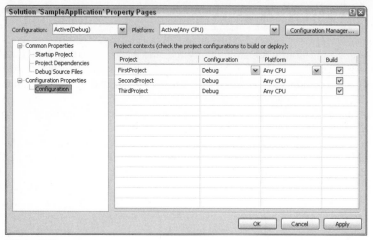

Figure 7-2

The following sections describe the Common and Configuration properties nodes in more detail.

Common Properties

There are three options when defining the Startup Project for an application, and they are somewhat self-explanatory. Selecting Current Selection will start the project that has current focus in the Solution Explorer. Single Startup will ensure that the same project starts up each time. This is the default selection, as most applications have only a single startup project. The last option, Multiple Startup Projects, allows for multiple projects to be started in a particular order. This can be useful if you have a client/server application specified in a single solution and you want them both to be running. When running multiple projects, it is also relevant to control the order in which they start up. Use the up and down arrows next to the project list to control the order in which projects are started.

The Project Dependencies section is used to indicate other projects on which a specific project is dependent. For the most part, Visual Studio will manage this for you as you add and remove project references for a given project. However, sometimes you may want to create dependencies between projects to ensure that they are built in the correct order. Visual Studio uses its list of dependencies to determine the order in which projects should be built. This window prevents you from inadvertently adding circular references and from removing necessary project dependencies.

In the Debug Source Files section, you can provide a list of directories through which Visual Studio can search for source files when debugging. This is the default list that is searched prior to the Find Source dialog being displayed. You can also list source files that Visual Studio should not try to locate. If you click Cancel when prompted to locate a source file, the file will be added to this list.

Configuration Properties

Both projects and solutions have build configurations associated with them that determine which items are built and how. Somewhat confusing is that there is actually no correlation between a project configuration, which essentially determines how things are built, and a solution configuration, which determines which projects are built, other than they might have the same name. A new solution will define both Debug and Release (solution) configurations, which correspond to building all projects within the solution in Debug or Release (project) configurations.

For example, a new solution configuration called Test can be created, which consists of two projects: MyClassLibrary and MyClassLibraryTest. When you build your application in Test configuration, you want MyClassLibary to be built in Release mode so you're testing as close to what you would release as possible. However, in order to be able to step through your test code, you want to build the test project in Debug mode.

When you build in Release mode, you don't want the Test solution to be built or deployed with your application. In this case, you can specify in the Test solution configuration that you want the MyClassLibrary project to be built in Release mode, and that the MyClassLibraryTest project should not be built.

Switching between configurations can be easily achieved via the Configuration drop-down on the standard toolbar. However, it is not as easy to switch between platforms, as the Platform drop-down is not on any of the toolbars. To make this available, select View⇨Toolbars⇨Customize. From the Build category on the Commands, the Solution Platforms item can be dragged onto a toolbar.

You will notice that when the Configuration Properties node is selected, the Configuration and Platform drop-down boxes are enabled. The Configuration drop-down contains each of the available solution configurations (Debug and Release by default), Active, and All. Similarly, the Platform drop-down contains each of the available platforms (Any CPU by default), Active, and All. Whenever these drop-downs appear and are enabled, you can specify the settings on that page on a per-configuration and/or per-platform basis. You can also use the Configuration Manager button to add additional solution configurations and/or platforms.

When adding additional solution configurations, there is an option (checked by default) to create corresponding project configurations for existing projects (projects will be set to build with this configuration by default for this new solution configuration), and the option to base the new configuration on an existing configuration. If the Create Project Configurations option is checked and the new configuration is based on an existing configuration, the new project configurations will copy the project configurations specified for the existing configuration.

The options available for creating new platform configurations are limited by the types of CPU available: Itanium, x86, and x64. Again, the new platform configuration can be based on existing configurations, and the option to create project platform configurations is also available.

The other thing you can specify in the solution configuration file is the type of CPU for which you are building. This is particularly relevant if you want to deploy to 64-bit architecture machines.

All these solution settings can be reached directly from the right-click context menu from the Solution node in the Solution Explorer window. While the Set Startup Projects menu item opens the solution configuration window, the Configuration Manager and Project Dependencies items open the Configuration Manager and Project Dependencies window. Interestingly, an additional option in the right-click context menu doesn't appear in the solution configuration, the Build Order. When selected, this opens the Project Dependencies window, which lists the build order in a separate tab. This tab is not particularly useful, as build order is actually controlled by dependency order, but it can be used to double-check that projects are being built in the correct order.

Project Types

Projects can be broadly classified into four categories. The first three appear as true projects within the Solution Explorer to the extent that they have a project file (for example, .vbproj or .csproj) that conforms to the MSBuild schema. The last project type is that of a web project (including web service projects). Due to the dynamic nature of web applications, significant effort has gone into making web applications less reliant on a project file. These project types do not necessarily correspond to the project templates that appear in the New Project dialog. Selecting a project template will create a new project, of a specific project type, and populate it with initial classes and settings. Following are the four project types:

❑ **Windows Application:** A Windows Application project type creates an executable (.exe) assembly that runs without a console window being displayed. This includes both Windows Forms and Windows Service applications.

❑ **Class Library:** As its name suggests, the Class Library project type creates an assembly that can easily be referenced by other projects. A class library reuses the familiar .dll extension.

❑ **Console Application:** Similar to the Windows Application, the Console Application creates an executable (.exe). However, this type of project runs with a console displayed for output purposes.

❑ **Web Applications:** As mentioned earlier, Web Applications no longer have a project file, as the dynamic compilation process enables the site to be updated without manually recompiling.

Project File Format

Visual Studio 2005 is the first IDE that uses the new build engine, MSBuild, which is controlled via an XML document. Each project file is now an XML document that conforms to the MSBuild schema (see C:\WINDOWS\Microsoft.NET\Framework\v2.0.50727\MSBuild\Microsoft.Build.Core.xsd). To view the project file in XML format, right-click the project and select Unload. Then right-click the project again and select Edit *<project name>*. This will display the project file in the XML editor, complete with IntelliSense.

Project Properties

The project properties can be reached by either right-clicking on the Project node in Solution Explorer and then selecting Properties, or by double-clicking on My Project (Properties in C#) just under the Project node. In contrast to solution properties, the project properties do not display in a modal dialog. Instead they appear as an additional tab alongside your code files. This was done in part to make it easier to navigate between code files and project properties, but it also makes it possible to open project properties of multiple projects at the same time. Figure 7-3 illustrates the project settings for a project called FirstProject. This section walks you through the vertical tabs on the project editor for a VB.NET project. C# projects have a different layout and use different terms for the properties, but they still generate a build file that conforms to the MSBuild schema.

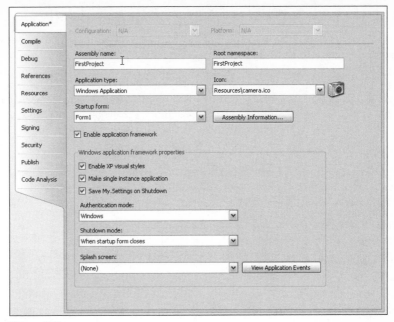

Figure 7-3

The project properties editor contains a series of vertical tabs that group the properties. As changes are made to properties in the tabs, a star is added to the corresponding vertical tab. This functionality is limited, however, as it does not indicate which fields within the tab have been modified.

Application

The Application tab, visible in Figure 7-3, enables the developer to set the information about the assembly that will be created when the project is compiled. These include attributes such as the output type (i.e., Windows or Console Application, Class Library, Windows Service, or a Web Control Library), application icon, and startup object.

Assembly Information

Attributes that previously had to be configured by hand in the AssemblyInfo file contained in the project can also be set via the Assembly Information button. This information is important, as it shows up when an application is installed and when the properties of a file are viewed in Windows Explorer. Figure 7-4 shows the assembly information for a sample application.

Each of the properties set in the Assembly Information dialog is represented by an attribute that is applied to the assembly. This means that the assembly can be queried in code to retrieve this information. Alternatively, the My namespace (covered in Chapter 24) can be used to retrieve this information.

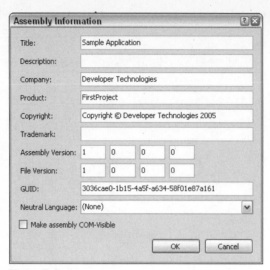

Figure 7-4

Application Framework (VB.NET Only)

Additional application settings are available for VB projects because they can use the Application Framework that is exclusive to VB.NET. This extends the standard event model to provide a series of application events and settings that control the behavior of the application. The Application Framework can be enabled by checking the Enable Application Framework checkbox. The following three checkboxes control the behavior of the Application Framework:

❑ **Enable XP visual styles:** XP visual styles are a feature that significantly improve the look and feel of Windows XP, as it provides a much smoother interface through the use of rounded buttons and controls that dynamically change color as the mouse passes over them. VB.NET applications enable XP styles by default and can be disabled from the Project Settings dialog, or controlled from within code.

❑ **Make single instance application:** Most applications support multiple instances running concurrently. However, an application opened more than two or three times may be only run once, with successive executions simply invoking the original application. Such an application could be a document editor, whereby successive executions simply open a different document. This functionality can be easily added by marking the application as a single instance.

❑ **Save My.Settings on Shutdown:** Selecting the Save My.Settings on Shutdown option will ensure that any changes made to user-scoped settings will be preserved, saving the settings provided prior to the application shutting down. It is also possible to select the authentication mode for the application.

Where an application is marked as a single instance, if a second instance of the application is run, then the request is rerouted to the existing application. If the application is being opened by double-clicking on a document, or via a shortcut whereby command arguments have been provided, it is important for the arguments to be passed through to the existing application. This process is handled by the *application events*.

Five application events are provided to give the developer information about the status of the application. These events can be accessed by clicking the View Application Events button (refer to the bottom-right corner of Figure 7-3). The following code snippet shows the contents of ApplicationEvents.vb, which is automatically created when the View Application Events button is pressed:

```
Namespace My
    ' The following events are available for MyApplication:
    '
    ' Startup:  Raised when the application starts, before the startup form is
    '           created.
    ' Shutdown: Raised after all application forms are closed.  This event is not
    '           raised if the application terminates abnormally.
    ' UnhandledException: Raised if an unhandled exception is raised.
    ' StartupNextInstance: Raised when launching a single-instance application
    '                      and the application is already active.
    ' NetworkAvailabilityChanged: Raised when the network connection is connected
    '                             or disconnected.
    Partial Friend Class MyApplication
        Private Sub MyApplication_StartupNextInstance _
                        (ByVal sender As Object, _
                        ByVal e As StartupNextInstanceEventArgs) _
                                Handles Me.StartupNextInstance
            For Each arg As String In e.CommandLine
                MsgBox("Command line arguement: " & arg)
            Next
        End Sub
    End Class
End Namespace
```

The Startup and Shutdown events are triggered when an application (only available to Windows Forms applications) is started for the first time and shut down, respectively. The NetworkAvailabilityChanged event is triggered when changes are made to network availability. This event is limited to detecting changes in the connectivity between the PC and the hub. Changes further along, such as between the hub and the rest of the network, will not be triggered.

If an exception is raised by the application that is not handled, an UnhandledException event will be raised. This enables the developer to easily log and handle these exceptions. Lastly, the StartupNext Instance event is raised when an application is marked as single instance and a second instance of the application is launched. The arguments passed into this event handler include a list of command-line arguments so that they can be processed by the existing application.

The Application Framework also gives the developer more control over what happens when the application starts and shuts down. Selecting a form as the splash screen ensures that this form is displayed when you start your application. By default, the splash screen will only remain visible while your application is loading. If your application loads quickly, you may not see the splash screen. A workaround is to handle the application Startup event and set the minimum display time for the splash screen:

```
Private Sub MyApplication_Startup _
            (ByVal sender As Object, ByVal e As StartupEventArgs) _
                Handles Me.Startup
    My.Application.MinimumSplashScreenDisplayTime = 2000
End Sub
```

Most applications are built around a main form that remains visible for the duration of the application. An alternative strategy is to have a manager class that manages which forms are visible. This is easily done by changing the shutdown mode for the application to When Last Form Closes.

Compile

The Compile section of the project settings, as shown in Figure 7-5, enables the developer to control how and where the project is built. For example, the output path can be modified so that it points to an alternative location. This might be important if the output is to be used elsewhere in the build process.

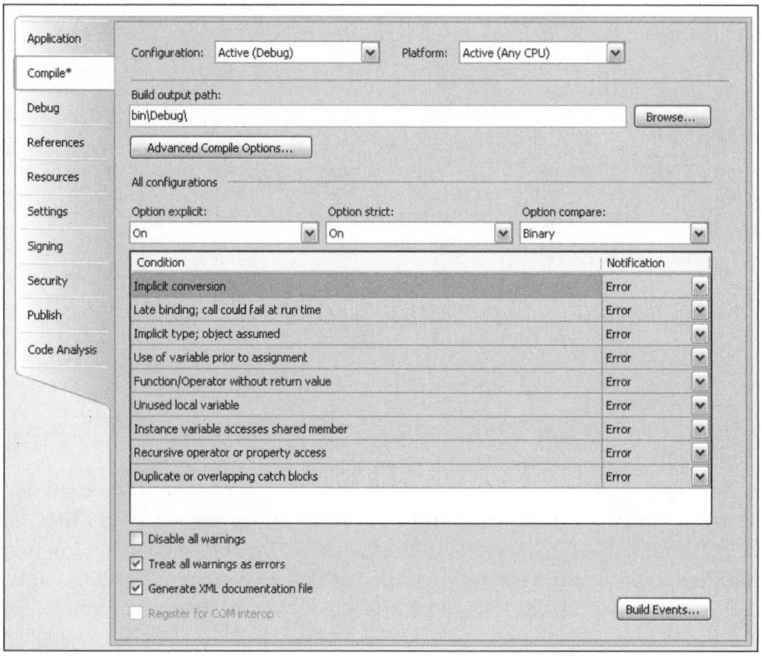

Figure 7-5

Within the Advanced Compile Options menu, various attributes can be adjusted, including the compilation constants. The Debug and Trace constants can be enabled here. Alternatively, you can easily define your own constant, which can then be queried. For example, the Debug constant can be queried as follows:

```
#If Debug Then
    MsgBox("Constant Defined")
#End If
```

Some VB.NET-specific properties can also be configured in the Compile pane. Option Explicit determines whether variables that are used in code have to be explicitly defined. Option Strict forces the type of variables to be defined, rather than it being late-bound. Finally, Option Compare determines whether strings are compared using binary or text comparison operators.

The Compile pane also defines a number of different compiler options that can be adjusted to improve the reliability of your code. For example, unused variables may only warrant a warning, whereas a path that doesn't return a value is more serious and should generate a build error. It is possible to either disable all of these warnings or treat all of them as errors.

VB developers now have the capability to generate XML documentation. Of course, as this will be generated for each build, it is beneficial to disable this option for debug builds. This will speed up the debugging cycle.

The last element of the Compile pane is the Build Events button. Click this button to view commands that can be executed prior to and after the build. Because not all builds are successful, the execution of the post-build event can depend on a successful build.

Debug

The debug tab, shown in Figure 7-6, determines how the application will be executed when run from within Visual Studio 2005.

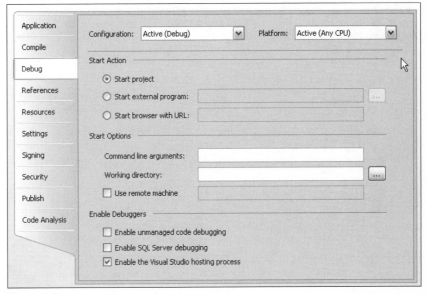

Figure 7-6

Start Action

When a project is set to start up, this set of radio buttons controls what actually happens when the application is run. Initially, this is set to start the project, which will call the Startup object specified on the Application tab. The other options are to either run an executable or launch a specific web site.

Startup Options

The options that can be specified when running an application are additional command-line arguments (generally used in conjunction with an executable start action) and the initial working directory. You can also specify to start the application on a remote computer. Of course, this is possible only when debugging is enabled on a remote machine.

Enable Debuggers

Debugging can be extended to include unmanaged code and SQL Server. The Visual Studio hosting process can also be enabled here. This process has a number of benefits associated with the performance and functionality of the debugger. The benefits fall into three categories. First, the hosting process acts as a background host for the application you are debugging. In order to debug a managed application, various administrative tasks must be performed, such as creating an AppDomain and associating the debugger, which take time. With the hosting process enabled, these tasks are handled in the background, resulting in a much quicker load time during debugging.

Second, in Visual Studio 2005, it is much easier to create, debug, and deploy applications that run under partial trust. The hosting process is an important tool in this process because it gives you the ability to run and debug an application in partial trust. Without this process, the application would run in full trust mode, preventing you from debugging the application in partial trust mode.

The last benefit that the hosting process provides is design-time evaluation of expressions. This is in effect an optical illusion, as the hosting process is actually running in the background. However, using the Immediate window as you're writing your code means that you can easily evaluate expressions, call methods, and even hit breakpoints without running up the entire application.

References

The references pane enables the developer to reference classes in other .NET assemblies, projects, and native DLLs. Once the project or DLL has been added to the references list, a class can be accessed either by its full name, including namespace, or the namespace can be imported into a code file so the class can be referenced by just the class name. Figure 7-7 shows the References tab for a project that has a reference to a number of framework assemblies, as well as a reference to a project entitled FirstProject.

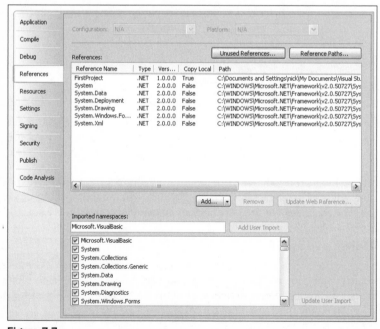

Figure 7-7

One of the added features of this tab for VB developers is the Unused References button, which performs a search to determine which references can be removed. It is also possible to add a reference path, which will include all assemblies in that location.

Once an assembly has been added to the reference list, any public class contained within that assembly can be referenced within the project. Where a class is embedded in a namespace (which might be a nested hierarchy), referencing a class requires the full class name. Both VB.NET and C# provide a mechanism for importing namespaces so that classes can be referenced directly. The References section allows namespaces to be globally imported for all classes in the project, without them being explicitly imported within the class file.

Resources

In the past, adding resources to a project required a lot of effort because required building a resource file. Project resources now can be added and removed via the Resources tab, shown in Figure 7-8, which illustrates an icon that has been added to this application. Resources can be images, text, icons, files, or any other serializable class.

Figure 7-8

This interface makes working with resource files at design time much easier than it has been in the past. Chapter 10 examines in more detail how resource files can be used to store application constants and internationalize your application.

Settings

Project settings can be of any type and simply reflect a name/value pair whose value can be retrieved at runtime. Previously, settings were only scoped to the application, which meant that they were specified in an `app.config` file. When the application is compiled this file is renamed according to the executable being generated — for example, `SampleApplication.exe.config`. Application scoped settings are assigned a value within the Settings tab, as shown in Figure 7-9, which is read-only at runtime.

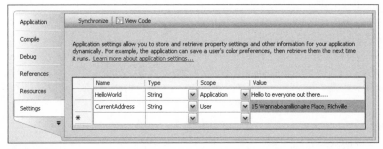

Figure 7-9

You can also define user-scoped settings. This means that although the default value is specified in the settings tab and will appear in the `app.config` file, it can be dynamically set at runtime. In addition to providing a rich user interface for defining application settings, Visual Studio 2005 also generates a designer file that gives developers a strongly typed wrapper to access the settings. The following snippet updates the user-scoped `CurrentAddress` setting. The `settings` class also generates `Reset` and `Reload` methods. `Reset` is used to restore the initial value of the setting, as found in the `app.config` file, whereas the `Reload` method returns the settings to the value stored within the user settings file:

```
My.Settings.CurrentAddress = "62 Regular Avenue, Smallville"
My.Settings.Save()
```

The Settings pane also provides a button entitled Synchronize. This removes any user settings that may have been saved by a previous execution of the application, synchronizing the settings to the default values.

Signing

Figure 7-10 shows the Signing tab, which provides developers with the capability to determine how assemblies are signed in preparation for deployment. An assembly can be signed by selecting a key file, as done previously.

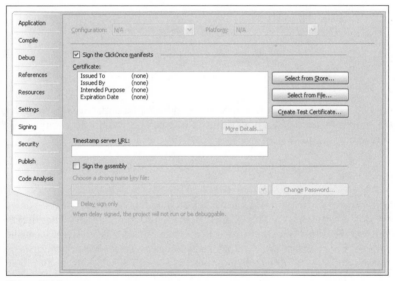

Figure 7-10

Visual Studio 2005 supports a new deployment model for applications called *ClickOnce*. In this model, an application can be published to a web site where a user can click once to download and install the application. Because this model is supposed to support deployment over the Internet, an organization must be able to sign the deployment package. The Signing tab provides an interface for specifying the certificate to use to sign the ClickOnce manifests.

Security

Applications deployed using the ClickOnce deployment model may be required to run under limited or partial trust. For example, if a low-privilege user selects a ClickOnce application from a web site across the Internet, the application will need to run with partial trust as defined by the Internet zone. This typically means that the application can't access the local file system, has limited networking ability, and can't access other local devices such as printers, databases, and computer ports.

In the past, developers had to build applications that ran under partial trust using an ad hoc trial-and-error. The Security tab, illustrated in Figure 7-11, has a Calculate Permissions buttons that will determine the permissions the application requires to operate correctly.

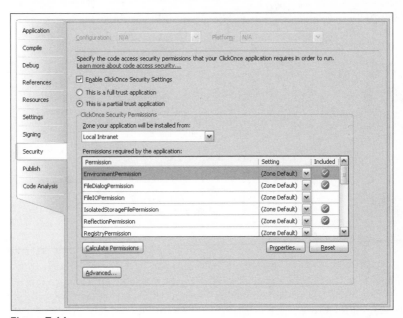

Figure 7-11

Modifying the permission set that is required for a ClickOnce application may limit who can download, install, and operate the application. For the widest audience, specify that an application should run in partial trust mode with security set to the defaults for the Internet zone. Alternatively, specifying that an application requires full trust will ensure that the application has full access to all local resources, but will necessarily limit the audience to local administrators.

One of the difficulties in building a partial trust application in the past was that it was difficult to debug the application while it was running in partial trust mode. Visual Studio 2005 runs the application using a separate hosting process, which, among other advantages, enables the application to be run in a limited security AppDomain. This closely simulates how a partial trust application would run. This feature can be disabled via the Advanced button on the Security tab.

Publish

The ClickOnce deployment model can be divided into two phases: initially publishing the application and publishing subsequent updates, and the download and installation of both the original application and subsequent revisions. Deploying an existing application using the ClickOnce model can be done using the Publish tab, shown in Figure 7-12.

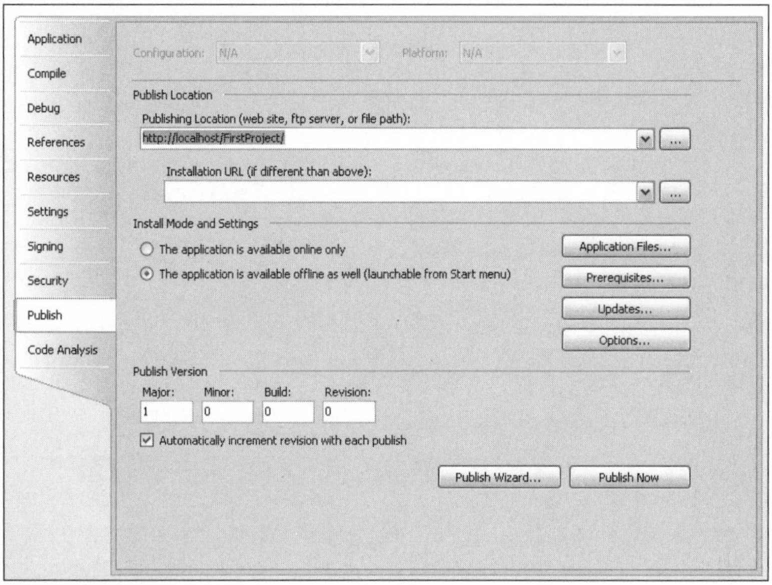

Figure 7-12

If the install mode for a ClickOnce application is set to be available offline when it is initially downloaded from the web site, it will be installed on the local computer. This will place the application in the Start menu and the Add/Remove Programs list. When the application is run and a connection to the original web site is available, the application will determine whether any updates are available. If there are updates, users will be prompted to determine whether they want the updates to be installed.

Deploying an application using this deployment model is much better than the traditional installer, as it allows the application to be dynamically updated as new versions become available. In an enterprise, this can eliminate the configuration nightmare that typically arises when multiple versions of an application are in use. ClickOnce incorporates features of the Application Updater block put together by the Patterns and Practices group at Microsoft (`http://msdn.microsoft.com/practices/`).

Code Analysis

Most developers who have ever worked in a team have had to work with an agreed upon set of coding standards. Organizations typically use an existing standard or create their own. Unfortunately, standards are only useful if they can be enforced, and the only way that this can be effectively done is using a tool. In the past this had to be done using an external utility, such as FXCoP. Visual Studio 2005 has the capability to carry out static code analysis from within the IDE. Code analysis incorporates the rules from FXCoP and includes new rules to support the new language enhancements.

The Code Analysis tab, shown in Figure 7-13, can be used to enable code analysis as part of the build process. Because this can be quite a time-consuming process, it may be included only in release or test build configurations. Regardless of whether code analysis has been enabled for a project, it can be manually invoked from the Build menu.

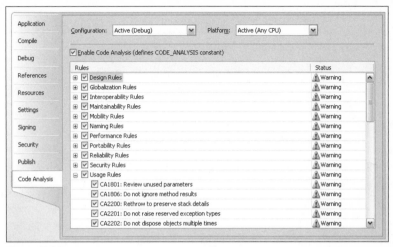

Figure 7-13

Not all rules defined in the Code Analysis pane are suitable for all organizations and/or applications. This pane gives the developer control over which rules are applied, and whether they generate a warning or a build error. Unchecking the rule in the Rules column will disable the rule. Double-clicking a cell in the Status column will toggle what happens when a rule fails to be met between a warning and a build error.

Creating a Custom Settings Provider

One of the limitations of storing data using settings is that only two Scope options are available: Application and User. For most scenarios this is sufficient, as settings are normally either static or variable on a per-user basis. However, there are times when an application setting needs to be changed, which can be achieved by creating a settings provider that stores this information in a user agnostic manager. For example, the value could be stored under the All Users folder or in the Local Computer section of the registry.

The current mechanism is also difficult to manage when an application is widely used. Every time an update is made, users' settings need to be replaced and/or upgraded. An alternative arrangement would see this information centrally recorded. Updating settings could be easily done, as this information can be centrally located. In this case, a settings provider that makes use of a web service to store settings information would be a good solution to this problem.

A settings provider can be created by inheriting from the framework class `SettingsProvider` and overriding the `Get` and `Set PropertyValue` methods. The arguments to these methods specify the context in which the application is running and the list of settings to be accessed. The following code provides an example:

```
Public Class RegistrySettingsProvider
    Inherits SettingsProvider

    ''' <summary>
    ''' Get the settings for this application
    ''' </summary>
    Public Overrides Function GetPropertyValues( _
                            ByVal context As SettingsContext, _
                            ByVal collection As SettingsPropertyCollection) _
                            As SettingsPropertyValueCollection
        Dim values As New SettingsPropertyValueCollection
        For Each settingProperty As SettingsProperty In collection
            Dim settingValue As New SettingsPropertyValue(settingProperty)
            settingValue.IsDirty = False

            settingValue.SerializedValue = _
                    My.WebServices.Settings.GetPropertyValue(settingProperty.Name)
            values.Add(settingValue)
        Next
        Return values
    End Function

    ''' <summary>
    ''' Update the settings that have changed.
    ''' </summary>
    Public Overrides Sub SetPropertyValues( _
                        ByVal context As SettingsContext, _
                        ByVal collection As SettingsPropertyValueCollection)
        For Each propertyValue As SettingsPropertyValue In collection
            My.WebServices.Settings.SetPropertyValue( _
                                    propertyValue.Name, _
                                    propertyValue.SerializedValue)

        Next
    End Sub
End Class
```

Summary

In this chapter you have seen how a solution and projects can be configured using the new user interfaces provided within Visual Studio 2005. In particular, this chapter showed you how to do the following:

❑   Configure application information

❑   Control how an application is compiled, debugged, and deployed

❑   Include resources and settings with an application

❑   Enforce good coding practices

❑   Extend the application using a custom settings provider

In subsequent chapters, some of these topics, such as ClickOnce deployment and the use of resource files, will be examined in more detail.

8

Source Control

There are many different methodologies for building software applications, and while the theories about team structure, work allocation, design, and testing often differ, the one point that they agree on is that there should be a single repository for all source code for an application. Source control is the process of storing source code (referred to as checking code in) and accessing it again (referred to as checking code out) for editing. When we refer to source code, we mean any resources, configuration files, code files, or even documentation that is required to build and deploy the application.

Source code repositories also vary in structure and interface. Basic repositories provide a limited interface through which files can be checked in and out. The storage mechanism can be as simple as a file share, and no history may be available. Yet this repository still has the advantage that all developers working on a project can access the same file, with no risk of changes being overwritten or lost. Most sophisticated repositories not only provide a rich interface for checking in and out, such as merging and other resolution options, they are also able to be used from within Visual Studio 2005 to manage the source code. Other functionality that a source control repository can provide includes versioning of files, branching, and remote access.

Most organizations start using a source control repository to provide a mechanism for sharing source code between participants in a project. Instead of developers having to manually copy code to and from a shared folder on a network, the repository can be queried to get the latest version of the source code. When a developer finishes his or her work, any changes can simply be checked in to the repository. This ensures that everyone in the team can access the latest code. Of course, having the source code checked into a single repository makes backing up the data easy.

One of the biggest benefits of using a source control repository comes from the history that it tracks of changes made to files. This is important for a number of reasons. Although most developers would like to think that they write perfect code, the reality is that quite often a change might break something else. Being able to review the history of changes made to a project makes it possible to identify which changes caused the breakage. Tracking changes to a project can also be used for reporting and reviewing purposes, as each change is date stamped and its author indicated.

Selecting a Source Control Repository

Visual Studio 2005 does not ship with a source control repository, but it does include rich support for checking files in and out, as well as merging and reviewing changes. To make use of a repository from within Visual Studio 2005, it is necessary to specify which repository to use. Previous versions have exclusively used the SCC API, published by Microsoft, to allow third-party source control repositories to be accessed from within Visual Studio. Any source control repository that exposes its functionality through this API can be used within the Visual Studio environment. Visual Studio 2005 still supports this API, although it also supports an interface to Team Foundation.

Feedback from customers using previous versions of Visual Studio has been focused around the need for a simpler and less cluttered IDE. To make Visual Studio 2005 easier to navigate and work with, functionality that is not used is removed from the menus. By default, Visual Studio 2005 does not display the source control menu item. In order to get this item to appear, you have to configure the source control provider information under the Options item on the Tools menu. The Options window, with the Source Control tab selected, is shown in Figure 8-1.

Initially, very few settings for source control appear. However, once a provider has been selected, additional nodes are added to the tree to control how source control behaves. It is worth noting that these options are specific to the source control provider that has been selected.

For the purposes of looking at source control within Visual Studio 2005, we will examine the integration of Visual SourceSafe. Later in the chapter we will cover the use of Team Foundation, as it offers a more comprehensive source control repository. As shown in Figure 8-1, there is also an Internet-based interface for Visual SourceSafe. This is a significant improvement in the latest version of SourceSafe that permits it to be used across a standard web interface.

Once a source control repository has been selected from the Plug-in menu, it is necessary to configure the repository for that machine. This includes specifying the path to the repository, the user with which to connect, and the settings to use when checking files in and out of the repository.

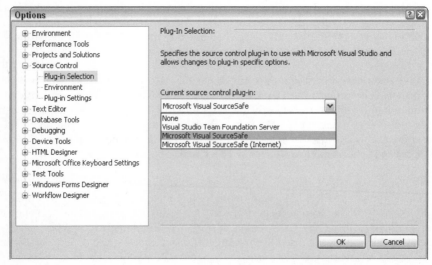

Figure 8-1

Environment Settings

Most source control repositories define a series of settings that must be configured in order for Visual Studio 2005 to connect to and access information from the repository. These settings are usually unique to the repository, although some apply across most repositories.

In Figure 8-2 the Environment tab is shown, illustrating the options that control when files are checked in and out of the repository. These options are available for most repositories. The drop-down menu at the top of the pane defines a couple of profiles, which provide suggestions for different types of developers.

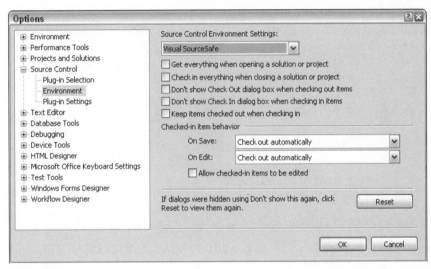

Figure 8-2

Plug-In Settings

Most source control repositories need some additional settings in order for Visual Studio 2005 to connect to the repository. These are specified in the Plug-in Settings pane, which is customized for each repository. Some repositories, such as SourceSafe, do not require specific information regarding the location of the repository until a solution is added to source control. At that point, SourceSafe requests the location of an existing repository or enables the developer to create a new repository.

Accessing Source Control

This section walks through the process of adding a solution to a new Visual SourceSafe 2005 repository, although the same principles apply regardless of the repository chosen. This process can be applied to any new or existing solution that is not already under source control. We also assume here that not only is SourceSafe installed, it has been selected as the source control repository within Visual Studio 2005.

Creating the Repository

The first step in placing a solution under source control is to create a repository in which to store the data. It is possible to place any number of solutions in the same repository, although this means that it is much harder to separate information pertaining to different projects. Furthermore, if a repository is corrupted, it may affect all solutions contained within that repository.

To begin the process of adding a solution to source control, navigate to the File menu and select Source Control⇨Add Solution to Source Control, as shown in Figure 8-3.

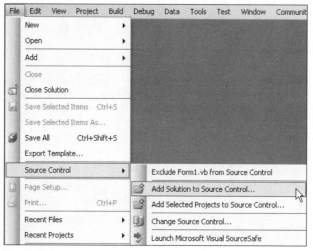

Figure 8-3

If this is the first time you have accessed SourceSafe, this will open a dialog box that lists the available databases, which at this stage will be empty. Clicking the Add button will initiate the Add SourceSafe Database Wizard, which will step you through either referencing an existing database, perhaps on a server or elsewhere on your hard disk, or creating a new database.

To create a new SourceSafe database you need to specify a location for the database and a name. You will also have to specify the type of locking that is used when checking files in and out. Selecting the Lock-Modify-Unlock model allows only a single developer to check out a file at any point in time. This prevents two people from making changes to the same file at the same time, which makes the check-in process very simple. However, this model can often lead to frustration if multiple developers need to adjust the same resource. Project files are a common example of a resource that multiple developers may need to be able to access at the same time. In order to add or remove files from a project, this file must be checked out. Unless developers are diligent about checking the project file back in after they add a new file, this can significantly slow down a team.

An alternative model, Copy-Modify-Merge, allows multiple developers to check out the same file. Of course, when they are ready to check the file back in, there must be a process of reconciliation to ensure that their changes do not overwrite any changes made by another developer. Merging changes can be a difficult process and can easily result in loss of changes or a final code set that neither compiles nor runs.

This model offers the luxury of allowing concurrent access to files, but suffers from the operational overhead during check in.

Adding the Solution

Once a SourceSafe repository has been created, the Add to SourceSafe dialog will appear, which prompts you for a location for your application and a name to give it in the repository. SourceSafe works very similarly to a network file share in that it creates folders under the root ($/) into which it places the files under source control. It doesn't matter what location you specify within the repository. In the past it has been recommended practice to align the SourceSafe folder structure to the directory structure on your computer. With SourceSafe 2005, the issues that preceded this recommendation have been addressed, although many developers will continue to use this rule as it encourages the use of good directory and folder structures.

After specifying a name and location in the repository, SourceSafe will proceed to add each file belonging to the solution into the source control repository. This initiates the process of tracking changes for these files.

Solution Explorer

The first difference that you will see after adding your solution to source control is that Visual Studio 2005 adjusts the icons within the Solution Explorer to indicate their source control status. Figure 8-4 illustrates three file states. When the solution is initially added to the source control repository, the files all appear with a little padlock icon next to the file type icon. This indicates that the file has been checked in and is not currently checked out by anyone. For example, the Solution file and Form1.vb have this icon.

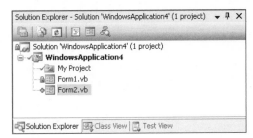

Figure 8-4

Once a solution is under source control, all changes are recorded. This includes when files are added and removed. Figure 8-4 illustrates the addition of Form2.vb to the solution. At the point this screen capture was taken, Form2.vb had been added to the solution, but this change was not yet updated in the repository. This is illustrated first by the plus sign next to Form2.vb, indicating that this is a new file, and second by the tick next to the WindowsApplication4 project (which includes the My Project node). The tick signifies that the file is currently checked out. In the rare case that two people have the same file checked out, this will be indicated with a double tick next to the appropriate item.

Checking In and Out

Files can be checked in and out using the right-click shortcut menu associated with an item in the Solution Explorer. When a solution is under source control, this menu expands to include the items shown on the left in Figure 8-5.

Figure 8-5

Prior to editing a file, it needs to be checked out. This can be done using the Check Out for Edit menu item. Once a file is checked out, the shortcut menu expands to include additional options, including Check In, View Pending Checkins, Undo Checkout, and more, as shown on the right in Figure 8-5.

Pending Changes

In a large application it can often be difficult to see at a glance which files have been checked out for editing, or recently added or removed from a project. The Pending Checkins window, shown in Figure 8-6, is very useful for seeing which files are waiting to be checked into the repository. It also provides a space into which a comment can be added. This comment is attached to the files when they are checked into the repository so that the reason for the change(s) can be reviewed at a later date.

Name	Change type	Container	Modified Time
Items below solution 'WindowsApplication4'			
Files below 'WindowsApplication4'			
WindowsApplication4		True	15/12/2005 11:08:33 PM
Form2.Designer.vb	Newly added file	False	15/12/2005 11:08:23 PM
Form2.vb	Newly added file	False	15/12/2005 11:08:23 PM
WindowsApplication4.vbproj	Content	False	15/12/2005 10:54:19 PM
My Project		True	15/12/2005 10:54:19 PM

Figure 8-6

To check a file back in, ensure that there is a check against the file in the list, add an appropriate comment in the space provided, and then select the Check In button. Depending on the options you have specified, you may also receive a confirmation dialog prior to the items being checked in.

One option that many developers prefer is to set Visual Studio to automatically check a file out when it is edited. This saves the often unnecessary step of having to check the file out prior to editing. However, it can result in files being checked out prematurely if a developer accidentally makes a change in the wrong file. Alternatively, a developer may decide that changes made previously are no longer required and wish to revert back to what is contained in the repository. The last button on the toolbar contained within the Pending Checkins window is an Undo Checkout button. This will retrieve the current version from the repository, in the process overwriting changes made by the developer. This option is also available via the right-click shortcut menu.

Prior to checking a file into the repository, it is a good idea for someone to review any changes that have been made. In fact, some organizations have a policy requiring that all changes be reviewed prior to being checked in. Selecting the Compare Versions menu item brings up an interface that highlights any differences between two versions of a file. Figure 8-7 shows that a Form Load event handler has been added to Form1.vb. Although not evident in Figure 8-7, these lines are marked in green. Red and blue lines indicate deleted and changed lines.

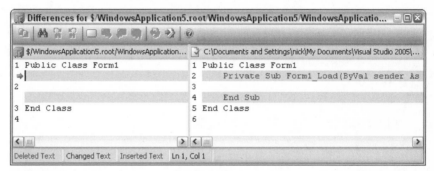

Figure 8-7

As source files can often get quite large, this window provides some basic navigation shortcuts. The Find option can be used to locate particular strings. Bookmarks can be placed to ease navigation forward and backward within a file. The most useful shortcuts are the Next and Previous difference buttons. These enable the developer to navigate through the differences without having to manually scroll up and down the file.

Merging Changes

Occasionally, changes might be made to the same file by multiple developers. In some cases these changes can be easily resolved if they are unrelated, such as adding methods to an existing class. However, when changes are made to the same portion of the file, there needs to be a process by which the changes can be mediated to determine the correct code.

Figure 8-8 illustrates the Merge dialog that is presented to developers when they attempt to check in a file that has been modified by another developer. The top half of the dialog shows the two versions of the file that are in conflict. Each pane indicates where that file differs from the original file that the developer checked out, which appears in the lower half of the screen. In this case, both versions had a message box inserted, and it is up to the developer to determine which of the messages is correct.

Unlike the Compare Versions dialog, the Merge dialog has been designed to facilitate developer interaction. From the top panes, changes made in either version can be accepted or rejected by simply clicking on the change. The highlighting changes to indicate that a change has been accepted, and that piece of code is inserted into the appropriate place in the code presented in the lower pane. The lower pane also allows the developer to enter code, although it does not support IntelliSense or error detection.

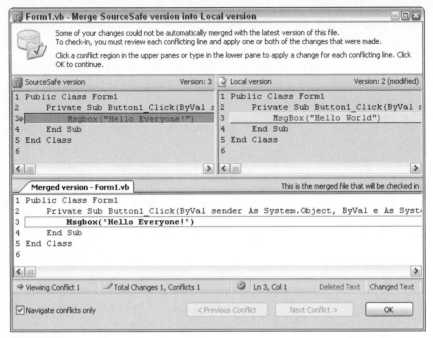

Figure 8-8

Once the conflicts have been resolved, clicking the OK button will ensure that the correct version is checked into the repository.

History

As a file is checked in and out of the SourceSafe repository, a history is recorded of each version of the file. Use the View History option on the right-click shortcut menu from the Solution Explorer to review this history. Figure 8-9 shows a brief history of a file that had three revisions checked in. This dialog enables developers to view previous versions, look at details (such as the comments), get the particular version (overwriting the current file), and check out the file. Additional functionality is provided to compare different versions of the file, pin a particular version, roll the file back to a previous version (which will erase newer versions), and report on the version history.

Pinning

The History window (refer to Figure 8-9) can be used to *pin* a version of the file. Pinning a version of a file makes that version the current version. When a developer gets the current source code from the repository, the pinned version is returned. Pinning a version of a file also prevents anyone from checking that file out. This can be useful if changes that have been checked are incomplete or are causing errors in the application. A previous version of the file can be pinned to ensure that other developers can continue to work while the problem is resolved.

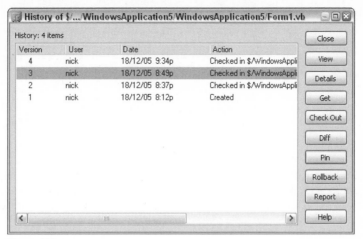

Figure 8-9

Source Control with Team Foundation

In early 2006, Microsoft will release Team Foundation Server, a server product that will support .NET developers through the provision of a project management solution. This product will include functionality such as work item tracking, build and test management, and a brand-new source control repository. Unlike SourceSafe, this product does not use the SCC API. Instead, in order to access the services exposed by the server, the Team Explorer plug-in needs to be installed for Visual Studio 2005. Once installed, the Visual Studio Team Foundation Server appears in the list of source control plug-ins. The settings exposed through the Options dialog are limited to providing the address of a proxy server and controlling whether deleted items are displayed in the list of files under source control.

The Team Foundation plug-in adds a number of windows and menu items that support the management of a software development process. Many of these fall outside the scope of this chapter and are covered in more detail in Chapter 56. Much of the source control interface is similar to that exposed by Visual SourceSafe. This section covers the additional functionality that Team Foundation provides over and above that provided by SourceSafe.

Source Control Explorer

The main addition to Visual Studio is the Source Control Explorer, shown in Figure 8-10, which can be found by selecting View⇨Other Windows. This window shows an interface similar to Windows Explorer, with a Folders list on the left and a file list on the right side. The Source Location drop-down box enables the developer to navigate between Team Foundation Servers.

Figure 8-10

Workspaces

The source control interface provided by Team Foundation uses a concept called a *workspace*. A workspace is simply a location on the local computer where files are placed when they are retrieved from the server. Whereas SourceSafe supports only a single mapping between the folder structure within the repository to a directory on the local computer, Team Foundation supports any number of workspaces.

Most developers use only a single workspace for any given project. However, an additional workspace can be useful if you are working on a new piece of functionality that is not complete and have to change tasks to fix a bug. Instead of putting the changes to one side a developer can switch to a different workspace, fix a bug, check in the changes, and then return to the original workspace.

Pending Changes

Visual SourceSafe uses the Pending Changes window to list files that have been checked out. As Team Foundation provides additional functionality when files are checked into the repository, it makes use of a new window also called Pending Changes. This window is divided into four vertical tabs that are used to associate additional data with the files being checked in:

❑ Source Files

❑ Work Items

❑ Check-in Notes

❑ Policy Warnings

Source Files

The Source Files tab (see Figure 8-11) shows the list of source files waiting to be checked in. This is similar to the Pending Changes window used by SourceSafe. It allows comments to be appended to a file being checked in, as well as provides an interface for rolling back any unwanted changes.

Figure 8-11

Work Items

The Work Items tab (see Figure 8-12) provides a list of outstanding tasks being tracked by the Team Foundation Server. When the tab is first selected, a query is run against the server and the list of tasks is retrieved. Changes being checked in can be assigned to a particular work item, providing information about what issue or functionality the change was addressing. As part of this process, the work item state can also be changed from Active to Resolved if appropriate.

Figure 8-12

Check-in Notes

Prior to a set of changes being checked in, the changes may have to be reviewed by a number of parties. In this case, the Check-in Notes tab (see Figure 8-13) provides space for comments to be added by a Code, Security, and Performance reviewer. These notes will also be associated with the changes for future reference.

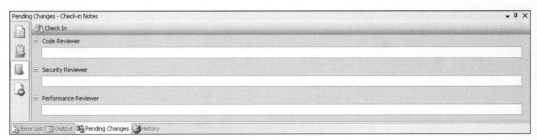

Figure 8-13

Policy Warnings

The last tab, Policy Warnings (see Figure 8-14), provides information about any policies that are currently being violated. In addition to providing a mechanism for tracking changes and work items, Team Foundation also provides some process guidance. One area where this can be applied is when files are checked in. Policies can be established that require each check in to be associated with a work item or to be reviewed prior to check in.

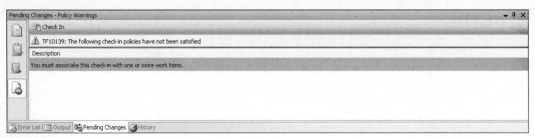

Figure 8-14

Shelving

The other area in which Team Foundation makes a significant improvement over SourceSafe is its ability to shelve changes. Quite often a developer will be working on one task and need to put those changes to one side while they do something else. Alternatively, they may need to hand a task over to someone else to complete it, or even for review and testing prior to being checked in. In each of these scenarios, shelving the changes into the source repository enables those changes to be retrieved at a later stage, perhaps by someone else, for work to continue.

Shelving changes can be done the same way as checking in changes — via either the Solution Explorer or the Source Control Explorer. When the Shelve Pending Changes item is selected, the Shelve – Source Files dialog appears, as illustrated in Figure 8-15. As per the check-in process, it is possible to associate work items and check-in comments with the change set.

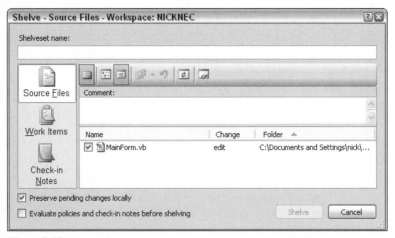

Figure 8-15

These changes can be retrieved from the repository via the Unshelve Pending Changes menu item. As there may be multiple change sets waiting to be unshelved, you will have to select the correct one to retrieve. To determine the appropriate change set, select the Details option to show the work items and check-in comments made when the change set was shelved. After unshelving, the files with changes will be shown in the Pending Changes window.

Summary

This chapter demonstrated Visual Studio 2005's rich interface for using a source control repository to manage files associated with an application. Checking files in and out can be done using the Solution Explorer window, and more advanced functionality is available via the Pending Changes window.

You have also seen some of the advantages that a more enterprise-ready source control repository, such as Team Foundation, provides. While SourceSafe is sufficient for small teams of developers, it has not been designed to scale for a large number of developers. Nor does it have the capability to track tasks or reviewer comments against a set of changes.

9

Application Configuration Files

One of the challenges of building applications is being able to adjust the way the application functions on-the-fly without having to rebuild it. There has been a long history of applications using configuration files to control the way an application runs. .NET applications use a series of XML configuration files that can be adjusted to determine application behavior. This chapter explores the structure of these configuration files and demonstrates how you can store custom information using a configuration section handler.

Config Files

The .NET Framework configuration system consists of several configuration files (discussed in the following sections) that can be used to adjust one or more applications on a computer system. Part of this system is an inheritance model that ensures that configurations can be applied at the appropriate level.

Machine.config

At the root of the inheritance model is the `machine.config` file (located in the `systemroot\Microsoft .NET\Framework\versionNumber\CONFIG\` folder), which defines configuration settings for the entire system. All configuration files inherit from this file and can override these settings.

Web.config

Web applications are configured via the `web.config` file. This file can be located in a number of locations depending on the scope to which the settings need to be applied. To apply a configuration to all web applications on a machine, place the `web.config` file in the same directory as the machine.config file. In most cases the settings need to be applied at a much finer granularity. As such, the web.config file can also be placed in any virtual directory or subdirectory to control web applications at that level. If placed in the root folder for a web site, the configuration will be applied to all ASP.NET applications in that web site.

A word of caution: When you are working with virtual directories that do not align with the directory model on the computer, it is possible to have an application with different configurations depending on how it is referenced. For example, consider c:\inetpub\wwwroot\MainApplication\Contacts\ Contact.aspx, which has been set up with both MainApplication and Contacts as virtual directories. You can reference the contact page as either

```
http://localhost/MainApplication/Contacts/Contact.aspx
```

or

```
http://localhost/Contacts/Contact.aspx
```

In the first case, the configuration settings that are applied are inherited from the MainApplication folder and may be overridden by a configuration file in the Contacts folder. However, in the second case, settings are applied only from the configuration file within the Contacts folder.

App.config

Windows applications can be configured using an application configuration file, which also inherits from machine.config. As the output assembly name is known only when an application is compiled, this file starts off as app.config and is renamed to <application>.exe.config as part of the build process. For example, an application with AccountingApplication.exe as the main executable would have a configuration file entitled AccountingApplication.exe.config. This configuration file is automatically loaded based on its name when the application is loaded.

Security.config

In conjunction with the application configuration files are a number of security configuration files. These also follow an inheritance path but across a different dimension. Instead of being application focused, the security configuration files are broken down into Enterprise (Enterprisesec.config), Machine (Security.config), and User (Security.config). The Enterprise- and Machine-level files are both stored in the same location as the machine.config file, while the User-level file is stored under the user-specific application data folder.

Configuration Schema

A configuration file, whether it is a machine.config, web.config, or an application configuration file, needs to adhere to the configuration schema that determines which elements should be included. The schema can be found at C:\Program Files\Microsoft Visual Studio 8\Xml\Schemas\ DotNetConfig.xsd and is broken down into a number of sections.

Configuration Attributes

All configuration elements can specify a `configSource`, which is simply a redirection to a separate file. This can be useful if a configuration file becomes unwieldy in length. The following code snippet illustrates how a section of a configuration file can be extracted and subsequently referenced using this attribute:

```
<!-- Original Configuration Section -->
<WindowsApplication1.My.MySettings">
    <setting name="Button1_Text" serializeAs="String">
        <value>Press Me!</value>
    </setting>
</WindowsApplication1.My.MySettings>
<!-- Reduced Configuration Section using configSource -->
<WindowsApplication1.My.MySettings configSource="MySettings.Config" />
<!-- Code from MySettings.Config -->
<WindowsApplication1.My.MySettings">
    <setting name="Button1_Text" serializeAs="String">
        <value>Press Me!</value>
    </setting>
</WindowsApplication1.My.MySettings>
```

Note a couple of limitations in using a `configSource`:

❑ There is no merging of configuration sections between the referenced file and the original configuration file.

❑ This attribute cannot be applied to configuration section groups. This can be a significant limitation, as the purpose of a section group is to group items that relate similar configuration sections. A logical separation could see all items in a particular section group in a separate configuration file.

Each element within the configuration file inherits a number of attributes that can be set to control whether that element can be overridden or not. To prevent an element, or even an entire section, from being overridden, that item can be locked. To reduce the number of attributes that are applied, five different locking attributes (outlined in the following table) can be used to specify any number of configuration attributes and elements that are to be locked.

Configuration Element	Description
LockItem	Locks the element to which this attribute is applied, including all other attributes provided on that element and all child elements
LockAttributes	Locks the comma-delimited list of attributes provided
LockAllAttributesExcept	Locks all attributes except those provided in the comma-delimited list
LockElements	Locks the comma-delimited list of child elements provided
LockAllElementsExcept	Locks all child elements except those provided in the comma-delimited list

Being able to lock configuration items is particularly relevant to web applications, which might contain a deep hierarchy of configuration inheritance. Windows applications inherit only from the `machine` `.config` file, so it is unlikely that the need will arise to lock items.

Section: startup

The startup configuration section determines the version of the framework that is either required (`<requiredRuntime>`) or supported (`<supportedRuntime>`) by the framework. By default, a .NET application will attempt to execute using the same version of the framework on which it was built. Any application being built with support for multiple versions of the framework should indicate this using the `supportedRuntime` element, defining the most preferred framework version first:

```
<configuration>
    <startup>
        <supportedRuntime version="v2.0.50727"/>
        <supportedRuntime version="v1.1.4322"/>
    </startup>
</configuration>
```

This configuration section would be used by an application that has been tested for both version 2.0 and 1.1 of the framework. Anomalies were detected in the testing for version 1.0 of the framework, so this has been omitted from the `supportedRuntime` list. The version number must correspond exactly to the installation directory for that framework version (for example, version 2.0 of the framework typically installs to `C:\WINDOWS\Microsoft.NET\Framework\v2.0.50727\`).

Section: runtime

Garbage collection is a feature of the .NET Framework that distinguishes it from nonmanaged environments. The process of collecting and disposing of unreferenced objects is usually done in parallel with the main application on a separate thread. This means that the user should not see any performance issues due to this process being run. However, there may be circumstances when this is not desirable and this process should be run inline with the main application. The runtime section of the configuration file can be used to provide limited control over how the .NET runtime engine operates. This includes specifying whether the garbage collection should be done concurrently with the main application.

This section can also be used to specify a location in which to search for assemblies that may be required by an application. This attribute can be useful if an application references assemblies. The following code illustrates the use of the `codeBase` attribute to locate the `ImportantAssembly.dll`, as well as to dictate that garbage collection be done inline with the main application thread:

```
<configuration>
    <runtime>
        <assemblyBinding xmlns="urn:schemas-microsoft-com:asm.v1">
            <dependentAssembly>
                <assemblyIdentity name="ImportantAssembly"
                            publicKeyToken="32ab4ba45e0a69a1"
                            culture="neutral" />
                <codeBase version="2.0.0.0" href="../ImportantAssembly.dll"/>
            </dependentAssembly>
```

```
        </assemblyBinding>
        <gcConcurrent enabled="false"/>
    </runtime>
</configuration>
```

Section: system.runtime.remoting

The `remoting` section of the configuration file can be used to specify information about remote objects and channels required by the application. For example, the default HTTP channel can be directed to listen to port 8080 using the following configuration snippet:

```
<configuration>
    <system.runtime.remoting>
        <application>
            <channels>
                <channel port="8080" ref="http"/>
            </channels>
        </application>
    </system.runtime.remoting>
</configuration>
```

Section: system.net

With the current demand for more secure operating environments, organizations often use proxies to monitor and protect traffic on their networks. This can often result in applications not functioning correctly unless they have been configured to use the appropriate proxy. The networking section of the configuration files can be used to adjust the proxy that is used by an application when making HTTP requests.

Version 2.0 of the .NET Framework ships with an `SmtpClient` class that can be used to send mail from within an application. Obviously, this requires information such as the server and the credentials to use when sending mail. Although this can be hard-coded within an application, a more flexible approach would be to specify this in a configuration file that can be adjusted when the application is deployed. The following configuration snippet illustrates the use of the default proxy (although it bypasses it for local addresses and the DeveloperNews web site) and specifies the default SMTP settings to be used by the SMTP client:

```
<configuration>
    <system.net>
        <defaultProxy>
            <proxy usesystemdefaults="true"
                   proxyaddress="http://192.168.200.222:3030"
                   bypassonlocal="true" />
            <bypasslist>
                <add address="[a-z]+\.developernews\.com" />
            </bypasslist>
        </defaultProxy>
        <mailSettings>
            <smtp deliveryMethod="network">
                <network host="smtp.developernews.com" port="25"
defaultCredentials="true" />
```

```
            </smtp>
        </mailSettings>
    </system.net>
</configuration>
```

Section: cryptographySettings

Although the framework contains base implementations for a number of cryptographic algorithms, such as the hashing function, there are times when it is necessary to override these algorithms. When this is required, the `cryptographySettings` section of the configuration file can be included to remap existing algorithm names, or map new names, to another implementation class.

Section: configurationSections

Configuration files can be customized to contain any structured XML data. In order to do this, a custom section has to be defined in the `configurationSections` block within the configuration file. This defines both the name of the configuration section as well as the class that is to be called in order to process the section.

The first `configurationSections` section in the `machine.config` file defines the handlers for each of the standard configuration sections discussed here. For example, the following code snippet defines the section handler for the `appSettings` configuration section (it is not recommended to override these section handlers as it may prevent your application from working properly):

```
<configuration>
    <configSections>
        <section name="appSettings"
                 type="System.Configuration.AppSettingsSection,
System.Configuration, Version=2.0.0.0, Culture=neutral,
PublicKeyToken=b03f5f7f11d50a3a" restartOnExternalChanges="false"
requirePermission="false" />
    </configSections>
</configuration>
```

Where used, this section must appear as the first child element within the configuration section.

Section: system.diagnostics

Debugging an application is always the hardest part of writing an application. It is made even more difficult when the application is in production and the error cannot be replicated in the debugging environment. One technique that is particularly important for debugging this type of issue is to use *trace statements*:

```
trace.writeline("The application made it this far before crashing.....")
```

Both trace and debug statements work very similarly to events and event handlers. For the preceding `writeline` statement to have any effect, an object must be listening for this `writeline`. This is typically done by a `TraceListener` class. The framework supports a number of default trace listeners that can be wired up to the application via the diagnostics section of the configuration file, as shown in the following section in which an `EventLog` trace listener has been attached to the application:

```
<configuration>
    <system.diagnostics>
        <trace autoflush="true" indentsize="0">
            <listeners>
                <add name="MyEventListener"
                    type="System.Diagnostics.EventLogTraceListener, system,
version=1.0.3300.0, Culture=neutral, PublicKeyToken=b77a5c561934e089"
initializeData="DeveloperApplicationEventLog"/>
            </listeners>
        </trace>
    </system.diagnostics>
</configuration>
```

The `initializeData` attribute specifies a text string to be passed into the constructor for the trace listener. In the case of the event log listener, this text corresponds to the name of the event log into which trace statements will be inserted.

Other elements can also be added to the diagnostics section of the configuration file—for example, to determine the level of trace logging to perform, which will determine how verbose the trace messages are; and to control whether the debug assertion dialog is displayed for an application or not.

Section: system.web

The `system.web` section of the configuration file is used to control how web applications behave. This is the section that can have quite a deep hierarchy, as configuration settings can be specified on a machine, web server, web site, web application, or even a subfolder basis. Because this section controls the security requirements for a web application, it is quite often used to restrict access to certain areas of the web application.

Section: webserver

Although web service applications use several configuration settings, such as authentication and impersonation sections, the `system.web` section of the configuration file contains some settings that are particular to the way that web services operate. For example, the following code snippet enables the use of Soap and Documentation protocols, but removes the Post and Get protocols for the application:

```
<configuration>
    <system.web>
        <webServices>
            <protocols>
                <add name="HttpSoap"/>
                <remove name="HttpPost"/>
                <remove name="HttpGet"/>
                <add name="Documentation"/>
            </protocols>
        </webServices>
    </system.web>
</configuration>
```

By default, only Soap and Documentation are enabled for web services. Quite often, for debugging purposes, it is convenient to allow the Post protocol so that the web service can be tested via a web browser. This should be done on an application basis by including the appropriate section in the configuration file within the application folder.

Section: compiler

The `compiler` section of the configuration file is used to list the compilers installed on a computer. The following snippet shows how the VB.NET compiler is referenced in the `machine.config` file. Within an application, this information can be accessed via the `CodeDomProvider` framework class.

```
<configuration>
    <system.codedom>
        <compilers>
            <compiler language="vb;vbs;visualbasic;vbscript" extension=".vb"
type="Microsoft.VisualBasic.VBCodeProvider, System, Version=2.0.0.0,
Culture=neutral, PublicKeyToken=b77a5c561934e089" />
        </compilers>
    </system.codedom>
</configuration>
```

Application Settings

Applications frequently have settings that do not fit into the default configuration schema. There are three mechanisms for storing this information.

Using appSettings

The first technique is to use the `appSettings` section of the configuration file. This section can be used to store simple name-value pairs of application settings, which might be useful for storing the name of the server, for example:

```
<configuration>
    <appSettings>
        <add key="ApplicationServer" value="http://DeveloperNews.com"/>
    </appSettings>
</configuration>
```

This value can easily be accessed within code using the `AppSettings` property of the new `ConfigurationManager` class:

```
Dim server As String = configurationmanager.AppSettings("ApplicationServer")
```

Dynamic Properties

The second mechanism for storing application-specific information is the use of dynamic properties. These are typically used to dynamically set designer properties. For example, the text on a `Button1` could be set using the following configuration block:

```
<configuration>
    <applicationSettings>
        <WindowsApplication1.My.MySettings>
            <setting name="Button1_Text" serializeAs="String">
                <value>Press Me Now!</value>
            </setting>
        </WindowsApplication1.My.MySettings>
    </applicationSettings>
</configuration>
```

When this application is deployed, the text displayed on Button1 is dynamically loaded from the configuration file. In the following steps, for example, we set the size of a control, Button1, to be dynamically loaded from the configuration file:

1. Select Button1 on the designer surface and press F4 to display the Properties window. Locate the Data category or the ApplicationSettings item in the alphabetic list, as shown in Figure 9-1.

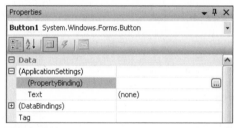

Figure 9-1

2. Press the Ellipses button (...) next to the PropertyBinding row. This will open a dialog that lists the available properties for Button1, along with any ApplicationSettings that have been assigned.

3. Select the drop-down next to the Size property and select New. This will open a dialog in which you can specify a default value, a name for the application setting, and the scope of the setting.

4. Specify a name for the application setting—for example, Button1_Size, and set the scope to Application. You can modify the default value or simply accept the value that has been extracted from the current properties of Button1.

5. Click OK on both dialogs. If you open the app.config file that will be available from the Solution Explorer window, you will see a section that defines this ApplicationSetting.

Custom Configuration Sections

Developers often want to include more structured information in the configuration file than can be stored in the AppSettings section. To solve this problem and eliminate any need for additional configuration files, you can create a custom configuration section. The new configuration section must be defined at the top of the configuration file, complete with a reference to a class that should be used to process that portion of the configuration file.

In the past this process was fairly complex, as the class needed to implement the IConfiguration SectionHandler interface. This exposed a simple method, Create, which was called the first time that section was referenced in code. There was little support from the framework to process the section, and a class implementing this interface often resorted to parsing the XML block to determine settings.

Visual Studio 2005 provides much better support for creating custom configuration sections via the ConfigurationSection and ConfigurationElement classes. These provide the basis for creating classes that map to the structure of the data being stored in the configuration files. Instead of mapping a class that processes the configuration section, we can now create a much simpler class that maps to the section. When the section is referenced in code, an instance of this class is returned with the appropriate data elements set. All the XML processing that would have been done in the past is now handled by the framework.

Although this mapping makes the process of writing a custom configuration section much easier, you may sometimes want more control over how the section is read. Two options can be used to provide this control.

❑ The first option is to go back to using a configuration section handler and manually process the XML file. This can be useful if the original XML representation is required. However, it still requires processing the XML file.

❑ The second strategy is to create an appropriate mapping class as an in-between measure. Instead of referencing this class directly, another class can be generated that exposes the configuration information in the appropriate manner.

If either of these options has to be pursued, then it might be worth taking a step back and determining whether the configuration section structure is actually in a format suited to the data being stored.

Of course, the best way to illustrate this is by example: Our application requires a list of registered entities with which to work. One type of entity is a company, and we need to be provided with both the company name and the date that they were registered. The XML snippet that we would like to have in the configuration file might look like the following:

```
<RegisteredEntities>
    <Companies>
        <add CompanyName="Random Inc" RegisteredDate="31/1/2005" />
        <add CompanyName="Developer Experience Inc" RegisteredDate="1/8/2004" />
    </Companies>
</RegisteredEntities>
```

Once generated, the corresponding classes that would map to the preceding snippet might look like the following:

```
Public Class RegisteredEntities
    Inherits ConfigurationSection

    <ConfigurationProperty("Companies")> _
    Public ReadOnly Property Companies() As Companies
        Get
            Return CType(MyBase.Item("Companies"),Companies)
        End Get
    End Property
```

```
    End Class

<ConfigurationCollectionAttribute(GetType(Company))> _
Public Class Companies
    Inherits ConfigurationElementCollection

    Protected Overrides Function CreateNewElement() As ConfigurationElement
        Return New Company
    End Function

    Protected Overrides Function GetElementKey _
                        (ByVal element As ConfigurationElement) As Object
        Return CType(element, Company).CompanyName
    End Function

    Public Sub Add(ByVal element As Company)
        Me.BaseAdd(element)
    End Sub

End Class

Public Class Company
    Inherits ConfigurationElement

    <ConfigurationProperty("CompanyName", DefaultValue:="Random Inc", IsKey:=true,
IsRequired:=true)> _
    Public Property CompanyName() As String
        Get
            Return CType(MyBase.Item("CompanyName"),String)
        End Get
        Set
            MyBase.Item("CompanyName") = value
        End Set
    End Property

    < ConfigurationProperty("RegisteredDate", DefaultValue:="31/1/2005",
IsKey:=false, IsRequired:=false)> _
    Public Property RegisteredDate() As String
        Get
            Return CType(MyBase.Item("RegisteredDate"),String)
        End Get
        Set
            MyBase.Item("RegisteredDate") = value
        End Set
    End Property
End Class
```

The code contains three classes that are required to correctly map the functionality of this section. The registered entities section corresponds to the RegisteredEntities class, which contains a single property that returns a company collection. A collection is required here because we want to be able to support the addition of multiple companies. This functionality could be extended to clear and/or remove companies, which might be useful if we had a web application for which we needed to control which companies were available to different portions of the application. Lastly, there is the Company class that maps to the individual company information being added.

To access this section from within code, we can simply call the appropriate section using the `configurationManager` framework class:

```
dim registered as RegisteredEntities= _
    ctype(configurationmanager.GetSection("RegisteredEntities"),RegisteredEntities)
```

Automation Using SCDL

You saw in the last section how custom configuration sections can be written and mapped to classes. Although this is a huge improvement over writing section handlers, it is still a fairly laborious process that is prone to error. Furthermore, debugging the configuration sections is nearly impossible because it is difficult to track what is going wrong.

As part of another project to support ASP.NET developers, Dmitryr, development manager for the ASP.NET team at Microsoft, recognized that the process of creating these mapping classes was rather a mundane task that could easily be automated. To this end he created a small application entitled SCDL (`http://blogs.msdn.com/dmitryr/archive/2005/12/07/501365.aspx`) that could take a snippet of configuration data, such as the `RegisteredEntities` section discussed previously, and output both the mapping classes and a schema file that represented the section supplied. Once generated, this code can be included in the application. Furthermore, if the snippet of configuration data is to be included as a noncompiled file within the solution, it is possible to automate the generation of the mapping classes via a prebuild `batch` command. If changes need to be made to the structure of the section, they could be made in the snippet. That way, the next time the solution is built, the mapping classes would be updated automatically.

IntelliSense

Even after you get the custom configuration sections correctly mapped, there is still no support provided by Visual Studio 2005 when adding the custom section to the configuration file. Unlike the rest of the configuration file, which has support for IntelliSense and will report validation issues, your custom section will not be able to be validated.

In order to get IntelliSense and validation for your custom configuration section, you need to indicate the structure of the configuration section to Visual Studio 2005. This can be done by placing an appropriate schema (as generated by the SCDL tool) in the XML Schemas folder, which is usually located at `C:\Program Files\Microsoft Visual Studio 8\Xml\Schemas\`. Unfortunately, this is where it gets a little bit more complex, as it is not enough to place the file in that folder; you also need to tell it that the schema should be included in the catalog used for parsing config files. To register your schema, follow these steps:

1. Generate your schema file from your configuration snippet:

```
Scdl.exe snippet.scdl snippet.vb snippet.xsd
```

2. Copy the schema file (in this case, `snippet.xsd`) to the schema folder.

3. Create a new text file called `Config.xsd` and include the following lines. Note that if your schema is called something different, update these lines appropriately. You may also add additional lines to include more than one schema. Do not remove the `DotNetConfig.xsd` line because that will remove validation for the standard configuration sections:

```
<?xml version="1.0" encoding="utf-8" ?>
<xs:schema xmlns:xs="http://www.w3.org/2001/XMLSchema">
    <xs:include schemaLocation="DotNetConfig.xsd"/>
    <xs:include schemaLocation="snippet.xsd"/>
</xs:schema>
```

4. Open `Catalog.xml` in a text editor and replace `DotNetConfig.xsd` with `Config.xsd`. This effectively remaps the validation, and IntelliSense, for config files to use `Config.xsd` instead of `DotNetConfig.xsd`. However, because this file sources both `DotNetConfig.xsd` and your schema information, you will get validation for both your configuration section and the standard configuration sections.

Summary

In this chapter you have learned how configuration files can be used not only to control how your application runs, but also to store settings that may need to be adjusted at runtime. You should now be able to store simple name-value information, as well as more structured information, within the configuration file.

Several security features of the .NET Framework can be tailored from the configuration file. The diagnostic section of the configuration file is covered in more detail in Chapter 37, in the discussion of event logs.

10

XML Resource Files

Developers quite often overlook the humble XML resource file, as it is often hidden by the IDE so as not to clutter the solution. Because their most common use is as a backing file for forms or web pages, it is possible to write large applications without interacting directly with resource files. However, resource files are an important tool that developers need to be able to use in order to write applications that can be easily maintained and translated into other languages. The first part of this chapter explains why resource files are important and describes the new IDE features that enable developers to work with them. The remainder of the chapter explains how resource files are used to localize an application for different languages and cultures.

Resourcing Your Application

Writing an application often requires data such as images, icons, or sounds (collectively known as *resources*) to enhance the appearance of the application. Furthermore, best coding practices suggest that the use of constant strings throughout your application should be avoided. In any of these cases we could put together a custom solution that stores these resources in files that need to be shipped with application.

An alternative is to include these resources in a resource file that can be compiled into your application. This way, you not only have the resources in a format that you can work with, they are automatically available within your application.

In Visual Studio 2005, forms are initially represented by two files: the generated designer file (for example, `form1.designer.vb`) and the code-beside file (for example, `form1.vb`). When a control, such as a button, is first added to the form, a resource file (for example, `form1.resx`) is automatically created for the form. By default, this resource file contains very little data, as most properties are hard-coded into the designer file. This file becomes very important when localization is turned on for the form. When this is done, via the properties grid shown in Figure 10-1, the designer properties for the controls on the form are persisted to the resource file.

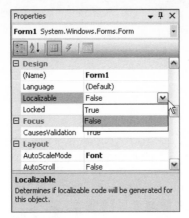

Figure 10-1

The following code snippet shows the designer-generated method `InitializeComponent`, which creates and sets properties on `Button1`. This is how the code would appear with the `Localizable` property on the form set to `False`:

```
Private Sub InitializeComponent()
    Me.Button1 = New Button
    '
    'Button1
    '
    Me.Button1.Location = New Point(71, 43)
    Me.Button1.Size = New Size(185, 166)
    Me.Button1.Text = "Button1"
    Me.Button1.TabIndex = 0
    Me.Button1.Name = "Button1"
    Me.Button1.UseVisualStyleBackColor = True
    '
    'Form1
    '
    Me.Controls.Add(Me.Button1)
End Sub
```

Once the `Localizable` property of the form has been set to `True`, the form uses the new `Component ResourceManager` class to load and apply properties found in the associated resource file (this framework class is covered in more detail later in this chapter):

```
Private Sub InitializeComponent()
    Dim resources As New componentResourceManager(GetType(Form1))
    Me.Button1 = New Button
    '
    'Button1
    '
    resources.ApplyResources(Me.Button1, "Button1")
    Me.Button1.Name = "Button1"
    Me.Button1.UseVisualStyleBackColor = True
    '
```

```
    'Form1
    '
    Me.Controls.Add(Me.Button1)
End Sub
```

Although the resource files generated by the forms designer can be manually edited, this is not encouraged because changes may be overwritten the next time the file is regenerated by the designer.

When resources files are used properly, they can provide a number of benefits because they are a convenient place to store strings, icons, images, and other data that might be referenced by an application. The use of resource files, both for tracking form properties and for application data, is a must for any application that needs to be translated for a foreign culture. We use the term "culture" here because it is more than language that can differ between countries and ethnic groups. Resource files enable developers to provide alternative data for different cultures. When the application is run, the .NET Framework uses the current culture information to determine which data to load based upon the resource fallback process. Common examples of information that might vary between cultures are prompts, titles, error messages, and button images.

What Are Resources?

A resource is any data required by an application, whether it is a string, an icon, an image, or even an audio clip. Resources are nonexecutable and support the running of the application through the provision of data such as location, size, and other physical properties of controls. While most resources are typically strings, images, audio, or icons, there is no reason why a resource could not be a more complex object that supports serialization.

Three types of resource files can be compiled into an application: text, resx (XML resource file), and resources (binary resource file) file formats. Whole files can also be embedded as application resources where needed. Most developers who use Visual Studio 2005 will use resx files and embedded file resources.

Text File Resources

Text files are the most basic sort of resource because they are limited to providing string values. In applications for which a large number of string literals need to be managed, a simple text file can be the easiest way to manage them because they are not cluttered among the other resources of the application.

The format of strings defined in a text resource file is a name-value pair, where the name is used to reference the resource in code, as shown in the following example:

```
Error_Unable_To_Connect = Unable to connect to specified server
```

Because each name-value pair is delimitated by a new line, this character cannot be added to the string. However C-style escape characters can be used to insert new lines (\n) or tabs (\t) into the text.

Comments can also be added to the resource file by prepending a line with a semicolon, as shown here:

```
;Error message to be displayed when a connection could not be made to the server
Error_Unable_To_Connect = Unable to connect to specified server
```

Text resource files should be saved with the file extension of `txt` or `restext`. The latter is useful when you want to distinguish text resource files from regular text files.

Although text resource files are easy to edit and update, it is harder to integrate them into your application. As text files, they cannot be directly compiled into an application; they must instead be converted into either resx or resources files. This can be achieved using the Resource Generator utility, `resgen .exe`, located in the `bin` folder of the Visual Studio 2005 SDK (located at C:\Program Files\Microsoft Visual Studio 8\SDK\v2.0\Bin):

```
resgen StringResources.txt StringResources.resources
```

The output file — in this case, StringResources.`resources` — can be included in your application to give you access to those resources.

A prebuild event can be used to convert text resource files into a resources file that can be compiled into the main application build. This will ensure that the resource files contained in the application are always up to date. To do this, include the text resource file in the application and set the build action property to None. Navigate to the Project Settings window and on the Compile tab select Build Events. In the prebuild events, enter the `resgen` command required to compile your text resource file:

```
"C:\Program Files\Microsoft Visual Studio 8\SDK\v2.0\Bin\resgen.exe"
"$(ProjectDir)StringResources.txt" "$(ProjectDir StringResources.resources"
```

Building the application will generate the resources file that needs to be included within your application as an embedded resource. Figure 10-2 illustrates how both the text and resources file are included within an application with appropriate build action properties.

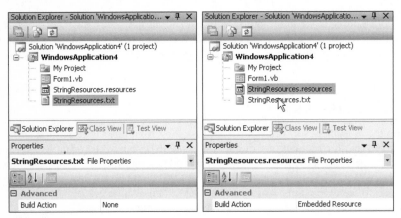

Figure 10-2

ResxResource Files

A much more user-friendly format for resources is the XML resource file, commonly referred to as a *resx file*. This is a simple XML data file that contains name-value pairs of XML nodes. The advantage of this format is that the value is not restricted to just a string; it can be any type that is serializable or can be represented as a string.

The following XML snippet shows a resource named `HelloWorld`, with associated value and comment. As you can see from the code, no information is available about the type of data contained within the resource, as this is a string resource:

```
<data name="HelloWorld">
  <value>Say Hello</value>
  <comment>This is how we say hello</comment>
</data>
```

The next snippet illustrates how a more complex data type can be stored in a resource file as a string representation. It also shows how an assembly alias can be used to reference an external assembly that contains type information. When this resource is accessed, the type information will be used to convert the string value to an object of this type:

```
<assembly alias="System.Drawing" name="System.Drawing, Version=2.0.0.0,
Culture=neutral, PublicKeyToken=b03f5f7f11d50a3a" />
  <data name="Button1.Location" type="System.Drawing.Point, System.Drawing">
    <value>71, 43</value>
  </data>
```

Although resx files can be included in an application without having to use the Resource File Generator (`resgen`), they are still converted prior to being compiled into the application. During the build process, resources files are generated for each resx file in the application. These are subsequently linked into the application.

Adding Resources

Visual Studio 2005 now supports a rich user interface for adding and modifying resource files. In the past it was possible to view the contents of a resource file within the IDE. However, unless the resource was a string, or had a string representation, it was not possible to modify the value within the resource file. The new resource editor provides support for strings, images, icons, audio, files, and more.

Double-clicking on a resx file within the Solution Explorer will bring up the resource editor. In the top left-hand corner of the resource editor is a drop-down list that navigates between resources of different types, as shown in Figure 10-3.

Figure 10-3

Depending on the resource type, the editor displays the resource in an appropriate format. For example, strings are presented in an editable textbox, whereas images are presented as thumbnail images that can be opened and edited. Adding new resources is as simple as selecting the Add Resource drop-down, choosing the appropriate resource type, and then adding the necessary information.

Embedding Files as Resources

It is often necessary to embed an entire file in an application. This can be done by including the file in the application and modifying the build action. Depending on the file type, when the item is included in the application, the build action (click on the file and open the Properties window) is normally set to either Compile or None. If this is changed to Embedded Resource, the entire file will be added to the application as an embedded resource.

When images, icons, and other files are added to an existing resource file, they are added as a *resxfileref* item. The file will appear in the resources directory, but the build action will be None. When the application is built, these files are compiled into the resources file prior to being linked into the application. In the past, the data from these files was pulled out and added to the resx file as a binary block. This meant that, once added, the data could not be easily modified. With the new file reference item, the data remains in an associated file and can easily be updated.

Accessing Resources

Resources can be accessed in code using a *resource manager*. A resource manager is easily created from the name of the resource file and a reference to the assembly from which the resource should be extracted:

```
Dim res As New ResourceManager ("MyProject.MyResources", GetType(Form1).Assembly)
```

Once created, resources can be extracted using either the GetObject or GetString functions:

```
res.GetObject("StringResource")
```

Resource Naming

Resources are named by combining the name of the resource file to which they belong and the root namespace. For example, if you have a resource file called Sample.resources in a project called MyProject, the full resource name will be MyProject.Sample.

This is particularly important to remember when you make a file an embedded resource. Each file can be accessed by prepending the project name to the filename. Unlike resource files, the name of the file retains the extension. For example, if you have a file called ASimpleDataDocument.doc in a project called MyProject, then it will need to be referenced as MyProject. ASimpleDataDocument.doc.

Satellite Resources

One of the big advantages of placing data in a resource file is the resulting capability to translate the data into foreign cultures. Instead of including all the languages in the single resource file, each culture is stored in a resource file that has a suffix defined by the culture.

Cultures

Cultures are defined by a combination of two lowercase letters, which represent the language, and two uppercase letters, which represent the country or region of the culture, separated by a hyphen. For example, U.S. English and Australian English are represented as en-US and en-AU, respectively. The corresponding resource files for these cultures would be `MyResource.en-US.resx` and `MyResource.en-AU.resx`. A full list of culture identifiers can be found at `http://msdn2.microsoft.com/en-us/library/system .globalization.cultureinfo.aspx`. For those who are curious, you can enumerate over all cultures available returned by `CultureInfo.GetCultures(CultureTypes.AllCultures)`.

This returns approximately 220 cultures that can be grouped as follows:

❑ **Invariant culture:** No language or country identifier (for example, `Form1.resx`). Data is not dependent upon culture. For example, this might be the company logo, which will not vary and is not dependent upon culture information.

❑ **Neutral culture:** Language identifier (for example, `Form1.en.resx`). Data is dependent upon language alone — for example, a simple warning message that merely needs to be translated.

❑ **Specific culture:** Language and country identifier (for example, `Form1.en-US.resx`). Data is dependent upon both language and country/region — for example, form layout, color, and prompts should all be translated and adjusted for a specific country.

Creating Culture Resources

If you are creating additional resource files for a form, then it is important to ensure that the `Localizable` property is set to `True`. There are three ways to create culture-specific resource files:

❑ If you know the identifier of the culture for which you want to generate a resource file, you can simply save the resx file to `<culture identifier>.resx`. For example, if you were converting the resource file `Form1.resx` to Australian English, you would save it as `Form1.en-AU.resx`. You will notice that when you do this, Visual Studio removes the original resx file from the solution and adds the new culture-specific resx file. In order to get both files to show up nested under the Form1 node, you actually need to exclude the new resx file, refresh the solution view (by closing and reopening the solution), and then include both files back into the project.

❑ Visual Studio supports a much better way to create culture-specific resource files for forms. From the Properties window for the form, you can select Language. The name of this property is slightly misleading because it adjusts not only the language, but also the country/region of the form in designer mode. This property is initially set to (Default) and should always be returned to this setting after you have finished generating or modifying specific culture resource files. To generate the resource file for Australian English, select English (Australia) from the Language drop-down and make appropriate changes to the form. Once you are comfortable with the new layout, save it and reset the Language property to (Default).

❑ The last way to generate culture-dependent resource files is to use `WinRes.exe`. Although it's not added to the Start menu, it is available under the .NET Framework SDK folder (`c:\program files\microsoft visual studio 8\sdk\v2.0\bin`) and is a graphical utility for generating resource files for forms. This utility can load an existing resource file, allow properties of all controls on the form to be modified, and then save the changes to a particular culture resource file. Before opening a form's resource file using this utility, make sure that the `Localizable` property is set to `True`; otherwise, the file will not load properly.

Loading Culture Resource Files

At this point you might be wondering how resource files interact, and whether culture-specific resource files have to be created and compiled at the same time as the main application. The answer to both of these questions lies in the resource *fallback process*, which is the mechanism by which the `ResourceManager` class loads resources.

The fallback process has three levels based upon the current user interface culture (UI culture) of the executing thread. This can be accessed in code via the `CultureInfo.CurrentUICulture` property. Be aware that this is different from `CultureInfo.CurrentCulture`, which is the current culture used in string comparisons, date formats, and so on. Unlike the current culture, which is based upon the regional settings of the computer (which can be adjusted using Control Panel⇨Regional Settings), the default UI Culture is dependent upon the Windows user interface language pack that is currently selected. Unless you have a Windows Multilingual User Interface Pack installed, you will not be able to modify the default UI culture for your applications.

Although you can't change the default user interface culture, you can adjust this property in code. A word of caution here, however: Without the interface pack installed, some cultures may not display correctly.

```
Thread.CurrentThread.CurrentUICulture = New CultureInfo("en-US")
```

Using the current user interface culture, the fallback process tries to locate resources based on a culture match. For example, if the UI culture is `en-US`, the process would start off by looking for specific culture resources that match both language (English) and country (U.S.). Where no resource can be located, the process falls back to neutral culture resources that match just the language (English). Finally, if still no resource can be located, then the process falls back to *invariant culture*, indicating there is no match on language or country.

Satellite Culture Resources

So far we have mentioned only how a resource can be converted into a new culture and added to an application. While this method gives you control over which cultures are deployed with your application, it would be better if you didn't have to rebuild your entire application whenever a culture resource needed to be modified, or when you decided to add support for a new culture.

When Visual Studio 2005 compiles culture resources, it splits the resource files into a hub-and-spoke arrangement, using satellite assemblies to contain culture resources. At the hub is the main assembly that would contain the invariant resources. Satellite assemblies are then created for each culture for which a resource has been created. The naming of the satellite assembly is of the form `MyApp.resources.dll` and it is located in a subdirectory named according to the culture under the main output path. Although there is an implicit relationship between specific cultures (for example, en-US) and neutral cultures (for example, en), satellite assemblies for these cultures should both reside in a subdirectory under the main output path.

Another alternative is for the main assembly and/or satellite assemblies to be installed into the Global Assembly Cache (GAC). In this case, each assembly must be strongly named so that it is unique within the cache.

Clearly, the resource fallback process needs to accommodate assemblies both in the GAC and in subdirectories. Hence, for each culture level (specific, neutral, and invariant) the GAC is checked first, followed by the culture subdirectory. Finally, if no resource is found, an exception is raised.

Note that culture resource files do not have to contain all the resources defined in the default resource file. The resource fallback process will load the resource from the default resource file if it is not located in a more specific resource file, so it makes sense to save only resources that are different in the specified culture.

Accessing Specifics

Numerous shortcuts have been built into the .NET Framework to support the most common tasks related to accessing resources. These include the My namespace (VB.NET only), single-line image loading, and the new ComponentResourceManager class.

My Namespace

VB.NET has introduced the concept of the My namespace, which serves several purposes, including providing wrapper functionality to projectwide resources. For example, an image resource called CompanyLogo can be accessed as follows:

```
Dim img As Image = My.Resources.CompanyLogo
```

This wrapper is an extension of the designer file generated by resgen, enabling such resources to be accessed using a single line. Although C# does not have the My Namespace, it does provide the designer file for project resources so that developers can easily access these resources in a strongly typed manner.

Bitmap and Icon Loading

Images and icons are two of the most common data types held in resource files. Therefore, both the Bitmap and Icon classes in the framework support a constructor that can create an instance directly from a resource without the need to use a resource manager:

```
Dim img As New Bitmap(gettype(ThisClass),"MyImage")
```

ComponentResourceManager

In the first example in this chapter, after localization was turned on, a ComponentResourceManager object was used to retrieve resources associated with the form. The ComponentResourceManager extends the base ResourceManager by providing additional functionality for retrieving and applying component properties. Here are the original four lines required to set the properties defined for Button1:

```
Me.Button1.Location = New Point(71, 43)
Me.Button1.Size = New Size(185, 166)
Me.Button1.Text = "Button1"
Me.Button1.TabIndex = 0
```

Using the `ComponentResourceManager`, this can be condensed to just one line:

```
resources.ApplyResources(Me.Button1, "Button1")
```

In previous versions of Visual Studio, the code that was generated when localization was turned on was much more verbose. For each property, a separate call was made to the `ResourcesManager` to retrieve the property by name, as shown in this code snippet:

```
Me.Button1.Location = CType(resources.GetObject("Button1.Location"), Point)
Me.Button1.Size = CType(resources.GetObject("Button1.Size"), Size)
Me.Button1.TabIndex = CType(resources.GetObject("Button1.TabIndex"), Integer)
Me.Button1.Text = resources.GetString("Button1.Text")
```

It is still possible to write this code because the `GetObject` method is still available on the `ComponentResourceManager`. The issue with writing this code is that each property that is going to be localized needs to be known at compile time. As such, every property on every control was added to the resource file. This added excess properties (even when they were no different from the default value) to the resource file. It also added huge overhead when loading up a form, as each property was set via a resource property.

The `ApplyResources` method in the `ComponentResourceManager` class works in reverse. By specifying a control name, which must be unique on a form, all resources that start with that prefix are extracted. The full resource name is then used to determine the property to set on the control. For example, a resource with the name `Button1.Location` would be extracted for the control called `Button1`, and the value used to set the `Location` property on that control.

This process eliminates the need to have all properties specified in a resource file. It also enables culture resource files to specify additional properties that perhaps were not defined in the default resource file.

You might be wondering whether there are any additional penalties in using the `ComponentResourceManager`. In order to set a property on a control using the name of the property, the `ComponentResourceManager` uses *reflection* to find the appropriate property. Once it has been retrieved, it can be invoked. Each search that is done in order to set the property is relatively expensive. However, given the reduced number of properties that are to be set, the trade-off is definitely worthwhile, as the application can easily be localized without recompilation of the main application.

Coding Resource Files

In addition to the rich visual tools that Visual Studio 2005 now provides for editing resource files, it is possible to create resource files from code. The .NET Framework provides support for reading and writing resource files using two interfaces: `IResourceReader` and `IResourceWriter`. Once the resource files have been created, they need to be added to the application or manually linked so that they can be referenced within the application.

❏   **IResource Reader:** The reader interface ensures that resource readers have the following methods:

    ❏   **GetEnumerator:** The `GetEnumerator` method retrieves an `IDictionaryEnumerator` object that permits the developer to iterate over each of the resources in the resource file.

    ❏   **Close:** The `Close` method is used to close the resource reader and release any associated resources.

❏   **IResource Writer:** The writer interface ensures that resource writers have the following methods:

    ❏   **AddResource:** There are three overloads to the `AddResource` method that support adding resources to the resource file. Both of the framework implementations of this interface have either an additional overload of this method or an alternative method for adding resources. The overloads that are part of this interface support adding resources in a name-value pair. Each method has the resource name as the first parameter; and takes a value, as a string, byte array, or object, as the second parameter. The final implementation that takes an object as a parameter may need to be serializable or converted to a string via a typeconverter.

    ❏   **Close:** The `Close` method writes resources out to the stream before closing it.

    ❏   **Generate:** Unlike the `Close` method, the `Generate` method simply writes the resources out to the stream without closing the stream. Once called, any other method will cause an exception to be raised.

ResourceReader and ResourceWriter

The `ResourceReader` and `ResourceWriter` are an implementation of the `IResource` interfaces to support reading and writing directly to resources files. Although reading and writing to this format is the most direct, as it reduces the need to use resgen to generate the resources file, it does limit the quality of information that can be retrieved when reading from the file. Each resource is treated as a series of bytes where the type is unknown.

ResxResourceReader and ResxResourceWriter

The `ResxResourceReader` and `ResxResourceWriter` are a more versatile implementation of the `IResource` interfaces. In addition to supporting the `IResource` interface, the `ResxResourceWriter` supports an additional overload of the `AddResource` method, whereby a `ResxDataNode` can be added. A `ResxDataNode` is very similar to a dictionary entry, as it has a key (in this case, the `Name` property) and a value (which needs to be set when the node is created). However, the difference is that this node can support additional properties such as a comment and, as an alternative to a value, a file reference (for example, where an image needs to be added to a resource file).

As mentioned previously, it is possible to add a file reference into a resx file so that the file is still editable yet has the benefit of being compiled into the resource file by `resgen.exe`. The supporting class in the framework is `ResxFileRef`. This can be instantiated and added as a resource using the `ResxResourceWriter`. This inserts an XML node similar to the following snippet:

```
<data name="Figure_11_2" type="ResXFileRef, System.Windows.Forms">
   <value>..\Resources\CompanyLogo.tif;System.Drawing.Bitmap, System.Drawing,
Version=2.0.0.0, Culture=neutral, PublicKeyToken=b03f5f7f11d50a3a</value>
   </data>
```

Resource Files: A Word of Caution

Resource files are the best strategy for storing static application data. Although resource files are linked into the application as part of the compilation process, the contents of the files can easily be extracted and made human readable. As such, resource files are not suitable for storing secure data such as passwords and credit card information.

Custom Resources

Although Visual Studio provides good support for international application development using resource files, there are times when it is not possible to get the level of control required using the default behavior. This section delves a little deeper into how you can serialize custom objects to the resource file and how you can generate designer files, which give you strongly typed accessor methods for resource files you have created.

Visual Studio 2005 enables you to store strings, images, icons, audio files, and other files within a resource file. This can all be done using the rich user interface provided. To store a more complex data type within a resource file, you need to serialize it into a string representation that can be included within the resource file.

The first step in adding any data type into a resource file is to make that data type serializable. This can be achieved easily by marking the class with the `Serializable` attribute. Once it is marked as serializable, the object can be added to a resource file using an implementation of the `IResourceWriter` interface—for example, the `ResXResourceWriter`:

```
<Serializable()> _
Public Class Person
    Public Name As String
    Public Height As Integer
    Public Weight As Double
End Class
Dim p As New Person
p.Name = "Bob"
p.Height = 167
p.Weight = 69.5

Dim rWriter As New ResXResourceWriter("foo.resx")
rWriter.AddResource("DefaultPerson", p)
rWriter.Close()
```

Serializing an object this way has a couple of drawbacks, however:

❑ Using code to write out this resource file needs to be done prior to the build process so that the resource file can be included in the application. Clearly, this becomes an administrative nightmare, as it is an additional stage in the build process.

❑ Furthermore, the serialized representation of the class is a binary blob and is not human readable. The assumption here is that what is written in the generating code is correct. Unfortunately, this is seldom the case, and it would be easier if the content could be human readable within Visual Studio 2005.

A workaround for both these issues is to define a `TypeConverter` for the class and use that to represent the class as a string. This way, the resource can be edited within the Visual Studio resource editor. `TypeConverters` provide a mechanism through which the framework can determine whether it is possible to represent a class (in this case, a `Person` class) as a different type (in this case, as a string). The first step is to create a `TypeConverter` as follows:

```
Imports System.ComponentModel
Imports System.ComponentModel.Design.Serialization
Imports System.Globalization

Public Class PersonConverter
    Inherits TypeConverter

    Public Overrides Function CanConvertFrom _
            (ByVal context As ITypeDescriptorContext, _
            ByVal sourceType As Type) As Boolean
        If (sourceType Is GetType(String)) Then
            Return True
        End If
        Return MyBase.CanConvertFrom(context, sourceType)
    End Function

    Public Overrides Function CanConvertTo _
            (ByVal context As ITypeDescriptorContext, _
             ByVal destinationType As Type) As Boolean
        If (destinationType Is GetType(InstanceDescriptor)) Then
            Return True
        End If
        Return MyBase.CanConvertTo(context, destinationType)
    End Function

    Public Overrides Function ConvertFrom _
            (ByVal context As ITypeDescriptorContext, _
             ByVal culture As CultureInfo, _
             ByVal value As Object) As Object
        Dim text1 As String = TryCast(value, String)
        If (text1 Is Nothing) Then
            Return MyBase.ConvertFrom(context, culture, value)
        End If
        Dim text2 As String = text1.Trim
        If (text2.Length = 0) Then
            Return Nothing
        End If
        If (culture Is Nothing) Then
            culture = CultureInfo.CurrentCulture
        End If
        Dim ch1 As Char = culture.TextInfo.ListSeparator.Chars(0)
        Dim chArray1 As Char() = New Char() {ch1}
        Dim textArray1 As String() = text2.Split(chArray1)
        If (textArray1.Length = 3) Then
            Dim o As New Person
            o.Name = textArray1(0)
            o.Height = CInt(textArray1(1))
            o.Weight = CDbl(textArray1(1))
            Return o
```

```
        End If
        Throw New ArgumentException("Unable to convert From")
    End Function

    Public Overrides Function GetCreateInstanceSupported _
            (ByVal context As ITypeDescriptorContext) As Boolean
        Return True
    End Function

    Public Overrides Function GetProperties _
            (ByVal context As ITypeDescriptorContext, _
             ByVal value As Object, _
             ByVal attributes As Attribute()) As PropertyDescriptorCollection
        Dim collection1 As PropertyDescriptorCollection = _
            TypeDescriptor.GetProperties(GetType(Person), attributes)
        Dim textArray1 As String() = New String() {"Name", "Height", "Weight"}
        Return collection1.Sort(textArray1)
    End Function

    Public Overrides Function ConvertTo _
            (ByVal context As ITypeDescriptorContext, _
             ByVal culture As CultureInfo, _
             ByVal value As Object, _
             ByVal destinationType As Type) As Object
        If (destinationType Is Nothing) Then
            Throw New ArgumentNullException("Unable to convert To")
        End If
        If TypeOf value Is Person Then
            If (destinationType Is GetType(Person)) Then
                Dim o As Person = CType(value, Person)
                If (culture Is Nothing) Then
                    culture = CultureInfo.CurrentCulture
                End If
                Dim text1 As String = (culture.TextInfo.ListSeparator & " ")
                Dim converter1 As TypeConverter = _
                    TypeDescriptor.GetConverter(GetType(Integer))
                Dim textArray1 As String() = New String(2) {}
                Dim num1 As Integer = 0
                textArray1(num1) = _
                    converter1.ConvertToString(context, culture, o.Name)
                num1 += 1
                textArray1(num1) = _
                    converter1.ConvertToString(context, culture, o.Height)
                num1 += 1
                textArray1(num1) = _
                    converter1.ConvertToString(context, culture, o.Weight)
                num1 += 1
                Return String.Join(text1, textArray1)
            End If
        End If
        Return MyBase.ConvertTo(context, culture, value, destinationType)
    End Function


    Public Overrides Function CreateInstance _
```

```
                (ByVal context As ITypeDescriptorContext, _
                  ByVal propertyValues As IDictionary) As Object
          If (propertyValues Is Nothing) Then
              Throw New ArgumentNullException("propertyValues")
          End If
          Dim obj1 As Object = propertyValues.Item("Name")
          Dim obj2 As Object = propertyValues.Item("Height")
          Dim obj3 As Object = propertyValues.Item("Weight")
          If ( _
              ((obj1 Is Nothing) OrElse _
                  (obj2 Is Nothing) OrElse _
                  (obj3 Is Nothing)) _
              OrElse _
              (Not TypeOf obj1 Is String OrElse _
                  Not TypeOf obj2 Is Integer OrElse _
                  Not TypeOf obj3 Is Double) _
              ) Then
              Throw New ArgumentException("Unable to Create Instance")
          End If
          Dim o As New Person
          o.Name = CType(obj1, String)
          o.Height = CType(obj2, Integer)
          o.Weight = CType(obj3, Double)
          Return o
      End Function

      Public Overrides Function GetPropertiesSupported _
              (ByVal context As ITypeDescriptorContext) As Boolean
          Return True
      End Function

  End Class
```

The class being represented also needs to be attributed with the `TypeConverter` attribute:

```
<System.ComponentModel.TypeConverter(GetType(PersonConverter))> _
<Serializable()> _
Public Class Person
    Public Name As String
    Public Height As Integer
    Public Weight As Double
End Class
```

Now this item can be added to a resource file using the string representation of the class. For example, an entry in the resx file might look like this:

```
    <assembly alias=" WindowsApplication1" name="WindowsApplication1,
  Version=1.0.0.0, Culture=neutral, PublicKeyToken=null" />
    <data name="Manager" type=" WindowsApplication1.Person, WindowsApplication1">
      <value>Joe, 175, 69.5</value>
    </data>
```

Designer Files

The resource generator utility, resgen, has a number of improvements that enable you to build strongly typed wrapper classes for your resource files. When you add a resx file to your application, Visual Studio will automatically create a designer file that wraps the process of creating a resource manager and accessing the resources by name. The accessor properties are all strongly typed and are generated by the designer to reduce the chance of invalid type conversions and references.

Unfortunately, Visual Studio 2005 does not automatically generate the designer file for text resource files, because text resource files cannot be explicitly added to the application. The process of generating a resource file from the text file can be extended to include the generation of the designer file.

A new argument has been added to resgen that facilitates the generation of this designer file:

```
resgen sample.txt sample.resources /str:vb
```

Both of the output files need to be added into the application so that the resources are accessible. In order to ensure that the resources can be correctly accessed, it is important to ensure that the naming used within the designer file matches the naming of the compiled resources. Additional parameters can be provided to control the namespace, class name, and output filename:

```
resgen sample.txt defaultnamespace.sample.resources
/str:vb,defaultnamespace,sample,sample.vb
```

In this case, the fully qualified output class would be `defaultnamespace.sample`, and the use of this file would allow access to resources without an exception being raised. Once the correct command has been determined, you can update your prebuild event to include the generation of the designer file. This way, every time the file is modified and saved and the application is compiled, the designer file will be current.

Summary

This chapter demonstrated how important XML resource files are to building an application that can both access static data and be easily localized into foreign languages and cultures. The rich user interface provided within Visual Studio 2005 allows resources such as images, icons, strings, audio, and other files to be easily added to an application.

The built-in support for localizing forms and generating satellite assemblies empowers developers to write applications that can target a global market. You have also seen that the user interface provided within Visual Studio 2005 is extensible, enabling you to modify it to interact with your own custom resource types.

Part III
Documentation and Research

Chapter 11: Help and Research

Chapter 12: XML Comments

Chapter 13: Control and Document Outline

Help and Research

Visual Studio 2005 is an immensely complex development environment that encompasses multiple languages based on an extensive framework of libraries and components. It's almost impossible to know everything about the IDE, let alone each of the languages or even the full extent of the .NET Framework.

This poses some challenges because all aspects of the development toolset have undergone significant changes since the last version. The .NET Framework has gone through a major revision with 2.0, the languages have evolved to synchronize with the Framework, and important features are introduced. The development environment has also been modified, as shown in Part I of this book.

The huge amount of knowledge required to fully understand every facet of this product is beyond the scope of a single book or course. More than likely, you'll periodically need to obtain more information on a specific topic. To help you in these situations, Visual Studio 2005 comes with comprehensive documentation in the form of the MSDN Library, Visual Studio 2005 Edition. This chapter walks through the methods of researching documentation associated with developing projects in Visual Studio 2005, and discusses the new interface for help that has been introduced in this latest version.

Accessing Help

The easiest way to get help for Visual Studio 2005 is to use the same method you would use for almost every Windows application ever created — press the F1 key, the universal shortcut key for help. If you do so, the first thing you'll notice is that help is contextual. For instance, if the cursor were currently positioned on or inside a class definition in a Visual Basic project, the help window would open immediately with a mini tutorial about what the `class` statement is and how it works, as shown in Figure 11-1.

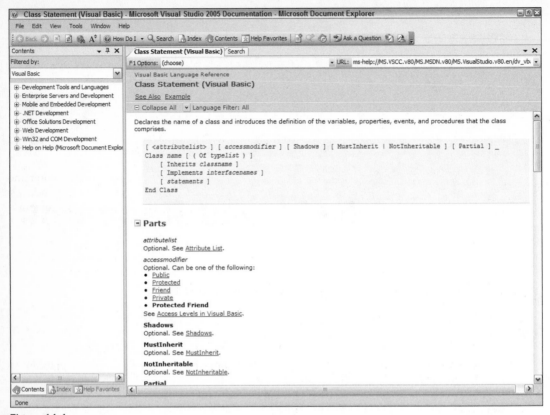

Figure 11-1

This is incredibly useful because more often than not you can go directly to a help topic in the documentation that deals with the problem you're currently researching simply by choosing the right context and pressing F1.

However, in some situations you will want to go directly to the table of contents, or the search page within the help system. Visual Studio 2005 provides the capability for doing this through its main Help menu (see Figure 11-2). The following table summarizes the commands related to help documentation (note the different keyboard shortcuts depending on your environment setup):

Menu Command	Visual Basic Shortcut	C# Shortcut	Action
How Do I	Ctrl+F1	Ctrl+F1, H	Opens a special set of documentation that introduces basic programming concepts for the language you're working in
Search	Ctrl+Alt+F3	Ctrl+F1, S	Opens the help Document Explorer, with the Search page active and ready for you to perform a research action

Menu Command	Visual Basic Shortcut	C# Shortcut	Action
Contents	Ctrl+Alt+F1	Ctrl+F1, C	Makes the Contents tab the active one in the help Document Explorer
Index	Ctrl+Alt+F2	Ctrl+F1, I	Shows the Index tab in the help Document Explorer
Help Favorites	Ctrl+Alt+F	Ctrl+F1, F	Opens the help Document Explorer with the Help Favorites tab active
Index Results	Shift+Alt+F2	Ctrl+F1, T	Opens the help Document Explorer and then opens the Index Results window so you can view the results of a previous search
Dynamic Help	Ctrl+Alt+F4	Ctrl+F1, D	Dynamic Help is a special tool window that dynamically changes its contents based on the context of what you're doing.

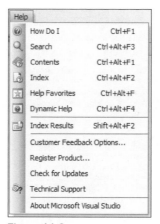

Figure 11-2

Document Explorer

The commands shown in the preceding table, with the exception of Dynamic Help, will open the main help documentation for Visual Studio 2005. With this latest version of Visual Studio, Microsoft has introduced a completely new help system, utilizing an interface known as the *Document Explorer*. Based on a combination of HTML Help, modern web browsers, and the Visual Studio 2005 IDE, the Document Explorer is a feature-rich application in its own right that can perform powerful functions.

Despite the revolutionary changes made to the documentation system, the Document Explorer still presents a familiar interface. It's constructed using regular Windows application standards: customizable menus, a toolbar at the top of the interface, a tabbed tool window docked by default to the left side of the main window, and a primary workspace that displays the documents you're working in, as well as the Search pane.

The phrase "tool window" was not used by accident in the previous paragraph. The pane on the left side of Figure 11-1 works in exactly the same way as the tool windows of Visual Studio 2005 itself. In fact, it's actually three tool windows: the Contents, Index, and Help Favorites tool windows. Each window can be repositioned independently — to float over the main interface, or be docked to any side of the Document Explorer user interface. The tool windows can be made to share the same space, as they do by default, or be docked above, below, or alongside each other, as the example in Figure 11-3 illustrates.

The help system can be used in a similar fashion to previous versions of Help. Utilizing the Contents tool window, you can browse through the hierarchy of topics until you locate the information you're seeking. Alternatively, the Index window gives you direct access to the full index generated by the currently compiled local documentation. Finally, just as in previous versions, a particular topic contains multiple hyperlinks to other parts of the documentation that are related to the given topic.

In addition to these traditional means of navigation, the Document Explorer also has a bar at the top of most help topics that provides other commands. Figure 11-1 illustrates this with the Class Statement topic; directly underneath the heading are two direct hotlinks to sections of the current topic, and two functions that can collapse the information or filter it based on a particular language, respectively.

Figure 11-4 shows the latter feature, Language Filter, in action. When the mouse pointer is placed over the Language Filter label, a drop-down list appears with the main Microsoft languages. If you know that the information you want to view is not related to specific languages, you can switch them off by unchecking their respective boxes.

Figure 11-3

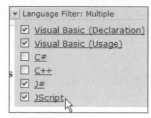

Figure 11-4

Dynamic Help

The only help-related command in the Help menu that does not display the Document Explorer interface is Dynamic Help. Using this command will display the Dynamic Help tool window, shown in Figure 11-5. By default, this window shares space with the Properties tool window, but it can be repositioned just like any other part of the Visual Studio IDE.

Figure 11-5

The Dynamic Help window contents are constantly updated based on the context in which you are working. This feature works regardless of what mode you're working under, so contextually it updates when you're working in Design or Class Diagram modes, changing as you select or add controls or classes.

However, the Dynamic Help window works most effectively when you're writing code. For instance, a simple class definition with one empty function will produce up to a dozen different sets of help information in the Dynamic Help window. To test this out yourself, create a class module and insert the following code:

```
Public Class Form1

    Public Function x() As Boolean
```

```
            Return False
        End Function

    End Class
```

Position the cursor at the start of the keyword `Public` and simply scroll through the code by pressing the right arrow key. As the cursor moves from `Public` to `Class` to `Form1`, you'll see the Dynamic Help window contents changing. Keep moving the cursor and you'll see the list change for the keywords `Function`, `Boolean`, `Return`, and even `False` and `End`.

Each of the links in the list will open the Document Explorer at the specific topic.

> *Using the Dynamic Help tool window has always been very CPU-intensive. With Visual Studio 2005, the performance of this window has noticeably improved but it can still adversely affect machines that only barely meet the system requirements of Visual Studio 2005.*

The Search Window

While these small features of the help system are appreciated, the real advance made in the help engine is the Search window. Figure 11-6 shows the Search window in its default state, with the local help documentation selected and abstracts for each topic result displayed.

Enter the search terms in the top text field and click the Search button. If you wish, you can filter the results before you perform the search, or afterward, or change the way the results will be sorted (both techniques are discussed in a moment).

The search engine starts searching all four main categories of documentation — the local help, MSDN Online, the community of developer web sites approved through Codezone, and the Question database. As it receives information from each group, the corresponding tab is populated with the number of results and the headings of the first three topics. In addition, the main area of the Search results window is populated with the topics that met the criteria, with a heading and brief abstract showing you the first chunk of documentation that will be found in the topic.

As well as these two items, depending on the category you're viewing, you'll find a footer line containing extra information. Figure 11-6 shows the footer information for local documentation searches — language information and documentation source — but MSDN Online and Codezone Community categories will display a rating value, while the Questions results will feature author and date information as well as the rating and source values.

To view a topic that met the search terms, locate it in the results list and click the heading, which is a hyperlink (or double-click anywhere in the abstract area). This will open a new tab if the Search tab is the only one open, or reuse the most recently accessed tab if other documents are already being viewed. To force the Document Explorer to open the topic in a new tab, right-click it and select the Open in New Window command.

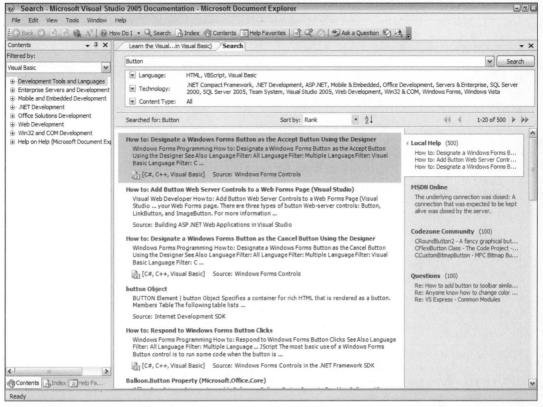

Figure 11-6

Sorting Results

Results can be sorted in a few different ways. Click the drop-down arrow in the Sort by list to choose from multiple options for sorting the results (see Figure 11-7). By default, results are sorted by rank, which tries to determine the most likely search result that you were looking for by comparing the number of times the search terms were found. If there are multiple terms, then results containing all of them will appear before results that only contain one.

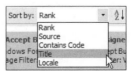

Figure 11-7

Chapter 11

The full list of sort options is itself filtered by the context of your search. For instance, if you're searching the local documentation, then several sort options, such as Rating and Author, are not available. The full list of sort options is shown in the following table:

Sort by	Effect
Rank	A calculated value based on how many search terms are found and how many hits for each, as well as the importance of the hit. For example, a search term found in a heading may be considered more important than one in a footnote or a See Also section.
Source	Sorts the results based on the set of documentation the topic comes from
Contains Code	Tries to determine whether each topic contains code or not
Title	Sorts based on the heading
Locale	The locale of the topic. Mostly these are English-U.S., but especially when you view topics online you may find other locales.
Rating	For online searches, you can sort the results based on ratings given to them by other users.
Author	Sorts results by their author
Topic Date	Sorts the results into date order

Filtering Results

In addition to sorting the results, you can also filter them based on particular technologies. Figure 11-8 shows the extensive list from which you can choose when filtering the search results. This list is incredibly useful when you know the information you need is only related to specific technologies, enabling you to avoid false positives when you search.

Figure 11-8

Keeping Favorites

There will be times when you find topics that you want to keep for later review. The Document Explorer includes a Help Favorites tool window (shown in Figure 11-9) that enables you to do just that.

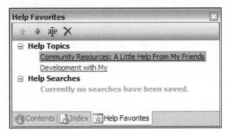

Figure 11-9

To add topics to the Help Favorites window, right-click on the result in the search results window and select the Add to Help Favorites command from the context menu. This menu is also available when you're viewing the actual topic, or you can access the command from the toolbar as well.

The Document Explorer also enables you to save common searches, as evidenced by the appropriately named Help Searches section (refer to Figure 11-9). To add a search, click the Save Search button on the toolbar.

From the Help Favorites list, you can rename both topics and searches by right-clicking the entry and choosing Rename or clicking the Rename command on the Help Favorites toolbar. This can be useful for excessively long headings or some of those esoterically named topics sometimes found in MSDN documentation.

Customizing Help

Just as with Visual Studio 2005, you can customize the way the help system works through a number of options. Rather than go through each one here, this section provides a summary of the options you may want to take a closer look at.

By default, the help system will look online for results and the contents of topics you're trying to look up. Only if it cannot find the results in the online system (or cannot contact the online documentation) does the Document Explorer try the local, offline version. The advantage of this is that you'll always have the most up-to-date information—a godsend for programmers who work with modern tools and find themselves frustrated with outdated documentation.

However, if you have a slow or intermittent Internet connection, you may want to change this option to use the local version of the documentation first, or even to not search the online documentation at all. Both of these options are available from the Online group in the Options window (see Figure 11-10). You can also filter the Codezone Community groups down to only the sites you prefer.

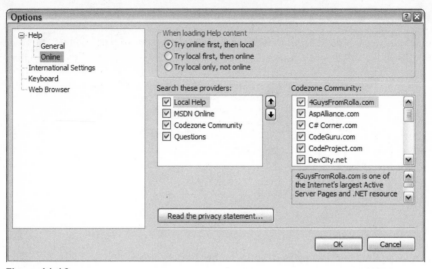

Figure 11-10

The other main options group you may want to take a look at is the Keyboard group. This should be immediately familiar to you because it is a direct clone of the Keyboard group of options in Visual Studio 2005. It enables you to set keyboard shortcuts for any commands that can be performed in the Document Explorer, which can be useful for actions you want to perform often that may be difficult to access. For instance, adding documentation topics to the Help Favorites window (View⇨AddToHelpFavorites) and saving commonly used searches to the same window (Help⇨SaveSearch) are actions to which you can assign keyboard shortcuts.

Ask a Question

The final aspect of the help system that's worth mentioning is the Ask a Question command. This is accessed via the Ask a Question button on the toolbar and redirects you to the main Microsoft Community Forums. From here you can perform searches against questions and answers others have submitted in a plain English format. The results are presented in a similar way to the Document Explorer, as shown in Figure 11-11. You may also choose to browse general groups of questions via the right-hand pane of the window.

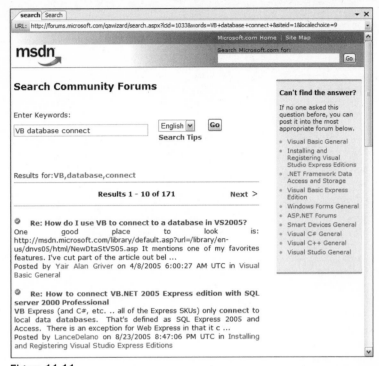

Figure 11-11

Summary

The new Document Explorer is a powerful interface to the documentation that comes with Visual Studio 2005. While it has some new features, the general presentation should be immediately familiar, so you can very easily get accustomed to researching your topics of interest. The ability to easily switch between online and local documentation ensures that you can balance the speed of offline searches with the up-to-date information found on the web; and the abstract paragraphs that are shown in all search results, regardless of their location, helps reduce the number of times you might click on a false positive.

All in all, the help and research engine for Visual Studio 2005 is more powerful than any other documentation system provided with Microsoft development tools. Of course, while getting help on the built-in functionality and features of Visual Studio 2005 is handy, it can be just as vital to keep track of your own applications and classes. The next chapter explains the Visual Studio 2005 XML comments system that enables you to create your own documentation.

12

XML Comments

Documentation is a critical, and often overlooked or abused, feature of the development process. Without documentation, other programmers, code reviewers, and management have a more difficult time analyzing the purpose and implementation of code. You can even have problems with your own code once it becomes complex, and having good internal documentation can aid in the development process.

XML comments are a way of providing that internal documentation for your code without having to go through the process of manually creating and maintaining documents. Instead, as you write your code, you include *metadata* at the top of every definition to explain what it is for, and let Visual Studio do the rest. Once the information has been included in your code, it can be consumed by Visual Studio in a variety of ways, such as providing additional IntelliSense information, or comprehensive documentation on an application solution.

What Are XML Comments?

XML comments are specialized comments that you include in your code listings. When the project goes through the build process, Visual Studio can optionally include a step to generate an XML file based on these comments to provide information about user-defined types such as classes and individual members of a class (user defined or not), including events, functions, and properties.

XML comments can contain any combination of XML and HTML tags, but Visual Studio will perform special processing on a particular set of predefined tags, as you'll see throughout the bulk of this chapter. Any other tags will be included in the generated documentation file as is.

In previous versions of Visual Studio, XML comments were available for C# only, leaving Visual Basic (and other languages) without an efficient way of producing documentation. Visual Studio 2005 rectifies this oversight for Visual Basic, with the two main Microsoft languages using very similar syntax.

How to Add XML Comments

XML comments are added immediately before the member or procedure they are associated with. To specify that a comment should be picked up by the XML comment processor in C#, use the /// prefix. By default, Visual Studio will automatically add the summary section when you first use the /// indicator for a member, and in some instances XML comments will already be present in code generated by the supplied project templates (see Figure 12-1).

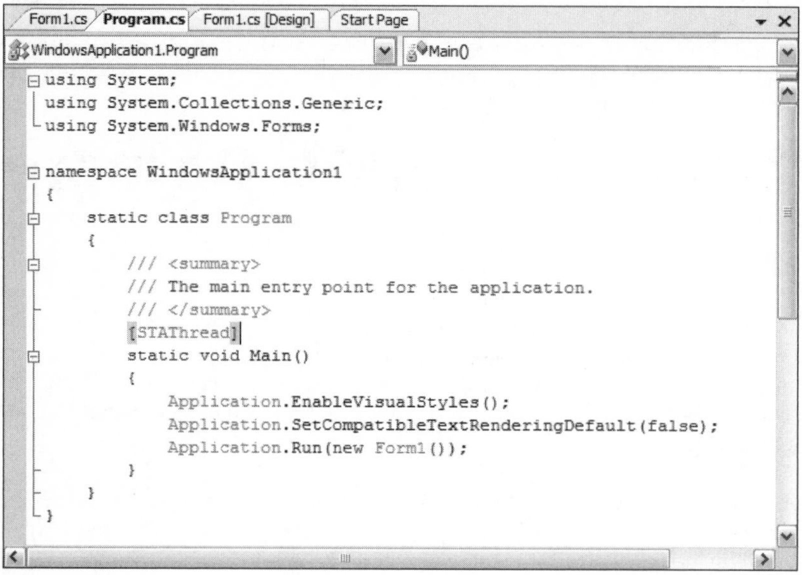

```
Form1.cs   Program.cs   Form1.cs [Design]   Start Page                    ▾ ✕
WindowsApplication1.Program              ▾    Main()                          ▾
using System;
using System.Collections.Generic;
using System.Windows.Forms;

namespace WindowsApplication1
{
    static class Program
    {
        /// <summary>
        /// The main entry point for the application.
        /// </summary>
        [STAThread]
        static void Main()
        {
            Application.EnableVisualStyles();
            Application.SetCompatibleTextRenderingDefault(false);
            Application.Run(new Form1());
        }
    }
}
```

Figure 12-1

The automatic insertion of the summary section can be turned off in the Advanced page for C# in the Text Editor group of options.

Adding XML comments to Visual Basic is achieved by using the triple apostrophe command, as a single apostrophe normally indicates comments. In this way it replicates the way C# documentation is generated.

In both languages, once the comments have been added, the Visual Studio IDE will automatically add a collapse button to the left margin so you can hide the documentation when you're busy writing code. Hovering over the collapsed area will display a tooltip message containing the first few lines of the comment block.

J# doesn't support XML comments in the same way C# and Visual Basic do. Instead, J# uses the Javadoc standard.

XML Comment Tags

While you can use any kind of XML comment structure you like, including your own custom XML tags, Visual Studio's XML comment processor recognizes a number of predefined tags and will automatically format them appropriately. You can supplement these with your own XML schema document so that tags not recognized by Visual Studio 2005 are also formatted in your reports, but using the default tags simplifies the process of creating elegant documentation.

Because documentation is so important, the bulk of this chapter details each of these predefined tags, their syntax, and how you would use them in your own documentation.

The <c> Tag

The <c> tag indicates that the enclosed text should be formatted as code, rather than normal text. It's used for code that is included in a normal text block. The structure of <c> is simple, with any text appearing between the opening and closing tags being marked for formatting in the code style:

```
<c>code-formatted text</c>
```

The following example shows how <c> might be used in the description of a subroutine in C#:

```
/// <summary>
/// The <c>sender</c> object is used to identify who invoked the procedure.
/// </summary>
/// <param name="sender"></param>
private void MyLoad(object sender)
{
    ...code...
}
```

The result of generating the documentation based on the summary section with a simple XSL definition could appear as follows:

> **The** `sender` **object is used to identify who invoked the procedure.**

The <code> Tag

If the amount of text in the documentation you need to format as code is more than just a phrase within a normal text block, you can use the <code> tag instead of <c>. This tag marks everything within it as code, but it's a block-level tag, rather than a character-level tag. The syntax of this tag is a simple opening and closing tag with the text to be formatted inside like so:

```
<code>
Code-formatted text
Code-formatted text
</code>
```

The <code> tag can be embedded inside any other XML comment tag. The following listing shows an example of how it could be used in the summary section of a property definition in Visual Basic:

```
''' <summary>
''' The <c>MyName</c> property is used in conjunction with other properties
''' to setup a user properly. Remember to include the <c>MyPassword</c> field too:
```

```
'''  <code>
'''  theObject.MyName = "Name"
'''  theObject.MyPassword = "x4*@v"
'''  </code>
'''  </summary>
Public ReadOnly Property MyName() As String
    Get
        Return mMyName
    End Get
End Property
```

Generating this documentation and viewing it with a basic transformation will produce something similar to what is shown in Figure 12-2.

Figure 12-2

The <example> Tag

A common requirement for internal documentation is to provide an example of how a particular procedure or member can be used. The <example> tags indicate that the enclosed block should be treated as a discrete section of the documentation, dealing with a sample for the associated member. Effectively, this doesn't do anything more than help organize the documentation, but used in conjunction with an appropriately designed XML style sheet or processing instructions, the example can be formatted properly.

The other XML comment tags, such as <c> and <code>, can be included in the text inside the <example> tags to give you a comprehensively documented sample. The syntax of this block-level tag is simple:

```
<example>
Any sample text goes here.
</example>
```

Using the example from the previous discussion, the following listing moves the <code> formatted text to an <example> section:

```
''' <summary>
''' The <c>MyName</c> property defines the name of the user logging on to the
system.
''' </summary>
''' <example>
''' The <c>MyName</c> property is used in conjunction with other properties
''' to setup a user properly. Remember to include the <c>MyPassword</c> field too:
''' <code>
''' theObject.MyName = "Name"
''' theObject.MyPassword = "x4*@v"
''' </code>
''' </example>
Public ReadOnly Property MyName() As String
    Get
        Return mMyName
    End Get
End Property
```

Figure 12-3 shows how this sample XML comment block could be formatted with an XSL transformation template that includes adding a heading for the Example section.

Figure 12-3

The <exception> Tag

The <exception> tag is used to define any exceptions that could be thrown from within the member associated with the current block of XML documentation. Each exception that can be thrown should be defined with its own <exception> block, with an attribute of cref identifying the type of exception that can occur. Note that the Visual Studio 2005 XML comment processor will check the syntax of the exception block to enforce the inclusion of this attribute. It will also ensure that you don't have multiple <exception> blocks with the same attribute value. The full syntax is as follows:

```
<exception cref="exceptionName">
Exception description.
</exception>
```

Extending the Visual Basic example from the previous tag discussions, the following listing adds two exception definitions to the XML comments associated with the `MyName` property: `System.TimeoutException`, and `System.UnauthorizedAccessException`. It would be expected that inside the associated member code, exceptions of these types would indeed be thrown at appropriate times:

```
''' <summary>
''' The <c>MyName</c> property defines the name of the user logging on to the
system.
''' </summary>
''' <exception cref="System.TimeoutException">
''' Thrown when the code cannot determine if the user is valid within a reasonable
''' amount of time.
''' </exception>
''' <exception cref="System.UnauthorizedAccessException">
''' Thrown when the user identifier is not valid within the current context.
''' </exception>
''' <example>
''' The <c>MyName</c> property is used in conjunction with other properties
''' to setup a user properly. Remember to include the <c>MyPassword</c> field too:
''' <code>
''' theObject.MyName = "Name"
''' theObject.MyPassword = "x4*@v"
''' </code>
''' </example>
Public ReadOnly Property MyName() As String
     Get
          Return mMyName
     End Get
End Property
```

Using the same XSL transformation as before, the documentation would be generated with an additional block containing an Exceptions heading, and each exception would be clearly formatted, as shown in Figure 12-4.

The <include> Tag

You'll often have documentation that needs to be shared across multiple projects. In other situations, one person may be responsible for the documentation while others are doing the coding. Either way, the `<include>` tag will prove useful. The `<include>` tag enables you to refer to comments in a separate XML file so they are brought inline with the rest of your documentation. Using this method, you can move the actual documentation out of the code listing, which can be handy when the comments are extensive.

The syntax of `<include>` requires that you specify which part of the external file is to be used in the current context. The `path` attribute is used to identify the path to the XML node, and uses standard XPath terminology:

```
<include file=="externalFile.xml" path="xmlNodePath[@name='nodeID']/*" />
```

Figure 12-4

The external XML file containing the additional documentation must have a path that can be navigated with the attribute you specify, with the end node containing an attribute of name to uniquely identify the specific section of the XML document to be included.

You can include files in either Visual Basic or C# using the same tag. The following listing takes the C# sample used in the `<c>` tag discussion and moves the documentation to an external file:

```
/// <include file="externalFile.xml" path="MyDoc/Procedures[@name='MyLoad']/*" />
private void MyLoad(object sender)
{
    ...code...
}
```

The external file's contents would be populated with the following XML document structure to synchronize it with what the `<include>` tag processing expects to find:

```
<MyDoc>
  <Procedures name="MyLoad">
    <summary>
      The <c>sender</c> object is used to identify who invoked the procedure.
    </summary>
    <param name="sender"></param>
  </Procedures>
</MyDoc>
```

The <list> Tag

Some documentation requires lists of various descriptions, and with the `<list>` tag you can generate numbered and unnumbered lists along with two-column tables. All three take two parameters for each entry in the list — a term and a description — represented by individual XML tags, but they instruct the processor to generate the documentation in different ways.

To create a list in the documentation, use the following syntax, where `type` can be one of the following values — `bullet`, `numbered`, or `table`:

```
<list type="type">
   <listheader>
      <term>termName</term>
      <description>description</description>
   </listheader>
   <item>
      <term>myTerm</term>
      <description>myDescription</description>
   </item>
</list>
```

The `<listheader>` block is optional, and is usually used for table-formatted lists. Depending on the list type, you can actually omit the `term` tag within each item as well.

The XML for each type of list can be formatted differently using an XML style sheet. An example of how to use the `<list>` tag in Visual Basic appears in the following code. Note how the sample has omitted the `listheader` tag, as it was unnecessary for the bullet list:

```
''' <summary>
''' Some function.
''' </summary>
''' <returns>
''' This function returns either:
''' <list type="bullet">
''' <item>
''' <term>True</term>
''' <description>Indicates that the routine was executed successfully.
''' </description>
''' </item>
''' <item>
''' <term>False</term>
''' <description>Indicates that the routine functionality failed.</description>
''' </item>
''' </list>
''' </returns>
Public Function MyFunction() As Boolean
    ...code...
    Return False
End Function
```

The results shown in Figure 12-5 used an XSL transformation file that included a heading to mark the Returns section.

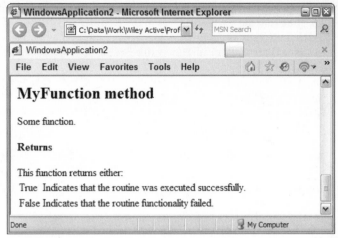

Figure 12-5

The <para> Tag

Without using the various internal block-level XML comments such as `<list>` and `<code>`, the text you add to the main `<summary>`, `<remarks>`, and `<returns>` sections all just runs together. To break it up into readable chunks, you can use the `<para>` tag, which simply indicates that the text enclosed should be treated as a discrete paragraph. The syntax is simple:

```
<para>This text will appear in a separate paragraph.</para>
```

The <param> Tag

To explain the purpose of any parameters in a function declaration, you can use the `<param>` tag. This tag will be processed by the Visual Studio XML comment processor with each instance requiring a `name` attribute that has a value equal to the name of one of the properties. Enclosed within the opening and closing `<param>` tags is the description of the parameter:

```
<param name="parameterName">Definition of parameter.</param>
```

The XML processor will not allow you to create multiple `<param>` tags for the one parameter, producing warnings that are added to the Error List in Visual Studio if you try. The following Visual Basic example shows how the `<param>` tag is used to describe two parameters of a function:

```
''' <param name="MyName">The Name of the user to log on.</param>
''' <param name="MyPassword">The Password of the user to log on.</param>
''' <remarks>Uses <see cref="MyName"/> and <see cref="MyPassword"/> to
''' attempt to log on to the system.
''' </remarks>
Public Function LoginProc(ByVal MyName As String, ByVal MyPassword As String) _
    As Boolean
    '...code...
    Return False
End Function
```

Generating the XML based on this definition with a simple XSL file will produce a result similar to that shown in Figure 12-6. Note that the `cref` attributes in the comment block refer to properties of the form elsewhere in the class definition. While they have the same name as the parameters of the function, the XML comment compiler will correctly resolve the values to the appropriate entry points, as shown in Figure 12-6.

Figure 12-6

The <paramref> Tag

If you are referring to the parameters of the method definition elsewhere in the documentation other than the `<param>` tag, you can use the `<paramref>` tag to format the value, or even link to the parameter information depending on how you code the XML transformation. The XML compiler does not require that the name of the parameter exist, but you must specify the text to be used in the `name` attribute, as the following syntax shows:

```
<paramref name="parameterName"
```

Normally, `<paramref>` tags are used when you are referring to parameters in the larger sections of documentation such as the `<summary>` or `<remarks>` tags, as the following C# example demonstrates:

```
/// <summary>
/// The <paramref name="sender" /> object is used to identify who
/// invoked the procedure.
/// </summary>
/// <param name="sender">Who invoked this routine</param>
/// <param name="e">Any additional arguments to this instance of the event.</param>
private void Form1_Load(object sender, EventArgs e)
{
}
```

The <permission> Tag

To describe the security permission set required by a particular method, use the `<permission>` tag. This tag requires a `cref` attribute to refer to a specific permission type:

```
''' <permission cref="permissionName">
''' description goes here
''' </permission>
```

If the function requires more than one permission, use multiple `<permission>` blocks, as shown in the following Visual Basic example:

```
''' <permission cref="System.Security.Permissions.RegistryPermission">
''' Needs full access to the Windows Registry.
''' </permission>
''' <permission cref="System.Security.Permissions.FileIOPermission">
''' Needs full access to the .config file containing application information.
''' </permission>
Public Function LoginProc(ByVal MyName As String, ByVal MyPassword As String) _
    As Boolean
    '...code...
    Return False
End Function
```

The <remarks> Tag

The `<remarks>` tag is used to add an additional comment block to the documentation associated with a particular method. Discussion on previous tags has shown the `<remarks>` tag in action, but the syntax is as follows:

```
<remarks>
Any further remarks go here
</remarks>
```

Normally, you would create a summary section, briefly outline the method or type, and then include the detailed information inside the `<remarks>` tag, explaining what each parameter is for along with the expected outcomes of accessing the member.

The <returns> Tag

When a method returns a value to the calling code, you can use the `<returns>` tag to describe what it could be. The syntax of `<returns>` is like most of the other block-level tags, consisting of an opening and closing tag with any information detailing the return value enclosed within:

```
<returns>
Description of the return value.
</returns>
```

A simple implementation of `<returns>` in Visual Basic might appear like the following code:

```
''' <returns>
''' This function returns either:
```

```
'''    <c>True</c> which indicates that the routine was executed successfully,
'''    or <c>False</c> which indicates that the routine functionality failed.
'''    </returns>
Public Function MyFunction() As Boolean
       '...code...
       Return False
End Function
```

The <see> Tag

You can add references to other items in the project using the <see> tag. Like some of the other tags already discussed, the <see> tag requires a cref attribute with a value equal to an existing member, whether it is a property or method definition. The XML processor will produce a warning if a member does not exist. The <see> tag is used inline with other areas of the documentation such as <summary> or <remarks>. The syntax is as follows:

```
<see cref="memberName" />
```

When Visual Studio processes the <see> tag it produces a fully qualified address that can then be used as the basis for a link in the documentation when transformed via style sheets. For example, referring to an application with a form containing a property named MyName would result in the following cref value:

```
<see cref="P:applicationName.formName.CheckUser"/>
```

The following example uses the <see> tag in a Visual Basic code listing to provide a link to another function called CheckUser. If this function does not exist, Visual Studio will use IntelliSense to display a warning and add it to the Error List:

```
'''    <param name="MyName">The name of the user to log in.</param>
'''    <param name="MyPassword">The password of the user to log in.</param>
'''    <returns><c>True</c> if login attempt was successful, otherwise returns
'''    <c>False</c>.</returns>
'''    <remarks>
'''    Use <see cref="CheckUser" /> to verify that the user exists
'''    before calling LoginProc.
'''    </remarks>
Public Function LoginProc(ByVal MyName As String, ByVal MyPassword As String) _
       As Boolean
       '...code...
       Return False
End Function
```

The <seealso> Tag

The <seealso> tag is used to generate a separate section containing information about related topics within the documentation. Rather than being inline like <see>, the <seealso> tags are defined outside the other XML comment blocks, with each instance of <seealso> requiring a cref attribute containing the name of the member to which to link. The full syntax appears like so:

```
<seealso cref="memberName" />
```

Modifying the previous example, the next listing shows how the `<seealso>` tag can be implemented in Visual Basic code:

```
''' <param name="MyName">The name of the user to log in.</param>
''' <param name="MyPassword">The password of the user to log in.</param>
''' <returns><c>True</c> if login attempt was successful, otherwise returns
''' <c>False</c>.</returns>
''' <remarks>
''' Use <see cref="CheckUser" /> to verify that the user exists
''' before calling LoginProc.
''' </remarks>
''' <seealso cref="MyName" />
''' <seealso cref="MyPassword" />
Public Function LoginProc(ByVal MyName As String, ByVal MyPassword As String) _
    As Boolean
    '...code...
    Return False
End Function
```

The result of this XML comment block transformed with a simple XSL file appears in Figure 12-7. Notice how the links for the `<see>` and `<seealso>` tags are formatted as hyperlinks and contain the full address to the specific member topic.

Figure 12-7

The <summary> Tag

The <summary> tag is used to provide the brief description that appears at the top of a specific topic in the documentation. In addition, the <summary> area is used for Visual Studio's IntelliSense engine when using your own custom-built code. The syntax to implement <summary> is as follows:

```
<summary>
Text goes here.
</summary>
```

The <typeparam> Tag

New to Visual Studio 2005, the <typeparam> tag provides information about the type parameters when dealing with a generic type or member definition. The <typeparam> tag expects an attribute of name containing the type parameter being referred to:

```
<typeparam name="typeName">
Description.
</typeparam>
```

You may use <typeparam> in either C# or Visual Basic, as the following listing shows:

```
''' <typeparam name="T">
''' Base item type (must implement IComparable).
''' </typeparam>
Public Class myList(Of T As IComparable)
    ' code.
End Class
```

The <value> Tag

Normally used to define a property's purpose, the <value> tag gives you another section in the XML where you can provide information about the associated member. When used in conjunction with a property, you would normally use the <summary> tag to describe what the property is for, whereas the <value> tag is used specifically to name what the property contains:

```
<value>The text to display</value>
```

Using XML Comments

Once you have the XML comments inline with your code, you'll most likely want to generate an XML file containing the documentation. In Visual Basic this setting is on by default, with an output path and filename specified with default values. However, C# has the option turned off as its default behavior, so if you want documentation you'll need to turn it on manually.

To ensure that your documentation is being generated where you require, open the property pages for the project through the Solution Explorer's right-click context menu. Locate the project for which you want documentation, right-click its entry in the Solution Explorer, and select Properties. Alternatively, in Visual Basic you can simply double-click the My Project entry in the Solution Explorer.

The XML documentation options are located in the Build section (see Figure 12-8). Below the general build options is an Output section containing a checkbox to generate the XML documentation file. When this checkbox is enabled, the text field next to it becomes available for you to specify the filename for the XML file that will be generated.

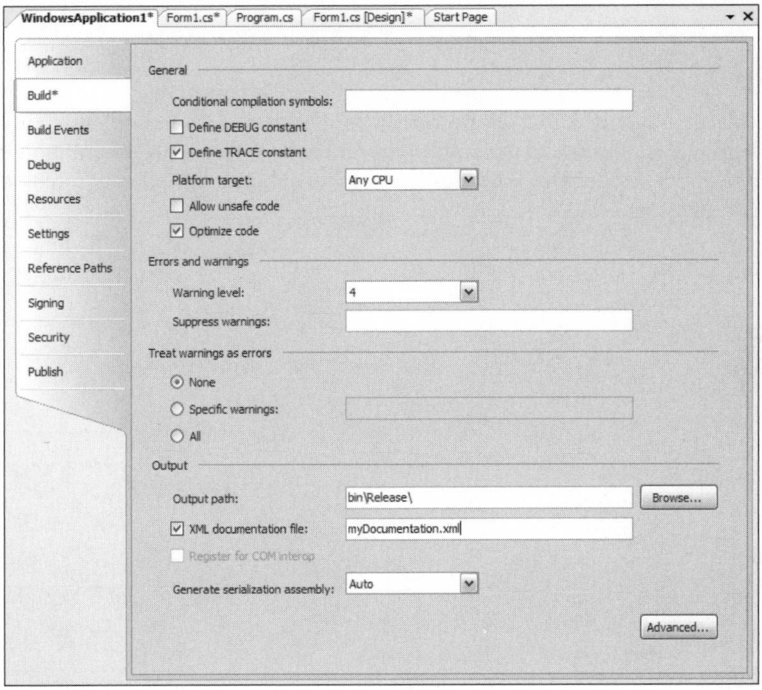

Figure 12-8

Once you've saved these options, the next time you perform a build, Visual Studio will add the /doc compiler option to the process so that the XML documentation is generated as specified.

The XML file that is generated will contain a full XML document that you can apply XSL transformations against, or process through another application using the XML Document Object Model. All references to exceptions, parameters, methods, and other "see also" links will be included as fully addressed information, including namespace, application, and class data.

IntelliSense Information

The other useful advantage of using XML comments is how Visual Studio 2005 consumes them in its own IntelliSense engine. As soon as you define the documentation tags that Visual Studio understands, it will generate the information into its IntelliSense, which means you can refer to the information elsewhere in your code.

IntelliSense can be accessed in two ways. If the member referred to is within the same project or is in another project within the same solution, you can access the information without having to build or generate the XML file. However, you can still take advantage of IntelliSense even when the project is external to your current application solution.

The trick is to ensure that when the XML file is generated by the build process, it must have the same name as the .NET assembly being built. For example, if the compiled output is `myApplication.exe`, then the associated XML file should be named `myApplication.xml`. In addition, this generated XML file should be in the same folder as the compiled assembly so that Visual Studio can locate it.

Summary

XML comments are not only extremely powerful, but also very easy to implement in a development project. Using them will enable you to generate comprehensive internal documentation for every member and class within your development solutions, as well as enhance the existing IntelliSense features by including your own custom-built tooltips and Quick Info data.

13

Control and
Document Outline

Sometimes your application source code is a little overwhelming to review and find exactly what you're looking for. Very large programs often have many modules containing just as many if not more classes, while forms can have upwards of hundreds of components on the form layout. When Visual Studio .NET first arrived on the scene, a feature known as *document outlining* came to at least partially save the day. This chapter introduces the Document Outline window and demonstrates how effective it can be at managing both source and design files.

Document Outline

The primary purpose of the Document Outline window was to present a navigable view of HTML pages so that you could easily locate the different HTML elements and the containers they were in. Because it was difficult to get HTML layouts correct, especially with the many .NET components that could be included on an ASP.NET page, the Document Outline view provided a handy way to find the correct position to place a specific component.

Figure 13-1 shows a typical HTML page with standard tags used in most web pages. DIV, TABLE, and other tags are used to define layout, while a FORM tag, along with its subordinate components for a login form, are also displayed.

Without the Document Outline window, the only way to determine the hierarchical position of a particular component is to select it and examine the bottom of the workspace area. Beside the Design and Source buttons is an area populated with the current hierarchy for the selected component. In the example shown in Figure 13-1, you can see that the selected item is an INPUT tag with a class of tbox login pass. In the current case, this helps locate the component, as that class value is unique, but a more logical property would be the ID or Name property so that you could be sure you had the correct HTML element.

As you click on each component, you can see where it sits in the HTML page's structure, but that's pretty much all the help you're going to have without something new added to the IDE, and that's where the Document Outline window comes into the picture.

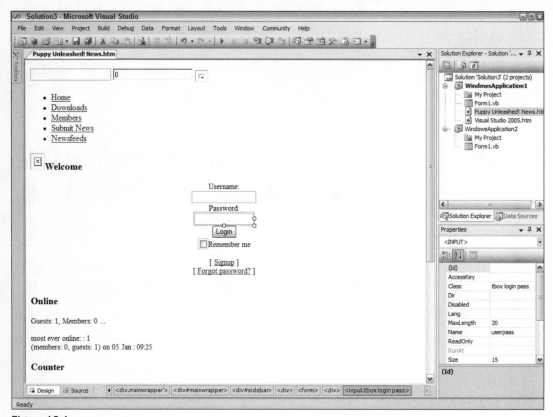

Figure 13-1

The Document Outline window presents that same information about the HTML page but does so exhaustively and with a much more intuitive interface. To use it, you must first have Visual Studio 2005 to display the tool window, which by default is docked to the left-hand side of the main IDE window. To do this, select View⇨Other Windows⇨Document Outline, or use the Ctrl+Alt+T keyboard shortcut.

When the Document Outline window is displayed, Visual Studio analyzes the content of the current active file and populates it with a tree view containing every element and its containers. Figure 13-2 shows the Document Outline view of the same HTML file shown in Figure 13-1. This time, the Name or ID value of each element is used to identify the component, while unnamed components are simply listed with their HTML tag. The password field selected above can be seen in the tree with its name userpass and an icon indicating that not only is it a form text entry field, but also that it is a password field — a lot more information!

As you select each entry in the Document Outline window, the Design view is updated to select the component and its children. In Figure 13-2, the DIV tag containing the login form's contents is selected, and it and all its contained HTML tags are highlighted in the Design view, giving you instant feedback as to what is included in that DIV area.

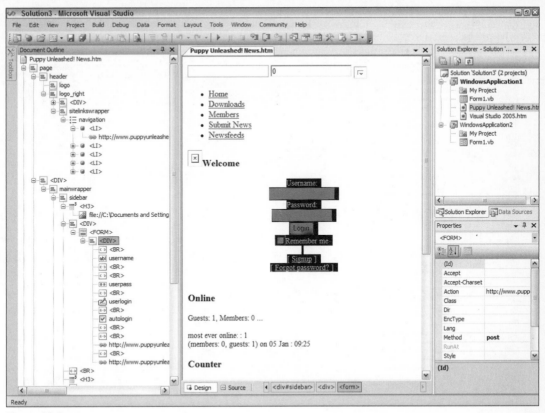

Figure 13-2

Control Outline

The Document Outline window has been available in Visual Studio since the first .NET version for HTML files but has been of little use for other file views. When Visual Studio 2003 was released, an add-in called the *Control view* was developed that allowed a similar kind of access to Windows forms.

The tool was so popular that Microsoft incorporated its functionality into the Document Outline tool window, so now you can browse Windows forms in the same way.

Figure 13-3 shows a typical complex form, with many panels to provide structure and controls to provide the visual elements. Each component is represented in the Document Outline by its name and component type. As each item is selected in the Document Outline window, the corresponding visual element is selected and displayed in the Design view.

This means that when the item is in a menu — as is the case in Figure 13-3 — Visual Studio will automatically open the menu and select the menu item ready for editing. As you can imagine, this is an incredibly useful way of navigating your form layouts, and it can often provide a shortcut way of locating wayward items.

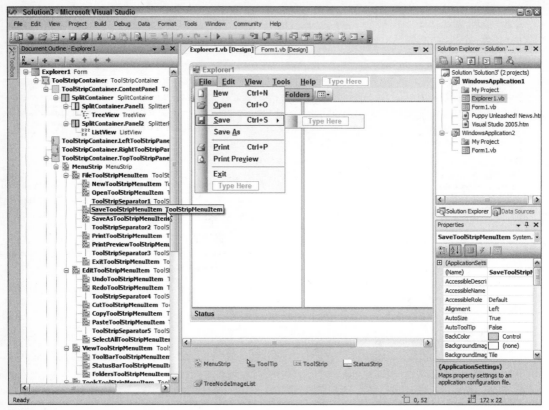

Figure 13-3

Extra Commands in Control Outline Mode

The Document Outline window has more functionality when used in Control Outline mode than just a simple navigation tool. Right-clicking an entry gives you a small context menu of actions that can be performed against the selected item. The most obvious is to access the Properties window.

One tedious chore is renaming components after you've added them to the form. You could select each one in turn and set its Name property in the Properties window, but using the Document Outline window, you can simply choose the Rename option in the context menu, and Visual Studio will automatically rename the component in the design code, thus updating the Name property for you without you needing to scroll through the Properties list.

Complex form design can sometimes produce unexpected results. This often happens when a component is placed in an incorrect or inappropriate container control. In such a case you'll need to move the component to the correct container. Of course, you have to locate the issue before you even know that there is a problem.

The Document Outline window can help with both of these activities. First, using the hierarchical view, you can easily locate each component and check its parent container elements. The example shown in Figure 13-3 indicates that the `TreeView` control is in `Panel1`, which in turn is in `SplitContainer`, which is itself contained in a `ContentPanel` object. In this way you can easily determine when a control is incorrectly placed on the form's design layout.

When you need to move a component it can be quite tricky to get the layout right. In the Document Outline window it's easy. Simply drag and drop the control to the correct position in the hierarchy. For example, dragging the `TreeView` control to `Panel2` results in it sharing the `Panel2` area with the `ListView` control.

You also have the option to cut, copy, and paste individual elements or whole sets of containers and their contents by using the right-click context menu. The copy and paste function is particularly useful, as you can duplicate whole chunks of your form design in other locations on the form without having to use trial and error to select the correct elements in the Design view, or resort to duplicating them in the code-behind in the `Designer.vb` file.

When you cut an item, remember to paste it immediately into the destination location.

Summary

The Document Outline window is a very useful but often overlooked tool. In Visual Studio 2005 it has become even more powerful, enabling you to control your form design intuitively and accurately by seeing each level of container and its children in a tree view so that you don't have to use guesswork to select them when editing forms.

Part IV
Security and Modeling

14

Code Generation

One of the core goals of Visual Studio 2005 is to reduce the amount of code that developers have to write. There are two ways that this can be done: either reduce the total amount of code that has to be written or reduce the amount that actually has to be written by developers. This chapter focuses on how Visual Studio 2005 generates code in order to reduce the amount of code that needs to be written. This in turn reduces the chances of error, while providing a much richer user interface through which to build your application.

This chapter looks in detail at the new Class Designer that comes with Visual Studio 2005 and explains how you can use it to design and refactor your class architecture. This chapter also examines other techniques for generating code within Visual Studio 2005.

Class Designer

The design process for an application typically involves at least a sketch of the classes that are going to be created and how they interact. Visual Studio 2005 provides a design surface, called the Class Designer, onto which classes can be drawn to form a class diagram. Fields, properties, and methods can then be added to the classes, and relationships can be established between classes. Although this design is called a class diagram, it supports classes, structures, enumeration, interfaces, abstract classes, and delegates.

Before you can start working with a class diagram, you need to add one to the project. This can be done by either adding a new class diagram to a project or by selecting the View Class Diagram menu item. A word of caution when using the second option to add a class diagram to a project: Using the View Class Diagram menu item will automatically add all the types defined within a project to the initial class diagram. Although this might be desirable, for a project that contains a large number of classes the process of creating and manipulating the diagram can be quite time consuming.

Unlike some tools that require all types within a project to be on the same diagram, the class diagram can include as many or as few of your types as you want. This makes it possible to add multiple class diagrams to a single solution.

The Class Designer can be divided into four components: the design surface, the Toolbox, the Class Details window, and the property grid. Changes made to the class diagram are saved in a .cd file, which works in parallel with the class code files to generate the visual layout shown in the Class Designer.

Design Surface

The design surface of the Class Designer enables the developer to interact with types using a drag-and-drop style interface. Existing types can be added to the design surface by dragging them from either the class view or the Solution Explorer. If a file in the Solution Explorer contains more than one type, they are all added to the design surface.

Figure 14-1 shows a simple class diagram that contains two classes: Customer and Order. Each class contains fields, properties, methods, and events. There is an association between the classes, as a Customer class contains a property called Orders that is a list of Order objects, and the Order class implements the IDataErrorInfo interface. All of this information is visible from this class diagram.

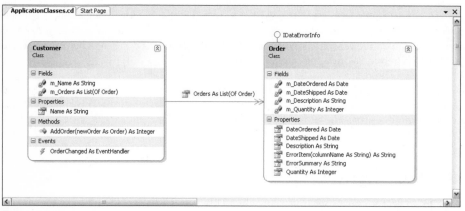

Figure 14-1

Each class appears as an entity on the class diagram, which can be dragged around the design surface and resized as required. A class is made up of fields, properties, methods, and events. In Figure 14-1, these components are grouped into compartments. Alternative layouts can be selected for the class diagram, which lists the components in alphabetical order or groups the components by accessibility.

The Class Designer is often used to view multiple classes to get an understanding of how they are associated. In this case, it is convenient to hide the components of a class to simplify the diagram. To hide all the components at once, use the toggle in the top-right corner of the class on the design surface. If only certain components need to be hidden they can be individually hidden, or the entire compartment can be hidden, by right-clicking on the appropriate element and selecting the Hide menu item.

Toolbox

To facilitate items being added to the class diagram there is a Class Designer tab in the Toolbox. To create an item, drag the item from the Toolbox onto the design surface or simply double-click it. Figure 14-2 shows the Toolbox with the Class Designer tab visible. The items in the Toolbox can be classified as either entities or connectors. Note the Comment item, which can be added to the Class Designer but does not appear in any of the code; it is there simply to aid documentation of the class diagram.

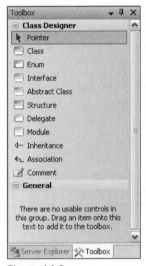

Figure 14-2

Entities

The entities that can be added to the class diagram all correspond to types in the .NET Framework. When a new entity is added to the design surface, it needs to be given a name. In addition, you need to indicate whether it should be added to a new file or an existing file.

Entities can be removed from the diagram by right-clicking and selecting the Remove From Diagram menu item. This will not remove the source code; it simply removes the entity from the diagram. In cases where it is desirable to delete the associated source code, select the Delete Code menu item.

The code associated with an entity can be viewed by either double-clicking on the entity or selecting View Code from the right-click context menu.

The following list explains each entity in the Toolbox:

❑ **Class:** Fields, properties, methods, events, and constants can all be added to a class via the right-click context menu or the Class Details window. Although a class can support nested types, they cannot be added using the Designer surface. Classes can also implement interfaces. In Figure 14-1, the `Order` class implements the `IDataErrorInfo` interface.

❑ **Enum:** An enumeration can only contain a list of members that can have a value assigned to them. Each member also has a summary and remark property, but these appear only as a comment against the member.

❑ **Interface:** Interfaces define properties, methods, and events that a class must implement. Interfaces can also contain nested types, but recall that adding a nested type is not supported by the Designer.

❑ **Abstract Class:** Abstract classes behave the same as classes except that they appear on the design surface with an italic name and are marked as `MustInherit`.

❑ **Structure:** A structure is the only entity, other than a comment, that appears on the Designer in a rectangle. Similar to a class, a structure supports fields, properties, methods, events, and constants. It too can contain nested types. However, unlike a class, a structure cannot have a destructor.

❑ **Delegate:** Although a delegate appears as an entity on the class diagram, it can't contain nested types. The only components it can contain are parameters that define the delegate signature.

❑ **Module:** A module can be used to group static methods. It can also contain nested types.

Connectors

Two types of relationships can be established between entities. These are illustrated on the class diagram using connectors, and are explained in the following list:

❑ **Inheritance:** The inheritance connector is used to show the relationship between classes that inherit from each other.

❑ **Association:** Where a class makes reference to another class, there is an association between the two classes. This is shown using the association connector. If that relationship is based around a collection — for example, a list of `Order` objects — this can be represented using a *collection association*. A collection association is shown in Figure 14-1 connecting the `Customer` and `Order` classes.

A *class association* can be represented as either a field or property of a class, or as an association link between the classes. The right-click context menu on either the field or property or the association can be used to toggle between the two representations.

Class Details

Components can be added to entities by right-clicking and selecting the appropriate component to add. Unfortunately, this is a time-consuming process and doesn't afford you the ability to add method parameters or return values. New to Visual Studio 2005 is a Class Details window, which provides a user interface that enables components to be quickly entered. This window is illustrated in Figure 14-3 for the `Customer` class previously shown in Figure 14-1.

On the left side of the window are buttons that can aid in navigating classes that contain a large number of components. The top button can be used to add methods, properties, fields, or events to the class. The remaining buttons can be used to bring any of the component groups into focus. For example, the second button is used to navigate to the list of methods for the class. You can navigate between components in the list using the up and down arrow keys.

Because Figure 14-3 shows the details for a class, the main region of the window is divided into four alphabetical lists: Methods, Properties, Fields, and Events. Other entity types may have other components, such as Members and Parameters. Each row is divided into five columns that show the name, the return type, the modifier or accessibility of the component, a summary, and whether the item is hidden on the design surface. In each case, the Summary field appears as an XML comment against the appropriate component. Events differ from the other components in that the Type column must be a delegate. You can navigate between columns using the left and right arrow keys, Tab (next column), and Shift+Tab (previous column).

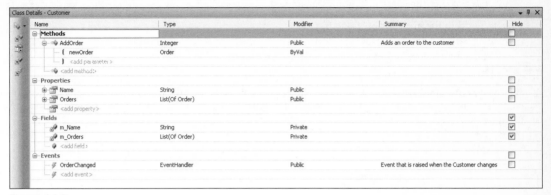

Figure 14-3

Methods and properties can both take parameters. To enter parameters, use the right arrow key to expand the method node so that a parameter list appears. Selecting the Add Parameter node will add a new parameter to the method. Once added, the new parameter can be navigated to using the arrow keys.

Properties Window

Although the Class Details window is useful it does not provide all the information required for entity components. For example, properties can be marked as read-only, which is not displayed in the Class Details window. The Properties window in Figure 14-4 shows the full list of attributes for the Orders property of the Customer class.

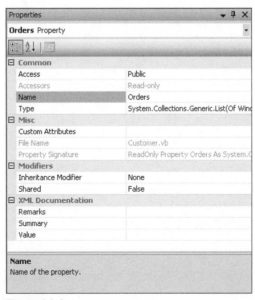

Figure 14-4

Figure 14-4 shows that the `Orders` property is read-only and that it is not shared. It also shows that this property is defined in the `Customer.vb` file. With the introduction of partial classes, a class may be separated over multiple files. When a partial class is selected, the `File Name` property will show all files defining that class as a comma-delimited list. As a result of an arbitrary decision made when implementing the Class Designer, some of these properties are read-only in the Designer. They can, of course, be adjusted within the appropriate code file.

Layout

As the class diagram is all about visualizing classes, you have several toolbar controls at your disposal to create the layout of the entities on the Designer. Figure 14-5 shows the toolbar that appears as part of the Designer surface.

Figure 14-5

The first three buttons control the layout of entity components. From left to right, the buttons are Group by Kind, Group by Access, and Sort Alphabetically.

The next two buttons are used to automate the process of arranging the entities on the design surface. On the left is the Layout Diagram button, which will automatically reposition the entities on the design surface. It will also minimize the entities, hiding all components. The right button, Adjust Shapes Width, adjusts the size of the entities so that all components are fully visible.

Entity components, such as fields, properties, and methods, can be hidden using the Hide Member button.

The display style of entity components can be adjusted using the next three buttons. The left button, Display Name, sets the display style to show only the name of the component. This can be extended to show both the name and the component type using the Display Name and Type button. The right button, Display Full Signature, sets the display style to be the full component signature. This is clearly the most useful, although it takes more space to display.

The remaining controls on the toolbar enable you to zoom in and out on the Class Designer, and to display the Class Details window.

Exporting

Quite often, the process of designing which classes will be part of the system architecture is a part of a much larger design or review process. Therefore, it is a common requirement to export the class diagram for inclusion in reports.

You can export a class diagram either by right-clicking the context menu from any space on the Class Designer or via the Class Diagram menu. Either way, selecting the Export Diagram as Image menu item opens a dialog prompting you to select an image format and filename for saving the diagram.

Other Code-Generation Techniques

Several other features within Visual Studio 2005 could be loosely classified as code-generation techniques, as they significantly reduce the code that you have to write. Because most of these are covered in more detail elsewhere in the book, this section can be used as a quick reference for those chapters.

Snippets

A large proportion of the code that developers have to write is mundane, such as writing property accessors for private member fields. You can often identify code blocks that you find yourself writing repeatedly. For these cases, you could have an electronic pin-board full of code snippets that you could include when you have to accomplish a particular task. Visual Studio 2005 ships with a large number of code snippets in all supported languages, and an editor has been built as a community project to create new snippets.

Figure 14-6 shows an example of a snippet being used to add a public property with an associated private backing field to the Customer class. The highlighted portions of the snippet (shown in green onscreen) indicate that sections should be replaced with custom values. In this case, three values need to be replaced: the name of the backing field, the type of the field and property, and the name of the property. Some developers choose to override this default snippet with their own snippet, which only requires two replacements. This can be done using the community-built Snippet Editor.

```
Public Class Customer

    Private newPropertyValue As Integer
    Public Property NewProperty() As Integer
        Get
            Return newPropertyValue
        End Get
        Set(ByVal value As Integer)
            newPropertyValue = value
        End Set
    End Property
```

Figure 14-6

Snippets are covered in more detail in Chapter 19.

Refactoring

With a lot of emphasis being placed on agile development methodologies, refactoring is an important technique for reviewing and simplifying code. The premise is that the simpler the code, the easier it is to test and the less likely it is to contain bugs. Out of the box, only C# really supports refactoring. VB.NET has basic support for renaming methods but requires a third-party product to provide real refactoring support.

An example of the refactoring support provided in C# is the Preview Changes dialog, shown in Figure 14-7, which is displayed when renaming a method. When electing to rename a method using C# refactoring, all uses of this method are located and you are presented with this dialog to either accept or reject changes to all code paths that might be affected by the name change.

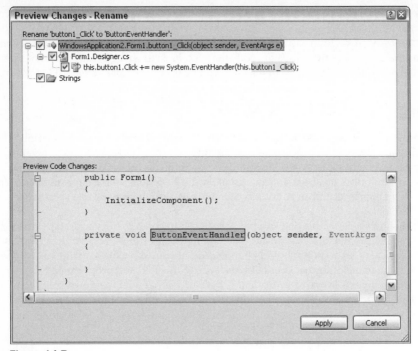

Figure 14-7

Refactoring can also be used to generate accessor properties for member fields, to extract blocks of code as separate methods, to encapsulate code in try-catch blocks, and for promotion of variables to method parameters. This is all covered in Chapter 21.

Project and Item Templates

Another mechanism for reducing the amount of mundane code that you have to write is to create your own set of project and item templates. Visual Studio 2005 now has the capability to export an existing project or item as a template that can be reused in future projects. More information on Visual Studio 2005 templates is covered in Chapter 25.

Strongly Typed Datasets

One of the easiest mechanisms for referencing data from a database is to use strongly typed datasets. As part of creating a data source for a project, a strongly typed dataset is added to the project. This can be edited directly using the Dataset design surface built into Visual Studio 2005.

Figure 14-8 shows a strongly typed dataset for a NorthwindDataSet that was generated from the Customers and Orders table from the Northwind database. When this was added as a data source to the project, it not only generated the dataset schema, which you see on the design surface, it also created a designer file and two additional support files. You don't need to know the details of how this is accomplished because everything is generated by the Custom tool MSDataSetGenerator, and can be controlled using the various wizards and property windows that support the Dataset Designer. Strongly typed datasets are covered in detail in Chapter 30.

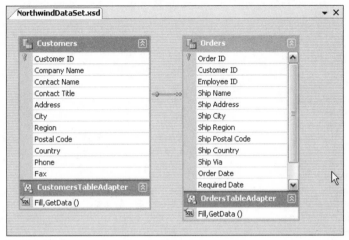

Figure 14-8

Forms

The Forms Designer within Visual Studio 2005 is one of the most heavily used code-generating tools because it dynamically generates all the code required to create and lay out the controls that have been added to the form in the Designer. Previously, all the code relating to a form had to be contained within the same file. A section at the beginning of the Form class was marked with a big Do Not Touch sign, as it was Designer-generated. With the introduction of partial classes, all the Designer-generated code has been moved into a designer file. For example, if you have a Form1, whereas in the past you would have just had Form1.vb, you now also have Form1.designer.vb. The contents of the designer file for Form1 that only has a single control, Button1, might look like the following:

```
<Global.Microsoft.VisualBasic.CompilerServices.DesignerGenerated()> _
Partial Class Form1
    Inherits System.Windows.Forms.Form

    'Form overrides dispose to clean up the component list.
    <System.Diagnostics.DebuggerNonUserCode()> _
    Protected Overrides Sub Dispose(ByVal disposing As Boolean)
        If disposing AndAlso components IsNot Nothing Then
            components.Dispose()
        End If
        MyBase.Dispose(disposing)
    End Sub

    'Required by the Windows Form Designer
    Private components As System.ComponentModel.IContainer

    'NOTE: The following procedure is required by the Windows Form Designer
```

```
           'It can be modified using the Windows Form Designer.
           'Do not modify it using the code editor.
           <System.Diagnostics.DebuggerStepThrough()> _
           Private Sub InitializeComponent()
               Me.Button1 = New System.Windows.Forms.Button
               Me.SuspendLayout()
               '
               'Button1
               '
               Me.Button1.Location = New System.Drawing.Point(60, 82)
               Me.Button1.Name = "Button1"
               Me.Button1.Size = New System.Drawing.Size(75, 23)
               Me.Button1.TabIndex = 1
               Me.Button1.Text = _
       Global.WindowsApplication1.My.MySettings.Default.Button1_Text
               Me.Button1.UseVisualStyleBackColor = True
               '
               'Form1
               '
               Me.AutoScaleDimensions = New System.Drawing.SizeF(6.0!, 13.0!)
               Me.AutoScaleMode = System.Windows.Forms.AutoScaleMode.Font
               Me.ClientSize = New System.Drawing.Size(292, 273)
               Me.Controls.Add(Me.Button1)
               Me.Name = "Form1"
               Me.Text = "Form1"
               Me.ResumeLayout(False)

           End Sub
           Friend WithEvents Button1 As System.Windows.Forms.Button

       End Class
```

By default, the designer file is hidden in the Solution Explorer. Selecting the Show All Files button will show that Form1 is made up of Form1.vb, Form1.designer.vb, and Form1.resx.

My Namespace

VB.NET developers have an additional code generator that is used to generate the My Namespace. The My Namespace achieves a number of goals, one of which is to provide quick accessors for forms and web services. When a VB.NET project is compiled, a series of fields, properties, and methods are dynamically created to allow forms and web services to be referenced via the My Namespace. This process does not generate a code file, as it is done as part of the build process.

Other parts of the My Namespace require actual code to be generated. This is the case for the strongly typed accessors for the application settings and resources. The following code illustrates the code that is generated to provide a strongly typed property for accessing the CompanyLogo resource from the application resource file:

```
   Namespace My.Resources
      <GeneratedCodeAttribute("StronglyTypedResourceBuilder", "2.0.0.0"), _
       DebuggerNonUserCodeAttribute(), _
       CompilerGeneratedAttribute(), _
```

```
        HideModuleNameAttribute()>  _
    Friend Module Resources
        Private resourceMan As Global.System.Resources.ResourceManager
        Private resourceCulture As Global.System.Globalization.CultureInfo

        <EditorBrowsableAttribute(EditorBrowsableState.Advanced)>  _
        Friend ReadOnly Property ResourceManager() As ResourceManager
            Get
                If Object.ReferenceEquals(resourceMan, Nothing) Then
                    Dim temp As ResourceManager = _
                            New ResourceManager("WindowsApplication1.Resources",
GetType(Resources).Assembly)
                    resourceMan = temp
                End If
                Return resourceMan
            End Get
        End Property

        <EditorBrowsableAttribute(EditorBrowsableState.Advanced)>  _
        Friend Property Culture() As CultureInfo
            Get
                Return resourceCulture
            End Get
            Set
                resourceCulture = value
            End Set
        End Property

        Friend ReadOnly Property CompanyLogo() As Bitmap
            Get
                Dim obj As Object = ResourceManager.GetObject("CompanyLogo",
resourceCulture)
                Return CType(obj, Bitmap)
            End Get
        End Property
    End Module
End Namespace
```

Taking Charge of the Class Designer

Now that you understand the basics of code generation within Visual Studio 2005, you can return to the Class Designer and work through some advanced features that can greatly improve the experience of designing, writing, and debugging code.

Earlier in this chapter, it was mentioned that the class diagram file is used in conjunction with the code file to generate the visual representation displayed on the class design surface. The question is, what exactly does the class diagram file contain? As with most files that are used by or generated by Visual Studio 2005, the class diagram file is an XML document that conforms to the class diagram schema.

Class Diagram Schema

Although the actual class diagram schema has not been made public, most of it can be inferred from the XML file that is generated from using the Class Designer. To view the class diagram file in XML format, right-click on the file in the Solution Explorer and select Open With from the context menu. When prompted for the program to open it with, select the XML Editor.

Taking the example class diagram from earlier in the chapter, you would expect to see an XML file similar to the following:

```xml
<?xml version="1.0" encoding="utf-8"?>
<ClassDiagram MajorVersion="1" MinorVersion="1" MembersFormat="FullSignature">
    <Font Name="Tahoma" Size="8.51" />
    <Class Name="WindowsApplication1.Customer">
        <Position X="0.5" Y="1.5" Width="2.5" />
        <TypeIdentifier>
            <FileName>Customer.vb</FileName>
            <HashCode>MAEAAAgAAAAAAAIAACACAQAAAAAAEACAAAAAAAAAA=</HashCode>
        </TypeIdentifier>
        <ShowAsCollectionAssociation>
            <Property Name="Orders" />
        </ShowAsCollectionAssociation>
        <Compartments>
            <Compartment Name="Events" Collapsed="true" />
        </Compartments>
    </Class>
    <Class Name="WindowsApplication1.Order" Collapsed="true">
        <Position X="5" Y="2.5" Width="1.5" />
        <TypeIdentifier>
            <FileName>Order.vb</FileName>
            <HashCode>AAAICAAAAAgAAAgAACAABAAAAAAAAAAAAAgABAwAA=</HashCode>
        </TypeIdentifier>
        <Lollipop Position="0.2" />
    </Class>
</ClassDiagram>
```

From this XML document you can see that the contents all relate to the layout of entities on the designer surface. One of the most significant points about the class diagram is that it contains no functional information about the class. Because the code file needs to contain this information for the code to function, there is no reason why it should be duplicated in the class diagram. This would only create the potential for the Designer to be out of sync with the code file. Changes made in either the Designer or the code file are immediately reflected in the other file.

Without going into every boring detail of the XML schema, note that each class to be contained on the class diagram is specified using a `Class` element. This element defines the full name of the class being referenced and whether it should be displayed in collapsed mode or not. Another optional parameter determines whether inheritance lines are shown where they are relevant. Sub-elements of the `Class` element are used to determine the position of the entity on the design surface and the code file in which the entity resides. Other elements are used to control relationships between entities and the appearance of interface (lollipop) markers.

IntelliSense Code Generation

When a class implements an interface or inherits from a base class it is highly probable that it will not initially implement or override all the methods. The Class Designer can provide a shortcut for creating methods that either implement an interface method or override an overridable base class method. For example, the steps to override a base class method are as follows:

1. Open the class diagram.

2. Right-click the class in which you want to override the method.

3. Select the IntelliSense item from the context menu, followed by the Override Members item.

4. Select the method from the base class you wish to override. This will add that method to the class you selected.

5. Double-click the method from the class diagram to edit that method in the code file.

Object Test Bench

Debugging classes can be quite a tedious process, especially when they are part of a large system that can take considerable time to start running. Visual Studio 2005 has what is known as the *object test bench*, which can be used to instantiate entities and invoke methods without having to load the entire application.

Invoking Static Methods

Starting from either the Class View window or the class diagram, static methods can be invoked. Right-clicking on the class will bring up the context menu from which you can select Invoke Static Method. This will bring up the Invoke Method dialog shown in Figure 14-9, which prompts you to provide parameters for the method.

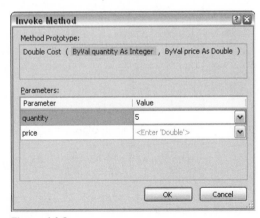

Figure 14-9

Specify values for each of the parameters and click OK to invoke the method. If there is a return method, a Method Call Result dialog will appear, returning the method output, as shown in Figure 14-10.

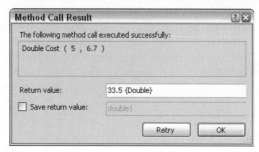

Figure 14-10

Instantiating Entities

You can use a similar technique to create an instance of an entity from either the Class View or the class diagram. Right-click on the class and select Create Instance from the context menu. This will prompt you for a name for the instance, as shown in Figure 14-11. The name you give the instance has no relationship to any property that may be called Name in your class. All it does is provide a user-friendly name for referring to the instance when working with it.

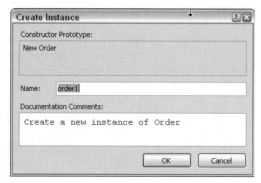

Figure 14-11

Clicking OK creates an instance of the Order class and places it in the object test bench. Figure 14-12 shows the newly created instance order1 alongside a previously created customer1 object. The friendly name that you gave the instance appears above the object type so that you can clearly distinguish it from any other objects of the same type that may have been created.

Figure 14-12

Accessing Fields and Properties

Within the object test bench you can access fields and properties using the same technique available during application debugging. In fact, it is exactly the same process, as Visual Studio 2005 is actually in debugging mode in the background to maintain the instances of the objects you are working with. As such, you can hover the mouse over the objects to access the properties of that object. When the mouse hovers over the object, an intelligent mouse-over tooltip appears that can be used to drill down to obtain the current values of both fields and properties, as shown in Figure 14-13. This tooltip also permits you to modify the public properties of the object to adjust the state of the object.

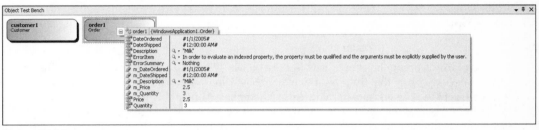

Figure 14-13

Invoking Instance Methods

The final step in working with items in the object test bench is to invoke instance, or nonstatic, methods. You can do this by right-clicking on the object on the test bench and selecting Invoke Method. In Figure 14-14, the AddOrder method has been invoked on the customer1 object off the test bench. The parameter for this method needs to be an Order. In the value column of the parameters list you can select from any object that appears on the object test bench. Because an Order is required, the order1 object seems a good candidate.

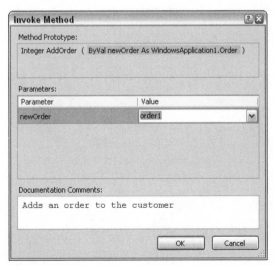

Figure 14-14

193

Invoking this method will return the number of orders that have been added to the customer. Referring back to Figure 14-10, note the checkbox to save the return value. Because this is going to be added to the object test bench it needs to have a friendly name so that it too can be referenced in future method invocations. If you assign the return value a name of orderCount, you end up with an object test bench that looks like what is shown in Figure 14-15.

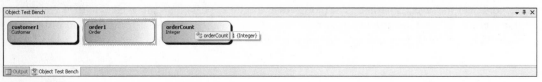

Figure 14-15

A couple of words of caution about the object test bench: To invoke a member or create an instance of a class you have to ensure that the project to which they belong is the startup project. This can be a pain when you want to access classes from different assemblies. Another big issue with the test bench is that it periodically decides that it needs to rebuild the project. Unfortunately, this process removes any objects you might have added to the work bench. The final issue is that there is no way to either access or set parameterized properties or methods with optional parameters. While none of these issues prevents you from using the object test bench, they can cause some frustration when a series of objects is removed due to a recompilation, or you wish to access classes from different assemblies.

Summary

This chapter focused on the Class Designer, one of the best tools built into Visual Studio 2005 for generating code. The design surface and supporting toolbars and windows provide a rich user interface with which complex class hierarchies and associations can be designed.

Other elements of Visual Studio 2005 where code is automatically generated for you were covered in the second half of the chapter. Most of these are covered in depth in later chapters, so this is merely a summary of code generation within Visual Studio 2005.

15

Security Concepts

In Chapter 16 you'll see how to secure your data by implementing cryptography, and in Chapter 17 protecting your source code is explained through the process of obfuscation. However, before you approach either feature within Visual Studio 2005 application programming, you should be familiar with the basic concepts that underpin how security works within the .NET environment.

Because security is such an important part of many applications, this chapter introduces these concepts, rather than examine any specific technical feature of the IDE.

Application Security

Applications and services can be executed in many different ways, mostly intentional. However, applications can also be run inadvertently, or with active malice toward gaining access to the functionality of the application's internals. With simple applications that do not provide anything particularly proprietary, such as common access functions (e.g., a simple text editor or calculator), you may not be concerned with who gains the capability to access it, or even if it is executed via another process.

However, in a situation where your application contains or processes sensitive data, you need a more proactive attitude regarding who can access the functionality within your application, and you may want to fine-tune the control over individual parts of it.

Code written in .NET enables you to decide who can execute what based on two different views. The first option is to look at what each individual function is and control access to parts of the application based on that particular set of code. This specific set of access to data and the underlying system is known as *code-based security*.

Alternatively, you can control access to the application or function based on the particular user, or rather, the user account being used to execute the application. This is known as *role-based security* because it interrogates the user account's authority to access the functions within your application code.

Code-Based Security

Code-based security, also known as code-access security, allows you to create applications that limit their functionality based on the code itself, relying on the access required by each statement for data and the system itself to control how the application can be executed.

You may want to look into code-based security because of two common computing environment scenarios. The first is the situation where a user is a member of the Administrators group in their particular Windows system. This is common for home users or small business owners, who tend to be the only user on their system and often need access to functionality that is otherwise locked down in the corporate environment. When they belong to a powerful user role such as this, role-based security can be next to useless, as they can perform almost any kind of activity, including some you may have implemented that destroy important data on the system.

The other situation is almost the complete opposite. Because of the rampant abuse of computer systems in larger companies, which can result in malicious code such as worms and viruses infecting massive networks, some systems are locked down so tightly that the end-user has very little access to the system. This can result in your application malfunctioning when it expects to have access to a particular feature to which the user is locked out.

This is compounded when you consider the variety of ways in which your application can be executed. Because Windows, in conjunction with the .NET CLR, doesn't allow programs executed from outside the local system (such as programs running from a web site or intranet site) to have full access to the system itself, you can again face difficulties when your application requires specific functionality to perform correctly.

The .NET Framework 2.0 includes code-access security functionality built directly into the system. Every function is signed with a specific set of access that it requires, which allows you to determine what each application and module will need to run successfully. For instance, if you know that your application can function successfully without access to the Windows registry or file system, you can specify that the application code access should exclude the requirement associated with that kind of security.

Having the ability to specify the kind of access your code will expect allows your users to understand what functionality will be performed. As a result, if your application were somehow infected with a virus that tried to access some feature that falls outside the code access points you've defined, then the attempt will fail completely before it can cause any damage.

> As a side effect, code-based security can aid you as well, because it can block inadvertent functionality in your code that tries to perform functions outside the scope of the code access you have defined for it.

When an application is deployed with an accurate code-access model, system administrators can configure a corresponding security policy for end-users, allowing them to execute the application with the required security access without exposing their system to other applications that also try to use the same security features, or even protect them from your own code trying to run functionality that extends beyond the security settings you've indicated.

In addition, when you use code-access security, you can handle permission exceptions gracefully. Whenever your application is about to perform a function that you know requires a specific security access, you can wrap it in a `Try-Catch` block to intercept situations where the application has not received sufficient security access.

In Chapter 47, you'll see how the ClickOnce functionality of Visual Studio 2005 uses code-access security to define what features your application requires for successful execution. You'll also learn how you can easily toggle specific code-access features on and off and then build this into the deployment model.

Role-Based Security

Role-based security, conversely, is all about the user accessing the application, or even individual parts of the application's functionality. It is based on the roles to which the user belongs. For instance, your application may need to provide full access to a database on sales tenders to only employees who are either managers or lead sales people. However, the supporting employees involved in a tender may need access to a subset of the information, which you want to be able to provide from within the same application.

Role-based security enables you to do this by explicitly specifying different levels of approval within the application functionality itself. You can even use this methodology to give different user roles access to the same functionality but with different behavior. For instance, managers may be able to approve all tenders, while lead sales people can only approve tenders under a certain amount.

You can implement role-based security in your application by retrieving information Windows provides about the current user. As mentioned previously, this isn't necessarily the user who is currently logged onto the system, because Windows allows an individual to execute different applications and services via different user accounts as long as they provide the correct credentials. This means that when your application asks for user information, Windows returns the details relating to the specific user account being used for your application process.

Visual Studio 2005 applications use the .NET Framework 2.0, which gives them access to the *identity* of a particular user account through a `Principal` object. This object contains the access privileges associated with the particular identity, consisting of the roles to which the identity belongs.

Every role in the system consists of a group of access privileges. When an identity is created, a set of roles is associated with it, which in turn define the total set of access privileges the identity has. For instance, you might have roles of ViewTenders, AuthorizeTenders, and RestrictTenderAmount in the example scenario used in this section. All employees associated with the sales process could be assigned the role of ViewTenders, while management and lead sales people have the AuthorizeTenders roles as well. Finally, lead sales people have a third role of RestrictTenderAmount, which your code can use later to determine whether they can authorize the particular tender being processed. Figure 15-1 shows how this could be represented visually.

The easiest way to implement the role-based security functionality in your application is to use the `My.User` object. You can use the `IsAuthenticated` property to determine whether there is a valid user context under which your application is executing. If there isn't, your role-based security code will not work, so you should use this property to handle that situation gracefully.

If you're using this code in a C# application, you'll need to add the references to the My namespace, as explained in Chapter 24.

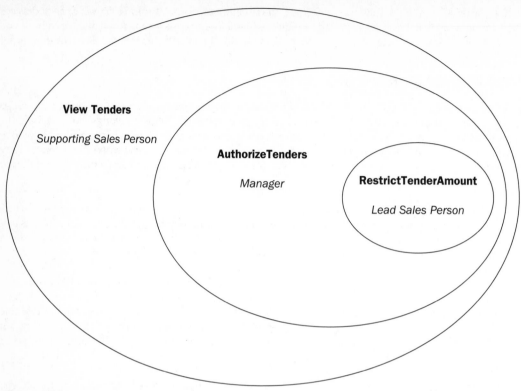

Figure 15-1

Once you've established that a proper user context is in use, use the `IsInRole` method to determine the methods to which the current user identity belongs. A simple implementation of the previous sample for a basic form is shown in the following code listing:

```
Private Sub Form1_Load(ByVal sender As System.Object, _
    ByVal e As System.EventArgs) Handles MyBase.Load

    With My.User
        If .IsAuthenticated Then
            txtTenderInfo.Visible = .IsInRole("ViewTenders")
            If .IsInRole("AuthorizeTenders") Then
                btnAuthorize.Enabled = True
                If .IsInRole("RestrictTenderAmount") And _
                    CInt(txtTenderAmount.Text) > 10000 Then
                    btnAuthorize.Enabled = False
                End If
            End If
        End If
    End With

End Sub
```

The result of a lead salesperson with properly defined roles running this code is shown in Figure 15-2.

Figure 15-2

In addition to using your own defined roles, you can also use the built-in roles that Windows creates.

This brief introduction to the differences between these two approaches to security is limited to a general discussion on how they are represented within the .NET Framework and how you might approach your particular project from either perspective. However, if you need more advanced coverage of program security, take a look at the *Visual Basic .NET Code Security Handbook* by Eric Lippert (Wrox Press, 2002). While this book is aimed at Visual Basic programmers and is now a couple of years old, it still serves as an excellent resource, offering great detail about how the different security practices can work in the .NET world.

Summary

Securing both your program code and your data is essential in today's computing environment. You need to inform the end-users of your applications what kind of access it requires to execute without encountering security issues. Once you understand the different types of security you can implement, you can use them to encrypt your data to protect your applications from unwanted use. Using a combination of role- and code-based security methodologies, you can ensure that the application only runs under the required permissions and that unauthorized usage will be blocked.

In the next chapter, you'll learn how to enhance the use of these concepts in a practical way by using the cryptography features of the .NET Framework to protect your data.

16

Cryptography

Security is an ongoing concern that all developers need to address, in particular when data is being stored or transmitted. This chapter covers the principles and practices of cryptography. The .NET Framework includes support for several of the standard algorithms. These algorithms can be combined to securely transfer data between two parties or securely store data.

General Principles

Cryptography focuses on four general principles to secure information that will be transferred between two parties. A secure application must apply a combination of these principles to protect any sensitive data:

- ❏ **Authentication:** Before information received from a foreign party can be trusted, the source of that information must be authenticated to prove the legitimacy of the foreign party's identity.

- ❏ **Non-Repudiation:** In addition to proving the identity of the information sender, there needs to be a mechanism to ensure that the sender did in fact send the information.

- ❏ **Data Integrity:** Once the authentication of the sender and the legitimacy of the correspondence have been confirmed, the data needs to be verified to ensure that it has not been modified.

- ❏ **Confidentiality:** Protecting the information from anyone who may intercept the transmission is the last principle of cryptography.

Techniques

Cryptographic techniques fall into four broad categories. In each of these categories, a number of algorithms are implemented in the .NET Framework using an inherited provider model. For each category there is typically an abstract class that provides common functionality. The specific providers implement the details of the algorithm.

Hashing

To achieve the goal of data integrity, a hashing algorithm can be applied to the data being transferred. This will generate a byte sequence that has a fixed length, referred to as the *hash value*. To ensure data integrity, the hash value has to be unique, and the algorithm should always produce the same hash value for a specific piece of data.

For example, if a piece of information is being sent from Susan to David, then the integrity of the information can be checked by comparing the hash value generated by Susan, from the original information, with the hash value generated by David, from the information he received. If the hash values match, the goal of data integrity has been achieved. Because the hash value cannot be converted back into the original information, both the information and hash value have to be sent. This is clearly a risk, as the information can easily be read. In addition, the information cannot be guaranteed to come from Susan because someone else could have used the same hashing algorithm prior to sending information to David.

The hashing algorithms included in the .NET Framework are as follows:

- HMACSHA1
- MACTripleDES
- MD5CryptoServiceProvider
- SHA1Managed
- SHA256Managed
- SHA384Managed
- SHA512Managed

Symmetric (Secret) Keys

To protect the confidentiality of the information being transferred, it can be encrypted by the sender and decrypted by the recipient. Both parties can use the same key to encrypt and decrypt the data using a symmetric encryption algorithm. The difficulty is that the key needs to be securely sent between the parties, as anyone with the key can access the information being transmitted.

A piece of information being sent from Susan to David, who both have access to the same encryption key, can be encrypted by Susan. Upon receiving the encrypted information, David can use the same algorithm to decrypt the information, thus preserving the confidentiality of the information. Due to the risk of the key being intercepted during transmission, the authentication of the sender, and hence the integrity of the data, may be at risk.

The following symmetric algorithms included in the .NET Framework all inherit from the `SymmetricAlgorithm` abstract class:

❏ DESCryptoServiceProvider

❏ RC2CryptoServiceProvider

❏ RijndaelManaged

❏ TripleDESCryptoServiceProvider

Asymmetric (Public/Private) Keys

Public-key, or asymmetric, cryptography algorithms can be used to overcome the difficulties associated with securely distributing a symmetric key. Instead of the same key being used to encrypt and decrypt data, an asymmetric algorithm has two keys: one public and one private. The public key can be distributed freely to anyone, whereas the private key should be closely guarded. In a typical scenario, the public key is used to encrypt some information. The only way that this information can be decrypted is with the private key.

Suppose Susan wants to ensure that only David can read the information she is transmitting. Using David's public key, which he has previously e-mailed her, she encrypts the information. Upon receiving the encrypted information, David uses his private key to decrypt the information. This guarantees data confidentiality. However, because David's public key can be easily intercepted, the authentication of the sender can't be confirmed.

The following asymmetric algorithms included in the .NET Framework all inherit from the `AsymmetricAlgorithm` abstract class:

❏ DSACryptoServiceProvider

❏ RSACryptoServiceProvider

Signing

The biggest problem with using an asymmetric key to encrypt information being transmitted is that the authentication of the sender can't be guaranteed. Using the asymmetric algorithm in reverse, the private key is used to encrypt data and the public key is used to decrypt the data, which guarantees authentication of the information sender. Of course, the confidentiality of the data is at risk, as anyone can decrypt the data. This process is known as *signing information*.

For example, prior to sending information to David, Susan can generate a hash value from the information and encrypt it using her private key to generate a signature. When David receives the information he can decrypt the signature using Susan's public key to get the hash value. Applying the hashing algorithm to the information and comparing the generated hash value with the value from the decrypted signature will guarantee the authentication of the sender and the integrity of the data. Because Susan must have sent the data, the goal of non-repudiation is achieved.

Signing information uses the same asymmetric algorithms that are used to encrypt data, and hence is supported in the .NET Framework with the same classes.

Chapter 16

Summary of Goals

Individually, none of these four techniques achieves all the goals of cryptography. To be able to securely transmit data between two parties, you need to use a combination. A commonly used scheme is for each party to generate an asymmetric key pair and to share the public keys. The parties can then generate a symmetric key that can be encrypted (using the public key of the receiving party) and signed (using the private key of the sending party). The receiving party needs to validate the signature (using the public key of the sending party) and decrypt the symmetric key (using the private key). Once the parties agree upon the symmetric key, it can be used to secure other information being transmitted.

Applying Cryptography

So far, you have seen the principles of cryptography and how they are achieved using hashing, encryption, and signing algorithms. In this section you'll walk through a sample that applies these algorithms and illustrates how the .NET Framework can be used to securely pass data between two parties.

Creating Asymmetric Key Pairs

Begin with a new Windows application and divide the form into two vertical columns. This can be achieved using a `TableLayoutPanel` with docked `Panel` controls. Into each of the two vertical columns place a button, which will be used to generate the asymmetric key, and two textboxes, which will be used to display the private and public keys. The result should be something similar to Figure 16-1. For reference, add a name label to each of the vertical panels.

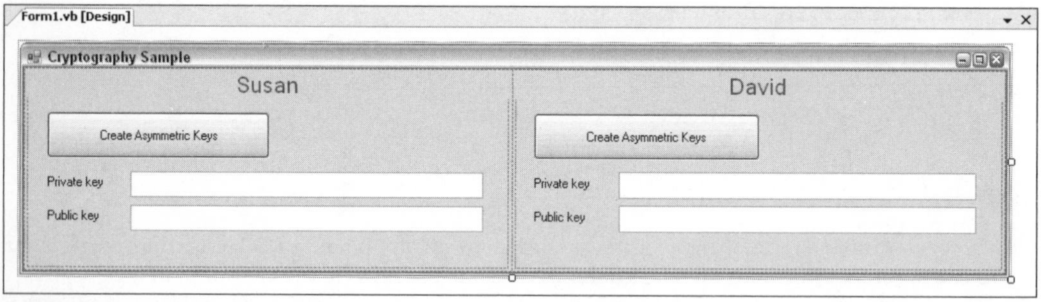

Figure 16-1

Double-clicking each of the buttons will create event handlers into which you need to add code to generate an asymmetric key pair. In this case, use the `RSACryptoServiceProvider` class, which is the default implementation of the RSA algorithm. Creating a new instance of this class automatically generates a new key pair that can be exported using the `ToXmlString` method, as shown in the following code. This method takes a Boolean parameter that determines whether the private key information should be exported:

```
Imports System
Imports System.IO
Imports System.Security.Cryptography
Imports System.Net.Sockets
Imports System.Text


Public Class Form1
```

```
#Region "Step 1 - Creating Asymmetric Keys"
    Private Sub BtnCreateAsmmetricKeys_Click(ByVal sender As System.Object, _
                                    ByVal e As System.EventArgs) _
                                    Handles BtnCreateAsmmetricKeys.Click
        CreateAsymmetricKey(Me.TxtPrivateKey1, Me.TxtPublicKey1)
    End Sub

    Private Sub BtnCreateAsmmetricKeys2_Click(ByVal sender As System.Object, _
                                    ByVal e As System.EventArgs) _
                                    Handles BtnCreateAsmmetricKeys2.Click
        CreateAsymmetricKey(Me.TxtPrivateKey2, Me.TxtPublicKey2)
    End Sub

    Private Sub CreateAsymmetricKey(ByVal txtPrivate As TextBox, _
                            ByVal txtPublic As TextBox)
        Dim RSA As New RSACryptoServiceProvider()
        txtPrivate.Text = RSA.ToXmlString(True)
        txtPublic.Text = RSA.ToXmlString(False)
    End Sub
#End Region
End Class
```

In the preceding example, note that a number of namespaces have been imported, which makes working with the cryptography classes much easier. When this application is run and the buttons are invoked, two new key pairs are created and displayed in the appropriate textboxes. Examining the text from one of the private key textboxes, you can see that it is an XML block that is broken up into a number of sections that represent the different components required by the RSA algorithm:

```
<RSAKeyValue>
    <Modulus>uUWTj5Ub+x+LN5xE63y8zLQf4JXNU0WAADsShaBK+jF/cDGdXc9VFcuDvRIX0oKLdUs1pH
cRcFh3VLi7djU+oRKAZUfs+75mMCCnoybPEHWWCsRHoIk8s4BAZuJ7KCQO+Jb9DxYQbeeCI9bYm2yYWtHRv
q7PJha5sbMvxkLOI1M=</Modulus>
    <Exponent>AQAB</Exponent>
    <P>79tcNXbc02ZVowH9qOuv3vrj6F009BSLdfSBtX6y8sosIAsLUfVqH+UEPKQbZO/gLDAyf3U65Qkj
5QZE03CFeQ==</P>
    <Q>xb28iwn6BPHqCaDPhxtea6p/OnYNTtJ8f/3Y/zHEl0Mc0aBjtY3Ci1ggnkUGvM4j/+BRTBwUOPKG
NP9DUE94Kw==</Q>
    <DP>0IkkYytjlLyNSfsKIho/vxrcmYKn7moKUlRxjW2JgcM6l+ViQzCewvonM93uH1TazzBcRyqSON0
4gv9vSXGz6Q==</DP>
    <DQ>j3bFICsw1f2dyzZ82o0kyAB/Ji8YIKPd6A6ILT4yX3w1oHE5ZjNffjGGGM4DwV/eBnr9ALcuhNK
QREsez1mY2Q==</DQ>
    <InverseQ>hS1ygkBiiYWyE7DjFgO1eOFhFQxOaLl1vPoqlAxw0YepbSQADBGmP8IB1ygzJjP3dmMEvQ
Zhwsbs6MAfPIe/gYQ==</InverseQ>
    <D>r4WC7pxNDfQsaFrb0F00YJqlOJezFhjZ014jhgT+A1mxahEXDTDHYwaToCPr/bs/c7f1yZIkK1Mk
elcpAiwfT8ssNgx2H97zhcHkcvCBO8yCgc0r+cSYlRNKLa+UPwsoXcc5NXGT0SHQG+GCVl7bywrtrWRryaW
OIpSwuHmjZYE=</D>
</RSAKeyValue>
```

In actual fact, this block shows both the public and private key components, which you can see if you look at the corresponding public key textbox:

```
<RSAKeyValue>
    <Modulus>uUWTj5Ub+x+LN5xE63y8zLQf4JXNU0WAADsShaBK+jF/cDGdXc9VFcuDvRIX0oKLdUs1pH
cRcFh3VLi7djU+oRKAZUfs+75mMCCnoybPEHWWCsRHoIk8s4BAZuJ7KCQO+Jb9DxYQbeeCI9bYm2yYWtHRv
q7PJha5sbMvxkLOI1M=</Modulus>
```

```
        <Exponent>AQAB</Exponent>
    </RSAKeyValue>
```

As you will learn later, this public key can be distributed so that it can be used to encrypt and sign information. Of course, the private key should be kept in a secure location.

Creating a Symmetric Key

In the example, only David is going to create a symmetric key that will be shared with Susan after being encrypted and signed using a combination of their asymmetric keys. A more secure approach would be for both parties to generate symmetric keys and for them to be shared and combined into a single key.

Before adding code to generate the symmetric key, extend the dialog so the key can be displayed. Figure 16-2 shows two textboxes that will contain the Initialization Vector and the Key. The data being encrypted is broken down into a series of individually encrypted input blocks. If two adjacent blocks are identical, the process of encrypting a stream of data using a simple key would result in two identical blocks in the encrypted output. Combined with knowledge of the input data, this can be used to recover the key. A solution to this is to use the previous input block as a seed for the encryption of the current block. Of course, at the beginning of the data there is no previous block, which is where the initialization vector is used. This vector can be as important as the key itself, so it should also be kept secure.

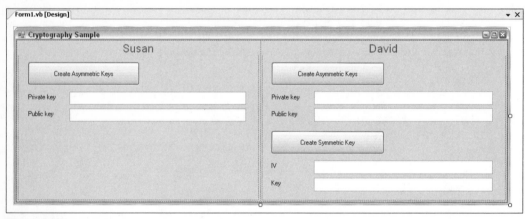

Figure 16-2

In the event handler for the Create Symmetric Key button, you need to create an instance of the `TripleDESCryptoServiceProvider` class, which is the default implementation of the TripleDES algorithm. Create a new instance of the class and then call the `GenerateIV` and `GenerateKey` methods to randomly generate a new key and initialization vector. Because these are both byte arrays, convert them to a base-64 string so they can be displayed in the textbox:

```
Public Class Form1
#Region "Step 1 - Creating Asymmetric Keys"
    '...
#End Region
#Region "Step 2 - Creating Symmetric Keys"
    Private Sub BtnCreateSymmetric_Click(ByVal sender As System.Object, _
                                ByVal e As System.EventArgs) _
```

```
                                                    Handles BtnCreateSymmetric.Click
        Dim TDES As New TripleDESCryptoServiceProvider()
        TDES.GenerateIV()
        TDES.GenerateKey()
        Me.TxtSymmetricIV.Text = Convert.ToBase64String(TDES.IV)
        Me.TxtSymmetricKey.Text = Convert.ToBase64String(TDES.Key)
    End Sub
#End Region
End Class
```

Encrypting and Signing the Key

Now that we have the symmetric key, we need to encrypt it using Susan's public key and generate a hash value that can be signed using David's private key. The encrypted key and signature can then be transmitted securely to Susan. Again, appropriate controls have been added to the dialog in Figure 16-3, so you can create and display the encrypted key, the hash value, and the signature.

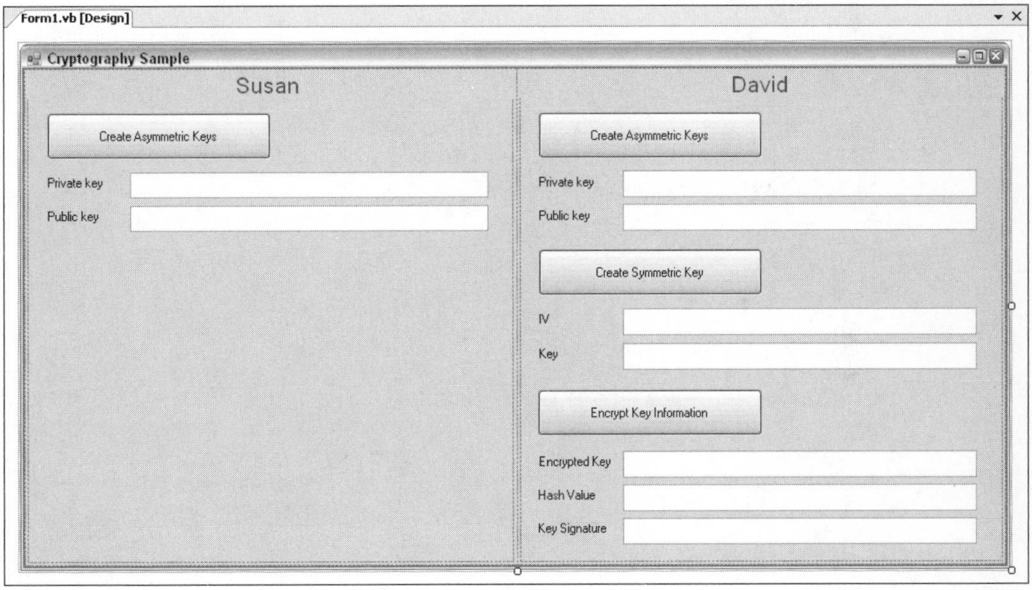

Figure 16-3

As discussed, this step involves three actions: encrypting the symmetric key, generating a hash value, and generating a signature. Encrypting the symmetric key is again done using an instance of the RSACrypto ServiceProvider class, which is initialized using Susan's public key. It is then used to encrypt both the initialization vector and the key into appropriate byte arrays. Because you want to create only a single hash and signature, these two byte arrays are combined into a single array, which is pre-pended with the lengths of the two arrays. This is done so the arrays can be separated prior to being decrypted.

The single-byte array created as part of encrypting the symmetric key is used to generate the hash value with the SHA1Managed algorithm. This hash value is then signed again using an instance of the RSACryptoServiceProvider, initialized this time with David's private key. An instance of the RSAP-KCS1SignatureFormatter class is also required to generate the signature from the hash value:

```
Public Class Form1
#Region "Step 1 & 2"
'...
#End Region
#Region "Step 3 - Encrypt, Hash and Sign Symmetric Key"
    Private Sub BtnEncryptKey_Click(ByVal sender As System.Object, _
                                ByVal e As System.EventArgs) _
                                                Handles BtnEncryptKey.Click

        EncryptSymmetricKey()
        Me.TxtHashValue.Text = Convert.ToBase64String _

(CreateSymmetricKeyHash(Me.TxtEncryptedKey.Text))
        SignSymmetricKeyHash()
    End Sub

    Private Sub EncryptSymmetricKey()
        Dim iv, key As Byte()
        Dim encryptedIV, encryptedkey As Byte()

        iv = Convert.FromBase64String(Me.TxtSymmetricIV.Text)
        key = Convert.FromBase64String(Me.TxtSymmetricKey.Text)

        'Load the RSACryptoServiceProvider class using
        'only the public key
        Dim RSA As New RSACryptoServiceProvider()
        RSA.FromXmlString(Me.TxtPublicKey1.Text)

        'Encrypt the Symmetric Key
        encryptedIV = RSA.Encrypt(iv, False)
        encryptedkey = RSA.Encrypt(key, False)

        'Create a single byte array containing both the IV and Key
        'so that we only need to encrypt and distribute a single value
        Dim keyOutput(2 * 4 - 1 + encryptedIV.Length + encryptedkey.Length) As Byte
        Array.Copy(BitConverter.GetBytes(encryptedIV.Length), 0, keyOutput, 0, 4)
        Array.Copy(BitConverter.GetBytes(encryptedkey.Length), 0, keyOutput, 4, 4)
        Array.Copy(encryptedIV, 0, keyOutput, 8, encryptedIV.Length)
        Array.Copy(encryptedkey, 0, keyOutput, 8 + encryptedIV.Length, _
                                                        encryptedkey.Length)

        Me.TxtEncryptedKey.Text = Convert.ToBase64String(keyOutput)
    End Sub

    Private Function CreateSymmetricKeyHash(ByVal inputString As String) As Byte()

        'Retrieve the bytes for this string
        Dim UE As New UnicodeEncoding()
        Dim MessageBytes As Byte() = UE.GetBytes(inputString)

        'Use the SHA1Managed provider to hash the input string
        Dim SHhash As New SHA1Managed()
        Return SHhash.ComputeHash(MessageBytes)
    End Function

    Private Sub SignSymmetricKeyHash()
        'The value to hold the signed value.
```

```
                  Dim SignedHashValue() As Byte

                  'Load the RSACryptoServiceProvider using the
                  'private key as we will be signing
                  Dim RSA As New RSACryptoServiceProvider
                  RSA.FromXmlString(Me.TxtPrivateKey2.Text)

                  'Create the signature formatter and generate the signature
                  Dim RSAFormatter As New RSAPKCS1SignatureFormatter(RSA)
                  RSAFormatter.SetHashAlgorithm("SHA1")
                  SignedHashValue = RSAFormatter.CreateSignature _
                                    (Convert.FromBase64String(Me.TxtHashValue.Text))

                  Me.TxtSymmetricSignature.Text = Convert.ToBase64String(SignedHashValue)
          End Sub
#End Region
End Class
```

At this stage, the encrypted key and signature are ready to be transferred from David to Susan.

Verifying Key and Signature

To simulate the encrypted key and signature being transferred, create additional controls on Susan's side of the dialog. Shown in Figure 16-4, the Retrieve Key Information button will retrieve the key, signature, and public key from David and populate the appropriate textboxes. In a real application, information could potentially be e-mailed, exported as a file and copied, or sent via a socket connection to a remote application. Essentially, it doesn't matter how the key and signature are transferred, as they are encrypted to prevent any unauthorized person from accessing the information.

Because the key and signature might have been sent via an unsecured channel, it is necessary to validate that the sender is who they claim to be. This can be done by validating the signature using the public key from the sender. Figure 16-4 shows what the form would look like if the Validate Public Key button is pressed and the signature received is successfully validated against the public key from the sender.

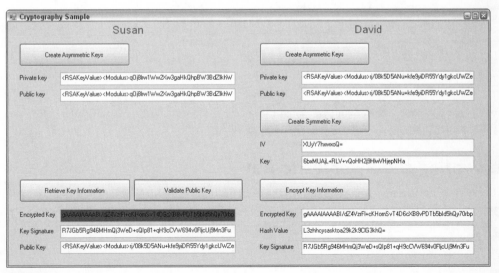

Figure 16-4

The code to validate the received signature is very similar to how the signature was created. A hash value is created from the encrypted key. Using the same algorithm used to create the received signature, a new signature is created. Finally, the two signatures are compared using the `VerifySignature` method, and the background color is adjusted accordingly:

```
Public Class Form1
#Region "Step 1 - 3"
'...
#End Region
#Region "Step 4 - Transfer and Validate Key Information"

    Private Sub BtnRetrieveKeyInfo_Click(ByVal sender As System.Object, _
                                  ByVal e As System.EventArgs) _
                                          Handles BtnRetrieveKeyInfo.Click
        Me.TxtRetrievedKey.Text = Me.TxtEncryptedKey.Text
        Me.TxtRetrievedSignature.Text = Me.TxtSymmetricSignature.Text
        Me.TxtRetrievedPublicKey.Text = Me.TxtPublicKey2.Text
    End Sub

    Private Sub BtnValidate_Click(ByVal sender As System.Object, _
                         ByVal e As System.EventArgs) _
                                           Handles BtnValidate.Click
        'Create the expected hash from the retrieved public key
        Dim HashValue, SignedHashValue As Byte()
        HashValue = CreateSymmetricKeyHash(Me.TxtRetrievedKey.Text)

        'Generate the expected signature
        Dim RSA As New RSACryptoServiceProvider()
        RSA.FromXmlString(Me.TxtRetrievedPublicKey.Text)
        Dim RSADeformatter As New RSAPKCS1SignatureDeformatter(RSA)
        RSADeformatter.SetHashAlgorithm("SHA1")
        SignedHashValue = Convert.FromBase64String(Me.TxtRetrievedSignature.Text)

        'Validate against received signature
        If RSADeformatter.VerifySignature(HashValue, SignedHashValue) Then
            Me.TxtRetrievedKey.BackColor = Color.Green
        Else
            Me.TxtRetrievedKey.BackColor = Color.Red
        End If
    End Sub
#End Region
End Class
```

Now that you have received and validated the encrypted key, the last remaining step before you can use the symmetric key to exchange data is to decrypt the key.

Decrypting the Symmetric Key

Decrypting the symmetric key will return the initialization vector and the key required to use the symmetric key. In Figure 16-5, the dialog has been updated to include the appropriate textboxes to display the decrypted values. These should match the initialization vector and key that were originally created by David.

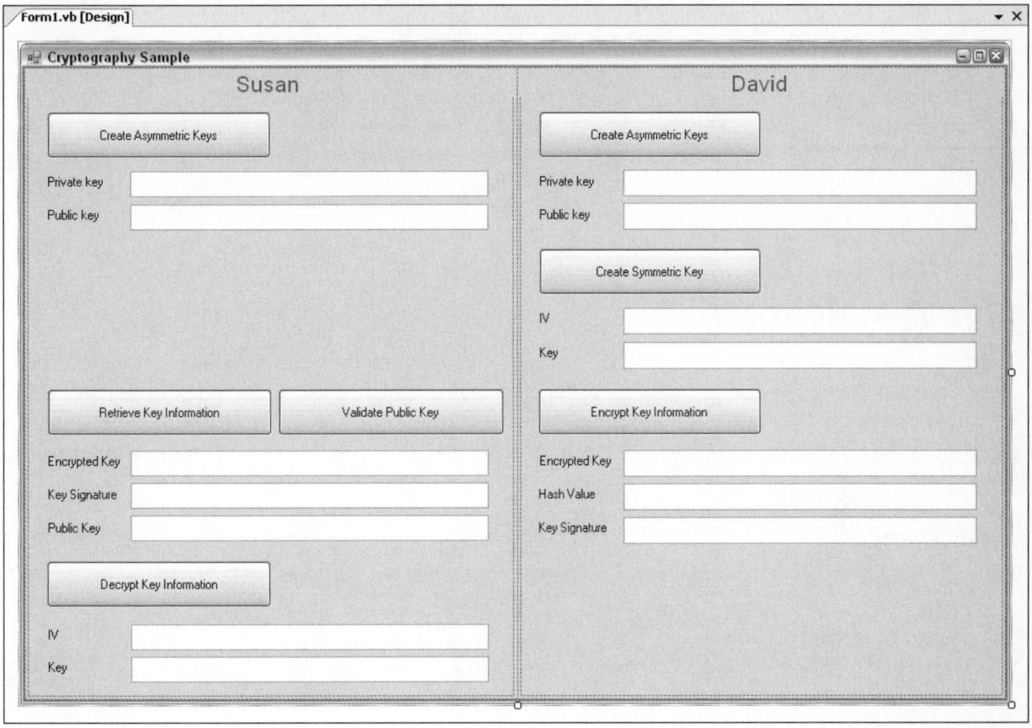

Figure 16-5

To decrypt the symmetric key, reverse the process for encrypting the symmetric key. Start by breaking up the single encrypted byte array into the iv and key byte arrays. To decrypt the key, you again need to create an instance of the RSACryptoServiceProvider class using Susan's private key. Because the data was encrypted using Susan's public key, the corresponding private key needs to be used to decrypt the data. This instance is then used to decrypt the initialization vector and the key:

```
Public Class Form1
#Region "Step 1 - 4"
'...
#End Region
#Region "Step 5 - Decrypt Symmetric key"
    Private Sub BtnDecryptKeyInformation_Click(ByVal sender As System.Object, _
                                        ByVal e As System.EventArgs) _
                                    Handles BtnDecryptKeyInformation.Click

        Dim iv, key As Byte()

        'Retrieve the iv and key arrays from the single array
        Dim keyOutput As Byte() = Convert.FromBase64String(Me.TxtRetrievedKey.Text)
        ReDim iv(BitConverter.ToInt32(keyOutput, 0) - 1)
        ReDim key(BitConverter.ToInt32(keyOutput, 4) - 1)
        Array.Copy(keyOutput, 8, iv, 0, iv.Length)
        Array.Copy(keyOutput, 8 + iv.Length, key, 0, key.Length)

        'Load the RSACryptoServiceProvider class using Susan's private key
```

```
            Dim RSA As New RSACryptoServiceProvider()
            RSA.FromXmlString(Me.TxtPrivateKey1.Text)

            'Decrypt the symmetric key and IV.
            Me.TxtDecryptedIV.Text = Convert.ToBase64String(RSA.Decrypt(iv, False))
            Me.TxtDecryptedKey.Text = Convert.ToBase64String(RSA.Decrypt(key, False))
      End Sub
#End Region
End Class
```

Sending a Message

Both Susan and David have access to the symmetric key, which they can now use to transmit secure data. In Figure 16-6, the dialog has been updated one last time to include three textboxes and a Send button. Text can be entered in the first textbox. Pressing the Send button will encrypt the text and place the encrypted data in the second textbox. The third textbox will be used to receive information from the other party.

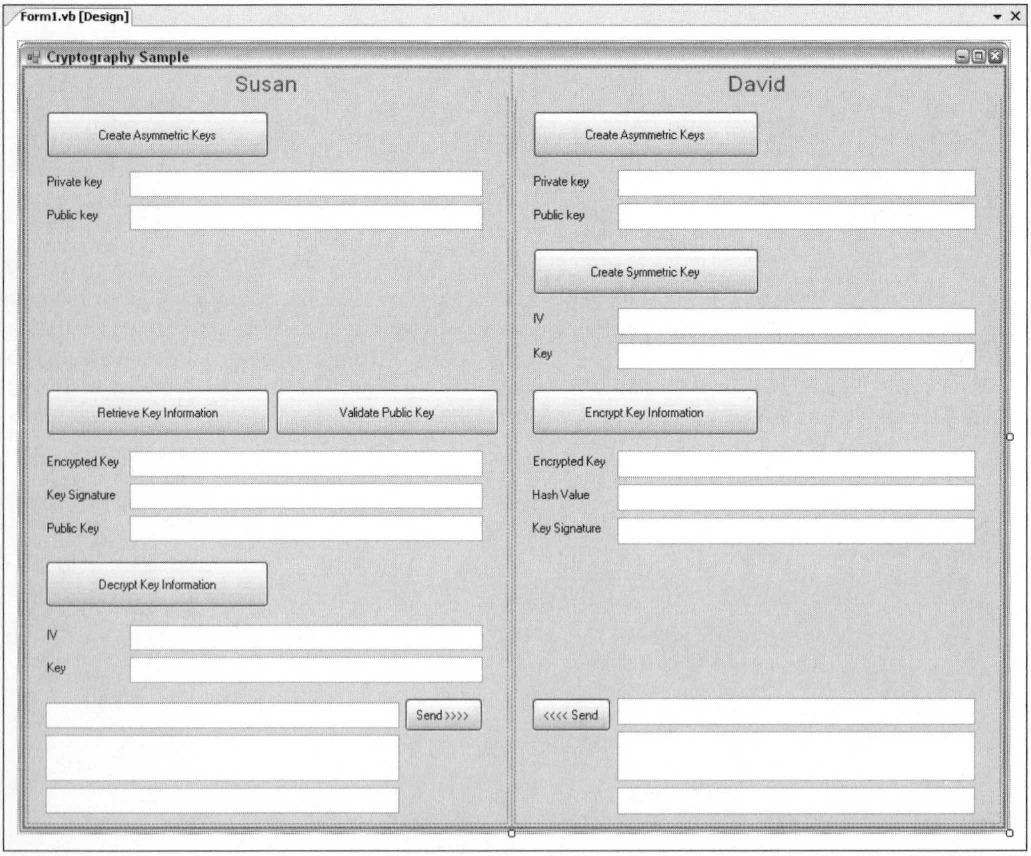

Figure 16-6

In the following code, the symmetric key is used to encrypt the text entered in the first textbox, placing the encrypted output in the second textbox. You will notice from the code that the process by which the data is encrypted is different from what you used with an asymmetric algorithm. Asymmetric algorithms are useful for encrypting short amounts of data, which means that they are typically used for keys and pass phrases. Conversely, symmetric algorithms can chain data together, enabling large amounts of data to be encrypted. For this reason they are suitable for a streaming model. When encrypting or decrypting, the input data can come from any stream, be it a file, the network, or an in-memory stream. Here is the code:

```vbnet
Public Class Form1
#Region "Step 1 - 5"
'...
#End Region
#Region "Step 6 - Sending a Message"
    Private Sub btnSendAToB_Click(ByVal sender As System.Object, _
                            ByVal e As System.EventArgs) _
                                            Handles btnSendAToB.Click
        Me.TxtMessageAEncrypted.Text = EncryptData(Me.TxtMessageA.Text, _
                                    Me.TxtDecryptedIV.Text, _
                                    Me.TxtDecryptedKey.Text)
    End Sub
    Private Sub BtnSendBToA_Click(ByVal sender As System.Object, _
                            ByVal e As System.EventArgs) _
                                            Handles BtnSendBToA.Click
        Me.TxtMessageBEncrypted.Text = EncryptData(Me.TxtMessageB.Text, _
                                    Me.TxtSymmetricIV.Text, _
                                    Me.TxtSymmetricKey.Text)

    End Sub

    Private Function EncryptData(ByVal data As String, ByVal iv As String, _
                                        ByVal key As String) As String
        Dim KeyBytes As Byte() = Convert.FromBase64String(key)
        Dim IVBytes As Byte() = Convert.FromBase64String(iv)

        'Create the output stream
        Dim strm As New IO.MemoryStream

        'Create the TripleDES class to do the encryption
        Dim Triple As New TripleDESCryptoServiceProvider()

        'Create a CryptoStream with the output stream and encryption algorithm
        Dim CryptStream As New CryptoStream(strm, _
                        Triple.CreateEncryptor(KeyBytes, IVBytes), _
                        CryptoStreamMode.Write)

        'Write the text to be encrypted
        Dim SWriter As New StreamWriter(CryptStream)
        SWriter.WriteLine(data)
        SWriter.Close()

        Return Convert.ToBase64String(strm.ToArray)
    End Function
#End Region
End Class
```

To encrypt the text message to be sent, create another instance of the `TripleDESCryptoService Provider`, which is the same provider you used to create the symmetric key. This, combined with the memory output stream, is used to create the `CryptoStream`. A `StreamWriter` is used to provide an interface for writing the data to the stream. The content of the memory stream is the encrypted data.

Receiving a Message

The final stage in this application is for the encrypted data to be transmitted and decrypted. To wire this up, trap the `TextChanged` event for the encrypted data textboxes. When this event is triggered, the encrypted data will be copied to the receiving side and decrypted, as shown in Figure 16-7. This simulates the information being sent over any unsecured channel.

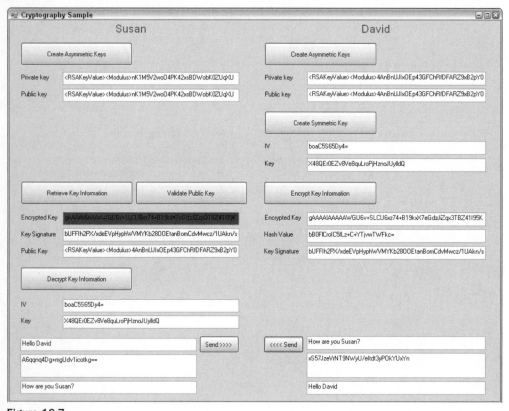

Figure 16-7

Decrypting the encrypted data is done the same way as the data was encrypted. An instance of the `TripleDESCryptoServiceProvider` is used in conjunction with the memory stream, based on the encrypted data, to create the `CryptoStream`. Using a `StreamReader`, the decrypted data can be read from the stream:

```
Public Class Form1
#Region "Step 1 - 6"
    '...
```

```
#End Region
#Region "Step 7 - Receiving a Message"
    Private Sub TxtMessageAEncrypted_TextChanged(ByVal sender As Object, _
                                        ByVal e As System.EventArgs) _
                              Handles TxtMessageAEncrypted.TextChanged
        Me.TxtReceivedMessageFromA.Text = DecryptData( _
                                  Me.TxtMessageAEncrypted.Text, _
                                  Me.TxtSymmetricIV.Text, _
                                  Me.TxtSymmetricKey.Text)
    End Sub

    Private Sub TxtMessageBEncrypted_TextChanged(ByVal sender As Object, _
                                        ByVal e As System.EventArgs) _
                              Handles TxtMessageBEncrypted.TextChanged
        Me.TxtReceivedMessageFromB.Text = DecryptData( _
                                  Me.TxtMessageBEncrypted.Text, _
                                  Me.TxtDecryptedIV.Text, _
                                  Me.TxtDecryptedKey.Text)
    End Sub

    Private Function DecryptData(ByVal data As String, ByVal iv As String, _
                                        ByVal key As String) As String
        Dim KeyBytes As Byte() = Convert.FromBase64String(key)
        Dim IVBytes As Byte() = Convert.FromBase64String(iv)

        'Create the input stream from the encrypted data
        Dim strm As New IO.MemoryStream(Convert.FromBase64String(data))

        'Create the TripleDES class to do the decryption
        Dim Triple As New TripleDESCryptoServiceProvider()

        'Create a CryptoStream with the input stream and decryption algorithm
        Dim CryptStream As New CryptoStream(strm, _
                              Triple.CreateDecryptor(KeyBytes, IVBytes), _
                              CryptoStreamMode.Read)

        'Read the stream.
        Dim SReader As New StreamReader(CryptStream)
        Return SReader.ReadToEnd
    End Function
#End Region
End Class
```

As demonstrated in this example, you can use asymmetric keys to authenticate the communicating parties and securely exchange a symmetric key. This ensures non-repudiation, as only the authenticated parties have access to the key, and the information is securely encrypted to achieve confidentiality and data integrity. Using a combination of algorithms you have achieved the goals of cryptography.

Miscellaneous

So far, this chapter has covered the principles and algorithms that make up the primary support for cryptography within the .NET Framework. To round out this discussion, the following sections describe both how to use the SecureString class and how to use a key container to store a private key.

SecureString

It's often necessary to prompt users for a password, which is typically held in a `String` variable. Any information held in the `String` will be contained within the String table. Because the information is stored in an unencrypted format, it can potentially be extracted from memory. To compound the problem, due to the immutable nature of the `String` class, there is no way to programmatically remove the information from memory. Using the `String` class to work with private encryption keys can be considered a security weakness.

An alternative is to use the `SecureString` class. Unlike the `String` class, the `SecureString` class is not immutable, so the information can be modified and cleared after use. The information is also encrypted, so it can be retrieved from memory. Because you never want the unencrypted form of the information to be visible, there is no way to retrieve a `String` representation of the encrypted data. The following sample code inherits from the standard `TextBox` control to create a `SecureTextbox` that will ensure that the password entered is never available as an unencrypted string in memory:

```
Imports System.Security
Imports System.Windows.Forms

Public Class SecureTextbox
    Inherits TextBox

    Private Const cHiddenCharacter As Char = "*"c
    Private m_SecureText As New SecureString

    Public Property SecureText() As SecureString
        Get
            Return m_SecureText
        End Get
        Set(ByVal value As SecureString)
            If value Is Nothing Then
                Me.m_SecureText.Clear()
            Else
                Me.m_SecureText = value
            End If
        End Set
    End Property

    Private Sub RefreshText(Optional ByVal index As Integer = -1)
        Me.Text = New String(cHiddenCharacter, Me.m_SecureText.Length)
        If index < 0 Then
            Me.SelectionStart = Me.Text.Length
        Else
            Me.SelectionStart = index
        End If
    End Sub

    Private Sub SecureTextbox_KeyPress(ByVal sender As Object, _
                            ByVal e As KeyPressEventArgs) _
                                                    Handles Me.KeyPress
        If Not Char.IsControl(e.KeyChar) Then
            If Me.SelectionStart >= 0 And Me.SelectionLength > 0 Then
                For i As Integer = Me.SelectionStart To _
```

```
                                      (Me.SelectionStart + Me.SelectionLength) - 1
                    Me.m_SecureText.RemoveAt(Me.SelectionStart)
            Next
        End If
    End If

    Select Case e.KeyChar
        Case Chr(Keys.Back)
            If Me.SelectionLength = 0 and Me.SelectionStart > 0 Then
                'If nothing selected, then just backspace a single character
                Me.m_SecureText.RemoveAt(Me.SelectionStart - 1)
            End If
        Case Chr(Keys.Delete)
            If Me.SelectionLength = 0 and _
                        Me.SelectionStart < Me.m_SecureText.Length Then
                Me.m_SecureText.RemoveAt(Me.SelectionStart)
            End If
        Case Else
            Me.m_SecureText.InsertAt(Me.SelectionStart, e.KeyChar)
    End Select
    e.Handled = True
    RefreshText(Me.SelectionStart + 1)
    End Sub
End Class
```

The `SecureTextbox` traps each `KeyPress` and adds any characters to the underlying `SecureString`. The `Text` property is updated to contain a `String` of * characters that is the same length as the `SecureString`. Once the text has been entered into the text box, the `SecureString` could be used to initiate another process, as shown in the following example:

```
Private Sub BtnStartNotepad_Click(ByVal sender As System.Object, _
                                  ByVal e As System.EventArgs) _
                                              Handles btnStartNotePad.Click

    Dim psi As New ProcessStartInfo()
    psi.Password = Me.SecureTextbox1.SecureText
    psi.UserName = Me.cboUsers.SelectedItem.ToString
    psi.UseShellExecute = False
    psi.FileName = "notepad"

    Dim p As New Process()
    p.StartInfo = psi
    p.Start()
End Sub
```

Key Containers

In the example application you have just worked through, both Susan and David have an asymmetric key pair, of which the public key was shared. Using this information, they shared a symmetric key that was used as a session key for transmitting data between parties. Given the limitations around authentication of a symmetric key once it has been shared to multiple parties, it is not advisable to maintain the same key for an extended period. Instead, a new symmetric key should be established for each transmission session.

Asymmetric key pairs, conversely, can be stored and reused to establish each new session. Given that only the public key is ever distributed, the chance of the private key falling into the wrong hands is greatly reduced. However, there is still a risk that the private key might be retrieved from the local computer if it is stored in an unencrypted format. This is where a *key container* can be used to preserve the key pair between sessions.

Working with a key container is relatively straightforward. Instead of importing and exporting the key information using methods such as ToXMLString and FromXMLString, you indicate that the asymmetric algorithm provider should use a key container by specifying a CspParameters class in the constructor. The following code snippet retrieves an instance of the AysmmetricAlgorithm class by specifying the container name. If no existing key pair exists in a container with that name, a new pair will be created and saved to a new container with that name:

```
Private Sub BtnLoadMyKeyPair_Click(ByVal sender As System.Object, _
                            ByVal e As System.EventArgs) _
                                        Handles BtnLoadMyKeyPair.Click
    Dim algorithm As AsymmetricAlgorithm = _
                        LoadAsymmetricAlgorithm(Me.TxtKeyContainerName.Text)
End Sub

Private Function LoadAsymmetricAlgorithm(ByVal container As String) _
                                        As AsymmetricAlgorithm
    'Create the CspParameters object using the container name
    Dim cp As New CspParameters()
    cp.KeyContainerName = container

    'Create or load the key information from the container
    Dim rsa As New RSACryptoServiceProvider(cp)
    Return rsa
End Function
```

If you need to remove a key pair from a key container, follow the same process to create the AsymmetricAlgorithm. You then need to set the PersistKeyInCsp to False, and execute the Clear method. This will ensure that the key is removed from both the key container and the AsymmetricAlgorithm object.

Summary

This chapter demonstrated how cryptography can play an important role in establishing a secure communication channel between multiple parties. Multiple steps are required to set up this channel, using a combination of symmetric and asymmetric algorithms. When deciding on a security scheme for your application, it is important to remember the four goals of cryptography: authentication, non-repudiation, integrity, and confidentiality. Not all applications require that all of these goals be achieved, and a piecemeal approach might be necessary to balance performance and usability against security.

Now that you have seen how to protect the data in your application, the next chapter shows you how to protect the embedded logic within your application from being stolen by a competitor.

17

Obfuscation

After wading through all the hype about the .NET Framework, you will have picked up on the fact that instead of compiling to machine language, .NET languages are compiled into the Microsoft Intermediary Language (MSIL, or just IL, for short). The IL is then just-in-time compiled as it is required for execution. This two-stage approach has a number of significant advantages, such as being able to dynamically query an assembly for a type and method information using reflection. However, this is a double-edged sword because this same flexibility means that once-hidden algorithms and business logic can easily be reverse engineered, legally or otherwise. This chapter introduces obfuscation and how it can be used to protect your application logic. Be forewarned, however: Obfuscation provides no guarantees, as the IL must still be executable and can thus be analyzed and potentially decompiled.

MSIL Disassembler

Before looking at how you can protect your code from other people, this section describes a couple of tools that can help you build better applications. The first tool is the MSIL Disassembler, or IL Dasm, which is installed with the .NET Framework SDK and can be found by clicking Start⇨All Programs⇨Microsoft .NET Framework SDK v2.0⇨Tools. In Figure 17-1, a small application has been opened using this tool, and you can immediately see the namespace and class information contained within this assembly.

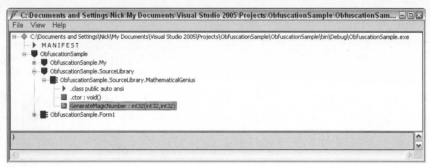

Figure 17-1

To compare the IL that is generated, the original source code for the `MathematicalGenius` class is as follows:

```
Namespace SourceLibrary
    Public Class MathematicalGenius
        Public Shared Function GenerateMagicNumber _
                        (ByVal age As Integer, ByVal height As Integer) As Integer
            Return age * height
        End Function
    End Class
End Namespace
```

Double-clicking on the `GenerateMagicNumber` method in IL Dasm will open up an additional window that shows the IL for that method. Figure 17-2 shows the IL for the `GenerateMagicNumber` method, which represents your patented algorithm. In actual fact, as you can roughly make out from the IL, the method expects two `int32` parameters, `age` and `height`, and multiplies them.

```
ObfuscationSample.SourceLibrary.MathematicalGenius::GenerateMagicNumber : int...
Find   Find Next
.method public static int32  GenerateMagicNumber(int32 age,
                                                 int32 height) cil managed
{
  // Code size       9 (0x9)
  .maxstack  2
  .locals init ([0] int32 GenerateMagicNumber)
  IL_0000:  nop
  IL_0001:  ldarg.0
  IL_0002:  ldarg.1
  IL_0003:  mul.ovf
  IL_0004:  stloc.0
  IL_0005:  br.s       IL_0007
  IL_0007:  ldloc.0
  IL_0008:  ret
} // end of method MathematicalGenius::GenerateMagicNumber
```

Figure 17-2

Anyone with a background in assembly programming will be at home reading the IL. For everyone else, a decompiler can convert this IL back into one or more .NET languages.

Decompilers

One of the most widely used decompilers is Reflector by Lutz Roeder (available for download at `www.aisto.com/roeder/dotnet/`). Reflector can be used to decompile any .NET assembly into C#, VB.NET, and even Delphi. In Figure 17-3, the same assembly you just accessed is opened using IL Dasm, in Reflector.

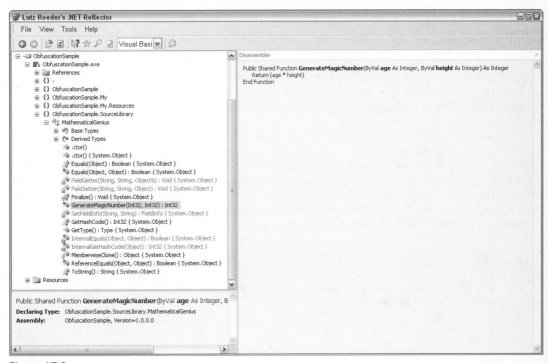

Figure 17-3

In the pane on the left of Figure 17-3, you can see the namespaces, type, and method information in a similar layout to IL Dasm. Double-clicking a method should open the Disassembler pane on the right, which will display the contents of that method in the language specified in the toolbar. In this case, you can see the VB.NET code that generates the magic number, which is almost identical to the original code.

If the generation of the magic number were a real secret on which your organization made money, the ability to decompile this application would pose a significant risk. This is made worse when you add the File Disassembler add-in, written by Denis Bauer (available at `www.denisbauer.com/NETTools/FileDisassembler.aspx`). With this add-in, an entire assembly can be decompiled into source files, complete with project file. There are some compatibility issues with the VB.NET output, but the generated C# can usually be compiled and executed without any adjustments.

Obfuscating Your Code

So far, this chapter has highlighted the need for better protection for the logic that is embedded in your applications. Obfuscation is the art of renaming symbols in an assembly so that the logic is unintelligible and can't be easily decompiled. Numerous products can obfuscate your code, each using its own tricks to make the output less likely to be decompiled. Visual Studio 2005 ships with the Community edition of Dotfuscator, which this chapter uses as an example of how you can apply obfuscation to your code.

Dotfuscator

Although Dotfuscator can be launched from the Tools menu within Visual Studio 2005, it is a separate product with its own licensing. The Community edition contains only a subset of the functionality of the Standard and Professional versions of the product. If you are serious about trying to hide the functionality embedded in your application, you should consider upgrading.

After starting Dotfuscator from the Tools menu, it prompts you to either create a new project or use an existing one. As Dotfuscator uses its own project format, create a new project that will be used to track which assemblies you are obfuscating and any options that you specify. Into the blank project, add the .NET assemblies that you want to obfuscate. Unlike other build activities that are typically run based on source files, obfuscating takes existing assemblies, applies the obfuscation algorithms, and generates a set of new assemblies. Figure 17-4 shows a new Dotfuscator project into which has been added the assembly for the ObfuscationSample application.

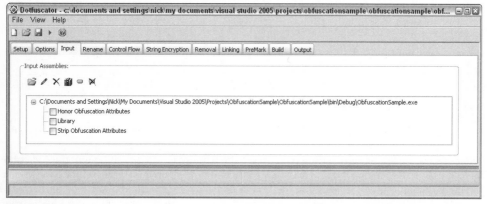

Figure 17-4

Without needing to adjust any other settings, you can select Build from the File menu, or click the play button (fourth from the left) on the toolbar, to obfuscate this application. The obfuscated assemblies will typically be added to a Dotfuscated folder. If you open this assembly using Reflector, as shown in Figure 17-5, you will notice that the `GenerateMagicNumber` method has been renamed, along with the input parameters. In addition, the namespace hierarchy has been removed and classes have been renamed. Although this is a rather contrived example, you can see how numerous methods with the same, or similar, non-intuitive names could cause confusion and make it difficult to decompile.

Figure 17-5

Unfortunately, this example obfuscated a public method. If you were to reference this assembly in another application, you would see a list of classes that have no apparent structure, relationship, or even naming convention. This would make working with this assembly very difficult. Luckily, Dotfuscator enables you to control what is renamed. Before going ahead, you need to refactor the code slightly to pull the functionality out of the public method. If you didn't do this and you excluded this method from being renamed, your secret algorithm would not be obfuscated. By separating the logic into another method, you can obfuscate that while keeping the public interface. The refactored code would look like the following:

```
Namespace SourceLibrary
    Public Class MathematicalGenius
        Public Shared Function GenerateMagicNumber _
                        (ByVal age As Integer, ByVal height As Integer) As Integer
            Return MultiplyAgeAndHeight(age, height)
        End Function


        Private Shared Function MultiplyAgeAndHeight _
                        (ByVal age As Integer, ByVal height As Integer) As Integer
            Return age * height
        End Function
    End Class
End Namespace
```

Chapter 17

After rebuilding the application and refreshing the Dotfuscator project (because there is no Refresh button, you need to reopen the project by selecting it from the Recent Projects list), the Rename tab will look like the one shown in Figure 17-6.

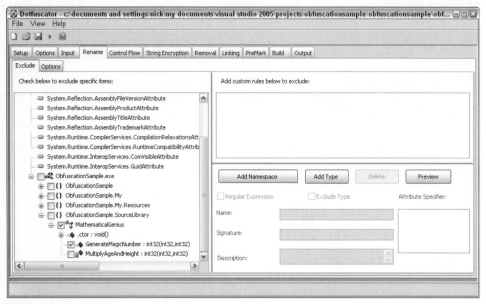

Figure 17-6

In the left pane you can see the familiar tree view of your assembly, with the attributes, namespaces, types, and methods listed. As the name of the tab suggests, this tree enables you to exclude symbols from being renamed. In Figure 17-6, the GenerateMagicNumber method, as well as the class that it is contained in, is excluded (otherwise, you would have ended up with something like b. `Generate MagicNumber`, where b is the renamed class). On the Options tab you also need to check the Keep Namespace checkbox. When you build the Dotfuscator project and look in the Output tab, you will see that the `MathematicalGenius` class and the `GenerateMagicNumber` method have not been renamed, as shown in Figure 17-7.

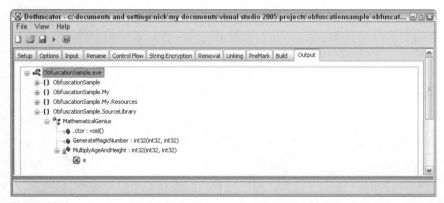

Figure 17-7

The `MultiplyAgeAndHeight` method has been renamed to `a`, as indicated by the subnode with the Dotfuscator icon.

Words of Caution

There are a couple of places where it is worth considering what will happen when obfuscation occurs, and how it will affect the workings of the application.

Reflection

The .NET Framework provides a rich reflection model through which types can be queried and instantiated dynamically. Unfortunately, some of the reflection methods use string lookups for type and method names. Clearly, the use of obfuscation will prevent these methods from working, and the only solution is not to mangle any symbols that may be invoked using reflection. Dotfuscator will attempt to determine a limited set of symbols to exclude based on how the reflection objects are used. For example, if you were to dynamically create an object based on the name of the class, and you then cast that object to a variable that matches an interface the class implements, Dotfuscator would be able to limit the excluded symbols to include only types that implemented that interface.

Strongly Named Assemblies

One of the purposes behind giving an assembly a strong name is that it prevents the assembly from being tampered with. Unfortunately, obfuscating relies on being able to take an existing assembly and mangle the names and code flow, before generating a new assembly. This would mean that the assembly is no longer strongly named. To allow obfuscation to occur you need to delay signing of your assembly by checking the Delay Sign Only checkbox on the Signing tab of the project properties window, as shown in Figure 17-8.

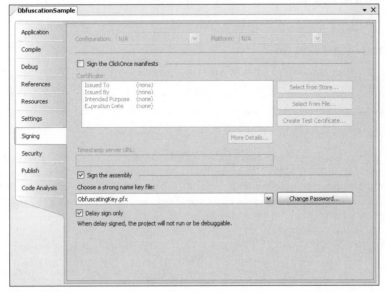

Figure 17-8

After building the assembly, you can then obfuscate it in the normal way. The only difference is that after obfuscating you need to sign the obfuscated assembly, which can be done manually using the `Strong Name` utility, as shown in this example:

```
sn -R ObfuscatingSample.exe ObfuscatingKey.pfx
```

Debugging with Delayed Signing

According to the project Properties window, checking the Delay Sign Only box will prevent the application from being able to be run or debugged. This is because the assembly will fail the strong name verification process. To enable debugging for an application with delayed signing, you can register the appropriate assemblies for verification skipping. This is also done using the `Strong Name` utility. For example, the following code will skip verification for the ObfuscatingSample application:

```
sn -Vr ObfuscatingSample.exe
```

Similarly, the following will reactivate verification for this application:

```
sn -Vu ObfuscatingSample.exe
```

This is a pain for you to have to do every time you build an application, so you can add the following lines to the post-build events for the application:

```
"$(DevEnvDir)..\..\SDK\v2.0\Bin\sn.exe" -Vr "$(TargetPath)"
"$(DevEnvDir)..\..\SDK\v2.0\Bin\sn.exe" -Vr
"$(TargetDir)$(TargetName).vshost$(TargetExt)"
```

The first line skips verification for the compiled application. However, Visual Studio 2005 uses an additional `vshost` file to bootstrap the application when it executes. This also needs to be registered to skip verification.

Where Did Those Attributes Go?

In the previous version of the .NET Framework, to sign an assembly you had to specify the appropriate attribute within the assemblyinfo file:

```
<Assembly: AssemblyKeyFile("MyKey.snk")>
<Assembly: AssemblyDelaySign(True)>
```

Because the location of the key was hard-coded into the assembly, it could be a security vulnerability; in addition, it could be difficult to configure, as the name had to match the physical location of the key. In Visual Studio 2005, the signing information specified in Figure 17-8 is included in the project file, as shown in the following code (this makes more sense than using attributes, as the signing process is just another part of the build process):

```
<?xml version="1.0" encoding="utf-8"?>
<Project DefaultTargets="Build"
xmlns="http://schemas.microsoft.com/developer/msbuild/2003">
    <PropertyGroup>
        <AssemblyName>ObfuscationSample</AssemblyName>
        ...
```

```
        <SignAssembly>true</SignAssembly>
        <AssemblyOriginatorKeyFile>ObfuscatingKey.pfx</AssemblyOriginatorKeyFile>
        <DelaySign>true</DelaySign>
    </PropertyGroup>
    ...
</Project>
```

As you can see from this code snippet, taken from the project file, both the attributes associated with signing the assembly are contained in the initial property group for the assembly being created. MSBuild uses this information to sign the assembly as part of the build process.

Attributes

In the previous example you saw how to choose which types and methods to obfuscate within Dotfuscator. Of course, if you were to move to an alternative obfuscating product you would have to configure it to exclude the public members. It would be more convenient to be able to annotate your code with attributes indicating whether a symbol should be obfuscated. You can do this by using the Obfuscation and ObfuscationAssembly attributes.

The default behavior in Dotfuscator is to ignore the obfuscation attributes in favor of any exclusions specified in the project. In Figure 17-4 there are a series of checkboxes for each assembly added to the project, of which the top checkbox is Honor Obfuscation Attributes. A limitation with the Community edition is that you can't control this feature for each assembly. You can apply this feature to all assemblies using the second button from the right on the toolbar.

ObfuscationAssembly

The ObfuscationAssembly attribute can be applied to an assembly to control whether it should be treated as a class library or as a private assembly. The distinction is that with a class library it is expected that other assemblies will be referencing the public types and methods it exposes. As such, the obfuscation tool needs to ensure that these symbols are not renamed. Alternatively, as a private assembly, every symbol can be potentially renamed.

```
<Assembly: Reflection.ObfuscateAssembly(False, StripAfterObfuscation:=True)>
```

The two arguments that this attribute takes indicate whether it is a private assembly and whether to strip the attribute off after obfuscation. The preceding snippet indicates that this is not a private assembly and that public symbols should not be renamed. In addition, the snippet indicates that the obfuscation attribute should be stripped off after obfuscation — after all, the less information available to anyone wishing to decompile the assembly, the better.

Adding this attribute to the assemblyinfo.vb file will automatically preserve the names of all public symbols in the ObfuscationSample application. This means that you can remove the exclusion you created earlier for the GenerateMagicNumber method.

Within Dotfuscator you can specify that you want to run all assemblies in library mode. Enabling this option has the same effect as applying this attribute to the assembly.

Obfuscation

The downside of the ObfuscationAssembly attribute is that it will expose all the public types and methods regardless of whether they existed for internal use only. The Obfuscation attribute can be applied to individual types and methods, so it provides a much finer level of control over what is obfuscated. To illustrate the use of this attribute, extend the example to include an additional public method, EvaluatePerson, and place the logic into another class, HiddenGenius:

```
Namespace SourceLibrary
    <Reflection.Obfuscation(applytomembers:=True, exclude:=True)> _
    Public Class MathematicalGenius

        Public Shared Function GenerateMagicNumber _
                    (ByVal age As Integer, ByVal height As Integer) As Integer
            Return HiddenGenius.MultiplyAgeAndHeight(age, height)
        End Function

        Public Shared Function EvaluatePerson _
                    (ByVal age As Integer, ByVal height As Integer) As Boolean
            Return HiddenGenius.QualifyPerson(age, height)
        End Function
    End Class

    <Reflection.Obfuscation(applytomembers:=False, exclude:=True)> _
    Public Class HiddenGenius
        Public Shared Function MultiplyAgeAndHeight _
                    (ByVal age As Integer, ByVal height As Integer) As Integer
            Return age * height
        End Function


        <Reflection.Obfuscation(Exclude:=True)> _
        Public Shared Function QualifyPerson _
                    (ByVal age As Integer, ByVal height As Integer) As Boolean
            Return (age / height) > 3
        End Function
    End Class
End Namespace
```

In this example, the MathematicalGenius class is the class that you want to expose outside of this library. As such, you want to exclude this class and all its methods from being obfuscated. This is done by applying the Obfuscation attribute with both the Exclude and ApplyToMembers parameters set to True.

The second class, HiddenGenius, is a hybrid class. As a result of some squabbling among the developers who wrote this class, the QualifyPerson method needs to be exposed, but all other methods in this class should be obfuscated. Again, the Obfuscation attribute is applied to the class so that the class does not get obfuscated. However, this time you want the default behavior to be such that symbols contained in the class are obfuscated, so the ApplyToMembers parameter is set to False. In addition, the Obfuscation attribute is applied to the QualityPerson method so that it will still be accessible.

Summary

In addition to learning about how to use obfuscation to protect your embedded application logic, this chapter reviewed two tools, IL Dasm and Reflector, which enable you to analyze and learn from what other developers have written. Although reusing code written by others without licensing their work is not condoned behavior, these tools can be used to learn techniques from other developers.

Part V
Coding

18

IntelliSense

One thing that Microsoft has long been good at is providing automated help as you write your code. Older versions of Visual Basic had a limited subset of this automated intelligence known as *IntelliSense,* but with the introduction of Visual Studio .NET, Microsoft firmly pushed the technology throughout the whole application development environment. With Visual Studio 2005, IntelliSense is even more pervasive than ever before, but you can also control it more than you could previously.

This chapter illustrates the many ways in which IntelliSense helps you write your code. Code snippets, using XML commenting in your own projects to create more IntelliSense information, and other features as simple as variable name completion are all covered.

IntelliSense Explained

IntelliSense is the general term for automated help and actions when you're using an application. The most commonly encountered IntelliSense is those wavy lines you see under words that are not spelled correctly in Microsoft Word, or small visual indicators in a Microsoft Excel spreadsheet to inform you that the contents of the particular cell do not conform to what was expected.

Even these basic visual feedback indicators provide you with a quick way of performing related actions. Right-clicking a word with red wavy underlining in Word will display a list of suggested words that you may have intended, and other applications work the same way.

This is just the tip of the IntelliSense iceberg. In more recent versions of Microsoft Office, advanced IntelliSense features include smart tag technology, which marks up recognized words and terms with additional indicators that you can then use to access appropriate actions, such as automatically adding an address into your Outlook Contacts folder from a recognized phrase in Word.

The good news is that Visual Studio has had similar functionality for a long time. In fact, the simplest IntelliSense features go back to tools such as Visual Basic 6. The even better news is that

Visual Studio 2005 has IntelliSense on overdrive, with many different features grouped under the IntelliSense banner. From visual feedback for bad code, smart tags while designing forms, to shortcuts that insert whole slabs of code, IntelliSense in Visual Studio 2005 provides greatly enhanced opportunities to improve your efficiency while creating applications.

General IntelliSense

The simplest feature of IntelliSense gives you immediate feedback about bad code in your module listings. Figure 18-1 shows one such example whereby an unknown data type is used to instantiate an object and then a second line of code tries to set a property. Because the data type is unknown in the context in which this code appears, Visual Studio draws a blue wavy line underneath it to indicate a problem.

The formatting of this color feedback can be adjusted in the Fonts and Colors group of Options.

Hovering the mouse pointer over the offending piece of code displays a tooltip to explain the problem. In this example, the cursor was placed over the data type with the resulting tooltip "Type 'PedoBear' is not defined." The second line of code also has an error because the enumeration is not present in this code context.

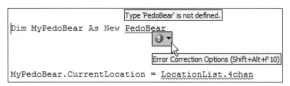

Figure 18-1

Visual Studio is able to look for this kind of error by continually precompiling the code you write in the background, looking for anything that will produce a compilation error. If you were to add a reference to the class containing the PedoBear definition, Visual Studio would automatically process this and remove the IntelliSense marker.

Figure 18-1 also displays a smart tag associated with the first error. This is a new feature for Visual Studio 2005 and applies only to errors for which the IDE can easily give you corrective actions. At the end of the problem code, a small yellow marker is displayed. Placing the mouse pointer over this marker will display the smart tag action menu associated with the type of error — in this case, it's an Error Correction Options list, which when activated will provide a list of possible data types that you meant to use instead of what's present.

The smart tag technology found in Visual Studio is not solely reserved for the code window. In fact, Visual Studio 2005 is the first Microsoft development tool to also include smart tags on visual components when you're editing a form or user control in Design view (see Figure 18-2).

When you select a control that has a smart tag, a small triangle will appear at the top-right corner of the control itself. Click this button to open the smart tag Tasks list — Figure 18-2 shows the Tasks list for a standard `TextBox` control.

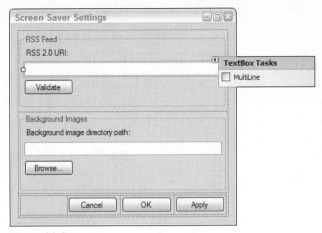

Figure 18-2

Completing Words and Phrases

The power of the IntelliSense in Visual Studio 2005 becomes apparent as you start creating your code. As you type, various drop-down lists are displayed to help you choose valid members, functions, and parameter types, thus reducing the number of potential compilation errors before you even finish writing your code.

List Members

The most common version of this feature is the member list. When you type the name of an object and then immediately follow it by a period (.) to indicate that you are going to refer to one of its members, Visual Studio will automatically display a list of members available to you for that object (see Figure 18-3). If this is the first time you've accessed the member list for a particular object, Visual Studio will highlight a default property or function, but if you've used it before, it will highlight the last member you accessed to shortcut the process for repetitive coding tasks.

Figure 18-3 also shows another helpful aspect of the member list for Visual Basic programmers. The Common and All tabs (at the bottom of the member list) enable you to view either just the commonly used members or a comprehensive list.

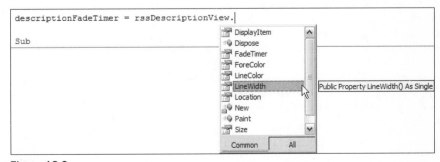

Figure 18-3

Only Visual Basic has the option to filter the member list down to commonly accessed properties, methods, and events.

You can also use a similar list to help you complete variable and object names. Simply type the initial few characters of the variable or object you need and use the keyboard shortcut Ctrl+Space. An extended list of all variables, objects, methods, data types, and more is displayed, with the first entry matching the characters you typed highlighted (see Figure 18-4). You can then navigate to the item you need.

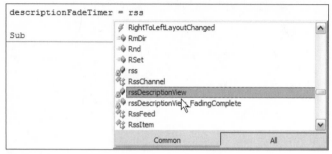

Figure 18-4

In this case, C# and other languages can automatically show the list without you typing the keyboard shortcut.

This list is also useful when you've encountered a compilation error. For instance, if you mistype an object name, Visual Studio will mark it with IntelliSense — the blue wavy line underneath the problematic name. Place the cursor anywhere in the bad name and press the keyboard shortcut Ctrl+Space to force Visual Studio 2005 to display the full member list from which you can choose the correct name.

Stub Completion

In addition to word and phrase completion, the IntelliSense engine has another feature known as *stub completion*. This feature can be seen in its basic form when you create a function by writing the declaration of the function and pressing Enter. Visual Studio will automatically reformat the line, including adding the appropriate `ByVal` keyword for parameters that don't explicitly define their context, and also adding an `End Function` line to enclose the function code.

Visual Studio 2005 takes this an extra step further by enabling you to do the same for interface and method overloading. When you add certain code constructs such as an interface in a C# class definition, Visual Studio will give you the opportunity to automatically generate the code necessary to implement the interface. To show you how this works, the following steps outline a task using the IntelliSense engine to generate an interface implementation in a simple class:

1. Start Visual Studio 2005 and create a C# WindowsApplication project. When the IDE has finished generating the initial code, open `Form1.cs` in Code view and navigate to the bottom of the namespace code structure.

2. At the top of the file, add a `using` statement to provide a shortcut to the `System.Collections` namespace:

```
using System.Collections;
```

3. Add the following line of code to start a new class definition:

```
public class MyCollection : IEnumerable
```

As you type the IEnumerable interface, Visual Studio will first add a red wavy line at the end to indicate that the class definition is missing its curly braces, and then add a smart tag indicator at the beginning of the interface name (see Figure 18-5).

```
public class MyCollection : IEnumerable
```

Figure 18-5

4. Hover your mouse pointer over the smart tag indicator. When the drop-down icon appears, click it to open the menu of possible actions. You should also see the tooltip explaining what the interface does, as shown in Figure 18-6.

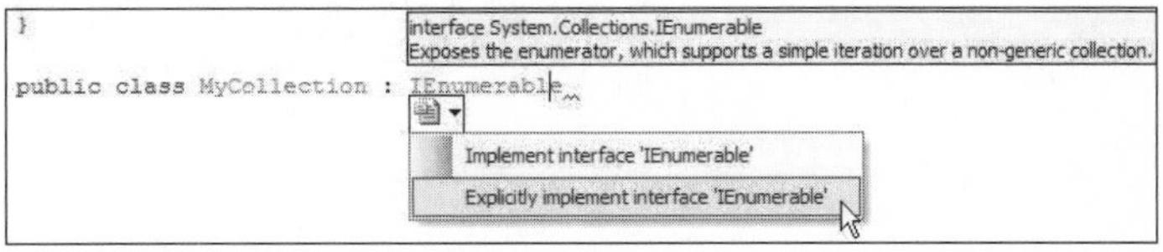

```
}

public class MyCollection : IEnumerable
```
interface System.Collections.IEnumerable
Exposes the enumerator, which supports a simple iteration over a non-generic collection.

Implement interface 'IEnumerable'
Explicitly implement interface 'IEnumerable'

Figure 18-6

5. Click the command "Explicitly implement interface 'IEnumerable'" and Visual Studio 2005 will automatically generate the rest of the code necessary to implement the minimum interface definition. Because it detects that the class definition itself isn't complete, it will also add the braces to correct that issue at the same time. Figure 18-7 shows what the final interface will look like.

```
public class MyCollection : IEnumerable
{
    #region IEnumerable Members

    IEnumerator IEnumerable.GetEnumerator()
    {
        throw new Exception("The method or operation is not implemented.");
    }

    #endregion
}
```

Figure 18-7

Event handlers can also be automatically generated by Visual Studio 2005. The IDE does this in a similar manner to interface implementation. When you write the first portion of the statement (for instance, myBase.OnClick +=), Visual Studio gives you a suggested completion that you can select by simply pressing Tab.

Parameter Information

In old versions of Microsoft development tools, such as Visual Basic 6, as you created the call to a function, IntelliSense would display the parameter information as you typed. Thankfully, this incredibly useful feature is still present in Visual Studio 2005.

The problem with the old way parameter information was displayed was that it would only be shown if you were actually modifying the function call. Therefore, you could see this helpful tooltip as you created the function call or when you changed it, but not if you were just viewing the code. The result was that programmers sometimes inadvertently introduced bugs into their code because they intentionally modified function calls so they could view the parameter information associated with the call.

Visual Studio 2005 eliminates that risk by providing an easily accessible command to display the information without modifying the code. Pressing the keyboard shortcut Ctrl+Shift+Space (or Ctrl+Shift+I) will display the information about the function call, as displayed in Figure 18-8. You can also access this information through the Edit➪IntelliSense➪Parameter Info menu command.

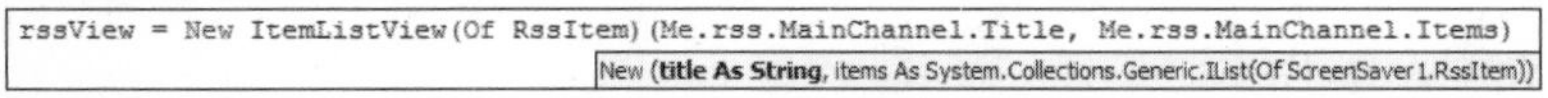

```
rssView = New ItemListView(Of RssItem)(Me.rss.MainChannel.Title, Me.rss.MainChannel.Items)
New (title As String, items As System.Collections.Generic.IList(Of ScreenSaver1.RssItem))
```

Figure 18-8

Quick Info

In a similar vein, sometimes you want to see the information about an object or interface without modifying the code. The Ctrl+I keyboard shortcut will display a brief tooltip explaining what the object is and how it was declared (see Figure 18-9).

You can also display this tooltip through the Edit➪IntelliSense➪Quick Info menu command.

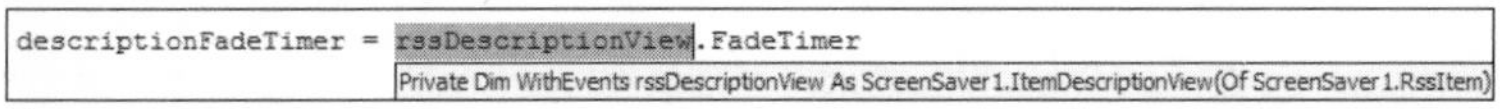

```
descriptionFadeTimer = rssDescriptionView.FadeTimer
Private Dim WithEvents rssDescriptionView As ScreenSaver1.ItemDescriptionView(Of ScreenSaver1.RssItem)
```

Figure 18-9

IntelliSense Options

Visual Studio 2005 sets up a number of default options for your experience with IntelliSense, but you can change many of these in the Options dialog if they don't suit your own way of doing things. Some of these items are specific to individual languages — for example, Visual Basic programmers tend to utilize IntelliSense features more than C# and C++ developers.

General Options

The first options to look at are found in the Environment section, under the Keyboard group. Every command available in Visual Studio has a specific entry in the keyboard mapping list (see Figure 18-10).

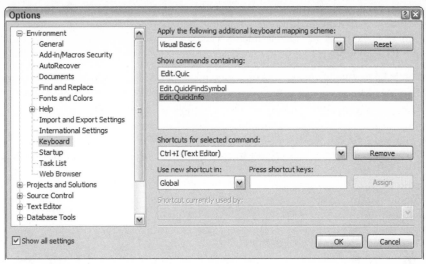

Figure 18-10

You can overwrite the predefined keyboard shortcuts, or add an additional keyboard shortcut. The commands for the IntelliSense commands are as follows:

Command Name	Default Shortcut	Command Description
Edit.QuickInfo	Ctrl+I	Displays the Quick Info information about the currently selected item
Edit.CompleteWord	Ctrl+Space	Attempts to complete a word if there is a single match, or displays a list to choose from if multiple terms match
Edit.ParameterInfo	Ctrl+Shift+Space or Ctrl+Shift+I	Displays the information about the parameter list in a function call
Edit.InsertSnippet	Ctrl+K, Ctrl+X	Invokes the Code Snippet dialog from which you can select a code snippet to insert code automatically
Edit.GenerateMethodStub	Ctrl+K, Ctrl+M	Generates the full method stub from a template
Edit.GenerateImplement AbstractClassStubs	None from a stub	Generates the abstract class definitions
Edit.GenerateImplement InterfaceStubsExplicitly	None	Generates the explicit implementation of an interface for a class definition
Edit.GenerateImplement InterfaceStubsImplicitly	None	Generates the implicit implementation of an interface for a class definition

Note that some of these shortcuts are the same kind of chords shown in Chapter 5. Use the techniques discussed in Chapter 5 to add additional keyboard shortcuts to any of these commands.

Statement Completion

You can control how IntelliSense works on a global language scale (see Figure 18-11) or per individual language. In the General tab of the language group, you want to change the Statement completion options to control how member lists should be displayed, if at all.

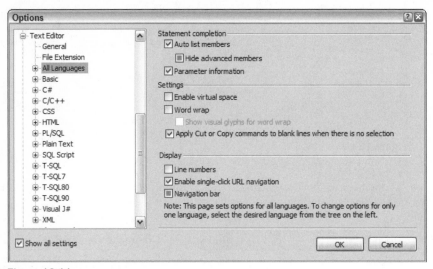

Figure 18-11

C#- and J#-Specific Options

Besides the general IDE and language options for IntelliSense, both C# and J# provide an additional IntelliSense tab in their own set of options. Displayed in Figure 18-12, the IntelliSense for these languages can be further customized to fine-tune how the IntelliSense features should be invoked and utilized.

First, you can turn off completion lists so they do not appear automatically, as discussed earlier in this chapter. Some developers prefer this so that the member lists don't get in the way of their code listings. If the completion list is not to be automatically displayed but instead only shown when you manually invoke it, you can choose what is to be included in the lists in addition to the normal entries, including keywords and code snippet shortcuts.

To select an entry in a member list, you can use any of the characters shown in the Selection In Completion List section, or optionally after the space bar is pressed. Finally, as mentioned previously, Visual Studio will automatically highlight the last used member in a list, which you can turn off for these languages or just clear the history.

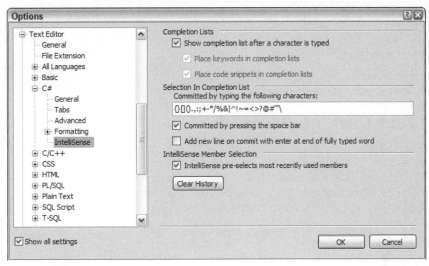

Figure 18-12

Extended IntelliSense

In addition to these aspects of IntelliSense, Visual Studio 2005 also implements extended IDE functionality that falls into the IntelliSense feature set. These features are discussed in detail in other chapters in this book, as referenced in the following discussion, but this chapter provides a quick summary of what's included in IntelliSense.

Code Snippets

Code snippets are sections of code that can be automatically generated and pasted into your own code, including associated references and `Imports` statements, and with variable phrases marked for easy replacement. To invoke the Code Snippets dialog, press the keyboard shortcut chord, Ctrl+K, Ctrl+X. Navigate the hierarchy of snippet folders until you find the one you need (as shown in Figure 18-13). If you know the shortcut for the snippet, you can simply type it and press Tab, and Visual Studio will invoke the snippet without the displaying the dialog. In Chapter 19, you'll see just how powerful code snippets are.

Figure 18-13

XML Comments

XML comments were discussed in Chapter 12 as a way of providing automated documentation for your projects and solutions. However, another advantage to using XML commenting in your program code is that Visual Studio can use it in its IntelliSense engine to display tooltips and parameter information beyond the simple variable-is-type information you see in normal user-defined classes.

Adding Your Own IntelliSense

You can also add your own IntelliSense schemas, normally useful for XML and HTML editing by creating a correctly formatted XML file and installing it into the `Common7\Packages\schemas\xml` subfolder inside your Visual Studio installation directory (the default location is `C:\Program Files\Microsoft Visual Studio 8`). The creation of such a schema file is beyond the scope of this book, but you can find schema files on the Internet by searching for IntelliSense Schema.

Summary

IntelliSense functionality extends beyond the main code window. Various other windows, such as the Command and Immediate tool windows, can harness the power of IntelliSense through statement and parameter completion. Any keywords, or even variables and objects, known in the current context during a debugging session can be accessed through the IntelliSense member lists.

In addition, Visual Studio 2005 loans the IntelliSense member lists to temporary objects. For example, consider inline string variables. When you use string literals in your code, you can access their properties and methods just as if they were string variables. Figure 18-14 illustrates this feature in action, displaying the member list for a string literal, complete with tooltip and parameter information about the currently highlighted member.

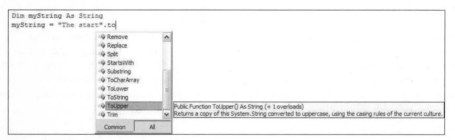

Figure 18-14

IntelliSense in all its forms enhances the Visual Studio experience beyond most other tools available to you. Constantly monitoring your keystrokes to give you visual feedback or automatic code completion and generation, IntelliSense enables to be extremely effective at writing code quickly and correctly the first time. In the next chapter, you'll dive into the details behind code snippets, a powerful addition to the IntelliSense lineup for Visual Studio 2005.

Code Snippets

Code snippets are small chunks of code that can be inserted into an application's code base and then customized to meet the application's specific requirements. They are usually generic in nature and serve one specific purpose. Code snippets do not generate full-blown applications or whole form definitions — project and item templates are used for such purposes. Instead, code snippets shortcut the programming task by automating frequently used code structures or obscure program code blocks that are not easy to remember.

In this chapter you'll see how code snippets have matured in Visual Studio 2005 to be powerful tools that can improve coding efficiency enormously, particularly for programmers who perform repetitive tasks with similar behaviors.

Code Snippets Revealed

Code snippet functionality has been around in many forms for a long time, but Microsoft has not included it in their development environments natively until the release of Visual Studio 2005, preferring to let third parties create various add-ins for languages such as Visual Basic 6 and the early versions of Visual Studio .NET.

Visual Studio 2005 marks the introduction of a proper code snippet feature built directly into the IDE. It allows code snippets that include not only blocks of code, but also multiple sections of code to be inserted in different locations within the module. In addition, a type of variable can be defined that makes it clear to see what parts of the snippet are to be customized and what sections can be left as is.

Original Code Snippets

The original code snippets from previous versions of Visual Studio were simple at best. These snippets were used to store a block of plain text that could be then inserted into a code module when desired. The process to create and use them was simple as well: Select a section of code and drag it over to the Toolbox. This creates an entry for it in the Toolbox with a default name equal to the first line of the code. You can rename it like any other element in the Toolbox, and to use it, simply drag the code to the desired location in the Code view and release the left mouse button (see Figure 19-1).

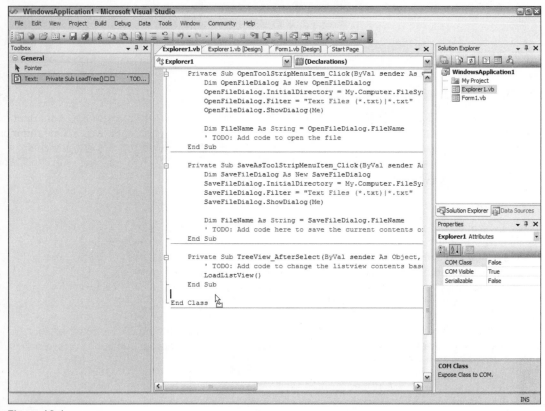

Figure 19-1

Many speakers used this simple technology to more easily display large code blocks in presentations, but in a real-world situation it was not as effective as it could have been, because often you had to remember to use multiple items to generate code that would compile.

It was also hard to share these so-called snippets, and equally hard to modify them. Nevertheless, this method of keeping small sections of code is still available to programmers in Visual Studio 2005, and it can prove useful when you don't need a permanent record of the code, but rather want to copy a series of code blocks for use immediately or in the near future.

"Real" Code Snippets

Now, in Visual Studio 2005, code snippet technology refers to something completely different. Code snippets are XML-based files containing sections of code that can include not only normal source code, but references and `Imports` statements and replaceable parameters as well.

Visual Studio 2005 ships with many predefined code snippets in the three main languages — Visual Basic, C#, and J#. These snippets are arranged hierarchically in a logical fashion so that you can easily locate the appropriate snippet. Rather than locate the snippet in the Toolbox, you can use menu commands or keyboard shortcuts to bring up the main list of groups.

New code snippets can be created to automate almost any coding task and then stored in this code snippet library. Because each snippet is stored in a special XML file, you can even share them with other developers.

Using Snippets in Visual Basic

Code snippets are a natural addition to the Visual Basic developer's toolset. They provide a shortcut way to insert code that either is difficult to remember or is used often with minor tweaks. One common problem some programmers have is remembering the correct references and Imports statements required to get a specific section of code working properly; code snippets in Visual Basic solve this problem by including all the necessary associations as well as the actual code.

To use a code snippet you should first locate where you want the generated code to be placed in the program listing and position the cursor at that point. You don't have to worry about the associated references and Imports statements, as they will be placed in the correct location.

There are three scopes under which a snippet can be inserted:

❑ **Class Declaration:** The snippet will actually include a class declaration, so it should not be inserted into an existing class definition.

❑ **Member Declaration:** This snippet scope will include code that defines members, such as functions and event handler routines. This means it should be inserted outside an existing member.

❑ **Member Body:** This scope is for snippets that are inserted into an already defined member, such as an event handler routine.

Once you've determined where the snippet is to be placed, the easiest way to bring up the Insert Snippet dialog is to use the keyboard shortcut chord of Ctrl+K, Ctrl+X (remember that a chord is a way of stringing multiple keyboard shortcuts together). There are two alternative methods to start the Insert Snippet process. The first is to right-click at the intended insertion point in the code window and select Insert Snippet from the context menu that is displayed. The other option is to use the Edit⇨IntelliSense⇨Insert Snippet menu command.

The Insert Snippet dialog is a special kind of IntelliSense (hence its location in the menu structure) that appears inline in the code window. Initially it displays the words Insert Snippet along with a drop-down list of code snippet groups from which to choose. Once you select the group that contains the snippet you require, it will show you the list of snippets from which you simply double-click the one you need.

Because you can organize the snippet library into many levels, you may find that the snippet you need is multiple levels deep in the Insert Snippet dialog. Figure 19-2 displays an Insert Snippet dialog in which the user has navigated through two levels of groups and then located a snippet named Draw a Pie Chart.

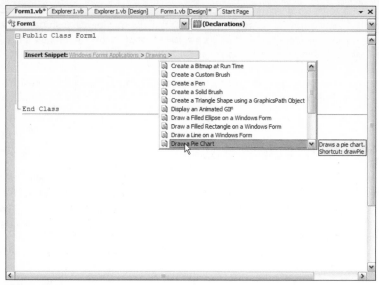

Figure 19-2

Double-clicking this entry will tell Visual Studio 2005 that you want the snippet to be generated at the current location. Figure 19-3 displays the result of selecting the Draw a Pie Chart snippet. This example shows a snippet with member declaration scope because it adds the definition of two subroutines to the code. To help you modify the code to your own requirements, the sections you would normally need to change are highlighted (the default is a green background).

When changing the variable sections of the generated code snippet, Visual Studio helps you even further. Select the first highlighted literal to be changed and enter the new value. Pressing the Tab key will move to the next literal and highlight it, ready for you to override the value with your own. Shift+Tab will navigate backward, so you have an easy way of accessing the sections of code that need changing without needing to manually select the next piece to modify.

Some code snippets use the same variable for multiple pieces of the code snippet logic. This means changing the value in one place will result in it changing in all other instances. A great example of this is can be found by selecting Windows Forms Applications⇨Forms⇨Add a Windows Forms Control At Run Time. The code that is generated through this snippet is shown in Figure 19-4, with all occurrences of `MyTest` referring to the same variable. Changing the first instance of `MyTest` in the line `Dim MyTest As New TextBox()` will result in the other two instances also changing automatically.

You might have noticed in Figure 19-2 that the tooltip text includes the words "Shortcut: drawPie." This text indicates that the selected code snippet has a text shortcut that you can use to automatically invoke the code snippet behavior without bringing up the IntelliSense dialog.

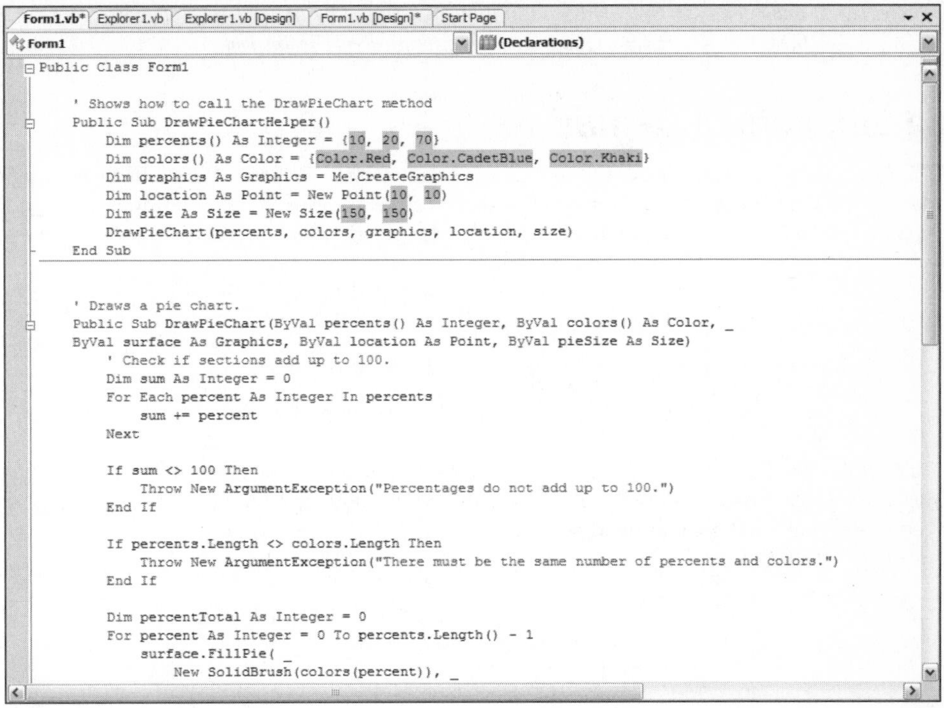

Figure 19-3

Of course, you need to know what the shortcut is before you can use this feature, but for those that you are aware of, all you need to do is type the shortcut into the code editor and press the Tab key. In Visual Basic the shortcut isn't even case sensitive, so this example can be generated by typing the term "draw-pie" and pressing Tab.

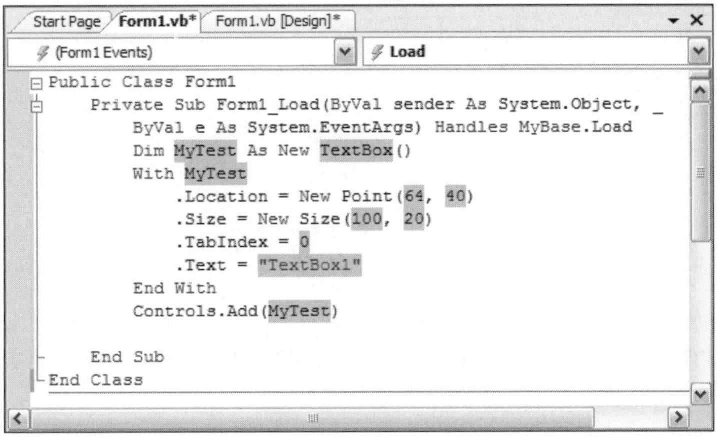

Figure 19-4

Note that in some instances the IntelliSense engine may not recognize this kind of shortcut. If this happens to you, press Ctrl+Tab to force the IntelliSense to intercept the Tab key.

Using Snippets in C# and J#

The code snippets in C# and J# are not as extensive as those available for Visual Basic but are inserted in the same way. Only Visual Basic supports the advanced features of the code snippet functionality, such as references and `Imports` statements. First, locate the position where you want to insert the generated code and then use one of the following methods:

❑ The keyboard chord Ctrl+K, Ctrl+X

❑ Right-click and choose Insert Snippet from the context menu

❑ Run the Edit⇨IntelliSense⇨Insert Snippet menu command

At this point, Visual Studio will bring up the Insert Snippet list for the current language, as Figure 19-5 shows. As you scroll through the list and hover the mouse pointer over each entry, a tooltip will be displayed to indicate what the snippet does.

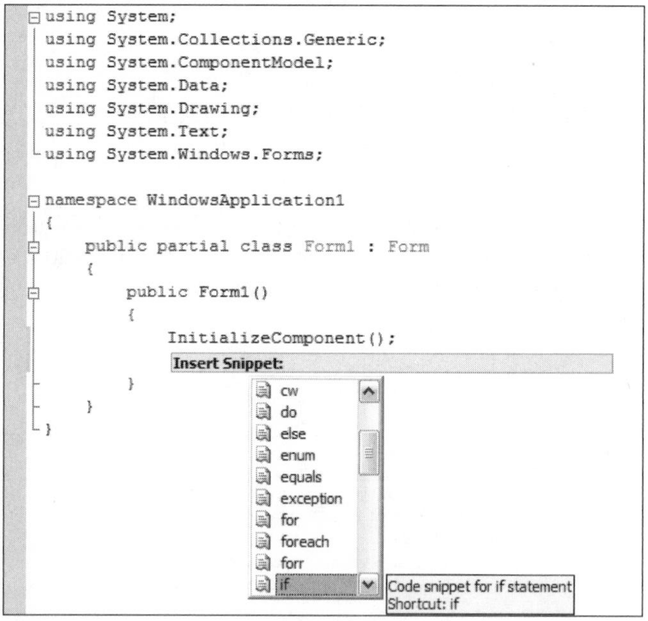

Figure 19-5

Although the predefined C# and J# snippets are limited in nature, you can create more functional and complex snippets for them.

Creating Snippets Manually

Visual Studio 2005 does not ship with a code snippet creator or editor. During the development of the IDE, Microsoft determined that a third-party tool, simply called the Snippet Editor, performed this functionality well enough that there was no reason to include a built-in editor in the IDE. Later in this chapter you'll learn how to use the Snippet Editor to create your own snippets, but it's worth taking a look at how code snippets are structured by looking at the manual method of creating one.

Each code snippet is simply an individual XML file with a file extension of `.snippet`. The contents of the file are written in plain text and follow the standard XML structure of a hierarchy of tags containing attributes and values. The remainder of this section deals with the structure of the code snippet XML schema.

Every snippet file must start with the `CodeSnippets` tag, identifying the namespace that defines the code snippet schema. This is written in the following form:

```
<CodeSnippets
    xmlns="http://schemas.microsoft.com/VisualStudio/2005/CodeSnippet">
</CodeSnippets>
```

Within these tags, each snippet is defined using the `CodeSnippet` tag, which will in turn contain the definition of the snippet itself:

```
<CodeSnippet Format="1.0.0">
</CodeSnippet>
```

Similar to HTML files, each code snippet has a header area and a body area, known as the `Header` and `Snippet`, respectively. The `Header` area can contain any combination of three separate tags, each defining a different attribute of the snippet:

- ❑   `Title`: The name of the snippet
- ❑   `Description`: The description of the snippet
- ❑   `Shortcut`: A shortcut term used to insert the snippet automatically

The `Header` layout looks like the following:

```
<Header>
  <Title>The Name Of The Snippet</Title>
  <Description>The description of the snippet. (Optional)</Description>
  <Shortcut>The shortcut for the snippet. (Optional)</Shortcut>
</Header>
```

Within the main `Snippet` tag you need to define the actual code to be inserted into the module. A `Code` tag is included with an attribute of `Language` (containing `VB`, `C#`, or `J#` depending on the language for which the snippet is intended). The actual code needs to be defined within a custom data tag with the format `<![CDATA[ code ]]>`. For example, the most basic `Snippet` tag looks like this:

```
<Snippet>
  <Code Language="VB">
    <![CDATA[The Code Goes Here]]>
  </Code>
</Snippet>
```

In addition to this code, you can define references and `Imports` statements in Visual Basic code snippets. Rather than insert the code at the selected entry point, Visual Studio will associate the references correctly as well as place the `Imports` statements at the top of the code module. These are placed at the top of the `Snippet` tag before the `Code` tag:

```
<Snippet>
  <References>
    <Reference>
      <Assembly>AssemblyName.dll</Assembly>
    </Reference>
  </References>
  <Imports>
    <Import>
      <Namespace>Namespace.Name</Namespace>
    </Import>
  </Imports>
  <Code Language="VB">
    <![CDATA[The Code Goes Here]]>
  </Code>
</Snippet>
```

As shown in the preceding example, code snippets can also have variable sections marked with special aliases so that the developer using the snippet knows which bits he or she should customize. To include such an alias, you first need to define it using a `Literal` tag. The `Literal` tag structure consists of the following:

❑   `ID`: An `ID` tag to uniquely identify the variable

❑   `Type`: The type of data to be inserted in this variable. This is optional.

❑   `ToolTip`: If defined, the user will see a tooltip containing this text. This is optional.

❑   `Default`: A default value to be placed in the automatically generated code. This is optional.

Following is a sample `Literal` tag:

```
<Literal>
  <ID>MyID</ID>
  <Type>String</Type>
  <ToolTip>The tooltip text</ToolTip>
  <Default>MyVarName</Default>
</Literal>
```

Object variables can also be included in the same way as literals, but use the `Object` tab instead.

To use `Object` and `Literal` aliases in the code to be inserted, enclose the ID of the required variable with dollar signs ($) and include it at the intended location in the code. The following code includes references to a literal and an object called `controlName` and `controlType`, respectively:

```
<Code Language="VB">
  <![CDATA[
      Dim $controlName$ As $controlType$
  ]]>
</Code>
```

You can use the same variable multiple times in the code. When you change the value after the code is generated, the code snippet IntelliSense engine will automatically update any other occurrences of the `Literal` or `Object` with the new value.

The final code snippet structure appears like this:

```
<CodeSnippets
    xmlns="http://schemas.microsoft.com/VisualStudio/2005/CodeSnippet">
  <CodeSnippet Format="1.0.0">
    <Header>
      <Title>The Name Of The Snippet</Title>
      <Description>The description of the snippet. (Optional)</Description>
      <Shortcut>The shortcut for the snippet. (Optional)</Shortcut>
    </Header>
     <Snippet>
     <References>
        <Reference>
          <Assembly>AssemblyName.dll</Assembly>
        </Reference>
      </References>
      <Imports>
        <Import>
          <Namespace>Namespace.Name</Namespace>
        </Import>
      </Imports>
        <Literal>
          <ID>MyID</ID>
          <Type>String</Type>
          <ToolTip>The tooltip text</ToolTip>
          <Default>MyVarName</Default>
        </Literal>
        <Object>
          <ID>MyType</ID>
          <Type>Control</Type>
          <ToolTip>The tooltip text</ToolTip>
          <Default>Button</Default>
        </Object>
      <Code Language="VB">
        <![CDATA[
            Dim $myID$ As $MyType$
        ]]>
      </Code>
    </Snippet>
  </CodeSnippet>
</CodeSnippets>
```

The best way to illustrate how code snippets can make your life easier is to walk through the creation of a simple example, adding it to the code snippets library and then using it in code. This next exercise does just that, creating a snippet that in turn creates three subroutines, including a helper subroutine that is intended to show the developer using the snippet how to call the functionality properly:

1. Start Notepad and add the following stub of XML (you're using Notepad to show that code snippets are simply XML written in plain text):

```xml
<?xml version="1.0"?>
<CodeSnippets xmlns="http://schemas.microsoft.com/VisualStudio/2005/CodeSnippet">
  <CodeSnippet Format="1.0.0">
  </CodeSnippet>
</CodeSnippets>
```

2. The first task is to define the header information. This is what's used to define the name of the snippet in the snippet library, and it also enables you to define a shortcut and a brief description of what the code snippet does. In between the CodeSnippet tags, insert the XML to create a Header tag that contains Title, Description, and Shortcut tags, like so:

```xml
<?xml version="1.0"?>
<CodeSnippets xmlns="http://schemas.microsoft.com/VisualStudio/2005/CodeSnippet">
  <CodeSnippet Format="1.0.0">
    <Header>
      <Title>CreateAButtonSample</Title>
      <Description>This snippet adds code to create a button control and
          hook an event handler to it.</Description>
      <Shortcut>createAButton</Shortcut>
    </Header>
  </CodeSnippet>
</CodeSnippets>
```

3. Now that the header information is present, you can begin creating the snippet itself. Start by defining the Snippet tag with a Declaration section and the main Code tag, setting attributes to VB (for Visual Basic) and method decl for the Kind so that Visual Studio knows that the scope of this snippet is a member declaration:

```xml
<?xml version="1.0"?>
<CodeSnippets xmlns="http://schemas.microsoft.com/VisualStudio/2005/CodeSnippet">
  <CodeSnippet Format="1.0.0">
    <Header>
      <Title>CreateAButtonSample</Title>
      <Description>This snippet adds code to create a button control and
          hook an event handler to it.</Description>
      <Shortcut>createAButton</Shortcut>
    </Header>
    <Snippet>
      <Declarations>
      </Declarations>
      <Code Language="VB" Kind="method decl">
      </Code>
    </Snippet>
  </CodeSnippet>
</CodeSnippets>
```

4. Define the Literal tags for the Name and Text properties that will be used to customize the button's creation. These properties will be used in the Helper subroutine so you know what you need to change to make the other subroutines work. Literal tags need an ID to identify

the alias used in the code snippet; and they can have a default value as well as an explanatory tooltip. You'll use all three tags to create your `Literal` tags, which should be included in the `Declarations` section:

```
<Declarations>
  <Literal>
    <ID>controlName</ID>
    <ToolTip>The name of the button.</ToolTip>
    <Default>"MyButton"</Default>
  </Literal>
  <Literal>
    <ID>controlText</ID>
    <ToolTip>The Text property of the button.</ToolTip>
    <Default>"Click Me!"</Default>
  </Literal>
</Declarations>
```

5. As mentioned earlier, the code to be inserted when this snippet is activated needs to be inserted in a custom data tag in the following form:

```
<![CDATA[code goes here]]>
```

Type the following code in between the opening and closing `Code` tags. It defines the three subroutines and is straight Visual Basic code other than the use of the aliased `Literal` tags. Note that these are enclosed by dollar signs ($) to tell Visual Studio that they are aliases — to use the `Literal` `controlName`, the alias `$controlName$` is used:

```
<Code Language="VB" Kind="method decl">
<![CDATA[Private Sub CreateButtonHelper
    CreateAButton($controlName$, $controlText$, Me)
End Sub

Private Sub CreateAButton(ButtonName As String, ButtonText As String, _
    Owner As Form)
    Dim MyButton As New Button

    MyButton.Name = ButtonName
    MyButton.Text = ButtonName
    Owner.Controls.Add(MyButton)

    MyButton.Top = 0
    MyButton.Left = 0
    MyButton.Text = ButtonText
    MyButton.Visible = True

    AddHandler MyButton.Click, AddressOf ButtonClickHandler
End Sub

Private Sub ButtonClickHandler(ByVal sender As System.Object, _
    ByVal e As System.EventArgs)
    MessageBox.Show("The " & sender.Name & " button was clicked")
End Sub
]]>
</Code>
```

6. Save the file as `CreateAButton.snippet` somewhere where you can locate it easily and switch to Visual Studio 2005. Bring up the code snippets library with the keyboard shortcut chord Ctrl+K, Ctrl+B. Once the library is displayed, click the Import button and browse to the snippet file you just saved.

7. Choose a suitable location for the snippet — the My Snippets group is the usual place for custom-built snippets — and click Finish. Click OK to close the library. Your snippet is now saved and stored in Visual Studio 2005, ready for use.

8. To test that the code snippet was properly defined and installed, create a new Windows Forms application and switch to the Code view of `Form1`. Display the Code Snippet IntelliSense dialog by using the keyboard chord Ctrl+K, Ctrl+X, and then browse to the CreateAButton snippet you just imported and double-click it. Visual Studio should insert the Visual Basic code to define three subroutines, with two variables highlighted.

9. Add the following code to the bottom of the `Form1` class definition:

```
Private Sub Form1_Load(ByVal sender As System.Object, _
    ByVal e As System.EventArgs) Handles MyBase.Load
    CreateButtonHelper()
End Sub
```

This will execute the `CreateButtonHelper` subroutine when the form is first loaded, which in turn will call the other subroutines generated by the code snippet and create a button with default text and a default behavior. Run the application and click the button that is created, and you should get similar results to those shown in Figure 19-6.

Figure 19-6

While this sample shows the creation of a simple code snippet, you can use the same technique to create complex snippets that include `Imports` statements, code definitions, and markup for sections within the code snippet text to be replaced by the developer using it.

Code Snippets Manager

The Code Snippets Manager is the central library for the code snippets known to Visual Studio 2005. You can access it via the Tools⇨Code Snippet Manager menu command or the keyboard shortcut chord, Ctrl+K, Ctrl+B.

When it is initially displayed, the Code Snippets Manager will show the snippets for the language you're currently using. Figure 19-7 shows how it will look when you're editing a Visual Basic project. The hierarchical folder structure follows the same set of folders on the PC by default, but as you add snippet files from different locations and insert them into the different groups, the new snippets slip into the appropriate folders.

If you have an entire folder of snippets to add to the library, such as when you have a corporate setup and need to import the company-developed snippets, you use the Add button. This brings up a dialog that you use to browse to the required folder. Folders added in this fashion will appear at the root level of the tree view — on the same level as the main groups of default snippets. However, you can add a folder that contains subfolders, which will be added as child nodes in the tree view.

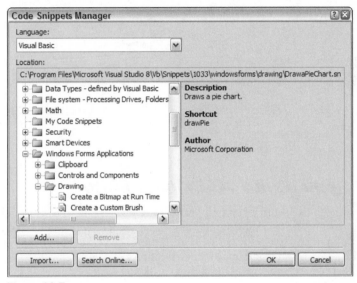

Figure 19-7

Removing a folder is just as easy — in fact, it's dangerously easy. Select the root node that you want to remove and click the Remove button. Instantly the node and all child nodes and snippets will be removed from the Snippets Manager without a confirmation window. You can add them back by following the steps explained in the previous walkthrough, but it can be frustrating trying to locate a default snippet folder that you inadvertently deleted from the list.

The location for the code snippets that are installed with Visual Studio 2005 is deep within the installation folder. By default, the code snippet library will be installed in `C:\Program Files\Microsoft Visual Studio 8\VB\Snippets\1033`.

Individual snippet files can be imported into the library using the Import button. The advantage of this method over the Add button is that you get the opportunity to specify the location of each snippet in the library structure.

Figure 19-8 shows the Import Code Snippet dialog for a sample snippet file `HelloPersonName` `.snippet`. By default, Visual Studio 2005 suggests that snippets added in this fashion be inserted into the custom My Code Snippets folder, but you can put the snippet in any folder that seems appropriate by finding it in the Location list.

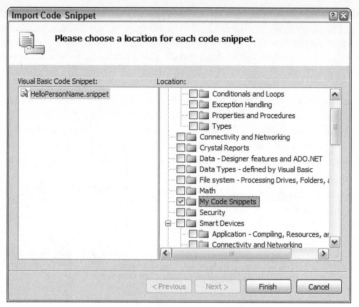

Figure 19-8

Creating Snippets with VB Snippet Editor

Creating code snippets by manually editing XML files can be tedious. It can also result in errors that are hard to track down. Fortunately, a third-party tool called Snippet Editor can make your life a lot easier. You'll find the Snippet Editor at `http://msdn.microsoft.com/vbasic/downloads/tools/snippeteditor/`. Download it and install it in a location that you can locate easily, as it doesn't create an entry in the Start menu. The default location is `C:\Documents and Settings\username\My Documents\MSDN\Code Snippet Editor`.

> *You may also want to create a desktop shortcut to the program if you'll be using it frequently.*

When you start the Snippet Editor, it will display a welcome screen showing you how to browse and create new snippets. The left side of the screen is populated with a tree view containing all the Visual Basic snippets defined in your system known to Visual Studio 2005. Initially the tree view is collapsed, but by expanding it you'll see a set of folders similar to those in the code snippet library (see Figure 19-9).

Reviewing Existing Snippets

An excellent feature of the Snippet Editor is the view it offers of the structure of any snippet file in the system. This means you can browse the default snippets installed with Visual Studio, which can provide insight into how to better build your own snippets.

Browse to the snippet you're interested in and double-click its entry to display it in the Editor window. Figure 19-9 shows a simple Hello World snippet. You'll notice two tabs at the top of the editing side of the form — Editor and Preview. Editor is where you'll do most of your work, while switching over to Preview shows how the snippet will look when you insert it into your application code.

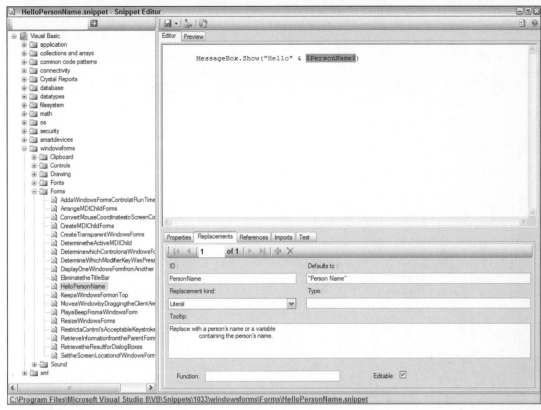

Figure 19-9

The lower area of the Editor pane contains all of the associated information about the snippet. From left to right, these tabs contain the following:

Tab	Function
Properties	The main properties for the snippet, including title, shortcut, and description
Replacements	All `Literal` and `Object` aliases are defined in this tab.
References	If your snippet will require system framework references, this tab allows you to define them.
Imports	Similar to the References tab, this tab enables you to define any `Imports` statements that are required in order for your snippet to function correctly.
Test	This tab attempts to analyze your snippet to confirm that it will work properly as is.

Browsing through these tabs enables you to analyze an existing snippet for its properties and replacement variables. In the example shown in Figure 19-9, the Replacements tab is displayed, showing that one replacement is defined as a `Literal` with an ID of `PersonName` and a default value of `"Person Name"`.

Be aware that the results shown in the Test tab are not always accurate. As shown in Figure 19-10, even the predefined snippet templates produce compilation errors when tested. This is because the Snippet Editor is not aware of the full context for which this snippet is intended. However, it's still a handy step to perform, as it will show you real errors in your code snippet as well.

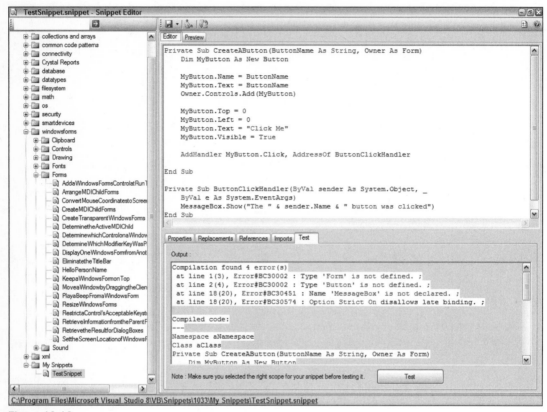

Figure 19-10

Both Figure 19-9 and Figure 19-10 show that editing snippets using the Snippet Editor is a much more pleasant process than editing the raw XML. The code to be inserted in the snippet is color-coded and formatted in a similar fashion to the Visual Basic editor in Visual Studio, giving you a familiar environment in which to write.

Replacements Explained

When defining `Literal` and `Object` aliases, you would normally define them in the XML using `Literal` and `Object` tags, and then refer to them in the code with special alias formatting. The Snippet Editor operates on a similar paradigm; use the Replacements tab to first define the replacement's properties. When the Add button is clicked in the Replacements tab, it will insert the default ID into the Editor window and populate the properties in the lower half.

You need to change the ID in the lower section, not in the Editor window.

To demonstrate how the Snippet Editor makes creating your own snippets a lot more straightforward, follow this next exercise in which you will create the same snippet you created earlier in this chapter, but this time taking advantage of the Snippet Editor's features:

1. Start the Snippet Editor and create a new snippet. To do this, locate the My Snippets folder in the tree view (or any other folder of your choice), right-click, and select Add New Snippet from the context menu that is displayed.

2. When prompted, name the snippet CreateAButtonSample2 and click OK. Double-click the new entry to open it in the Editor pane.

Note that creating the snippet will not automatically open the new snippet in the Editor — don't over-write the properties of another snippet by mistake!

3. The first thing you need to do is edit the Title, Description and Shortcut fields so they match the previous sample (see Figure 19-11):

- ❑ `Title`: CreateAButtonSample2

- ❑ `Description`: This snippet adds code to create a button control and hook an event handler to it.

- ❑ `Shortcut`: createAButton

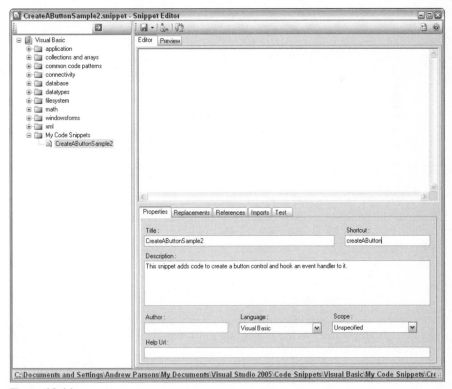

Figure 19-11

4. Because this snippet contains member definitions, set the Scope to `Member declaration`.

5. In the Editor window, insert the code necessary to create the three subroutines as before. Note that you don't have to include the custom data tag CDATA, as the Snippet Editor will do that for you in the background:

```
Private Sub CreateButtonHelper
    CreateAButton(, , Me)
End Sub

Private Sub CreateAButton(ButtonName As String, ButtonText As String, Owner As
Form)
    Dim MyButton As New Button

    MyButton.Name = ButtonName
    MyButton.Text = ButtonName
    Owner.Controls.Add(MyButton)

    MyButton.Top = 0
    MyButton.Left = 0
    MyButton.Text = ButtonText
    MyButton.Visible = True

    AddHandler MyButton.Click, AddressOf ButtonClickHandler
End Sub

Private Sub ButtonClickHandler(ByVal sender As System.Object, _
    ByVal e As System.EventArgs)
    MessageBox.Show("The " & sender.Name & " button was clicked")
End Sub
```

6. You'll notice that the call to CreateAButton is incomplete, because you haven't defined the `Literal` aliases yet, so switch over to the Replacements tab. Position the cursor immediately after the opening parenthesis on the CreateAButton function call and click the Add button to create a new replacement.

The Snippet Editor will immediately insert the default name for the new replacement in the code, but don't worry: It will be changed when you set the ID.

7. Change the replacement properties like so (note that the default values should include the quotes (") so they are generated in the snippet:

    ❑   ID: `controlName`

    ❑   Defaults to: `"MyButton"`

    ❑   Tooltip: The name of the button

8. Notice that the code window changed the alias to the new ID. Position the cursor after the first comma and repeat the process of creating a new replacement. Set the properties of the new replacement as follows:

    ❑   ID: `controlText`

    ❑   Defaults to: `"Click Me!"`

    ❑   Tooltip: The text property of the button

Your snippet is now done and ready to be used (compare it to Figure 19-12). You can use the Preview tab to check it against the code generated by the previous code snippet exercise or use Visual Studio 2005 to insert the snippet into a code window.

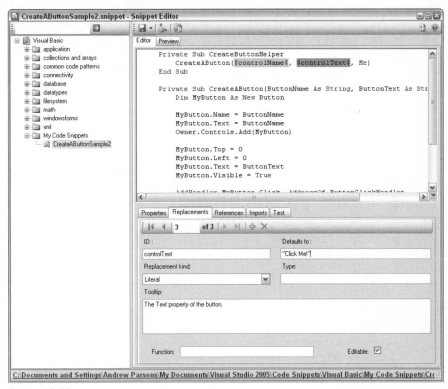

Figure 19-12

Note that if you added your snippet to a known folder, Visual Studio 2005 will automatically find it and recognize its shortcut without you needing to import it manually.

Summary

Code snippets are a valuable inclusion in the Visual Studio 2005 feature set. You learned in this chapter how to use them, and, more important, how to create your own, including variable substitution and `Imports` and reference associations for Visual Basic snippets. With this information you'll be able to create your own library of code snippets from functionality that you use frequently, saving you time in coding similar constructs later.

20

Regions and Bookmarks

Visual Studio 2005 comes with many visual indicators in the development environment interface to give you feedback about what you're doing, as well as shortcuts to manage your code. In the previous two chapters, you saw in detail how a lot of that worked with the various IntelliSense automated features.

However, some of the visual aspects of the editors that can be used in the IDE are created manually, rather than being automatically generated by Visual Studio itself. Features such as regionalizing code and creating bookmarks for easy navigation are included in this subset of available tools in the main IDE. These features are the subject of this chapter. As well as regions and bookmarks, you'll also learn some of the other visual indicators that the IDE provides for you so that you know what's going on.

Regions

Code regions are a concept that provides you with the ability to logically break up your Visual Basic or C# code and present it in a way that makes it more manageable. When not needed, regions of code can be collapsed down to a single line in the editor. Similarly, an expand button enables you to easily display them again.

For example, the code shown in Figure 20-1 has been collapsed down to a few region headlines that can be digested immediately — there is a class called ScreenSaverForm that consists of three sections: class-level constant and variable definitions, the code you created, and the code generated automatically by the wizard that instantiated the form.

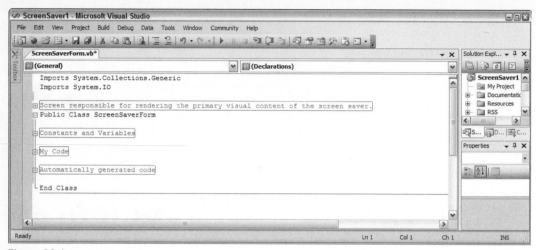

Figure 20-1

Figure 20-1 also shows two additional code regions that Visual Studio automatically added to the editor. The first is a collapsed region containing the XML comments defined for the class. The last region is the entire class definition itself. Clicking the small collapse button next to the definition of the `Public Class ScreenSaverForm` line will collapse the whole class definition down to a single line in the editor.

Creating Regions

Creating manual code regions in Visual Basic is easy. To define a region, use the compiler directive-like command words `#Region` and `#End Region`. In Visual Basic you must specify a title for the region, like so:

```
#Region "Name of Region Here"
    VB code here
#End Region
```

As soon as Visual Studio detects a valid pairing of the two commands, it will add the collapse button to the start of the region's area. Clicking this button will collapse the code editor down to a single line labeled with the title you specified. Figure 20-2 shows how a region definition might look to contain a section of code.

Figure 20-2

Creating regions in C# is done in a similar fashion but isn't as restrictive. The command words are `#region` and `#endregion` and there is no need for a title to the region, so the following definition is valid:

```
#region
    C# code here
#endregion
```

This results in a single line with the text #region when the region is collapsed, so you may find it more appropriate to include a title even though it isn't required. Unlike Visual Basic, in which the title must be a string constant (i.e., must be enclosed with quotes), C# regions can have the title string tacked onto the #region statement without quotes:

```
#region My Code Region
    C# code here
#endregion
```

Using Regions

Regardless of whether a region is created automatically by Visual Studio or manually by you, it is used in the same way. When a region is collapsed, it is represented by a single line of text in the code editor window along with an expand button so you can view and edit the code within the region. This single line of text can be one of the following:

❑ **The Summary Line:** This is used for XML comment blocks.

❑ **The First Line of Code:** Automatic regions, such as class and procedure definitions, will display this.

❑ **The Title of the region:** Manually defined regions will display the title that was specified (or the phrase #region if untitled in C# code).

Hovering your mouse pointer over a collapsed region will display an expanded tooltip containing the first few lines of code, similar to the example shown in Figure 20-3. This works only if the mouse pointer is placed over an outlined section of the region title — in Visual Basic, this section is the entire line, but in other languages such as C#, it may only be represented by an ellipsis at the end of the visible line.

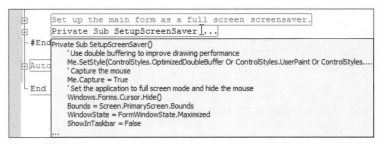

Figure 20-3

If you prefer to use keyboard shortcuts, the shortcut chord Ctrl+M, Ctrl+M will toggle the collapsed/expanded state of the region containing the current insertion point. Alternatively, if you want to collapse all regions down to their region stubs, you can use the Ctrl+M, Ctrl+L chord.

In addition, you can hide a section of code temporarily if you're using C# or J#. The keyboard shortcut chord Ctrl+M, Ctrl+H will hide the code currently selected in the editor window. This shortcut is only available when Visual Studio is not outlining the code into automatic regions based on class and procedural definitions.

In previous versions of Visual Studio, you could also perform this function in Visual Basic code, but you can no longer do this with Visual Studio 2005.

Introducing Outlining Commands

The automated regionalizing of class and procedural definitions is available courtesy of Visual Studio 2005's outlining feature. By default, this functionality constantly analyzes the code and determines when valid regional areas are defined. As soon as a new area has been defined and is capable of being made into a region, the IDE will mark it as such. Conversely, the automated outlining functionality detects immediately when a regionalized area is no longer capable of being a region. For example, Visual Studio will detect the following code as a valid region:

```
Function MyFunction() As Boolean
    Some VB Code
End Function
```

However, the following code snippet will not be recognized as a region, because the function definition hasn't been coded correctly (the End Function statement is incomplete):

```
Function MyFunction2() As Boolean
    Some VB Code
End Funct
```

This automated outlining can be turned off using the keyboard chord Ctrl+M, Ctrl+P. When automated outlining is inactive, only manually defined regions created using the techniques discussed earlier in this chapter can be used to organize the code.

The Collapse to Definitions function is used to collapse the automated regions (and manually defined regions) down to their closed state. You'll most likely find this more useful than the Collapse All command discussed earlier because you can still see the function definitions within a function, rather than having them hidden inside a collapsed class definition. To invoke Collapse to Definitions, use the Ctrl+M, Ctrl+O keyboard chord.

If you turn outlining off and find that you want it back on, you need to have Visual Studio recreate the automated regions for existing code by first using the Collapse to Definitions command and then expanding the code with the expand all chord, Ctrl+M, Ctrl+L.

The Outlining menu provides an alternative access point to all of these commands. You can access it via the Edit menu (see Figure 20-4) or by right-clicking in the code editor window.

Figure 20-4

Visual Indicators

The code editor windows in the IDE also provide several visual indicators along with the IntelliSense and automated formatting features of Visual Studio 2005. These include color-coding of the margin and icons to represent breakpoints, bookmarks, and search results. The following sections explain what each of these indicators mean.

Color Coding

When code is first opened or generated in the IDE, the side margin is left as is to indicate that the code is original code. However, as you edit the code, and build and debug the solutions, the margins change color to show that changes have occurred.

When code is added or changed in a module, the margin will turn yellow. Once the changed code has passed through the build process and has been compiled successfully, the margin color changes to green. Figure 20-5 shows the results of a subroutine that was first created and compiled, with an additional line added subsequent to the build.

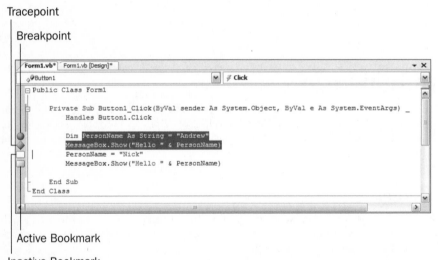

Figure 20-5

Note that color-coding remains only for as long as the editor window is open. Once you close the editor window and reopen it, the margin will be reset to its default state.

Margin Icons

Figure 20-6 shows the Code view for a form with a number of icons in the left margin. Each of these represents a different indicator so you can see at a glance what's significant about the particular line.

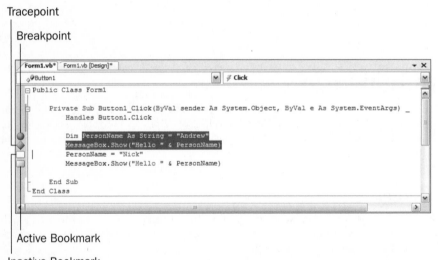

Figure 20-6

From top to bottom, the icons represent a breakpoint, a tracepoint, an inactive bookmark, and an active bookmark.

Because lines of code can have multiple states, these icons can be overlaid on top of each other. Figure 20-7 shows the same code window during a debug session with an additional icon indicating the current line of code being executed. Note how this icon overlays the pre-existing tracepoint icon.

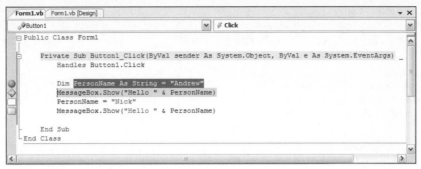

Figure 20-7

Breakpoints and tracepoints are discussed in Chapter 49.

Bookmarks and the Bookmark Window

Bookmarks in Visual Studio 2005 enable you to mark places in your code modules so you can easily return to them later. As mentioned in the previous discussion, they are represented by a visual indicator in the left margin of the code, but they are also listed together in a Bookmarks tool window (discussed in a moment).

To toggle a bookmark, use the keyboard shortcut chord Ctrl+K, T. Ctrl+K indicates to Visual Studio that the chord is related to bookmarks, while the T invokes the toggle command. Alternatively, you can use the Edit➪Bookmarks➪Toggle Bookmark menu command to achieve the same goal.

Remember that toggle means just that. If you use this command on a line already bookmarked, it will remove the bookmark.

Figure 20-8 shows a section of the code editor window with two bookmarks. The top bookmark is in its normal state, represented by a shaded blue rectangle. The lower bookmark has been disabled and is represented by a solid white rectangle. Disabling bookmarks enables you to keep the bookmark for later use while excluding it from the normal bookmark navigation functions.

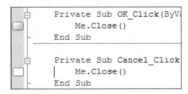

Figure 20-8

To disable a bookmark, use the Edit➪Bookmarks➪Enable Bookmark toggle menu command. Use the same command to re-enable the bookmark.

You may want to set up a shortcut for this if you plan on using bookmarks a lot in your code manage-ment. To do so, access the Keyboard options page in the Environment group in Options and look for Edit.EnableBookmark. *A good shortcut to use is* Ctrl+K, E, *as it is consistent with the standard Ctrl+K chords for bookmarks and is easy to remember.*

Along with the capability to add and remove bookmarks, Visual Studio provides a Bookmarks tool win-dow, as displayed in Figure 20-9. By default, this window is docked to the bottom of the IDE and shares space with other tool windows such as the Task List and Find Results windows.

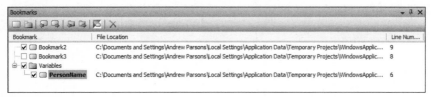

Figure 20-9

Figure 20-9 illustrates some useful features of bookmarks in Visual Studio 2005. The first is the capability to create folders that can logically group the bookmarks. In the example list, notice a folder named Variables with a bookmark named PersonName (presumably marking a variable of the same name) inside it.

To create a folder of bookmarks, click the New Folder icon in the toolbar along the top of the Bookmarks window (it's the second button from the left). This will create an empty folder (using a default name of Folder1, Folder2, and so on). Right-click the entry and select Rename from the context menu to choose a different name.

Move bookmarks into the folder by selecting their entry in the list and dragging them into the desired folder. Note that you cannot create a hierarchy of folders, but it's unlikely that you'll want to. Bookmarks can be renamed in the same way as folders, and for permanent bookmarks this can be use-ful, rather than accepting the default names of Bookmark1, Bookmark2, and so forth.

To navigate to a bookmark, double-click its entry in the list. Alternatively, if you want to cycle through all of the bookmarks defined in the project, use the Previous Bookmark and Next Bookmark commands. You can restrict this navigation to only the bookmarks in a particular folder by first selecting a bookmark in the folder and then using the Previous Bookmark in Folder and Next Bookmark in Folder commands.

The last two buttons in the Bookmarks window are the Toggle All Bookmarks command, which can be used to disable (or re-enable) all of the bookmarks defined in a project, and the Delete command, which can be used to delete a folder or bookmark from the list.

Deleting a folder will also remove all of the bookmarks contained in the folder. Visual Studio will pro-vide a confirmation dialog to safeguard accidental loss of bookmarks. Deleting a bookmark is the same as toggling a bookmark off.

Bookmarks can also be controlled via the Bookmarks submenu, which is found in the Edit main menu.

Unlike previous versions of Visual Studio, bookmarks in Visual Studio 2005 are retained between ses-sions, making permanent bookmarks a much more viable option for managing your code organization.

Task Lists are a customized version of Bookmarks that are now displayed in their own tool window. The only connection that still exists is that there is an Add Task List Shortcut command still in the Bookmarks menu. Be aware that this does not add the shortcut to the Bookmarks window, but instead to the Shortcuts list in the Task List window.

Summary

In this chapter you've seen how Visual Studio can provide even more visual cues for you to work with: automated ones such as the color-coded margins, manually instigated indicators such as margin icons for bookmarks and breakpoints, and code regions for easier code management. Using these techniques will help improve your coding efficiency in simple ways.

21
Refactoring

One of the techniques that has received a lot of attention recently is *refactoring*, the process of reworking code to improve it without changing its functionality. This might entail simplifying a method, extracting a commonly used code pattern, or even optimizing a section of code to make it more efficient. This chapter reviews the refactoring support offered by Visual Studio 2005. Unfortunately, because of the massive list of functionality that the VB.NET team tried to squeeze into the product, support for a wide range of refactoring actions just didn't make the cut. Luckily for VB.NET developers, Microsoft has come to an arrangement with Developer Express to license the VB version of their Refactor! product for anyone using Visual Studio 2005. Refactor! can be downloaded from the Visual Basic developer center at `http://msdn.microsoft.com/vbasic/`, as illustrated in Figure 21-1.

Figure 21-1

Refactor! provides a range of refactoring support that complements the integrated support available for C# developers. However, this chapter's discussion is restricted to the refactoring support provided within Visual Studio 2005 and the Refactor! product.

Accessing Refactoring Support

Visual Studio 2005 makes use of both the main menu and the right-click context menu to invoke the refactoring actions. Refactor! only uses the context menu to invoke actions, although it does offer hints while you're working.

C# — Visual Studio 2005

Refactor support for C# developers is available via the Refactor menu or the right-click context menu, as shown in Figure 21-2.

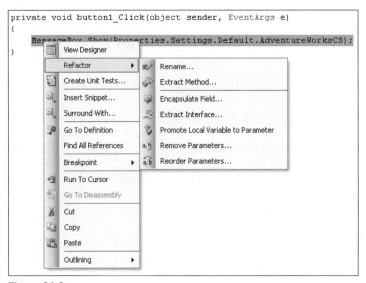

Figure 21-2

The full list of refactoring actions available to C# developers within Visual Studio 2005 includes Rename, Extract Method, Encapsulate Field, Extract Interface, Promote Local Variable to Parameter, Remove Parameters, and Reorder Parameters. You can also use Generate Method Stub, and Surround with Snippet, which can be loosely classified as refactoring.

VB.NET — Refactor!

Refactor support for VB.NET developers is available via the right-click context menu, as shown in Figure 21-3.

As you work with your code, Refactor! is busy in the background. The context menu is dynamically changed so that only valid refactoring actions are displayed. Refactor! also offers useful hints that can be used to invoke refactoring actions, as shown in Figure 21-4.

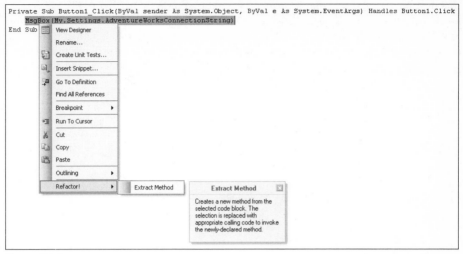

Figure 21-3

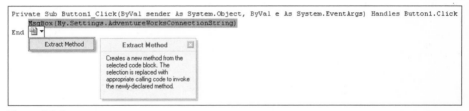

Figure 21-4

The limited refactoring support provided by Visual Studio 2005 for VB.NET developers includes Rename and Surround with Snippet. Refactor! adds support for much, much more: Create an overload, Encapsulate a field, Extract a method, Extract a property, Flatten conditional statement, Inline temporary variable, Introduce a constant, Introduce local variable, Move declaration near reference, Move initialization to declaration, Remove assignments to parameters, Rename, Reorder parameters, Replace temporary variable with method, Reverse conditional statement, Safe rename, Simplify conditional statement, Split initialization from declaration, and Split temporary variable.

Refactoring Actions

The following sections describe each of the refactoring options and provide examples of how to use built-in support for both C# and Refactor!

Extract Method

One of the easiest ways to refactor a long method is to break it up into several smaller methods. The Extract Method refactoring action is invoked by selecting the region of code you want moved out of the original method and selecting Extract Method from the context menu. In C#, this will prompt you to enter a new method name, as shown in Figure 21-5. If there are variables within the block of code to be extracted that were used earlier in the original method, they will automatically appear as variables in the method signature. Once the name has been confirmed, the new method will be created immediately after the original method. A call to the new method will replace the extracted code block.

Figure 21-5

For example, in the following code snippet, if you wanted to extract the conditional logic into a separate method, then you would select the code, shown with a gray background, and choose Extract Method from the right-click context menu:

```
private void button1_Click(object sender, EventArgs e)
{
    string output = Properties.Settings.Default.AdventureWorksCS;
    if (output == null)
    {
        output = "DefaultConnectionString";
    }
    MessageBox.Show(output);
    /* ... Much longer method ... */
}
```

This would automatically generate the following code in its place:

```
Private void button1_Click(object sender, EventArgs e)
{
    string output = Properties.Settings.Default.AdventureWorksCS;
    output = ValidateConnectionString(output);
    MessageBox.Show(output);
}

private static string ValidateConnectionString(string output)
{
    if (output == null)
    {
        output = "DefaultConnectionString";
    }
    return output;
}
```

Refactor! handles this refactoring action slightly differently. After you select the code you want to replace, Refactor! prompts you to select a place in your code where you want to insert the new method. This can help developers organize their methods in groups, either alphabetically or according to functionality. Figure 21-6 illustrates the aid that appears to enable you to position, using the cursor keys, the insert location.

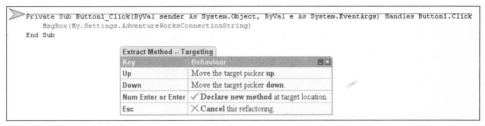

```
Private Sub Button1_Click(ByVal sender As System.Object, ByVal e As System.EventArgs) Handles Button1.Click
    MsgBox(My.Settings.AdventureWorksConnectionString)
End Sub
```

Extract Method -- Targeting	
Key	**Behaviour**
Up	Move the target picker up.
Down	Move the target picker down.
Num Enter or Enter	✓ Declare new method at target location.
Esc	✗ Cancel this refactoring.

Figure 21-6

After selecting the insert location, Refactor! will insert the new method, giving it an arbitrary name. In doing so it will highlight the method name, enabling you to rename the method either at the insert location or where the method is called (see Figure 21-7).

```
Private Sub Button1_Click(ByVal sender As System.Object, ByVal e As System.EventArgs) Handles Button1.Click
    Dim output As String = My.Settings.AdventureWorksConnectionString
    ValidataConnectionString(output)
    MsgBox(My.Settings.AdventureWorksConnectionString)
End Sub

Private Sub ValidataConnectionString(ByVal output As String)
    If output = "" Then
        output = "DefaultConnectionString"
    End If
End Sub
```

Figure 21-7

Encapsulate Field

Another common task when refactoring is to encapsulate an existing class variable with a property. This is what the Encapsulate Field refactor action does. To invoke this action, select the variable you want to encapsulate and select the appropriate refactor action from the context menu. This will give you the opportunity to name the property and elect where to search for references to the variable, as shown in Figure 21-8.

The next step after specifying the new property name is to determine which references to the class variable should be replaced with a reference to the new property. Figure 21-9 shows the preview window that is returned after the reference search has completed. In the top pane is a tree indicating which files and methods have references to the variable. The checkbox beside each row indicates whether a replacement will be made. Selecting a row in the top pane brings that line of code into focus in the lower pane. Once each of the references has been validated, the encapsulation can proceed. The class variable is updated to be private, and the appropriate references are updated as well.

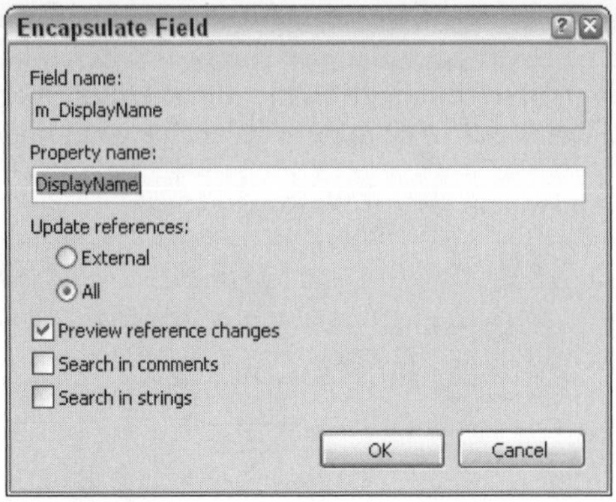

Figure 21-8

The Encapsulate Field refactoring action using Refactor! works in a similar way, except that it automatically assigns the name of the property based on the name of the class variable. The interface for updating references is also different, as shown in Figure 21-10. Instead of a modal dialog, Refactor! presents a visual aid that can be used to navigate through the references. Where a replacement is required, click the check mark. Unlike the C# dialog box, in which the checkboxes can be checked and unchecked as many times as needed, once you click the check mark, there is no way to undo this action.

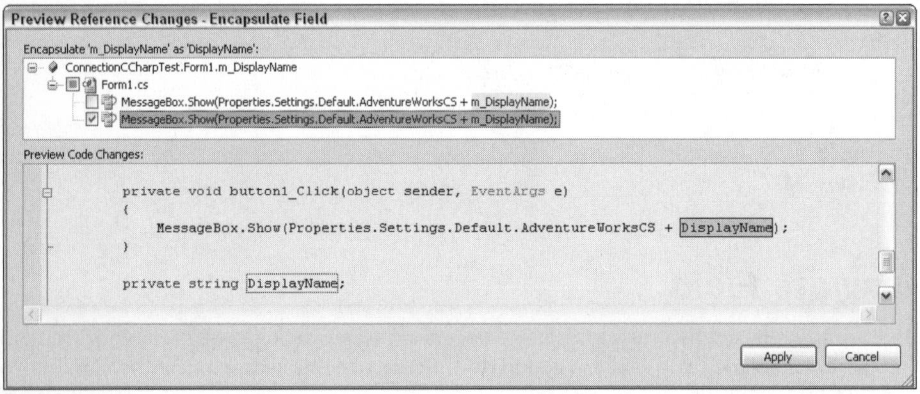

Figure 21-9

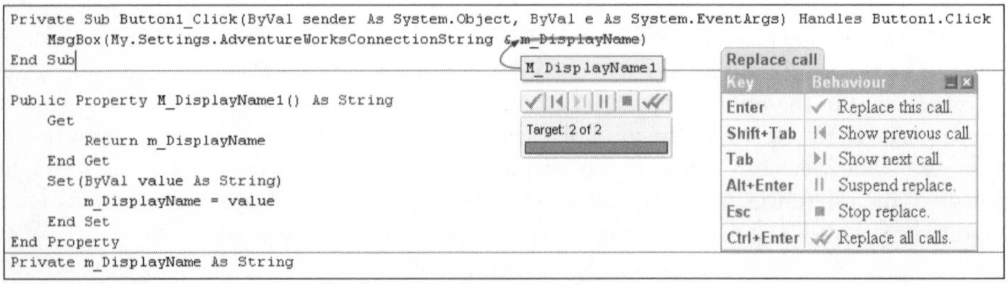

Figure 21-10

Extract Interface

As a project goes from prototype or early-stage development through to a full implementation or growth phase, it is often necessary to extract the core methods for a class into an interface to enable other implementations or to define a boundary between disjointed systems. In the past you could do this by copying the entire method to a new file and removing the method contents so you were just left with the interface stub. The Extract Interface refactoring action enables you to extract an interface based on any number of methods within a class. When this refactoring action is invoked on a class, the dialog in Figure 21-11 is displayed, which enables you to select which methods are included in the interface. Once selected, those methods are added to the new interface. The new interface is also added to the original class.

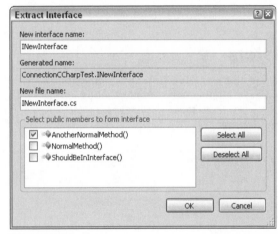

Figure 21-11

In the following example, the first method needs to be extracted into an interface:

```
public class ConcreteClass1
{
    public void ShouldBeInInterface()
    { /* ... */ }

    public void NormalMethod(int ParameterA, string ParameterB)
    { /* ... */ }

    public void AnotherNormalMethod()
    { /* ... */ }
}
```

Selecting Extract Interface from the right-click context menu will introduce a new interface and update the original class as follows:

```
interface IConcreteClass11
{
    void ShouldBeInInterface();
}
```

```
public class ConcreteClass1 : ConnectionCCharpTest.IConcreteClass11
{
    public void ShouldBeInInterface()
    { /* ... */ }

    public void NormalMethod(int ParameterA, string ParameterB)
    { /* ... */ }

    public void AnotherNormalMethod()
    { /* ... */ }
}
```

Extracting an interface is not available within Refactor!.

Reorder Parameters

Sometimes it is necessary to reorder parameters. This is often for cosmetic reasons, but it can also aid readability and is sometimes warranted when implementing interfaces. The Reorder Parameters dialog, shown in Figure 21-12, enables you to move parameters up and down in the list according to the order in which you wish them to appear.

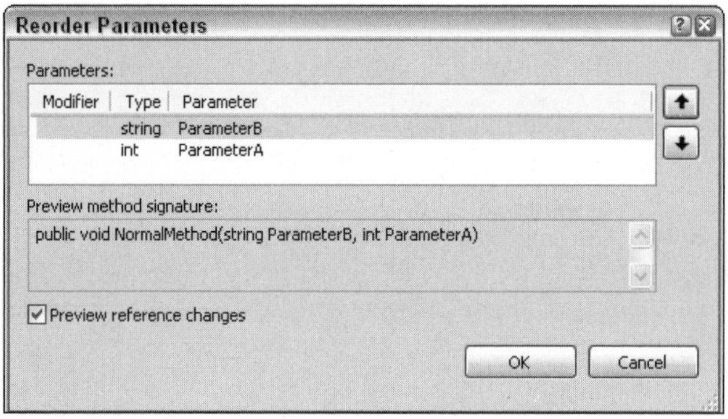

Figure 21-12

Once you establish the correct order, you're given the opportunity to preview the changes. By default, the parameters in every reference to this method will be reordered according to the new order. The preview dialog, similar to the one shown in Figure 21-9, enables you to control which references are updated.

The Refactor! interface for reordering parameters is one of the most intuitive on the market. Again, Design Express has opted for visual aids instead of a modal dialog, as shown in Figure 21-13. You can move the selected parameter left or right in the parameter list and navigate between parameters with the Tab key. Once the parameters are in the desired order, the search and replace interface illustrated in Figure 21-10 enables the developer to verify all updates.

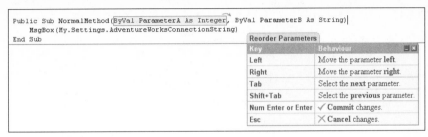

Figure 21-13

Remove Parameters

It is unusual to have to remove a parameter while refactoring, as it usually means that the functionality of the method has changed. However, having support for this action considerably reduces the amount of searching that has to be done for compile errors that can occur when a parameter is removed. The other time this action is particularly useful is when there are multiple overloads for a method. Removing a parameter may not generate compile errors; however, there may be runtime errors caused by semantic, rather than syntactical, mistakes.

Figure 21-14 illustrates the Remove Parameters dialog that is used to remove parameters from the parameters list. If a parameter is accidentally removed, it can be easily restored until the correct parameter list is arranged. As the warning on this dialog indicates, removing parameters can often result in unexpected functional errors, so it is important to review the changes made. Again, the preview window can be used to validate the proposed changes.

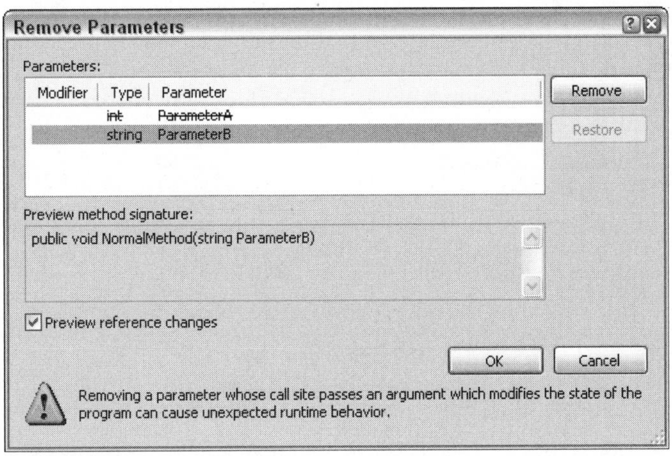

Figure 21-14

You cannot remove a parameter with Refactor!.

Rename

Visual Studio 2005 provides rename support in both C# and VB.NET. The rename dialog for C# is shown in Figure 21-15; it is similar in VB.NET.

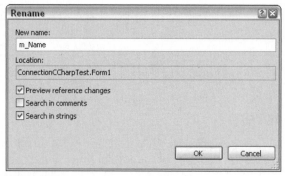

Figure 21-15

Unlike the C# rename support, which uses the preview window so you can confirm your changes, the rename capability in VB.NET simply renames all references to that variable.

Promote to Paramet4er

One of the most common refactoring techniques is to adapt an existing method to accept an additional parameter. By promoting a method variable to a parameter, the method can be made more general. It also promotes code reuse. Intuitively, this operation would introduce compile errors wherever the method was referenced. However, the catch is that the variable you are promoting to a parameter must have an initial constant value. This constant is added to all the method references to prevent any changes to functionality. Starting with the following snippet, if the method variable `output` is promoted, then you end up with the second snippet:

```
public void MethodA()
{
    MethodB();
}
public void MethodB()
{
    string output = "Test String";
    MessageBox.Show( output);
}
```

After the variable is promoted, you can see that the initial constant value has been applied where this method is referenced:

```
public void MethodA()
{
    MethodB("Test String");
}
public void MethodB(string output)
```

```
    {
        MessageBox.Show( output);
    }
```

Promoting a variable to a parameter is not available within Refactor!.

Generate Method Stub

As you write code, you may realize that you need a method that generates a value, triggers an event, or evaluates an expression. For example, the following snippet illustrates a new method that you need to generate at some later stage:

```
public void MethodA()
{
    string InputA;
    double InputB;
    int OutputC = NewMethodIJustThoughtOf(InputA, InputB);
}
```

Of course, the preceding code will generate a build error because this method has not been defined. Using the Generate Method Stub refactoring action, you can generate a method stub. As you can see from the following sample, the method stub is complete with input parameters and output type:

```
private int NewMethodIJustThoughtOf(string InputA, double InputB)
{
    throw new Exception("The method or operation is not implemented.");
}
```

Generating a method stub is not available within Refactor!.

Surround with Snippet

The last refactoring action, available in both C# and VB.NET, is the capability to surround an existing block of code with a code snippet. Figure 21-16 shows the list of surrounding snippets that are available to wrap the selected line of code.

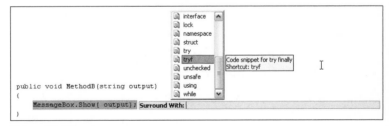

Figure 21-16

Selecting the `tryf` snippet results in the following code:

```
public void MethodB(string output)
{
    try
    {
        MessageBox.Show(output);
    }
    finally
    { /* ... */ }
}
```

Summary

This chapter provided examples of each of the refactoring actions available within Visual Studio 2005. Although VB.NET developers do not get complete refactoring support out of the box, Refactor! provides a wide range of refactoring actions that complement the editor they already have.

Generics, Nullable Types, and Partial Types

When the .NET Framework was initially released, many C++ developers cited the lack of code templates as a primary reason for not moving to one of the .NET languages. Visual Studio 2005 and the .NET Framework 2.0 introduce generics, which are more than simply design-time templates, as they offer first-class support within the CLR. This chapter explores the syntax, in both C# and VB.NET, for consuming and creating generics. The chapter also looks at nullable types, which help bridge the logical gap between database and object data; partial types, which help effectively partition code to promote code generation; and operator overloading.

Generics

For anyone unfamiliar with templates in C++ or the concept of a generic type, this section begins with a simple example that illustrates where a generic can replace a significant amount of coding, while also maintaining strongly typed code. This example stores and retrieves integers from a collection. As you can see from the following code snippet, there are two ways to do this: either using a non-typed `ArrayList`, which can contain any type, or using a custom-written collection:

```
'Option 1 - Non-typed Arraylist
'Creation - unable to see what types this list contain
Dim nonTypedList As New ArrayList
'Adding - no type checking, so can add any type
nonTypedList.Add(1)
nonTypedList.Add("Hello")
nonTypedList.Add(5.334)
'Retrieving - no type checking, must cast (should do type checking too)
Dim output As Integer = CInt(nonTypedList.Item(1))

'Option 2 - Strongly typed custom written collection
```

```
'Creation - custom collection
Dim myList As New IntegerCollection
'Adding - type checking, so can only add integers
myList.Add(1)
'Retrieving - type checking, so no casting required
output = myList.Item(0)
```

Clearly, the second approach is preferable because it ensures that you put only integers into the collection. However, the downside of this approach is that you have to create collection classes for each type you want to put in a collection. You can rewrite this example using the Generic List class:

```
'Creation - generic list, specifying the type of objects it contains
Dim genericList As New List(Of Integer)
'Adding - type checking
genericList.Add(1)
'Retrieving - type checking
output = genericList.Item(0)
```

This example has the benefits of the strongly typed collection without the overhead of having to rewrite the collection for each type. To create a collection that holds strings, all you have to do is change the type argument of the List — for example, List(Of String).

In summary, generic types have one or more type parameters that will be defined when an instance of the type is declared. From the example you just saw, the class List has a type parameter, T, which, when specified, determines the type of items in the collection. The following sections describe in more detail how to consume, create, and constrain generic types.

Consumption

You have just seen a VB.NET example of how to consume the Generic List to provide either a collection of integers or a collection of strings. You can accomplish this by supplying the type parameter as part of the declaration. The following code snippets illustrate the consumption of generic types for both VB.NET and C#:

C#
```
Dictionary<String,double> scores = new Dictionary<String,double>();
```

VB.NET
```
Dim scores As New Dictionary(Of String, Double)
```

There are also generic methods, which also have a type parameter that must be supplied when the method is invoked. This is illustrated in calling the Choose method, which randomly picks one of the two arguments passed in:

C#
```
newValue=Chooser.Choose<int>(5, 6);
newValue=Chooser.Choose(7, 8);
```

VB.NET
```
newValue = Chooser.Choose(of Integer)(5,6)
newValue = Chooser.Choose(7,8)
```

In these examples, you can see that a `type` argument has been supplied in the first line but omitted in the second line. You're able to do this because the type inference process kicks in to determine what the `type` argument should be.

Creation

To create a generic type, you need to define the `type` parameters that must be provided when the type is constructed, performed as part of the type signature. In the following example, the `ObjectMapper` class defines two type parameters, `TSource` and `TDestination`, that need to be supplied when an instance of this class is declared:

C#
```
public class ObjectMapper<TSource, TDestination>
{
    private TSource source;
    private TDestination destination;

    public ObjectMapper(TSource src , TDestination dest )
    {
        source = src;
        destination = dest;
    }
}
```

VB.NET
```
Public Class ObjectMapper(Of TSource, TDestination)
    Private source As TSource
    Private destination As TDestination

    Public Sub New(ByVal src As TSource, ByVal dest As TDestination)
        source = src
        destination = dest
    End Sub
End Class
```

A naming convention for `type` parameters is to begin them with the letter T, followed by some sort of descriptive name if there is more than one `type` parameter. In this case, the two parameters define the type of `source` and `destination` objects to be provided in the mapping.

Generic methods are defined using a similar syntax as part of the method signature. Although generic methods may often be placed within a generic type, that is not a requirement; in fact, they can exist anywhere a non-generic method can be written. The following `CreateObjectMapper` method takes two objects of different types and returns a new `ObjectMapper` object, passing the `type` arguments for the method through to the constructor:

C#
```
public static ObjectMapper<TCreateSrc, TCreateDest>
                            CreateObjectMapper<TCreateSrc, TCreateDest>
                                (TCreateSrc src, TCreateDest dest)
{
    return new ObjectMapper<TCreateSrc, TCreateDest>(src, dest);
}
```

VB.NET

```
Public Shared Function CreateObjectMapper(Of TCreateSrc, TCreateDest) _
                    (ByVal src As TCreateSrc, ByVal dest As TCreateDest) _
                            As ObjectMapper(Of TCreateSrc, TCreateDest)
    Return New ObjectMapper(Of TCreateSrc, TCreateDest)(src, dest)
End Function
```

Constraints

So far, you have seen how to create and consume generic types and methods. However, having `type` parameters limits what you can do with the parameter because you only have access to the basic object methods such as `GetType`, `Equals`, and `ToString`. Without more information about the `type` parameter, you are limited to building simple lists and collections. To make generics more useful, you can place constraints on the `type` parameters to ensure that they have a basic set of functionality. The following example places constraints on both parameters:

C#

```
public class ObjectMapper<TSource, TDestination>
                    : IComparable<ObjectMapper<TSource,TDestination>>
                    where TSource: IComparable<TSource>
                    where TDestination: new()
{
    private TSource source;
    private TDestination destination;

    public ObjectMapper(TSource src)
    {
        source = src;
        destination = new TDestination();
    }
    public int CompareTo(ObjectMapper<TSource,TDestination> mapper)
    {
        return source.CompareTo(mapper.source);
    }
}
```

VB.NET

```
Public Class ObjectMapper(Of TSource As IComparable(Of TSource), _
                    TDestination As New)
    Implements IComparable(Of ObjectMapper(Of TSource, TDestination))

    Private source As TSource
    Private destination As TDestination

    Public Sub New(ByVal src As TSource)
        source = src
        destination = new TDestination
    End Sub
    Public Function CompareTo _
            (ByVal other As ObjectMapper(Of TSource, TDestination)) As Integer _
                Implements System.IComparable(Of ObjectMapper _
                                    (Of TSource, TDestination)).CompareTo
        Return source.CompareTo(other.source)
    End Function
End Class
```

The `TSource` parameter is required to implement the `IComparable` interface so that an object of that type can be compared to another object of the same type. This is used in the `CompareTo`, which implements the `IComparable` interface for the `ObjectMapper` class, to compare the two source objects. The `TDestination` parameter requires a constructor that takes no arguments. The constructor is changed so that instead of a `destination` object being provided, it is created as part of the constructor.

This example covered interface and constructor constraints. The full list of constraints is as follows:

- ❑ **Base class:** Constrains the `type` parameter to be, or be derived from, the class specified

- ❑ **Class or Structure:** Constrains the `type` parameter to be a class or a structure (a struct in C#)

- ❑ **Interface:** Constrains the `type` parameter to implement the interface specified

- ❑ **Constructor:** Constrains the `type` parameter to expose a no-parameter constructor

Multiple constraints can be supplied by separating the constraints with a comma, as shown in these snippets:

C#

```
public class MultipleConstraintClass<T>
                              where IComparable, new()
{...}
```

VB.NET

```
Public Class MultipleConstraintClass(Of T As {IComparable,new})
...
End Class
```

Nullable Types

Any developer who has worked with a database understands some of the pain that goes into aligning business objects with database schemas. One of the difficulties has been that the default value for a database column could be nothing (as in not specified), even if the column was an integer. In .NET, value types, such as integers, always have a value. When pulling information from the database, it was necessary to add additional logic that would maintain state for the database columns to indicate whether a value had been set. Two of the most prominent solutions to this problem were to either adjust the database schema to prevent nothing values, which can be an issue where a field is optional, or to add a Boolean flag for every field that could be nothing, which added considerable amounts of code to even a simple application.

Generic types provide a mechanism to bridge this divide in quite an efficient manner, using the generic `Nullable` type. The `Nullable` type is a generic structure that has a single `type` parameter, which is the type it will be wrapping. It also contains a flag indicating whether a value exists, as shown in the following snippet:

```
Public Structure Nullable(Of T As Structure)
    Private m_hasValue As Boolean
    Private m_value As T

    Public Sub New(ByVal value As T)
        Me.m_value = value
```

```
            Me.m_hasValue = True
        End Sub

        Public ReadOnly Property HasValue() As Boolean
            Get
                Return Me.m_hasValue
            End Get
        End Property

        Public ReadOnly Property Value() As T
            Get
                If Not Me.HasValue Then
                    Throw new Exception("...")
                End If
                Return Me.m_value
            End Get
        End Property

        Public Function GetValueOrDefault() As T
            Return Me.m_value
        End Function

        Public Function GetValueOrDefault(ByVal defaultValue As T) As T
            If Not Me.HasValue Then
                Return defaultValue
            End If
            Return Me.m_value
        End Function

        Public Shared Narrowing Operator CType(ByVal value As Nullable(Of T)) As T
            Return value.get_Value
        End Operator

        Public Shared Widening Operator CType(ByVal value As T) As Nullable(Of T)
            Return New Nullable(Of T)(value)
        End Operator
    End Structure
```

This code indicates how you can create a new `Nullable` type by specifying a `type` argument and calling the constructor. However, the last two methods in this structure are operators that allow conversion between the `Nullable` type and the `type` argument provided. Conversion operators are covered later in this chapter, but for now it is sufficient to understand that conversion from the `type` argument to a `Nullable` type is allowed using implicit conversion, whereas the reverse requires explicit casting. You can also see that the `type` parameter, `T`, is constrained to be a structure. Because class variables are object references, they are implicitly nullable.

The following example creates and uses a `Nullable` type. You can see that C# has additional support for `Nullable` types with an abbreviated syntax:

C#
```
Nullable<int>x=5;
int? y,z;
if (x.HasValue)
    y=x.Value;
```

```
    else
        y=8;
    z=x?? + y??7;
    int? w = x + y;
```

VB.NET
```
Dim x, y, z As Nullable(Of Integer)
x = 5
If x.HasValue Then
    y = x.Value
Else
    y = 8
End If
z = x.GetValueOrDefault + y.GetValueOrDefault(7)
```

In these examples, both languages can use the `HasValue` property to determine whether a value has been assigned to the `Nullable` type. If it has, the `Value` property can be used to retrieve the underlying value. The `Value` property throws an exception if no value has been specified. Having to test before you access the value property is rather tedious, so the `GetValueOrDefault` function was added. This retrieves the value if one has been supplied; otherwise, it returns the default value. There are two overloads to this method, with and without an alternative value. If an alternative value is supplied, this is the default value that is returned if no value has been supplied. Alternatively, the default value is defined as the zero-initialized underlying type. For example, if the underlying type were a `Point`, made up of two double values, the default value would be a `Point` with both values set to zero.

C# uses two abbreviations to make working with `Nullable` types easier. First, `Nullable<int>` can be abbreviated as `int?`, which defines a `Nullable` integer variable. The second abbreviation is the null coalescing operator, `??`. This is used to abbreviate the `GetValueOrDefault` function. The last line of the C# snippet shows an interesting feature, which is that C# supports null propagation. If either `x` or `y` are null, the null value propagates to `w`. This is the equivalent of the following:

```
    int? w = x.HasValue && y.HasValue ? x.Value + y.Value : (int?)null;
```

Partial Types

`Partial` types are a simple concept that enable a single type to be split across multiple files. The files are combined at compile time into a single type. As such, `Partial` types cannot be used to add or modify functionality in existing types. The most common reason to use `Partial` types is to separate generated code. In the past, elaborate class hierarchies had to be created to add additional functionality to a generated class due to fear of that code being overwritten when the class was regenerated. Using `Partial` types, the generated code can be partitioned into a separate file, and additional code added to a file where it will not be overwritten by the generator.

`Partial` classes are defined by using the `Partial` keyword in the type definition. The following example defines a `Person` class across two files:

```
'File 1 - fields and constructor
Partial Public Class Person
    Private m_Name As String
    Private m_Age As Integer
```

```
        Public Sub New(ByVal name As String, ByVal age As Integer)
            Me.m_Name = name
            Me.m_Age = age
        End Sub
    End Class
    'File 2 - public properties
    Public Class Person
        Public ReadOnly Property Age() As Integer
            Get
                Return Me.m_Age
            End Get
        End Property
        Public ReadOnly Property Name() As String
            Get
                Return Me.m_Name
            End Get
        End Property
    End Class
```

You will notice that the `Partial` keyword is used only in one of the files. This is specific to VB.NET, as C# requires all partial classes to use this keyword. The disadvantage there is that the `Partial` keyword needs to be added to the generated file. The other difference in C# is that the `Partial` keyword appears after the class accessibility keyword (in this case, `Public`).

Form Designers

Both the Windows and Web Forms designer make use of `Partial` types to separate the designer code from event handlers and other code written by the developer. The Windows Forms designer generates code into an associated designer file. For example, for `Form1.vb` there would also be `Form1.designer.vb`. In addition to protecting your code so that it isn't overwritten by the generated code, having the designer code in a separate file also trims down the code files for each form. Typically, the code file would only contain event handlers and other custom code.

In the previous version of Visual Studio, web forms were split across two files where controls had to be defined in both the designer file and the code-behind files so event handlers could be wired up. The designer file inherited from the code-behind file, which introduced another level of complexity. With `Partial` types, this has been simplified, with controls being defined in the designer file and only event handlers being defined in the code file. The code file is now a code-beside file, as both the code and designer information belong to the same class.

Operator Overloading

Both VB.NET and C# now support operator overloading, which means that you can define the behavior for standard operators such as +, -, / and *. You can also define type conversion operators that control how casting is handled between different types.

Operators

The syntax for operator overloading is very similar to a static method except that it includes the `Operator` keyword, as shown in the following example:

C#

```csharp
public class OperatorBaseClass{
    private int m_value;

    public static OperatorBaseClass operator +(OperatorBaseClass op1 ,
                                                OperatorBaseClass op2 )
    {
        OperatorBaseClass obc =new OperatorBaseClass();
        obc.m_value = op1.m_value + op2.m_value;
        return obc;
    }
}
```

VB.NET

```vbnet
Public Class OperatorBaseClass
    Private m_value As Integer

    Public Shared Operator +(ByVal op1 As OperatorBaseClass, _
                             ByVal op2 As OperatorBaseClass) As OperatorBaseClass
        Dim obc As New OperatorBaseClass
        obc.m_value = op1.m_value + op2.m_value
        Return obc
    End Operator
End Class
```

In both languages, a binary operator overload requires two parameters and a return value. The first value, op1, appears to the left of the operator, with the second on the right side. Clearly, the return value is substituted into the equation in place of all three input symbols. Although it makes more sense to make both input parameters and the return value the same type, this is not necessarily the case, and this syntax can be used to define the effect of the operator on any pair of types. The one condition is that one of the input parameters must be of the same type that contains the overloaded operator.

Type Conversions

A type conversion is the process of converting a value of one type to another type. These can be broadly categorized into *widening* and *narrowing* conversions. In a widening conversion, the original type has all the necessary information to produce the new type. As such, this conversion can be done implicitly and should never fail. An example would be casting a derived type to its base type. Conversely, in a narrowing conversion, the original type may not have all the necessary information to produce the new type. An example would be casting a base type to a derived type. This conversion cannot be guaranteed, and needs to be done via an explicit cast.

The following example illustrates conversions between two classes, Person and Employee. Converting from a Person to an Employee is a well-known conversion, as an employee's initial wage can be defined as a multiple of their age (for example, when they are employed). However, converting an Employee to a Person is not necessarily correct, as an employee's current wage may no longer be a reflection on their age:

C#

```csharp
public class Employee
{
    ...
```

```
        static public implicit operator Employee(Person p)
        {
            Employee emp=new Employee();
            emp.m_Name=p.Name;
            emp.m_Wage = p.Age * 1000;
            return emp;
        }
        static public explicit operator Person(Employee emp)
        {
            Person p = new Person();
            p.Name = emp.m_Name;
            p.Age=(int)emp.m_Wage/1000;
            return p;
        }
}
```

VB.NET

```
Public Class Employee
    ...
    Public Shared Widening Operator CType(ByVal p As Person) As Employee
        Dim emp As New Employee
        emp.m_Name = p.Name
        emp.m_Wage = p.Age * 1000
        Return emp
    End Operator
    Public Shared Narrowing Operator CType(ByVal emp As Employee) As Person
        Dim p As New Person
        p.Name = emp.m_Name
        p.Age = CInt(emp.m_Wage / 1000)
        Return p
    End Operator
End Class
```

Why Static Methods Are Bad

Now that you know how to overload operators and create your own type conversions, this section
serves as a disclaimer stating that static methods should be avoided at all costs. Because both type con-
versions and operator overloads are static methods, they are only relevant for the type for which they
are defined. This can cause all manner of grief and unexpected results when you have complex inheri-
tance trees. To illustrate how you can get unexpected results, consider the following example:

C#

```
Public Class FirstTier
    Public Value As Integer
    Public Shared Widening Operator CType(ByVal obj As FirstTier) As String
        Return "First Tier: " & obj.Value.ToString
    End Operator
    Public Overrides Function ToString() As String
        Return "First Tier: " & Me.Value.ToString
    End Function
End Class

Public Class SecondTier
```

```
        Inherits FirstTier
        Public Overloads Shared Widening Operator CType(ByVal obj As SecondTier) _
                                                                      As String
            Return "Second Tier: " & obj.Value.ToString
        End Operator

        Public Overrides Function ToString() As String
            Return "Second Tier: " & Me.Value.ToString
        End Function
End Class
```

VB.NET

```
'Sample code to call conversion and tostring functions
Public Class Form1
    Private Sub BtnLanguageClick(ByVal sender As System.Object, _
                        ByVal e As System.EventArgs) Handles BtnLanguage.Click

        Dim foo As New SecondTier
        foo.Value = 5
        Dim bar As FirstTier = foo

        Console.WriteLine("<SecondTier> ToString " & vbTab & foo.ToString)
        Console.WriteLine("<SecondTier> CStr " & vbTab & CStr(foo))

        Console.WriteLine("<FirstTier> ToString " & vbTab & bar.ToString)
        Console.WriteLine("<FirstTier> CStr " & vbTab & CStr(bar))
    End Sub
End Class
```

The output from this sample is as follows:

```
<SecondTier> ToString    Second Tier: 5
<SecondTier> CStr        Second Tier: 5
<FirstTier> ToString     Second Tier: 5
<FirstTier> CStr         First Tier: 5
```

As you can see from the sample, the last cast gives an unusual response. In the first two casts, you are dealing with a `SecondTier` variable, so both `ToString` and `CStr` operations are called from the `SecondTier` class. When you cast the object to a `FirstTier` variable, the `ToString` operation is still routed to the `SecondTier` class, as this overrides the functionality in the `FirstTier`. However, because the `CStr` operation is a static function, it is routed to the `FirstTier` class, as this is the type of variable. Clearly, the safest option here is to ensure that you implement and call the `ToString` method on the instance variable. This rule holds for other operators such as equals, which can be overridden instead of defining the = operator. In cases where you need a +, -, / or * operator, consider using non-static Add, Subtract, Divide, and Multiply operators that can be run on an instance.

Predefined Delegates

The event-driven model that forms an integral part of the .NET Framework is built around the concept of a *delegate*, or *function pointer*. In fact, an event, as you will see later, is no more than a multicast delegate, or a delegate that when invoked triggers multiple functions (such as listeners or event handlers).

With this in mind, one of the most well-known delegates is the `EventHandler` delegate, which is defined within the .NET Framework and can be used in place of defining your own event type.

With the introduction of generics, and in particular generic methods, it is no surprise that you can also have generic delegates. This makes possible the addition of a number of predefined delegates to the .NET Framework to support common tasks such as find, comparison, and conversion operations. This section offers a brief summary of some of the predefined delegates at your disposal.

Action

The `Action` delegate is useful for performing a specific action on a list of items using the `Array.ForEach` or `List.ForEach` methods. The syntax is as follows:

```
Public Delegate Sub Action(Of T) (obj As T)
```

For example, the following sample gives each employee a $2,000 pay raise. Because you know that `employees` is a `List(Of Employees)`, when you call the `ForEach` method it is expecting a delegate, `Action(Of Employee)`, which both `PrintEmployee` and `IncreaseSalary` match:

```
Private Sub BtnLanguageClick(ByVal sender As System.Object, _
                             ByVal e As System.EventArgs) Handles BtnLanguage.Click
    Dim employees As List(Of Employee) = GetEmployees()

    employees.ForEach(AddressOf PrintEmployee)
    employees.ForEach(AddressOf IncreaseSalary)
    employees.ForEach(AddressOf PrintEmployee)
End Sub

Private Sub PrintEmployee(ByVal emp As Employee)
    Console.WriteLine("Employee: {0} - ${1}", emp.Name, emp.Wage)
End Sub
Private Sub IncreaseSalary(ByVal emp As Employee)
    emp.Wage += 2000
End Sub
```

Comparison

The `Comparison` delegate accepts two parameters of the same type and returns a value indicating how those items are relative to each other (Less than 0⇨x before y, 0⇨x is the same as y; More than 0⇨x after y). The syntax for the `Comparison` delegate is as follows:

```
Public Delegate Function Comparison(Of T) (x As T, y As T) As Integer
```

This delegate is most commonly used by the `Array.Sort` and `List.Sort` methods, as shown in the following example in which employees are sorted by wage and then name:

```
Private Sub BtnLanguageClick(ByVal sender As System.Object, _
                             ByVal e As System.EventArgs) Handles BtnLanguage.Click
    Dim employees As List(Of Employee) = GetEmployees()

    employees.ForEach(AddressOf PrintEmployee)
```

```
            employees.Sort(AddressOf CompareEmployees)
            employees.ForEach(AddressOf PrintEmployee)
    End Sub

    Private Function CompareEmployees(ByVal emp1 As Employee, _
                                ByVal emp2 As Employee) As Integer
        If emp1.Wage = emp2.Wage Then Return String.Compare(emp1.Name, emp2.Name, True)
        If emp1.Wage > emp2.Wage Then Return -1 Else Return 1
    End Function
```

Converter

The `Converter` delegate is used to convert one type to another. Its syntax is as follows:

```
    Public Delegate Function Converter(Of TInput, TOutput) (input As TInput) As TOutput
```

The `Converter` delegate is usually applied to an entire collection using `Array.ConvertAll` or `List.ConvertAll`, as shown in the following example in which a list of formatted strings is generated from the employees list:

```
    Private Sub BtnLanguageClick(ByVal sender As System.Object, _
                            ByVal e As System.EventArgs) Handles BtnLanguage.Click
        Dim employees As List(Of Employee) = GetEmployees()

        employees.ForEach(AddressOf PrintEmployee)
        Dim mainFrameInput As List(Of String) = _
                        employees.ConvertAll(Of String)(AddressOf ConvertToString)
        mainFrameInput.ForEach(AddressOf PrintMainFrameInput)
    End Sub

    Private Function ConvertToString(ByVal emp As Employee) As String
        Return String.Format("KEY-{0} AMT-{1}", emp.Name, emp.Wage)
    End Function
    Private Sub PrintMainFrameInput(ByVal str As String)
        Console.WriteLine(str)
    End Sub
```

Predicate

The `Predicate` delegate is used to query an item to determine whether it meets a search criterion:

```
    Public Delegate Function Predicate(Of T) (obj As T) As Boolean
```

`Predicate` is used by the `List` and `Array` types in a number of methods, particularly those such as `Find` and `FindAll`, which query the collection and return items that meet the criterion. The following example looks for all employees who are below the threshold value, as they all deserve a pay raise:

```
    Private Sub BtnLanguageClick(ByVal sender As System.Object, _
                            ByVal e As System.EventArgs) Handles BtnLanguage.Click
        Dim employees As List(Of Employee) = GetEmployees()

        employees.ForEach(AddressOf PrintEmployee)
```

```
        Dim lowWageEmployees As List(Of Employee) = _
                            employees.FindAll(AddressOf BelowWageThreshold)
    lowWageEmployees.ForEach(AddressOf IncreaseSalary)
    employees.ForEach(AddressOf PrintEmployee)
End Sub

Private Function BelowWageThreshold(ByVal emp As Employee) As Boolean
    Return emp.Wage < 50000
End Function
```

EventHandler

The last delegate to discuss in this section is the `EventHandler` delegate; its syntax is as follows:

```
Public Delegate Sub EventHandler(Of TEventArgs As EventArgs) _
                            (sender As Object, e As TEventArgs)
```

Most developers are familiar with the non-generic version of this delegate, which expects an `EventArgs` object as the second parameter. In the generic form, the second parameter can be any class so long as it derives from the `EventArgs` class, meaning that event handlers can be strongly typed without having to declare a new delegate for each event:

```
Private Sub BtnLanguageClick(ByVal sender As System.Object, _
                        ByVal e As System.EventArgs) Handles BtnLanguage.Click
    Dim employees As List(Of Employee) = GetEmployees()

    employees.ForEach(AddressOf PrintEmployee)
    employees.ForEach(AddressOf SubscribeToEmployeeEvents)
    Dim lowWageEmployees As List(Of Employee) = _
                            employees.FindAll(AddressOf BelowWageThreshold)
    lowWageEmployees.ForEach(AddressOf IncreaseSalary)
End Sub

Private Sub SubscribeToEmployeeEvents(ByVal emp As Employee)
    AddHandler emp.EmployeeChanged, AddressOf EmployeeChangedEventHandler
End Sub
Private Sub EmployeeChangedEventHandler(ByVal sender As Object, _
                            ByVal e As Employee.EmployeeEventArgs)
    Console.WriteLine("Employee '{0}' wage changed from ${1} to ${2}", _
                        e.Employee.Name, e.OldWage, e.Employee.Wage)
End Sub

Partial Class Employee
    Public Class EmployeeEventArgs
        Inherits EventArgs

        Private m_OldWage As Integer
        Private m_Employee As Employee

        Public Sub New(ByVal emp As Employee, ByVal oldWage As Integer)
            Me.m_Employee = emp
            Me.m_OldWage = oldWage
        End Sub
        Public ReadOnly Property Employee() As Employee
```

```
            Get
                Return Me.m_Employee
            End Get
        End Property
        Public ReadOnly Property OldWage() As Integer
            Get
                Return Me.m_OldWage
            End Get
        End Property
    End Class

    Public Event EmployeeChanged As EventHandler(Of EmployeeEventArgs)

    Public Property Wage() As Integer
        Get
            Return Me.m_Wage
        End Get
        Set(ByVal value As Integer)
            If Not Me.m_Wage = value Then
                Dim oldWage As Integer = Me.m_Wage
                Me.m_Wage = value
                RaiseEvent EmployeeChanged(Me, New EmployeeEventArgs(Me, oldWage))
            End If
        End Set
    End Property
End Class
```

This example has modified the `Employee` class to raise an `EmployeeChangedEvent` when the employee's wage is changed. Although the `Employee` object is passed as the sender of the event, it is also passed into the `EmployeeChangedEventArgs` so there is strongly typed support when handling the event. The main routine subscribes to the change event for each of the `Employee` objects before searching for those that need a pay raise. When those employees are given a pay raise, the `EmployeeChangedEvent` is raised and the event handler is used to print the list of employees who received a pay raise.

Property Accessibility

Good coding practices state that fields should be private and wrapped with a property. This property should be used to access the backing field, rather than to refer to the field itself. However, one of the difficulties has been exposing a public read property so that other classes can read the value, but also making the write part of the property either private or at least protected, preventing other classes from making changes to the value of the field. The only workaround for this was to declare two properties, a public read-only property and a private, or protected, read-write, or just write-only, property. Visual Studio 2005 now lets you define properties with different levels of accessibility for the read and write components. For example, the `Name` property has a public read method and a protected write method:

C#
```
public string Name
{
    get { return m_Name; }
    protected set { m_Name = value; }
}
```

VB.NET

```
Public Property Name() As String
    Get
        Return Me.m_Name
    End Get
    Protected Set(ByVal value As String)
        Me.m_Name = value
    End Set
End Property
```

The limitation on this is that the individual read or write components cannot have an accessibility that is more open than the property itself. For example, if you define the property to be protected, you cannot make the read component public. Instead, you need to make the property public and the write component protected.

Custom Events

Both C# and VB.NET can declare custom events that determine what happens when someone subscribes or unsubscribes from an event, and how the subscribers list is stored. Note that the VB.NET example is more verbose, but it enables you to control how the event is actually raised. In this case, each handler is called asynchronously for concurrent access. The `RaiseEvent` waits for all events to be fully raised before resuming:

C#

```csharp
List<EventHandler> EventHandlerList = new List<EventHandler>();

public event EventHandler Click{
    add{EventHandlerList.Add(value);}
    remove{EventHandlerList.Remove(value);}
}
```

VB.NET

```vbnet
Private EventHandlerList As New ArrayList

Public Custom Event Click As EventHandler
    AddHandler(ByVal value As EventHandler)
        EventHandlerList.Add(value)
    End AddHandler
    RemoveHandler(ByVal value As EventHandler)
        EventHandlerList.Remove(value)
    End RemoveHandler
    RaiseEvent(ByVal sender As Object, ByVal e As EventArgs)
        Dim results As New List(Of IAsyncResult)
        For Each handler As EventHandler In EventHandlerList
            If handler IsNot Nothing Then
                results.Add(handler.BeginInvoke(sender, e, Nothing, Nothing))
            End If
        Next
        While results.Find(AddressOf IsFinished) IsNot Nothing
            Threading.Thread.Sleep(250)
        End While
```

```
        End RaiseEvent
    End Event
    Private Function IsFinished(ByVal async As IAsyncResult) As Boolean
        Return async.IsCompleted
    End Function
```

Summary

This chapter explained how generic types, methods, and delegates can significantly improve the efficiency with which you can write and maintain code. You were also introduced to features — such as property accessibility and custom events — that give you full control over your code and the way it executes.

The following chapter examines C# and VB.NET specifics and the support they have within Visual Studio 2005.

23

Language-Specific Features

One of the hotly debated topics among developers is which .NET language is the best for performance, efficient programming, readability, and so on. While each of the .NET languages has a different objective and target market, developers are continually seeing long-term feature parity. In fact, there are very few circumstances where it is impossible to do something in one language that can be done in another. This chapter examines some features that are specific to either C# or VB.NET. It is likely that in the next release of Visual Studio you will see these features adopted by other .NET languages.

C#

The C# language has always been at the forefront of language innovation, with a focus on writing efficient code. Version 2.0 of the language includes anonymous methods, iterators, and static classes that help tidy up your code make it more efficient.

Anonymous Methods

Anonymous methods are essentially methods that do not have a name, and at surface level they appear and behave the same way as a normal method. A common use for an anonymous method is writing event handlers. Instead of declaring a method and adding a new delegate instance to the event, this can be condensed into a single statement, with the anonymous method appearing inline. This is illustrated in the following example:

```
private void Form1_Load(object sender, EventArgs e)
{
    this.button1.Click += new EventHandler(OldStyleEventHandler);

    this.button1.Click += delegate{
                            Console.WriteLine("Button pressed - new
school!");
```

```
                                        };
    }
    private void OldStyleEventHandler(object sender, EventArgs e){
        Console.WriteLine("Button pressed - old school!");
    }
```

The true power of anonymous methods is that they can reference variables declared in the method in which the anonymous method appears. The following example searches a list of employees, as you did in the previous chapter, for all employees that have a salary less than $40,000. The difference here is that instead of defining this threshold in the predicate method, the amount is held in a method variable. This dramatically reduces the amount of code you have to write to pass variables to a predicate method. The alternative is to define a class variable and use that to pass in the value to the predicate method.

```
    private void ButtonClick(object sender, EventArgs e)
    {

        List<Employee> employees = GetEmployees();
        int wage = 0;
        bool reverse = false;
        Predicate<Employee> employeeSearch = delegate(Employee emp)
        {
            if (reverse==false)
                return (emp.Wage < wage);
            else
                return !(emp.Wage < wage);
        };

        wage = 40000;
        List<Employee> lowWageEmployees = employees.FindAll(employeeSearch);
        wage=60000;
        List<Employee> mediumWageEmployees = employees.FindAll(employeeSearch);
        reverse = true;
        List<Employee> highWageEmployees = employees.FindAll(employeeSearch);
    }
```

In this example, you can see that an anonymous method has been declared within the ButtonClick method. The anonymous method references two variables from the containing method: wage and reverse. Although the anonymous method is declared early in the method, when it is evaluated it uses the current values of these variables.

Iterators

Prior to generics, you not only had to write your own custom collections, you also had to write enumerators that could be used to iterate through the collection. In addition, if you wanted to define an enumerator that iterated through the collection in a different order, you had to generate an entire class that maintained state information. Writing an iterator in C# dramatically reduces the amount of code you have to write in order to iterate through a collection, as illustrated in the following example:

```
    public class ListIterator<T> : IEnumerable<T>
    {
        List<T> myList;
        public ListIterator(List<T> listToIterate){
```

```
            myList=listToIterate;
    }

    public IEnumerator<T> GetEnumerator() {
        foreach (T x in myList) yield return x;
    }

    System.Collections.IEnumerator System.Collections.IEnumerable.GetEnumerator()
    {
        return GetEnumerator();
    }

    public IEnumerable<T> Top5OddItems {
        get {
            int cnt = 0;
            for (int i = 0; i < myList.Count - 1; i++){
                if (i % 2 == 0){
                    cnt += 1;
                    yield return myList[i];
                }
                if (cnt == 5) yield break;
            }
        }
    }
}
```

In this example, the keyword `yield` is used to return a particular value in the collection. At the end of the collection, you can either allow the method to return, as the first iterator does, or you can use `yield break` to indicate the end of the collection. Both the `GetEnumerator` and `Top5OddItems` iterators can be used to cycle through the items in the `List`, as shown in the following snippet:

```
public static void PrintNumbers()
{
    List<int> randomNumbers = GetNumbers();

    Console.WriteLine("Normal Enumeration");
    foreach (int x in (new ListIterator<int>(randomNumbers)))
    {
        Console.WriteLine("{0}", x.ToString());
    }

    Console.WriteLine("Top 5 Odd Values");
    foreach (int x in (new ListIterator<int>(randomNumbers)).Top5OddItems)
    {
        Console.WriteLine("{0}", x.ToString());
    }
}
```

Static Classes

At some stage most of you have written a class that only contains static methods. In the past there was always the danger that someone would create an instance of this class. The only way to prevent this was to create a private constructor and make the class non-inheritable. In the future, however, an instance method might accidentally be added to this class, which of course could not be called, as an instance of the class could not be created. C# now permits a class to be marked as static, which not only prevents an instance of the class being created, it also prevents any class from inheriting from it and provides design-time checking to ensure that all methods contained in the class are static methods:

```
public static class HelperMethods
{
    static Random rand = new Random();
    public static int RandomNumber(int min,int max)
    {
        return rand.Next(min, max);
    }
}
```

In this code snippet, the static keyword in the first line indicates that this is a static class. As such, it cannot contain instance variables or methods.

Naming Conflicts

An issue that crops up occasionally is how to deal with naming conflicts. Of course, good design practices are one of the best ways to minimize the chance of a conflict. However, this alone is not enough, as quite often you don't have control over how types in third-party libraries are named. This section covers three techniques to eliminate naming conflicts. To illustrate them, we'll start from the scenario in which you have a naming conflict for the class BadlyNamedClass in two namespaces:

```
namespace NamingConflict1
{
    public class BadlyNamedClass
    {
        public static string HelloWorld()
        {
            return "Hi everyone! - class2";
        }
    }
}

namespace NamingConflict2
{
    public class BadlyNamedClass
    {

        public static string HelloWorld()
        {
            return "Hi everyone! - class1";
        }


    }
}
```

Clearly, if you import both NamingConflict1 and NamingConflict2, you will end up with a naming conflict when you try to reference the class BadlyNamedClass.

Namespace Alias Qualifier

When namespaces are imported into a source file with the `using` statement, the namespaces can be assigned an alias. In addition to minimizing the code you have to write when accessing a type contained within the referenced namespace, providing an alias means that types with the same name in different imported namespaces can be distinguished using the alias. The following example uses a namespace alias to resolve the conflict illustrated in the opener to this section:

```
using NCF1 = NamingConflict2;
using NCF2 = NamingConflict1;
public class Naming
{
    public static string SayHelloWorldVersion1()
    {
        return NCF1.BadlyNamedClass.HelloWorld();
    }
    public static string SayHelloWorldVersion2()
    {
        return NCF2.BadlyNamedClass.HelloWorld();
    }
}
```

This resolves the current conflict, but what happens when you introduce a class called either `NCF1` or `NCF2`? You end up with a naming conflict between the introduced class and the alias. The namespace alias qualifier `::` was added so this conflict could be resolved without changing the alias. To fix the code snippet, you would insert the qualifier whenever you reference `NCF1` or `NCF2`:

```
using NCF1 = NamingConflict2;
using NCF2 = NamingConflict1;
public class Naming
{
    public static string SayHelloWorldVersion1()
    {
        return NCF1::BadlyNamedClass.HelloWorld();
    }
}
public class NCF1 {/*...*/}
public class NCF2 {/*...*/}
```

The namespace alias qualifier can only be preceded by a `using` alias (as shown here), the `global` keyword, or an `extern` alias (both to be covered in the next sections).

Global

The `global` identifier is a reference to the `global` namespace that encompasses all types and namespaces. When used with the namespace alias qualifier, `global` ensures a full hierarchy match between the referenced type and any imported types. For example, you can modify the sample to use the global identifier:

```
public class Naming
{
    public static string SayHelloWorldVersion1()
    {
```

```
            return global::NamingConflict1.BadlyNamedClass.HelloWorld();
    }
}
public class NCF1 {/*...*/}
public class NCF2 {/*...*/}
```

Extern Aliases

Despite both the namespace alias qualifier and the `global` identifier, it is still possible to introduce conflicts. For example, adding a class called `NamingConflict1` would clash with the namespace you were trying to import. An alternative is to use an *extern alias*. When a reference is added to a project, by default it is assigned to the global namespace and is subsequently available throughout the project. However, this can be modified by assigning the reference to an alternative alias. In Figure 23-1, the conflicting assembly has been assigned an external alias of X.

Figure 23-1

Types and namespaces that exist in references that are added to the `global` namespace can be used without explicitly importing them into a source file using their fully qualified name. When an alternative alias is specified, as shown in Figure 23-1, this reference must be imported into every source file that needs to use types or namespaces defined within it. This is done with the `extern alias` statement, as shown in the following example:

```
extern alias X;

public class Naming
{
    public static string SayHelloWorldVersion1()
    {
        return X::NamingConflict1.BadlyNamedClass.HelloWorld();
    }
}
public class NCF1 {/*...*/}
public class NamingConflict1 {/*...*/}
```

This example added a reference to the assembly that contains the `NamingConflict1` namespace, and set the `Aliases` property to `X`, as shown in Figure 23-1. To reference classes within this assembly, use the namespace alias qualifier, preceded by the `extern alias` defined at the top of the source file.

Pragma

Occasionally you would like to ignore compile warnings. This can be done for superficial reasons — perhaps you don't want a warning to appear in the build log. Occasionally, you have a legitimate need to suppress a compile warning; it might be necessary to use a method that has been marked obsolete during a transition phase of a project. Some teams have the compile process set to treat all warnings as errors; in this case, you can use the `Pragma` statement to disable and then restore warnings:

```
[Obsolete]
public static string AnOldMethod()
{ return "Old code...."; }

#pragma warning disable 168
public static string CodeToBeUpgraded()
{
    int x;
    #pragma warning disable 612
    return AnOldMethod();
    #pragma warning restore 612
}
#pragma warning restore 168
```

Two warnings are disabled in this code. The first, warning 168, is raised because you have not used the variable x. The second, warning 612, is raised because you are referencing a method marked with the `Obsolete` attribute. These warning numbers are very cryptic and your code would benefit from some comments describing each warning and why it is disabled. You might be wondering how you know which warnings you need to disable. The easiest way to determine the warning number is to examine the build output, as shown in Figure 23-2. Here, the warnings CS0612 and CS0168 are highlighted (in yellow), with a description accompanying the warning.

Figure 23-2

VB.NET

Very few new language features are only available in VB.NET, the most significant being the `My` namespace, which is covered in detail in the next chapter. The other additions are a number of keywords that make the language more powerful and easier to work with.

Continue

The Continue statement is used to move the point of execution to the end of the loop it is contained in, bypassing all remaining code in the block, without prematurely terminating the loop. This is illustrated in the following snippet that prints out the contents of the people list except for any Person with the name Bob:

```
Public Sub Example()
    Dim people As New List(Of Person)
    For Each p As Person In people
        If p.Name = "Bob" Then Continue For
        Console.WriteLine(String.Format("{0} has {1} relatives", _
                                            p.Name, p.Relatives.Count))
    Next
End Sub
```

The Continue statement can be used to break out of multiple loops. However, as there is no way to label a loop, the loops must be of different types. The following example replaces a second For loop with a Do While loop instead:

```
Public Sub Example()
    Dim people As New List(Of Person)
    Dim relativeCounter
    For Each p As Person In people
        If p.Name = "Bob" Then Continue For
        Console.WriteLine(String.Format("{0} has {1} relatives", _
                                            p.Name, p.Relatives.Count))
        relativeCounter = 0
        While relativeCounter < p.Relatives.Count
            If p.Relatives(relativeCounter).Name = "Bob" Then Continue While
            Console.WriteLine(String.Format("{0} is a relative of {1}", _
                                    p.Relatives(relativeCounter).Name, p.Name))
            relativeCounter += 1
            If relativeCounter = 10 Then Continue For
        End While
    Next
End Sub
```

IsNot

The IsNot operator is the counterpart to the Is operator that is used for reference equality comparisons. Whereas the Is operator will evaluate to True if the references are equal, the IsNot operator will evaluate to True if the references are not equal. Although a minor improvement, this keyword can save a considerable amount of typing, eliminating the need to go back to the beginning of a conditional statement and insert the Not operator:

```
Dim aPerson As New Person
Dim bPerson As New Person
If Not aPerson Is bPerson Then
    Console.WriteLine("This is the old way of doing this kind of check")
End If
If aPerson IsNot bPerson Then
```

```
        Console.WriteLine("This is the old way of doing this kind of check")
    End If
```

Not only does the `IsNot` operator make it more efficient to write the code; it also makes it easier to read. Instead of the "Yoda-speak" expression `If Not aPerson Is bPerson Then`, you have the much more readable expression `If aPerson IsNot bPerson Then`.

Global

The VB.NET `Global` keyword is very similar to the C# identifier with the same name. Both are used to escape to the outermost namespace, and both are used to remove any ambiguity when resolving namespace and type names. In the following snippet, both `Namespace1` and `Namespace2` declare a class called `AmbiguousClass`. The `Global` keyword is used to distinguish between them:

```
Imports Namespace1
Imports Namespace2

Public Class Test
    Public Sub Example()
        Dim x As New Global.Namespace1.AmbiguousClass
        Dim y As New Global.Namespace2.AmbiguousClass
    End Sub
End Class
```

TryCast

In an ideal world you would always work with interfaces and there would never be a need to cast between object types. However, the reality is that you build complex applications and often have to break some of the rules of object-orientated programming to get the job done. To this end, one of the most commonly used code snippets is the *test-and-cast technique,* whereby you test an object to determine whether it is of a certain type before casting it to that type so you can work with it. The problem with this approach is that you are in fact doing two casts, as the `TypeOf` expression attempts to convert the object to the test type. The result of the conversion is either nothing or an object that matches the test type, so the `TypeOf` expression then does a check to determine whether the result is nothing. If the result is not nothing, and the conditional statement is true, then the second cast is performed to retrieve the variable that matches the test type. The following example illustrates both the original syntax, using `TypeOf`, and the improved syntax, using `TryCast`, for working with objects of unknown type:

```
Dim fred As Object = New Person
If TypeOf (fred) Is Employee Then
    Dim emp As Employee = CType(fred, Employee)
    'Do actions with employee
End If

Dim joe As Object = New Person
Dim anotherEmployee As Employee = TryCast(joe, Employee)
If anotherEmployee IsNot Nothing Then
    'Do actions with another employee
End If
```

The TryCast expression, as illustrated in the second half of this example, maps directly to the isinst CLR instruction, which will return either nothing or an object that matches the test type. The result can then be compared with nothing before performing operations on the object.

Summary

This chapter described the features that differentiate C# and VB.NET. Although C# with anonymous methods and iterators is slightly ahead of the game, you are likely to see these differences disappear in the next iteration of the framework and Visual Studio 2005. However, not being able to write anonymous methods and iterators does not limit the code that a VB.NET developer can write. The two primary .NET languages, C# and VB.NET, do have different objectives, but despite their best attempts to differentiate themselves they are constrained by the direction of the .NET Framework itself. In the long run there will be language parity, with differences only in the syntax and the functionality within Visual Studio.

The next chapter looks at the My namespace, which combines a rich class library with a powerful application model to deliver a framework with which developers can truly be more productive.

24

The My Namespace

Many namespaces make up the classes of the .NET Framework. One of the most popular introduced with the release of version 2.0 is the My namespace collection, created specifically to address the needs of Visual Basic programmers who were concerned with the complexity of the original .NET Framework and how difficult it was to develop Windows applications with Visual Basic .NET — applications that were previously easy to create in Visual Basic 6.

For clarity, when referring to the entire My feature, it will be referred to as a namespace even though it's not a true namespace, as you'll see in the next section.

This, of course, is a concern. After all, creating applications, particularly Windows applications, was meant to be easier and more straightforward with the introduction of the whole fabric of .NET technology components. For Visual Basic programmers, however, many tasks did indeed become more complex and a lot harder to understand. For example, where previously you could use a simple Print command to send a document to the default printer, you now needed to create a whole bunch of objects, and trap events to determine when and what they could print.

When the sheer number of developers clamoring for a solution became obvious, Microsoft began work on providing a way for Visual Basic programmers to achieve results in the efficient manner they were used to without needing to worry about creating whole sets of classes. Thus, the My namespace was born.

This chapter examines the My namespace and describes how you can harness it to simplify the creation of applications. As you'll see, the My namespace actually encompasses web development as well, bringing the ease of development that Visual Basic 6 programmers were used to in Windows development to web applications and services. Even C# developers can take advantage of My, which can be handy for achieving simple tasks that don't warrant the extra effort of writing masses of class-based code.

What Is the My Namespace?

The My feature is not a true namespace like the other parts of the .NET Framework, but it does act just like a namespace in many respects, containing a hierarchy of classes and method definitions that you can utilize in your own applications.

However, My is actually a set of wrapper classes and structures that encapsulate complete sets of .NET classes and automated object instantiations and initializations. The structure of My, shown in Figure 24-1, shows that it is similar to real namespace architecture.

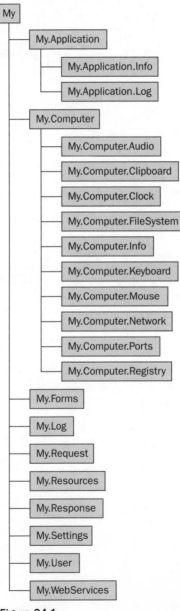

Figure 24-1

This means that rather than defining a particular object of a system class, instantiating it, initializing it with the values you need, and then using it for the specific purpose you need it for, you can simply refer to the corresponding My class and let .NET work out what needs to happen behind the scenes to achieve the same result. Consider more complex tasks that require you to create up to dozens of classes to achieve something simple, such as establishing user credentials or navigating through the file system efficiently, and compare them to the same one-class access that My provides for such functions and you begin to see the power of what can be achieved.

The Main Components

Ten major classes comprise the top level of My. Each class has a number of methods and properties that you can use in your application, and two of them, My.Application and My.Computer, have additional subordinate classes in the namespace-like structure, which in turn have their own methods and properties. In a moment you'll see what each of them can do in detail, but here's a quick reference:

My Object	Purpose
My.Application	Used to access information about the application, My.Application also exposes certain events that are applicationwide. In addition, this class also has two subordinate My classes: My.Application.Log and My.Application.Info.
My.Computer	Deals with the computer system in which the application is running, and is the most extensive My object. In fact, the My.Computer class has a total of ten subordinate My classes, ranging from My.Computer.Audio to My.Computer.Registry, with classes in between that deal with things such as the file system and the network.
My.Forms	Provides quick access to the forms in the current application project
My.Log	Gives you direct access to the application log so you can interact with it more easily than before
My.Request	Related to web page calls, the My.Request class, along with My.Response and My.WebServices, can be used to simplify your calls and interactions in web-based applications, and is the class used to hold the call to the web service
My.Resources	Allows you to easily access the various resources in your application
My.Response	Holds the web page response. See My.Request for more information.
My.Settings	Used to access both applicationwide and user-specific settings
My.User	Used to determine the user's current login profile, including security information
My.WebServices	Gives you easy access to all the web services referenced in the current application project

Using My in Code

Utilizing the My objects in your application code is straightforward in most Windows and web-based projects (see the "Contextual My" section later in this chapter). Because the underlying real namespace is implicitly referenced and any necessary objects are created for you automatically, all you need to do is reference the object property or method you wish to use.

> *The fully qualified name is documented as* `Microsoft.VisualBasic.MyServices,` *but as you'll see in a moment, for project types that do not implicitly support* My, *you can still use it through the* `Microsoft.VisualBasic.Devices` *namespace.*

As an example, consider the following code snippet that evaluates the user identity and role attached to the thread running an application:

```
Private Sub OK_Click(ByVal sender As System.Object, _
    ByVal e As System.EventArgs) Handles OK.Click
    If My.User.IsAuthenticated Then
        If My.User.IsInRole("Administrators") Then
            My.Application.Log.WriteEntry("User " & My.User.Name & _
                " logged in as Administrator", TraceEventType.Information)
        Else
            My.Application.Log.WriteEntry("User " & My.User.Name & _
                " does not have correct priveleges.", TraceEventType.Error)
        End If
    End If
    ...
End Sub
```

The code is fairly straightforward, with the various My object properties and methods defined with readable terms such as `IsAuthenticated` and `WriteEntry`. However, the code to attach to the current principal, extract the authentication state, determine what roles it belongs to, and then write to an application log were all reasonably nontrivial tasks prior to the introduction of My to the developer's toolbox.

Every My object provides vital shortcuts to solve commonly faced scenarios by both Windows and web developers, as this example intimates. Microsoft did a great job in creating this namespace for developers and has definitely brought the concept of ease of use back home to Visual Basic programmers in particular.

Using My in C#

Although My is widely available in Visual Basic projects, other languages such as C# can take advantage of the shortcuts as well. As previously mentioned, this is because the My namespace actually sits on a real .NET Framework 2.0 namespace called `Microsoft.VisualBasic.Devices` for most of its objects. For example, if you want to use the My.Audio or My.Keyboard objects in a Windows application being developed in C# you can.

To access the My objects, you will first need to add a reference to the main Visual Basic library (which also contains other commonly used Visual Basic constructs such as enumerations and classes) in your project. The simplest way to do this is to right-click the References node in the Solution Explorer for the project to which you're adding My support, and choose Add Reference from the context menu.

After a moment, the References dialog window will be displayed, defaulting to the .NET components. Scroll through the list until you locate `Microsoft.VisualBasic` and click OK to add the reference. At this point you're ready to use `My`, but you'll need to prefix all of your references to `My` objects with the rather wordy `Microsoft.VisualBasic.Devices` namespace prefix. To keep your coding to a minimum, you can add a `using` statement to implicitly reference the objects. The result is code similar to the following listing:

```
using System;
...
using System.Windows.Forms;
using Microsoft.VisualBasic.Devices;

namespace WindowsApplication1
{
    public partial class Form1 : Form
    {
        ...
        private void Form1_Load(object sender, EventArgs e)
        {
            Keyboard MyKeyboard = new Keyboard();
            if (MyKeyboard.ScrollLock == true)
            {
                MessageBox.Show("Scroll Lock Is On!");
            }
        }
    }
}
```

Note that not all `My` objects are available outside Visual Basic. However, there is usually a way to access the functionality through other standard Visual Basic namespace objects. A prime example of this issue is the `FileSystemProxy`, which is used by the `My.Computer` object to provide more efficient access to the `FileSystem` object.

Unfortunately for C# developers, this proxy class is not available to their code (although interestingly J# programmers can harness it). Rather than utilize `My` for this purpose, C# programmers still can take advantage of Visual Basic's specialized namespace objects. In this case, C# code should simply use the `Microsoft.VisualBasic.FileIO.FileSystem` object to achieve the same results.

Contextual My

While ten `My` objects are available for your use, only a subset is ever available in any given project. In addition, some of the `My` classes have a variety of forms that provide different information and methods depending on the context.

By dividing application development projects into three broad categories, you can see how the `My` classes logically fit into different project types. The first category of development scenarios is Windows-based applications. Three kinds of projects fall into this area — Windows applications for general application development, Windows Control Libraries used to create custom user controls for use in Windows applications, and Windows Services that are designed to run in the services environment of Windows itself. The following table shows which classes these project types can access:

My Class	Applications	Control Libraries	Services
My.Application	Available	Available	Available
My.Computer	Available	Available	Available
My.Forms	Available	Available	
My.Log			
My.Request			
My.Resources	Available	Available	Available
My.Response			
My.Settings	Available	Available	Available
My.User	Available	Available	Available
My.WebServices	Available	Available	Available

As you can see, the available classes are logical — for example, there's no reason why Windows Services applications need general access to a My.Forms collection, as they do not have Windows Forms.

All three project types use a variant of the My.Computer class related to Windows applications. It is based on the server-based version of My.Computer, which is used for web development but includes additional objects usually found on client machines, such as keyboard and mouse classes. The My.User class is also a Windows version, which is based on the current user authentication (well, to be accurate, it's actually based on the current *thread's* authentication).

However, each of the three project types for Windows development uses different variations of the My.Application class. The lowest common denominator is the Library version of My.Application, which provides you with access to fundamental features in the application such as version information and the application log. The Windows Control Library projects use this version.

Windows Services projects use a customized version of My.Application that inherits from this Library version and add extra methods for accessing information such as command-line arguments. Windows Application projects take this console version and add even more information for accessing the forms found in the application, among other things.

Web development projects can use a very different set of My classes. It doesn't make sense for them to have My.Application or My.Forms, for instance, as they cannot have this Windows client-based information. Instead, you have access to the web-based My objects, as indicated in the following table:

My Class	Sites	Control Libraries
My.Application		
My.Computer	Available	Available
My.Forms		
My.Log	Available	

My Class	Sites	Control Libraries
My.Request	Available	
My.Resources		Available
My.Response	Available	
My.Settings		Available
My.User	Available	Available
My.WebServices		Available

The Web Project styles use a different version of the My.Computer object. In these cases, the information is quite basic and excludes all the normal Windows-oriented properties and methods. In fact, these two project types use the same My.Computer version as Windows Services.

My.User is also different from the Windows version. It associates its properties with the identity of the application context.

Finally, some project types don't fit directly into either the Windows-based application development model or the web-based projects. Project types such as console applications and general class libraries (DLLs) fall into this category, as do solutions that begin empty or fit into any other type not covered by the previous categories. Empty solutions do not have access to any part of the My namespace, while these other project types have access to another set of My objects, as shown in the following table:

My Class	Class Library	Console App
My.Application	Y* 2	Y*3
My.Computer	Available	Available
My.Forms		
My.Log		
My.Request		
My.Resources	Available	Available
My.Response		
My.Settings	Available	Available
My.User	Available	Available
My.WebServices	Available	Available

The first thing you'll notice in this table is that projects that don't fit into any of the standard types do not have direct access to any of the My objects at all. This doesn't prevent you from using them in a similar fashion, as discussed earlier with C# usage of My.

The `My.Computer` object that is exposed to class libraries and console applications is the same version as the one used by the Windows project types — you get access to all the Windows properties and methods associated with the `My.Computer` object. The same goes for `My.User`, with any user information being accessed relating to the thread's associated user identity.

What can these different objects do for you? The next section delves into each of the main `My` objects and describes how they can be used in your projects to make your coding much more efficient.

Default Instances

Several of the `My` objects use *default instances* of the objects in your project. A default instance is an object that is automatically instantiated by the .NET runtime, which you can then reference in your code. For example, instead of defining and creating a new instance of a form, you can simply refer to its default instance in the `My.Forms` form collection. `My.Resources` works in a similar fashion by giving you direct references to each resource object in your solution, while `My.WebServices` provides proxy objects for each web service reference added to your project so you don't even need to create those.

Using the default instances is straightforward — simply refer to the object by name in the appropriate collection. To show a form named `Form1`, you would use `My.Forms.Form1.Show`, while calling a web service named `CalcWS` would be achieved by using the `My.WebServices.CalcWS` object.

My.Application

The `My.Application` object gives you immediate access to various pieces of information about the application. At the lowest level, `My.Application` allows you to write to the application log through the subordinate `My.Application.Log` as well as to add general information that is common to all Windows-based projects in the `My.Application.Info` object.

As mentioned earlier, if the *context* of `My.Application` is a Windows service, it also includes information related to the command-line arguments and the method of deployment. Windows Forms applications have all this information in the contextual form `My.Application` and enable the accessing of various forms-related data.

Prior to `My`, all of this information was accessible through a variety of methods but it was difficult to determine where some of the information was. Now the information is all consolidated into one easy-to-use location. To demonstrate the kind of data you can access through `My.Application`, try the following sample task:

1. Start Visual Studio 2005 and create a basic Windows application. Add a button to the form. You'll use the button to display information about the application.

2. Double-click the My Project node in the Solution Explorer to access the Solution properties. In the Application page, click Assembly Information and set the Title, Copyright, and Assembly Version fields to something you'll recognize and click OK to save the settings.

3. Return to the `Form1` Design view and double-click it to have Visual Studio automatically generate a stub for the button's `Click` event. Add the following code:

```
Private Sub Button1_Click(ByVal sender As System.Object, _
    ByVal e As System.EventArgs) Handles Button1.Click
```

```
        Dim ApplicationMessage As String = vbNullString
        With My.Application
            With .Info
                ApplicationMessage &= .Title & vbCrLf
                ApplicationMessage &= .Version.ToString & vbCrLf
                ApplicationMessage &= .Copyright & vbCrLf
            End With
            ApplicationMessage &= .CommandLineArgs.Count & vbCrLf
            ApplicationMessage &= .OpenForms(0).Name
        End With
        MessageBox.Show(ApplicationMessage)
    End Sub
```

This demonstrates the use of properties available to all My-compatible applications in the My.Application.Info object, then to Windows Services and Windows Forms applications with the CommandLineArgs property, and then finally information that's only accessible in Windows Forms applications.

4. Run the application and click the button on the form and you will get a dialog similar to the one shown in Figure 24-2.

Figure 24-2

Using the information in My.Application is especially useful when you need to give feedback to your users about what version of the solution is running. It can also be used internally to make logical decisions about what functionality should be performed based on active forms and version information.

My.Computer

My.Computer is by far the largest object in the My namespace. In fact, it has ten subordinate objects that can be used to access various parts of the computer system, such as keyboard, mouse, and network. Besides these ten objects, the main property that My.Computer exposes is the machine name, through the conveniently named Name property.

My.Computer.Audio

The My.Computer.Audio object gives you the capability to play system and user sound files without needing to create objects and use various API calls. There are two main functions within this object:

❑ PlaySystemSound will play one of the five basic system sounds.

❑ Play will play a specified audio file. You can optionally choose to have the sound file play in the background and even loop continuously. You can halt a background loop with the Stop method.

The following snippet of code illustrates how to use these functions:

```
My.Computer.Audio.PlaySystemSound(Media.SystemSounds.Beep)
My.Computer.Audio.Play("C:\MySoundFile.wav", AudioPlayMode.BackgroundLoop)
My.Computer.Audio.Stop()
```

My.Computer.Clipboard

The Windows clipboard has come a long way since the days when it could only store simple text. Now you can copy and paste images, audio files, file and folder lists, and text. The My.Computer.Clipboard object provides access to all of this functionality, giving you the ability to store and retrieve items of the aforementioned types as well as custom data specific to your particular application.

Three main groups of methods are used in My.Computer.Clipboard—Contains, Get, and Set. The Contains methods are used to check the clipboard for a specific type of data. For example, ContainsAudio will have a value of True if the clipboard contains audio data. GetAudio will retrieve the audio data in the clipboard (if there is some), and the other Get methods are similar in functionality for their own types. Finally, SetAudio stores audio data in the clipboard, while the other Set methods will do the same for the other types of data.

The only exceptions to this are the ContainsData, GetData, and SetData methods. These three methods enable you to store and retrieve custom data for your application in any format you like, taking a parameter identifying the custom data type. The advantage of using these is that if you have sensitive data that you allow the user to copy and paste within your application, you can preclude it from being accidentally pasted into other applications by using your own format.

To reset the clipboard entirely, use the Clear method.

My.Computer.Clock

Previously, an often frustrating task for some developers was converting the current system time to a standard GMT time, but with My.Computer.Clock it's easy. This object exposes the current time in both local and GMT formats as Date type variables with LocalTime and GmtTime properties.

In addition, you can retrieve the system timer of the computer with the TickCount property.

My.Computer.FileSystem

Accessing the computer file system usually involves creating multiple objects and having them all refer to each other in ways that sometimes appear illogical. The `My.Computer.FileSystem` object does away with all the confusion with a central location for all file activities, whether it's just file manipulation such as copying, renaming, or deleting files or directories, or reading and writing to a file's contents.

The following sample routine searches for files containing the word `loser` in the `C:\Temp` directory, deleting each file that's found:

```
Dim foundList As System.Collections.ObjectModel.ReadOnlyCollection (Of String)
foundList = My.Computer.FileSystem.FindInFiles("C:\Temp", "loser", True, _
    FileIO.SearchOption.SearchTopLevelOnly)

For Each thisFileName As String In foundList
    My.Computer.FileSystem.DeleteFile(thisFileName)
Next
```

My.Computer.Info

Similar to the `Info` object that is part of `My.Application`, the `My.Computer.Info` object exposes information about the computer system. Notably, it returns memory status information about the computer and the installed operating system. The important properties are listed in the following table:

Property	Description
AvailablePhysicalMemory	The amount of physical memory free on the computer
TotalPhysicalMemory	The total amount of physical memory on the computer
AvailableVirtualMemory	The amount of virtual addressing space available
TotalVirtualMemory	The total amount of virtual addressable space
OSFullName	The full operating system, such as Microsoft Windows XP Professional
OSPlatform	The platform identifier, such as Win32NT
OSVersion	The full version of the operating system

My.Computer.Keyboard and My.Computer.Mouse

The `My.Computer.Keyboard` and `My.Computer.Mouse` objects return information about the currently installed keyboard and mouse on your computer, respectively. The `Mouse` object will let you know if there is a scroll wheel, how much the screen should scroll if it's used, and whether the mouse buttons have been swapped.

`My.Computer.Keyboard` provides information about the various control keys such as Shift, Alt, and Ctrl, as well as keyboard states such as Caps Lock, Num Lock, and Scroll Lock. You can use this information to affect the behavior of your application in response to the specific combination of keys.

The `My.Computer.Keyboard` object also exposes the `SendKeys` method that many Visual Basic programmers use to simulate keystrokes.

My.Computer.Network

At first glance, the `My.Computer.Network` object may look underwhelming. It has only a single property that indicates whether the network is available or not — `IsAvailable`. However, in addition to this property, `My.Computer.Network` has three methods that can be used to send and retrieve files across the network or web:

- ❑　`Ping`: Use Ping to determine whether the remote location you intend to use is reachable with the current network state.

- ❑　`DownloadFile`: Specify the remote location and where you want the file to be downloaded.

- ❑　`UploadFile`: Specify the file to be uploaded and the remote location's address.

Of course, networks can be unstable, particularly if you're talking about the web; and that's where the `NetworkAvailabilityChanged` event comes to the rescue. The `My.Computer.Network` object exposes this event for you to handle in your application, which you can do by defining an event handler routine and attaching it to the event:

```
Public Sub MyNetworkAvailabilityChangedHandler( ByVal sender As Object, _
    ByVal e As Devices.NetworkAvailableEventArgs)
    ... do your code.
End Sub

Private Sub Form1_Load(ByVal sender As System.Object, _
    ByVal e As System.EventArgs) Handles MyBase.Load
    AddHandler My.Computer.Network.NetworkAvailabilityChanged, _
        AddressOf MyNetworkAvailabilityChangedHandler
End Sub
```

You can then address any network work your application might be doing when the network goes down, or even kick off background transfers when your application detects that the network has become available again.

My.Computer.Ports

The `My.Computer.Ports` object exposes any serial ports available on the computer through the `SerialPortNames` property. You can then use `OpenSerialPort` to open a specific port and write to it using standard I/O methods.

My.Computer.Registry

Traditionally, the Windows registry has been dangerous to play around with — so much so, in fact, that Microsoft originally cordoned off Visual Basic programmers' access to only a small subset of the entire registry key set.

`My.Computer.Registry` provides a reasonably safe way to access the entire registry. You can still mess things up, but because its methods and properties are easy to use, there's less likelihood of such a mistake happening.

Each of the main root keys in the registry is referenced by a specific property of `My.Computer.Registry`, and you can use `GetValue` and `SetValue` in conjunction with these root properties to enable your application access to any data that the end user can access.

For instance, to determine whether a particular registry key exists, you can use the following snippet:

```
If My.Computer.Registry.GetValue("HKEY_LOCAL_MACHINE\MyApp", "Value", Nothing) _
    Is Nothing Then
    MessageBox.Show("Value not there.")
End If
```

My.Forms and My.WebServices

`My.Forms` gives you access to the forms in your application. The advantage this object has over the old way of using your forms is that it provides a default instance of each form so you don't need to define and instantiate them manually. Whereas before you would write

```
Dim mMyForm As New Form1
mMyForm.Show
```

now you can simply code

```
My.Forms.Form1.Show
```

Each form has a corresponding property exposed in the `My.Forms` object. You can determine which forms are currently open using the `My.Application.OpenForms` collection.

`My.WebServices` performs a similar function but for, you guessed it, the web services you've defined in your project. If you add a reference to a web service and name the reference `MyCalcWS`, you can use the `My.WebServices.MyCalcWS` instance of the web service proxy, rather than instantiate your own each time you need to call it.

My For the Web

When building web applications, you can use the `My.Request` and `My.Response` objects to set and retrieve the HTTP request and HTTP response information. This is a godsend to any developer who has tried to maintain these objects in the past and found it difficult to remember where the information was located.

These objects are basically `System.Web.HTTPRequest` and `System.Web.HTTPResponse` classes, but you don't have to worry about the context of which page has what data because they're referring to the current page.

My.Resources

.NET applications can have many types of embedded resource objects. Visual Studio 2005 has an easy way of adding resource objects in the form of the Resources page of My Project in Visual Basic, or the corresponding Properties area in C#. `My.Resources` makes using these resources in code just as easy.

Each resource added to the project has a unique name assigned to it (normally the filename for audio and graphic files that are inserted into the resource file), which you can refer to in code. These names are rendered to object properties exposed by the `My.Resources` object. For example, if you have an image resource called `MainFormBackground`, then the shortcut way of accessing this resource is `My.Resources` `.MainFormBackground`.

Use the following sample task to verify how `My.Resources` works:

1. Start Visual Studio 2005 and create a new Visual Basic WindowsApplication. Double-click the My Project node in the Solution Explorer and navigate to the Resources tab.

2. Click the Add Resource drop-down and choose New Image⇨BMP Image. When prompted, name the new image MainFormBackground and click OK to add it to the project's resource file.

3. Visual Studio 2005 automatically opens the image editor view for the new image. A standard Windows form is 300 × 300 pixels, so set the image's `Width` and `Height` properties to 300.

4. Draw something in the image that you want to use as the background for the form. The sample shown in Figure 24-3 draws some rounded rectangles to simulate a custom-built form interface. Once you're satisfied, save the project so the resource file has the new image updated into the project.

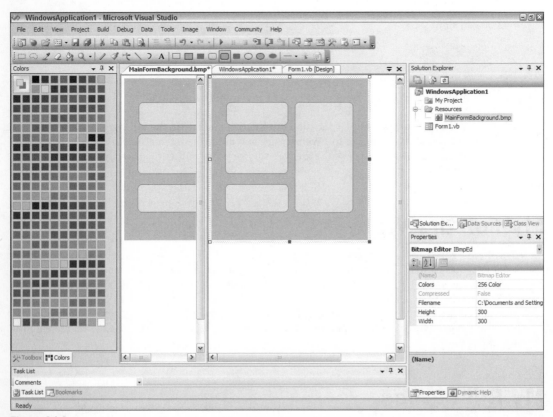

Figure 24-3

5. Open Form1 in Design view and double-click on the form's design surface so that Visual Studio automatically inserts the default stub subroutine for the `Form_Load` event. Add a single line to the procedure as follows:

```
Private Sub Form1_Load(ByVal sender As System.Object, _
    ByVal e As System.EventArgs) Handles MyBase.Load
    Me.BackgroundImage = My.Resources.MainFormBackground
End Sub
```

This line of code sets the `BackgroundImage` property of the form to the resource image you added earlier. Note how the name of the resource object can be referred to directly in code. You could even interrogate the resource file's properties and correspondingly act on them.

6. Run the application. The form will be displayed with a background of the resource image. Notice that as you type the line of code, IntelliSense will show you the list of available resources in the `My.Resources` list, as illustrated in Figure 24-4.

Figure 24-4

Other My Classes

The other `My` classes are fairly basic in their usage. The `My.User` class is used to determine information about the current user. When using role-based security, this includes the Current Principal, but as you saw earlier in this chapter, you can also retrieve the user's login name and whether they belong to specific roles.

`My.Settings` exposes the `Settings` strings in your application, enabling you to edit or retrieve the information in the same way that `My.Forms` exposes the application form objects and `My.Resources` exposes the resource file contents. Settings can be either applicationwide or userwide, and can be persisted between sessions with the `My.Settings.Save` method.

Finally, `My.Log` is an alternative way of addressing the application log.

Summary

The `My` namespace is an extremely powerful feature introduced with Visual Studio 2005. Although it was originally intended for Visual Basic programmers, J# and C# developers can also harness the efficiencies it offers in the code they write.

The `My.Application` and `My.Computer` objects expose a large array of information about the current application process and the computer it's running on, enabling you to quickly determine what situation your application is in and respond effectively.

Part VI
Automation

25

Code Generation Templates

Most development teams build a set of standards that specifies how they build applications. This means that every time you start a new project or add an item to an existing project, you have to go through a process to ensure that it conforms to the standard. Visual Studio 2005 enables you to create templates that can be reused, without having to modify the standard item templates that it ships with. This chapter describes how you can create simple templates and then extend them using the `IWizard` interface. It also examines how you can create a multi-project template that can greatly save you some time when starting a new application.

Creating Templates

There are two types of templates: those that create new project items and those that create entire projects. Both types of templates essentially have the same structure, as you will see later, except that they are placed in different template folders. The project templates appear in the Add New Project dialog, whereas the item templates appear in the Add New Item dialog.

Item Template

Although it is possible to build a template manually, it is much quicker to create a template from an existing sample and make changes as required. This section begins by looking at a project item template — in this case, an About form that contains some basic information, such as who the application was written by and the version of the application. The About screen, shown in Figure 25-1, has been created in an existing project.

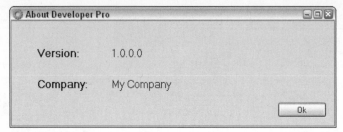

Figure 25-1

To make a template out of the About form, select the Export Template item from the File menu. This starts the Export Template Wizard, shown in Figure 25-2. The first step is to determine what type of template you want to create. In this case, select the Item Template radio button and make sure that the project in which the About form resides is selected in the drop-down list.

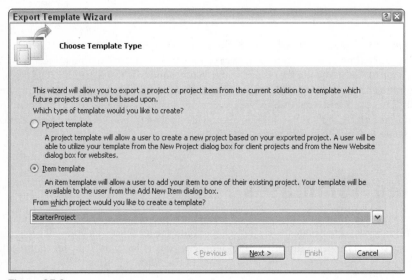

Figure 25-2

Click Next. You will be prompted to select the item on which you want to base the template. In this case, select the About form. The use of checkboxes is slightly deceiving, as you can only select a single item on which to base the template. After making your selection and clicking Next, the dialog shown in Figure 25-3 enables you to include any project references that you may require. This list is based on the list of references in the project in which that item resides. Because this is a form, include a reference to the System .Windows.Forms library. If you did not, and a new item of this type were added to a class library, it is highly possible that the project would not compile, as it would not have a reference to this assembly.

The final step in the Export Template Wizard is to specify some properties of the template to be generated, such as the name, description, and icon that will appear in the Add New Item dialog. Figure 25-4 shows the final dialog in the wizard. As you can see, there are a couple of options to display the output folder upon completion and whether to automatically import the new template into Visual Studio 2005.

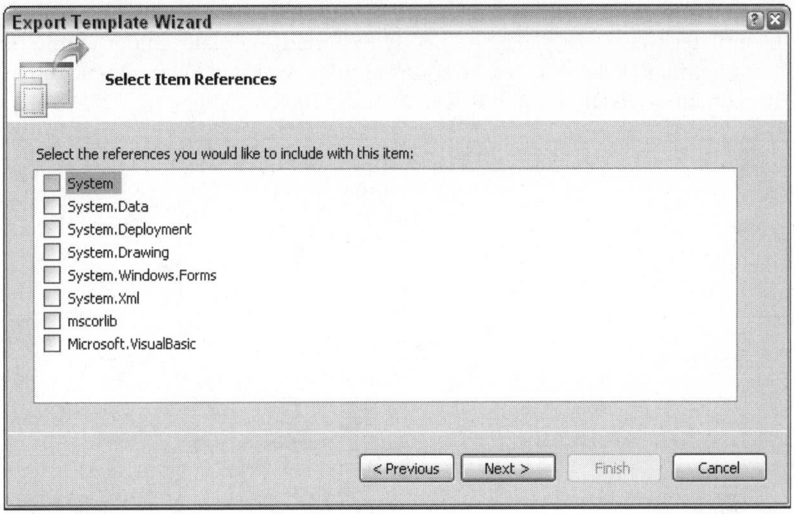

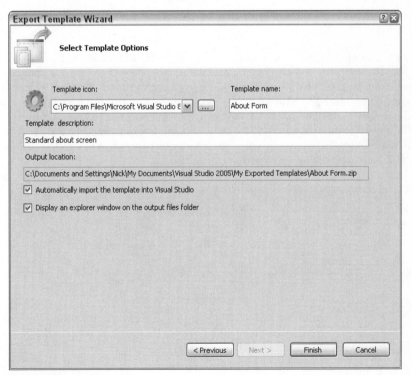

Figure 25-3

Figure 25-4

For some reason the team who wrote this feature decided that the output location could not be editable, and that all templates were to be placed in the My Exported Templates folder within the current user's Documents and Settings folder. If you take a look at this folder (see Figure 25-5), you can see a number of folders that contain user settings about Visual Studio 2005.

Figure 25-5

Also notice the Templates folder in Figure 25-5. Visual Studio 2005 looks in this folder for additional templates to display when you are creating new items. Not shown here are two subfolders beneath the Templates folder that hold Item templates and Project templates, respectively. These in turn are divided by language. If you check the "Automatically import the template into Visual Studio" option on the final page of the Export Template Wizard, the new template will not only be placed in the output folder; it will also be copied to the relevant location, depending on language and template type, within the Templates folder. Visual Studio 2005 will automatically display this item template the next time you display the Add New Item dialog, as shown in Figure 25-6.

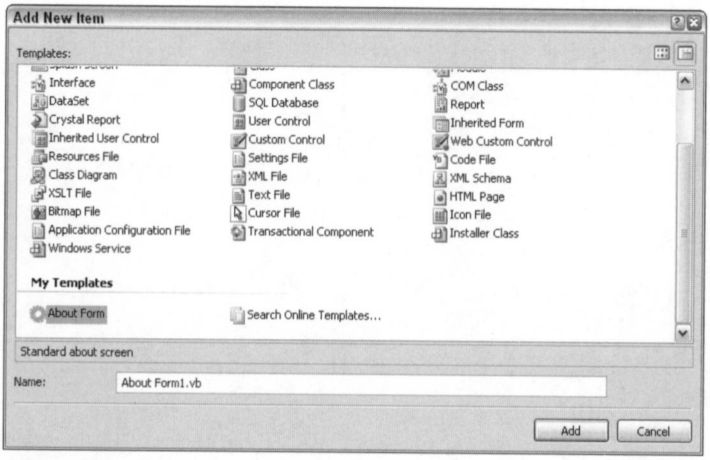

Figure 25-6

Project Template

You build a project template the same way you build an item template but with one difference. Whereas the item template is based on an existing item, the project template needs to be based on an entire project. For example, you might have a simple project, as shown in Figure 25-7, that has a main form, complete with menu bar, an About form, and a splash screen.

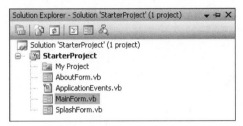

Figure 25-7

To generate a template from this project, you follow the same steps you took to generate an item template, except you need to select Project Template when asked what type of template to generate. After completing the Export Template Wizard, the new project template will appear in the New Project dialog, shown in Figure 25-8.

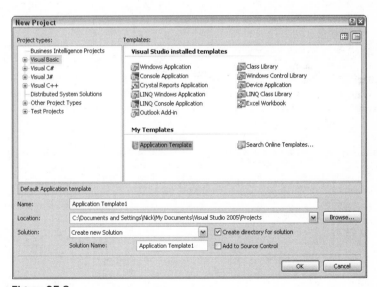

Figure 25-8

Template Structure

Before examining how to build more complex templates, you need to understand what is produced by the Export Template Wizard. If you look in the My Exported Templates folder, you will see that all the templates are exported as compressed zip folders. The zip folder can contain any number of files or folders, depending on whether they are a template for a single file or a full project. However, the one common element between all template folders is that they contain a .vstemplate file. This file is an XML document that determines what happens when the template is used:

```xml
<VSTemplate Version="2.0.0"
xmlns="http://schemas.microsoft.com/developer/vstemplate/2005" Type="Project">
  <TemplateData>
    <Name>Application Template</Name>
    <Description>Default Application template</Description>
    <ProjectType>VisualBasic</ProjectType>
    <SortOrder>1000</SortOrder>
    <CreateNewFolder>true</CreateNewFolder>
    <DefaultName>Application Template</DefaultName>
    <ProvideDefaultName>true</ProvideDefaultName>
    <LocationField>Enabled</LocationField>
    <EnableLocationBrowseButton>true</EnableLocationBrowseButton>
    <Icon>__TemplateIcon.ico</Icon>
  </TemplateData>
  <TemplateContent>
    <Project TargetFileName="StarterProject.vbproj" File="StarterProject.vbproj"
ReplaceParameters="true">
      <ProjectItem ReplaceParameters="true"
TargetFileName="AboutForm.vb">AboutForm.vb</ProjectItem>
      <ProjectItem ReplaceParameters="true"
TargetFileName="AboutForm.Designer.vb">AboutForm.Designer.vb</ProjectItem>
      <ProjectItem ReplaceParameters="true"
TargetFileName="AboutForm.resx">AboutForm.resx</ProjectItem>
      <ProjectItem ReplaceParameters="true"
TargetFileName="ApplicationEvents.vb">ApplicationEvents.vb</ProjectItem>
      <ProjectItem ReplaceParameters="true"
TargetFileName="MainForm.vb">MainForm.vb</ProjectItem>
      <ProjectItem ReplaceParameters="true"
TargetFileName="MainForm.Designer.vb">MainForm.Designer.vb</ProjectItem>
      <ProjectItem ReplaceParameters="true"
TargetFileName="MainForm.resx">MainForm.resx</ProjectItem>
      <Folder Name="My Project" TargetFolderName="My Project">
        <ProjectItem ReplaceParameters="true"
TargetFileName="Application.myapp">Application.myapp</ProjectItem>
        <ProjectItem ReplaceParameters="true"
TargetFileName="Application.Designer.vb">Application.Designer.vb</ProjectItem>
        <ProjectItem ReplaceParameters="true"
TargetFileName="AssemblyInfo.vb">AssemblyInfo.vb</ProjectItem>
        <ProjectItem ReplaceParameters="true"
TargetFileName="Resources.resx">Resources.resx</ProjectItem>
        <ProjectItem ReplaceParameters="true"
TargetFileName="Resources.Designer.vb">Resources.Designer.vb</ProjectItem>
        <ProjectItem ReplaceParameters="true"
TargetFileName="Settings.settings">Settings.settings</ProjectItem>
        <ProjectItem ReplaceParameters="true"
TargetFileName="Settings.Designer.vb">Settings.Designer.vb</ProjectItem>
      </Folder>
      <ProjectItem ReplaceParameters="true"
TargetFileName="SplashForm.vb">SplashForm.vb</ProjectItem>
```

```
        <ProjectItem ReplaceParameters="true"
   TargetFileName="SplashForm.Designer.vb">SplashForm.Designer.vb</ProjectItem>
      </Project>
   </TemplateContent>
</VSTemplate>
```

This sample illustrates the `MyTemplate.vstemplate` that was generated for the project template created earlier. At the top of the sample, the `VSTemplate` node contains a `Type` attribute that determines whether this is an Item template (`"Item"`), a Project template (`"Project"`), or a Multiple Project template (`"ProjectGroup"`). The remainder of the sample is divided into `TemplateData` and `TemplateContent`. The `TemplateData` block includes information about the template itself, such as the name, description, and icon that will be used to represent the template in the New Project dialog, whereas the `Template Content` block defines the structure of the template.

In the preceding example, the content starts with a `Project` node, which indicates the project file to use. The files contained in this template are listed using the `ProjectItem` nodes. Each node contains a `Target FileName` attribute that can be used to specify the name of the file as it will appear in the project created from this template. In the case of an Item template, the `Project` node is missing and `ProjectItems` are contained within the `TemplateContent` node.

For more information on the `vstemplate` file, the full schema is available at `C:\Program Files\ Microsoft Visual Studio 8\Xml\Schemas\1033\vstemplate.xsd`.

Extending Templates

Building templates based on existing items and projects limits what you can do because it assumes that every project or scenario will require exactly the same items. Instead of creating multiple templates for each different scenario (for example, one that has a main form with a black background and another that has a white background), with a bit of user interaction you can accommodate multiple scenarios from a single template. Therefore, this section takes the project template created earlier and tweaks it so users can specify the background color for the main form. In addition, you'll build an installer for both the template and the wizard that you will create for the user interaction.

To add user interaction into a template, you need to implement the `IWizard` interface in a class library that is then strongly signed and placed in the GAC on the machine on which the template will be executed. Earlier releases of Visual Studio 2005 had the capability to use a nonsigned assembly placed within the template zip folder. However, despite being an incredibly useful way to deploy templates, this was deemed a security risk and removed. As such, to deploy a template that uses a wizard, you also need to deploy the wizard assembly to the GAC.

Template Project Setup

Before plunging in and implementing the `IWizard` interface, follow these steps to set up your solution so you have all the bits and pieces in the same location, which will make it easy to make changes, perform a build, and then run the installer:

1. As you did earlier, start with the StarterProject solution on which you based the initial project template. Make sure that this solution builds and runs successfully before proceeding. Any issues with this solution will be harder to detect later, as the error messages that appear when a template is used are somewhat cryptic.

2. Into this solution add a Class Library project, in which you will place the IWizard implementation. You will also need to add a Setup project to the solution. To do this, select the Setup Wizard template and follow the prompts so that the Primary Output from the Class Library is included in the installer.

3. To access the IWizard interface, add references to the Class Library project to both EnvDTE.dll and Microsoft.VisualStudio.TemplateWizardInterface.dll, both located at C:\Program Files\Microsoft Visual Studio 8\Common7\IDE\PublicAssemblies\.

   This should result in a solution that looks similar to what is shown in Figure 25-9.

Figure 25-9

As shown in Figure 25-9, both the primary output and content files from the Class Library project have been added to the installer. This action also adds a number of dependencies to the installer. Because the template will only be used on a machine with Visual Studio 2005, you don't need any of these dependencies. Exclude them by clicking the Exclude menu item on the right-click context menu.

4. By default, when you add project outputs to the installer, they are added to the Application folder. In this case, add the primary output of the class library to the GAC, and place the content files for the class library into the user's Visual Studio Templates folder. Before you can move these files, right-click the Installer project and select View⇨File System from the context menu to open the File System view.

5. By default, the File System view contains the Application Folder (which can't be deleted), the User's Desktop, and the User's Programs Menu. Remove the two User folders by selecting Delete from the right-click context menu.

6. Add both the Global Assembly Cache (GAC) folder and the User's Personal Data folder (My Documents) to the file system by right-clicking the File System on Target Machine node and selecting these folders from the list.

7. Into the User's Personal Data folder, add a Visual Studio 2005 folder, followed by a Templates folder, followed by a ProjectTemplates folder. The result should look like what is shown in Figure 25-10.

Figure 25-10

8. To complete the installer, move the primary output from the Application folder into the Global Assembly Cache folder, and then move the content files from the Application folder to the ProjectTemplates folder (simply drag the files between folders in the File System view).

IWizard

Now that you've completed the installer, you can work back to the wizard class library. As shown in Figure 25-9, you have a form, `ColorPickerForm`, and a class, `MyWizard`. The former is a simple form that can be used to specify the color the background of the main form, as shown in Figure 25-11.

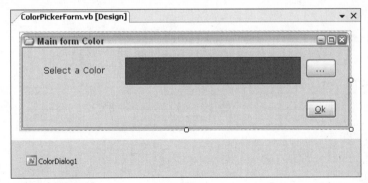

Figure 25-11

The event handler for the ellipses button opens the ColorDialog that is used to select a color, as shown in the following code snippet:

```vb
Public Class ColorPickerForm
    Private Sub BtnPickColor_Click(ByVal sender As System.Object, _
                      ByVal e As System.EventArgs) Handles BtnPickColor.Click
        Me.ColorDialog1.Color = Me.PnlColor.BackColor
        If Me.ColorDialog1.ShowDialog() = Windows.Forms.DialogResult.OK Then
```

```
                Me.PnlColor.BackColor = Me.ColorDialog1.Color
            End If
        End Sub

        Public ReadOnly Property SelectedColor() As Drawing.Color
            Get
                Return Me.PnlColor.BackColor
            End Get
        End Property
    End Class
```

The MyWizard class implements the IWizard interface, which provides a number of opportunities for user interaction throughout the template process. In this case, add code to the RunStarted method, which will be called just after the project creation process is started. This provides the perfect opportunity to select and apply a new background color for the main form:

```
Imports Microsoft.VisualStudio.TemplateWizard
Imports System.Collections.Generic
Imports System.Windows.Forms
Public Class MyWizard
    Implements IWizard


    Public Sub BeforeOpeningFile(ByVal projectItem As EnvDTE.ProjectItem) _
                                        Implements IWizard.BeforeOpeningFile
    End Sub

    Public Sub ProjectFinishedGenerating(ByVal project As EnvDTE.Project) _
                                    Implements IWizard.ProjectFinishedGenerating
    End Sub

    Public Sub ProjectItemFinishedGenerating _
                        (ByVal projectItem As EnvDTE.ProjectItem) _
                        Implements IWizard.ProjectItemFinishedGenerating
    End Sub

    Public Sub RunFinished() Implements IWizard.RunFinished

    End Sub

    Public Sub RunStarted(ByVal automationObject As Object, _
                    ByVal replacementsDictionary As _
                                            Dictionary(Of String, String), _
                    ByVal runKind As WizardRunKind, _
                    ByVal customParams() As Object) _
                                        Implements IWizard.RunStarted
        Dim selector As New ColorPickerForm
        If selector.ShowDialog = DialogResult.OK Then
            Dim c As Drawing.Color = selector.SelectedColor
            Dim colorString As String = "System.Drawing.Color.FromArgb(" & _
                                        c.R.ToString & "," & _
                                        c.G.ToString & "," & _
                                        c.B.ToString & ")"
```

```
            replacementsDictionary.Add _
                                ("Me.BackColor = System.Drawing.Color.Silver", _
                                "Me.BackColor = " & colorString)
        End If
    End Sub

    Public Function ShouldAddProjectItem(ByVal filePath As String) As Boolean _
                                    Implements IWizard.ShouldAddProjectItem
        Return True
    End Function
End Class
```

In the `RunStarted` method, you prompt the user to select a new color and then use that response to add a new entry into the replacements dictionary. In this case, you are replacing `"Me.BackColor = System.Drawing.Color.Silver"` with a concatenated string made up of the RGB values of the color specified by the user. The replacements dictionary is used when the files are created for the new project, as they will be searched for the replacement keys. Upon finding any instances of these keys, they will be replaced by the appropriate replacement value. In this case, you're looking for the line specifying that the `BackColor` is `Silver`, replacing it with the new color supplied by the user.

The class library containing the implementation of the `IWizard` interface must a strongly named assembly capable of being placed into the GAC. To accomplish this, use the Signing tab of the project properties dialog to generate a new signing key, as shown in Figure 25-12.

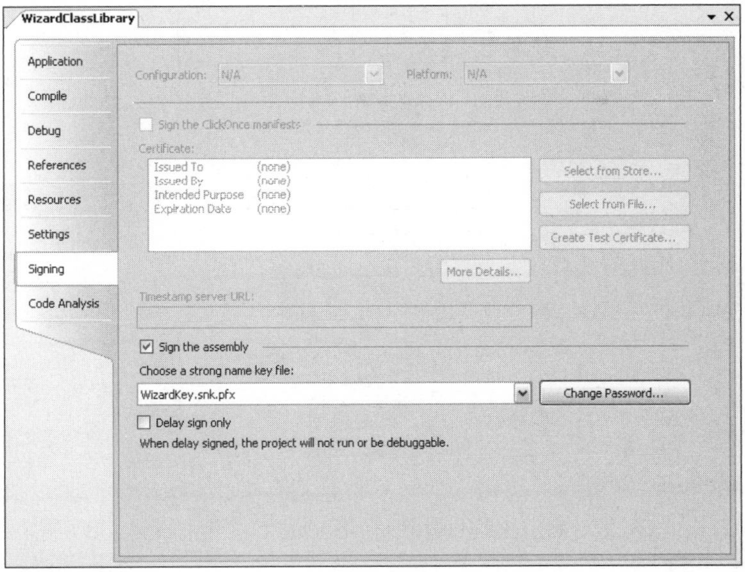

Figure 25-12

After checking the Sign the Assembly checkbox, there will be no default value for the key file. To create a new key, select <New...> from the drop-down list. Alternatively, you can use an existing key file using the <Browse...> item in the drop-down list.

Starter Template

You're basing the template for this example on the StarterProject, and you need only make minor changes in order for the wizard you just built to work correctly. In the previous section you added an entry in the replacements dictionary, which searches for instances where the BackColor is set to Silver. If you want the MainForm to have the BackColor specified during the wizard, you need to ensure that the replacement value is found. To do this, simply set the BackColor property of the MainForm to Silver. This will add the line "Me.BackColor = System.Drawing.Color.Silver" to the MainForm.Designer.vb file so that it is found during the replacement phase.

Instead of exporting the StarterProject as a new template each time and manually adding a reference to the wizard, use a command-line zip utility (in this case, 7-zip, available at www.7-zip.org, was used, but any command-line zip utility will work) to build the template. This makes the process easier to automate from within Visual Studio 2005. If you zip the StarterProject folder, you would have all the content files for the template, but you would be missing the VSTemplate file and the associated icon file. This can easily be fixed by adding the VSTemplate file (created when you exported the project template) to the StarterProject folder. You can also add the icon file to this folder. Make sure that you do *not* include these files in the StarterProject itself; they should appear as excluded files, as shown in Figure 25-13.

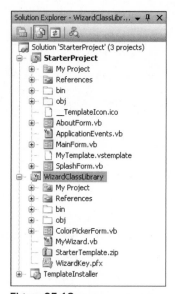

Figure 25-13

To have the wizard triggered when creating a project from this template, add some additional lines to the VSTemplate file:

```
<VSTemplate Version="2.0.0"
xmlns="http://schemas.microsoft.com/developer/vstemplate/2005" Type="Project">
  <TemplateData>
  ...
  </TemplateData>
  <TemplateContent>
```

```
    ...
  </TemplateContent>
  <WizardExtension>
    <Assembly>WizardClassLibrary, Version=1.0.0.0, Culture=neutral,
PublicKeyToken=d2bbc1a3dd199c27, Custom=null</Assembly>
    <FullClassName>WizardClassLibrary.MyWizard</FullClassName>
  </WizardExtension>
</VSTemplate>
```

The `<WizardExtension>` node added in the following sample indicates the class name of the wizard and the strong named assembly in which it resides. You have already signed the wizard assembly, so all you need to do is determine the `PublicKeyToken` by opening the assembly using Lutz Roeder's .NET Reflector (available at `www.aisto.com/roeder/dotnet/`). If you haven't already built the WizardLibrary, you will have to build the project so you have an assembly to open with Reflector. Once you have opened the assembly in Reflector, you can see the `PublicKeyToken` of the assembly by selecting the assembly in the tree, as shown in Figure 25-14. The `PublicKeyToken` value in the `VSTemplate` file needs to be replaced with the actual value found using Reflector.

Figure 25-14

The last change you need to make to the StarterProject is to add a post-build event command that will zip this project into a Project template. In this case, the command to be executed is a call to the 7-zip executable, which will zip the entire contents of the StarterProject folder, recursively, into `StarterTemplate.zip`, placed in the WizardClassLibrary folder. Note that you may need to supply the full path for your zip utility:

```
7z.exe a -tzip ..\..\..\WizardClassLibrary\StarterTemplate.zip ..\..\*.* -r
```

Referring to Figure 25-13, notice that the generated zip file (`StarterTemplate.zip`) is included in the Class Library project. The `Build Action` property for this item is set to `Content`. This aligns with the installer you set up earlier, which will place the Content files from the class library into the templates folder as part of the installation process.

You have now completed the individual projects required to create the project template (StarterProject), added a user interface wizard (WizardClassLibrary), and built an installer to deploy your template. One last addition is to correct the solution dependency list to ensure that the StarterProject is rebuilt (and hence the template zip file recreated) prior to the installer being built. Because there is no direct dependency between the installer project and the StarterProject, you need to open the solution properties and indicate that there is a dependency, as illustrated in Figure 25-15.

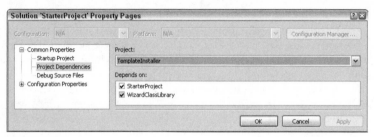

Figure 25-15

Your solution is now complete and can be used to install the StarterTemplate and associated IWizard implementation. Once installed, you can create a new project from the StarterTemplate you have just created.

Summary

This chapter provided an overview of how to create both Item and Project templates with Visual Studio 2005. Existing projects or items can be exported into templates that you can deploy to your colleagues. Alternatively, you can build a template manually and add a user interface using the IWizard interface. From what you learned in this chapter, you should be able to build a template solution that can create the template, build and integrate a wizard interface, and finally build an installer for your template.

26

Macros

Macros are a great way to automate simple tasks, and with Visual Studio 2005 you can easily create and maintain a full library of macros to perform all kinds of functions. Even better, the default installation comes with dozens of pre-built macros that you can immediately use in the Visual Studio IDE.

A *macro* is a set of commands grouped together into a batchlike, interpretative function. Instead of manually performing each of the commands in turn, you can run one macro function that will invoke the commands in sequence. Visual Studio 2005 macros are organized into complete Macro projects, which can contain multiple modules that in turn can contain multiple macros.

This organizational structure enables you to group macros into logical categories as well as divide your macro collection into manageable blocks. Keeping the macros organized into separate projects also enables you to share groups of macros with other developers more easily.

In this chapter you'll take a look at the structure of a macro and learn how to create and use them effectively.

The Macro Explorer

To review the macros currently defined in an instance of Visual Studio, you can use the Macro Explorer tool window (see Figure 26-1). This window shares space with the Solution Explorer by default and can be accessed with the Tools⇨Macros⇨Macro Explorer menu command.

Each macros project loaded in Visual Studio 2005 is represented by a root node in the tree view, with the macros themselves divided into the modules that contain them. You can use the Macro Explorer to load or create additional macros projects by right-clicking the top level Macros node and choosing Load Macro Project or New Macro Project from the context menu.

Macro projects, modules, and individual macros can all be renamed by right-clicking their entry in the Macro Explorer and choosing Rename. Modules and macros can also be deleted from within this tool window, while macro projects can be unloaded with the same context menu.

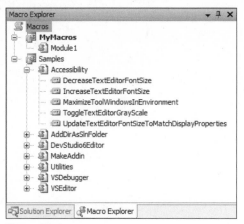

Figure 26-1

The Load Macro Project command displays the Add Macro Project dialog in which you can browse the file system for .vsmacros project files. Each one you load will be added to the top level of the tree view.

Figure 26-1 shows the MyMacros project in bold in the Macro Explorer. This is because it has been set as the Recording Project, which is where any temporary macros are placed when you record them. You'll learn how to record macros later in this chapter.

Running Macros

The most direct method to run a macro is to double-click its entry in the Macro Explorer. You can optionally right-click and select the Run menu command (see Figure 26-2), but given that macros are meant to make the developer's life easier, this method is rarely used.

Figure 26-2

As the macro is executed, the macro engine will display an icon depicting a cassette tape, and an accompanying tooltip in the system notification area of the Windows taskbar (shown in Figure 26-3).

This information is useful for longer running macros, and can be used to stop the execution of a macro that is behaving in an unexpected way (e.g., stuck in an endless loop). As the tooltip indicates, just double-click the icon to stop the macro's execution.

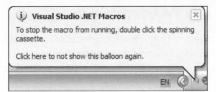

Figure 26-3

You can also run macros directly from the command window by entering in the macro name and pressing Enter. However, the easiest way to run macros that you use often is to assign them to keyboard shortcuts. Because Visual Studio uses proper reflection techniques, the Keyboard options page in the Environment section will include any macros that are currently loaded into the IDE (see Figure 26-4).

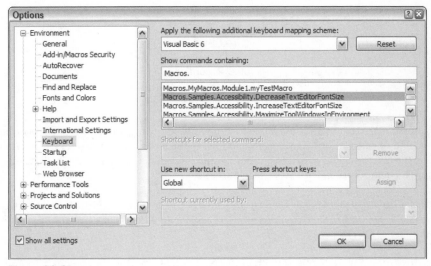

Figure 26-4

Note that the Show All Settings checkbox at the lower-left corner of the Options dialog is only visible for Visual Basic environment setups.

All macro commands consist of the prefix `Macros` followed by the project, module, and macro names, so to easily find them you can filter the list with the term `Macros`. Note that if you change a macro's name, then any keyboard shortcut you assign to it will remain; and if you delete the macro entirely, Visual Studio will clean up keyboard shortcut mappings for you.

Creating Macros

Macros can be created in two main ways: by recording a series of actions you perform to a temporary macro and then saving it to convert it to permanent status, or by creating a macro from scratch in the Visual Studio Macros IDE.

Recording Temporary Macros

Recording a macro is the quickest way to create a simple macro, but it cannot be used to create complex macros that use referenced namespaces and programming logic blocks to dictate what actions should be performed. Instead, recording simply records a series of commands as you perform them within the IDE, storing them in a straight sequential manner.

To begin recording a macro, use the Tools⇨Macros⇨Record Temporary Macro menu command or use the keyboard shortcut Ctrl+Shift+R. An extra toolbar will be displayed containing the three macro recording functions you have available (shown in Figure 26-5). This toolbar is only visible while you're recording the temporary macro; it will not appear in the regular toolbar.

Pause Recording

Cancel Recording

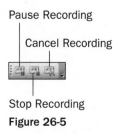

Stop Recording

Figure 26-5

The additional macro commands available to you while recording are to pause the recording, to stop the recording, and to cancel it or save the command list to the temporary macro function. When you stop the recording, the macro will be added to a module called `RecordingModule` in whichever macro project is set to store the temporary macro.

> To change the macro project to which temporary macros will be stored, right-click on the required macro project in the Solution Explorer and choose the Set as Recording Project menu command from the context menu.

Because a recorded macro is considered temporary, if you record a second macro before saving the first one, the first macro will be overwritten — only one temporary macro entry is possible at a time. Therefore, to save the sequence of commands you performed in a recording session, use the Tools⇨Macros⇨Save Temporary Macro menu command. Using this command will prompt you to set a new macro name.

Recording Issues

When recording a macro, the Visual Studio IDE keeps track of any text you change and any menu items or keyboard shortcuts that invoke standard Visual Studio commands. However, you can perform a number of actions within the IDE that are not included in the recording session. Two major features not included are any actions you perform with the mouse and any user interface changes you make.

These unrecorded user interface changes include adding or moving controls on a Windows form, setting properties on controls, navigating the contents of tool windows, and opening or closing windows. In addition, mouse input is generally not recorded unless it is used to activate different windows in the environment. In some systems (it depends on your mouse driver), you won't even be able to use your mouse to change the insert marker or select blocks of text.

If you perform any of these functions while recording, they simply will be ignored, and your resulting macro will only have the commands on either side of the omitted function, which could cause unexpected problems.

Remember that recording will save everything you do, including typing errors and cursor movements. Therefore, if you are creating a macro that is designed to work on a single code statement, make sure you position the cursor where you want the macro to start before recording, rather than position it after the recording has commenced.

With these issues in mind, using the Record Macro feature can give you a good head start in creating your macro; a combination of recording and manual editing of the macro code usually results in the most efficient way of creating what you need.

The Visual Studio Macros Editor

The other way to create a macro is to use the Visual Studio Macros editor directly, or to first create the macro stub in the Macro Explorer and then switch to the Visual Studio Macros editor to create the commands to perform. The advantage of using the Visual Studio Macros editor is that you have full control over the macro code, and can include functionality that cannot be recorded, such as conditional code and loops.

You can access the Visual Studio Macros IDE through the Tools⇨Macros submenu or by right-clicking the macro you want to edit in the Macro Explorer and selecting the Edit command. Either way, the Visual Studio Macros environment will be loaded and displayed with the current macro active (see Figure 26-6).

Although macros have their own standalone development environment, it shares many features with its bigger cousin, Visual Studio 2005. Many of the menus and toolbars are replicated, and the macro code is automatically outlined, formatted, and syntax colored in the same way as Visual Basic code is in the main IDE.

The Macros IDE also has a subset of the tool windows available in Visual Studio 2005, including a Project Explorer that loosely combines the Macro Explorer and Solution Explorer, along with Toolbox and Properties tool windows. Like the Visual Studio IDE, these windows can be docked, pinned, moved, and resized in whatever configuration you want. The IDE in Figure 26-6 shows the default configuration, with the Project Explorer docked to the left side of the main workspace area and the Toolbox and Properties windows pinned to the same side but hidden.

The Macros IDE also shares the IntelliSense engine, enabling you to find members of objects through the Member List as well as providing feedback about parameters in function calls. With the same features present in Visual Studio 2005, you can use the descriptions in the appropriate chapters to customize the appearance and performance of the Macros IDE with the Options pages, including project locations and text editor settings, as discussed in Chapter 2, as well as customize toolbars and menus, covered in Chapter 5.

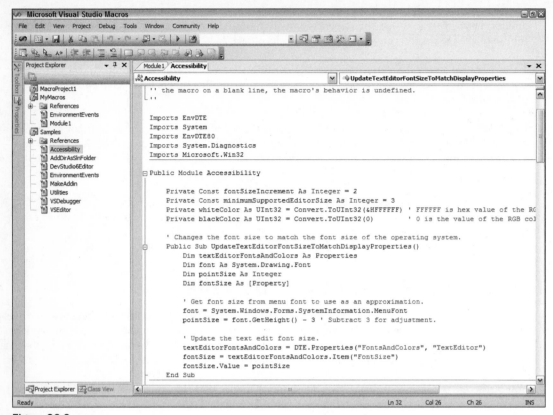

Figure 26-6

The Project Explorer gives you the same kind of options as the Solution Explorer, including the ability to create new items such as classes and modules. Macro projects have their own set of item templates that you can use to create new items. In a default installation, using the Add New Item command will give you access to new modules, classes, and blank code modules (see Figure 26-7).

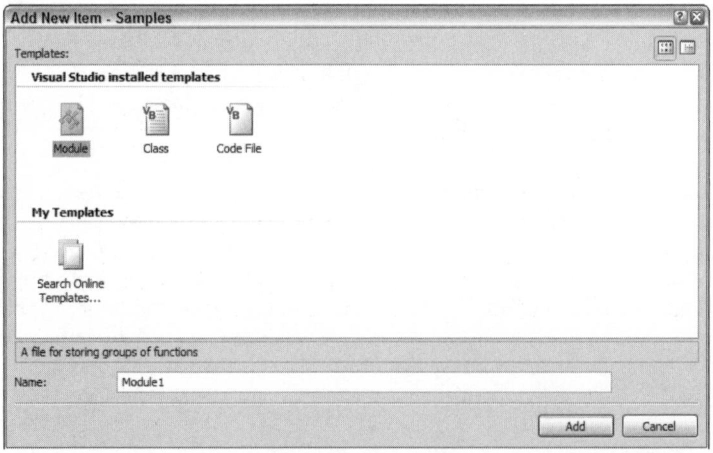

Figure 26-7

Generally, macros are stored in standard modules instead of class definitions because they are executed directly, so the main purpose for classes in your macro projects is when you require them internally.

The DTE Object

Every standard macro module includes several `Imports` statements to bring in line the namespaces normally used in macro code. Besides the familiar `System` and `System.Diagnostics` namespaces, the other two mandatory namespaces to be included are the `EnvDTE` and `EnvDTE80` namespaces shared by the Visual Studio add-in extensibility model discussed in Chapter 32.

Along with these namespaces are some implicitly defined objects that you can use to access the components of Visual Studio. Primary in this set is the `DTE` object, which represents the top-level object in the Visual Studio 2005 automation model. The `DTE` object actually implements the `EnvDTE80.DTE2` interface as well as the `EnvDTE` interface, and provides access to the following useful members in your code:

Member	Description
ActiveDocument	Returns the currently active document in the main workspace of Visual Studio 2005. You'll generally need this object to manipulate code directly.
ActiveWindow	Contains the currently active window, which is not necessarily the currently active document
CommandBars	Returns a collection of `CommandBar` objects equivalent to the `CommandBars` collection in Visual Studio 2005
CommandLineArguments	Contains a string with the command-line arguments of the current execution of the Visual Studio 2005 environment
DisplayMode	Returns the current display mode, which can be either MDI or Tabbed Documents. You can also use this member to change the display mode programmatically in the macro.
Documents	Returns a collection of all open documents in the IDE. Note that this isn't all documents in the currently loaded solution.
LocaleID	Allows you to interrogate the locale under which the IDE is running and adjust your code accordingly
MainWindow	Returns a `Window` object that represents the main IDE window
Mode	Determines whether the IDE is in design or debug mode
Properties	Contains all available properties in the Options dialog of Visual Studio 2005. It does this by storing the individual properties as items in a two-dimensional collection that is keyed by category and individual Options pages.
Solution	Contains the `Solution` object for the currently open solution and returns all associated projects in that solution

Table continued on following page

Member	Description
StatusBar	Provides access to the main status bar of the Visual Studio IDE, enabling you to provide information as your macro executes
ToolWindows	Enables you to quickly find the main tool windows. You can also use the more generic Windows collection to get to the tool windows by name. Tool windows accessible in this collection include Command, Error List, Solution Explorer, Task List, and Toolbox.
Windows	A complete collection of all windows that belong to the Visual Studio IDE. Each window is referenced through the Item property of the Windows collection, rather than being explicitly named as they are in the ToolWindows collection, but this means you can reference any window currently available in the IDE.

In addition to these members, several other members exposed by the interface can be quite useful in your macro code. The GetObject method enables you to late bind to any object that the extensibility model can interface with at runtime.

ExecuteCommand will run any Visual Studio 2005 command with the following syntax:

```
DTE.ExecuteCommand(commandName, commandArgs)
```

The commandName argument should be a string containing a single command that you could enter in the Command window — for example, File.NewFile or Tools.Options. commandArgs are used to pass over any parameters that the command might require.

The ItemOperations object provides shortcuts to common file-related actions such as NewFile or AddNewItem. The following two statements are equivalent:

```
DTE.ExecuteCommand("File.FileNew")
DTE.ItemOperations.NewFile
```

Typically, the members of the ItemOperations object accept parameters to customize their behavior. For example, to create a plain text file with the name myFile.txt, you could amend the previous statement as follows:

```
DTE.ItemOperations.NewFile("General\Text File", "myFile.txt")
```

Your macro code can also be used to intercept most of the Visual Studio IDE events as they occur. Every macro project includes an additional module named EnvironmentEvents. Within this module is a section that defines most of the event objects you can use in your macros, in the following form:

```
<System.ContextStaticAttribute()> _
Public WithEvents DTEEvents As EnvDTE.DTEEvents
```

If the event you want to trap is not included in the event objects automatically inserted — for example, if the event were in the CommandEvents object — you can add it using the same syntax as the existing events, remembering to prefix the event declaration with the System.ContextStaticAttribute attribute. You can also use this method to define the IDE event objects in other modules in your code.

Once the appropriate events object is added to the module, you can define event handler routines for the events in the same way as you would in a normal Visual Basic project. First, select the appropriate event object from the Class list, and then the event you want to handle from the Method Name list. The Macros IDE will automatically generate the event handler. For example, choosing first the `TaskListEvents` object from the Class list, and then the `TaskAdded` event from the Method Name list will generate the following code:

```
Private Sub TaskListEvents_TaskAdded(ByVal TaskItem As EnvDTE.TaskItem) _
    Handles TaskListEvents.TaskAdded

End Sub
```

Sample Macros

As mentioned previously, Visual Studio 2005 ships with a collection of sample macros. You can use these macros as a basis for your own functionality and to review common programming tasks. If you're serious about building macros, it's worth your while to take a look through the samples; there is a good chance that the very solution you're trying to implement is already present in one form or another.

The following sample macros come from the Accessibility group and are used in Chapter 40 in the discussion about how to tweak your environment through the use of keyboard shortcuts. Each of the macros discussed in that section uses the Visual Studio IDE's `Properties` object to customize the `FontSize` setting for the Text Editor (the main code editor). The easiest to follow is `IncreaseTextEditorFontSize()`:

```
' Increases the font size used within the editor.
Public Sub IncreaseTextEditorFontSize()
    Dim textEditorFontsAndColors As Properties

    textEditorFontsAndColors = DTE.Properties("FontsAndColors", "TextEditor")
    textEditorFontsAndColors.Item("FontSize").Value += fontSizeIncrement
End Sub
```

As mentioned in the previous discussion about the `DTE` object, the `Properties` collection provides direct access to every property setting available from the Options dialog of Visual Studio 2005. In this case, the code accesses the `TextEditor` settings found within the Fonts and Colors page in the Options dialog, increasing the `FontSize` setting by a preset constant (defined elsewhere in the macro code module).

The functionality of this macro could have easily been achieved with a single line instead of expanding it out into multiple statements, but this way you can more easily customize it with additional code if needed. If you do prefer brevity, the shortened version of the function looks like this:

```
Public Sub IncreaseTextEditorFontSize()
    DTE.Properties("FontsAndColors", "TextEditor").Item("FontSize").Value += _
        fontSizeIncrement
End Sub
```

The `DecreaseTextEditorFontSize` macro extends the functionality of the Increase macro by adding a condition to the logic. This is to avoid situations where the macro tries to set the font size too small. The full macro appears in the following listing:

```
' Decreases the font size used within the editor.
Public Sub DecreaseTextEditorFontSize()
```

```
        Dim textEditorFontsAndColors As Properties
        Dim fontSize As [Property]

        textEditorFontsAndColors = DTE.Properties("FontsAndColors", "TextEditor")
        fontSize = textEditorFontsAndColors.Item("FontSize")
        If fontSize.Value >= minimumSupportedEditorSize Then
            fontSize.Value -= fontSizeIncrement
        End If
    End Sub
```

This code also illustrates another way of referring to individual properties. By using the `Property` object, you can directly assign a reference to a property to your own variables and then change the variable instead of having to fully specify the property each time.

The third sample macro resets the font size to match the system font. In addition to setting the `FontSize` property value in a similar way to the previous two macros, the `UpdateTextEditorFontSizeTo MatchDisplayProperties` macro also demonstrates how you can use the normal .NET Framework objects to gain information about the system and user. In this case, the code retrieves the setting for the size of the menu font used by the system:

```
    ' Changes the font size to match the font size of the operating system.
    Public Sub UpdateTextEditorFontSizeToMatchDisplayProperties()
        Dim textEditorFontsAndColors As Properties
        Dim font As System.Drawing.Font
        Dim pointSize As Integer
        Dim fontSize As [Property]

        ' Get font size from menu font to use as an approximation.
        font = System.Windows.Forms.SystemInformation.MenuFont
        pointSize = font.GetHeight() - 3 ' Subtract 3 for adjustment.

        ' Update the text edit font size.
        textEditorFontsAndColors = DTE.Properties("FontsAndColors", "TextEditor")
        fontSize = textEditorFontsAndColors.Item("FontSize")
        fontSize.Value = pointSize
    End Sub
```

Building and Deploying

When you're ready to build your macro project, you can customize the way the build process will work by accessing the Build Property Pages (see Figure 26-8). To access the Build options, right-click the project you want to customize in the Project Explorer and choose Properties.

The Build options for macros are a simplified version of the Visual Basic 2005 settings, with Option Strict, Option Explicit, and Option Compare represented, as well as a simple customization of how warnings are dealt with during the compilation of the macro code. In addition, by default the macro project will have the Generate Debugging Information option enabled, which will allow you to debug any macros that have runtime errors.

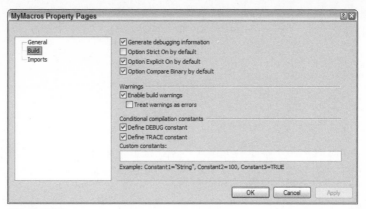

Figure 26-8

When debugging symbols are included, if the macro is executed in Visual Studio and an error occurs, then the code will switch over to the Macros IDE, where you can step through the code and examine the various objects using the fully featured debugging windows provided by Visual Studio 2005. Because macros are built on the Visual Basic engine, you can use the Edit-and-Continue feature of the language to quickly amend any problems encountered while you're debugging the macro.

Summary

The macros functionality in Visual Studio 2005 is a fully featured set of tools, including the capability to create temporary macros on-the-fly by recording keystrokes and certain actions in the IDE, as well as quickly load or remove entire macro projects that can contain dozens of macros grouped into logical categories. Supporting this, Visual Studio 2005 provides a number of interfaces to the macros feature, including a Macro Explorer window and a full Macros submenu accessible from the Tools menu.

The macros you create can be extensive, complete with program conditional and looping logic; have access to the majority of the IDE's objects; and have the capability to intercept the events raised from Visual Studio 2005. However, while this will deal with most repetitive tasks in the IDE, in some cases it won't suffice. Chapters 32 through 34 deal with extending Visual Studio 2005 further with third-party tools and add-ins that you can create yourself.

Connection Strings

A large proportion of applications need to persist data, and the obvious candidate for enterprise software is a relational database. The .NET Framework provides support for working with SQL Server, Oracle, ODBC, and OLE DB databases. To connect to any of these databases you need to specify a connection string that determines the location, the database, authentication information, and other connection parameters. This chapter explains how to create and store connection strings. In addition, you'll learn about encrypting and working with connection strings in code.

Data Source Configuration Wizard

Connection strings are similar to XML in that although they can be read, it is neither an enjoyable experience nor recommended to work with them directly. Because connection strings are strings, it is easy to introduce errors, misspell words, or even omit a parameter. Unlike XML, which can easily be validated against a schema, connection strings are harder to validate. The Data Source Configuration Wizard built into Visual Studio 2005 enables you to specify database connections without having to manually edit the connection string itself.

You can invoke the Data Source Configuration Wizard in a number of ways, as you will experience when you start working with any of the data controls in either the Windows form or web form designers. For the purposes of illustrating the wizard, follow these steps to add a new data source to an existing Windows Forms application. You'll connect to the sample AdventureWorks database, which you will need to download from the Microsoft web site (www.microsoft.com).

1. From the Data menu within Visual Studio 2005, select Add New Data Source, which opens the Data Source Configuration Wizard.

2. Selecting Database enables you to determine the database connection to use. If a connection already exists, you can select it from the drop-down and the associated connection string will appear in the lower portion of the window, as shown in Figure 27-1.

Figure 27-1

In this case, the connection string is stored in the application settings file (indicated by MySettings next to the connection name) and is used to connect to the AdventureWorks database on the sqlexpress database server on machine nickibm.

Later in this chapter you'll look at the properties of a SQL Server connection string in more detail.

3. Click the New Connection button to open the Add Connection dialog in which you can specify the properties of the connection string. Figure 27-2 shows the dialog as it would appear for a SQL Server database connection.

   Notice in Figure 27-2 that only the basic connection properties (such as server name, database name, and authentication information) are presented.

4. Click the Advanced button to open the Advanced Properties window, shown in Figure 27-3, where you can configure all properties for a SQL Server connection. At the bottom of this window is the connection string being constructed. The default values are omitted from the connection string. Once a value is set, it appears in the connection string and in bold in the Properties window.

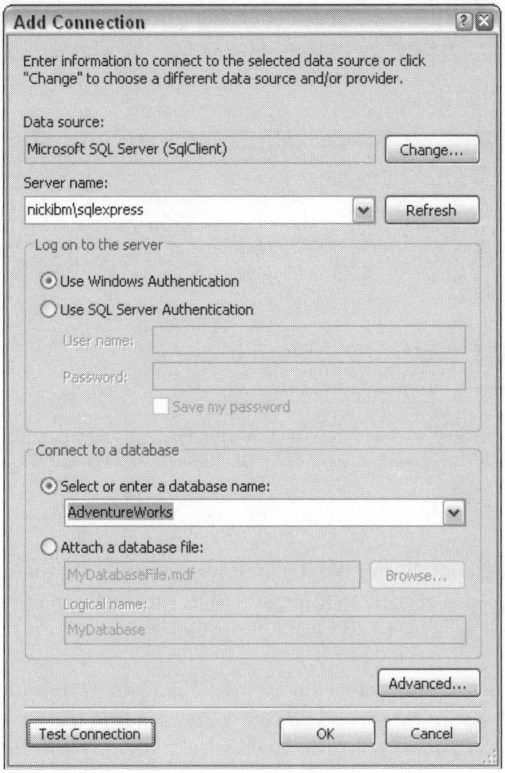

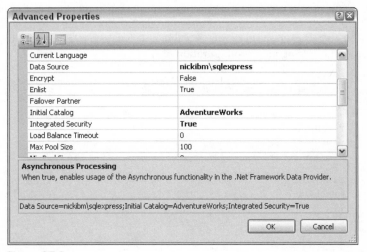

Figure 27-2

Figure 27-3

5. Click OK to return to the Add Connection window, where you can change the type of data source by clicking the Change button. This opens the Change Data Source dialog, shown in Figure 27-4.

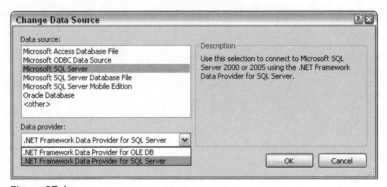

Figure 27-4

The list on the left contains all the data sources currently registered in the `machine.config` file. For a given data source, such as Microsoft SQL Server, there may be multiple data providers — in this case, the SQL Server and OLE DB providers.

Selecting an alternative data source-data provider combination will result in a different Add Connection dialog, displaying parameters that are relevant to that database connection. In most cases it is necessary to open the Advanced properties window to configure the connection itself.

6. After specifying the data source and connection settings using the Add Connection dialog, return to the Data Source Configuration Wizard. If you are creating a new connection, you will be given the option to save the connection string in the application configuration file, as shown in Figure 27-5. Unless you can guarantee that the location of the database, the authentication mode, or any other connection property will not change at a later stage, it is a good idea to store the connection string in the configuration file.

Figure 27-5

If you don't save the connection string to the configuration file, it is explicitly assigned to the connection object you are creating, which makes reuse difficult. Alternatively, saving the connection string in the configuration file means that other connection objects can access the same string. If the database connection changes at a later stage, you can easily update it in a single location.

When you save the connection string to the configuration file, it is added to the `connectionStrings` configuration section, as illustrated in the following snippet from an `app.config` file (the same section can exist in a `web.config` file for a web application):

```
<?xml version="1.0" encoding="utf-8" ?>
<configuration>
    <appSettings />
    <connectionStrings>
        <add name="AdventureWorksConnectionString"
            connectionString="Data Source=nickibm\sqlexpress;Initial
Catalog=AdventureWorks;Integrated Security=True"
            providerName="System.Data.SqlClient" />
    </connectionStrings>
</configuration>
```

The `connectionStrings` section of a configuration file uses the standard element collection pattern, which allows multiple connection strings to be specified and then referenced in code. For example, the preceding connection string can be accessed in code as follows:

```
Private Sub OpenConnectionClick(ByVal sender As System.Object, _
                                ByVal e As System.EventArgs) _
                                            Handles BtnOpenConnection.Click
    Dim sqlCon As New SqlClient.SqlConnection
    sqlCon.ConnectionString = ConfigurationManager.ConnectionStrings _
                            ("AdventureWorksConnectionString").ConnectionString
    sqlCon.Open()
End Sub
```

A nice artifact of working with the Data Source Connection Wizard is that it also adds strongly typed support for accessing the connection string from within your code. This means that you can access the connection string using the following strongly typed methods, rather than call them using a string constant:

C#
```
Properties.Settings.Default.AdventureWorksCS;
```

VB.NET
```
My.Settings.AdventureWorksConnectionString
```

The other advantage of saving the connection string in the configuration file is that when you are editing the project settings, the connection strings are listed alongside other settings for the project. Not only can you modify the connection string directly; you also have a shortcut to the Data Source Connection Wizard, which enables you to adjust the connection properties without fear of corrupting the connection string.

SQL Server Format

In order to concentrate on the connections themselves, the remainder of the Data Source Configuration Wizard is covered in a later chapter. Probably the most familiar data provider is the SQL Server database provider, so the following table details some of the common connection properties you may need to specify to connect to your database server:

Connection Property	Description
Asynchronous Processing	Determines whether the connection will support asynchronous database calls. Most applications try to deliver a responsive user interface, so it is important for it not to freeze when retrieving data. In the past this could only be achieved by doing the data processing in a separate thread from the user interface. The data access methods, such as `ExecuteNonQuery`, now support calls using the `Begin` and `End` asynchronous pattern. For example, `BeginExecuteNonQuery` will return immediately so the user interface does not block while the data access is performed.
AttachDBFilename	New to SQL Server 2005, you can work with databases that aren't permanently attached to a SQL Server instance. This property is a path reference to the primary database file that contains the database. Specifying `AttachDBFilename` effectively attaches and detaches the database when required.
Connect Timeout	Determines the maximum length of time that the `Open` method will block when attempting to connect to the database. This should not be confused with the `Timeout` property on the `SQLCommand` class, which determines the timeout for a given command to execute.
Data Source	The host name or IP address of the instance of SQL Server that the connection will be accessing. In cases where multiple instances exist on a given machine, or where SQL Server has been assigned an instance name other than the default instance, this needs to be specified as part of the Data Source field, e.g., `192.168.205.223\InstanceName`.
Initial Catalog	Specifies the name of the database to connect to.
Integrated Security	If `Integrated Security` is used, the Windows credentials of the current user will be used to connect to the database server. To provide user ID and password, this property must be set to `false`. Also be aware that when working with ASP.NET using Windows authentication without impersonation, if `Integrated Security` is enabled, then the authenticated web user's credentials will be used to access the database server.

Connection Property	Description
`MultipleActiveResultSets`	Allows multiple result sets to be returned across a given connection. For example, a single database command might contain two SELECT statements. If the `MultipleActiveResultSets` property is enabled, the results of both SELECT statements will be returned and can be used to populate a dataset. This property is only compatible with SQL Server 2005.
`Password`	Used for the SQL Server user account used to access the database server
`User ID`	Specifies the SQL Server account used to access the database server. Mixed-mode authentication for the SQL Server must be enabled, and the `Integrated Security` property must be set to `false`.

Each connection string property must be specified as it appears in the preceding table, but they can be in any order in the connection string. A semicolon is used to separate each property. An example connection string might be as follows:

```
Data Source=nickibm\sqlexpress;Initial Catalog=AdventureWorks;Integrated
Security=True;MultipleActiveResultSets=True
```

In-Code Construction

Although the Data Source Connection Wizard in Visual Studio 2005 provides a convenient tool for writing connection strings, it is often necessary to build one dynamically — a feat easily done with the `SqlConnectionStringBuilder` class. In fact, there are also string builder classes for Oracle, ODBC, and OLE DB, and they all derive from the generic `DBConnectionStringBuilder` class, which exposes the `ConnectionString` property.

This example demonstrates creating a connection builder object, based on an existing connection string, changing the authentication mode to use the user ID and password provided by the user before assigning the new connection string to the connection object. In addition, the example demonstrates the use of the `MultipleActiveResultSets` property to retrieve multiple tables from the database using a single command object:

```
Private Sub LoadDataClick(ByVal sender As System.Object, _
                          ByVal e As System.EventArgs) Handles Button1.Click
    'Update the connection string based on user settings
    Dim sqlbuilder As New SqlClient.SqlConnectionStringBuilder _
                          (My.Settings.AdventureWorksConnectionString)
    If Not Me.TxtUserId.Text = "" Then
        sqlbuilder.IntegratedSecurity = False
        sqlbuilder.UserID = Me.TxtUserId.Text
        sqlbuilder.Password = Me.TxtPassword.Text
    End If
```

```
        sqlbuilder.MultipleActiveResultSets = True

        'Create the connection based on the updated connection string
        Dim sqlCon As New SqlClient.SqlConnection
        sqlCon.ConnectionString = sqlbuilder.ConnectionString

        'Set the command and create the dataset to load the data into
        Dim sqlcmd As New SqlClient.SqlCommand("SELECT * FROM Person.Contact;" & _
                                        "select * from Person.ContactType", _
                                        sqlCon)

        Dim ds As New DataSet
        Dim rds As New SqlClient.SqlDataAdapter(sqlcmd)

        'Open connection, retrieve data, and close connection
        sqlCon.Open()
        rds.Fill(ds)
        sqlCon.Close()
    End Sub
```

The important thing to note about this code sample is that the `MultipleActiveResultSets` property is enabled, which means that multiple `Select` statements can be specified in the `SqlCommand` object. The `SqlCommand` object is then used by the `SqlDataAdapter` object to fill the `DataSet`. The `DataSet` object will contain two data tables, each populated by one of the `Select` statements.

Encrypting Connection Strings

Although best practices state that you should use windows authentication and integrated security wherever possible, this is not always the case; sometimes you have to resort to specifying a user ID and password in a connection string. It is recommended that this information not be hard-coded into your application, as it can easily be extracted from the assembly. As such, this information needs to be either specified by the users each time they use the system, or added to the connection string in the configuration file. The upshot of this is that you need a mechanism for encrypting configuration sections. This walkthrough shows you how to encrypt a section of a configuration file for a web application, StagingWebsite, which has a `web.config` file as follows:

```
<?xml version="1.0"?>
<configuration>
    <connectionStrings>
        <add name="AdventureWorksConnectionString" connectionString="Data
Source=.\sqlexpress;Initial Catalog=AdventureWorks;Integrated Security=True"
            providerName="System.Data.SqlClient" />
    </connectionStrings>
    <!--
        ...
    -->
</configuration>
```

Using the command prompt, execute the following commands in sequence, replacing *UserName* with the name of the account that the web application will run as (for example, the AspNet account):

1. `cd\WINDOWS\Microsoft.NET\Framework\v2.0.50727`

2. `aspnet_regiis -pa "NetFrameworkConfigurationKey" "UserName"`

3. `aspnet_regiis -pe "connectionStrings" -app "/StagingWebsite"`

Executing these commands modifies the web.config file as follows:

```xml
<?xml version="1.0"?>
<configuration>
 <connectionStrings configProtectionProvider="RsaProtectedConfigurationProvider">
  <EncryptedData Type="http://www.w3.org/2001/04/xmlenc#Element"
  xmlns="http://www.w3.org/2001/04/xmlenc#">
  <EncryptionMethod Algorithm="http://www.w3.org/2001/04/xmlenc#tripledes-cbc" />
  <KeyInfo xmlns="http://www.w3.org/2000/09/xmldsig#">
   <EncryptedKey xmlns="http://www.w3.org/2001/04/xmlenc#">
   <EncryptionMethod Algorithm="http://www.w3.org/2001/04/xmlenc#rsa-1_5" />
   <KeyInfo xmlns="http://www.w3.org/2000/09/xmldsig#">
    <KeyName>Rsa Key</KeyName>
   </KeyInfo>
   <CipherData>
<CipherValue>Y4Be/ND8fXTK13r0CASBK0oaOSvbyijYCVUudf1AuQlpU2HRsTyEpR2sVpxrOukiBhvcGy
Wlv4EM0AB9p3Ms8FgIA3Ou6mGORhxfO9eIUGD+M5tJSe6wn/9op8mFV4W7YQZ4WIqLaAAu7MKVI6KKK/ANI
KpV8l2NdMBT3uPOPi8=</CipherValue>
   </CipherData>
   </EncryptedKey>
  </KeyInfo>
  <CipherData>

<CipherValue>BeKnN/kQIMw9rFbck6IwX9NZA6WyOCSQlziWzCLA8Ff/JdA0W/dWIidnjae1vgpS8ghouY
n7BQocjvc0uGsGgXlPfvsLq18//1ArZDgiHVLAXjW6b+eKbE5vaf5ss6psJdCRRB0ab5xaoNAPHH/Db9UKM
ycWVqP0badN+qCQzYyU2cQFvK1S7Rum8VwgZ85Qt+FGExYpG06YqVR9tfWwqZmYwtW8izr7fijvspm/oRK4
Yd+DGBRKuXxD6EN4kFgJUil7ktzOJAwWly4bVpmwzwJT9N6yig54lobhOahZDP05gtkLor/HwD9IKmRvO1j
v</CipherValue>
   </CipherData>
  </EncryptedData>
 </connectionStrings>
   <!--
       ...
   -->
</configuration>
```

As you can see from this example, the connection string is no longer readable in the configuration file. The commands you executed did two things. Ignoring the first command (because it simply changes the directory so you can access the asp_regiis executable), the second command permits access to the key container NetFrameworkConfigurationKey for the user Nick. This key container is the default container for the RSAProtectedConfigurationProvider, which is specified in the machine.config file. In order for your application to be able to decrypt data from the configuration file, the user that the application is running as must be able to access the key container. To determine the identity of this user, execute the following command:

```
System.Security.Principal.WindowsIdentity.GetCurrent().Name
```

The third command encrypts the connectionStrings section of the configuration file for the web application StagingWebsite. Other sections of the configuration file can also be encrypted using the same command. If at some later stage you need to decrypt the configuration section, execute the same command, but with –pd instead of –pe. For example:

```
aspnet_regiis -pd "connectionStrings" -app "/StagingWebsite"
```

Summary

This chapter showed you how to use Visual Studio 2005 to take charge of your application and configure it to connect to a database using a connection string. With the built-in support of the data classes in the .NET Framework, connection strings can be dynamically created and modified so you never have to handcraft a connection string again.

Upcoming chapters continue the data access story, as you learn how to work with strongly typed datasets and a raft of new data controls.

28

Assembly Signing

When you create your .NET projects, they compile down to an assembly. By default, this assembly is open and doesn't have any security on it to ensure that your users are consuming the correct version of the binary file. However, signing your assembly can rectify that issue by providing a strong name to the compiled application or component, which can then uniquely identify it to other applications and even system administrators who can apply a security policy against it.

Before you take a look at how to sign your solution's output, you need to understand a couple of concepts — namely, strong-named assemblies and the Global Assembly Cache.

Strong-Named Assemblies

A strong name consists of the parts that uniquely identify an assembly's identity. This includes the plain-text name and a version number. Added to these elements are a public key and a digital signature. These are generated with a corresponding private key. Because of this private/public key system coupled with a digital signature, strong names can be relied on to be completely unique.

Using a strong name can also ensure that the version of your assembly is the one that has been shipped. No modification can be made to it without affecting its signature and thus breaking its compatibility with the generated strong name.

As mentioned previously, using strong names also gives administrators the ability to explicitly set security policy against your solutions by referring to their unique names. This can give a corporation confidence that once deployed, the software will run as expected because it cannot be tampered with without affecting the signing of the strong name.

Once you start using strong-named assemblies in your solution, you will have to use strong-named files right down the chain of references because allowing an unsigned assembly as part of the chain would break the very security that strong-naming your assembly was intended to implement.

The Global Assembly Cache

If you've been programming with .NET for a while, you're already familiar with the Global Assembly Cache, but if you're new to the world of .NET this might be a new concept. Every computer that has the .NET Framework installed has a systemwide cache that stores all assemblies that are to be shared by multiple applications.

In this cache (usually stored in a folder within the Windows directory) you'll find the common language runtime components as well as other globally registered binary files that you, and anyone else, can consume. If an assembly is only going to be used by a single application, then it should be deployed in that application's folder.

However, if you are going to share the assembly between applications and want to store it in this Global Assembly Cache (known as the GAC), then your assembly must be strong-named. You don't have a choice in the matter, because the cache interrogates all files to ensure that their integrity is valid; hence, it needs the strong-name versioning to compare against.

Signing an Assembly in VS 2005

Previously, signing an assembly in Visual Studio required the generation of a strong-name key (.snk) file via an external utility and then editing the assembly attributes of your application's configuration file. Thankfully, Visual Studio 2005 changes all that for managed code projects by introducing an additional page in the Project Designer specifically for signing the output of your project.

The Signing tab (see Figure 28-1) enables you to sign the assembly in the lower half of the page. You first should select the Sign the Assembly checkbox to indicate that you will be generating a strong name. You will then need to select the strong name key file to use when signing the assembly.

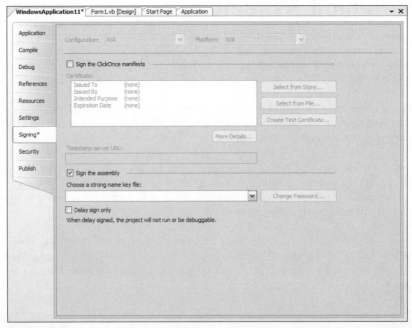

Figure 28-1

Sometimes you won't have access to the private key to successfully sign the assembly. When you're in this situation, you can still dictate that the application will ultimately be digitally signed, but also select the Delay Sign Only option as well.

While you are deferring the signing process, you won't be able to debug or even run the application, but you can at least build it to be ready for the signing phase.

Existing key files in either the older .snk paired key file format or the new .pfx format can be used. From the drop-down list, select the Browse option to locate the file in your file system and click OK in the dialog to save the key file to the Signing page settings.

Alternatively, you can create a new strong-named key by selecting the New option from the drop-down list. When you choose New, you will be able to create a new .pfx formatted strong-named file. Figure 28-2 shows the Create Strong Name Key dialog. You can simply choose a filename to use for the key or additionally protect the key file with a password.

Figure 28-2

Either way, once you've created and selected the .pfx file, it will be added to your project in the Solution Explorer, enabling you to easily include it for deployment projects.

Summary

Strong-naming your application and thus safeguarding it from improper use is now straightforward to implement, and can be done completely from within the Visual Studio 2005 IDE. The Signing page gives you the ability to both create and set the key file without having to edit the application's assembly attributes directly.

Preemptive Error Correction

It's obviously a good idea to deal with errors as soon as they pop up in your program code. Unfortunately, some issues don't show up at design time in an obvious way that you can deal with because they're marked as only warnings, while other issues aren't even marked up as such by default. In this chapter, you'll learn how to customize your compilation experience so you can deal with issues before getting too far into the development cycle. You'll also learn how Visual Studio 2005 tries to help you when you encounter certain types of errors by prompting you with suggested solutions.

Smart Compile Auto Correction

Chapter 18 briefly touched on a feature of Visual Studio 2005 that offered error correction via smart tags. The full name for this feature is *Smart Compile Auto Correction*, and it is available to both Visual Basic and C# developers as they write the program code for an application.

As you write your code, Visual Studio 2005 continuously performs a background compilation of the program logic to look for errors. As errors occur, the IntelliSense engine marks up the code with different types of messages and errors so you're made aware of them.

Some detected errors have a set of easily implemented solutions. With these errors, the Visual Studio IDE determines the possible answers for the given issue that could be added to the program code and presents you with a list from which to choose.

It does this with the Smart Compile Auto Correction feature of IntelliSense, adding an extra visual indicator to the end of the compilation error in question. This small glyph — by default, a small yellow and maroon line drawn underneath the last character of the statement in error — can be used to access the Error Correction Options smart tag dialog.

Hovering your mouse pointer over this indicator displays the smart tag button. When clicked, the Error Correction Options dialog will appear, enabling you to select the desired solution. Figure 29-1 shows a typical error that falls into the category of easily correctable.

Figure 29-1

In this case, an object was defined of a type that doesn't exist or is not immediately known to the program in its current context. Visual Studio 2005 first background-compiles the statement and determines that it is in error. Using its normal behavior, it first provides feedback by marking up the section of the statement in error with the wavy underline (blue by default).

Visual Studio 2005 then checks to see whether the error is in its list of easily rectified issues. When it finds that undefined object types often have easy fixes, it paints the additional glyph at the end of the statement (which is hidden in Figure 29-1 by the smart tag button).

Typically, placing your mouse pointer over a statement that has been marked as an error results in a tooltip displaying a summary of the problem. In this example, the tooltip indicates that the `Type 'XmlDocument' is not defined` and must be of a known type. Errors that fall under the purview of the Smart Compile Auto Correction feature display an additional button to access the smart tag.

In Visual Basic, this button consists of an icon with an exclamation mark and a down arrow. In addition, as you can see in Figure 29-1, it displays a tooltip containing the Error Correction Options text and the assigned keyboard shortcut for the feature.

Opening the smart tag dialog displays the error message along with suggestions for how to fix it. Figure 29-2 shows the result of opening the smart tag dialog for the undefined `XmlDocument` object type. The dialog repeats the error text and offers four possible solutions to the error.

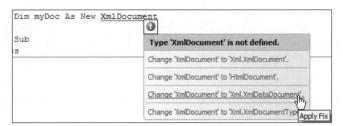

Figure 29-2

As you can see in this example, Visual Studio tries to guess what you meant when you wrote the code, so it not only provides a fully specified `Xml.XmlDocument` object definition, but also the `HtmlDocument` object type that doesn't need to be qualified.

To implement a particular solution, click its corresponding link in the list. Doing so applies the fix to the code (as the tooltip will inform you), performing whatever actions are necessary to correct it.

In some cases, the suggested fix might need further explanation than a simple one-line description. In these situations, the smart tag dialog extends to include a preview pane for each possible solution it has found. These preview panes can be expanded and collapsed as needed, with an option at the bottom of the dialog window to Expand All Previews simultaneously (see Figure 29-3).

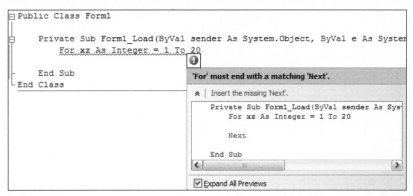

Figure 29-3

Figure 29-3 shows a compilation error and a pre-defined solution available for it. Because the `For` loop requires a matching `Next` statement to close the block of code that will be looped, IntelliSense marks it up as a compilation error. However, the problem has a straightforward solution — to insert the corresponding `Next` statement, so the Smart Compile Auto Correction feature displays the smart tag dialog.

In this case, the solution is displayed with a preview of what will happen if you select the particular option, enabling you to confirm what actions will be taken before they occur, and implement your own solution if the suggestion is incorrect.

C# developers will have a slightly different experience with the Smart Compile Auto Correction feature because of the way errors are displayed when working in the code. Because errors are not normally marked up through the background compilation process, C# programmers may not even realize that they have coded an error in the program logic.

Despite this, Visual Studio 2005 still identifies certain easily correctable errors and marks them up with the error correction smart tag visual indicator. Placing your mouse pointer over this indicator displays the C# version of the smart tag button, as shown in Figure 29-4.

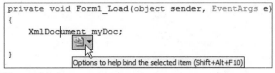

Figure 29-4

In this case, the tooltip that accompanies the smart tag is modified to include more meaningful information about what actions can be performed. As this sample implies, the suggested solutions are not necessarily marked as error corrections, but instead are portrayed as helper functions.

What's interesting is that the two languages have different sets of problem statements that can be rectified, and even different lists of corrections that can be implemented to fix an issue. The example shown in Figure 29-4 is the C# equivalent of the Visual Basic example shown earlier, with a variable defined as the `XmlDocument` object type without fully qualifying it in the code. However, in the case of C# code, only two suggestions are made, as displayed in Figure 29-5.

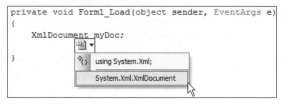

```
private void Form1_Load(object sender, EventArgs e)
{
    XmlDocument myDoc;

}
            using System.Xml;

            System.Xml.XmlDocument
```

Figure 29-5

These suggestions accurately reflect the typical responses that a C# developer might take, and assume that the programmer knew what object was wanted. Note that the first suggestion is to add a `using` statement at the top of the program logic. Because the solution involves inserting code in another part of the program, an additional icon is displayed next to the link.

Customizing Warnings in Visual Basic

Although Smart Compile Auto Correction is an incredibly useful feature of Visual Studio 2005 that bolsters the value of using the IDE in addition to the valuable information provided by other aspects of IntelliSense, you may not be aware that some warnings are more important than others. In fact, some commonly encountered situations in code are overlooked by default, leaving you without a clue as to why your program might be failing.

It all comes down to the warning levels of your program, and what situations are considered warnings or errors. To customize the way warnings are dealt with in a specific project, open the My Project page for the project. You can do this by either right-clicking the project's entry in the Solution Explorer and choosing the Properties command, double-clicking the My Project entry in the Solution Explorer, or executing the Project⇨*Project Name* Properties menu command.

The warning settings are all accessible from the Compile page of My Project, as shown in Figure 29-6.

The first settings to look at are the compile options. By default, Option Explicit is turned on, requiring you to explicitly define any variables that you use in your program code. However, Option Strict is turned off. Option Strict forces you to properly convert variables of one type to another, rather than let the compilation engine implicitly convert them for you.

Because this can cause a large number of errors you may not want to deal with (it will even report the conversion of an `Integer` to a `String` as an error), the option is turned off by default. For commercial applications, it's worth turning the option on and reviewing the errors that are generated with the setting enabled.

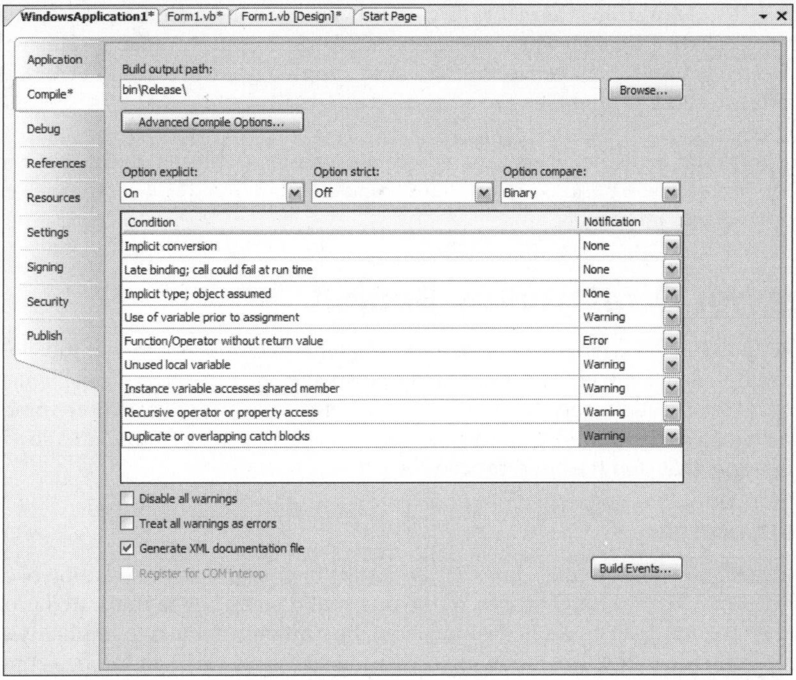

Figure 29-6

When using Option Strict, the Smart Compile Auto Correction feature is activated for any implicit conversions you might have in your code, giving you quick access to the correct conversion statement required for the situation. For example, the following code would be fine with Option Strict off, but will generate a compilation error for each line when Option Strict is active:

```
Dim myDocObject As Object = New Xml.XmlDocument
Dim myDoc As Xml.XmlDocument
myDoc = myDocObject

Dim myString As String
Dim myInteger As Integer = 3
myString = myInteger
```

Using the Smart Compile Auto Correction feature, with a couple of mouse clicks this code is converted to properly coded type conversions. The assignment statements for the myDoc and myString variables are flagged as errors that have possible solutions. Using the Smart Compile Auto Correction links that are added to these errors, you can select from the suggestions, which results in the following code block:

```
Dim myDocObject As Object = New Xml.XmlDocument
Dim myDoc As Xml.XmlDocument
myDoc = CType(myDocObject, Xml.XmlDocument)

Dim myString As String
Dim myInteger As Integer = 3
myString = CStr(myInteger)
```

375

If you want to treat all warnings as errors so you can be sure of the cleanest compilation of your solution, you can check the "Treat all warnings as errors" checkbox (off by default). This will consider all warnings except for implicit conversions of `Integer` types to `String` types as errors, and will not allow the compilation to succeed until they are addressed as errors.

If, however, you want to do the reverse and ignore the warnings, you can do this by checking the Disable All Warnings option. These options are mutually exclusive; and if you have both checked, the Disable All Warnings option takes precedence.

Warnings Not Displayed by Default

A number of individual warnings can have their behavior set independently of the global option for treating warnings. Some of these warnings are not displayed by default, but can be the source of issues in your program's execution. You should review each of these warnings and determine whether they should be activated as either warnings (displaying a warning at compilation but allowing the build to continue) or errors that stop the build process, or left deactivated.

Implicit conversion

Implicit conversion issues can cause unexpected results in your program execution because the different variable objects may be of different types, or the information may not be translated properly across types. When you don't code an explicit conversion, the runtime attempts to implicitly convert the source object to the destination type. The following code shows an example of an implicit conversion:

```
Dim myDocObject As Object = New Xml.XmlDocument
Dim myDoc As Xml.XmlDocument
myDoc = myDocObject
```

By default, this option is turned off and any implicit conversions are ignored in the compilation of your program. Turning this option on to `Warning` will mark any type conversions as warnings so you are informed about them. If you don't want the program to build with implicit conversions present in your code, set the option to Error.

To avoid warnings or errors when this condition is activated, always explicitly convert your object types. The preceding sample code could be amended to explicitly convert the `Object` to an `XmlDocument` type like so:

```
Dim myDocObject As Object = New Xml.XmlDocument
Dim myDoc As Xml.XmlDocument
myDoc = CType(myDocObject, Xml.XmlDocument)
```

This condition is slightly different from Option Strict, as it ignores the implicit conversion of numeric types such as an `Integer` to a `String`, so it may be a better option for your environment than activating Option Strict.

Late binding; call could fail at run time

Some applications require late binding of objects, but the actual process of late binding has risks because at runtime the application may fail when it tries to instantiate the late-bound object. The usual reason for late-binding failures is that the object type doesn't exist on the system or is not registered correctly. To avoid these issues, make sure you always write code to handle the unexpected situation.

By default, this condition is turned off, meaning you won't be informed of any late binding in your code, but you may want to set it to `Warning` level so you will always be aware of any late binding in your application code.

Implicit type; object assumed

An old programming practice was to simply define objects without identifying their type. In Visual Basic 6 this would result in variables of the `Variant` type, but in Visual Basic 2005 the result is a generic `Object` type. Object variables can contain almost any other type of object but they do not provide you with the safe compilation option of ensuring that you only use valid members of the object.

In Visual Basic 2005, this kind of definition is accepted by default, but it can be changed through the `Implicit type; object assumed` condition. It is good programming practice to explicitly define your variables to be a specific type, so you may want to set this option to either `Warning` or `Error`. The following definition would generate an `Error` or a `Warning` if you activate this condition:

```
Dim myObject
```

Other Customizable Warnings

In addition to the previous list of warnings that are not processed by default, a number of other warnings in the Conditions list are set to a warning level by default. Changing their individual settings enables you to mark them as compilation errors, or to be reduced to informational conditions that do not display in the compilation output or Error List.

Use of variable prior to assignment

Most commonly, you'll see this condition displayed when you define an object or `String` and then assign it to another variable without first initializing it to a value. The following code demonstrates when this warning will be displayed:

```
Dim myString As String
Dim myString2 As String
myString2 = myString
```

Because the code tries to assign the value of `myString` to the `myString2` variable, without `myString` being set to a value first, a warning is displayed.

If you want to ensure that your objects are always initialized with a proper value before assigning them, set this condition to `Error`.

Function/Operator without return value

The old way of writing functions in Visual Basic was to set an implicitly defined variable of the same name as the function to whatever value you needed to return. Once the value was set, the function would continue until it reached the end of the function definition or it encountered an `Exit Function` statement.

It was possible to perform code in the function without explicitly setting this return value, which would result in a default value being returned. The following function definition illustrates how a simple function might look in Visual Basic 6:

```
Public Function myTest(theVariable As Integer) As Boolean
    If theVariable > 10 Then myTest = True
End Function
```

With Visual Basic 2005, values are returned to the calling code by using the `Return` statement. As soon as the processing of the function encounters a `Return` statement, it returns to the calling code with the value specified, and ignores the remainder of the function. While the situation can occur where the return value is not set, Visual Basic 2005 regards this as poor programming form that can result in unexpected results (which was not the case in Visual Basic 6).

To ensure that you're aware of any functions that do not return values on all logic paths, this condition is set to `Warning` by default. However, if you feel that you should explicitly set a return value under all circumstances, you can set this to `Error` and stop the solution from building if the return value isn't set. The following function illustrates how the Visual Basic 6 definition would be converted to Visual Basic 2005:

```
Public Function myTest(theVariable As Integer) As Boolean
    If theVariable > 10 Then Return True
End Function
```

To stop this condition from being processed, you would need to add an additional `Return` statement in the event that `theVariable` was 10 or less, as the following listing demonstrates:

```
Public Function myTest(theVariable As Integer) As Boolean
    If theVariable > 10 Then Return True
    Return False
End Function
```

Unused local variable

The `Unused local variable` condition is self-explanatory. Whenever the compiler identifies a variable that has been defined but not used in the associated code block, it will generate a warning by default. This is a very handy feature for reviewing large programs for variables that are not used.

To quickly locate and remove all unused variables from your code, set this condition to `Error` and step through the compilation errors on the Error List.

Instance variable accesses shared member

You may get unexpected results when performing a shared method in a class definition from an instance. For example, you might have a class `theClass` with a shared function of `myFunc`. When you create an instance of `theClass`, it appears that you can call the `myFunc` from the instance, as the following code demonstrates:

```
Public Class theClass
    Shared Function myFunc() As Boolean
        ' some code
    End Function
End Class

...elsewhere in the code

Dim xx As New theClass
xx.myFunc()
```

However, this practice obscures the functionality of shared members, which provide a single access for all instances of the method or property. Better programming practice is to use the class definition to call upon shared members, which means that instead of using the `xx.myFunc()` statement, you would program `theClass.myFunc()` in its place.

To ensure that you always review these kinds of situations, the `Instance variable accesses shared member` condition is set to `Warning`, but you can either turn it off, if your in-house programming style requires that you always call shared members through an instance, or set it to the `Error` level so the solution won't be built when such instances are encountered in the code.

When this condition is set to `Error` or `Warning`, the Smart Compile Auto Correction feature will display a suggested solution that involves converting the access to the class instead of an instance.

Recursive operator or property access

The `Recursive operator or property access` condition is set to `Warning` by default, and flags any instances where your code refers to the function or property that contains the code itself. The following code demonstrates this problem by defining a `Property` called `myProp`, and then attempting to set and return `myProp` in the `Get` and `Set` accessors of the property definition:

```
Public Property myProp() As String
    Get
        Return myProp
    End Get
    Set(ByVal value As String)
        myProp = value
    End Set
End Property
```

You will most likely want to set this to an `Error` level so you can fix the code — recursively calling a property in this way is never going to work.

Setting this property to `Warning` or `Error` won't flag recursive functions — which is a good thing because a lot of programming techniques use them!

Duplicate or overlapping catch blocks

The `Duplicate or overlapping catch blocks` condition deals with situations in which multiple `Catch` blocks consume the same errors, resulting in one `Catch` block never being reached. The following code snippet shows an instance of where this might occur — the generic `Exception` `Catch` block appears before the more specific `ApplicationException` block:

```
Try
    ...some code...
Catch ex As Exception
    MessageBox.Show(ex.Message)
Catch exApp As ApplicationException
    MessageBox.Show(exApp.Message)
End Try
```

By default, this condition is set to `Warning`, but you will most likely want to set it to `Error` to ensure that you're always aware of exception `Catch` blocks that cannot be processed.

Customizing Warnings in C#

C# developers also have a way of customizing how warnings are treated in their code. As in the case of Visual Basic projects, a simple toggle option is available to treat all, some, or no warnings as errors (see Figure 29-7). The default option is to assume that all warnings are just that — warnings — allowing the compilation to complete.

However, if you want to stop the solution from being built in the event of a warning, you can change this option to either `All` or `Specific` warnings. If you are only concerned about specific warnings, you should provide a list of warning numbers separated by commas or semicolons.

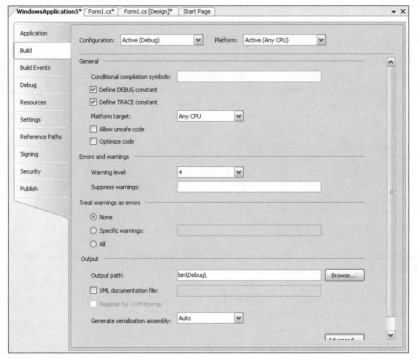

Figure 29-7

You can suppress individual warnings completely by entering them in the Suppress Warnings text box. Again, you should separate the warning numbers with commas or semicolons. Any warnings entered in this area will not be displayed regardless of what other options you set.

The final way of customizing your compilation output for warnings is to set the warning level. By default this option is set to 4, which will result in all errors, warnings, and even informational messages being displayed in the output of the build process. You can fine-tune the amount of information generated in the compilation by changing this setting to a value of 0 through to 3. A value of 0 will suppress all warnings and informational messages completely, resulting in only compilation errors being displayed, while a value of 3 will display all errors and warnings but not purely informational messages.

Using a combination of these settings, you can achieve a "perfect" compilation for your particular requirements. The idea is to set any warnings that must be dealt with as errors in the Specific Warnings option, and then suppress the less important messages and warnings. The result, once you've dealt with the required errors and warnings, will be a build process with a clean output.

Summary

This chapter described the additional features Visual Studio 2005 provides to help you preempt problems in your programs. Using the Smart Compile Auto Correction feature in conjunction with customizing which warnings are displayed and how they are treated, you can build an environment that highlights the issues that are most important to you, while suppressing issues that you do not need to worry about for the particular application.

30

Strongly Typed DataSets

A large proportion of applications use some form of data storage. This might be in the form of serialized objects or XML data, but for long-term storage that supports concurrent access by a large number of users, most applications use a database. The .NET Framework includes strong support for working with databases and other data sources. This chapter examines how to use strongly typed DataSets to build applications that work with data from a database.

This examples in this chapter are based on the sample AdventureWorks database that is available as a download from www.microsoft.com.

DataSet Overview

The .NET Framework *DataSet* is a complex object that is approximately equivalent to an in-memory representation of a database. It contains *DataTables* that correlate to database tables. These in turn contain a series of *Columns* that define the composition of each *DataRow*. The DataRow correlates to a row in a database table. Of course, it is possible to establish relationships between DataTables within the DataSet in the same way that a database has relationships between tables.

One of the ongoing challenges for the object-oriented programming paradigm is that it does not align smoothly with the relational database model. The DataSet object goes a long way toward bridging this gap, as it can be used to represent and work with relational data in an object-oriented fashion. However, the biggest issue with a raw DataSet is that it is weakly typed. Although the type of each column can be queried prior to accessing data elements, this adds overhead and can make code very unreadable. Strongly typed DataSets combine the advantages of a DataSet with strong typing to ensure that data is accessed correctly at design time. This is done with the custom tool MSDataSetGenerator, which converts an XML schema into a strongly typed DataSet. In the following code snippet, you can see the difference between using a raw DataSet, in the first half of the snippet, and a strongly typed DataSet, in the second half:

```
'Raw DataSet
Dim nontypedAwds As DataSet = RetrieveData()
Dim nontypedcontacts As DataTable = nontypedAwds.Tables("Contact")
Dim nontypedfirstContact As DataRow = nontypedcontacts.Rows(0)
MsgBox(nontypedfirstContact.Item("FirstName"))

'Strongly typed DataSet
Dim awds As AdventureWorksDataSet = RetrieveData()
Dim contacts As AdventureWorksDataSet.ContactDataTable = awds.Contact
Dim firstContact As AdventureWorksDataSet.ContactRow = contacts.Rows(0)
MsgBox(firstContact.FirstName)
```

Using the raw DataSet, both the table lookup and the column name lookup are done using string literals. As you are likely aware, string literals can be a source of much frustration and should only be used within generated code, although preferably not at all.

Adding a Data Source

You can manually create a strongly typed DataSet by creating an XSD using the XML schema editor. To create the DataSet you set the custom tool value for the XSD file to be the MSDataSetGenerator. This will create the designer code file that is needed for strongly typed access to the DataSet. In most cases, the source of your data will be a database, in which case Visual Studio 2005 provides a wizard that you can use to generate the necessary schema based on the structure of your database.

To create a strongly typed DataSet from an existing database, start by selecting Add New Data Source from the Data menu, and following these steps:

Although this functionality is not available for ASP.NET projects, a workaround is to perform all data access via a class library.

1. The first step in the Data Source Configuration Wizard is to select the type of data source to work with, as shown in Figure 30-1. In this case, you want to work with data from a database, so select the Database icon and click Next.

2. The next screen prompts you to select the database connection to use. To create a new connection, click the New Connection button, which opens the Add Connection dialog. The attributes displayed in this dialog are dependent on the type of database you are connecting to. By default the SQL Server provider is selected, as illustrated in Figure 30-2.

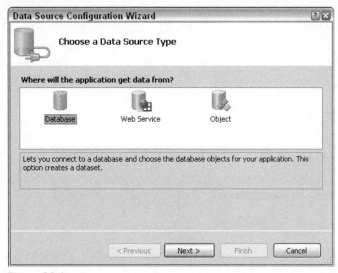

Figure 30-1

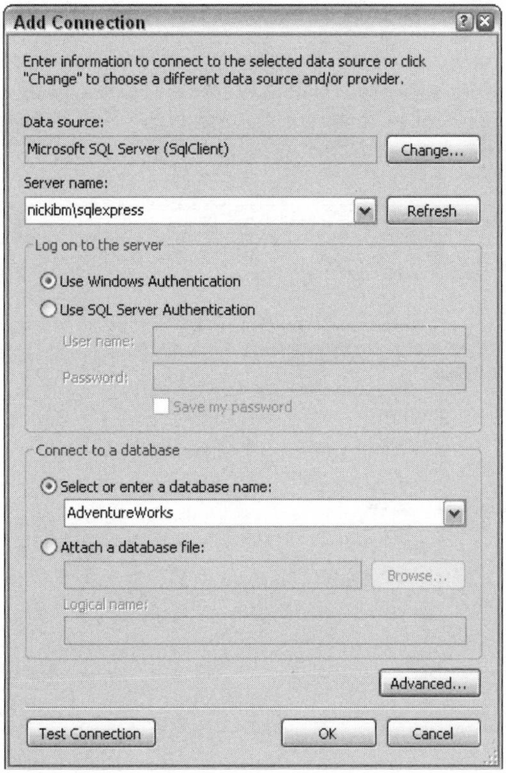

Figure 30-2

3. After you specify a connection, it will be saved as an application setting in the application configuration file.

   When the application is later deployed, the connection string can be modified to point to the production database. This process can often take longer than expected to ensure that various security permissions line up. Because the connection string is stored in the configuration file as a string without any schema, it is quite easy to make a mistake when making changes to it.

   A little-known utility within Windows can be used to create connection strings, even if Visual Studio is not installed. Known as the Data Link Properties dialog, you can use it to edit Universal Data Link files, files that end in .udl. When you need to create or test a connection string, you can simply create a new text document, rename it to something.udl *and then double-click it. This opens the Data Link Properties dialog, which enables you to create and test connection strings for a variety of providers. Once you have selected the appropriate connection, this information will be written to the UDL file as a connection string, which can be retrieved by opening the same file in Notepad. This can be particularly useful if you need to test security permissions and resolve other data connectivity issues.*

4. After specifying the connection, the next stage is to specify the data to be extracted. At this stage you will be presented with a list of tables, views, stored procedures, and functions from which you can select what to include in the DataSet. Figure 30-3 shows the final stage of the Data Source Configuration Wizard with a selection of columns from the Contact table in the AdventureWorks database.

   You will probably want to constrain the DataSet so it doesn't return all the records for a particular table. You can do this after creating the DataSet, so for the time being simply select the information you want to return. The editor's design makes it is easier to select more information here and then delete it from the designer, rather than create it afterwards.

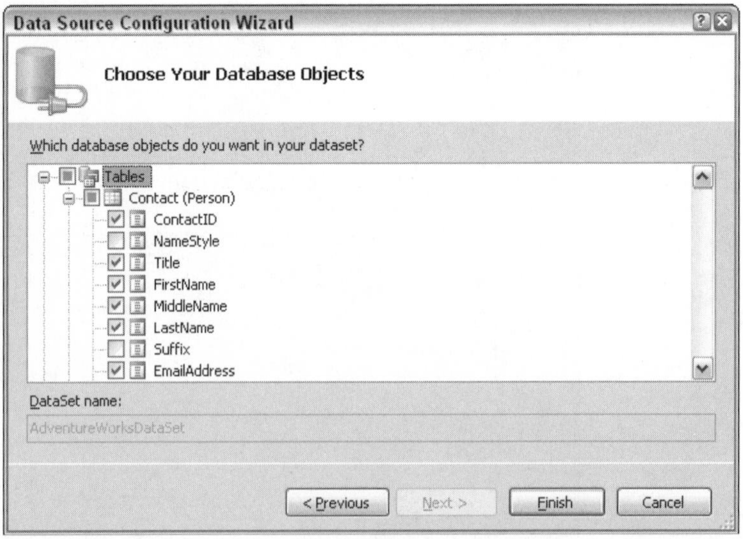

Figure 30-3

5.   Click Finish to add the new DataSet to the Data Sources window, shown in Figure 30-4, where you can view all the information to be retrieved for the DataSet. Each column is identified with an icon that reflects the type of data. For example, the Contact ID and EmailPromotion fields are numeric, whereas the Name fields are clearly text.

Figure 30-4

DataSet Designer

The Data Source Configuration Wizard uses the database schema to guess the appropriate .NET type to use for the DataTable columns. In cases where the wizard gets information wrong, it can be useful to edit the DataSet without the wizard. To edit without the wizard, right-click the DataSet in the Data Sources window and select Edit DataSet with Designer from the context menu. Alternatively, you can open the Data Sources window by double-clicking on the XSD file in the Solution Explorer window. This will open the DataSet editor in the main window, as shown in the example in Figure 30-5.

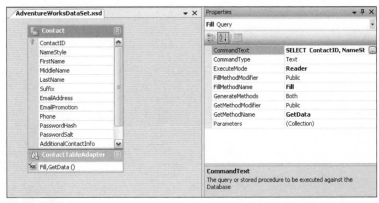

Figure 30-5

Here you start to see some of the power of using strongly typed DataSets. Not only has a strongly typed table (Contact) been added to the DataSet, you also have a ContactTableAdapter. This TableAdapter is used for selecting from and updating the database for the DataTable to which it is attached. If you have multiple tables included in the DataSet, you will have a TableAdapter for each. Although a single TableAdapter can easily handle returning information from multiple tables in the database, it becomes difficult to update, insert, and delete records.

As you can see in Figure 30-5, the strongly typed TableAdapter also has `Fill` and `GetData` methods, which are called to extract data from the database. The following code shows how you can use the `Fill` method to populate an existing strongly typed DataTable, perhaps within a DataSet. Alternatively, the `GetData` method creates a new instance of a strongly typed DataTable:

```
Dim ta As New AdventureWorksDataSetTableAdapters.ContactTableAdapter
Dim contacts1 As New AdventureWorksDataSet.ContactDataTable
ta.Fill(contacts1)

Dim contacts2 As AdventureWorksDataSet.ContactDataTable = ta.GetData
```

In Figure 30-5, the `Fill` and `GetData` methods appear as a pair because they make use of the same query. The Properties window can be used to configure this query. A query can return data in one of three ways: using a text command (as the example illustrates), a stored procedure, or tabledirect (where the contents of the table name specified in the `CommandText` are retrieved). This is specified in the CommandType field. Although the `CommandText` can be edited directly in the Properties window, it is difficult to see the whole query and easy to make mistakes. Clicking the ellipses button (at the top-right of Figure 30-5) opens the Query Builder window, shown in Figure 30-6.

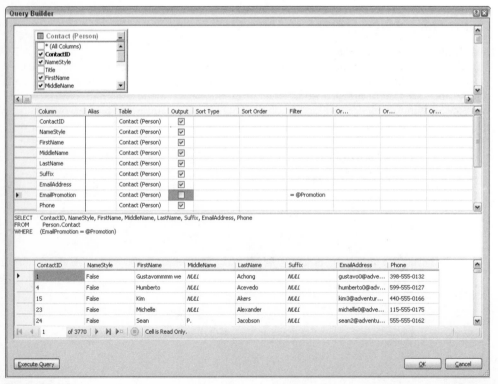

Figure 30-6

The Query Builder dialog is divided into four panes. In the top pane is a diagram of the tables involved in the query, and the selected columns. The second pane shows a list of columns related to the query. These columns are either output columns, such as FirstName and LastName, or a condition, such as the EmailPromotion field, or both. The third pane is, of course, the SQL command that is to be executed. The final pane includes sample data that can be retrieved by clicking the Execute Query button (in the bottom-left corner of Figure 30-6). If there are parameters to the SQL statement (in this case, @Promotion), a dialog will be displayed, prompting for values to use when executing the statement (see Figure 30-7).

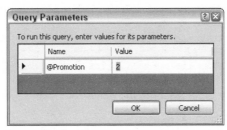

Figure 30-7

To change the query, you can make changes in any of the first three panes. As you move between panes, changes in one field are reflected in the others. You can hide any of the panes by unchecking that pane from the Panes item of the right-click context menu. Conditions can be added using the Filter column. These can include parameters (such as @Promotion), which must start with the at (@) symbol.

Returning to the DataSet designer, and the properties window associated with the Fill method, click the ellipses to examine the list of parameters. This shows the Parameters Collection Editor, as shown in Figure 30-8. Occasionally, the Query Builder doesn't get the data type correct for a parameter, and you may need to modify it using this dialog.

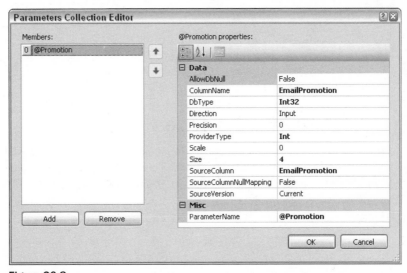

Figure 30-8

Also from the properties window for the query, you can specify whether the `Fill` and/or `GetData` methods are created, using the `GenerateMethods` property. You can also specify the names of the generated methods.

The other window that is occasionally useful when working with the DataSet designer is the Preview Data window. This is similar to the fourth pane in the Query Builder where parameters can be supplied and a query executed to preview the results, as shown in Figure 30-9. Open the Preview Data window by selecting Preview Data from the right-click context menu on any of the DataTables or TableAdapters on the DataSet designer.

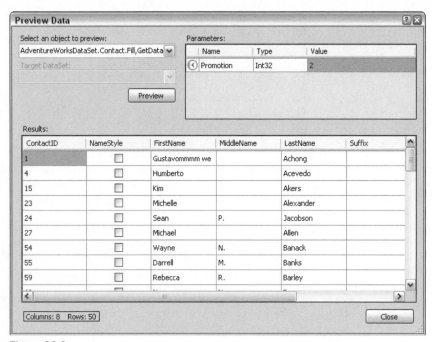

Figure 30-9

Working with Data Sources

So far you have created a strongly typed DataSet that contains a number of rows from the Contact table, based on a `Promotion` parameter. The DataSet is contained within a class library that you are going to expose to your application via a web service. To do this, you need to add a Windows application and an ASP.NET web service application to your solution.

In the Web Service project, you will add a reference to the class library. You also need to modify the `Service` class file so it has two methods, in place of the default `HelloWorld` web method:

```
Imports System.Web
Imports System.Web.Services
Imports System.Web.Services.Protocols
Imports DataTierLibrary

<WebService(Namespace:="http://tempuri.org/")> _
<WebServiceBinding(ConformsTo:=WsiProfiles.BasicProfile1_1)> _
<Global.Microsoft.VisualBasic.CompilerServices.DesignerGenerated()> _
Public Class Service
    Inherits System.Web.Services.WebService

    <WebMethod()> _
    Public Function RetrieveContacts(ByVal PromotionalCategory As Integer) _
                    As DataTierLibrary.AdventureWorksDataSet.ContactDataTable
        Dim ta As New AdventureWorksDataSetTableAdapters.ContactTableAdapter
        return ta.GetData(promotionalcategory)
    End Function

    <WebMethod()> _
    Public Sub SaveContacts(ByVal changes As Data.DataSet)
        Dim changesTable as Data.DataTable = changes.Tables(0)
        Dim ta As New AdventureWorksDataSetTableAdapters.ContactTableAdapter
        ta.Update(changesTable.Select)
    End Sub
End Class
```

The first web method, as the name suggests, retrieves the list of contacts based on the `promotional-category` that is passed in. In this method, you create a new instance of the strongly typed TableAdapter and return the DataTable retrieved by the `GetData` method. The second web method is used to save changes to a DataTable, again using the strongly typed TableAdapter. As you will notice, the DataSet that is passed in as a parameter to this method is not strongly typed. Unfortunately, the generated strongly typed DataSet doesn't provide a strongly typed `GetChanges` method, which will be used later to generate a DataSet containing only data that has changed. This new DataSet is passed into the `SaveContacts` method so that only changed data needs to be sent to the web service.

Web Service Data Source

These changes to the web service complete the server side of the process, but your application still doesn't have access to this data. To access the data from your application, you need to add a Data Source to the application. Again, use the Add New Data Source Wizard, but this time select a web service from the Data Source Type screen. To add a Web Service Data Source, you need to specify a URL from which the Web Service schema can be deduced. Add the Web Service Data Source via the Add Web Reference dialog that is displayed after you select the web service Data Source type, as shown in Figure 30-10.

Clicking the "Web services in this solution" link displays a list of web services available in your solution. The web service that you have just been working on should appear in this list. When you click the hyperlink for that web service, the Add Reference button is enabled. Clicking the Add Reference button will add an AdventureWorksDataSet to the Data Sources window under the localhost node (which you should rename via the Properties window, as it is not a very practical namespace). Expanding this node, you will see that the Data Source is very similar to the Data Source you had in the class library.

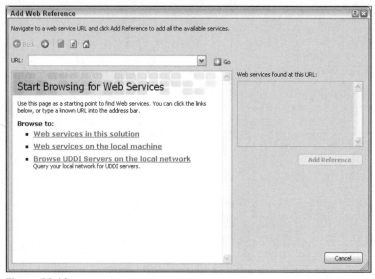

Figure 30-10

Browsing Data

To actually view the data being returned via the web service, you need to add some controls to your form. Open the form so the designer appears in the main window. In the Data Sources window, click the Contact node and select Details from the drop-down. This indicates that when you drag the Contact node onto the Form, Visual Studio 2005 will create controls to display the details of the Contact table (for example, the row contents), instead of the default `DataGridView`. Next, select the attributes you want to display by clicking on them and selecting the control type to use. For this scenario, select None for NameStyle, Suffix, and Phone. When you drag the Contact node onto the Form, you should end up with the layout shown in Figure 30-11.

In addition to adding controls for the information to be displayed and edited, a navigator control has also been added to the top of the form (this isn't generated if a `DataGridView` is selected), and an Adventure WorksDataSet and a ContactBindingSource have been added to the nonvisual area of the form.

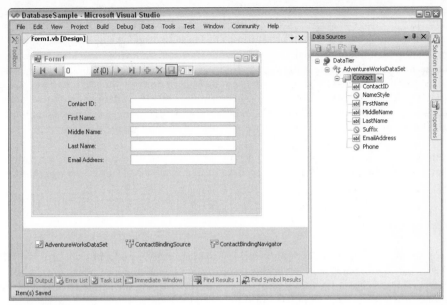

Figure 30-11

The final stage is to wire up the Load event of the form to retrieve data from the web service, and to add the Save button on the navigator to save changes. Right-click on the save icon and select Enabled to enable the Save button on the navigator control, and then double-click on the save icon to generate the stub event handler. Add the following code to load data and save changes via the web service you created earlier:

```vb
Public Class Form1

    Private Sub Form1_Load(ByVal sender As System.Object, _
                              ByVal e As System.EventArgs) Handles MyBase.Load
        Me.ContactBindingSource.DataSource = _
                              My.WebServices.Service.RetrieveContacts(2)

    End Sub

    Private Sub ContactBindingNavigatorSaveItem_Click _
                (ByVal sender As System.Object, ByVal e As System.EventArgs) _
                          Handles ContactBindingNavigatorSaveItem.Click
        Me.ContactBindingSource.EndEdit()
        Dim ds As DataTier.AdventureWorksDataSet.ContactDataTable = _
                       CType(Me.ContactBindingSource.DataSource, _
                          DataTier.AdventureWorksDataSet.ContactDataTable)
        Dim changesTable As DataTable = ds.GetChanges()
        Dim changes as New DataSet
        changes.Tables.Add(changesTable)
        My.WebServices.Service.SaveContacts(changes)
    End Sub
End Class
```

To retrieve the list of contacts from the web service, all you need to do is call the appropriate web method — in this case, RetrieveContacts. Pass in a parameter of 2, which indicates that only contacts with a promotional code of 2 should be returned. The Save method is slightly more complex, as you have to end the current edit (to make sure all changes are saved), retrieve the DataTable, and then extract the changes as a new DataTable. Although it would be simpler to pass a DataTable to the SaveContacts web service, only DataSets can be specified as parameters or return values to a web service. As such, you can create a new DataSet and add the changes DataTable to the list of tables. The new DataSet is then passed into the SaveContacts method. As mentioned previously, the GetChanges method returns a raw DataTable, which is unfortunate because it limits the strongly typed data scenario.

This completes the chapter's coverage of the strongly typed DataSet scenario, and provides you with a two-tiered solution for accessing and editing data from a database via a web service interface.

Summary

This chapter provided an introduction to working with strongly typed DataSets. Support within Visual Studio 2005 for creating and working with strongly typed DataSets simplifies the rapid building of applications. This is clearly the first step in the process of bridging the gap between the object-oriented programming world and the relational world in which the data is stored.

The following chapter looks in more detail at some of the controls this chapter merely introduced, such as the bindingsource and navigator controls. In addition, it explains how you can use the third type of Data Source — Objects — to persist and work with data.

31

Data Binding and Object Data Sources

Chapter 30 looked at strongly typed DataSets as an introduction to working with data in Visual Studio 2005. This chapter examines the data-binding controls in more detail, showing how they interact and how you can use the designers to control how data is displayed.

Data Binding

Data binding has often been the bane of a developer's existence. Most developers at some stage or another have resorted to writing their own wrappers to ensure that data is correctly bound to the controls on the screen. Visual Studio 2005 dramatically reduces the pain of getting two-way data binding to work. The examples used in the following sections work with the AdventureWorks sample database, and as in the previous chapter you will add this as a Data Source to your application. For simplicity, you'll work with a single Windows application, but the concepts discussed here can be extended over multiple tiers.

In this example, you build an application to assist you in managing the customers for AdventureWorks. To begin, you need to ensure that the `AdventureWorksDataSet` contains the Customer, SalesTerritory, Individual, Contact, and SalesOrderHeader tables. With the form designer and Data Sources window open, set the mode for the Customer table to Details using the drop-down list. Before creating the editing controls, tweak the list of columns for the Customer table. You're not that interested in the CustomerID or rowguid fields, so set them to None (again using the drop-down list for those nodes in the Data Sources window). AccountNumber is a generated field, and ModifiedDate should be automatically set when changes are made, so both of these fields should appear as labels, preventing them from being edited.

Now you're ready to drag the Customer node onto the form design surface. This will automatically add controls for each of the columns you have specified. It will also add a BindingSource, a BindingNavigator, the AdventureWorksDataSet, and a CustomerTableAdapter to the form—Figure 31-1 shows the basic layout of the form, as well as the nonvisual controls.

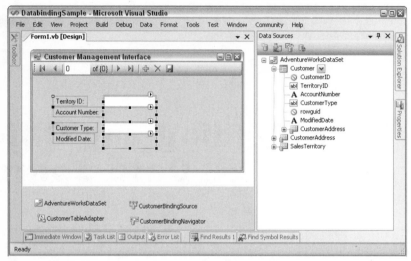

Figure 31-1

At this point you can build and run this application and navigate through the records using the navigation control, and you can also take the components apart to understand how they interact. Start with the AdventureWorksDataSet and the CustomerTableAdapter, as they carry out the background grunt work of retrieving information and persisting changes to the database. The AdventureWorksDataSet that is added to this form is actually an instance of the AdventureWorksDataSet class that was created by the Data Source Configuration Wizard. This instance will be used to store information for all the tables on this form. To populate the DataSet, call the Fill method. If you open the code file for the form, you will see that the Fill command has been added to the form's Load event handler. There is no requirement for this to occur while the form is loading—for example, if parameters need to be passed to the SELECT command, then you might need to input values before clicking a button to populate the DataSet.

```
Private Sub Form1_Load(ByVal sender As System.Object, _
                    ByVal e As System.EventArgs) Handles MyBase.Load
        Me.CustomerTableAdapter.Fill(Me.AdventureWorksDataSet.Customer)
End Sub
```

As you add information to this form, you'll also add TableAdapters to work with different tables within the AdventureWorksDataSet.

BindingSource

The next item of interest is the `CustomerBindingSource` that was automatically added to the nonvisual part of the form designer. This control is used to wire up each of the controls on the design surface with the relevant data item. In fact, this control is just a wrapper for the CurrencyManager. However, using a `BindingSource` considerably reduces the number of event handlers and custom code that you have to write. Unlike the `AdventureWorksDataSet` and the `CustomerTableAdapter` — which are instances of the strongly typed classes with the same names — the `CustomerBindingSource` is just an instance of the regular `BindingSource` class that ships with the .NET Framework.

Take a look at the properties of the `CustomerBindingSource` so you can see what it does. Figure 31-2 shows the Properties window for the `CustomerBindingSource`. The two items of particular interest are the `DataSource` and `DataMember` properties. The drop-down list for the `DataSource` property is expanded to illustrate the list of available Data Sources. The instance of the `AdventureWorksDataSet` that was added to the form is listed under Form1 List Instances. Selecting the `AdventureWorksDataSet` type under the Project Data Sources node creates another instance on the form instead of reusing the existing `DataSet`. In the `DataMember` field, you need to specify the table to use for data binding. Later, you'll see how the `DataMember` field can be used to specify a foreign key relationship so you can show linked data.

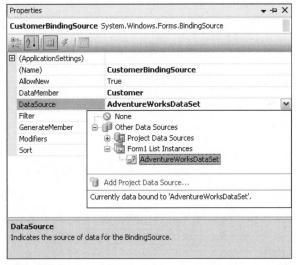

Figure 31-2

So far you have specified that the `CustomerBindingSource` will bind data in the Customer table of the `AdventureWorksDataSet`. What remains is to bind the individual controls on the form to the `BindingSource` and the appropriate column in the Customer table. To do this you need to specify a DataBinding for each control. Figure 31-3 shows the Properties grid for the TerritoryID textbox, with the DataBindings node expanded to show the binding for the `Text` property.

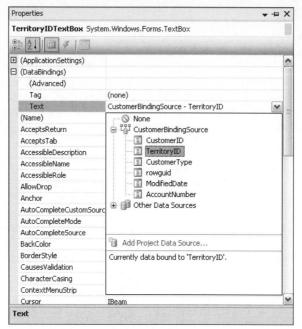

Figure 31-3

Again, enable the drop-down list so you can see that the Text property is being bound to the TerritoryID field of the CustomerBindingSource. Because the CustomerBindingSource is bound to the Customer table, this is actually the TerritoryID column in that table. If you look at the designer file for the form, you can see that this binding is set up using a new Binding, as shown in the following snippet:

```
Me.TerritoryIDTextBox.DataBindings.Add( _
            New System.Windows.Forms.Binding("Text", _
                                    Me.CustomerBindingSource, _
                                    "TerritoryID", True) _
        )
```

A Binding is used to ensure that two-way binding is set up between the Text field of the TerritoryID textbox and the TerritoryID field of the CustomerBindingSource. The controls for AccountNumber, CustomerType, and ModifiedDate all have similar bindings between their Text properties and the appropriate fields on the CustomerBindingSource.

BindingNavigator

The last control to cover is the CustomerBindingNavigator component, which is an instance of the BindingNavigator class. Although this control appears in the nonvisual area of the design surface, it has a visual representation in the form of the navigation toolstrip that is initially docked to the top of the form. As with regular toolstrips, this control can be docked to any edge of the form. In fact, in many ways the BindingNavigator behaves the same way as a toolstrip in that buttons and other controls can be added to the Items list. When the BindingNavigator is initially added to the form, a series of buttons are added for standard data functionality, such as moving to the first or last item, moving to the next or previous item, and adding, removing, and saving items.

What is neat about the `BindingNavigator` is that it not only creates these standard controls, but also wires them up for you. Figure 31-4 shows the Properties window for the `BindingNavigator`, with the Data and Items sections expanded. In the Data section you can see that the associated `BindingSource` is the `CustomerBindingSource`, which will be used to perform all the actions implied by the various button clicks. The Items section plays an important role, as each property defines an action, such as `AddNewItem`. The value of the property defines the `ToolStripItem` to which it will be assigned — in this case, the `BindingNavigatorAddNewItem` button.

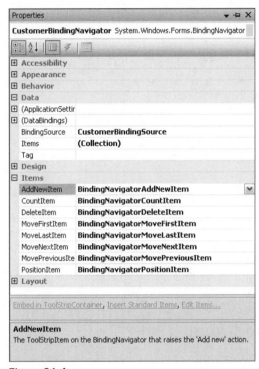

Figure 31-4

Behind the scenes, when this application is run and this button is assigned to the `AddNewItem` property, the `OnAddNew` method is wired up to the `Click` event of the button. This is shown in the following snippet, extracted using Reflector from the `BindingNavigator` class. The `AddNewItem` property calls the `WireUpButton` method, passing in a delegate to the `OnAddNew` method:

```
Public Property AddNewItem As ToolStripItem
    Get
        If ((Not Me.addNewItem Is Nothing) AndAlso Me.addNewItem.IsDisposed) Then
            Me.addNewItem = Nothing
        End If
        Return Me.addNewItem
    End Get
    Set(ByVal value As ToolStripItem)
        Me.WireUpButton(Me.addNewItem, value, _
                                    New EventHandler(AddressOf Me.OnAddNew))
    End Set
```

```
End Property

Private Sub OnAddNew(ByVal sender As Object, ByVal e As EventArgs)
      If (Me.Validate AndAlso (Not Me.bindingSource Is Nothing)) Then
            Me.bindingSource.AddNew
            Me.RefreshItemsInternal
      End If
End Sub

Private Sub WireUpButton(ByRef oldButton As ToolStripItem, _
                         ByVal newButton As ToolStripItem, _
                         ByVal clickHandler As EventHandler)
      If (Not oldButton Is newButton) Then
            If (Not oldButton Is Nothing) Then
                  RemoveHandler oldButton.Click, clickHandler
            End If
            If (Not newButton Is Nothing) Then
                  AddHandler newButton.Click, clickHandler
            End If
            oldButton = newButton
            Me.RefreshItemsInternal
      End If
End Sub
```

The OnAddNew method performs a couple of important actions. First, it forces validation of the active field, which is examined later in this chapter. Second, and the most important aspect of the OnAddNew method, it calls the AddNew method on the BindingSource. The other properties on the Binding Navigator also map to corresponding methods on the BindingSource, and it is important to remember that the BindingSource, rather than the BindingNavigator, does the work when it comes to working with the Data Source.

Data Source Selections

Now that you have seen how the BindingSource works, it's time to improve the user interface. At the moment, the TerritoryID is being displayed as a text box, but this is in fact a foreign key to the Sales Territory table. This means that if a user enters random text, then an error will be thrown when you try to commit the changes. Because the list of territories is defined in the database, it would make sense to present a drop-down list that enables users to select the territory, rather than specify the ID. To add the drop-down, replace the TextBox control with a ComboBox control, and bind the list of items in the drop-down to the SalesTerritory table in the database.

Start by removing the TerritoryID TextBox. Next, add a ComboBox control from the toolbar. With the new ComboBox selected, note that a smart tag is attached to the control. Expanding this tag and checking the "Use data bound items" checkbox will open the Data Binding Mode options, as shown in Figure 31-5. Take this opportunity to rearrange the form slightly so the controls line up.

You need to define four things to get the data binding to work properly. The first is the Data Source. In this case, select the existing AdventureWorksDataSet that was previously added to the form. Within this Data Source, set the Display Member, the field that is to be displayed, to be equal to the Name column of the SalesTerritory table. The Value Member, which is the field used to select which item to display, is set to the TerritoryID column. These three properties configure the contents of the drop-down list. The last property you need to set determines which item will be selected and what property to update when the selected item changes in the drop-down list. This is the Selected Value property; in this case, set it equal to the TerritoryID field on the existing `CustomerBindingSource` object.

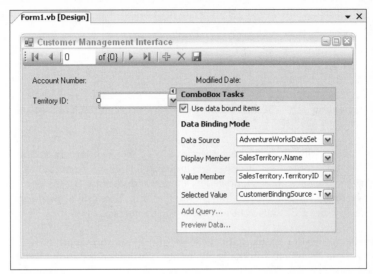

Figure 31-5

In the earlier discussion about the `DataSet` and the `TableAdapter`, recall that to populate the Customer table in the `AdventureWorksDataSet`, you need to call the `Fill` method on the `CustomerTableAdapter`. Although you have wired up the TerritoryID drop-down list, if you run what you currently have, there would be no items in this list, as you haven't populated the DataSet with any values for the SalesTerritory table. To retrieve these items from the database, add a `TableAdapter` to the form and call the `Fill` method when the form loads. When you added the `AdventureWorksDataSet` to the data source list, it not only created a set of strongly typed tables, it also created a set of table adapters. These are automatically added to the Toolbox under the Components tab. In this case, drag the `SalesTerritoryTableAdapter` onto the form and add a call to the `Fill` method to the `Load` event handler for the form. You should end up with the following:

```
Private Sub Form1_Load(ByVal sender As System.Object, _
                ByVal e As System.EventArgs) Handles MyBase.Load
    Me.SalesTerritoryTableAdapter.Fill(Me.AdventureWorksDataSet.SalesTerritory)
    Me.CustomerTableAdapter.Fill(Me.AdventureWorksDataSet.Customer)
End Sub
```

Now when you run the application, instead of having a text box with a numeric value, you have a convenient drop-down list from which to select the Territory.

BindingSource Chains

At the moment, you have a form that displays some basic information about a customer, such as Account Number, Sales Territory ID, and Customer Type. This information by itself is not very interesting, as it really doesn't tell you who the customer is or how to contact them. Before adding more information to

401

this form, you need to limit the customer list. There are actually two types of customers in the database, Individuals and Stores, as indicated by the Customer Type field. For this example, you are only interested in Individuals, as Stores have a different set of information stored in the database. The first task is to open the `AdventureWorksDataSet` in the design window, click on the `CustomerTableAdapter`, select the `SelectCommand` property, and change the query to read as follows:

```
SELECT     CustomerID, CustomerType, TerritoryID, rowguid,
           ModifiedDate, AccountNumber
FROM       Sales.Customer
WHERE      (CustomerType = 'I')
```

Now that you're dealing only with individual customers, you can remove the Customer Type information from the form.

To present more information about the customers, you need to add information from the Individual and Contact tables. The only column of interest in the Individual table is Demographics. From the Data Sources window, expand the Customer node, followed by the Individual node. Set the Demographics node to Textbox using the drop-down and then drag it onto the form. This will also add an `Individual` `BindingSource` and an `IndividualTableAdapter` to the form.

When you run the application in this state, the demographics information for each Customer is displayed. What is going on here to automatically link the Customer and Individual tables? The trick is in the new `BindingSource`. The `DataSource` property of the `IndividualBindingSource` is the `CustomerBindingSource`. In the DataMember field, you can see that the `IndividualBindingSource` is binding to the `FK_Individual_Customer_CustomerID` relationship, which of course is the relationship between the Customer table and the Individual table. This relationship will return the collection of rows in the Individual table that relate to the current Customer. In this case, there will only ever be a single Individual record, but, for example, if you look at the relationship between an Order and the OrderDetails table, there might be a number of entries in the OrderDetails table for any given Order.

As you probably have noticed, the Individual table is actually a many-to-many joining table for the Customer and Contact tables. On the Customer side, this is done because a Customer might be either an Individual or a Store; and similarly on the Contact side, not all Contacts are individual customers. The Data Sources window doesn't handle this many-to-many relationship very well, as it can only display parent-child (one-to-many) relationships in the tree hierarchy. Under the Contact node there is a link to the Individual table, but this won't help because dragging this onto the form will not link the `BindingSources` correctly. Unfortunately, there is no out-of-the-box solution to this problem within Visual Studio 2005. However, the following paragraphs introduce a simple component that you can use to give you designer support for many-to-many table relationships.

Begin by completing the layout of the form. For each of the fields under the Contact node, you need to specify whether you want them to be displayed or not. Then set the Contact node to Details, and drag the node onto the form. This will again add a `ContactBindingSource` and a `ContactTableAdapter` to the form.

To establish the binding between the `IndividualBindingSource` and the `ContactBindingSource`, you need to trap the `ListChanged` and `BindingComplete` events on the `IndividualBindingSource`. Then, using the current record of the `IndividualBindingSource`, apply a filter to the `Contact` `BindingSource` so only related records are displayed. Instead of manually writing this code every time you have to work with a many-to-many relationship, it's wise to create a component to do the work for you, as well as give you design-time support. The following code is divided into three regions. The opening section declares the fields, the constructor, and the `Dispose` method. This is followed by the Designer Support region, which declares the properties and helper methods that will be invoked to give you design-time support for this component. Lastly, the remaining code traps the two events and places the filter on the appropriate `BindingSource`:

```
Imports System.ComponentModel
Imports System.Drawing.Design

Public Class ManyToMany
    Inherits Component

    Private WithEvents m_LinkingBindingSource As BindingSource
    Private m_Relationship As String
    Private m_TargetBindingSource As BindingSource


    Public Sub New(ByVal container As IContainer)
        MyBase.New()
        container.Add(Me)
    End Sub

    Protected Overrides Sub Dispose(ByVal disposing As Boolean)
        If disposing Then
            Me.TargetBindingSource = Nothing
            Me.Relationship = Nothing
        End If
        MyBase.Dispose(disposing)
    End Sub

#Region "Designer Support"
    Public Property LinkingBindingSource() As BindingSource
        Get
            Return m_LinkingBindingSource
        End Get
        Set(ByVal value As BindingSource)
            If Not m_LinkingBindingSource Is value Then
                m_LinkingBindingSource = value
            End If
        End Set
    End Property

    <RefreshProperties(RefreshProperties.Repaint), _
    Editor("System.Windows.Forms.Design.DataMemberListEditor, System.Design, _
Version=2.0.0.0, Culture=neutral, PublicKeyToken=b03f5f7f11d50a3a", _
    GetType(UITypeEditor)), DefaultValue("")> _
    Public Property Relationship() As String
        Get
            Return Me.m_Relationship
        End Get
        Set(ByVal value As String)
            If (value Is Nothing) Then
                value = String.Empty
            End If
```

```vbnet
                If Me.m_Relationship Is Nothing OrElse _
                                        Not Me.m_Relationship.Equals(value) Then
                    Me.m_Relationship = value
                End If
            End Set
        End Property


        <AttributeProvider(GetType(IListSource)), _
        RefreshProperties(RefreshProperties.Repaint), _
        DefaultValue(CType(Nothing, String))> _
        Public Property TargetBindingSource() As BindingSource
            Get
                Return Me.m_TargetBindingSource
            End Get
            Set(ByVal value As BindingSource)
                If (Me.m_TargetBindingSource IsNot value) Then
                    Me.m_TargetBindingSource = value
                    Me.ClearInvalidDataMember()
                End If
            End Set
        End Property


        <Browsable(False)> _
        Public ReadOnly Property DataSource() As BindingSource
            Get
                Return Me.TargetBindingSource
            End Get
        End Property

        Private Sub ClearInvalidDataMember()
            If Not Me.IsDataMemberValid Then
                Me.Relationship = ""
            End If
        End Sub

        Private Function IsDataMemberValid() As Boolean
            If String.IsNullOrEmpty(Me.Relationship) Then
                Return True
            End If
            Dim collection1 As PropertyDescriptorCollection = _
                    ListBindingHelper.GetListItemProperties(Me.TargetBindingSource)
            Dim descriptor1 As PropertyDescriptor = collection1.Item(Me.Relationship)
            If (Not descriptor1 Is Nothing) Then
                Return True
            End If
            Return False
        End Function
#End Region


#Region "Filtering"
    Private Sub BindingComplete(ByVal sender As System.Object, _
                    ByVal e As System.Windows.Forms.BindingCompleteEventArgs) _
                            Handles m_LinkingBindingSource.BindingComplete
        BindNow()
```

```
        End Sub

    Private Sub ListChanged(ByVal sender As System.Object, _
                    ByVal e As System.ComponentModel.ListChangedEventArgs) _
                            Handles m_LinkingBindingSource.ListChanged
        BindNow()
    End Sub

    Private Sub BindNow()
        If Me.DesignMode Then Return

        If Me.TargetBindingSource Is Nothing OrElse _
                        Me.TargetBindingSource.List.Count <= 0 Then Return
        Dim childColumn As String = CType(Me.TargetBindingSource.List, _
DataView).Table.ChildRelations(Me.Relationship).ChildColumns(0).ColumnName
        Dim parentColumn As String = CType(Me.TargetBindingSource.List, _
DataView).Table.ChildRelations(Me.Relationship).ParentColumns(0).ColumnName

        Dim filterString As String = ""
        For Each row As DataRowView In LinkingBindingSource.List

            If Not filterString = "" Then filterString &= " OR "
            filterString &= childColumn & "= '" & row(parentColumn) & "'"
        Next
        Me.m_TargetBindingSource.Filter = filterString
        Me.m_TargetBindingSource.EndEdit()
    End Sub
#End Region

End Class
```

Adding this component to your solution will add it to the Toolbox, from which it can be dragged onto the nonvisual area on the designer surface. In Figure 31-6, you can see that you can now set the LinkingBindingSource property to be the BindingSource for the linking table — in this case, the IndividualBindingSource. You also have designer support for selecting the TargetBindingSource — the ContactBindingSource — and the Relationship, which in this case is FK_Individual_Contact_ ContactId. The events on the LinkingBindingSource are automatically wired up using the Handles keyword, and when triggered they invoke the BindNow method, which sets the filter on the Target BindingSource.

When you run this application, you can easily navigate between customer records. In addition, not only is the data from the Customer table displayed; you can also see the information from both the Individual table and the Contact table, as shown in Figure 31-7. Notice that the text box for the Email Promotion column has been replaced with a checkbox. This can be done the same way that you replaced the TerritoryID text box: by dragging the checkbox from the Toolbox and then using the DataBindings node in the Properties window to assign the EmailPromotion field to the checked state of the checkbox.

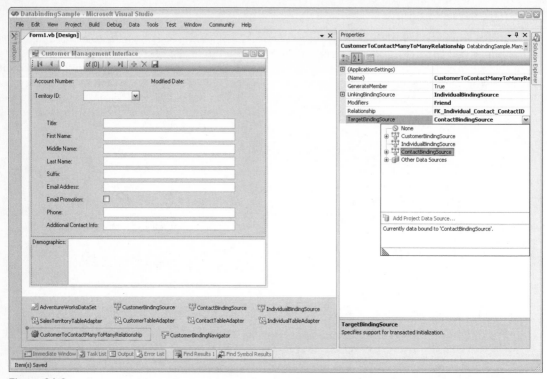

Figure 31-6

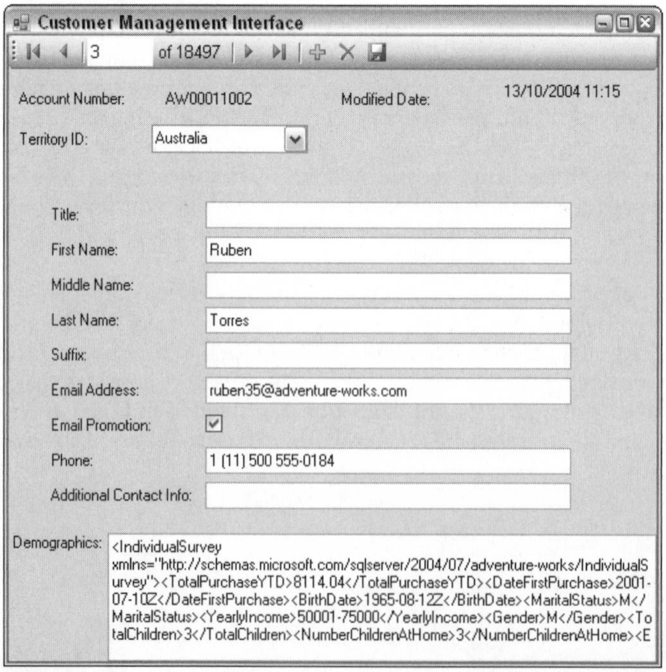

Figure 31-7

Saving Changes

Now that you have a usable interface, you need to add support for making changes and adding new records. If you double-click the Save icon on the CustomerBindingNavigator toolstrip, the code window opens with a code stub that would normally save changes to the Customer table. Clearly, you need to modify this method to save changes made to both the Individual table and the Contact table. The result is a method that looks like the following snippet. Remember that because Individual is a linking table between Customer and Contact, it needs to be saved last to ensure that there are no conflicts when changes are sent to the database:

```
Private Sub CustomerBindingNavigatorSaveItem_Click(ByVal sender As System.Object, _
                                    ByVal e As System.EventArgs) _
                            Handles CustomerBindingNavigatorSaveItem.Click
    Me.Validate()
    Me.ContactBindingSource.EndEdit()
    Me.ContactTableAdapter.Update(Me.AdventureWorksDataSet.Contact)
    Me.CustomerBindingSource.EndEdit()
    Me.CustomerTableAdapter.Update(Me.AdventureWorksDataSet.Customer)
    Me.IndividualBindingSource.EndEdit()
    Me.IndividualTableAdapter.Update(Me.AdventureWorksDataSet.Individual)
End Sub
```

If you run this, make changes to a customer, and click the Save button, an exception will be thrown because you're currently trying to update calculated fields. You need to correct the Update and Insert methods used by the CustomerTableAdapter to prevent updates to the Account Number column, because it is a calculated field, and to automatically update the Modified Date field. Using the DataSet Designer, select the CustomerTableAdapter, open the Properties window, expand the UpdateCommand node, and click the ellipses button next to the CommandText field. This opens the Query Builder dialog that you used in the previous chapter. Uncheck the boxes in the Set column for the rowguid and AccountNumber rows. In the New Value column, change @ModifiedDate to getdate(), to automatically set the modified date to the date on which the query was executed. This should give you a query similar to the one shown in Figure 31-8.

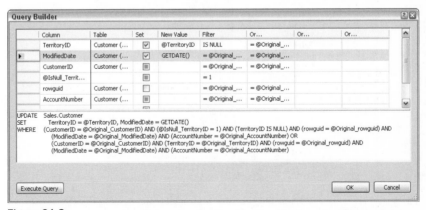

Figure 31-8

Unfortunately, the process of making this change to the Update command causes the parameter list for this command to be reset. Most of the parameters are regenerated correctly except for the IsNull_

TerritoryId parameter, which is used to handle cases where the TerritoryID field can be null in the database. To fix this problem, open the Parameter Collection Editor for the Update command and update the settings for the @IsNull_TerritoryId parameter as outlined in the following table (see Figure 31-9):

Property	Value
AllowObNull	True
ColumnName	
DbType	Int32
Direction	Input
ParameterName	@IsNull_TerritoryID
Precision	0
ProviderType	Int
Scale	0
Size	0
SourceColumn	TerritoryID
SourceColumnNullMapping	False
SourceVersion	Original

Now that you've completed the Update command, not only can you navigate the customers; you can also make changes.

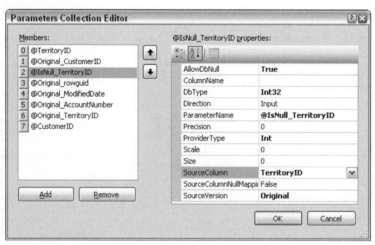

Figure 31-9

You also need to update the `Insert` command so it automatically generates both the modification date and the rowguid. Using the Query Builder, update the `Insert` command using the following table as a guide (see Figure 31-10):

Column	New Value
TerritoryID	@TerritoryID
Customer Type	@CustomerType
rowguid	NEWID()
ModifiedDate	GETDATE()

Unlike the `Update` method, you don't need to change any of the parameters for this query. Both the `Update` and `Insert` queries for the Individual and Customer tables should work without modifications.

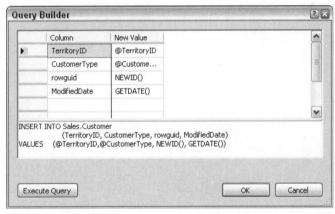

Figure 31-10

Inserting New Items

You now have a sample application that enables you to browse and make changes to an existing set of individual customers. The one missing piece is the capability to create a new customer. By default, the Add button on the `BindingNavigator` is automatically wired up to the `AddNew` method on the `BindingSource`, as shown earlier in this chapter. In this case, you actually need to set some default values and create entries in both the Individual and Contact tables in addition to the record that is created in the Customer table. To do this, you need to write our own logic behind the Add button.

The first step is to double-click the Add button to create an event handler for it. Make sure that you also remove the automatic wiring by setting the `AddNewItem` property to `(None)`; otherwise, you will end up with two records being created every time you press the Add button. You can then modify the default event handler as follows to set initial values for the new Customer, as well as create records in the other two tables:

```
Private Const cCustomerType As String = "I"
Private Sub BindingNavigatorAddNewItem_Click(ByVal sender As System.Object, _
                                    ByVal e As System.EventArgs) _
                                Handles BindingNavigatorAddNewItem.Click

    Dim drv As DataRowView

    'Create record in the Customer table
    drv = TryCast(Me.CustomerBindingSource.AddNew, DataRowView)
    If drv Is Nothing Then Return
    Dim cr As AdventureWorksDataSet.CustomerRow = _
                        TryCast(drv.Row, AdventureWorksDataSet.CustomerRow)
    If cr Is Nothing Then Return
    cr.rowguid = Guid.NewGuid
    cr.CustomerType = cCustomerType
    cr.ModifiedDate = Now

    'Create record in the Contact table
    drv = TryCast(Me.ContactBindingSource.AddNew, DataRowView)
    If drv Is Nothing Then Return
    Dim ct As AdventureWorksDataSet.ContactRow = _
                        TryCast(drv.Row, AdventureWorksDataSet.ContactRow)
    If ct Is Nothing Then Return
    ct.NameStyle = True
    ct.PasswordSalt = ""
    ct.PasswordHash = ""
    ct.rowguid = Guid.NewGuid
    ct.ModifiedDate = Now

    'Create record in the Individual table
    drv = TryCast(Me.IndividualBindingSource.AddNew, DataRowView)
    If drv Is Nothing Then Return
    Dim indiv As AdventureWorksDataSet.IndividualRow =
                        TryCast(drv.Row, AdventureWorksDataSet.IndividualRow)
    indiv.CustomerRow = cr
    indiv.ContactRow = ct
    indiv.ModifiedDate = Now
End Sub
```

From this example, it seems that you are unnecessarily setting some of the properties — for example, PasswordSalt and PasswordHash being equal to an empty string. This is necessary to ensure that the new row meets the constraints established by the database. Because these fields cannot be set by the user, you need to ensure that they are initially set to a value that can be accepted by the database. Clearly, for a secure application, the PasswordSalt and PasswordHash would be set to appropriate values.

Running the application with this method instead of the automatically wired event handler enables you to create a new Customer record using the Add button. If you enter values for each of the fields, you can save the changes.

Validation

In the previous section, you added functionality to create a new customer record. If you don't enter appropriate data upon creating a new record — for example, you don't enter a first name — this record will be rejected when you click the Save button. In fact, an exception will be raised if you try to move away from this record. The schema for the AdventureWorksDataSet contains a number of constraints, such as FirstName can't be null, which are checked when you perform certain actions, such as saving or moving between records. If these checks fail, an exception is raised. You have two options. One, you can trap these exceptions, which is poor programming practice, as exceptions should not be used for execution control. Alternatively, you can pre-empt this by validating the data prior to the schema being checked. Earlier in the chapter, when you learned how the `BindingNavigator` automatically wires the `AddNew` method on the `BindingSource`, you saw that the `OnAddNew` method contains a call to a `Validate` method. This method propagates up and calls the `Validate` method on the active control, which returns a Boolean value that determines whether the action will proceed. This pattern is used by all the automatically wired events and should be used in the event handlers you write for the navigation buttons.

The `Validate` method on the active control triggers two events — `Validating` and `Validated` — that occur before and after the validation process, respectively. Because you want to control the validation process, add an event handler for the `Validating` event. For example, you could add an event handler for the `Validating` event of the First Name `TextBox`:

```
Private Sub FirstNameTextBox_Validating(ByVal sender As System.Object, _
                         ByVal e As System.ComponentModel.CancelEventArgs) _
                                        Handles FirstNameTextBox.Validating
    Dim firstNameTxt As TextBox = TryCast(sender, TextBox)
    If firstNameTxt Is Nothing Then Return
    e.Cancel = firstNameTxt.Text = ""
End Sub
```

While this prevents users from leaving the text box until a value has been added, it doesn't give them any idea why the application prevents them from proceeding. Luckily, the .NET Framework includes an `ErrorProvider` control that can be dragged onto the form from the Toolbox. This control behaves in a similar manner to the Tooltip control. For each control on the form, you can specify an Error string, which, when set, causes an icon to appear alongside the relevant control, with a suitable tooltip displaying the Error string. This is illustrated in Figure 31-11, where the Error string is set for the First Name text box.

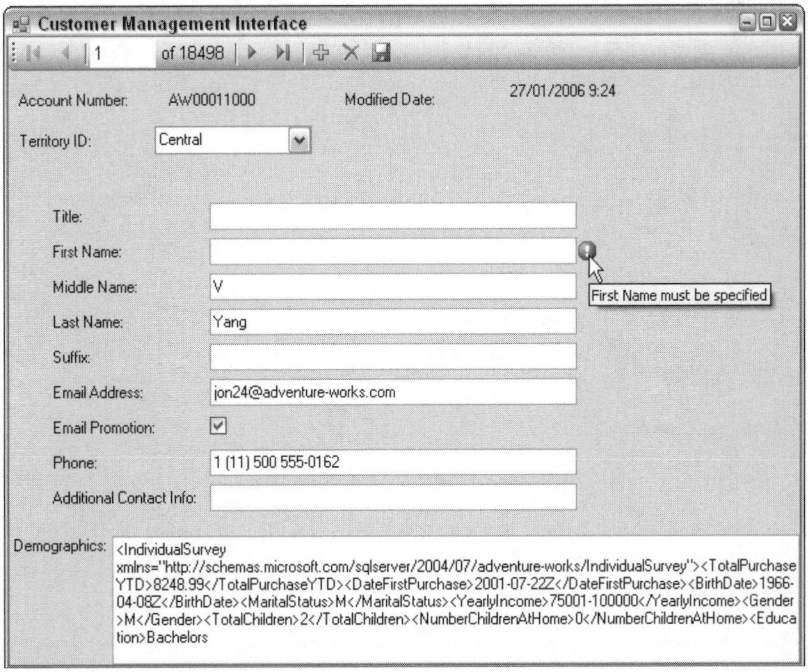

Figure 31-11

Clearly, you want only to set the Error string property for the First Name text box when there is no text. Following from the earlier example in which you added the event handler for the `Validating` event, you can modify this code to include setting the Error string:

```
Private Sub FirstNameTextBox_Validating(ByVal sender As System.Object, _
                            ByVal e As System.ComponentModel.CancelEventArgs) _
                                        Handles FirstNameTextBox.Validating
    Dim firstNameTxt As TextBox = TryCast(sender, TextBox)
    If firstNameTxt Is Nothing Then Return
    e.Cancel = firstNameTxt.Text = ""
    If firstNameTxt.Text = "" Then
        Me.ErrorProvider1.SetError(firstNameTxt, "First Name must be specified")
    Else
        Me.ErrorProvider1.SetError(firstNameTxt, Nothing)
    End If
End Sub
```

You can imagine that having to write event handlers that validate and set the error information for each of the controls can be quite a lengthy process, so the following component, for the most part, gives you designer support:

```
Imports System.ComponentModel
Imports System.Drawing.Design

<ProvideProperty("Validate", GetType(Control))> _
Public Class ControlValidator
    Inherits Component
    Implements IExtenderProvider

#Region "Rules Validator"
    Private Structure Validator
        Public Rule As Predicate(Of IRulesList.RuleParams)
        Public Information As ValidationAttribute
        Public Sub New(ByVal r As Predicate(Of IRulesList.RuleParams), _
                    ByVal info As ValidationAttribute)
            Me.Rule = r
            Me.Information = info
        End Sub
    End Structure
#End Region


    Private m_ErrorProvider As ErrorProvider
    Private rulesHash As New Dictionary(Of String, Validator)
    Public controlHash As New Dictionary(Of Control, Boolean)

    Public Sub New(ByVal container As IContainer)
        MyBase.New()
        container.Add(Me)
    End Sub


#Region "Error provider and Rules"

    Public Property ErrorProvider() As ErrorProvider
```

```vb
            Get
                Return m_ErrorProvider
            End Get
            Set(ByVal value As ErrorProvider)
                m_ErrorProvider = value
            End Set
        End Property


        Public Sub AddRules(ByVal ruleslist As IRulesList)
            For Each rule As Predicate(Of IRulesList.RuleParams) In ruleslist.Rules
                Dim attributes As ValidationAttribute() = _
                            TryCast(rule.Method.GetCustomAttributes _
                                        (GetType(ValidationAttribute), True), _
                                                ValidationAttribute())
                If Not attributes Is Nothing Then
                    For Each attrib As ValidationAttribute In attributes
                        rulesHash.Add(attrib.ColumnName.ToLower, _
                                            New Validator(rule, attrib))
                    Next
                End If
            Next
        End Sub
#End Region

#Region "Extender Provider to turn validation on"
        Public Function CanExtend(ByVal extendee As Object) As Boolean _
                        Implements System.ComponentModel.IExtenderProvider.CanExtend
            Return TypeOf (extendee) Is Control
        End Function

        Public Sub SetValidate(ByVal control As Control, _
                            ByVal shouldValidate As Boolean)
            If shouldValidate Then
                AddHandler control.Validating, AddressOf Validating
            End If
            controlHash.Item(control) = shouldValidate
        End Sub

        Public Function GetValidate(ByVal control As Control) As Boolean
            If controlHash.ContainsKey(control) Then
                Return controlHash.Item(control)
            End If
            Return False
        End Function
#End Region

#Region "Validation"
        Private ReadOnly Property ItemError(ByVal ctrl As Control) As String
            Get
                Try
                    If ctrl.DataBindings.Count = 0 Then Return ""
                    Dim key As String =
ctrl.DataBindings.Item(0).BindingMemberInfo.BindingField
                    Dim bs As BindingSource =
TryCast(ctrl.DataBindings.Item(0).DataSource, BindingSource)
```

```
                    If bs Is Nothing Then Return ""
                    Dim drv As DataRowView = TryCast(bs.Current, DataRowView)
                    If drv Is Nothing Then Return ""

                    Dim valfield As String = ctrl.DataBindings.Item(0).PropertyName
                    Dim val As Object = ctrl.GetType.GetProperty(valfield, _
                                                New Type() {}).GetValue(ctrl, Nothing)
                    Return ItemError(drv, key, val)
                Catch ex As Exception
                    Return ""
                End Try
            End Get
        End Property

        Private ReadOnly Property ItemError(ByVal drv As DataRowView, ByVal columnName _
    As String, ByVal newValue As Object) As String
            Get
                columnName = columnName.ToLower
                If Not rulesHash.ContainsKey(columnName) Then Return ""
                Dim p As Validator = rulesHash.Item(columnName)
                If p.Rule Is Nothing Then Return ""
                If p.Rule(New IRulesList.RuleParams(drv.Row, newValue)) Then Return ""

                If p.Information Is Nothing Then Return ""
                Return p.Information.ErrorString
            End Get
        End Property

        Private Sub Validating(ByVal sender As Object, ByVal e As CancelEventArgs)
            Dim err As String = InternalValidate(sender)
            e.Cancel = Not (err = "")
        End Sub

        Private Function InternalValidate(ByVal sender As Object) As String
            If Me.m_ErrorProvider Is Nothing Then Return ""
            Dim ctrl As Control = TryCast(sender, Control)
            If ctrl Is Nothing Then Return ""
            If Not Me.controlHash.ContainsKey(ctrl) OrElse Not _
    Me.controlHash.Item(ctrl) Then Return ""
            Dim err As String = Me.ItemError(ctrl)
            Me.m_ErrorProvider.SetError(ctrl, err)
            Return err
        End Function

        Private Sub ChangedItem(ByVal sender As Object, ByVal e As EventArgs)
            InternalValidate(sender)
        End Sub
#End Region

#Region "Validation Attribute"
        <AttributeUsage(AttributeTargets.Method)> _
        Public Class ValidationAttribute
            Inherits Attribute

            Private m_ColumnName As String
```

```vb
            Private m_ErrorString As String

            Public Sub New(ByVal columnName As String, ByVal errorString As String)
                Me.ColumnName = columnName
                Me.ErrorString = errorString
            End Sub

            Public Property ColumnName() As String
                Get
                    Return m_ColumnName
                End Get
                Set(ByVal value As String)
                    m_ColumnName = value
                End Set
            End Property

            Public Property ErrorString() As String
                Get
                    Return m_ErrorString
                End Get
                Set(ByVal value As String)
                    m_ErrorString = value
                End Set
            End Property
        End Class
#End Region

#Region "Rules Interface"
    Public Interface IRulesList

        Structure RuleParams
            Public ExistingData As DataRow
            Public NewData As Object
            Public Sub New(ByVal data As DataRow, ByVal newStuff As Object)
                Me.ExistingData = data
                Me.NewData = newStuff
            End Sub
        End Structure

        ReadOnly Property Rules() As Predicate(Of RuleParams)()

    End Interface
#End Region

End Class
```

The `ControlValidator` has a number of parts that work together to validate and provide error information. First, to enable validation of a control, the `ControlValidator` exposes an `Extender Provider`, which allows you to indicate whether the `ControlValidator` on the form should be used for validation. The right pane in Figure 31-12 shows the Properties window for the First Name text box, in which the `Validate` property has been set to `True`. When the First Name text box is validated, the `ControlValidator1` control will be given the opportunity to validate the `FirstName` property.

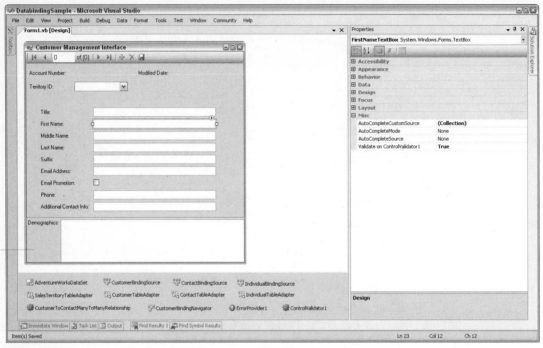

Figure 31-12

The `ControlValidator` has an `ErrorProvider` property that can be used to specify an `ErrorProvider` control on the form. This is not a requirement, however, and validation will proceed without one being specified. If this property is set, the validation process will automatically set the Error string property for the control being validated.

What you're currently missing is a set of business rules to use for validation. This is accomplished using a rules class that implements the `IRulesList` interface. Each rule is a predicate — in other words, a method that returns true or false based on a condition. The following code defines a `CustomerValidationRules` class that exposes two rules that determine whether the First Name and TerritoryID fields contain valid data. Each rule is attributed with the `ValidationAttribute`, which determines the column that the rule validates, and the Error string, which can be displayed if the validation fails. The column specified in the `Validation` attribute needs to match the field to which the control is data bound:

```
Imports System
Imports DatabindingSample.ControlValidator
Public Class CustomerValidationRules
    Implements IRulesList

    Public Shared ReadOnly Property Instance() As CustomerValidationRules
        Get
            Return New CustomerValidationRules
        End Get
    End Property

    Public ReadOnly Property Rules() As Predicate(Of IRulesList.RuleParams)() _
```

```
                                                    Implements IRulesList.Rules
        Get
            Return New Predicate(Of IRulesList.RuleParams)() { _
                                              AddressOf TerritoryId, _
                                              AddressOf FirstName}
        End Get
    End Property

    <Validation("TerritoryID", "TerritoryID must be >0")> _
        Public Function TerritoryId(ByVal data As IRulesList.RuleParams) As Boolean
        Try
            If Not TypeOf (data.NewData) Is Integer Then Return False
            Dim newVal As Integer = CInt(data.NewData)
            If newVal > 0 Then Return True
            Return False
        Catch ex As Exception
            Return False
        End Try
    End Function

    <Validation("FirstName", "First Name must be specified")> _
    Public Function FirstName(ByVal data As IRulesList.RuleParams) As Boolean
        Try
            Dim newVal As String = TryCast(data.NewData, String)
            If newVal = "" Then Return False
            Return True
        Catch ex As Exception
            Return False
        End Try
    End Function
End Class
```

The last task that remains is to add the following line to the form's Load method to associate this rules class to the ControlValidator:

```
Me.ControlValidator1.AddRules(CustomerValidationRules.Instance)
```

To add more rules to this form, all you need to do is add the rule to the CustomerValidationRules class and enable validation for the appropriate control.

DataGridView

So far you've been working with standard controls, and you've seen how the BindingNavigator enables you to scroll through a list of items. Sometimes it is more convenient to display a list of items in a grid. This is where the DataGridView is useful, as it enables you to combine the power of the BindingSource with a grid layout.

Extending the Customer Management Interface, add the list of orders to the form using the DataGridView. Returning to the Data Sources window, select the SalesOrderHeader node from under the Customer node. From the drop-down list, select DataGridView and drag the node into an empty area on the form. This adds the appropriate BindingSource and TableAdapter to the form, as well as a DataGridView showing each of the columns in the SalesOrderHeader table, as shown in Figure 31-13.

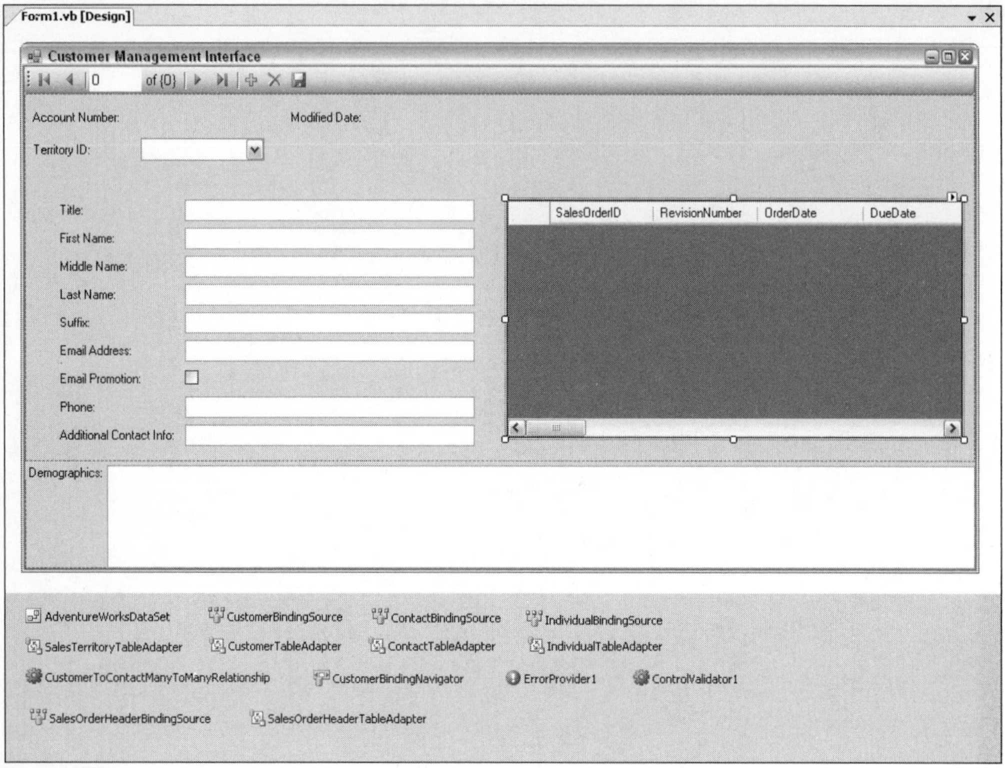

Figure 31-13

Unlike working with the Details layout, when you drag the `DataGridView` onto the form it ignores any settings you might have specified for the individual columns. Instead, every column is added to the grid as a simple text field. To modify the list of columns that are displayed, you can either use the smart tag for the newly added `DataGridView` or select Edit Columns from the right-click context menu. This will open the Edit Columns dialog (shown in Figure 31-14), in which columns can be added, removed, and reordered.

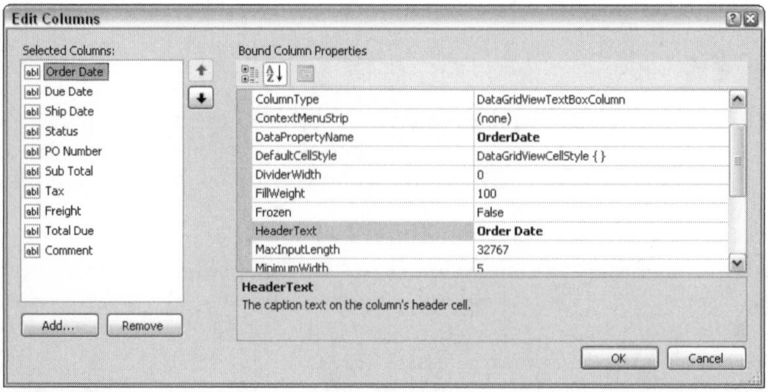

Figure 31-14

After specifying the appropriate columns, the finished application can be run; and the list of orders will be visible for each of the customers in the database. The final version is illustrated in Figure 31-15.

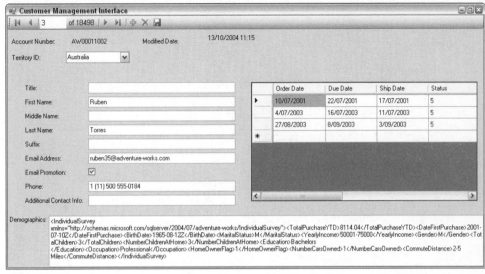

Figure 31-15

Object Data Source

In a number of projects, an application is broken up into multiple tiers. Quite often it is not possible to pass around strongly typed DataSets, as they may be quite large, or perhaps the project requires custom business objects. In either case, it is possible to take the data-binding techniques you just learned for DataSets and apply them to objects. For the purposes of this discussion, use the following `Customer` and `SalesOrder` classes:

```
Public Class Customer
    Private m_Name As String
    Public Property Name() As String
        Get
            Return m_Name
        End Get
        Set(ByVal value As String)
            m_Name = value
        End Set
    End Property


    Private m_Orders As New List(Of SalesOrder)
    Public Property Orders() As List(Of SalesOrder)
        Get
            Return m_Orders
        End Get
```

```vbnet
            Set(ByVal value As List(Of SalesOrder))
                m_Orders = value
            End Set
        End Property
End Class
Public Class SalesOrder
    Implements System.ComponentModel.IDataErrorInfo

    Private m_Description As String
    Public Property Description() As String
        Get
            Return m_Description
        End Get
        Set(ByVal value As String)
            m_Description = value
        End Set
    End Property


    Private m_Quantity As Integer
    Public Property Quantity() As Integer
        Get
            Return m_Quantity
        End Get
        Set(ByVal value As Integer)
            m_Quantity = value
        End Set
    End Property


    Private m_DateOrdered As Date
    Public Property DateOrdered() As Date
        Get
            Return m_DateOrdered
        End Get
        Set(ByVal value As Date)
            m_DateOrdered = value
        End Set
    End Property

    Public ReadOnly Property ErrorSummary() As String _
                          Implements System.ComponentModel.IDataErrorInfo.Error
        Get
            Dim summary As New System.Text.StringBuilder
            Dim err As String = ErrorItem("Description")
            If Not err = "" Then summary.AppendLine(err)
            err = ErrorItem("Quantity")
            If Not err = "" Then summary.AppendLine(err)
            err = ErrorItem("DateOrdered")
            If Not err = "" Then summary.AppendLine(err)
            Return summary.ToString
        End Get
```

```
        End Property

        Default Public ReadOnly Property ErrorItem(ByVal columnName As String) _
                    As String Implements System.ComponentModel.IDataErrorInfo.Item
            Get
                Select Case columnName
                    Case "Description"
                        If Me.m_Description = "" Then _
                            Return "Need to order item description"
                    Case "Quantity"
                        If Me.m_Quantity <= 0 Then _
                            Return "Need to supply quantity of order"
                    Case "DateOrdered"
                        If Me.m_DateOrdered > Now Then _
                            Return "Need to specify a date in the past"
                End Select
                Return ""
            End Get
        End Property
    End Class
```

To use data binding with custom objects, follow roughly the same process as you did with DataSets. Add a new Data Source via the Data Sources window. This time, select an Object Data Source type. Doing so will display a list of available classes within the solution, as shown in Figure 31-16.

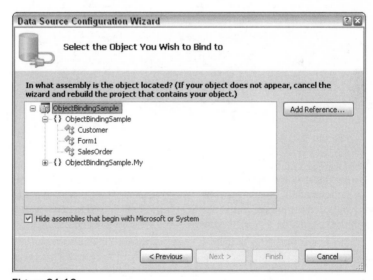

Figure 31-16

Select the Customer class and complete the wizard to add the Customer class, along with the nested list of orders, to the Data Sources window, as shown in Figure 31-17.

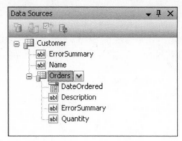

Figure 31-17

As you did previously, you can select the type of control you want for each of the fields before dragging the Customer node onto the form. Doing so adds a `CustomerBindingSource` and a `CustomerNavigator` to the form. If you set the Orders list to be a `DataGridView` and drag that onto the form, you will end up with the layout shown in Figure 31-18. As you did previously with the `DataGridView`, again opt to modify the default list of columns using the Edit Columns dialog accessible from the smart tag dialog.

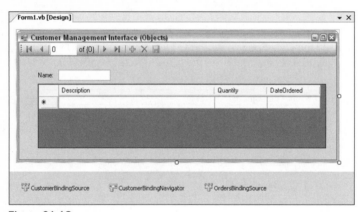

Figure 31-18

Unlike binding to a `DataSet` that has a series of `TableAdapters` to extract data from a database, there is no automatically generated fill mechanism for custom objects. The process of generating the `Customer` objects is usually handled elsewhere in the application. All you have to do here is issue the following code snippet to link the existing list of customers to the `CustomerBindingSource` so they can be displayed:

```
Private Sub Form1_Load(ByVal sender As System.Object, _
                    ByVal e As System.EventArgs) Handles MyBase.Load
    Me.CustomerBindingSource.DataSource = GetCustomers()
End Sub

Public Function GetCustomers() As List(Of Customer)
```

```
         Dim cust As New List(Of Customer)
         'Populate customers list..... eg from webservice
         Return cust
End Function
```

Running this application provides a simple interface for working with customer objects.

IDataErrorInfo

You will notice in the code provided earlier that the SalesOrder object implements the IDataErrorInfo interface. This is an interface that is understood by the DataGridView and can be used to validate custom objects. As you did in the earlier application, you need to add an ErrorProvider to the form. Instead of manually wiring up events in the ErrorProvider control, in conjunction with the DataGridView use the IDataErrorInfo interface to validate the SalesOrder objects. The running application is shown in Figure 31-19, where an invalid date and no quantity have been specified for a SalesOrder.

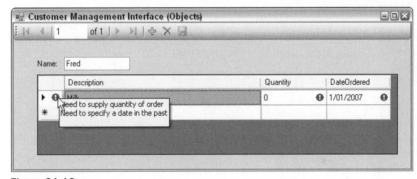

Figure 31-19

The icon at the end of the row provides a summary of all the errors. This is determined by calling the Error property of the IDataError interface. Each of the columns in turn provides an icon to indicate which cells are in error. This is determined by calling the Item property of the IDataError interface.

Application Settings

Visual Studio 2005 also provides support for binding application settings to control properties. This section illustrates this concept with the Text property of the form, but it could be any property on any control. Open the form designer, expand the Application Settings node in the Properties window, and select the Property Bindings node. This opens the Application Settings dialog, shown in Figure 31-20.

The left column indicates the properties to which you can bind an application setting. In Figure 31-20, the down arrow next to the Text property has been clicked. At the moment, there are no application settings, so click the New link to open the New Application Setting dialog shown in Figure 31-21, which enables you to create an application setting to which the Text property can be bound.

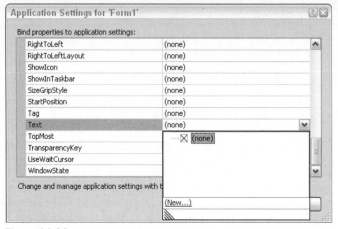

Figure 31-20

Once you complete the application setting, you can dynamically change the text on this form by changing the FormTitle setting in the Application Settings file.

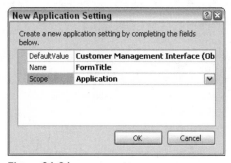

Figure 31-21

Summary

It is hoped that this chapter has given you an appreciation for how the BindingSource, Binding Navigator, and other data controls work together to give you the ability to rapidly build data applications. Because the new controls support working with either DataSets or your own custom objects, they can significantly reduce the amount of time it takes you to write an application.

In subsequent chapters you will return to working with some of the data controls that work with device applications, and you'll learn how to build mobile applications that work with SQL Mobile.

32

Add-Ins

Visual Studio 2005 has an enormous set of features right out of the box. In addition, for automating repetitive tasks, the development environment comes with a comprehensive macro system, including a standalone IDE and debugging environment. Occasionally, however, you'll encounter a situation where the existing toolset doesn't quite meet your requirements. Fortunately, Visual Studio 2005 doesn't leave you hanging, as it provides a full extensibility model that you can program against to create your own add-ins.

In this chapter you'll learn how to manage any third-party add-ins you have installed, as well as create new add-ins for your own use. The discussion covers some of the more commonly used objects and methods, and explains how to debug and deploy your add-ins successfully.

The Add-In Manager

The Add-in Manager is a utility that controls the loaded state of any add-ins defined to the Visual Studio 2005 IDE. To access the Add-in Manager, use the Tools⇨Add-In Manager menu command. All add-ins available to the particular application will be displayed in a list along with their current loading status and availability (see Figure 32-1).

Locate the add-in you wish to load and tick the checkbox next to it. If you want the add-in to start whenever the IDE is loaded, then check the Startup box, whereas if the add-in is to be loaded when the Visual Studio environment is run through the command line (such as when performing command-line builds), then you should check the Command Line box.

The lower half of the dialog displays any descriptive text associated with the add-in so you can verify the functionality that will be made available.

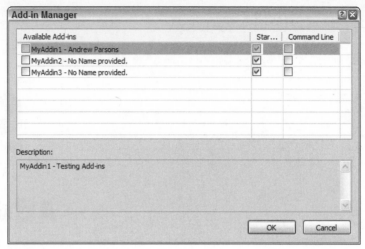

Figure 32-1

Using the Add-in Manager, you can also deactivate add-ins that may be performing abnormally or causing the IDE to function improperly even if they were loaded at startup.

You can also bypass all add-in loading when the IDE starts by holding the left Shift key down when starting Visual Studio.

Types of Add-Ins

Although using third-party add-ins is fine, the real power of Visual Studio's extensibility model lies in the capability it provides for creating your own custom-built additions to the Visual Studio 2005 IDE and command-line processes. When you create an add-in project, two options are available to you: Visual Studio add-ins and shared add-ins.

Visual Studio add-ins harness the additional functionality exposed by Visual Studio 2005's own extensibility model and are not compatible with other application hosts such as Microsoft Word. This is because in previous versions of Visual Studio, the add-in functionality was partially provided by the `Microsoft.Office.Core` namespace (particularly access to the command bars such as menus and toolbars). Visual Studio 2005 introduces a new assembly, `Microsoft.VisualStudio.CommandBars`, which is used instead, and has additional features specific to the Visual Studio IDE.

If you are building add-ins for other applications, you should choose the Shared Add-In project template. When Visual Studio walks you through the associated wizard process, you can choose which application hosts should be able to use your add-in. This list is derived from your own system setup, so make sure you have already installed the application for which you intend to program the add-in.

Visual Studio add-ins can be targeted specifically at the main Visual Studio 2005 IDE or also include the independent Macros IDE.

Creating a Simple Add-In with the Wizard

The best way to illustrate the ease of setting up an Add-In project is to walk through the project wizard creation process. This wizard enables you to include common requirements for add-ins, such as an entry on the Tools menu, and to customize where the add-in can be used.

The following exercise creates an add-in, with Visual Basic as the core language, that performs the age-old Hello World functionality when executed from the Tools menu:

1. To create an add-in, start Visual Studio 2005 and create a new project. Assuming you have the Visual Basic environmental set up, use File⇨New Project; otherwise, it will be File⇨New⇨ Project. When the New Project dialog is displayed, navigate to the Other Project Types⇨ Extensibility project group and select the Visual Studio Add-in project type. Set the project name and location as you would for any other project and click OK to have Visual Studio launch the Visual Studio Add-in Wizard.

You are presented with a welcome screen explaining what the wizard will do; simply click Next to get to the first interactive screen of the wizard.

2. The first choice you have to make is which programming language to use. For Visual Studio add-ins, you can use either managed code or native C++/ATL code, as shown in Figure 32-2. For this sample, choose "Create an Add-in using Visual Basic" and click Next to continue.

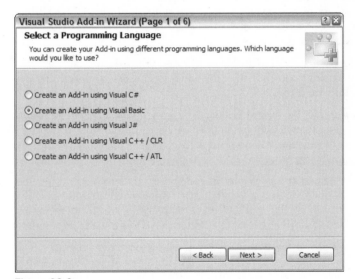

Figure 32-2

Shared add-ins, used for application hosts other than Visual Studio, don't have as many language options, with only Visual Basic, C#, and C++/ATL available.

3. Once you set the language, the next step is to choose where the add-in will be available. This step enables you to select from either the main Visual Studio 2005 IDE, the Macros IDE, or both environments to host the add-in's functionality (see Figure 32-3). Click Next after making your selection.

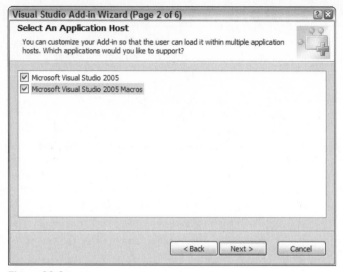

Figure 32-3

4. Step 3 of the wizard enables you to set the name and description for your add-in. These two pieces of text are displayed when configuring the add-in via the Add-in Manager dialog. By default, the name consists of the registered name of the user who installed Visual Studio 2005, along with the project name.

   This name will appear in the list of add-ins in the Add-in Manager dialog, while the description text appears in the lower half of the window so users can determine what general functionality your add-in performs.

5. The next step of the wizard is the most useful. If you accept the wizard's default settings, the project template will only create the most basic routine stubs necessary for registration of your add-in to the hosts you nominated in step 2. However, you can automate the generation of additional code by checking the options on page 4 of the wizard (see Figure 32-4).

   ❑ The first option creates the code necessary for your add-in to be added to the Tools menu. As you'll see later in this chapter, you can easily change this to any other menu within the IDE, but the code to actually hook into any menu initially is not necessarily straightforward, and it's useful to have this initialization code generated for you.

   ❑ Choosing the second option enables you to have your add-in automatically loaded when the host application is started. Again, the code necessary to have this feature implemented is automatically created for you, leaving you to concentrate on the functionality you wish to implement in the add-in itself.

   ❑ Finally, you can also indicate whether your add-in will use any modal user interface elements such as modal dialog windows. As explained in the wizard screen, modal dialogs can interfere with unattended application execution or when you're using Visual Studio from the command line to build solutions.

   If you do have modal dialogs, you can always customize the way the add-in is loaded depending on how Visual Studio itself is loaded. The OnConnection *method of the add-in includes a parameter,* connectMode, *that indicates what mode Visual Studio is in. For instance, a* connectMode *value of* ext_ConnectMode.ext_cm_CommandLine *indicates that Visual Studio is running in command-line mode, so it does not expect any user interface elements to be loaded.*

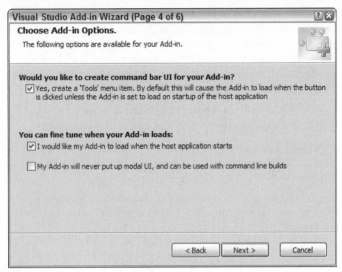

Figure 32-4

6.   The next step of the wizard enables you to specify the inclusion of information for the About dialog box for the add-in. You can specify an extended block of text to direct the users of your add-in to technical support and other information (see Figure 32-5).

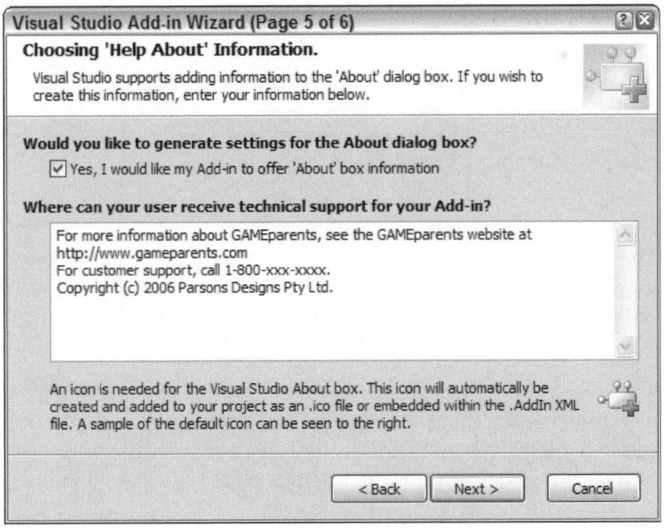

Figure 32-5

This information will be displayed in the About dialog of Visual Studio 2005 along with any other installed add-ins and products. The icon is displayed alongside the text in the Product Details pane of the About window when a user selects your add-in. You can exclude your add-in from appearing in the About dialog by unchecking the checkbox in this step.

7. Once you've entered your details for the About dialog, click Next to view a summary page detailing everything the wizard is going to do in creating your add-in. Review the settings to ensure all of the following: your add-in will be created with the Visual Basic language, it will be registered for both Visual Studio 2005 and Visual Studio 2005 Macros, the Tools menu item will be created, the add-in will be loaded when the host application starts up, and About dialog box information will be included in the add-in file.

When you're satisfied with the settings, click Finish to have the wizard generate all the associated code and configuration files to implement this functionality.

8. Without doing any customization to the project, run it by pressing F5. Because of the default debug settings, a new instance of the Visual Studio 2005 IDE will be launched with the add-in loaded automatically.

You can ensure that your add-in has loaded by looking for its entry in the Tools menu. The default entry appears at the top of the Tools menu and will have a smiley face icon associated with it (see Figure 32-6).

Figure 32-6

You can also confirm that the About dialog box information was also included by displaying the main About box (Help➪About) and scrolling the products list until you locate your add-in. Select the entry and review the product details pane to confirm that your information was included.

9. The add-in doesn't do anything at the moment, so close this extra instance of the Visual Studio IDE and return to the add-in project. Reviewing the files in the Solution Explorer, you can see that the wizard created the standard `Connect.vb` module containing the main processing of an add-in, as well as two `.AddIn` files used for deploying the add-in in either debugging or real modes.

You can customize many of the settings that were created for you in the wizard process by editing this file directly. The following listing shows a sample .AddIn file for a typical add-in. Note how multiple valid host applications are defined to the add-in, as well as the informational data for the component, such as the name and description. The LoadBehavior property controls when the add-in will be loaded, with a value of 1 representing load-at-startup functionality:

```xml
<?xml version="1.0" encoding="UTF-16" standalone="no"?>
<Extensibility xmlns="http://schemas.microsoft.com/AutomationExtensibility">
    <HostApplication>
        <Name>Microsoft Visual Studio Macros</Name>
        <Version>8.0</Version>
    </HostApplication>
    <HostApplication>
        <Name>Microsoft Visual Studio</Name>
        <Version>8.0</Version>
    </HostApplication>
    <Addin>
        <FriendlyName>MyAddin1 - Andrew Parsons</FriendlyName>
        <Description>MyAddin1 - Testing Add-ins</Description>
        <AboutBoxDetails>For more information about GAMEparents, see the
GAMEparents website at\r\nhttp://www.gameparents.com\r\nFor customer support, call
1-800-xxx-xxxx.\r\nCopyright (c) 2006 Parsons Designs Pty Ltd.</AboutBoxDetails>
        <AboutIconData>0000010006002020100000000000E802000066000000101010000000000
            ...
            FE3F0000FE3F0000FE3F0000FFFF0000</AboutIconData>
        <Assembly>MyAddin1.dll</Assembly>
        <FullClassName>MyAddin1.Connect</FullClassName>
        <LoadBehavior>1</LoadBehavior>
        <CommandPreload>1</CommandPreload>
        <CommandLineSafe>0</CommandLineSafe>
    </Addin>
</Extensibility>
```

10. Open the Connect.vb code module to add the simple "Hello World" functionality. Whenever a user clicks the menu item that corresponds to your add-in on the Tools menu, it will invoke the Exec method of the add-in, so locate the Exec routine and add a single line to display a message box like so:

```vb
Public Sub Exec(ByVal commandName As String, ByVal executeOption As _
    vsCommandExecOption, ByRef varIn As Object, ByRef varOut As Object, _
    ByRef handled As Boolean) Implements IDTCommandTarget.Exec

    handled = False
    If executeOption = vsCommandExecOption.vsCommandExecOptionDoDefault Then
        If commandName = "MyAddin1.Connect.MyAddin1" Then
            Msgbox("hello")
            handled = True
            Exit Sub
        End If
    End If
End Sub
```

Note how the Exec method works: A commandName is passed in to indicate which command the user is trying to perform. This name will equate to the value you equated with the menu item in the OnConnection startup routine, enabling you to code complex add-ins with multiple commands for your users.

You should always set the `handled` flag to `True` once you've processed the command so Visual Studio knows the menu item was processed and will stop trying to process it any further.

11. While you're editing the `Connect.vb` code, you can also change the icon to display on the Tools menu by modifying the `OnConnection` routine. Locate the statement that is used to add the item to the menu by searching for the `AddNamedCommand2` method. The sixth parameter to the function call specifies the index of the icon to use. By default, the wizard generates a value of `59`, which equates to the smiley face icon.

Change this index value to match a more suitable icon for your add-in. For instance, if your add-in were somehow related to table formatting, you might use a value of `203`, which displays a small table grid icon. The statement should now appear like the following:

```
Dim command As Command = commands.AddNamedCommand2(_addInInstance, "MyAddin1", _
    "MyAddin1", "Executes the command for MyAddin1", True, 203, Nothing, _
    CType(vsCommandStatus.vsCommandStatusSupported, Integer) + _
    CType(vsCommandStatus.vsCommandStatusEnabled, Integer), _
    vsCommandStyle.vsCommandStylePictAndText, _
    vsCommandControlType.vsCommandControlTypeButton)
```

12. Run the add-in again. This time, the icon in the Tools menu will be the table grid icon, and when you select the command from the menu, a message box is displayed with the words "Hello World."

Common Classes, Objects, and Methods

The extensibility model that accompanies Visual Studio 2005 is comprehensive, with many classes and methods available to you as you create add-ins. However, you will tend to use some members more often than others. The next few sections provide a summary of these more common members and explain how they can be used to implement the functionality you might require in your add-in.

IDTExtensibility2

The `IDTExtensibility2` interface is the core implementation of add-in projects. Every project that is defined as an add-in will have this interface included in its definition. `IDTExtensibility2` contains all of the events you can implement in your add-in that Visual Studio will raise. When you create an add-in using the Add-in Wizard, the association with this interface will be automatically included, along with the stubs for all necessary methods, such as `OnConnection`.

When added to a class in Visual Basic, the IDE will automatically generate the stubs for required methods, so simply adding the `Implements` statement and pressing Enter will provide you with the routines you must implement. However, for C# projects, you must manually create the subroutines that implement the different required members of the interface (although even here Visual Studio helps you by providing a smart tag action to implement the interface automatically). The included routines are as follows:

❑ OnAddInsUpdate

❑ OnBeginShutdown

❑ OnConnection

- ❏ OnDisconnection

- ❏ OnStartupComplete

Of these, only OnConnection is essential to initialize how your add-in will interact with the IDE and the user.

OnConnection is invoked when the hosting application adds the add-in to its collection of components. When invoked, OnConnection includes parameters identifying the application that is hosting the add-in along with how the hosting application is connecting to the add-in. This was mentioned earlier for controlling your add-in's functionality depending on whether Visual Studio was started in UI mode or command-line mode.

You should always keep a local reference to the application object and the instance of the add-in itself in module-level object variables. Again, the Add-in Wizard will generate this code for you automatically to ensure that you have the objects for later program execution. A minimal OnConnection routine would look like this:

```
Public Sub OnConnection(ByVal application As Object, _
    ByVal connectMode As ext_ConnectMode, ByVal addInInst As Object, _
    ByRef custom As Array) Implements IDTExtensibility2.OnConnection

    _applicationObject = CType(application, DTE2)
    _addInInstance = CType(addInInst, AddIn)
End Sub
```

IDTCommandTarget

If you want to integrate your add-in with the user interface of Visual Studio itself, you'll need to implement an additional interface called IDTCommandTarget. This interface belongs to the EnvDTE namespace and provides the members you will need to intercept user events and uniquely identify any commands in the add-in.

Once implemented, named commands can then be used throughout the Visual Studio IDE, including assigning keyboard shortcuts and Command Window execution. Most important, named commands can also be added to toolbars and menus.

QueryStatus

The QueryStatus method of IDTCommandTarget retrieves the current status for the specific named command. It should be used to reject any commands unknown to your add-in to avoid improper execution. The function requires the name of the command accompanied by a parameter that indicates what kind of query is to be performed. You should return a status value indicating whether or not the command is supported and whether it's even enabled (under some circumstances you may want to temporarily disable a particular command while retaining its supported status).

A typical QueryStatus method definition is shown in the following listing. This example uses the neededText property to first determine whether the calling application should retrieve the availability of the specified command:

```
Public Sub QueryStatus(ByVal commandName As String, _
    ByVal neededText As vsCommandStatusTextWanted, _
    ByRef status As vsCommandStatus, _
    ByRef commandText As Object) Implements IDTCommandTarget.QueryStatus

    If neededText = vsCommandStatusTextWanted.vsCommandStatusTextWantedNone Then
        If commandName = "MyAddin3.Connect.MyAddin3" Then
            status = CType(vsCommandStatus.vsCommandStatusEnabled + _
                vsCommandStatus.vsCommandStatusSupported, vsCommandStatus)
        Else
            status = vsCommandStatus.vsCommandStatusUnsupported
        End If
    End If
End Sub
```

Once `QueryStatus` determines that the command should be analyzed, it checks the `commandName` parameter value against the known named commands. If it is a match, `QueryStatus` returns the `status` value, identifying that the command is supported, along with a hard-coded `enabled` value as well, which dictates that the command is always available.

This `commandName` value directly correlates to the name you specify when creating a named command with the `AddNamedCommand2` method (shown later in this chapter). The set of status values you can use is as follows:

❑   `enabled`: The command is enabled and available for use.

❑   `invisible`: The command is invisible. It is up to the calling application to determine whether the command can still be executed if it is currently hidden.

❑   `supported`: The command is supported in the current context. You must include this value if the command is supported by your application, regardless of any other status values you return.

❑   `unsupported`: The command name passed to your add-in is unknown to your add-in code and is not supported. You can also use this value to indicate that the command is not supported in the particular context; for instance, a command might only be supported at design time, so while debugging you could return this value so the command is not processed.

Exec

The `Exec` method is used to execute the specified command. Once the hosting application determines via the `QueryStatus` function that a particular command is supported and available to be executed, the `Exec` command will be invoked with the named command.

You should always set the `handled` flag to `True` once you've processed a command so Visual Studio will know that the command was successfully executed according to the add-in. You can use the `execute Option` parameter to customize how the command should be performed, but Visual Studio will always call the method with a value of `vsCommandExecOptionDoDefault`, which will leave it up to the add-in to decide whether or not to use user interface elements in the processing of the specified command.

Like the `QueryStatus` function, you should use the `commandName` parameter to determine which command is being executed. In simple add-ins that only have one known command (such as the sample you walked through earlier in this chapter), it is still advisable to ensure that the `Exec` method is called with your defined command so you can avoid malfunctioning code.

AddNamedCommand2

To create named commands, use the `AddNamedCommand2` method. Any commands made known to Visual Studio via this method will be available even if the add-in itself is not loaded when the hosting application starts, meaning you can still reference the command in keyboard shortcuts and the Command Window.

Once created, a named command can then be assigned to a menu or toolbar. The following code listing is a snippet from code automatically generated after a developer inserts a newly created add-in into the Tools menu:

```
Dim commands As Commands2 = CType(_applicationObject.Commands, Commands2)
Dim toolsMenuName As String
Try
    Dim resourceManager As System.Resources.ResourceManager = _
        New System.Resources.ResourceManager("MyAddin3.CommandBar", _
        System.Reflection.Assembly.GetExecutingAssembly())
    Dim cultureInfo As System.Globalization.CultureInfo = _
        New System.Globalization.CultureInfo(_applicationObject.LocaleID)
    toolsMenuName = _
    resourceManager.GetString(String.Concat(cultureInfo.TwoLetterISOLanguageName, _
        "Tools"))
Catch e As Exception
    toolsMenuName = "Tools"
End Try
Dim commandBars As CommandBars = CType(_applicationObject.CommandBars, CommandBars)
Dim menuBarCommandBar As CommandBar = commandBars.Item("MenuBar")
Dim toolsControl As CommandBarControl = _
    menuBarCommandBar.Controls.Item(toolsMenuName)
Dim toolsPopup As CommandBarPopup = CType(toolsControl, CommandBarPopup)
Try
    Dim command As Command = commands.AddNamedCommand2(_addInInstance, "MyAddin3", _
        "MyAddin3", "Executes the command for MyAddin3", True, 59, Nothing, _
        CType(vsCommandStatus.vsCommandStatusSupported, Integer) + _
        CType(vsCommandStatus.vsCommandStatusEnabled, Integer), _
        vsCommandStyle.vsCommandStylePictAndText, _
        vsCommandControlType.vsCommandControlTypeButton)
    command.AddControl(toolsPopup.CommandBar, 1)
Catch argumentException As System.ArgumentException
End Try
```

The `AddNamedCommand2` method is used to create the `MyAddin3` named command for the `MyAddin3` add-in project. It includes the description of the command and an icon index, and defines the command as being both supported and enabled. The `commandStyle` parameter dictates how the command should appear by default, while the `commandControlType` indicates what kind of control should be used for this command's implementation.

To add this to the Tools menu, the code first uses the Resource Manager to find the current culture string representation of the Tools menu name and then uses the hosting application object's `CommandBars` collection to locate the menu bar that corresponds to that name.

Once it has been located, it drills down into the menu bar object to find the object into which the add-in command will be inserted, which in this case is a `CommandBarPopup` object. Once it has this information and the named command has been created, you can use the command's `AddControl` method to connect the command and menu.

You can use a similar method to place your command anywhere within the IDE's collection of menus and toolbars. Simply replace the string `"Tools"` with the English string representing the menu you want to hook into.

CreateToolWindow2

You can even create your own tool windows that are used as part of your add-in. The `CreateTool Window2` method forms the basis for creating a new tool window in the IDE, and requires that you first create a (standard) user control to be hosted inside its container space. This capability to host a user control means you can build complex user interfaces that reside within the IDE's workspace, and they can be docked, resized, and moved just like all the other tool windows that come with Visual Studio.

Debugging

Because add-ins are created with managed code right within Visual Studio, you can use all the same debugging procedures available to you for any other Windows application. Remember that the Debug property page for the project will default to starting up an additional instance of Visual Studio 2005 and host the debugged version of the add-in in that, so if you need to test out the add-in in the Macros IDE, changing the startup settings on that page.

Refer to Section IX for more information on debugging Windows projects.

Registration and Deployment

Add-in registration is performed with the new `.AddIn` configuration file mentioned earlier in this chapter. Within this XML-based file you specify the various settings that control how your add-in should be loaded and which hosting applications can use it. To deploy it, simply place this `.AddIn` file in the Addins folder so Visual Studio 2005 can find it. You can specify that the add-in should be available to all users or a specific user by placing it in the appropriate folder. For all users, the location is `\Documents and Settings\All Users\My Documents\Visual Studio 2005\Addins`. Replace the `All Users` string with the specific user name if you want to restrict it to a particular user.

When Visual Studio 2005 starts, it will look in this folder for any add-ins that should be loaded. When it locates an `.AddIn` file, it reads through the XML to locate the `Assembly` tag, which dictates where the actual add-in DLL is to be found.

You no longer need to register your add-in through COM as you did with previous versions of Visual Studio .NET!

Summary

Add-ins are a great way to enhance the functionality of Visual Studio 2005 with your own unique tools. To help you get started, Microsoft provides a set of example projects you can download from their site that illustrate some of the more advanced concepts in creating complex add-ins. Go to `http://msdn .microsoft.com/downloads` and search for "Visual Studio 2005 Automation Samples" to locate the current download location.

In the next chapter you'll see how the capability to customize the functionality of Visual Studio 2005 extends beyond the use of add-ins, with an introduction to creating your own custom tools and code generators.

Third-Party Extensions

The last few chapters have discussed the concepts behind creating your own extensions to the Visual Studio 2005 IDE to address scenarios you encounter where the default toolset doesn't do what you require. However, there is an alternative to spending time creating your own tools: download and use other people's creations. Over the next few pages, you will see some of the best add-ins and extensions that are currently available for Visual Studio 2005.

Most of these tools are free for personal use (in fact, a lot of them are free for corporate use too). But even those you have to pay for are worth considering because they can often reduce your workload to an extent that far outweighs the small monetary investment required to use them beyond the trial period.

> These tools are not owned or distributed by Microsoft. They are true third-party tools created and distributed by a variety of individuals and vendors. You are encouraged to visit the web site links provided in the description of the particular extension you're interested in to find out more and download (and register, if necessary) the tool from the creator/vendor directly.

Development Environment Enhancements

Sometimes you'll find yourself wishing the IDE could help you in the design of your projects and forms. While you could write a macro or more comprehensive add-in for the purpose, the two tools described here eliminate the time and effort it takes to create your own.

CoolCommands for VS2005

CoolCommands for VS2005 is a tiny set of tools that integrate directly into the IDE with no obvious interface difference. However, the small size belies two very powerful utilities that are added into the context menu of the Solution Explorer.

Resolve Project References automatically attempts to check all references to other projects and assemblies from within the active project. It enables you to ensure that you have correctly identified the associated projects for your solution, and will flag any missing files for you to fix.

The other feature that makes CoolCommands for VS2005 worth including in this list is the capability to copy and paste references between projects. Simply locate the reference in the source project, right-click, and select Copy. Then open the destination project's References folder, right-click, and select Paste. The tool will automatically add the reference correctly for you, without you needing to browse the Reference dialog to add the association.

CoolCommands for VS2005 can be downloaded from the designer's site at `http://weblogs.asp.net/GMilano/archive/2006/02/27/439208.aspx`.

MZ-Tools

MZ-Tools was first released as a free add-in for Visual Basic 6 and became one of the most popular add-in toolsets for that development environment. It boasted a huge number of features, from automated control naming and tab index allocation to code sorting and generation. Now MZ-Tools is available for Visual Studio 2005 and offers even more features and improvements that will make your development life much easier, no matter what part of the IDE you normally work in

MZ-Tools has a lot going for it as a package even though the Visual Studio 2005 version must be purchased after a 30-day trial. The small set of tool windows shown in Figure 33-1 are a great example of how MZ-Tools can make form design more efficient:

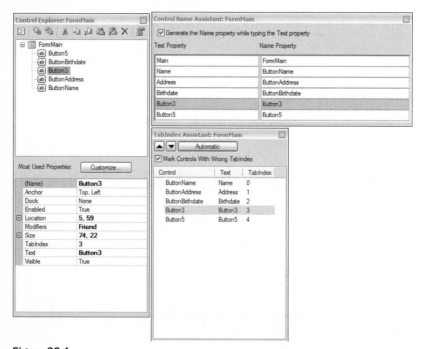

Figure 33-1

❏ The Control Explorer lists all controls currently sited on the active form layout, along with a set of commonly used properties. This enables you to quickly locate each component in the hierarchy of controls and containers and then set the properties you most often access. The Customize button gives you the capability to set which properties should be displayed.

❏ The Control Name Assistant tool window is an even more direct way of accessing the two most commonly accessed properties on a form: Name and Text. Because often the two are related, this window updates the Name property as you change the Text property so they are kept synchronized. You can customize the control prefix in the options pages for the toolset.

❏ The TabIndex Assistant has been part of MZ-Tools since its first release on Visual Basic 6. It provides a simple list of every control that can receive focus and its tab order. You can have MZ-Tools automatically reassign the tab order for the entire form using left to right, top to bottom logic.

Along with the many tool windows, MZ-Tools also comes with many other design-time enhancements, including the capability to customize default properties such as height and width for Button controls, and then to have those properties automatically assigned to the associated control type; an enhanced automatic control-positioning tool that aligns and positions controls on the form layout when you double-click them in the Toolbox; and the capability to copy all associated code (mostly in any explicitly defined event handler routines) along with a control when it is copied and pasted to another form.

Most functions are available from the toolbar, which you can customize to include only the commands you most often use (see Figure 33-2). So many options are available to you that they have been split up into Personal and Corporate options. The latter are intended to contain settings that are applied right across your company or development team, while the former include options specific to your own editing experience. Both Options screens can be accessed from the MZ-Tools toolbar or menu.

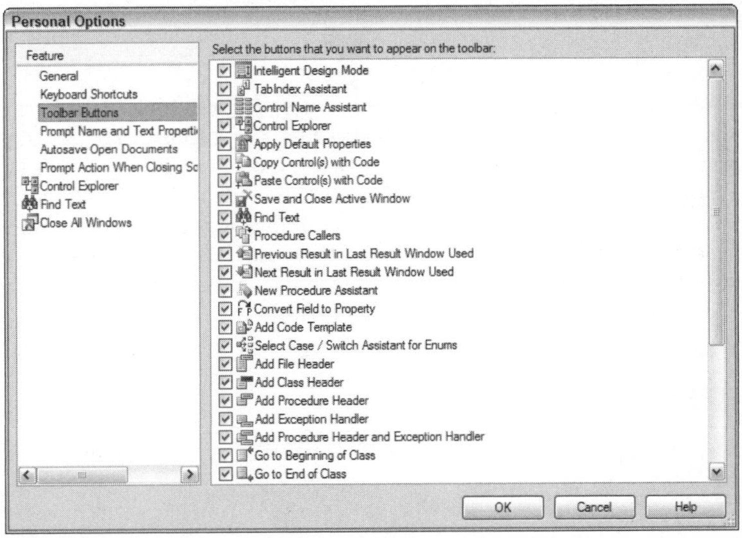

Figure 33-2

All of the commands appear on the extra menu that MZ-Tools adds to the IDE.

The Corporate options store all the customization settings for the tools. This is where you can set control prefixes, default properties, and the definitions of a variety of code stubs that can be automatically added to your modules — from file, class, and method headers to automatic exception handlers, as shown in Figure 33-3.

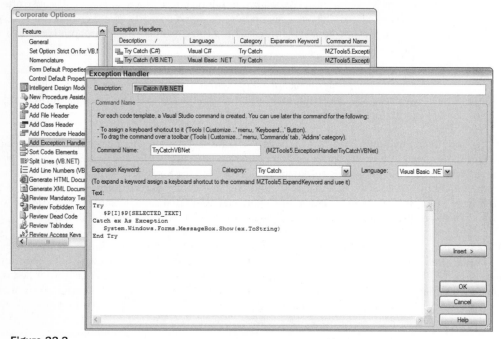

Figure 33-3

These settings and commands are just the tip of the iceberg for MZ-Tools, which also includes additional functionality that can sort your code into alphabetical order, and split and rejoin lines for Visual Basic code. In addition, a set of review functions can check for improper usage of access keys or even dead code. While some of the tools replace existing functionality with a slightly different implementation (such as the Find Text dialog), they usually include additional features that you might find useful (for example, the Find Text dialog comes with much finer scope). The best way to explore everything that MZ-Tools has to offer is to try it for yourself. Download the trial version from www.mztools.com.

Code Aids

Some tools are available just to help keep your code organized or enhance the way you write it. Here are two add-ins that integrate into your code editor window.

Imports Sorter

If you liked the idea of being able to sort code, as mentioned in the MZ-Tools description, this nifty little add-in should prove useful. The Imports Sorter has a single self-explanatory purpose — to sort the `Imports` statements in your code into a logical order so that it is consistent across all of your projects.

Using the Imports Sorter is just as simple after you've installed it. Once you add the `Imports` statements to your code, right-click anywhere in the code window and select the new Sort the Imports Block command from the context menu (see Figure 33-4).

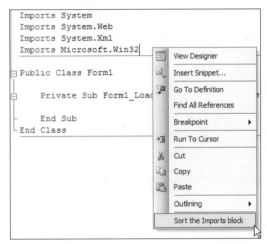

Figure 33-4

As shown in Figure 33-4, the sorted list isn't in alphabetical order, but in a predefined order that makes sense — `System` namespaces have precedence over `Microsoft` namespaces, for instance. You can change the order via the Tools menu to indicate that all of your `Imports` code blocks will always appear in the manner specified. Download this tool from `http://bordecal.mvps.org/Nicole/ImportsSorter/`.

CodeKeep

The code snippet library that comes with Visual Studio 2005 is only a small set of functions that either are commonly required or illustrate lesser-known techniques. You can, of course, add your own snippets to the library, as explained in Chapter 19, but there is no easy way of sharing your snippets with other developers, or delving into their collections of code blocks for useful snippets for your own use.

CodeKeep is a utility that integrates into the Visual Studio 2005 IDE but uses a central repository on the Internet to store any code snippets you might want to keep. You first need to create a user account on the associated web site and then use those credentials when you first install the add-in.

CodeKeep enables you to submit your own snippets, search for specific keywords in the public snippet database, or simply browse the entire database by language or author (see Figure 33-5). This window is defined as a standard tool window, which means it can be docked anywhere in the IDE, providing you with quick access to the snippet library as you work.

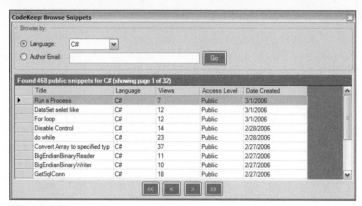

Figure 33-5

When you double-click a snippet entry, CodeKeep displays a detailed view of the code included in the snippet, along with description, usage, and a notes section (see Figure 33-6). This enables you to see exactly what will be included if you use the snippet. From this View Snippet dialog, you use the Copy button to copy the code into your module or class.

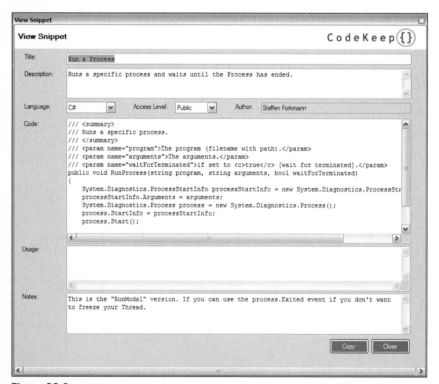

Figure 33-6

You can get started with CodeKeep by browsing the database of snippets and downloading the Visual Studio 2005 add-in found at www.codekeep.net.

Documentation

Documentation is an important part of the design process, and although it is provided for in Visual Studio 2005 with the inclusion of XML comment blocks, it's still not an easy process to implement. The golden rule of "if it's easy the developer will have more inclination to do it" means that any additional enhancements to the documentation side of development will encourage more people to use it properly.

GhostDoc is an add-in for Visual Studio that attempts to do just that, providing the capability to set up a keyboard shortcut that will automatically insert the XML comment block for a class or member. However, the true power of GhostDoc is not in the capability to create the basic stub, but to automate a good part of the documentation itself.

Through a series of lists that customize how different parts of member and variable names should be interpreted, GhostDoc will generate simple phrases that get you started in creating your own documentation. For example, consider the list shown in Figure 33-7, where words are defined as trigger points for "Of the" phrases. Whenever a variable or member name has the string "color" as part of its name, GhostDoc will attempt to create a phrase that can be used in the XML documentation. The bottom list of adjectives is used to describe the member name.

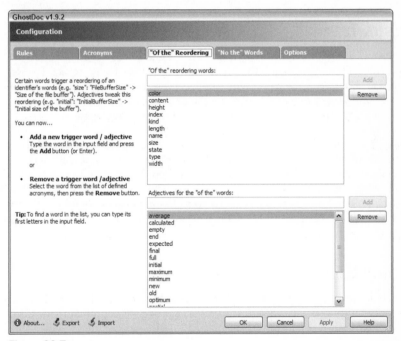

Figure 33-7

For instance, a variable name of `NewBackgroundColor` will generate a complete phrase of `New color of the background`. The functionality of GhostDoc also recognizes common parameter names and their purpose. Figure 33-8 shows this in action with a default `Load` event handler for a form. The `sender` and `e` parameters were recognized as particular types in the context of an event handler, and the documentation that was generated by GhostDoc reflects this accordingly.

```
/// <summary>
/// Handles the Load event of the Form1 control.
/// </summary>
/// <param name="sender">The source of the event.</param>
/// <param name="e">The <see cref="T:System.EventArgs"/> instance containing the event data.</param>
private void Form1_Load(object sender, EventArgs e)
{

}
```

Figure 33-8

GhostDoc is an excellent resource for those who find documentation difficult. You can find it at its official web site, www.roland-weigelt.de/ghostdoc.

Testing and Debugging

Many components of Visual Studio 2005 help you to test and debug your solutions, but not surprisingly, you can also find some very good third-party components that can enhance your experience in this area too. The following tools vary in size and functionality, but both will aid you as you test your applications.

Regex Visualizer

Regular expressions can sometimes be hard to decipher and understand, and often the time it hits hardest is when debugging an application that isn't behaving as you would expect. The Regex Visualizer builds on the capability to create your own visualizers for debugging purposes (which is explained in Chapter 50) by providing a descriptive explanation of a regular expression string and, when used in conjunction with regular expression objects, any matches that met the criteria.

Figure 33-9 demonstrates the visualizer in action with a simple regular expression of (The) *book. The visualizer hooks into the String variable and adds an extra option of how to view the data, with the Matches Details dialog being displayed when it is invoked. The Pattern Desc tab provides an English translation of what the regular expression is trying to match on; in this case, it has determined that the criteria specify looking for zero or more occurrences of The immediately followed by book. To download the visualizer, visit the author's web site at http://weblogs.asp.net/rosherove/archive/2005/11/26/AnnoucingRegexKit10.aspx.

TestDriven.NET

No discussion of third-party tools for Visual Studio would be complete without a mention of TestDriven .NET. This tool enables you to run a series of unit tests as well as coordinate code coverage testing with a variety of testing frameworks, including NUnit and Visual Studio Team System.

In addition, you can build your own tests with its built-in ad hoc testing framework, and run them as easily as right clicking in the code window and selecting Run Test(s) from the context menu. As you run the tests through their paces, the chosen framework will be invoked, presenting the results in its own way. Get started with TestDriven.NET by visiting the official product web site at www.testdriven.net.

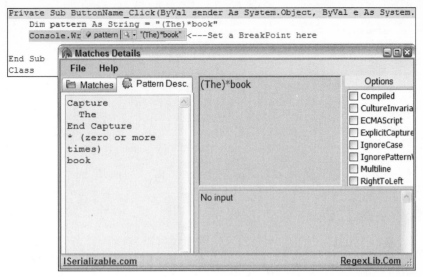

Figure 33-9

Summary

Dozens of add-ins are available for Visual Studio 2005, but the products highlighted in this chapter describe tools that are either simple but effective, or of a very high quality, enabling you to avoid wading through the murky waters of unknown extensions.

Using third-party add-ins enables you to extend the development experience of Visual Studio 2005 beyond the initial environment setup without having to invest time in creating your own tools. The tools in this chapter cover a wide range of functionality, from assisting you in creating documentation and testing cycles to small helper commands and whole tool suites, such as MZ-Tools. The one thing they do have in common, however, is that they are all excellent additions to a Visual Studio 2005 developer's toolbox.

34

Starter Kits

Visual Studio 2005 comes with a wide array of project templates from which you can start building applications. However, each project type does the absolute minimum, creating a blank form, control, or page, leaving the rest up to you. Starter kits take the concept of a project template and add a whole bunch of functionality into the generated output.

Each starter kit shows you best practices for different programming and design concepts, and can be used as a basis for creating your own applications and solutions that share similar features. Perhaps one of the best uses for the official starter kits is to look through the code that is included in the default project generation to see how Microsoft recommends you implement the various techniques, including new programming concepts such as generics, and design elements such as SQL Server database files.

This chapters completes the Automation part of this book by introducing you to each of the four main starter kits that are installed with Visual Studio 2005, describing their purpose and what functionality you can find in them for use with your own applications.

Working with starter kits is easy because they work the same way that normal project templates do and are integrated into the New Project dialog for each language that you can use. Locate the starter kit you want to implement in the New Project dialog, select a name for your instance of it, and click OK to have Visual Studio 2005 process the template and generate all of the required code and data files.

> While there is a Starter Kit subcategory within the C#, J#, and Visual Basic project groups, unfortunately not all starter kits will appear in that location. For instance, the Card Game Starter Kit appears only at the root project group for C# and Visual Basic. While it is frustrating that some of the starter kits were implemented incorrectly by Microsoft, there's no question of the value they provide to developers in getting a handle on different techniques, as explained in this chapter.

The Card Game Starter Kit

The Card Game Starter Kit is the most basic kit, covering the use of graphics in Windows Forms applications, using the new settings and resources designers, and introducing programming techniques found in the new 2.0 version of C# and Visual Basic, such as generics.

The default project comes ready to compile and run with the game of Black Jack. It uses a series of forms that contain numerous components such as `Button` and `TextBox` controls, which have their properties customized so they appear to be graphically drawn, rather than standard Windows Forms controls (see Figure 34-1).

The form graphics are stored in the resources file that accompanies the project and can be browsed through the Resources page of the Project Designer, while the graphics associated with the player object and card background are saved in separate files, which are then connected to their appropriate component through the Settings page. Keeping the files separate like this shows you how you might best approach building a similar application — with some graphical elements hard-coded into the design, and others easily changed by changing the external image file.

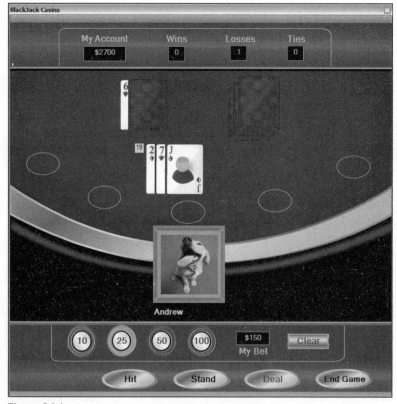

Figure 34-1

In addition to showing you how to use settings and resources, the project builds a set of classes that interact with each other to create a deck of cards, as well as a collection of players. If you were to create your own card game application, you could easily use these classes as a starting point, including the use of generic collections, which are new to .NET 2.0.

The Screensaver Starter Kit

The Screensaver Starter Kit goes an extra step beyond the project based on a card game. It teaches you how to harness the GDI+ engine to draw various graphical and textual objects onscreen, as well as consume RSS feeds from the web and process XML using the `System.XML` namespace.

When the project is compiled and started in its default configuration, it will invoke the screensaver with an empty RSS feed and a series of default images (as shown in Figure 34-2). However, the project shows you how to take advantage of command-line arguments with the `/c` parameter, invoking an options form that can be used to customize the directory for background images as well as the location for an RSS feed to consume.

Figure 34-2

The code uses the `OnPaint` and `OnPaintBackground` events to draw the graphics on the screensaver form, harnessing the power of the GDI+ engine for the different components. Using these events means that every component needs to be manually painted, but it also provides you with total control over what appears.

In addition to the graphics-based coding blocks illustrated throughout the project, the Screensaver Starter Kit also shows you how to use the `WebClient` class to connect to and download information (an RSS feed) from the Internet. It uses `WebClient` in conjunction with `XmlTextReader` and `XmlNode` objects to extract the information from the RSS feed into a human-readable form and presents it on the screensaver form.

The Movie Collection Starter Kit

With the Movie Collection Starter Kit, you can see how data binding works, with the project building a single form that connects to a database file to store a collection of movie DVDs. The standard kit only allows you to enter the information manually and view your existing data, but is still a useful project because it demonstrates how easy it is to implement a project using a SQL Server database file without having to resort to using an instance of SQL Server.

The main form is actually empty and hosts two user controls, each of which contains its own set of user interface components and business logic. This implementation illustrates how you can achieve easy customization of the user interface for your own projects, with many of the components obtaining their appearance from a resources file of images (see Figure 34-3).

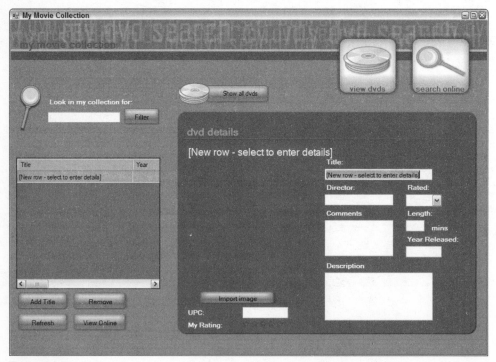

Figure 34-3

However, the primary purpose of this starter kit is to show you how to connect different components to a database, and the code fully documents this process so you can reuse the techniques of populating data-bound controls at runtime in your own applications.

A web-enabled version of the Movie Collection Starter Kit is available for download. This version implements the online search capabilities of the application and introduces additional techniques for connecting to web services and consuming the information they expose in a Windows Forms environment. To download the latest version of the starter kit, refer to the documentation that comes with the kit in Visual Studio 2005.

The Personal Web Site Starter Kit

The Personal Web Site Starter Kit introduces you to a wide array of web-specific functionality. The accompanying documentation walks you through the process of setting up the security and basic user configuration for a user-based site.

A number of the new components available in ASP.NET 2.0 are covered with this starter kit, including the ability to create master pages that can then be used to contain details pages and control their appearance. Figure 34-4 shows the default configuration of the project as it appears in Internet Explorer. The top part of the page is part of the master page, while the rest is defined in a details page that inherits the style and structure of the master.

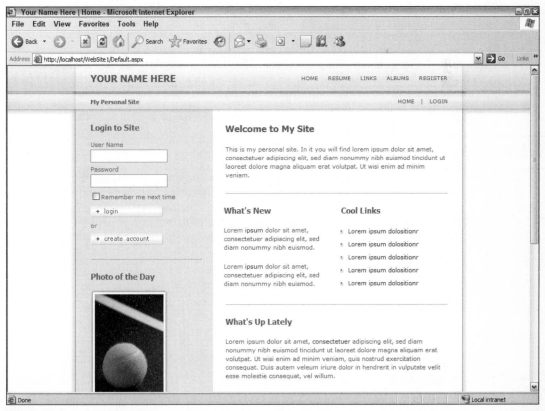

Figure 34-4

The kit also illustrates how to implement user management for a site (with functionality being activated and deactivated based on which user is logged in), and includes a number of common functions found in a personal site, such as photo albums and common links.

Creating Your Own Starter Kit

Creating your own starter kit is actually quite easy. Because starter kits are basically just project templates with pre-generated code, all you need to do is follow the same steps you would follow if you were creating a project template, including the additional form design, components and properties, and all underlying code.

You can include as many files as you require, including documentation like the official starter kits. You can even have Visual Studio automatically open the files you want to display. Chapter 25 has a complete discussion about creating your own project templates for use as a starting point. Once you have created your project and tested it to ensure that it will build without error, you should export it as a project template.

To open files automatically, edit the .vstemplate file for the project template and locate the ProjectItem node that corresponds to each file you want to display to developers using the starter kit, and add an OpenInEditor attribute with a value of true. You can also use the OpenOrder attribute to specify the order in which the files should be opened, as shown in the following example:

```
<ProjectItem OpenInEditor="true" OpenOrder="10">MyForm.vb</ProjectItem>
<ProjectItem OpenInEditor="true" OpenOrder="20">ReadMe.html</ProjectItem>
```

Using these official starter kits in conjunction with the walkthrough for creating project templates in Chapter 25 as a basis, you will be able to create good, strongly built starter kits of your own, which can be used as a basis for starting complex projects with a set of corporate standards-compliant classes and objects such as user controls and forms. Even solo developers should benefit from the ability to create starter kits in this fashion.

Summary

The Automation part of this book has shown you many techniques that can be used through the Visual Studio 2005 IDE to minimize the amount of work you need to perform for a variety of tasks that were previously difficult to implement, including assembly signing, creating your own add-ins, item and project templates, and strongly typing DataSets and creating macros to minimize repetition. Section VII continues with this theme, demonstrating additional ways to save time in Visual Studio 2005.

Part VII
Other Time Savers

35

Workspace Control

The opening chapters of this book described several of the windows that are built into Visual Studio 2005 to help you visualize your application. This chapter provides a summary of all the available windows and their functionality. Where these windows are covered in more detail in other chapters, cross-references are provided so information isn't duplicated. In addition, several shortcuts and techniques are presented in this chapter to help you build applications with Visual Studio 2005.

Visual Studio 2005 Windows

Visual Studio 2005 has numerous windows that can help you visualize your application, or aid in writing or debugging code. This section provides an outline of most of these windows. A cross-reference is provided where a windows is covered in more detail in another chapter. Not all of these windows are available in the Professional version of Visual Studio 2005. Windows available only in the Team Suite version are appropriately marked.

Start Page

Figure 35-1 shows the Start page that is initially displayed when you open Visual Studio 2005. Depending on your selected profile, different articles are loaded from MSDN.

The Start page is available for all versions of Visual Studio 2005. It can be disabled via the Options item on the Tools menu.

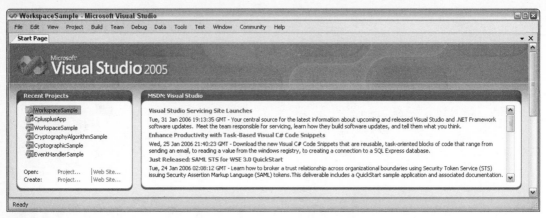

Figure 35-1

Code/Designer

The main window, which appears in the center of Visual Studio 2005 and is shown in Figure 35-2, houses code files, the design surface for windows forms, web forms, components, and data designers. The main window is also used by default by some of the other Visual Studio 2005 windows. With the new window docking feature, any window can be displayed in the main window, pinned to an edge, or left floating.

Figure 35-2

Further information about the code window can be found in Chapter 1 and Chapter 5, in the discussion on customizing window layout.

Solution Explorer

The Solution Explorer shows the layout of the files that make up your application. In Visual Studio 2005, the default view hides many of the designer-generated files so the solution appears less cluttered. In Figure 35-3, the Show All Files button has been toggled so you can see all the files associated with this application.

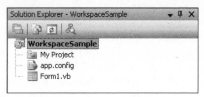

Figure 35-3

More information on the Solution Explorer is available in Chapters 1 and 4.

Properties

Properties associated with the currently selected object are displayed in the Properties window shown in Figure 35-4. This window provides a visual interface to the code that ultimately sets these properties at runtime.

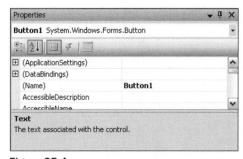

Figure 35-4

More information on the Properties window is available in Chapter 1.

Toolbox

Figure 35-5 shows the Toolbox that is displayed when editing a file using the designer surface. Different designers have different sets of controls, so the Toolbox is dynamically adjusted to include items relevant in the current context.

Figure 35-5

More information on the Toolbox is available in Chapter 1.

Server Explorer

The Server Explorer, shown in Figure 35-6, provides a link between Visual Studio 2005 and your computer. The first node shows the list of data connections that have been used in the past. Each data connection is represented by a separate node through which that database can be manipulated. The second node lists the servers that have been connected. By default, the local computer appears in this list, but any other computer that you have permissions to access can be connected to. Each computer has a series of nodes that represent the hardware and services available. For example, the Event Viewer can be launched from the right-click context menu off the Event Logs node.

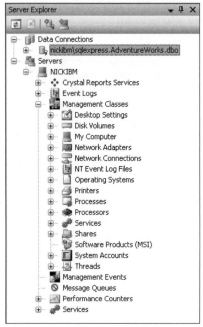

Figure 35-6

Other nodes can be dragged onto the designer surface to create a component that can be used to interact with that node. For example, dragging a service from the Services list onto a form will add a Service Controller component to the nonvisual area on the design surface. This enables the service to be controlled from the form.

Error List

Any errors or warnings that occur during compilation are added to the Error List, as shown in Figure 35-7. Toggling the buttons will show or hide errors, warnings, and messages so you can work through any issues in your application. The list of columns can be adjusted to customize the Error List to provide the information you need.

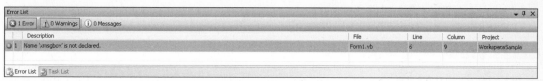

Figure 35-7

More information on the Error List is available in Chapter 1.

Object Browser

Figure 35-8 shows the Object Browser, which you can use to search or navigate the list of referenced types. This can be useful for locating a type when you only remember part of the name or for determining what methods are available for a particular type.

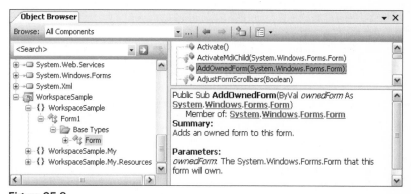

Figure 35-8

In the lower-right pane, information about the selected method is provided, including a summary of the method and a list of the parameters it expects.

Task List

Visual Studio 2005 has a separate Task List that you can use to track outstanding tasks. Tasks can be added using special TODO comments, which will appear to all users making changes to the code, as shown in Figure 35-9. Alternative tasks can be added directly into the task pane but will only be available to that user. The user tasks can be seen by selecting User Tasks from the drop-down box.

Figure 35-9

More information on working with the Task List is available in Chapter 2.

Class View

In Figure 35-10 the Class View shows part of the inheritance hierarchy for Form1 in the `WorkspaceSample` namespace. This view is useful if you have a deep inheritance model or need to remember a method name.

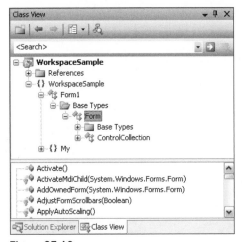

Figure 35-10

The Class View window can also be used to open the class diagram or to create an instance of a class using the Object Test Bench.

Code Definition

Figure 35-11 shows the Code Definition window, which appears underneath the code window and displays the definition of the symbol that was last selected. Although the code can't be edited in the Code Definition window, the code window can be moved to the definition line from the right-click context menu.

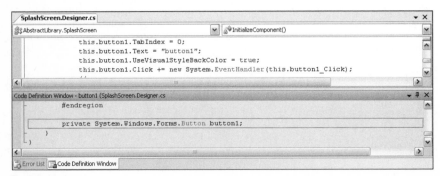

Figure 35-11

This feature works only for C# and C++ code files.

Output

The Output window has a dual purpose — first, to show the status during compilation; and second, to display any output that the application may have written to the console. Errors during the build process will be displayed in the Build output, while application output will display in the Debug output. This can be selected using the drop-down shown in Figure 35-12.

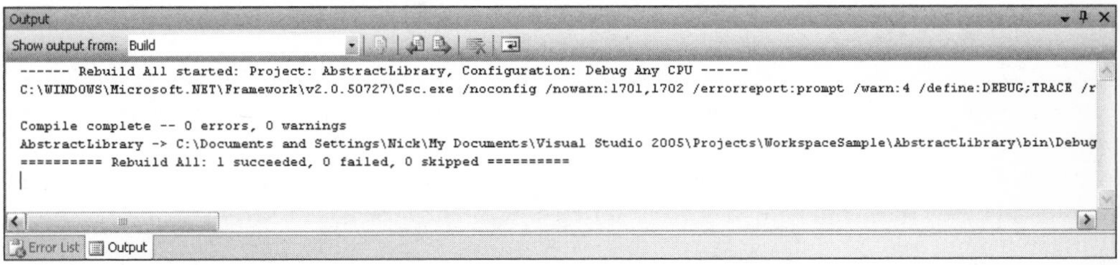

Figure 35-12

More information on the Output window is available in Chapter 49.

Find Results

The Find Results window, shown in Figure 35-13, displays the results of a search, using Find in Files. Double-clicking a line in the results window will open the appropriate code window.

Figure 35-13

There are multiple Find Results windows, and the find results can be directed to the appropriate window from the Find and Replace dialog under the Result options. This window is covered in more detail in the next chapter.

Call Browser

The Call Browser, available to C++ developers, can be used to locate where a method is being called from, as shown in Figure 35-14, and to navigate to other methods it calls.

To launch the Call Browser, select either Show Callers Graph or Show Call Graph from the Call Browser item on the right-click context menu for the method you are interested in.

Figure 35-14

Command Window

Most macros and built-in commands can be invoked using either a key combination or a menu. The Command Window can be used to invoke a Visual Studio 2005 command or macro by name.

In Figure 35-15, the `View.SolutionExplorer` command was executed to display the Solution Explorer. On the last line, a new command has been started and IntelliSense has kicked in to provide auto-completion once a command or macro with the correct name has been located.

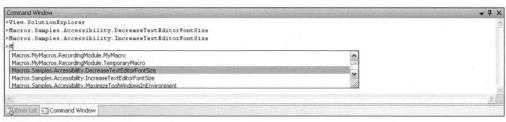

Figure 35-15

Document Outline

Most ASP.NET developers will be familiar with the Document Outline window, which displays the hierarchy of HTML tags. This window can now be used by Windows application developers to show the nesting of controls on a form, as shown in Figure 35-16.

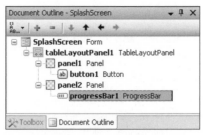

Figure 35-16

More information on the Document Outline window is available in Chapter 13.

Object Test Bench

When coding a class, we often want to create an instance without running the entire application. This is where the Object Test Bench can be used to house an instance of the class and enable you to invoke methods. Figure 35-17 shows an instance of the SplashScreen form, and from the right-click context menu you can invoke the button1_Click method.

Figure 35-17

More information on using the Object Test Bench is provided in Chapter 14.

Performance Explorer

Once the Performance Wizard has been run, the options can be configured via the Performance Explorer window, shown in Figure 35-18. Each time the performance tool is executed, a new report is generated, which can be used to analyze memory allocation, object lifetime, and garbage collection performance.

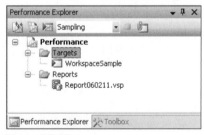

Figure 35-18

More information on the Performance Explorer is available in Chapter 56. This window is only available as part of the Team Suite version of Visual Studio 2005.

Property Manager

Unlike C# and VB.NET, which use the new Project Properties window, C++ projects use the Property Manager to configure property sheets that can be applied to one or more project configurations. Figure 35-19 shows debug and release configurations for a project, with an additional property sheet being applied to the debug configuration.

Figure 35-19

Property sheets can inherit from other property sheets, making it possible to build a hierarchy, which makes the tree format for this window very appropriate.

Resource View

The Resource View, only applicable to C++ developers, can be used to navigate the resources that are associated with a particular project, as shown in Figure 35-20. Resources can be edited within Visual Studio 2005 by double-clicking on them from this view.

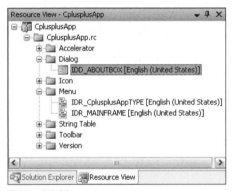

Figure 35-20

C# and VB.NET applications use the Resources tab on the Project Properties window, which is covered in Chapter 10.

History

A change history for a file that is under source control with Team Foundation Server can be reviewed using the History window, shown in Figure 35-21. Alternatively, a modal dialog is available for those working with another source control provider.

Figure 35-21

More information on working with source control is available in Chapter 8. This window is only available as part of the Team Suite version of Visual Studio 2005.

Source Control Explorer

In Figure 35-22 the Source Control Explorer appears in the main window. This can be used to navigate the repository built into Team Foundation Server. Files can be checked in and out, versions can be compared, and merge operations can be carried out using this window.

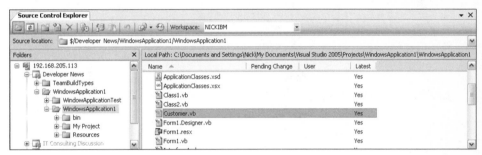

Figure 35-22

More information on the Source Control Explorer is available in Chapter 8. This window is only available as part of the Team Suite version of Visual Studio 2005.

Pending Changes

When a file is checked out of the source control repository, it appears in the Pending Changes window shown in Figure 35-23. This interface can be used to incrementally check files in, roll back changes, or compare the controlled version with the version being worked on.

Figure 35-23

More information on the Pending Changes window is available in Chapter 8. This window varies between versions of Visual Studio 2005; the Team Suite version, shown here, permits association between pending changes and work items.

Macro Explorer

Figure 35-24 shows the Macro Explorer, which can be used to browse and execute macros. Macros can also be modified by selecting the Edit item from the right-click context menu.

Figure 35-24

Web Browser

Visual Studio 2005 has a built-in web browser, shown in Figure 35-25, that can be used instead of opening another application.

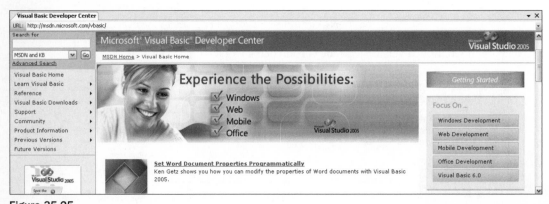

Figure 35-25

Each .NET language has its own developer center, accessible via the MSDN site at `http://msdn.microsoft.com`, which provides updates on best practices and information on how to work efficiently with Visual Studio 2005.

Team Explorer

Navigating information held in a Team Foundation Server can be done using the Team Explorer, shown in Figure 35-26. This window provides access to queries that can be used to return work items, available build types, and the source control repository.

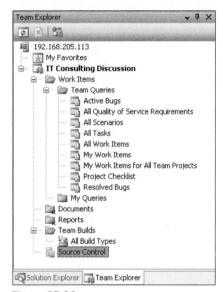

Figure 35-26

More information on the Team Explorer is available in Chapter 56. This window is only available after the Team Foundation Client has been installed on top of the Team Suite version of Visual Studio 2005.

Breakpoints

The Breakpoints window is useful for navigating between breakpoints and reviewing any breakpoint conditions. Figure 35-27 shows a breakpoint that will break the fifth time the line of code is executed.

Figure 35-27

More information on the Breakpoints window is available in Chapter 49.

Immediate

The Immediate window, shown in Figure 35-28, can be used to evaluate expressions without having to run the application. This can be useful if you are unsure of how a method functions or would like to test a method you are currently implementing.

Immediate Window
y=7
z=x+y
debug.Print(z)
13
Breakpoints
Immediate Window

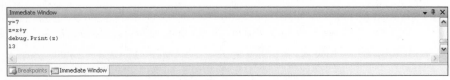

Figure 35-28

More information on the Immediate window is available in Chapter 49.

Script Explorer

Developers who have to work with scripts (JavaScript or VBScript) embedded in their ASP.NET applications can use the Script Explorer, shown in Figure 35-29, to help them navigate and debug their code.

Script Explorer
Microsoft Internet Explorer (NICKIBM)
Default.aspx

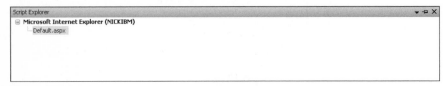

Figure 35-29

More information on the Script Explorer window is available in Chapter 49.

Registers

Figure 35-30 shows the Registers window, which can be used to monitor the values held in the Registers as the application executes.

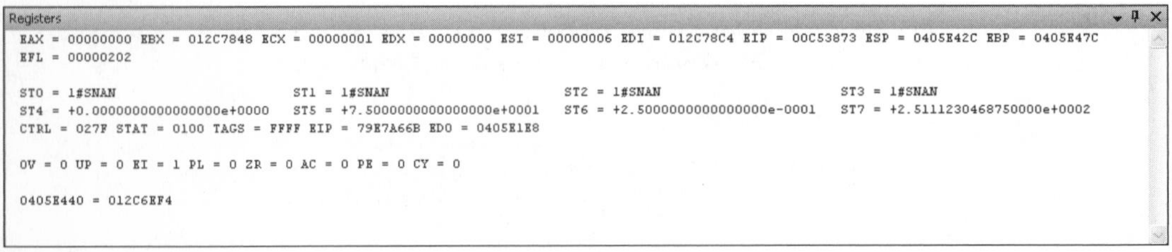
Registers
EAX = 00000000 EBX = 012C7848 ECX = 00000001 EDX = 00000000 ESI = 00000006 EDI = 012C78C4 EIP = 00C53873 ESP = 0405E42C EBP = 0405E47C
EFL = 00000202
ST0 = 1#SNAN
ST1 = 1#SNAN
ST2 = 1#SNAN
ST3 = 1#SNAN
ST4 = +0.0000000000000000e+0000
ST5 = +7.5000000000000000e+0001
ST6 = +2.5000000000000000e-0001
ST7 = +2.5111230468750000e+0002
CTRL = 027F STAT = 0100 TAGS = FFFF EIP = 79E7A66B EDO = 0405E1E8
OV = 0 UP = 0 EI = 1 PL = 0 ZR = 0 AC = 0 PE = 0 CY = 0
0405E440 = 012C6EF4

Figure 35-30

More information on the Registers window is available in Chapter 49.

Disassembly

The Disassembly window, shown in Figure 35-31, can be used to step through code at a micro level. It is rare to have to debug at this level, but reviewing the execution of the IL statements can reveal performance and other issues that might otherwise have been overlooked.

Disassembly
Address: n2_Click(Object, System.EventArgs)
00000029 xor ebx,ebx
0000002b xor edx,edx
0000002d mov dword ptr [ebp-4Ch],edx
00000030 nop
testMethod()
00000031 mov ecx,dword ptr [ebp-3Ch]
00000034 cmp dword ptr [ecx],ecx
00000036 call 005F12B4
0000003b nop

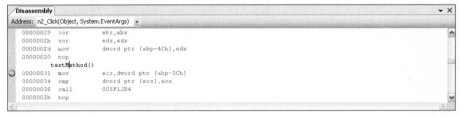

Figure 35-31

More information on the Disassembly window is available in Chapter 49.

Memory

The Memory window, shown in Figure 35-32, can be used to monitor memory during execution.

Memory 1
Address: 0x022730C8
Columns: Auto

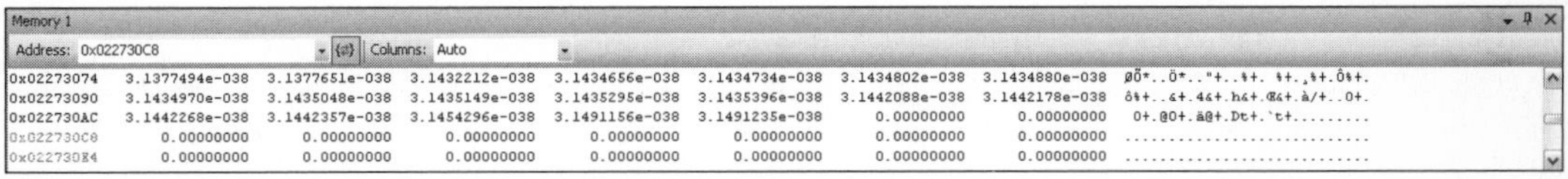

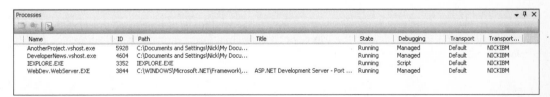

Figure 35-32

More information on the Memory window is available in Chapter 49.

Processes

In Figure 35-33, the Processes window displays a list of the processes that the debugger is currently attached to and their state.

Processes
Name
ID
Path
Title
State
Debugging
Transport
Transport...
AnotherProject.vshost.exe 5928 C:\Documents and Settings\Nick\My Docu... Running Managed Default NICKIBM
DeveloperNews.vshost.exe 4604 C:\Documents and Settings\Nick\My Docu... Running Managed Default NICKIBM
IEXPLORE.EXE 3352 IEXPLORE.EXE Running Script Default NICKIBM
WebDev.WebServer.EXE 3844 C:\WINDOWS\Microsoft.NET\Framework\... ASP.NET Development Server - Port ... Running Managed Default NICKIBM

Figure 35-33

More information on the Processes window is available in Chapter 49.

Modules

The Modules window, shown in Figure 35-34, shows which assemblies have been loaded and whether their symbols have also been loaded. In order for the debugger to step into the assembly code, an appropriate symbol file must be located.

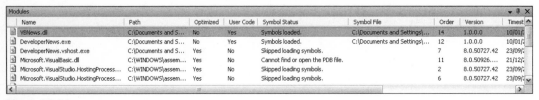

Name	Path	Optimized	User Code	Symbol Status	Symbol File	Order	Version	Timest
VBNews.dll	C:\Documents and S...	No	Yes	Symbols loaded.	C:\Documents and Settings\...	14	1.0.0.0	10/01/
DeveloperNews.exe	C:\Documents and S...	No	Yes	Symbols loaded.	C:\Documents and Settings\...	12	1.0.0.0	10/01/
DeveloperNews.vshost.exe	C:\Documents and S...	Yes	No	Skipped loading symbols.		7	8.0.50727.42	23/09/
Microsoft.VisualBasic.dll	C:\WINDOWS\assem...	Yes	No	Cannot find or open the PDB file.		11	8.0.50926....	21/12/
Microsoft.VisualStudio.HostingProcess...	C:\WINDOWS\assem...	Yes	No	Skipped loading symbols.		2	8.0.50727.42	23/09/
Microsoft.VisualStudio.HostingProcess...	C:\WINDOWS\assem...	Yes	No	Skipped loading symbols.		6	8.0.50727.42	23/09/

Figure 35-34

More information on the Modules window is available in Chapter 49.

Threads

In building a multi-threaded application, it is essential to be able to switch between threads. The Threads window can be used to show the execution point for each running thread (see Figure 35-35). It also displays the priority, name, and ID of each thread.

ID	Name	Location	Priority	Suspend
5128	<No Name>		Normal	0
6032	.NET SystemEvents		Normal	0
4980	Main Application Thread	VBNews.Customer.set_Name	Normal	0
5836	Thread 0	VBNews.Customer.threadRun	Normal	0
4788	Thread 1	VBNews.Customer.threadRun	Normal	0
5584	Thread 2	VBNews.Customer.threadRun	Normal	0
1908	Thread 3	VBNews.Customer.threadRun	Normal	0
2872	Thread 4	VBNews.Customer.threadRun	Normal	0
3128	Thread 5		Normal	0

Figure 35-35

More information on the Threads window is available in Chapter 49.

Call Stack

Figure 35-36 shows the Call Stack window, which can be used to determine a call graph. This can be important when trying to identify the source of an issue. In a multi-threaded application, you can display the call stack for the currently selected thread in the Threads window.

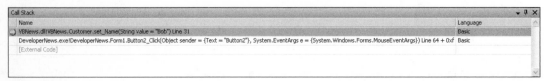

Name	Language
VBNews.dll!VBNews.Customer.set_Name(String value = "Bob") Line 31	Basic
DeveloperNews.exe!DeveloperNews.Form1.Button2_Click(Object sender = {Text = "Button2"}, System.EventArgs e = {System.Windows.Forms.MouseEventArgs}) Line 64 + 0xf	Basic
[External Code]	

Figure 35-36

More information on the Call Stack window is available in Chapter 49.

Autos, Locals, and Watch

The multiple Watch windows — which include the Autos, Locals, and a number of additional user-configurable Watch windows — are used to display the value of variables when the application is in break mode (see Figure 35-37). Nested properties can be navigated by expanding the plus (+) symbol.

Figure 35-37

More information on the Watch windows is available in Chapter 49.

Code Coverage

Testing is a difficult art and being able to determine the percentage of your application that has been tested is nearly impossible. One metric that can be used is how much of your code has been executed — in other words, the code coverage of your test cases. The Code Coverage window shown in Figure 35-38 illustrates a method that is yet to be tested. Other methods are completely covered by the existing test cases.

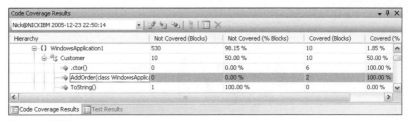

Figure 35-38

More information on the Code Coverage window is available in Chapters 55 and 56. This window is only available as part of the Team Suite version of Visual Studio 2005.

Test Results

Figure 35-39 shows the Test Results window, which displays the results of the set of tests that were executed. Clicking on any of the results will open a more detailed analysis of the test.

Figure 35-39

More information on the Test Results window is available in Chapters 55 and 56. This window is only available as part of the Team Suite version of Visual Studio 2005.

Test Manager

The Test Manager, illustrated in Figure 35-40, is used to create a list of tests that can be scheduled or run as a group. This is useful if an application has a large set of tests. A subset of the tests pertaining to the area of the application being worked on can be created so developers can continuously run the tests to ensure they don't break anything. The full set of tests should also be run as frequently as possible.

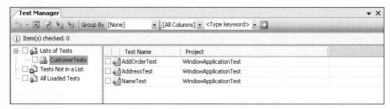

Figure 35-40

More information on the Test Manager is available in Chapter 56. This window is only available as part of the Team Suite version of Visual Studio 2005.

Test View

Figure 35-41 shows the Test View window, which can be used to select and run individual test cases.

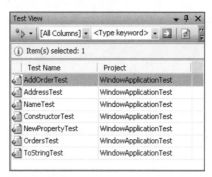

Figure 35-41

More information on the Test View window is available in Chapters 55 and 56. This window is only available as part of the Team Suite version of Visual Studio 2005.

Team Builds

The Team Builds window (see Figure 35-42) is available only as part of the Team Suite version of Visual Studio 2005.

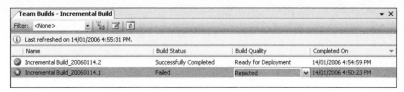

Figure 35-42

More information on this window is available in Chapter 56.

Test Runs

Team Foundation Server can be used to schedule a set of tests, perhaps as part of the build process. These test runs can be reviewed using the Test Runs window, shown in Figure 35-43.

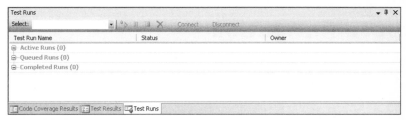

Figure 35-43

More information on the Test Runs window is available in Chapter 56. This window is only available as part of the Team Suite version of Visual Studio 2005.

Bookmarks

The Bookmarks window, shown in Figure 35-44, can be used to navigate, enable, and disable bookmarks throughout your code.

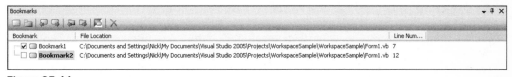

Figure 35-44

Data Sources

Figure 35-45 shows the Data Sources window, which is used to generate strongly typed data access code and to provide drag-and-drop support for building data-bound user interfaces.

Figure 35-45

More information on using the Data Sources window is covered in Chapters 30 and 31.

Workspace Navigation

This section describes a few tricks you can employ when navigating within Visual Studio 2005 that can help you write and debug your application.

Full Screen Mode

Most developers at some stage or another have cursed because no matter how big their monitor is, they can't quite fit everything onto the screen. Visual Studio 2005 supports running in full screen mode, which will give you back those lost centimeters. This can be invoked from the View menu, and a Full Screen release button appears in the menu bar. By default, none of the extra windows, such as the Toolbox or the Solution Explorer, are visible. These can be displayed from the View menu, and the configuration will be automatically saved for the next time you work in full screen mode.

In Figure 35-46 you can see the Full Screen release button at the top of the window. Notice that, as you would expect, Visual Studio 2005 takes up the entire screen.

Navigation Keys

Although using the mouse is good for dragging around controls on a form or designing an XML schema using the visual designer, when you write code it is inconvenient to have to switch back to the mouse to navigate. This section shares a couple of shortcuts that can make navigating with the keyboard easier than with the mouse. In some cases the keyboard shortcuts are modified as part of the profile you have selected. If the shortcuts mentioned in this section do not work, use the Keyboard node in the Options window to find the command and the associated keyboard shortcut.

Forward/Backward

As you move within and between files, Visual Studio 2005 tracks where you have been, in a similar way that a web browser tracks the sites you have visited. Using the Navigate Forward and Navigate Backward items from the View menu you can easily go back and forth between files that you are working on. The keyboard shortcut to navigate backward is Ctrl+−. To navigate forward again it is Ctrl+Shift+−.

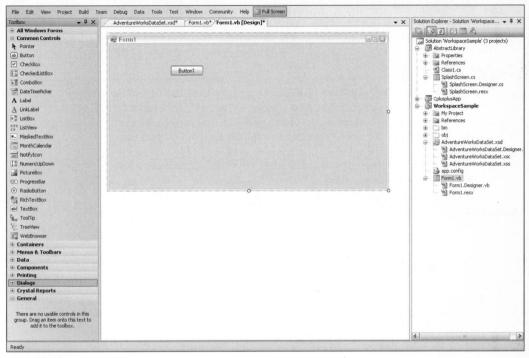

Figure 35-46

Next/Previous Task

The View menu has items to move to the Next and Previous tasks. In fact, there are also commands to move to the Next and Previous error. If the profile you selected has a keyboard shortcut assigned to these commands, they will appear next to the command in the View menu. To specify a shortcut, or to reassign the command to another keyboard combination, select the Keyboard node from the Options dialog, shown in Figure 35-47.

Figure 35-47

In the "Show commands containing" text box, enter part of the command you are looking for — in this case, the NextTask command. Once the correct command has been located, you can assign a keyboard shortcut by pressing the new combination followed by the Assign button.

Between Windows

In a similar style to navigating between running programs using the Alt+Tab combination, you can use Ctrl+Tab to navigate between open files and windows within Visual Studio 2005. Once the navigation window is displayed, shown in the center of Figure 35-48, you can release the Tab key (keep holding the Ctrl key, though) and use the arrow keys to select the file or window you want.

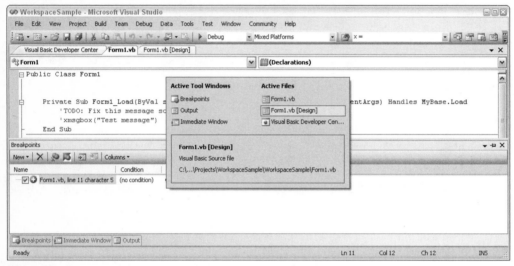

Figure 35-48

Summary

This chapter provided an overview of the numerous windows available in Visual Studio 2005. You also learned how to navigate using a couple of keyboard shortcuts, which will make you a more efficient developer.

The rest of this part of the book focuses on other aspects of Visual Studio 2005 that can save you time when building an application, such as Find and Replace, the topic of the next chapter.

36

Find and Replace

In the current wave of development technology, find and replace functionality is expected as a fundamental part of the toolset, and Visual Studio 2005 delivers on that expectation. However, unlike other development environments that enable you to perform only simple searches against the active code module, the Visual Studio IDE includes the capability to perform rapid find and replace actions on the active code module, the active project, or right across the solution.

It then goes an extra step by giving you the capability to search external files and even whole folder hierarchies for different kinds of search terms and to perform replacement actions on the results automatically. This chapter shows you how to invoke and control this powerful tool.

Introducing Find and Replace

The find and replace functionality in Visual Studio 2005 is split into two broad tiers with a shared dialog and similar features: *Quick Find*, and the associated *Quick Replace*, is for searches that you need to perform quickly on the document or project currently open in the IDE. The two tools have limited options to filter and extend the search, but as you'll see in a moment, even those options provide a powerful search engine that is beyond that you'll find in most applications.

The second, extended tier is the *Find in Files* and *Replace in Files* commands. These functions enable you to broaden the search beyond the current solution to whole folders and folder structures, and even perform mass replacements on any matches for the given criteria and filters. Additional options are available to you when using these commands, and search results can be placed in one of two tool windows so you can easily navigate them.

In addition to these two groups of find and replace tools, Visual Studio also offers two other ways to navigate code:

❑ **Find Symbols:** Rather than strings of text, you can use Find Symbols to locate the symbols of various objects and members within your code.

❑ **Bookmarks:** You can bookmark any location throughout your code and then easily go back to it, either with the Bookmarks window or by using the Bookmark menu and toolbar commands.

Quick Find

Quick Find is the term that Visual Studio 2005 uses to refer to the most basic search functionality. By default, it enables you to search for a simple word or phrase of text within the current document, but even Quick Find has additional options that can extend the search beyond the active module, or even to use wildcards and regular expressions in the search criteria.

To start a find action, press the standard keyboard shortcut Ctrl+F or select the Edit⇨Quick Find menu command. Visual Studio will display the basic Find and Replace dialog, with the default Quick Find action selected (see Figure 36-1).

Figure 36-1

Type the search criteria into the Find What text box, or select from previous searches by clicking on the drop-down arrow and scrolling through the list of criteria that have been used. By default, the scope of the search is restricted to the current document or window you're editing, but the Look In drop-down list gives you additional options based on the context of the search itself. For instance, if you're editing a Visual Basic code module, you'll see additional scopes such as Current Block, while searching within a tool window will display a Current Window option.

The various scopes available to you in a typical search action are as follows:

❑ **Selection:** Only available when you have a section of text selected, this option restricts the search to only selected text in the active document.

❑ **Current Block:** Searches the current block of code. This could be a subroutine or other procedure, a class definition, or even an entire module file, depending on where the current cursor is.

❑ **Current Document:** Allows you to search the active document in its entirety

❑ **Current Window:** Used for tool window searches

❑ **All Open Documents:** Use this option to restrict the search to all documents that you currently have open in the workspace.

❑ **Current Project:** Searches with this option selected will be conducted against every file (visible or not) in the project to which the active document belongs.

Find and replace actions will always wrap around the selected scope looking for the search terms, stopping only when the find process has reached the starting point again. As Visual Studio finds each result, it will highlight the match and scroll the code window so you can view it.

If the match is already visible in the code window, Visual Studio will not scroll the code. Instead, it will just highlight the new match. However, if it does need to scroll the window, it will attempt to position the listing so the match is in the middle of the code editor window.

If the next match happens to be in a document other than the active one, Visual Studio will open the new document in a new tab in the workspace.

Quick Replace

Performing a Quick Replace action is similar to performing a Quick Find. You can switch between Quick Find and Quick Replace by clicking their respective buttons at the top of the dialog window. If you want to go directly to Quick Replace, you can do so with the keyboard shortcut Ctrl+H or the menu command Edit⇨Quick Replace. The Quick Replace options (see Figure 36-2) are the same as those for Quick Find, but with an additional field to allow you to specify what text should be used in the replacement.

Figure 36-2

The Replace With field works in the same way as Find What — you can either type a new replacement string or choose one from any you've previously entered with the drop-down list provided.

Quick Find and Replace Dialog Options

Sometimes you will want to filter the search results in different ways, and that's where the find options come into play. First, to display the options section (available in all find and replace actions), click the expand icon next to Find Options. The dialog will expand to show a set of checkbox options and drop-down lists from which you can choose, as shown in Figure 36-3.

Figure 36-3

These options enable you to filter the search results as follows:

Option	Purpose
Match case	The match will only be made if it meets the exact case that you enter for the criteria.
Match whole word	Only finds matches that are made up of exactly the term you enter. This allows you to filter out embedded words; for example, searching for *the* won't return *then* or *there*.
Search up	Search from the current point and up. This mode will still wrap around, but allows you to find previous matches easily.
Search hidden text	Searches in collapsed regions of the code. By default, this option is inactive, and any matches that are in collapsed sections of the document are not returned.
Use	In addition to regular text searches, you can choose to perform searches that include either regular expressions or wildcards.

Wildcards

Wildcards are simple text symbols that represent one or more characters, and are familiar to many users of Windows applications. The following table lists wildcard characters and what they represent:

Wildcard Symbol	Expression	Purpose
? (Question Mark)	Single character	Matches any single character. It must match at least one.
# (Hash)	Single digit	Same as ? but only matches digits

Wildcard Symbol	Expression	Purpose
* (Asterisk)	Zero or more	Matches any number of characters, including zero. For example, my*car will find mycar, my car, and my own car.
[ ] (Square Brackets)	Any one character in the set	Matches any one character listed between the square braces. Use [!] to invert the match to only find characters not in the list.
\ (Backslash)	Escape	Indicates that the next character should be treated as a literal. For example, \? will match a question mark.

Regular Expressions

Regular expressions take searching to a whole new level, with the capability to do complex text matching based on the full RegEx engine built into Visual Studio 2005. Chapter 39 deals with regular expressions in depth, so you're encouraged to read through that chapter if you want to use this mode.

However, it's worth mentioning the additional help provided by the Find and Replace dialog if you choose to use regular expressions in your search terms. When regular expressions are active, a small right-pointing arrow is enabled next to the Find What area (and Replace With if the dialog is in Replace mode). Clicking on this arrow shows the expression builder menu shown in Figure 36-4. From here you can easily build your regular expressions with the most commonly used regular expression phrases and symbols, with English descriptions of each in the menu.

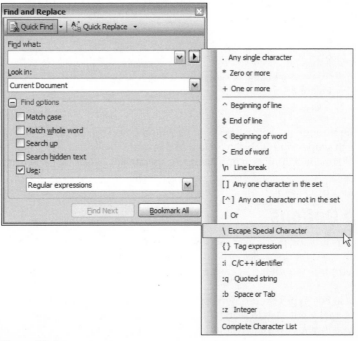

Figure 36-4

Find in Files

The really powerful part of the search engine built into Visual Studio is found in the Find in Files command. Rather than restrict yourself to a single document or project, Find in Files gives you the ability to search entire folders (along with all of their subfolders), looking for files that contain the search criteria.

The Find in Files dialog can be invoked via the menu command Edit⇨Quick Find. Initially, the Quick Find dialog is shown, as described previously in this chapter. To switch over to the Find in Files mode, click the small drop-down arrow next to Quick Find and choose Find in Files. Alternatively, a much quicker method to show the dialog is to use the keyboard shortcut Ctrl+Shift+F.

Most of the Quick Find options are still available to you (see Figure 36-3), including the wildcard and regular expression searching, but instead of choosing a scope from the project or solution, the Look In field is used to specify where the search is to be performed. Either type the location you wish to search or click the ellipses to display the Choose Search Folders dialog, shown in Figure 36-5.

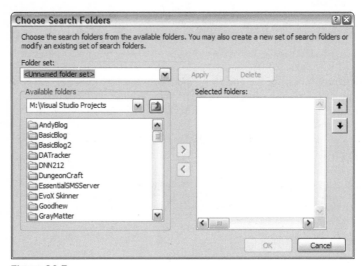

Figure 36-5

You can navigate through the entire file system, including networked drives, and add the folders you want to the search scope. This enables you to add disparate folder hierarchies to the one single search action, and, as Figure 36-5 implies, name them as a specific folder set that you can retrieve for future searches.

Find Dialog Options

Because the search is being performed on files that are not normally open within the IDE, the two find options normally used for open files—namely, Search up and Search hidden text—are not present. However, in their place is a filter that can be used to search only on specific file types.

The Look at These File Types drop-down list contains several extension sets, each associated with a particular language, making it easy to search for code in Visual Basic, C#, J#, and other language-based projects. You can type in your own extensions too, so if you're working in a non-Microsoft language, or just want to use the Find in Files feature for non-development purposes, you can still filter the search results only to those that correspond to the file types you want.

In addition to the Find options, there are also configuration settings for how the results should be displayed. For searching only, you can choose one of two different results windows, which enables you to perform a subsequent search without losing your initial action. The results can be quite lengthy if you show the full output of the search, but if you're interested only in finding out which files contain the information you're looking for, check the Display File Names Only option and the results window will only be populated with one line per file, as shown in Figure 36-6.

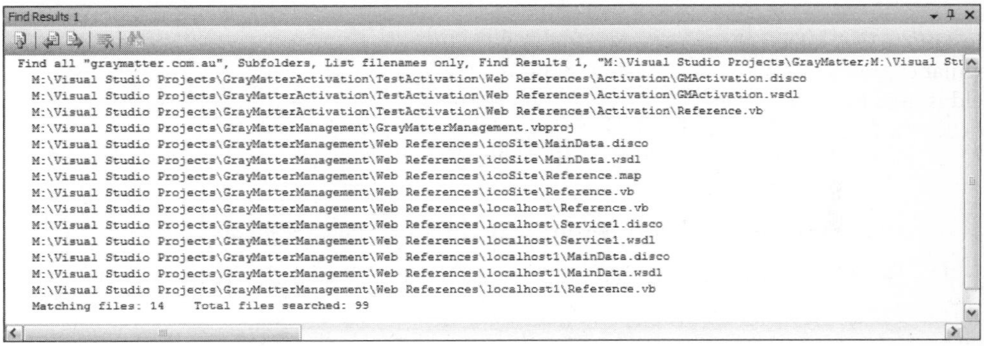

Figure 36-6

Results Window

When performing a Find in Files action, results are displayed in one of two Find Results windows. These windows appear as open tool windows docked to the bottom of the IDE workspace. For each line that contained the search criteria, the results window displays a full line of information, containing the filename and path, the line number that contained the match, and the actual line of text itself so you can instantly see the context (see Figure 36-7).

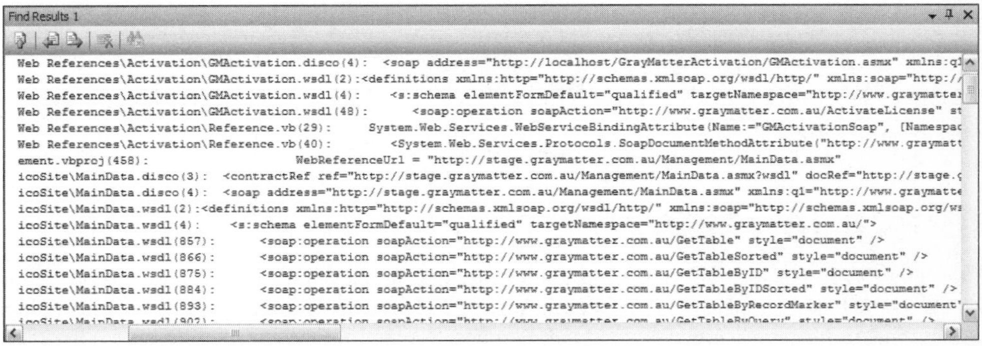

Figure 36-7

Along the top of each results window is a small toolbar (shown in Figure 36-8) for navigation within the results themselves. From left to right, these buttons perform the following commands:

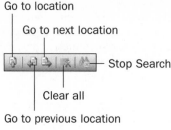

Figure 36-8

❑ **Go To Location:** Opens the file containing the current match, and locates the cursor at the specific match

❑ **Go to Previous Location:** Navigates to the previous match's location

❑ **Go to Next Location:** Navigates to the next match's location

❑ **Clear All:** Clears the results window

❑ **Stop Search:** Stops an incremental search

These commands are also accessible through a context menu (see Figure 36-9). Right-click on the particular match you want to look at and choose the Go To Location command. Alternatively, double-clicking on a specific match will also perform this function.

Figure 36-9

Replace in Files

Although it's useful to search a large number of files and find a number of matches to your search criteria, even better is the Replace in Files action. Accessed via the keyboard shortcut Ctrl+Shift+H, or by clicking the drop-down arrow next to Quick Replace, Replace in Files performs in much the same way as Find in Files, with all the same options.

The main difference is that you can enable an additional Results option when you're replacing files. When performing a mass replacement action like this, it can be handy to have a final confirmation before committing the changes that occurred. To have this sanity check available to you, enable the :Keep modified files open after Replace All: checkbox (shown at the bottom of Figure 36-10).

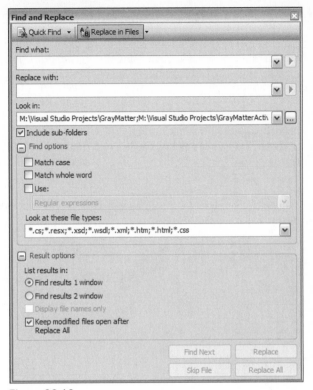

Figure 36-10

Note that this feature works only when using Replace All; if you just click Replace, Visual Studio will open the file containing the next match and leave the file open in the IDE anyway.

> *Important: If you leave this option unchecked and perform a mass replacement on a large number of files, they will be changed permanently without any recourse for an undo action. Be very sure that you know what you're doing.*

Whether you have this option checked or not, after performing a Replace All action, Visual Studio will report back to you how many occurrences were changed (see Figure 36-11). If you're familiar with the process and don't care how many, you can uncheck the "Always show this message" option for future searches. However, be aware that you don't get any other visual feedback indicating when a mass replacement has finished processing, so you may want to leave this dialog window displayed.

Figure 36-11

Incremental Search

If you're looking for something in the current code window and don't want to bring up a dialog, the Incremental Search function might be what you need. Invoked by either the Edit⇨Advanced⇨Incremental Search menu command (see Figure 36-12), or using the keyboard shortcut Alt+I, Incremental Search locates the next match based on what you type.

Immediately after invoking Incremental Search, simply begin typing the text you need to find. The mouse pointer will change to a set of binoculars and a down arrow. As you type each character, the editor will move to the next match. For example, typing *f* would find the first word containing an *f* — for example, *offer*. Typing an *o* would then move the cursor to the first word containing *fo* — for example, *form*, and so on.

Using this feature is an incredibly efficient way of navigating through long code blocks when you want to quickly locate the next place you need to work.

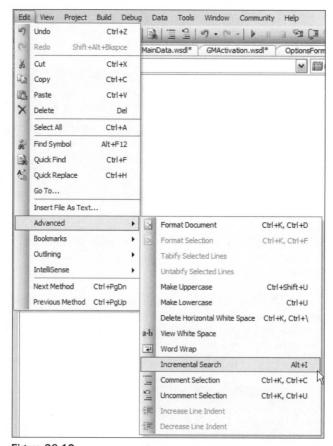

Figure 36-12

Find Symbol

In addition to these already comprehensive find and replace tools, there is an additional search feature in Visual Studio 2005. You can now search for symbols that are objects, classes, and procedural names. The Find Symbol dialog is invoked by the keyboard shortcut Alt+F12, or through the menu command Edit⇨Find Symbol. Alternatively, you can switch the normal Find and Replace dialog over to Find Symbol by clicking the drop-down arrow next to Quick Find or Find in Files.

The Find Symbol dialog (see Figure 36-13) has slightly different options from the other Find actions. Rather than scope based on a current document or solution like Quick Find, or the file system like Find in Files, Find Symbol can search through your whole solution, a full component list, or even the entire .NET Framework. In addition, you can include any references added to the solution as part of the scope. To create your own set of components in which to search, click the ellipses next to the Look In field, and browse through and select the .NET and COM components registered in the system, or browse to files or projects.

> *The Find options are also simplified. You can only search for whole words, substrings (the default option), or a prefix.*

After clicking Find All, the search results are compiled and presented in a special tool window entitled Find Symbol Results. By default, this window shares space with the Find Results windows at the bottom of the IDE, and displays each result with any references to the particular object or component. This is extremely handy when you're trying to determine where and how a particular object is used or referenced from within your project.

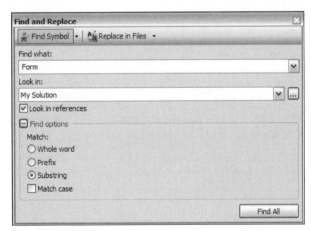

Figure 36-13

Find and Replace Options

Believe it or not, you can further customize the find and replace functionality with its own set of options in the main Options dialog. Found in the Environment group, the Find and Replace options (see Figure 36-14) enable you to reset informational and warning message settings as well as indicate whether the Find What field should be automatically filled with the current selection in the editor window.

Chapter 36

The final option in the list of checkboxes is inactive by default to allow you to perform subsequent Quick Find or Quick Replace actions, but if you often use Quick Find to find one instance and then want to be able to edit or view that instance, you may want to check this option to hide the dialog after it navigates to the first match.

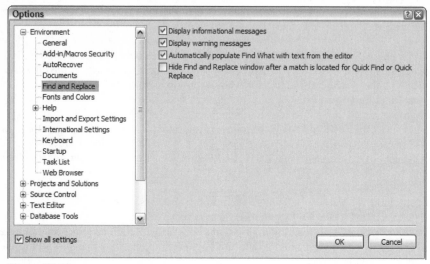

Figure 36-14

Summary

As you've seen in this chapter, Visual Studio 2005 comes with an excellent set of search and replacement functionality that makes your job a lot easier, even if you need to search entire computer file systems for regular expressions. The additional features such as Find Symbol and Incremental Search also add to your toolset, simplifying the location of code and objects as well.

37

Server Explorer

In Chapter 35 you learned about the numerous windows available in Visual Studio 2005. One of these, the Server Explorer, exposes hardware and services for you to query and work with in your application. This window is divided into two main sections: Servers, which is covered in this chapter, and Data Connections, which is covered in the next chapter.

The Server Explorer, shown in Figure 37-1, has two top-level nodes. The first, Data Connections, enables you to work with all aspects of data connections, including the capability to create databases, add and modify tables, build relationships, and even execute queries. Chapter 38 goes into more detail about setting up and working with data connections.

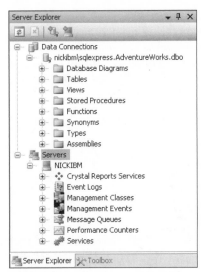

Figure 37-1

The Servers Node

The Servers node would be better named Computers, as it can be used to attach to and interrogate any computer to which you have access. Under each node (for example, the NICKIBM node) is a list of the hardware, services, and other components that belong to that computer. Each of these nodes contains a number of activities or tasks that can be performed. Some software vendors have components that plug into the Server Explorer.

By default, the local computer appears in the Servers list. To add computers, right-click the Servers node and select Add Server from the context menu. This opens the Add Server dialog shown in Figure 37-2.

Figure 37-2

Entering a computer name or IP address will initiate an attempt to connect to the machine using your credentials. If you do not have sufficient privileges, you can elect to connect using a different user name by clicking on the appropriate link. The link appears to be disabled, but clicking it does bring up a dialog in which you can provide an alternative user name and password.

Event Logs

The Event Logs node gives you access to the machine event logs. You can launch the Event Viewer from the right-click context menu. Alternatively, as shown in Figure 37-3, you can drill into the list of event logs to view the events for a particular application. Clicking on any of the events displays the full information about the event in the Properties window. You can also clear each of the event logs by selecting Clear Event Log from the right-click context menu.

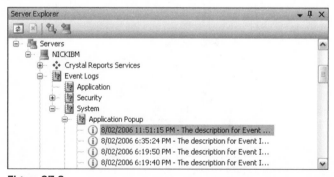

Figure 37-3

Although the Server Explorer is useful for interrogating a machine while writing your code, the true power comes with the component creation you get when you drag particular nodes onto a Windows form. For example, in this case, if you drag the Application node onto a Windows form, you get an instance of the `System.Diagnostic.EventLog` class added to the nonvisual area of the designer. You can then write an entry to this event log using the following code:

```
Private Sub ButtonClick(ByVal sender As Object, ByVal e As EventArgs) _
                                                    Handles Button1.Click
    Me.EventLog1.Source = My.Settings.EventLogName
    Me.EventLog1.WriteEntry("Button Clicked", EventLogEntryType.Information)
End Sub
```

You can also write exception information using the `WriteException` method, which accepts an exception and a string that may provide additional debugging information. Unfortunately, you still have to manually set the `Source` property before calling the `WriteEntry` method. Of course, this could have been set using the Properties window for the `EventLog1` component, but doing so would make it hard-coded into the application. Instead, this is provided as a setting in the configuration file.

An alternative to adding an `EventLog` class to your code is to use the built-in logging provided by the `My` namespace. For example, you can modify the previous code snippet to write a log entry using the `Application.Log` property:

```
Private Sub ButtonClick(ByVal sender As Object, ByVal e As EventArgs) _
                                                    Handles Button1.Click
    My.Application.Log.WriteEntry("Button Clicked", EventLogEntryType.Information)
End Sub
```

This is equivalent to the previous code, even to the extent of having the event source specified in the configuration file. Using the `My` namespace to write logging information also has a number of additional benefits. In the following configuration file, an `EventLogTraceListener` is specified to route log information to the event log. However, you can specify other trace listeners — for example, the `FileLog TraceListener`, which writes information to a log file by adding it to the `SharedListeners` and `Listeners` collections:

```
<?xml version="1.0" encoding="utf-8" ?>
<configuration>
    <system.diagnostics>
        <sources>
            <source name="DefaultSource" switchName="DefaultSwitch">
                <listeners>
                    <add name="EventLog"/>
                </listeners>
            </source>
        </sources>
        <switches>
            <add name="DefaultSwitch" value="Information" />
        </switches>
        <sharedListeners>
            <add name="EventLog"
                type="System.Diagnostics.EventLogTraceListener"
                initializeData="ApplicationEventLog"/>
        </sharedListeners>
    </system.diagnostics>
</configuration>
```

This configuration also specifies a switch called `DefaultSwitch`. This switch is associated with the trace information source via the `switchName` attribute and defines the minimum event type that will be sent to the listed listeners. For example, if the value of this switch were `Critical`, then events with the type `Information` would not be written to the event log. The possible values of this switch are as follows:

DefaultSwitch	Event Types Written to Log
`Off`	No events
`Critical`	`Critical` events
`Error`	`Critical` and `Error` events
`Warning`	`Critical`, `Error`, and `Warning` events
`Information`	`Critical`, `Error`, `Warning`, and `Information` events
`Verbose`	`Critical`, `Error`, `Warning`, `Information`, and `Verbose` events
`ActivityTracing`	`Start`, `Stop`, `Suspend`, `Resume`, and `Transfer` events
`All`	All events

Note that there are overloads for both `WriteEntry` and `WriteException` that do not require an event type to be specified. These methods will default to `Information` and `Error`.

Management Classes

Figure 37-4 shows the full list of management classes available via the Server Explorer. Each node exposes a set of functionality specific to that device or application. For example, right-clicking the Printers node enables you to add a new printer connection, whereas right-clicking the named node under My Computer enables you to add the computer to a domain or workgroup. The one thing common to all these nodes is that they provide a strongly typed wrapper around the Windows Management Instrumentation (WMI) infrastructure. In most cases, it is simply a matter of dragging the node representing the information you are interested in across to the form. From your code you can then access and manipulate that information.

To give you an idea of how these wrappers can be used, this section walks through how you can use the management classes to retrieve information about a user. Start by dragging a user node onto a form. Under the System Accounts node, you can drill down into Authenticated Users⇨Groups⇨Users⇨Users and Accounts. In this node you should see a list of users. Selecting a node and dragging it onto the form will give you a UserAccount component in the nonvisual area of the form, as shown in Figure 37-5.

If you look in the Solution Explorer, you will see that it has also added a custom component called root.CIMV2.Win32_UserAccount.vb (or similar depending on the computer configuration). This custom component is generated by the Management Strongly Typed Class Generator (`Mgmtclassgen.exe`) and includes the `UserAccount` and other classes, which will enable you to expose WMI information.

Figure 37-4

Figure 37-5

If you click on the `UserAccount1` object on the form, you can see the information about that user in the Properties window. In this application, however, you're not that interested in that particular user; that user was selected as a template to create the `UserAccount` class. The `UserAccount1` object can be deleted, but before deleting it, copy the `Path` property of the object, as you need to use this information, combined with the user name entered in the form in Figure 37-5, to load the information about that user. Add the following code to handle the button click event for the Load User Information button:

```
Public Class MainForm
    Private Const CUserPath As String = _
        "\\NICKIBM\root\CIMV2:Win32_UserAccount.Domain=""NICKIBM"",Name=""{0}"""

    Private Sub BtnRetriveCounters_Click(ByVal sender As System.Object, _
```

```
                              ByVal e As System.EventArgs) _
                                   Handles BtnRetriveCounters.Click
        If Not Me.TxtUserName.Text = "" Then
            Dim userName as string = Me.TxtUserName.Text
            Dim pathString as String = String.Format(CUserPath,userName)
            Dim path as New System.Management.ManagementPath(pathString)
            Dim cu As New ROOT.CIMV2.UserAccount(path)

            My.Forms.UserInformation.UserPropertyGrid.SelectedObject = cu
            My.Forms.UserInformation.ShowDialog()
        End If
    End Sub
End Class
```

In this example, the Path property is taken from the UserAccount1 object and the user name component is replaced with a string replacement token, {0}. When the button is clicked, the user name entered into the text box is combined with this path using String.Format to generate the full WMI path. The path is then used to instantiate a new UserAccount object, which is in turn passed to the UserInformation form. The UserInformation form is a simple form that contains a docked PropertyGrid through which the user can change attributes of the UserAccount object. This is shown in Figure 37-6.

Figure 37-6

Changes made in this form are immediately committed to the computer, although you can alter this behavior by changing the AutoCommit property on the UserAccount class.

This is only a single example of how you can work with the management classes to retrieve and work with computer information using the WMI interface.

Management Events

In the previous section you learned how you can drag a management class from the Server Explorer onto the form and then work with the generated classes. The other way to work with the WMI interface is through the Management Events node. A management event enables you to monitor any WMI data type and have an event raised if an object of that type is created, modified, or deleted. By default, this node will be empty, but you can create your own by selecting Add Event Query, which will invoke the dialog shown in Figure 37-7.

Use this dialog to locate the WMI data type in which you are interested. Because there are literally thousands of these, it is useful to use the Find box. In Figure 37-7, the search term "user account" was entered, and it was found under the root\CIMV2 node. You are interested in all event types, so select "Object creation, modification or deletion" from the drop-down menu.

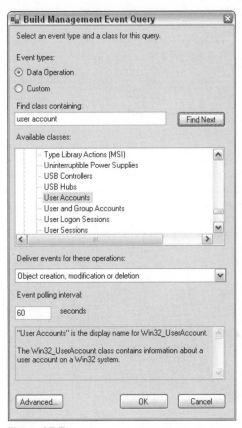

Figure 37-7

After clicking OK, a User Accounts Event Query node is added to the Management Events node. If you use Computer Management to enable or disable a user, you will see events being progressively added to this node. In the Build Management Event Query dialog shown in Figure 37-7, the default polling interval was set to 60 seconds, so you may need to wait up to 60 seconds for the event to show up in the tree once you have made the change.

When the event does finally show up, it will appear along with the date and time in the Server Explorer, and it will also appear in the Output window, as shown in the lower pane of Figure 37-8. If you select the event, you will notice that the Properties window is populated with a large number of properties that don't really make any sense. This is where the management classes become really useful, as you can use the information contained in the management event to populate an instance of the class you generated earlier.

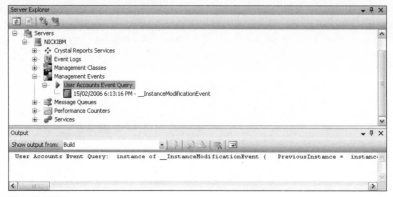

Figure 37-8

To continue the example, drag the User Accounts Event Query node onto a form. This generates an instance of the `System.Management.ManagementEventWatcher` class, with properties configured so it will listen for changes to user account information. The actual query can be accessed via the `QueryString` property of the nested `ManagementQuery` object. As with most watcher classes, the `ManagementEventWatch` class triggers an event when the watch conditions are met—in this case, the `EventArrived` event. To generate an event handler, double-click the event in the Properties window and add the following code:

```
Private Sub ManagementEventWatcher1_EventArrived(ByVal sender As System.Object, _
                    ByVal e As System.Management.EventArrivedEventArgs) _
                          Handles ManagementEventWatcher1.EventArrived
    For Each p As System.Management.PropertyData In e.NewEvent.Properties
        If p.Name = "TargetInstance" Then
            Dim mbo As System.Management.ManagementBaseObject = _
                        CType(p.Value, System.Management.ManagementBaseObject)
            Dim msp As New ROOT.CIMV2.UserAccount.ManagementSystemProperties(mbo)
            Dim path As New System.Management.ManagementPath(msp.PATH)
            Dim cu As New ROOT.CIMV2.UserAccount(path)
            My.Forms.UserInformation.UserPropertyGrid.SelectedObject = cu
            My.Forms.UserInformation.ShowDialog()
            Return
        End If
    Next
End Sub

Private Sub ChkUserMonitor_CheckedChanged(ByVal sender As System.Object, _
                    ByVal e As System.EventArgs) _
                    Handles ChkUserMonitor.CheckedChanged
    If Me.ChkUserMonitor.Checked Then
        Me.ManagementEventWatcher1.Start()
    Else
        Me.ManagementEventWatcher1.Stop()
    End If
End Sub
```

In the event handler, you need to iterate through the `Properties` collection on the `NewEvent` object. Where an object has changed, two instances are returned: `PreviousInstance`, which holds the state at the beginning of the polling interval, and `TargetInstance`, which holds the state at the end of the polling interval. It is possible for the object to change state multiple times within the same polling period. If this is the case, an event will only be triggered when the state at the end of the period differs from the state at the beginning of the period. For example, no event is raised if a user account is enabled and then disabled within a single polling interval.

Notice also from this code snippet the addition of a checkbox to the form to control whether the form is watching for user events. The generated code for the event watcher does not automatically start the watcher.

Message Queues

The Message Queues node, expanded in Figure 37-9, gives you access to the message queues available on your computer. You can use three types of queues: private, which will not appear when a foreign computer queries your computer; public, which will appear; and system, which is used for unsent messages and other exception reporting. In order for the Message Queues node to be successfully expanded, you need to ensure that MSMQ is installed on your computer. This can be done via Add/Remove Windows Components accessible from Start⇨Settings⇨Control Panel⇨Add or Remove Programs. Some features of MSMQ are only available when a queue is created on a computer that is a member of a domain.

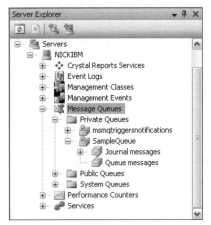

Figure 37-9

In Figure 37-9, the SampleQueue has been added to the Private Queues node by selecting Create Queue from the right-click context menu. Once you have created a queue, you can create a properly configured instance of the `MessageQueue` class by dragging the queue onto your form. To demonstrate the functionality of the `MessageQueue` object, use the following code to add a couple of text boxes and a Send button. The Send button is wired up to use the `MessageQueue` object to send the message entered in the first text box. In the `Load` event for the form, a background thread is created that continually polls the queue to retrieve messages, which will populate the second text box:

```
Public Class MessagingForm
    Private Sub BtnSend_Click(ByVal sender As System.Object, _
                        ByVal e As System.EventArgs) Handles BtnSend.Click
        Me.TheQueue.Send(Me.TxtMessageToSend.Text, "Message: " & _
                        Now.ToShortDateString & " " & Now.ToShortTimeString)
    End Sub

    Private Sub MessagingForm_Load(ByVal sender As System.Object, _
                        ByVal e As System.EventArgs) Handles MyBase.Load
        Dim monitorThread As New Threading.Thread(AddressOf MonitorMessageQueue)
        monitorThread.IsBackground = True
        monitorThread.Start()
    End Sub

    Private Sub MonitorMessageQueue()
        Dim m As Messaging.Message
        While True
            Try
                m = Me.TheQueue.Receive(New TimeSpan(0, 0, 0, 0, 50))
                Me.ReceiveMessage(m.Label, m.Body)
            Catch ex As Messaging.MessageQueueException
                If Not ex.MessageQueueErrorCode = _
                            Messaging.MessageQueueErrorCode.IOTimeout Then
                    Throw ex
                End If
            End Try
            Threading.Thread.Sleep(10000)
        End While
    End Sub

    Private Delegate Sub MessageDel(ByVal lbl As String, ByVal msg As String)
    Private Sub ReceiveMessage(ByVal lbl As String, ByVal msg As String)
        If Me.InvokeRequired Then
            Me.Invoke(New MessageDel (AddressOf ReceiveMessage), lbl, msg)
            Return
        End If
        Me.TxtReceived.Text = msg
        Me.LblMessageLabel.Text = lbl
    End Sub

End Class
```

Note in this code snippet that the background thread is never explicitly closed. Because the thread has the IsBackGround property set to True, it will automatically be terminated when the application exits. Because the message processing is done in a background thread, you also need to switch threads when you update the user interface. This is done via the Invoke method. Putting this all together, you get a form like the one shown in Figure 37-10.

As messages are sent to the message queue, they will appear under the appropriate queue in Server Explorer. Clicking on the message will display its contents in the Properties window.

Figure 37-10

Performance Counters

One of the most common things developers forget to consider when building an application is how it will be maintained and managed. For example, consider an application that was installed a year ago and has been operating without any issues. All of a sudden, requests start taking an unacceptable amount of time. It is clear that the application is not behaving correctly, but there is no way to determine the cause of the misbehavior. One strategy for identifying where the performance issues are is to use performance counters. Windows has many built-in performance counters that can be used to monitor operating system activity, and a lot of third-party software also installs performance counters so administrators can identify any rogue behavior.

The Performance Counters node in the Server Explorer tree, expanded in Figure 37-11, has two primary functions. First, it enables you to view and retrieve information about the currently installed counters. You can also create new performance counters, as well as edit or delete existing counters. As you can see in Figure 37-11, under the Performance Counters node is a list of categories, and under those is a list of counters.

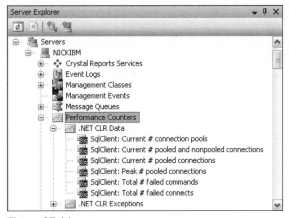

Figure 37-11

To edit either the category or the counters, select Edit Category from the right-click context menu for the category. To add a new category and associated counters, right-click the Performance Counters node and select Create New Category from the context menu. Both of these operations use the dialog shown in Figure 37-12. Here, a new performance counter category has been created that will be used to track a form's open and close events.

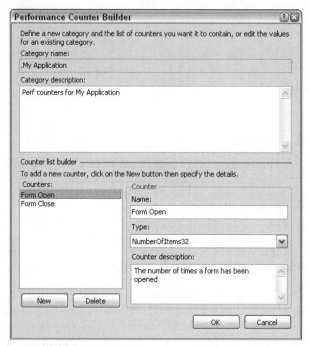

Figure 37-12

The second function of the Performance Counters section is to provide an easy way for you to access performance counters via your code. By dragging a performance counter category onto a form, you gain access to read and write to that performance counter. To continue with this chapter's example, drag the new .My Application performance counters, Form Open and Form Close, onto your form. Also add a couple of text boxes and a button so you can display the performance counter values. Finally, rename the performance counters so they have a friendly name. This should give you a form similar to the one shown in Figure 37-13.

In the properties for the selected performance counter, you can see that the appropriate counter — in this case, Form Close — has been selected from the .My Application category. You will also notice a `Machine Name` property, which is the computer from which you are retrieving the counter information, and a `Read| Only` property, which needs to be set to `False` if you want to update the counter. (By default, the `ReadOnly` property is set to `True`.) To complete this form, add the following code to the Retrieve Counters button:

```
Private Sub BtnRetriveCountersClick(ByVal sender As System.Object, _
                        ByVal e As System.EventArgs) _
                                    Handles BtnRetriveCounters.Click
    Me.TxtFormOpen.Text = Me.PerfCounterFormOpen.RawValue
    Me.TxtFormClose.Text = Me.PerfCounterFormClose.RawValue
End Sub
```

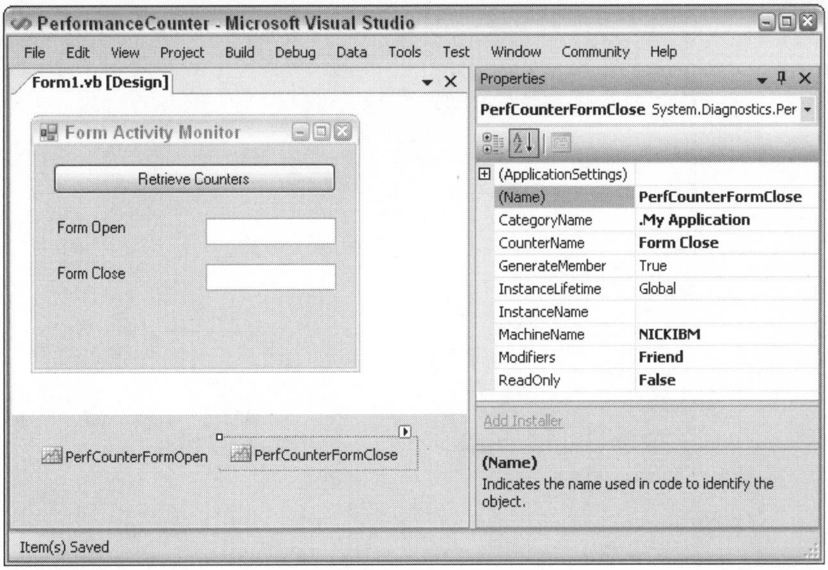

Figure 37-13

You also need to add code to the main application to update the performance counters. For example, you might have the following code in the Load and FormClosing event handlers:

```
Private Sub MainFormClosing(ByVal sender As Object, _
                          ByVal e As System.Windows.Forms.FormClosingEventArgs) _
                                                          Handles Me.FormClosing
    Me.PerfCounterFormOpen.Increment()
End Sub

Private Sub MainFormLoad(ByVal sender As Object, _
                       ByVal e As System.EventArgs) Handles Me.Load
    Me.PerfCounterFormClose.Increment()
End Sub
```

When you dragged the performance counter onto the form, you may have noticed a smart tag on the performance counter component that had a single item, Add Installer. When the component is selected, as in Figure 37-13, you will notice the same action at the bottom of the Properties window. Clicking this action in either place adds an Installer class to your solution that can be used to install the performance counter as part of your installation process. Of course, for this installer to be called, the assembly it belongs to must be added as a custom action for the deployment project (for more information on custom actions, see Chapter 47).

A word of caution when you have multiple performance counters in the same application: If you try to click the Add Installer shortcut for each of the performance counters, Visual Studio 2005 will simply direct you back to the first installer that was created. It is then up to you to modify this installer to create multiple installers, which can be done by selecting the PerformanceCounterInstaller component on the design surface for the PerformanceInstaller. In the Properties window, selecting the Counters property will open the Collection Editor, shown in Figure 37-14, enabling you to add counters in the same category.

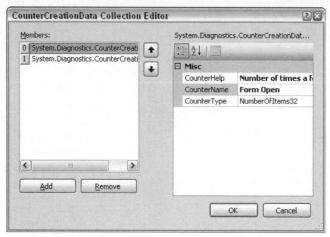

Figure 37-14

You can also add counters in other categories by adding additional `PerformanceCounterInstaller` components to the design surface. You are now ready to deploy your application with the knowledge that you will be able to use a tool such as perfmon to monitor how your application is behaving.

Services

It's often necessary to stop and start services while developing an application — for example, you might want to start the SQL Server service if you don't have it running by default. The Services node, expanded in Figure 37-15, shows the registered services for the computer. Each node indicates the state of that service in the bottom-right corner of the icon. Possible states are stopped, running, or paused, and you can start, stop, or pause a service from its right-click context menu. Some services can't be paused or stopped, in which case these options will be disabled.

Figure 37-15

As with other nodes in the Server Explorer, each service can be dragged onto the design surface of a form. This generates a ServiceController component in the nonvisual area of the form. By default, the ServiceName property is set to the service that you dragged across from the Server Explorer, but this can be changed to access information and control any service. Similarly, the MachineName property can be changed to connect to any computer to which you have access. The following code shows some of properties and methods that can be invoked on a ServiceController component:

```
Private Sub ServiceControlClick(ByVal sender As System.Object, _
                    ByVal e As System.EventArgs) _
                                          Handles BtnServiceControl.Click
    Console.WriteLine("Service: " & Me.ServiceController1.DisplayName)
    Console.WriteLine("Service Name: " & Me.ServiceController1.ServiceName)
    Console.WriteLine("Type: " & Me.ServiceController1.ServiceType.ToString)
    Console.WriteLine("Machine: " & Me.ServiceController1.MachineName)
    Console.WriteLine("Status: " & Me.ServiceController1.Status.ToString)

    Console.WriteLine("Can be Paused = " & _
                                      Me.ServiceController1.CanPauseAndContinue)
    Console.WriteLine("Can be Stopped = " & Me.ServiceController1.CanStop)
    Console.WriteLine("Should be notified on system Shutdown = " & _
                                      Me.ServiceController1.CanShutdown)

    Console.WriteLine("Service dependent on")
    For Each srv As System.ServiceProcess.ServiceController _
                                      In Me.ServiceController1.DependentServices
        Console.WriteLine("< {0} >" & srv.DisplayName)
    Next

    If Me.ServiceController1.CanPauseAndContinue And _
Me.ServiceController1.Status = ServiceProcess.ServiceControllerStatus.Running Then
        Me.ServiceController1.Pause()
        Me.ServiceController1.Continue()
    End If

    If Me.ServiceController1.CanStop And _
Me.ServiceController1.Status = ServiceProcess.ServiceControllerStatus.Running Then
        Me.ServiceController1.Stop()
        Me.ServiceController1.Start()
    End If
End Sub
```

In addition to the three main states — running, paused, or stopped — there are additional transition states: ContinuePending, PausePending, StartPending, and StopPending. If you are about to start a service that may be dependent on another service that is in one of these transition states, you can call the WaitForStatus method to ensure that the service will start properly.

Summary

In this chapter you learned how the Server Explorer can be used to manage and work with computer information. The next chapter continues with the Server Explorer, covering the Data Connections node in more detail.

Visual Database Tools

Database connectivity is almost essential in every application you create, regardless of whether it's a Windows-based program or a web-based site or service. When Visual Studio .NET was first introduced, it provided developers with a great set of options to navigate to the database files on their file system and local servers, with a Server Explorer, data controls, and data-bound components. The underlying .NET Framework included ADO.NET, a retooled database engine that works most efficiently in a disconnected world, which is becoming more prevalent today.

Visual Studio 2005 took those features and smoothed out the kinks, adding tools and functionality to the IDE to give you more direct access to the data in your application. This chapter looks at how you can implement data-based solutions with the tools provided in Visual Studio 2005, collectively termed the *Visual Database Tools*.

Database Windows in Visual Studio 2005

There are a number of windows that specifically deal with databases and their components. From the Data Sources window that shows project-related data files and the Data Connections node in the Server Explorer to the Database Diagram Editor and the visual designer for database schema, you'll find most of what you need directly within the IDE. In fact, it's unlikely that you'll need to venture outside of Visual Studio for most application solutions to edit database settings.

Figure 38-1 shows the Visual Studio 2005 IDE with a current database editing session. Notice how the windows, toolbars, and menus all update to match the particular context of editing a database table. The next few pages take a look at each of these windows and describe their purpose so you can use them effectively.

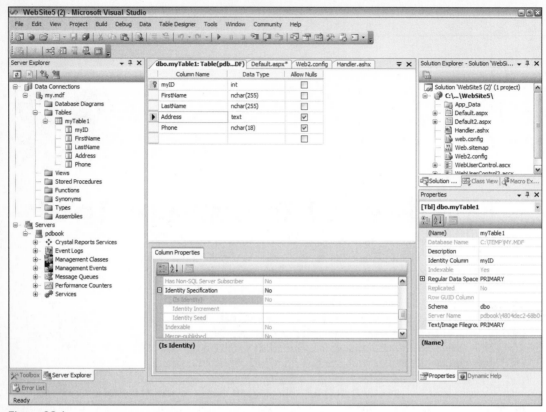

Figure 38-1

Server Explorer

In the last chapter you saw how the Server Explorer can be used to navigate the components that make up your system (or indeed the components of any server to which you can connect). One component of this tool window that was omitted from that discussion is the Data Connections node, where the databases known to Visual Studio 2005 appear.

Contrary to Microsoft's own current set of documentation, the Servers node does not display a child node containing SQL Servers running on each server. Instead, you're forced to create a direct connection to the database and server you need through the Data Connections node.

Figure 38-2 shows the Server Explorer window with an active database connection open. The database icon displays whether you are actively connected to the database or not, and contains a number of child nodes dealing with the typical components of a modern database.

The database node provides you with a hierarchical view of your database schema. Each of the main sections not only lists the primary items, but also provides as detailed a view as possible. The screenshot in Figure 38-2 shows the Customers table expanded to show its fields. The Views, Stored Procedures, and Functions folders are similar, with extra nodes shown for each parameter and field in every component.

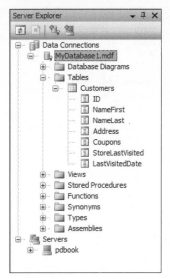

Figure 38-2

To add a new database connection to the Server Explorer window, click the Connect to Database button at the top of the Server Explorer, or right-click on the Data Connections root node and select the Add Connection command from the context menu.

If this is the first time you have added a connection, Visual Studio will ask you what type of Data Source you are connecting to. Visual Studio 2005 comes packaged with a number of data source connectors, including Access and Oracle as well as a generic ODBC driver.

Two new additions with the introduction of Visual Studio 2005 and SQL Server 2005 are Microsoft SQL Server Database File and Microsoft SQL Server Mobile Edition. The Mobile Edition entry is self-explanatory; it connects to mobile device–based SQL Server databases.

However, the Database File option is a new concept for SQL Server that borrows on the easy deployment model of its lesser cousins, Microsoft Access and MSDE. With SQL Server Database File, you can create a flat file for an individual database. This means you don't need to store it in the SQL Server database repository, and it's highly portable — you simply deliver the .mdf file containing the database along with your application.

Once you've chosen the Data Source type to use, the Add Connection dialog appears. Figure 38-3 shows this dialog for a SQL Server Database File connection, with the settings appropriate to that data source type. You are taken directly to this dialog if you already have data connections defined in Visual Studio.

The Change button returns you to the Data Sources page, enabling you to add multiple types of database connections to your Visual Studio session. Note how easy it is to create a SQL Server Database File. Just type or browse to the location where you want the file and specify the database name for a new database. If you want to connect to an existing database, use the Browse button to locate it on the file system.

Figure 38-3

Generally, the only other task you need to perform is to specify whether your SQL Server configuration is using Windows or SQL Server Authentication. The default installation of Visual Studio 2005 includes an installation of SQL Server Express, which uses Windows Authentication as its base authentication model.

> *The Test Connection button displays an error message if you try to connect to a new database. This is because it doesn't exist until you click OK, so there's nothing to connect to!*

When you click OK, Visual Studio attempts to connect to the database. If successful, it adds it to the Data Connections node, including the children nodes for the main data types in the database, as discussed earlier.

> *If the database doesn't exist and you've chosen a connection type such as SQL Server Database File, Visual Studio 2005 will also attempt to create the database file for you.*

Table Editing

The easiest way to edit a table in the database is to double-click its entry in the Server Explorer. An editing window is displayed in the main workspace, consisting of two components. The top section is where you specify each field name, data type, and key information such as length for text fields, and whether the field is nullable.

Right-clicking a field gives you access to a set of commands that you can perform against that field, as shown in Figure 38-4. This context menu is actually the same as the Table Designer menu that is displayed while you're editing a table, but it is usually easier to use the context menu because you can easily determine which field you're referring to with the menu commands.

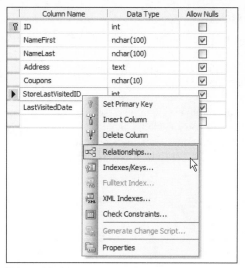

Figure 38-4

The lower half of the table editing workspace contains the Column Properties window for the currently selected column. You can use this section to specify the same set of properties available in the top grid area along with additional database setting such as auto-number fields.

Shown in Figure 38-5 is a sample Column Properties window for a field that has been defined with an Identity clause that is automatically incremented by 1 for each new record added to the table.

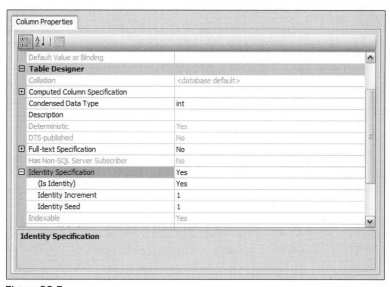

Figure 38-5

Relationship Editing

Most databases that are likely to be used by your .NET solutions are relational in nature, which means you connect tables together by defining relationships. To create a relationship, select one of the tables that you need to connect and click the Relationships button on the toolbar, or use the Table Designer⇨Relationships menu command.

The Foreign Key Relationships dialog is displayed (see Figure 38-6), containing any existing relationships that are bound to the table you selected. Click the Add button to create a new relationship, or select one of the existing relationships to edit. Locate the Tables and Columns Specification entry in the property grid and click its associated ellipses to set the tables and columns that should connect to each other.

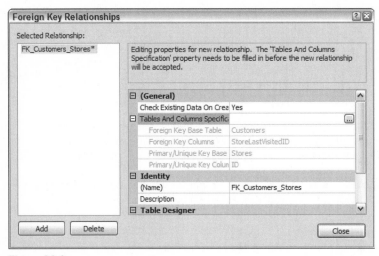

Figure 38-6

In the Tables and Columns dialog, first choose which table contains the primary key to which the table you selected will connect. Note that the Foreign Key table field is populated with the current table name and is disabled.

Once you have the primary key table, you then connect the fields in each table that should bind to each other. You can add multiple fields to the relationship by clicking in the blank row that is added as you add the previous field. When you are satisfied with the relationship settings, click OK to save it and return to the Foreign Key Relationships dialog.

Add any additional relationships for the selected table until you have met the requirements of your database design and then click the Close button to return to the main IDE.

Views

Views are predefined queries that can appear like tables to your application and can be made up of multiple tables. Use the Data⇨Add New⇨View menu command or right-click on the Views node in Server Explorer and choose Add New View from the context menu.

The first task is to choose which tables, other views, functions, and synonyms will be included in the current view. When you've chosen which components will be added, the View editor window is displayed (see Figure 38-7).

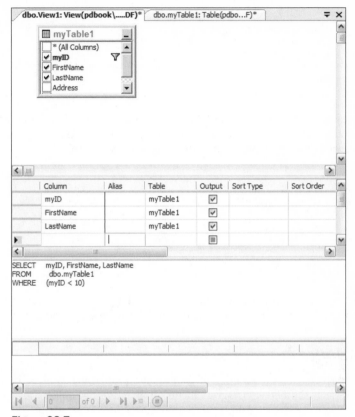

Figure 38-7

This editor should be familiar to anyone who has worked with a visual database designer such as Access. The tables and other components are visible in the top area, where you can select the fields you want included. The top area also shows connections between any functions and tables.

The middle area shows a tabular representation of your current selection, and adds columns for sorting and filtering properties, while the area directly beneath the tabular representation shows the SQL that is used to achieve the view you've specified. The bottom part of the view designer can be used to execute the view SQL and preview the results.

Stored Procedures and Functions

To create and modify stored procedures and functions, Visual Studio 2005 uses a text editor such as the one shown in Figure 38-8. While there is no IntelliSense to help you create your procedure and function definitions, Visual Studio doesn't allow you to save your code if it detects an error.

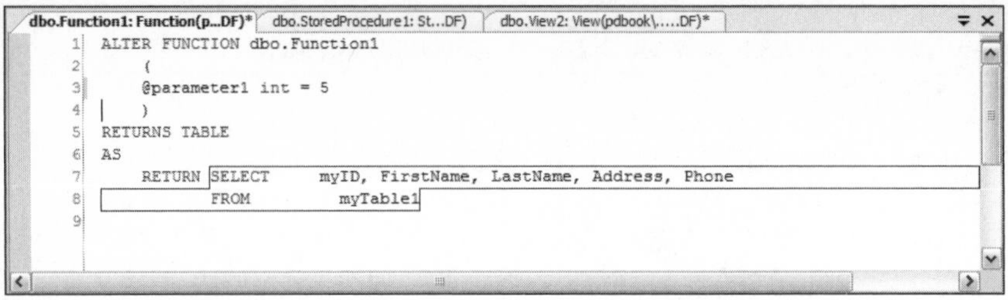

Figure 38-8

For instance, if the SQL function in Figure 38-8 were written as shown in the following code listing, Visual Studio would display a dialog upon an attempted save, indicating a syntax error near the closing parenthesis because of the extra comma after the parameter definition:

```
alter function dbo.function1
    (
    @parameter1 int = 5,
    )
returns table
as
    return select      myid, firstname, lastname, address, phone
              from      mytable1
```

You can use the Edit⇔Advanced menu in the IDE to format the text with commonly required tasks such as setting the code to all uppercase or lowercase, and to swap between using tab characters and spaces.

Database Diagrams

You can also create a visual representation of your database tables via database diagrams. To create a diagram, use the Data⇔Add New⇔Diagram menu command or right-click the Database Diagrams node in the Server Explorer and choose Add New Diagram from the context menu.

When you create your first diagram in a database, Visual Studio may prompt you to allow it to automatically add necessary system tables and data to the database. If you disallow this action, you won't be able to create diagrams at all, so it's just a notification, rather than an optional action to take.

The initial process of creating a diagram enables you to choose which tables you want in the diagram but you can add tables later through the Database Diagram menu that is added to the IDE. You can use this menu to affect the appearance of your diagram within the editor too, with zoom and page break preview functionality as well as being able to toggle relationship names on and off.

Because database diagrams can be quite large, the IDE has an easy way of navigating around the diagram. In the lower-right corner of the Database Diagram editor in the workspace is an icon displaying a four-way arrow. Click this icon and a thumbnail view of the diagram appears, as shown in Figure 38-9.

Just click and drag the mouse point around the thumbnail until you position the components you need to view and work with in the viewable area of the IDE (which is updated in real time).

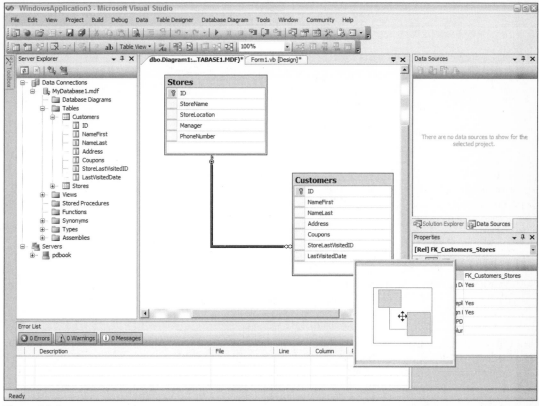

Figure 38-9

Data Sources Window

One more window deserves explanation before you move on to actually using the database in your projects and solutions. The Data Sources window, which shares space with the Solution Explorer in the IDE, contains any active data sources known to the project (as opposed to the Data Connections in the Server Explorer, which are known to Visual Studio overall). To display the Data Sources tool window, use the Data⇨Show Data Sources menu command.

The Data Sources window has two main views, depending on the active document in the workspace area of the IDE. When you are editing code, the Data Sources window will display tables and fields with icons representing their types. This aids you as you write code because you can quickly reference the type without having to look at the table definition. This view is shown on the left-hand side of Figure 38-10.

When you're editing a form in Design view, however, the Data Sources view changes to display the tables and fields with icons representing their current default control type (initially set in the Data UI Customization page of Options). On the right-hand side of Figure 38-10, you can see that both text fields and integer-based fields use TextBox controls, whereas the Date field will use a DateTimePicker control. The icons for the tables indicate that all tables will be inserted as DataGridView components by default.

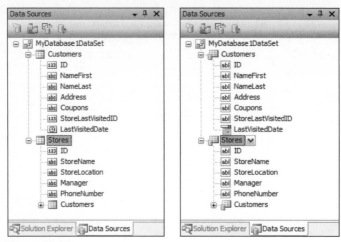

Figure 38-10

Adding a data source is straightforward. If the Data Sources window is currently empty, the main space will contain an Add a New Data Source link. Otherwise, click the Add New Data Source button at the top of the tool window, or use the Data⊃Add New Data Source menu command.

In the Data Source Configuration Wizard that is displayed, you must first choose the type of data source to which you're connecting. Use the obvious database type and click Next to go to the Choose Your Data Connection page (see Figure 38-11).

Figure 38-11

The Choose Your Data Connection page of the wizard is where you select the database to which you'll be connecting the data source. The drop-down list is populated with all data connections already defined in both the application and the Server Explorer, but you can use the New Connection button to link to a database that is not listed. (Clicking the New Connection button displays the Add Connection dialog described previously.)

When you select the connection that Visual Studio is to use for the data source, the full connection string is displayed in the lower pane, enabling you to confirm that the database file you're connecting to is the one you intended.

When you're connecting to a SQL Server database file outside your project structure, Visual Studio warns you that it is outside the project definition. At this point, you can choose to copy the file to the project directory or use the existing file (see Figure 38-12).

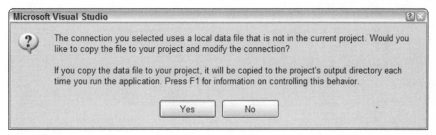

Figure 38-12

The choice you make here has direct consequences on the execution of your application. If you choose to copy the file to the project directory, be aware that the database file will be included as part of the build process and copied to the project's output folder every time you compile and run the application. This enables you to define a default set of data in the table, which can then be used as a basis for your testing of the application, rather than having to manually reset any changes you make during a debug session.

Conversely, if you choose not to copy the file, any changes you make during a debugging session are saved permanently to the database. If you choose to copy the database file into the project but do not want the database copied over each time you run the application, you can change the Copy to Output property of the database.

You can access the Properties page for a database file in your project via the Solution Explorer.

The last step is to choose which database objects should be included in the Data Source (see Figure 38-13). Expand the object types you wish to include and select the individual items that are to make up your Data Source.

As demonstrated in Figure 38-13, you can select a subset of fields from within a table (or a view), and you can include stored procedures and functions. You can access this page at a later stage by clicking the Configure DataSet with Wizard button at the top of the Data Sources window. When you've selected the objects, click Finish to have Visual Studio build the Data Source XML schema definition that controls how the data is used in your application.

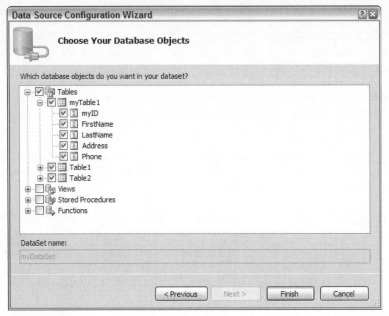

Figure 38-13

Using Databases

Data Sources can be used in code, bound to individual controls, or used to automate creating entire visual interfaces to your data. This section looks at the ways Visual Studio 2005 helps you define these data connections from a visual standpoint. If you want to investigate further how to manage the connections in code, please take a look at *Professional ADO.NET 2: Programming with SQL Server 2005, Oracle, and MySQL* (Wrox, 2005).

Editing Data Source Schema

If you need to edit your Data Source schema once you have added it to the project, you can do so with the schema designer. Shown in Figure 38-14, this editor window displays a visual representation of each of the tables and views defined in the Data Source, along with any relationships that connect them.

In this example, two tables named Customers and Stores are connected by the `Store.ID` and `Customers.StoreLastVisitedID` fields. You can easily see which fields are the primary keys for each table; and to reduce clutter while you're editing the tables, you can collapse either the field list or the queries list in the `TableAdapter` defined for the table.

To perform actions against a table, either right-click the table or individual field and choose the appropriate command from the context menu, or use the main Data menu that is added to the menu bar of the IDE while you're editing the database schema.

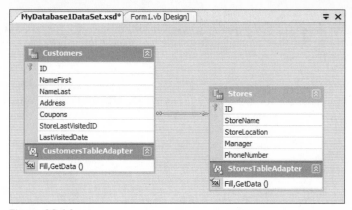

Figure 38-14

To change the SQL for a query that you've added to the `TableAdapter`, first select the query you wish to modify and the use the Data⇨Configure menu command. The TableAdapter Configuration Wizard will appear, displaying a text representation of the existing query string (see Figure 38-15). You can either use the Query Builder to visually create a new query or simply overwrite the text with your own query.

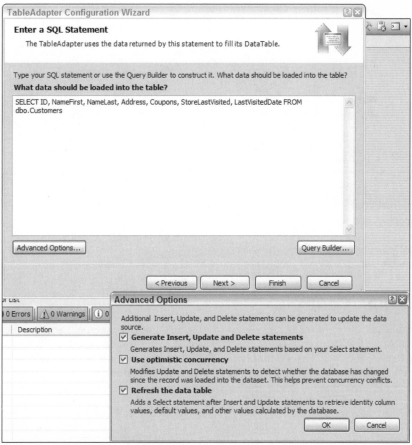

Figure 38-15

You can optionally have additional, associated queries for insert, delete, and update functionality gener-
ated along with the default SELECT query. To add this option, click the Advanced Options button and
check the first option. The other options here enable you to customize how the queries will handle data
during modification queries.

Figure 38-16 shows a sample Query Builder, which works in the same way as the View designer dis-
cussed earlier in this chapter. You can add tables to the query by right-clicking in the top area and choos-
ing Add Table from the context menu, or by editing the SELECT statement in the text field.

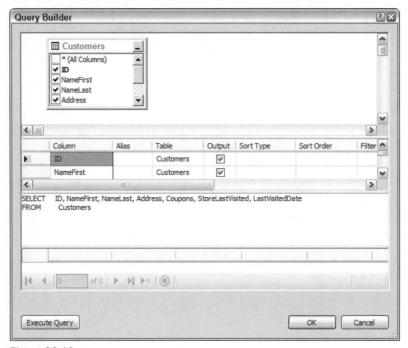

Figure 38-16

To confirm that your query will run properly, use the Execute Query button to preview the results in the
dialog before saving it.

These functions also work when adding a new query to a TableAdapter except that you can choose to
use SQL statements or a stored procedure for the final query definition.

Data Binding Controls

Most Windows Forms controls can be bound to a Data Source once the Data Source has been added to
the project. Add the control to the form and then access the Properties window for the control and locate
the (Data Bindings) group. The commonly used properties for the particular field will be displayed,
enabling you to browse to a field in your Data Source (or an existing TableBindingSource object). For
example, a TextBox will have entries for both the Text and Tag properties.

When you click the drop-down arrow next to the property you want to bind to a data element, the data bindings property editor will be displayed (see Figure 38-17). Any data sources defined in your project appear under the Other Data Sources⇨Project Data Sources node. Expand the Data Source and table until you locate the field you want to bind to the property.

Figure 38-17

Visual Studio then automatically creates a `TableBindingSource` component and adds it to the form's designer view (it will be added to the tray area for nonvisual controls) along with the other data-specific components necessary to bind the Data Source to the form. This is a huge advance since the last version of Visual Studio, in which you had to first define the data adapters and connections on the form before you could bind the fields to controls.

If you need to bind a control to a property that is not listed as a common property for that control type, select the (Advanced) property from within the (Data Bindings) entry in the Properties window and click the ellipsis button to display the Formatting and Advanced Binding dialog, shown in Figure 38-18 for a `TextBox` control.

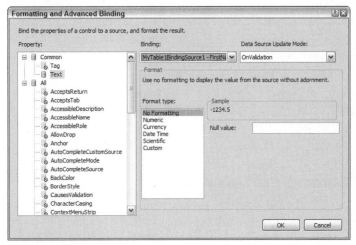

Figure 38-18

Locate the field you wish to bind, and then select the corresponding binding setting from either a Data Source or existing `TableBindingSource` owned by the form. You can also customize the formatting of the data at this point, even for the common properties.

Data Controls

The Toolbox has a whole group of controls that are directly related to databases. The Data controls are used to bind a Data Source to your form, and include the easy-to-use `DataGridView`. Previous versions of Visual Studio had two components that you used in conjunction with each other to create a tabular view of the data in a table: `DataGrid` and `DataView`. The `DataGridView` combines the functionality of these two controls into one component that can connect to a Data Source, define what data editing features can be performed, and customize the view in the grid area.

All of these settings can be controlled through the smart tag task pane associated with the `DataGridView` component (see Figure 38-19). You can select which columns from the Data Source should be shown, and whether a user can add, edit, or delete data or even move the columns around. You can change the query that will be used to populate the grid with data and preview how the data will fill the grid at design time.

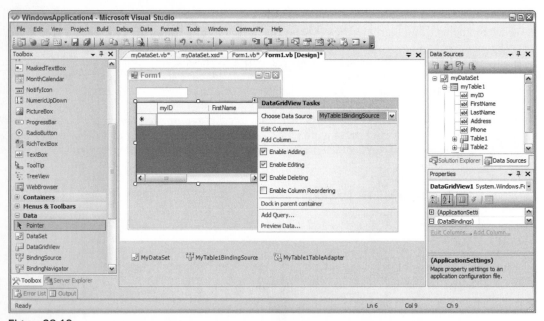

Figure 38-19

Data Binding Controls the Easy Way

While you may have thought the previous walkthrough showing how to add data-bound fields to your forms was straightforward, there's an even easier way that takes a lot of the guesswork out of binding the data to the controls. You may recall from the discussion about data sources that there are two views of the tables and fields in that tool window (refer to Figure 38-10).

The second view mentioned is used specifically to ease data-bound forms development. To implement this feature, simply drag and drop the table or individual field you need onto the form's design surface. Visual Studio automatically generates a control based on the type specified in the corresponding node in the Data Sources window and binds it to a `DataSet` and `TableBindingSource` (also creating them if it needs to) on the form.

> *If the form already has* `DataSet` *and* `TableBindingSource` *components, Visual Studio will ask you which ones you want to use.*

If you're not happy with the default control type for a particular field, first select the field in the Data Sources window, and then access the drop-down list and choose the control type you want to use instead. The drop-down list only displays the control types that have been chosen to work for that data type (see the section "Changing the Default Control Type" a bit later in this chapter).

If Visual Studio has to create the underlying data components to connect the control to the Data Source instead of using existing controls, it will also automatically add a `BindingNavigator` control to the form's design surface, which is automatically docked to the top of the form. This `BindingNavigator` control provides the data navigation and editing tools required to view and change the data.

The complex form design shown in Figure 38-20 was performed through two simple operations. First, the sample Stores table was added to the form by selecting the Details view in the Data Sources list and dragging the whole table to the form. This added the `BindingNavigator` along with the associated `DataSet`, `BindingSource`, and `TableAdapter` components, in addition to the `Label` and `TextBox` combinations for the fields belonging to the Store table.

Figure 38-20

Second, the Customers table was added to the form using the default `DataGridView` control type, with its own associated data components. The controls were then resized and repositioned, and the form layout was done—without any code needing to be written or even any data binding properties being set manually.

In fact, if you take a look at the Properties window for any of the `TextBox` controls, you'll see that Visual Studio automatically creates the appropriate (Data Binding) values to connect them without you lifting a finger.

Changing the Default Control Type

You can change the default control for each data type by going into the Data UI Customization page in the Visual Studio Options dialog. This options page is located under the Windows Forms Designer group (see Figure 38-21).

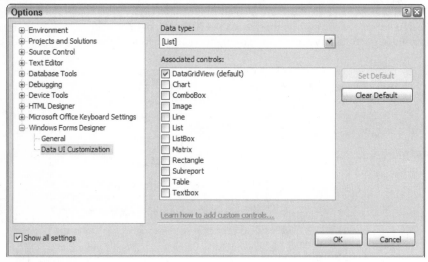

Figure 38-21

From the drop-down, select the data type you want to change and then pick which control type is to be associated with that kind of data. Note that you can select multiple control types to associate with the data type, but only one can be the default used by the Data Sources to set the initial control types for the fields and tables.

Managing Test Data

Visual Studio 2005 also has the capability to view and edit the data contained in your database tables. To edit the information, use the Data⇨Show Table Data menu command after you highlight the table you want to view in the Server Explorer.

You will be presented with a tabular representation of the data in the table, enabling you to edit it to contain whatever default or test data you need to include. As you edit information, the table editor will display indicators next to fields that have changed (see Figure 38-22).

Figure 38-22

You can also show the diagram, criteria, and SQL panes associated with the table data you're editing by right-clicking anywhere in the table and choosing the appropriate command from the Pane submenu.

Previewing Data

You can preview data for different Data Sources to ensure that the associated query will return the information you expect. In the database schema designer, right-click on the query you want to test and choose Preview Data from the context menu.

The Preview Data dialog is displayed with the object list defaulted to the query you want to test. Click the Preview button to view the sample data, shown in Figure 38-23. A small status bar provides information about the total number of data rows that were returned from the query, as well as how many columns of data were included.

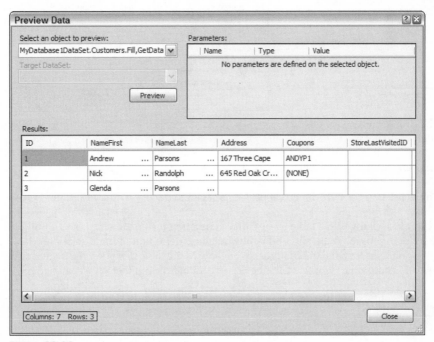

Figure 38-23

If you want to change to a different query, you can do so with the "Select an object to preview" drop-down list. If the query you're previewing requires parameters, you can set their values in the Parameters list in the top-right pane of the dialog.

Database Projects

If you're just creating a database and don't require any other type of project, Visual Studio 2005 has a Database Project template you can use to define a simple SQL Server 2005 database project. This offers the additional benefit of being able to create stored procedures and functions in either Visual Basic or C#, rather than in straight SQL form.

Script-Based Database Projects

You can create script-based SQL Server 2005 projects via the Other Project Types⇨Database Project Template group in the New Project dialog. When you define this type of project, you still define your queries and scripts in standard SQL language and use the various data designers discussed throughout this chapter to create tables, views, and stored procedures.

You can add scripts to programmatically create your database tables by right-clicking the table you need in the Server Explorer and choosing Generate Create Script from the context menu. Doing so creates the script, stores it in the database, and then adds it to the Solution Explorer (see Figure 38-24).

Figure 38-24

The Generate Create Script option is only available for script-based project types.

Everything else you do in the database project is saved in database query files and SQL definitions.

When you make changes to a table layout after generating the create script, you should generate a change script to programmatically update the database definition in the SQL Server database. The easiest way to do this is to make the changes to the table in the table designer, right-click anywhere in the designer, and choose the Generate Change Script command from the context menu.

At this point, you're given the option to save the script to a text file as well as to the database.

Even here, Visual Studio provides you with additional aid by including a set of item templates specific to script-based database projects. This ranges from an SQL script file stub to a database query or stored procedure (see Figure 38-25).

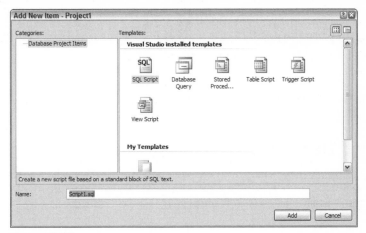

Figure 38-25

Managed Code Language-Based Database Projects

Managed code database projects are found in their respective language groups in the New Project dialog. Rather than being script-based, your functions and stored procedures are defined in managed code (either Visual Basic or C#) and can be debugged with the CLR debugger (discussed in Chapter 52).

When you add items to this kind of database project, Visual Studio presents you with a combination of database-specific templates such as Stored Procedure and User-Defined Function, and regular code files, including class and module definitions.

The following listing shows a sample managed code stored procedure written in Visual Basic. The `Microsoft.SqlServer.Server.SqlProcedure` attribute is prefixed to the subroutine's definition to identify it as a stored procedure to the build process, but internally the routine appears as normal managed code:

```
<Microsoft.SqlServer.Server.SqlProcedure()> _
Public Shared Sub PriceSum(<Runtime.InteropServices.Out()> ByRef value As SqlInt32)
    Using connection As New SqlConnection("context connection=true")
        value = 0
        connection.Open()
        Dim command As New SqlCommand("SELECT Price FROM Products", connection)
        Dim reader As SqlDataReader
        reader = command.ExecuteReader()

        Using reader
            While reader.Read()
                value += reader.GetSqlInt32(0)
            End While
        End Using
    End Using
End Sub
```

Summary

With the variety of tools and windows available to you in Visual Studio 2005, you can easily create and maintain databases without having to leave the IDE. You can manipulate data as well as define database schema visually using the Properties tool window in conjunction with the Schema Designer view.

Once you have your data where you want it, Visual Studio keeps helping you by providing a set of drag-and-drop components that can be bound to a Data Source. These can be as simple as a checkbox or textbox, or as feature rich as a `DataGridView` component with complete table views. The ability to drag whole tables or individual fields from the Data Sources window onto the design surface of a form and have Visual Studio automatically create the appropriate controls for you is a major advantage for rapid application development.

Finally, you can use Visual Studio 2005 to create whole database projects in SQL Server 2005 that use managed code for stored procedures and functions. All in all, Visual Studio 2005 brings the ease-of-use factor firmly into the database editing area of development and will be a benefit to all developers.

39

Regular Expressions

Regular expressions are a great way to retrieve a set of matches for complex search criteria, but they're underused because they can be quite complex and appear almost unintelligible to a lot of developers. With Visual Studio 2005, regular expressions are now not only usable in the normal program code, but also featured in other areas of the environment such as the Find and Replace dialog.

To help more programmers understand how to use them, this chapter introduces regular expressions and shows how they can be used in different situations. It discusses the particular implementation of regular expressions in Visual Studio 2005, along with descriptions of the major components of regular expression syntax so you can begin to build your own expressions confidently regardless of the situation.

At their core, regular expressions are a series of pattern-matching strings that use an extensive set of pattern constructs to control how strings of text can be matched. The character patterns can be used to find and then extract, replace, or remove substrings within large blocks of text, and are used often to extract information from large files with a defined syntax, such as HTML pages or even XML files and header information on e-mails.

Visual Studio 2005 provides an implementation of regular expressions through its use of the .NET Framework's `System.Text.RegularExpressions` namespace, which includes several members that can be used in your code to perform the various functions of the regular expression engine using typical programming practices. Note that while the regular expression engine in Visual Studio is extensive, there may be differences between its implementation and that of other languages that use regular expressions, such as PHP or awk. In addition, the regular expressions that can be built in the Find and Replace dialog are a subset of the full set of functionality. Only syntactical elements appropriate in the context of finding and replacing text in files are available.

Where Can Regular Expressions Be Used?

Using regular expressions can aid you in three primary areas of Visual Studio 2005: normal program code, with full access to the .NET Framework regular expression classes; the Find and Replace dialog, which has a subset of the regular expression syntax but also comes with a regular expression builder to make creating regular expression strings easier; and Visual Studio Tools for Office Smart Tags, which includes an Expressions collection that uses regular expressions to build smart tag search patterns.

Regular Expression Programming

Using regular expressions in program code has been around for a long time, with languages such as Visual Basic 6 able to take advantage of COM components such as MSXML to perform regular expression functionality. The introduction of the first version of Visual Studio .NET included a managed code namespace called System.Text.RegularExpressions that exposed a number of methods and members, most notably the Regex object, which is used to store the actual pattern matching string along with a series of members relating to the string, including any matching results.

A typical use of the namespace in program logic is shown in the following code listing. The code creates a new Regex object containing the pattern TextToMatch. It then uses a Match object to store the first instance of the pattern, which is returned by the Match method exposed by the Regex object. Finally, it determines whether there was a match and then outputs a message to the console, including the position at which the string was found:

```
Dim myRegex As New Regex("TextToMatch")
Dim myMatch As Match = myRegex.Match("Search string containing TextToMatch")
If myMatch.Success Then
    Console.WriteLine("Found match at position " & myMatch.Index.ToString())
End If
```

While this example is simple, it illustrates how the different regular expression objects can be used in familiar programming techniques. Later in this chapter you'll see a variety of additional techniques you can use with regular expression objects in your code.

Note that this code assumes you have the RegularExpressions namespace explicitly imported into your code. You can do this in your own project with the following line at the top of the module containing the regular expression code:

```
Imports System.Text.RegularExpressions
```

Find and Replace

Regular expression matching in the Find and Replace dialog was present in Visual Studio 2003, but the IDE left it up to you to write your own pattern matching strings without giving you any feedback to indicate whether the regular expression was even correctly formatted. With Visual Studio 2005, the implementation of regular expression searching changed to include a regular expression builder that takes away a lot of the guesswork when creating your strings.

Regular expression matching is available in both the Quick Find and Quick Replace functions, as well as the more extensive Find in Files and Replace in Files modes, but it is disabled by default. To use regular expression matching in a search or replace action, you'll first need to activate them by expanding the Find Options section of the Find and Replace dialog. Check the Use option and then select Regular Expressions from the associated drop-down list (which defaults to Wildcards).

Once regular expression matching is enabled, the right-facing triangular buttons next to the Find What and Replace With text boxes enable you to pick from a set of regular expression syntactical elements (see Figure 39-1).

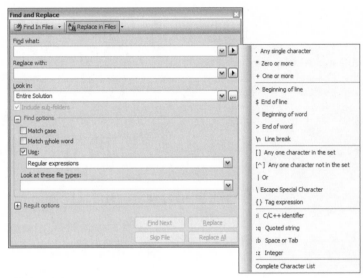

Figure 39-1

Note that these options are only a subset of the pattern constructs you can use in your searches. However, most searches will be possible using the lists in these menus. The regular expression element list available to the replace text is different, containing shortcuts to the tagged expression constructs.

When using a construct that encapsulates a set of characters such as the set constructs, you can either add the regular expression syntax first and then fill it out with the characters, or first add the characters, highlight them, and then add the regular expression, which will automatically wrap the selection you made.

There are minor syntactical differences between regular expression patterns in the Find and Replace dialog compared to the Regex object of the .NET Framework. Mostly these are minor, but there is one significant difference in the way they use the braces construct. Braces ({}) are used in .NET regular expressions to denote multiple instances of the previous search text. For instance, the{2} will find one or two occurrences of the letter e, resulting in a match for thee but not for them. However, in the Find and Replace dialog, braces represent tags instead of multiple instances. To replicate this behavior you would need to specify the(e)^2.

Visual Studio Tools for Office Smart Tags

The other main area for using regular expressions in Visual Studio is in the new Visual Studio Tools for Office 2005 toolkit that integrates Visual Studio 2005 and Microsoft Office 2003 with advanced managed code solutions for Microsoft Excel, Outlook, and Word.

One of the new features of VSTO with the 2005 release of the toolkit is the capability to add document-centric smart tags that use managed code to perform their recognition and action components. Recognition in VSTO smart tags can be performed by adding strings of text to the `Terms` collection, which will match the text exactly, including case, or by adding pattern matching strings to the `Expressions` collection object. While the smart tag object model doesn't help you create regular expressions, once you've figured out the correct pattern it's to easy to add it to the smart tag's `Expressions` collection, as the following sample code demonstrates:

```
Private Sub AddCompanySmartTag()
    Dim CompanyDetails As New Microsoft.Office.Tools.Word.SmartTag( _
        "www.test.com/CompanyDetails#CompanyDetailsSample", "Company Details")

    CompanyDetails.Expressions.Add("regular expression goes here")

    SaveCompanyName = New Microsoft.Office.Tools.Word.Action("Save Name")

    CompanyDetails.Actions = New Microsoft.Office.Tools.Word.Action() _
        {SaveCompanyName}

    Me.VstoSmartTags.Add(CompanyDetails)
End Sub
```

Because the `Expressions` member is a collection object, you can build and store multiple expressions to match against.

VSTO2005 is discussed at length in Chapter 55, including how to add smart tags to documents.

What Are Regular Expressions?

Now that you know how regular expressions are used in different parts of Visual Studio 2005, you may still be wondering how you construct a regular expression. Well, a regular expression consists of a series of characters, or a string, including special characters, that identify different ways of performing pattern matching. The simplest regular expression is plain text and is identical to searching for the characters directly — for example, the statement `Dim myRegex As New Regex("TextToMatch")` creates a regular expression that finds any instances in a block of text that match the string `TextToMatch`.

The next step is the introduction of simple constructs, such as the asterisk to represent multiple instances or a period to indicate any single character except a line break. Using these two constructs in combination, you can locate a string that includes other information. For example, the following code looks for any instance of the string `Text` followed by the string `ToMatch`, regardless of how far apart they are:

```
Dim myRegex As New Regex("Text.*ToMatch")
Dim myMatches As MatchCollection = _
    myRegex.Matches("Search string containing Text Other Information ToMatch")
For Each myMatch As Match In myMatches
    Console.WriteLine("Found match at position " & myMatch.Index.ToString() & _
        ": " & myMatch.Value)
Next
```

Regular expression constructs can also be used to mark special conditions such as the start or end of a line or word, as well as to provide alternative search terms. For example, the regular expression

(This|That) will match any instance of This or That in the search text. Advanced forms of this kind of optional searching are also available to your pattern construction, such as classes of characters represented by square brackets; for example, [abc] will find any instance of a, b, or c.

Using Regular Expressions to Replace Data

When using regular expressions to modify data, such as replacing it with other information or removing it from the source text, additional pattern constructs are used. These extra syntactical elements relate to the parts of the text that were found in the pattern matching part of the process and how they should be treated — for example, when the text is found, you save parts of it with aliased variables that you can then use in the replacement phase with your new text.

Consider the following example in which the elements of a string containing a date are swapped around:

```
NewDateYMD = Regex.Replace(OldDateMDY, _
    "\b(?<month>\d{1,2})/(?<day>\d{1,2})/(?<year>\d{2,4})\b", _
    "${year}-${month}-${day}")
```

The Replace method of the Regex object takes three parameters: an input string that is used as the source for the replacement action, the search pattern to find the string to replace, and the replacement pattern for the required outcome. In this case, the search pattern looks for the following:

❑   A one- or two-digit number, stored in memory with the alias month, followed by

❑   A forward slash character, followed by

❑   A one- or two-digit number, stored in memory with the alias day, followed by

❑   A forward slash character, followed by

❑   A two- or four-digit number, stored in memory with the alias year

The \b elements at the beginning and end of the pattern indicate a word boundary. When the regular expression finds a match for this search pattern, it then replaces it with the following string:

❑   Whatever text was stored in the year alias, which will be a two- or four-digit number, followed by

❑   A hyphen character, followed by

❑   Whatever text was stored in the month alias, which will be a one- or two-digit number, followed by

❑   A hyphen character, followed by

❑   Whatever text was stored in the day alias, which will be a one- or two-digit number

The following table shows several input strings and what is produced as the output of this command:

Original String	New String
12/31/05	05-12-31
The date is 12/31/05.	The date is 05-12-31.
3/1/2005	2005-3-1

Note how the replacement functionality leaves the remainder of the string unchanged because it is only replacing the matched portion of the original text.

Regular Expression Syntax

While complex regular expressions can be daunting, once you understand the syntax of each matching pattern, it becomes straightforward to interpret. The following table introduces you to the patterns you can use in constructing your regular expressions:

Pattern Syntax	Description
{}	In Find and Replace, a tagged portion of text. However, in code, braces are used to indicate a number of occurrences of the previous expression. For example, `is(my){2}book` will only match the string `ismymybook`.
*	An asterisk will match any number of occurrences of the previous expression or character, including none. It is equivalent to `{0,}`. For example, `is(my)*book` will match the strings `isbook`, `ismybook`, and `ismymybook`, but not `isyourbook`.
+	Similar to the asterisk, this will match a number of occurrences of the previous expression, but requires at least one. This pattern is equivalent to `{1,}`. In the previous example, using + instead of * would result in `isbook` being omitted from the matches.
?	Takes the previous expression one step further and restricts the pattern to match one instance only, but will also pass if there is no instance of the pattern. This pattern is the equivalent of `{0,1}`. Using an example pattern of `is(my)?book` would match `isbook`, `ismybook` but not `ismymybook`.
^ and $	Marks the start and end positions of a line of text
< and >	Marks the start and end positions of a word. You can also use \b as a word boundary escape character.
^digit	Find and Replace uses this nomenclature for finding a set number of instances of an expression. If you were looking for the string `ismymybook` in your code listing, you would use the pattern `is(my)^2book`.
()	Parentheses are used to group an expression. In the previous examples the phrase `my` was grouped for subsequent constructs by enclosing it in parentheses. If you used a pattern of `ismy*book` it would return only text that contained 0 to many instances of the letter y, such as `ismyyybook`.
[]	A class of characters from which the pattern can match one. That set of characters can have a range of characters specified by using a hyphen. For example, `[a-cm-p]` will find any one character that is any of the alphabetic characters, a, b, c, m, n, o, or p. You can also include the ^ character in the set to indicate that the pattern should not match the following characters. For example, changing the preceding example pattern to `[^a-cm-p]` will find any one character that is not in the range of alphabetic characters listed.

Pattern Syntax	Description
.	Matches any single character except a line break special character, so `b..k` will match the strings `book` and `back`, but not `brick`.
|	Indicates an either-or situation and is usually used in a group expression to provide alternate strings that can be matched. For example `book(case|end)` will match either bookcase or bookend.
~	Preceding an expression in the Find and Replace dialog with the tilde character indicates that that the expression will be used to exclude matches. For example, `is~(your)book` will find the strings `ismybook` and `ishisbook`, but not `isyourbook`.
\	Used as an escape character, the backslash indicates that the following regular expression character is to be considered literally, so `\~` will find the tilde character, rather than assume it is an exclusion construct.
\n	Indicates a line break character
\e	Indicates the escape character
\h	Represents the backspace character
\t	Used to indicate the tab character

In addition to these rules, there are also a number of regular expression aliases that allow you to shortcut some complex patterns. These expressions are available only in the Find and Replace dialog:

Expression	Description
:b	Matches either a space or tab character
:z	Matches a number and is equivalent to a pattern of `([0-9]+)`
:d	Matches a single digit, which is the same as the pattern `([0-9])`
:c	Matches an alphabetic character and is equivalent to `([a-zA-Z])`
:a	Matches an alphanumeric character and is equivalent to `([0-9a-zA-Z])`
:w	Matches an alphabetic string, thereby replacing the pattern `([a-zA-Z]+)`
:h	Matches all hexadecimal numbers, which is equivalent to `([0-9a-fA-F]+)`
:q	Matches a quoted string with either quotation marks or apostrophes. To write this out explicitly as a pattern, you would need to specify `(("[^"]*")|('[^']*'))`.

Regular Expressions in .NET Programming

The `System.Text.RegularExpressions` namespace contains a number of classes representing regular expressions and objects used in regular expression programming. You can use these to implement various search and replace functions in your applications, starting with the `Regex` object, which contains a single regular expression, and then using the objects that represent match results on various forms.

The next couple of pages detail the main objects in the `RegularExpressions` namespace and how you can best use them in your own Visual Studio 2005 projects.

Regex

The `Regex` class represents a single regular expression. It is immutable, which means once you create it, you cannot change it. However, you can perform a series of functions against the regular expression within the `Regex` object to achieve your searching (and replacement) goals.

To create a `Regex` object in C#, you can first define it and then instantiate it with the regular expression pattern, as shown here:

```
Regex myRegex;
myRegex = new Regex("regularExpressionPattern");
```

As mentioned with the earlier example, you'll need to add a reference to the `System.Text.RegularExpressions` *namespace to the top of the module that contains this code.*

Once instantiated, you can call upon a variety of methods and properties to establish the state of the regular expression against a search string. The list of methods includes the following:

❑ `Match`: Searches a given string and returns a single `Match` object for the first text that is matched by the regular expression pattern

❑ `Matches`: Searches a given string and returns a `MatchCollection` object for all locations that are matched by the pattern stored in the `Regex` object

❑ `IsMatch`: Returns `True` if the provided string contains the pattern

❑ `Split`: Splits the given string into an array of substrings using the regular expression pattern as the delimiter

❑ `Replace`: Replaces any instances of text that match the pattern in the `Regex` object with the provided expression

The following function returns true if the string provided as an argument is in the U.S. date format of month/day/year by using the `IsMatch` method of the `Regex` class:

```
Boolean IsUSDate(String input)
{
    return Regex.IsMatch(input,
        ""\b(?<month>\d{1,2})/(?<day>\d{1,2})/(?<year>\d{2,4})\b ");
}
```

You can provide additional options to the constructor of the `Regex` object that will affect how it is created and used. For example, you can choose to have the regular expression compiled rather than left as a pattern. This will result in faster execution during the majority of the application, but will slow down the startup process as it compiles the expression.

Other useful `Regex` options include `IgnoreCase` to enforce case-insensitive matching, `Multiline`, which will interpret `^` and `$` as the beginning of lines as well as the entire string, and `Singleline`, which will interpret the period (`.`) to match any character.

To specify options during the construction of the `Regex` object, change the instantiation to take a second parameter that consists of the options you need. For example:

```
Dim myRegEx As New Regex("regularExpressionPattern", _
    RegexOptions.Compiled Or RegexOptions.Multiline)
```

Match

The `Match` object is used to represent a single match of the regular expression. When the `Match` method of the `Regex` object is used, it returns a `Match` object that contains the matching text. You can use the `Success` property of the `Match` object to determine whether there was a match or not, and access the substring that matched the pattern with the `ToString` property.

The following code shows how a `Match` object can be used in C# to find the word *book* in a string:

```
Regex myReg = new Regex("book");
// Find a single match in the string.
Match myMatch = myReg.Match("This book is great");
if (myMatch.Success)
{
    Console.WriteLine("Found match " + myMatch.ToString() + " at position " +
        myMatch.Index);
}
```

You can use the `NextMatch` method to search the string from the point of the last matched substring to retrieve the next substring that matches the regular expression pattern.

MatchCollection

When dealing with a search string that could result in multiple matches, however, you're better off using the `Matches` method of the `Regex` object and assigning the result to a `MatchCollection`. The `MatchCollection` object contains a series of `Match` objects, each representing a single substring from the string searched.

You can use this class to navigate through a series of matches in a given string, as the following Visual Basic sample demonstrates:

```
Dim myMatches As MatchCollection
Dim myRegex As New Regex("book")
```

```
myMatches = myRegex.Matches("This book is OK, but that book is better.")

For Each myMatch As Match In MyMatches
    Console.WriteLine("Match found at " + myMatch.Index.ToString)
Next
```

Running this code will produce the following output:

```
Match found at 5
Match found at 26
```

Replacing Substrings

The `Replace` method of `Regex` is used to replace matched portions of a given string with the specified replacement. While the most simplistic form of this function can just replace the substrings with a literal string, the value of the `Replace` method becomes evident when you use it in conjunction with *backreferences*.

A backreference is a way of finding a repeating group of text. Once implemented in a regular expression, every subsequent use of the `backreference` alias will use the same substring that was matched.

Returning to the sample code used earlier to convert a date format, you can see the way `backreferences` can be used:

```
NewDateYMD = Regex.Replace(OldDateMDY, _
    "\b(?<month>\d{1,2})/(?<day>\d{1,2})/(?<year>\d{2,4})\b", _
    "${year}-${month}-${day}")
```

In this example, the three required parts of the matched substring are assigned `backreference` aliases of month, day, and year. When these backreferences are subsequently used further along in the regular expression's `Replace` functionality, the regular expression engine takes whatever content was stored in the `backreference` variables and replaces the references with the substring.

Summary

Regular expressions are a woefully underutilized yet powerful resource for the Visual Studio developer. Whether you need to perform complex searches on your code or data, regular expressions provide you with a way to match extensive patterns that can include conditional and repeating blocks without sacrificing performance with lengthy code. In addition, with the introduction of the Expression Builder options in the Find and Replace dialog, you can now easily create search criteria for looking through your projects and solutions.

Tips, Hacks, and Tweaks

Ever wondered if you can color-code different code files other than the ones supplied by Visual Studio 2005? Maybe you wished you could paint vertical guidelines on your code editor to ensure that your code blocks are lining up the way you want them to. What about those of you using dual-monitor setups — is there a way to manage the layout of the IDE to use them effectively?

These questions and others are answered in this chapter, where you'll dive into the Windows registry and play around with different settings to achieve exactly the system you want. In addition, you'll learn some techniques that will reduce the tedium of performing common tasks by replacing them with keyboard shortcuts and lesser-known features of the IDE.

IDE Shortcuts

The integrated development environment of Visual Studio 2005 is a perfect place to start. The next set of tips let you in on features that are either undocumented or often overlooked in the documentation to the degree that you will likely never notice them.

The Open With Dialog

Visual Studio comes with a number of built-in editors, and it tries to open each file type with the appropriate editor. There are editors for XML and HTML as well as a general code editor for Visual Basic and C# and other languages, and specialized editors for visual form design, binary files, and resource files.

What you may not be aware of is that you can easily choose a different editor for a file. To open a file with a different editor, right-click its entry in the Solution Explorer and choose the Open With command from the context menu. This displays the Open With dialog (shown in Figure 40-1), in which you can choose from the various editors registered in Visual Studio 2005.

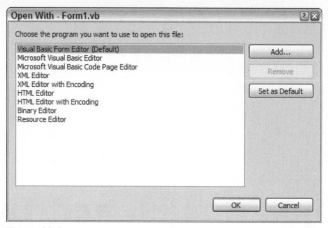

Figure 40-1

You're not restricted to the built-in editors, however; you can add as many other editors as you require. The following walkthrough shows you how to add the standard Windows Notepad as an additional editor for Visual Basic code:

1. Locate a Visual Basic code file in the Solution Explorer (any file that has an extension of .vb). Right-click its entry and select Open With.

2. When the Open With dialog window is displayed, click the Add button to add a new editor to the list.

3. Click the ellipsis button next to the Program Name text box to browse the file system on the computer. Navigate to your Windows installation directory (by default, C:\Windows), select NOTEPAD.EXE, and click Open.

4. The Friendly Name field defaults to NOTEPAD.EXE, so overtype this with the friendlier "Notepad." Click OK to save the entry to the editor list.

5. Select the Notepad entry in the editor list and click OK. Visual Studio starts up an instance of Notepad and uses it to open the selected file.

The Open With command will display a set of editors that are registered for the particular file type, so if you add Notepad for Visual Basic code files (.vb), you'll also need to add it to other file types if you want it available in their Open With list.

Accessing the Active Files List

When you have many files open, sometimes it can be hard to keep track of where each file is in the tabbed list along the top of the main workspace area. In most cases, you'll only be able to see three or four tabs at a time, with the rest shown in the Active Files drop-down list. This list is accessed through the button next to the close button in the top-right corner of the workspace (see Figure 40-2).

The frustrating aspect of this way of organizing your files is that it can interrupt your workflow when you have to access the list using your mouse. Fortunately, even this list has a keyboard shortcut bound to it. Press Ctrl+Alt+the down arrow and the Active Files list will be displayed. Once displayed, it then retains the focus for you to use the arrow keys to scroll up and down the list to choose which file you want to view.

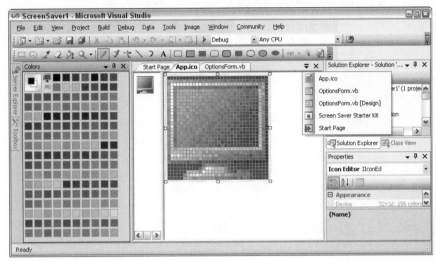

Figure 40-2

Changing Font Size

In Chapter 26 you saw how macros work in Visual Studio 2005. Along with building your own macros, Visual Studio ships with dozens of pre-defined macros ready for your use. What you may not realize is that you can assign keyboard shortcuts to macros and make them even more useful.

One common problem for some development teams is the different font size requirements when editing code. Some developers prefer as much code on screen as possible, and therefore keep the font size small, while others require the font size to be larger than average. Previous versions of Visual Studio relied on third-party add-ins to provide a font zooming feature to the IDE, similar to that found in Microsoft Word.

However, with the macros supplied with Visual Studio 2005, and the capability to bind them to keyboard shortcuts, you don't need to go digging around the Internet looking for a suitable add-in. Follow this task list to bind shortcut keystrokes to macros to increase and decrease the font size in the editor windows:

1. Open the Keyboard page in the main options window by using Tools⇨Options to bring up the Options dialog, and then navigate to the Keyboard page in the Environment group. This won't be visible if your Options dialog is only showing the basic set, so check the Show All Settings checkbox if you need to (for Visual Basic environmental setups only).

2. Filter the command list by entering the text **fontsize**. As a result, the command list is reduced to three entries. These three entries represent macros that perform the following functionality:

    ❏ Macros.Samples.Accessibility.DecreaseTextEditorFontSize: Decreases the font size in the text editor by 2 points.

❏ Macros.Samples.Accessibility.IncreaseTextEditorFontSize: Increases the font size in the text editor by 2 points.

❏ Macros.Samples.Accessibility.UpdateTextEditorFontSizeToMatchDisplayProperties: Sets the font size to match the Windows system setting.

3. Now you need to assign the keystrokes. Because the shortcuts are to be available only within the text editor, change the Use New Shortcut In drop-down list to Text Editor (this also avoids clashes with other areas of the IDE that use some of the shortcut combinations you're about to implement). Select the first entry in the command list, position the cursor in the Press Shortcut Keys text box, and press Ctrl, Shift, and the down arrow simultaneously. Click the Assign button to bind the shortcut.

4. Repeat this process with the second entry in the command list but this time use Ctrl, Shift, and the up arrow.

5. Finally, repeat the process one more time with the last entry, setting the shortcut to Ctrl+Shift+=. Click OK to save the settings and you're ready to zoom in and out on your code window any time. Use the Ctrl+Shift+= shortcut to return the font size to the default setting.

Making Rectangular Selections

You may wonder when you would use the next tip, but chances are good that once you've used it, you'll realize how handy it can be. You can make a rectangular selection in your code listing that selects a part of a section of lines. The sample shown in Figure 40-3 illustrates the feature in action, with the `Private` keyword selected on four successive lines.

This block can be deleted, cut, or copied to another section of your program. The behavior is inherited from similar functionality in Microsoft Word, and you can access it in the same way. First, press and hold the Alt key. Now, simply click and drag your mouse pointer from one corner of the intended area to select to the opposing corner.

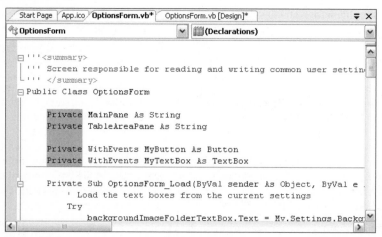

Figure 40-3

Go To Find Combo

The Go To Find Combo (yes, that's what it's called!) is one of the more useful features found on the tool-bars of Visual Studio, and one of the least used. The Go To Find Combo is part of the default standard toolbar in most configurations (see Figure 40-4), but Visual Basic developers were left out and will need to add it manually to the toolbar.

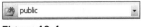

Figure 40-4

In its standard mode, you can use it to find simple strings of text. Type the string you're looking for and press Enter, and Visual Studio will attempt to locate the search text in the active document. You can cycle through the instances of the search criteria by repeatedly pressing Enter.

However, there are less obvious ways to use the Go To Find Combo (although the name does give them away). Here are some other uses for the Combo:

Text Entered	Shortcut Keys	Effect
Number	Ctrl+G	Replicates the Go To command to navigate directly to a given line number without the need for an additional dialog box
Filename	Ctrl+Shift+G	Locates the file in the Solution Explorer
Programming Keyword	F1	Opens the Document Explorer and navigates to the help topic associated with the keyword that was entered
Function Name	F9	Adds or removes a breakpoint from the start of the function with the name that was entered
> any command	Enter	The > character indicates that the text should be interpreted as a command alias, just as it would be in the Command Window

You can access the Go To Find Combo by using the Ctrl+/ keyboard shortcut.

As mentioned previously, this feature is not active by default in the Visual Basic configuration of the IDE. You can customize the standard toolbar to include the Go To Find Combo just as you would any modern toolbar. Right-click in the toolbar region of the IDE and select Customize from the context menu. Display the Commands tab and then select the Edit category. Scroll through the list of commands until you locate the Go To Find Combo and then click and drag it to the position you want it to occupy on the toolbar.

You'll also want to set up keyboard shortcuts for some of the functionality shown in the preceding table (for instance, Ctrl+G is set up to display the Immediate window, rather than the Go To Line Number dialog). In addition, to access the Go To Find Combo from the keyboard, Visual Basic programmers will find that the Ctrl+/ shortcut is unassigned, so it can be used to replicate the behavior of the other IDE configurations.

To assign any of these shortcuts, follow the steps shown in the previous walkthrough, which outlines how to assign shortcuts to macros.

Forced Reformat

Visual Studio 2005 does a good job at applying formatting to your code automatically (much better than previous versions), but every now and then it will get out of sync and lose track of your code indentation levels and stop formatting it in other ways too.

You can always perform a forced reformat of your code by using the Edit⇨Advanced⇨Format Document menu command (which in Visual Basic has a keyboard shortcut chord of Ctrl+K, Ctrl+D), or just a segment of the code by first selecting it and then using Edit⇨Advanced⇨Format Selection (or the chord Ctrl+K, Ctrl+F).

If you perform a forced reformat and the code remains unformatted, you likely have a syntactical compilation error obstructing the Visual Studio IDE from applying formatting. Fix any errors in the Error List and perform the forced reformat again.

Word Wrapping

Those long lines of code can be hard to read when they trail off the screen. Visual Studio 2005 provides an option to wrap the lines so they are visible in their entirety. This setting can be found in the Text Editor group of options and can be set for all or specific languages on the General page.

Underneath the Word Wrap option is an additional option to show visual glyphs when lines are wrapped. While this option is not enabled by default, you may find it useful to display the glyphs if you're used to a language such as Visual Basic in which code statements must reside on a single line without a specific line continuation character.

Registry Hacks

This next set of tips enables you to customize the appearance and functionality of Visual Studio 2005 by delving into the Windows registry. As with any other advice you may have read concerning the Windows registry, you must be careful with your changes, as doing the wrong thing can have disastrous results.

However, if you're comfortable with adding entries to the registry, you will find these extra features easy to implement.

Vertical Guidelines

Ever needed to line up blocks of code that are so far apart that they are not visible on the screen at the same time? This can happen in large functions when dealing with enclosing blocks such as loops and conditional blocks in which you want indenting to occur consistently.

While Visual Studio does a good job of automatically indenting, sometimes it gets it wrong, and other times it doesn't do it at all (such as in text files). This tweak enables you to add vertical guidelines to the text editor code windows so that you can easily line up code when desired.

Sara Ford of Microsoft was the first person to bring this to the general developer community's attention, although she insists on not taking credit for the discovery, saying that the internal editor team gave her the tip first. Her blog can be found at `http://blogs.msdn.com/saraford/default.aspx`.

1. Shut down Visual Studio 2005 if it's currently active and open the Windows Registry Editor by running regedit.

2. Locate the key `[HKEY_CURRENT_USER]\Software\Microsoft\VisualStudio\8.0\Text Editor`. Create a new `String` value with a name of `Guides`.

3. Set the value of this new `String` to the following text:

```
RGB(255,0,0) 4, 20, 50
```

This sets vertical guidelines at columns 5, 21, and 51 (the values are zero-based) and colors them red. Start Visual Studio 2005, open a module for editing, and check how the vertical guidelines displayed (Figure 40-5 shows the guidelines with this setting applied).

You can customize the appearance of the guidelines by changing the RGB value to your own preferred color scheme. Each column number should be separated by commas, and you can have up to 13 guidelines defined at any one time.

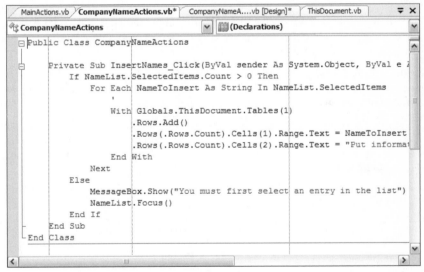

Figure 40-5

To remove the guidelines, simply delete the entry from the Windows registry.

Right-Click New Solution

Some developers prefer to create their solution file and associated folder structure prior to creating the individual projects. However, Visual Studio 2005 doesn't really allow for that kind of behavior, preferring to control creation of files and defaulting to a set location. You can change this location, of course, but it could be handy to be able to easily create your own solution files where you want first.

It's remarkably easy to do and only requires creating a small text file and adding a single entry to the Windows registry. The following walkthrough creates a blank solution file that is used as a template for creating new solutions. It then binds that template to Visual Studio's solution handling in the Windows registry, enabling you to easily create solution files in your file system.

While it is remarkably easy, Peter Provost was first to blog about this shortcut on his site www.peter provost.org/.

1. Open Notepad or any other text editor you prefer and add the following text:

```
Microsoft Visual Studio Solution File, Format Version 9.00
# Visual Studio 2005
Global
    GlobalSection(SolutionProperties) = preSolution
        HideSolutionNode = FALSE
    EndGlobalSection
EndGlobal
```

2. This text is all you need for an absolute bare-bones definition for a Visual Studio 2005 solution, so save the file as Visual Studio Solution.sln. This filename will be used to generate what appears in the right-click New menu, so make sure you name it something that you'll recognize. Save the file to the Windows\ShellNew directory.

3. Edit the Windows registry by running regedit. Navigate to the [HKEY_CLASSES_ROOT]\.sln node in the tree. This is used to specify how Windows (and Visual Studio) will handle .sln files. Add a new Key entry and name it ShellNew.

4. In the ShellNew key, add a new String value named FileName. Set the value of this String to be the same as the filename you used earlier, so if you've been following along exactly, you should enter the value Visual Studio Solution.sln.

That's all you need to do. Open Windows Explorer and navigate to a folder in which you want to create a new Visual Studio solution. Right-click and open the New submenu from the context menu. You should find a new entry to choose, which will create a new, empty solution file (see Figure 40-6).

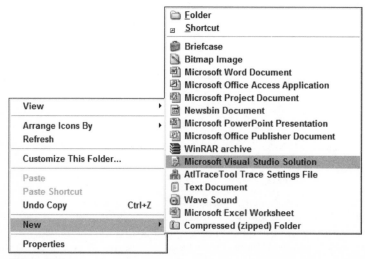

Figure 40-6

Keyword Color-Coding

Visual Studio 2005 color-codes your code modules with different colors based on the syntax. Keywords, literals, and other special phrases and words are marked up with different colors to make it easier for you to determine which code is doing what. However, code contained in files that have an unusual extension, or that is written in a completely different language, does not have the automatic benefit of this coloring.

Fortunately, through a back door you can add your own file types and keywords to Visual Studio 2005 so that keywords will be color-coded in your specialized files. Like the previous tip, this undocumented feature requires the creation of a text file and an entry in the Windows registry. The following walk-through shows you how to perform all the steps necessary to provide color-coding to a special file type.

1. The first task in providing color-coding is to specify which words should be recognized by Visual Studio as keywords. Create a new text file in Notepad and type each keyword on its own line. For this example, create a fictitious file type called .pd that only has two keywords: `MyKeyWord` and `HerKeyWord`. The file contents should appear as shown here:

```
MyKeyWord
HerKeyWord
```

2. Save this file with a name of `usertype.dat` in the `Common7\IDE` subfolder of your Visual Studio 2005 installation directory. By default, the full path will be `C:\Program Files\Microsoft Visual Studio 8\Common7\IDE`. The file `usertype.dat` can be used to specify any additional keywords for the existing languages too, such as the many C++ MFC classes.

3. Now you need to add an entry to the Windows registry for the new file type. Edit the registry by running regedit and navigate to `HKEY_LOCAL_MACHINE\SOFTWARE\ Microsoft\VisualStudio\8.0\Languages\File Extensions`.

4. Add a new key named .pd. Set the `Default` value to the following GUID:

```
{B2F072B0-ABC1-11D0-9D62-00C04FD9DFD9}
```

    This is the secret to enabling Visual Studio's proper processing of the file. Because C++ can have many different file types, which sometimes don't have proper language formatting, you can "borrow" the C++ GUID for your own file types. Compare the GUID listed here to the one found in the .cpp key and you'll find that they're the same.

5. You're now good to go. Create a text file and name it `myTest.pd`. Add the following lines of "code" to it:

```
MyKeyWord varName As MyType
HerKeyWord = varName
```

6. Save the file and open it in Visual Studio 2005. You should see that the two keywords have been color-coded with your default keyword color (see Figure 40-7 for an example).

    Because the figures in this book are grayscale, you'll have to take it on trust that the keywords are, in fact, color-coded.

You can use this technique to add file types of other programming languages such as PHP and their associated keywords to Visual Studio's color-coding format engine.

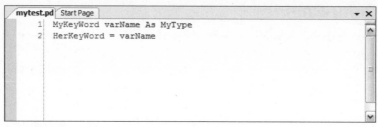

Figure 40-7

Other Tips

The following two tips are worth mentioning, but didn't fit into either of the preceding major categories.

Disable Add-Ins Loading on Startup

Sometimes an add-in may be malfunctioning and cause unexpected issues in your Visual Studio 2005 experience, or you may just want to bypass an add-in that you're currently working on yourself.

Either way, you can cause Visual Studio to bypass its add-in loading at startup by holding the left Shift key down when you start the IDE. When started this way, no add-ins at all will be loaded.

Alternatively, you can allow Visual Studio to load the add-ins at startup and then disable them individually in the Add-in Manager, which is accessible from the Tools menu.

Add-ins are discussed at length in Chapters 32 and 33.

Multi-Monitor Layouts

An ever-growing number of developers are using multiple-monitor setups for their development efforts. Visual Studio 2005 has a number of features that enable you to customize its layout to suit a multiple-monitor setup. These features are discussed elsewhere in this book, but it's worth listing the different aspects of the IDE that could be used:

IDE Feature	Multi-Monitor Usage
Undockable Tool Windows	You can undock any of the tool windows within the IDE and position them anywhere in the desktop setup. This enables you to maximize your code editing and form design workspace on one screen while floating the windows in your preferred order on the other screen.
Vertical Tab Group	You can have multiple documents open at the same time. If you position the split of the editors along the monitor joins, then you'll effectively have two editors side by side without any awkward monitor joins in the middle of code.

IDE Feature	Multi-Monitor Usage
Debugging	Have your Visual Studio IDE open on the secondary monitor when working on Windows applications. When debugged, at startup these will show by default on the primary monitor, providing you with a full view of both application and code at all times. You can do the same thing when debugging web applications, or position your web browser on the secondary monitor and your IDE on the primary one so that you get the same effect.

Summary

This chapter showed you a multitude of tips and tweaks to get the most out of your Visual Studio 2005 setup. Along the way, you were introduced to other settings, keyboard shortcuts, and even intriguing entries in the Windows registry. Why not take a closer look at these additional features and see what else you can do to customize your experience?

41

Creating Web Applications

When Microsoft released the first version of Visual Studio .NET, one of the most talked about features was the capability to create full-blown web applications in a very similar way to Windows applications. This arrival introduced the concept of developing feature-rich applications that ran over the web in a wholly integrated way. However, Microsoft went a little too far in making web development the same as Windows development, and some programmers were confused about how to create web applications.

Visual Studio 2005 rectifies that by separating the creation of web-based solutions from the Windows-based project types, but it still provides the integrated development environment. Therefore, you get the best of both worlds — a single consistent development experience coupled with a distinction between Windows and web application programming. In this chapter you'll learn how to create web applications in Visual Studio 2005 as well as look at some of the new web components that Microsoft has introduced to make your development life a little (and in some cases, a lot) easier.

Creating Web Projects

Creating a web project in Visual Studio 2005 is slightly different from creating a regular Windows-type project. With normal Windows applications and services, you pick the type of project, name the solution, and click OK. Each language has its own set of project templates and there are no real options related to creating the project. Web development is different because you can now create the development project in different locations, from the local file system to a variety of FTP and HTTP locations that are defined in your system setup, including the local IIS server or remote FTP folders.

Because of this major difference in creating web-based applications and services, Microsoft has separated out the web project types into their own command and dialog. On the File menu of Visual Studio 2005 is a new command called New Web Site. Invoking this command displays the New Web Site dialog, where you can choose the type of project template you want to use (see Figure 41-1).

In some languages, the File menu structure is slightly different. Instead of having File⇨New Project and File⇨New Web Site, languages such as C# will have a File⇨New submenu that contains Project and Web Site as options.

Most likely, you'll use two main types of project: the ASP.NET Web Site and ASP.NET Web Service templates. The other templates provide variations on the Web Site template. Regardless of which type of web project you're creating, the lower section of the dialog enables you to choose where to create the project as well as what language should be used as a base for the project.

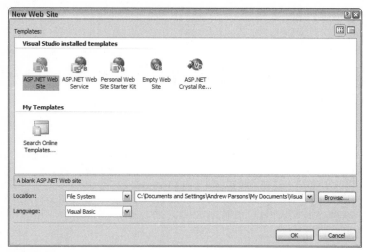

Figure 41-1

You have a choice of Visual Basic, C#, and J#, but Visual Studio will default to the language you chose when first configuring the IDE's layout. If you are using the general developer environment or a language other than these three, the dialog will default to Visual Basic.

The more important choice you have to make is where the web project will be created. By default, Visual Studio expects you to develop the web site or service locally using the normal file system. The default location is in the My Documents folder for the current user, but you can change this by overtyping the value, selecting an alternative location from the drop-down list, or clicking the Browse button.

The Location drop-down list also contains HTTP and FTP as options. Selecting HTTP will change the value in the Filename area to a default location in the `localhost` web server, while FTP provides a blank `ftp://` prefix ready for you to type in the destination folder. Either way, you can also overtype the value or click the Browse button to change the intended location of the project.

The Choose Location dialog (shown in Figure 41-2) enables you to specify where the project should be stored. Note that this isn't necessarily where the project will be deployed, as you can specify a different destination for that when you're ready to ship, so don't expect that you are specifying the ultimate final destination here.

The File System option enables you to browse through the folder structure known to the system, including the My Network Places folders, and gives you the option to create subfolders where you need them. This is the easiest way of specifying where you want the web project files, and the easiest to locate later, but most local web development is normally saved to the `//localhost` folder (normally `C:\Inetpub\wwwroot`).

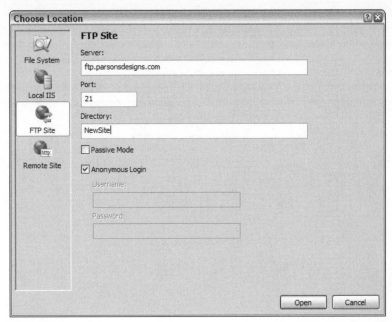

Figure 41-2

While you could specify this folder with the File System option, a better option is to use the Local IIS location type and browse through the `//localhost` server Default Web Site folders. This is because it will also contain virtual directory entries that point to web sites not physically located within the folder structure within `//localhost`, but aliases to elsewhere in the file system or network. You can create your application in a new web application folder or create a new virtual directory entry in which you browse to the physical file location and specify an alias to appear in the web site list.

The FTP Site location type is shown in Figure 41-2, which gives you the option to log in to a remote FTP site anonymously or with a specified user. When you click Open, Visual Studio saves the FTP settings for when you create the project, so be aware that it won't test whether the settings are correct until it's ready to actually create the project files and save them to the specified destination.

> *You can save your project files to any FTP server to which you have access, even if that FTP site doesn't have .NET installed. However, you will not be able to run it without .NET, so you will only be able to use it as a file store.*

The last location type is Remote Site, which enables you to connect to a remote server that has FrontPage extensions installed on it. If you have such a site, you can simply specify the location where you want the new project to be saved and Visual Studio 2005 will confirm that it can create the folder through the FrontPage extensions.

Once you've chosen the intended location for your project, clicking the OK button tells Visual Studio 2005 to create the project files and propagate them to the desired location. After the web application has finished initializing, Visual Studio opens the `Default.aspx` page and populates the Toolbox with the components available to you for web development (remember that you can customize the Toolbox to include additional components, as explained in Chapter 3).

The first thing you should notice with the main workspace area in the IDE is that below the design surface for the web page is a toolstrip containing buttons to switch between Design and Source view of the ASPX page and a text hierarchical notation indicating where you are currently positioned in the HTML (see Figure 41-3). As you navigate around the HTML, this text area will change to highlight the current HTML element.

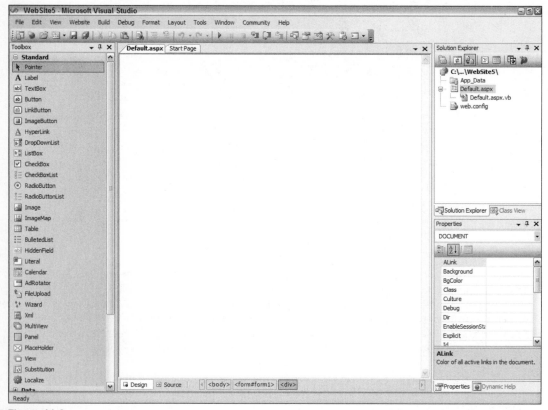

Figure 41-3

When you are finished editing your site's pages, you can use the normal functionality of Visual Studio 2005 to run the web page into the browser. By default, the Web.config file that controls how the web site will run will have debugging turned off. To run the web site without debugging from within Visual Studio, press the Ctrl+F5 keyboard shortcut.

Dynamic Compilation

Perhaps one of the biggest changes in Visual Studio 2005 web development is that the compilation of the code behind the web pages is actually done as needed. Previously, the code had to be compiled into a binary DLL, which would then be invoked by the ASP.NET services when .NET components needed the code.

The new method of compiling the code behind dynamically is much preferred, as it enables you to directly edit the code without having to recompile in Visual Studio. As long as the files are saved, the .NET services on the web server will do the rest.

Web Services

Creating a web services project is done in much the same way, with the same location options for placing the project files. Like previous versions of Visual Studio, the default ASMX page is generated with a sample "Hello World" web method defined for you to use as a template. However, be aware that unlike previous versions, the sample is not commented out and will be published as an available method in your web service unless you delete it.

Personal Web Site Starter Kit

An excellent resource to investigate for best practices and good use of a lot of the new features found in ASP.NET 2.0 components and design is the Personal Web Site Starter Kit project. This is one of the derivatives of the main Web Site project type but generates everything you need to build a personal website, complete with SQL Server Express database, multiple CSS themes, master-detail pages, user management, and more.

Figure 41-4 shows the Personal Web Site Starter Kit in action, with the dark theme applied in its default configuration. The photo of the day section is a great example of the kind of effect you can achieve with normal web controls and two lines of code.

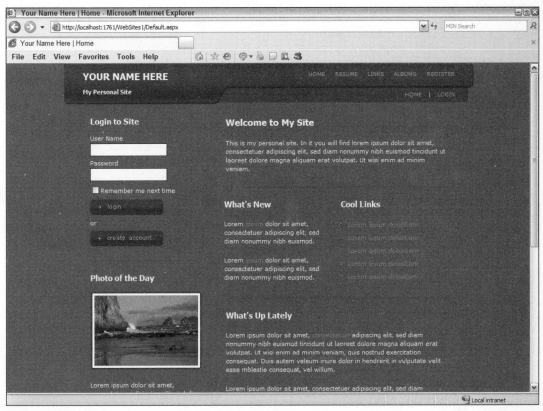

Figure 41-4

Features shown in the Starter Kit, such as user authentication and master pages, are discussed in the next several pages, but remember that this great example project is available for you to look through to gain an insight about how the various controls and components are meant to be used. The Personal Web Site Starter Kit is available for all three Microsoft languages — Visual Basic, C# and J#.

Web Development Options

Before you take a look at how to customize the web pages in your site with the many components and features offered in Visual Studio 2005, it's worth taking a look at some of the web-development-specific options within the IDE that can make your life easier in the long run.

The options related to web development can be found in two places — the HTML text editor and the HTML Designer groups of options. Each of these deals with a different aspect of how you can configure the IDE to suit your own working style.

HTML Text Editor Options

The text editor options group has a section of parameters for each language that Visual Studio 2005 understands, and HTML is no exception. Within the HTML text editor, you'll find the normal pages of options for tabbing and autocompletion. In addition to these are three pages of HTML-specific options: Format, Miscellaneous, and Validation.

Format options specify how the HTML tags should be capitalized and how the internal attributes on each element should be formatted. Additional formatting options can be specified for each individual HTML tag by clicking the Tag Specific Options button. The tag list includes both straight HTML and ASP.NET control tags, and for each tag you can specify whether it requires a closing tag and whether the contents within the opening and closing tags should be indented. It also enables you to control the color of each tag.

The Miscellaneous page has two innocuous looking options that can have profound effects on your HTML code if you're unaware of them. The first is "Auto ID elements on paste" in Source view. By default this option is turned on and will assign an ID attribute on every element that is pasted into the source of a web page. This can be both good and bad. It's great when you're pasting a whole section of HTML with many elements that you're going to need to refer to in code because the IDs will be guaranteed to be unique. However, the problem with this is that it will overwrite any pre-existing ID values, so if your HTML and program code depend on the IDs having specific values, you'll also need to update those places with the newly assigned ID values.

The second option is turned off by default but can be handy in the same situation. "Format HTML on paste" will reformat the HTML source code to fit in with the existing HTML structure in your source, including indentation and spacing. Leaving this option disabled means that the HTML is pasted as is without any reformatting occurring.

The last page of options for the HTML editor is the Validation options set. With this page you can have Visual Studio 2005 analyze the HTML source and validate it against a particular standard. Figure 41-5 shows this page with the HTML 4.01 standard selected, but you can also pick browser-specific standards, or XHTML 1.0 and 1.1 standards, for comparing your code.

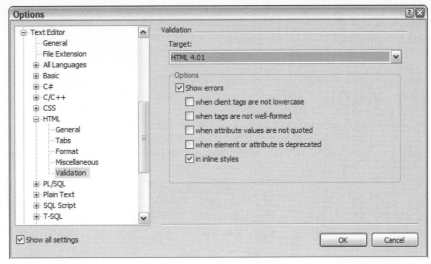

Figure 41-5

HTML Designer Options

The HTML Designer group contains a number of options related to the graphical designer for web pages. The General options page only has a couple of simple options that come into play when you open an HTML page for editing or when you place a component on the page. The Display options page supplements these with some extra settings specifying how various controls should be drawn in Design view.

The most important option to be aware of is the positioning setting in the CSS Positioning options page (see Figure 41-6). By default, positioning is specified as absolute, which is great when you want to hardcode a particular layout. However, Visual Studio 2005 takes absolute positioning to the extreme, and can insert absolute values for individual cells in tables and other childlike elements. As a result, you can sometimes find yourself modifying multiple values where one would have sufficed.

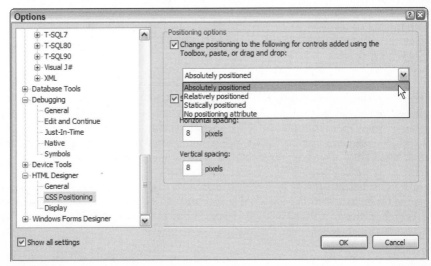

Figure 41-6

Other situations call for the more flexible relative positioning whereby elements are positioned relative to other elements and the page itself, or are even statically positioned. Use this page to choose the type of positioning you need for your specific project.

Website Menu

One last topic worthy of mention is the Website menu (see Figure 41-7) that appears in the main menu list when you're editing a web project. From this menu you can control how the Solution Explorer displays the files and folders in your project, adds new pages and elements to your project, and adds references.

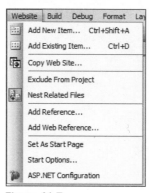

Figure 41-7

In addition, the Website menu is where you can publish your website from a local set of files to a remote destination. Later in this chapter you'll learn how to deploy a site using this method. Two other important commands are the Start Options and ASP.NET Configuration menu commands. Start Options enables you to set how your website should be started, including startup page and debugging options, while the ASP.NET Configuration command invokes the Web Site Administration Tool with which you can add users, roles, security, and other application-specific settings. Both of these topics are also discussed later in this chapter.

Web Controls

So, you have your first web site project with a single blank page named `default.aspx`. You can start editing the HTML straight away, using the Visual Studio 2005 IDE as a normal HTML editor, with both Design and Source views. The Design view enables you to start writing content directly onto the page much like any other WYSIWYG web editor. You can add HTML-specific elements such as tables, images, and `div` tags to the page through the HTML group on the Toolbox. Formatting text with bold and italic, coloring, and setting its size and alignment are all done through the Format menu.

It is also worth noting here that all of the HTML tags in the page layout can have their properties edited just like the .NET components that are added to the design. This can save you time because you don't need to switch between Design and Source views of the page just to change a simple property.

The result is a fairly basic but sturdy editor for your HTML. Of course, there will still be times when you need to edit the HTML directly, which is where the Source view comes in to play. Visual Studio's HTML text editor color-codes tags, attributes, and values, as well as automatically indents your source code for legibility. The IntelliSense engine also works in HTML, so when you add an opening tag that requires a corresponding closing tag, the editor will automatically add it.

Similarly, when you add an attribute to a tag, the IDE displays a list of available attributes from which you can choose; and if the attribute has a proscribed set of values, you are also presented with those options.

IntelliSense also marks HTML with potential problems, such as an `<img>` tag without an `alt` attribute, or elements that don't meet the HTML standard you chose in the settings discussed earlier.

General Property Settings

Before taking a look at some of the new web components you can harness in your web development projects, note a couple of new dialogs in Visual Studio 2005 that are shared among the web controls you add to your page designs.

The new Color Picker dialog (shown in Figure 41-8) is a lot larger and easier to navigate than the Color dialog that Windows projects use. You can manually create a color irrespective of whether or not it falls into the official web palette through the Custom Color tab, or choose from web-safe colors in either the Web Palette or Named Colors tab.

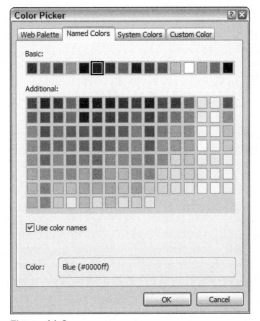

Figure 41-8

If you choose the Named Colors tab you can choose to insert either the hexadecimal value or the color name, by checking the Use Color Names checkbox. Note that the default behavior is to insert the color name, so if you prefer to know the exact value of CornflowerBlue or DarkSalmon, uncheck this option to insert the corresponding literal value (#6495ED and #E9967A, respectively).

Any component that can have a style applied to it directly can take advantage of the Style Builder (see Figure 41-9). The Style Builder enables you to interactively create a style on-the-fly. There are eight groups of options for every element, giving you control over borders, padding, coloring, and font styles (including the capability to assign multiple font names as is standard practice in professional web design), layout and positioning rules, and even the capability to set the mouse cursor or where print page breaks should occur.

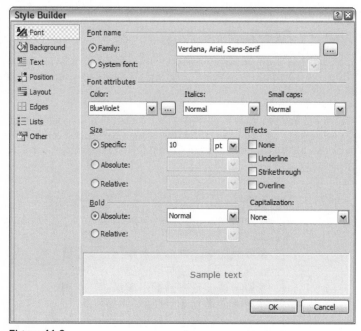

Figure 41-9

When you're done creating the style and click OK, the values are populated as a text string into the `Style` property, which you can edit directly, or even copy to an external CSS file so it can be shared among multiple components.

> *This same Style Builder dialog is available when creating or editing styles in a CSS file. You can display the Style Builder in a CSS file by either using the Styles⇨Build Style menu command or right-clicking anywhere within the style rule you want to change and selecting Build Style from the context menu.*

The Controls

When Visual Studio .NET (2002) was first released a whole new way of building web applications was enabled for Microsoft developers. Instead of using strictly server-based components in ASP or similar languages, and having to deal with the sequential way page code was processed, ASP.NET introduced the concept of feature-rich controls for web pages that acted in similar ways to their Windows counterparts.

Web controls such as button and text box components have familiar properties such as `Text`, `Left`, and `Width`, along with just as recognizable methods and events such as `Click`, `TextChanged`, and `ToString`. In addition to these was a limited set of web-specific components, some dealing with data-based information, such as the `DataGrid` control, and others providing common web tasks, such as an `ErrorProvider` to give feedback to users about problems with information they entered into a web form.

Visual Studio 2005 introduces a host of new web-based components to the Toolbox. Some of these components — such as the `ImageMap` and `FileUpload` controls — are straightforward and immediately fill a need faced by developers creating web applications. However, some of the new components are special enough to warrant individual mention.

The Wizard Component

The ASP.NET Wizard component is a complex object that encapsulates an entire step-by-step wizard process. In a Windows wizard, a single dialog window is used to contain the contents of each step, with the necessary text and input fields being displayed as the user navigates through the stages of the wizard. The web-based component replicates this behavior with a user interface comprised of two areas.

The left-hand side contains the list of steps in the wizard, formatted as hyperlinks, while the main right-hand pane contains the objects for each step. The smart tag Tasks list (displayed in Figure 41-10) enables you to switch the design-time view between the available steps, pick a preset formatting set, and manage the number of steps you have in the wizard.

Each step can be defined as a starting, finishing, or intermediate stage of the wizard, which affects how ASP.NET renders the navigation buttons.

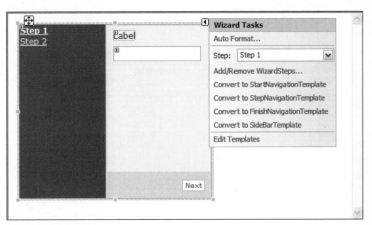

Figure 41-10

This component also illustrates the introduction of templatized component design. This style of component development enables you to design one single layout (as complex as you require) and set it as a template to be used in other parts of your design. Template design is derived from the master-detail page concept discussed later in this chapter.

Simple Navigation Components

The Toolbox has a separate section for navigation controls, appropriately named Navigation. This group contains three components by default: Sitemap, Menu, and TreeView. The Sitemap control is discussed in the next chapter, which deals with advanced web techniques, but the other two are both useful enough to be covered here.

The Menu component enables you to create complex nested menus for your web page that do not require server-based processing for the user to navigate. As Figure 41-11 demonstrates, the default view state for a menu is Static, which means ASP.NET expects the menu to be a fixed set of options such as those shown in the figure. Each menu item can contain a set of submenu items to create as much depth as you require. As users hover their mouse pointers over a menu item, the appropriate submenu is displayed without having to go back to the server for more information.

> *Alternatively, you can have the menu build its contents dynamically as it receives the request, or even from a Data Source such as a sitemap or XML file.*

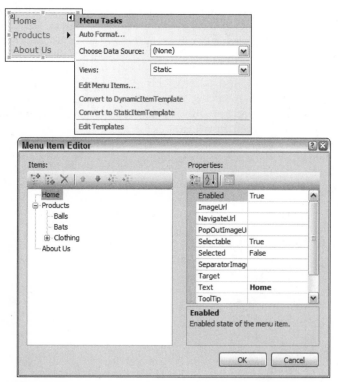

Figure 41-11

Menus can be displayed vertically as shown in Figure 41-11, or horizontally for the top or bottom of a web page; this is set through the Orientation property of the Menu object itself.

The TreeView component enables you to replicate the TreeView control on many Windows applications. It works in much the same way, with a root node that contains a series of child nodes, which in turn have their own children, and so on.

`TreeView` components can be collapsed or expanded as the user requires, and Visual Studio 2005 comes bundled with a series of preset formats that emulate common Windows applications such as Messenger and Outlook, as shown in Figure 41-12.

Besides formatting the `TreeView` to look like various Windows applications, you can bind the control to a Data Source in the same way you can with `Menu` components, even right down to the detail of formatting the lines that join the nodes with color, thickness, and style.

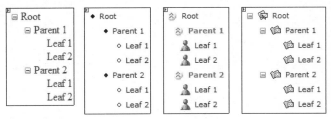

Figure 41-12

User Authentication Components

Perhaps the most significant additions to the web components in terms of functionality are the seven user authentication and login components. With these you can quickly and easily create the user-based parts of your web application without having to worry about how to format them and what controls are necessary.

By default, every web application you create has an automatic Data Source added to its ASP.NET configuration (see the section entitled "Site Administration" later in this chapter). The Data Source is a SQL Server Express database with a default name pointing to a local file system location. This Data Source is used as the default location for your user authentication processing, storing information about users and their current settings.

The benefit of having this automated data store generated for each web site is that Visual Studio can have an array of user-bound web components that can automatically save user information without requiring you to write any code.

Before you can sign in as a user on a particular site, you first need to create one. Initially, you can do that in the administration and configuration of ASP.NET, but you will also want to allow visitors of the site to create their own user accounts. The `CreateUserWizard` component does just that, containing two wizard pages with information about creating an account, and indicating when the account is successful.

The default behavior for this control is shown in Figure 41-13 with a simple formatting scheme applied to it for greater legibility. You can see that the initial step allows the site visitor to enter a username, a password (and confirmation of the password), an e-mail address, and some security information for retrieving forgotten passwords. The text below these input fields is a custom control inherited from an `ErrorProvider` component that is displayed when the password fields don't match.

Other messages can be customized as well, dealing with situations such as passwords not being long enough or duplicate usernames being detected. Although the component is obviously made up of subcomponents such as `Label`, `TextBox`, and `Button` controls, all the complexity is hidden away behind individual settings that control only the properties of each child control you need to change.

Alternatively, you can select the Customize Create User Step or Customize Complete Step commands from the smart tag Tasks list, also shown in Figure 41-13, and gain direct access to the individual child controls.

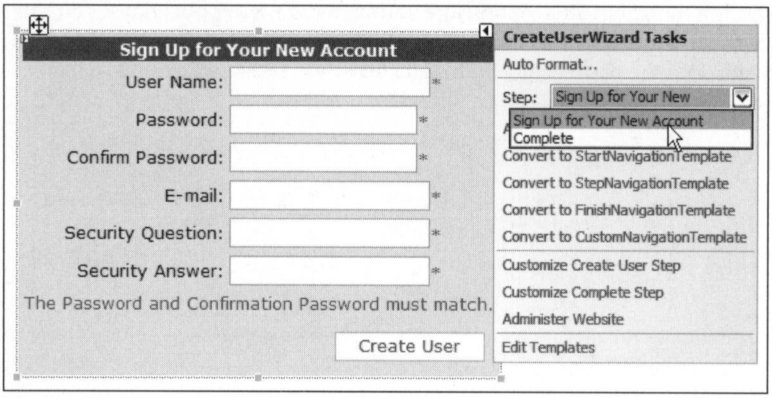

Figure 41-13

The major advantage of using this CreateUserWizard component over building your own is that it does everything for you, including the database access to verify that the user can be added, and the actual saving of user information. You don't have to do a single thing to have this work. As a test, create a new ASP.NET web application and drag an instance of the CreateUserWizard component from the Login group on the Toolbox onto the page and start the application with the Ctrl+F5 keyboard shortcut (to bypass debugging). After Visual Studio saves the files, a virtual server is created and the new page is loaded. You can then test the various error-checking features of the component (such as validation of the password fields) and even create multiple users for the site.

Of course, once users have created their account, they need to be able to log in to the site, and the Login control fills this need. Adding the Login component to your page creates a small form containing User Name and Password fields, along with the option to remember the login credentials, and a Log In button (see Figure 41-14).

Figure 41-14

You can customize the appearance of the component to include a link (including icon and text) to create a user account in the event that the visitor hasn't previously registered, or even turn off the "Remember me next time" checkbox, forcing users of your web site to log in each time they visit.

The one trick to getting this to work straight away is to edit your Web.config file and change authentication to Forms. This is because the default authentication type is Windows, and the web site authenticates you as per the Windows user you are currently logged in as. Obviously, some web applications require Windows authentication, but for a simple web site that you plan to deploy on the Internet, this is the only change you need to make in order for the Login control to work properly.

The LoginStatus control is a simple bi-state component that displays one set of content when the site detects that a user is currently logged in, and a different set of content when there is no logged in user. Conveniently, the default configuration of this control generates hyperlinks to log in or log out of the site depending on the current status. For example, if the user is logged in, then the hyperlink enables the user to log out; and if the user is not currently logged in, then the hyperlink tries to log the user in using saved login information, or redirects the user to the defined login page in the Web.config file.

The LoginName component is also simple. It just returns the name of the logged in user. If your site is using Windows authentication mode, this is the fully qualified username, including server/machine details; otherwise, it will be the registered username.

You may want to implement a policy that forces your site's registered users to change their password regularly, or you might want to simply allow them to change it when they want to. Either way, the ChangePassword component works in conjunction with the other automatic user-based components to enable users to change their password. The default view of the control asks users for their current password as well as the new password (entered twice), and provides Change Password and Cancel buttons (see Figure 41-15).

Figure 41-15

This component does the same password validation as the CreateUserWizard object, enforcing the minimum length and special character requirements. The component also has a second view to indicate success, or you can optionally specify a SuccessPageUrl property value that tells ASP.NET to redirect to a new page when the password has been changed successfully.

Sometimes users forget their password, and that's where the PasswordRecovery control comes into play. This component, shown in Figure 41-16, has three views: UserName, Question, and Success. The idea is that users first enter their username so the application can determine and display the security question, and then wait for an answer. If the answer is correct, then the component moves to the Success page and sends an e-mail to the registered e-mail address.

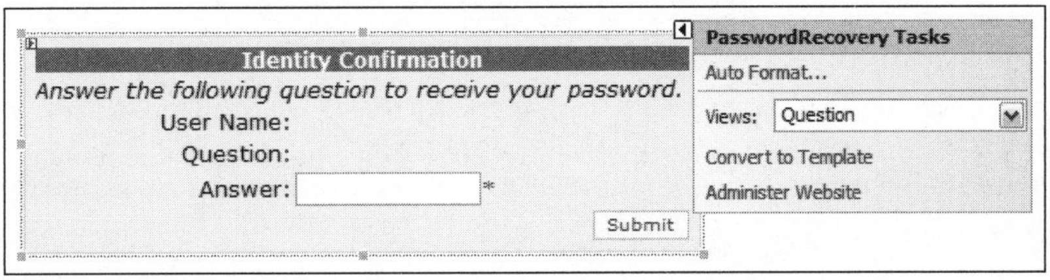

Figure 41-16

Because this process involves sending an e-mail, you need to set up a couple of properties and settings to make it work. First, e-mail messages must have a From e-mail address set. You'll find this in the Mail Definition section of properties for the `PasswordRecovery` component; along with From you can also set the Subject line and specify the importance of the e-mail that will be sent.

The other change you'll need to make is to add a new section of settings in the `Web.config` file. Because sending e-mail requires a default SMTP server, you'll need to save this in the `Web.config` file; the SMTP information is kept in the `system.net` settings area. The following listing provides an example of the minimum code you'll need to add to the `Web.config` file:

```
<system.net>
  <mailSettings>
    <smtp deliveryMethod="network">
      <network
        host="mail.mymailserver.com"
        port="25"
        defaultCredentials="true"
      />
    </smtp>
  </mailSettings>
</system.net>
```

The `system.net` node resides at the same level as `system.web` inside `configuration`.

The last component in the Login group on the Toolbox is the `LoginView` object. `LoginView` enables you to create whole sections on your web page that are only visible under certain conditions related to who is (or isn't) logged in. By default, you have two views: the `AnonymousTemplate`, which is used when no user is logged in, and the `LoggedInTemplate`, used when any user is logged in. Both templates have an editable area that is initially completely empty.

However, because you can define specialized roles and assign users to these roles, you can also create templates for each role you have defined in your site (see Figure 41-17). The Edit RoleGroups command on the smart tag Tasks list associated with `LoginView` displays the typical collection editor and enables you to build role groups that can contain one or multiple roles. When the site detects that the user logs in with a certain role, the display area of the `LoginView` component will be populated with that particular template's content.

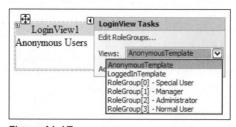

Figure 41-17

See the "Site Administration" section later in this chapter for more information about roles.

What's amazing about all of these controls is that with only a couple of manual property changes and a few extra entries in the `Web.config` file you can build a complete user authentication system into your web application. In fact, as you'll see in the "Site Administration" section later in this chapter, you can edit all these settings without needing to edit the `Web.config` file directly. Now that's efficient coding!

Data Controls

Data controls were introduced to Microsoft web developers with the first version of Visual Studio .NET, but have evolved to be even more powerful with Visual Studio 2005. Each data control has a smart tag Tasks list associated with it that enables you to edit the individual templates for each part of the displayable area. For example, the `DataList` has seven templates in all, which can be individually customized (see Figure 41-18).

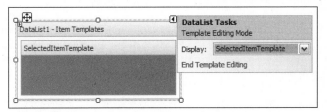

Figure 41-18

The `DataList` also has a property builder that gives you total control over the formatting of individual items. Figure 41-19 shows the Properties dialog with the Format page open, with all possible element types displayed. However, you can turn off unneeded components in the General page, such as hiding the header or footer, and specify whether to use the default vertical orientation for the data or to flip it to horizontal data viewing.

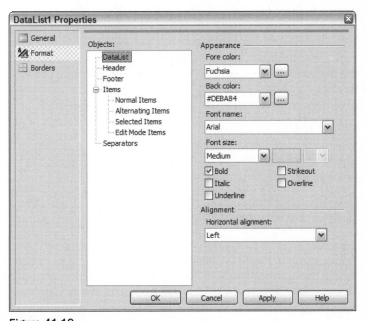

Figure 41-19

Master/Detail Content Pages

A new feature of web development in Visual Studio 2005 is the capability to create *master pages* that define sections that can be customized. This enables you to create a single page design that contains the common elements that should be shared across your entire site, specify areas that can house individual-ized content, and inherit it for each of the pages on the site.

To add a master page to your web application project, use the Add New Item command from the Website menu or from the context menu in the Solution Explorer. This displays the Add New Item dia-log, which contains a large number of item templates that can be added to a web application (see Figure 41-20). You'll notice that besides Web Forms (.aspx) pages and Web User Controls, you can also add plain HTML files, XML files and schema, and other web-related file types. To add a master page, select the Master Page template, choose a name for the file, and click OK.

When a master page is added to your web site, it starts out empty except for a single ContentPlaceHolder component. This is where the detail information can be placed for each individ-ual page. You can create the master page in the same way as any other web form page, complete with ASP.NET and HTML elements, CSS style sheets, and theming.

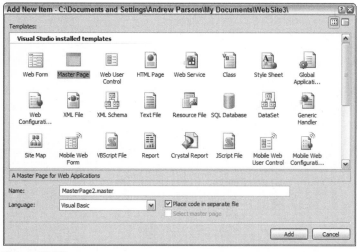

Figure 41-20

If your design requires more than one area for detail information, you'll need to switch to Source view and add the following tags where you need the additional area:

```
<asp:contentplaceholder id="aUniqueId" runat="server">
</asp:contentplaceholder>
```

Once the design of your master page has been finalized, you can use it for the detail pages by adding new web forms to your project. Figure 41-20 shows an extra option of Select Master Page, which is grayed out because in the current context the developer is creating a master page item. However, this checkbox becomes available when you select the Web Form template.

Visual Studio 2005 will remember the state of this checkbox when you add additional web forms.

When you check the Select Master Page option, you'll be presented with an additional dialog listing the master pages currently defined in your web application. Select the master page to be applied to the detail page and click OK. The new web form page that is added to the project will inherit the design and layout of its master page. However, you'll be able to edit only the areas defined as `ContentPlaceHolders`; any other area of the page will be locked. The only place you can edit those areas is in the master page itself.

Finalizing and Deployment

Once you have your site designed and working in a development environment, you're going to want to finalize the site settings so that it works in a way the user will expect. The Start Options page of the site properties contains settings that control how the site will be started. To display the Start Options, either use the Website⇨Start Options menu command or right-click on the web project you want to configure and select Property Pages from the context menu.

Either way, you'll gain access to the Start Options section of the project properties, as displayed in Figure 41-21. The default behavior specifies that running the site will use the current page as its startup page. This is actually really handy when developing sites. Previously you needed to run the site and always go to the default page as defined in the `Web.config` file. Then you would navigate to the page you were actively developing, which could be inefficient depending on the complexity of your site.

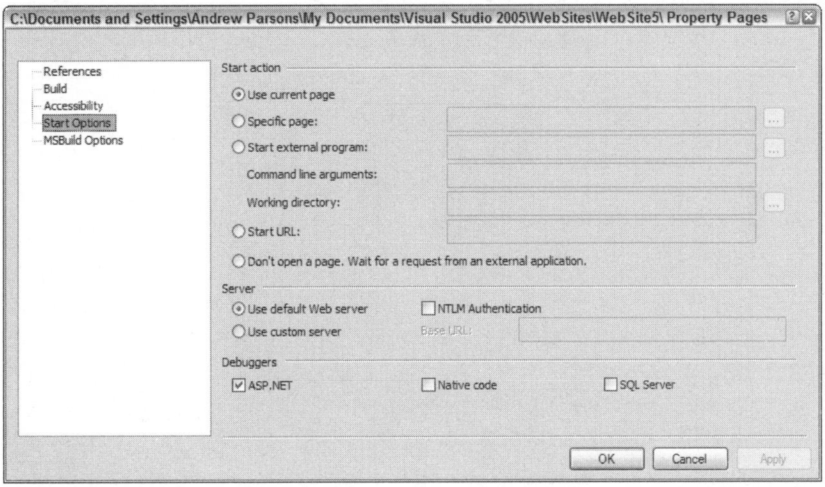

Figure 41-21

With Visual Studio 2005's default start behavior, you can go directly to the page you're currently editing, which enables you to be more efficient in testing and debugging your web applications.

However, when deploying the site, you're going to want to set a specific page or external application to start the site so users always have a consistent viewing experience when they access it. You can specify a starting URL or a specific page that is relative to the root folder of the application. Alternatively, you can specify an application that will control how your web application starts, and even define a different web server to run the project.

At the bottom of the Start Options page is a section where you can specify what debuggers are to be activated. Note that while the ASP.NET debugger is turned on by default, you can only debug your application if the `Web.config` file is edited to allow debugging. Unlike previous versions of Visual Studio .NET, the default `Web.config` file has debugging disabled so you don't accidentally deploy an application to the web with debugging on.

Deploying the Site

If the site is already on a remote server, whether it was an HTTP, FTP, or FrontPage server, you don't need to do anything else for it to be up and running for your users. However, if you created the web application in the local file system, you'll need to deploy it to the final destination.

To copy your web application to the deployment destination, use the Website⇨Copy Web Site menu command. This will display the Copy Web interface in the main workspace area (see Figure 41-22).

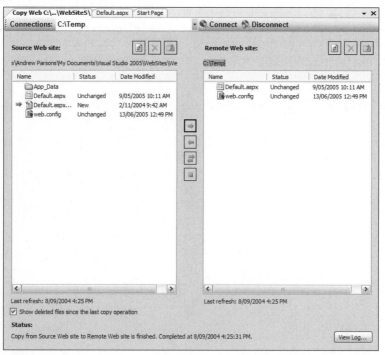

Figure 41-22

If you have previously copied the site to another destination, the Connections textbox will be populated with the previous location. Click the Connect button to bring up the Connections dialog, which is similar to the Browse dialog displayed when you're first creating a web solution, with options for local file system, HTTP, and FTP locations.

Once you've specified the required destination location, Visual Studio connects to the remote site and lists the files that are present. You can then select the individual files or folders you want to copy over to the site and click either the Copy or Synchronize buttons that are situated between the Source Web site and Remote Web site views.

Synchronize checks both locations to ensure they have the same version of the selected file. If the file versions are different, whichever location is deemed to be the most recent is used as the source and is copied to the other location.

Site Administration

While running your web application with default behavior will work in most situations, sometimes you'll need to manage the application settings beyond simply setting the properties of components and page items. The Web Site Administration Tool provides you with a web-based configuration application that enables you to define various security-related settings, including defining users and roles, as well as applicationwide settings that can come in handy, such as a default error page and the SMTP mail settings that were mentioned earlier in the discussion about the `PasswordRecovery` component.

To start the Administration Tool, use the Website⇨ASP.NET Configuration menu command. If necessary, Visual Studio 2005 instantiates a temporary web server on a unique port and starts the tool itself, pointing it to the application you're currently administering.

You can determine whether the web server is active by looking in the notification area of your taskbar and finding the Development Server icon connected to the port Visual Studio 2005 allocated when it was started up. You can stop an active web server by right-clicking its icon in the notification area and selecting Show Details. When the server information is displayed (see Figure 41-23), click the Stop button to stop the specific instance of the development web server.

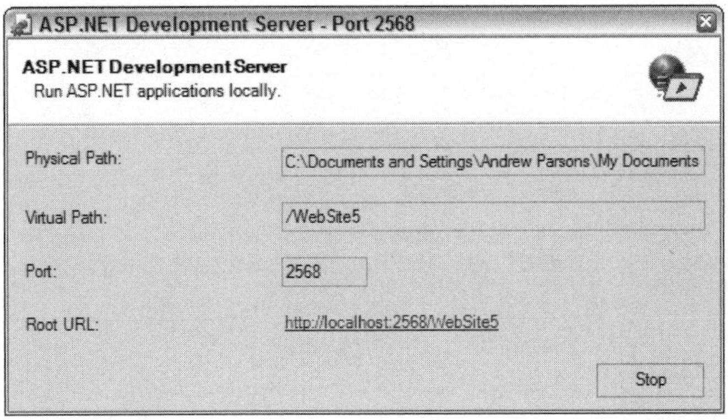

Figure 41-23

Note that this won't affect any other development servers that are currently running.

When the Administration Tool is displayed in your web browser, it will show the application name, accompanied by the current Windows-based authenticated user. There are three main sections to the tool: security to create and maintain users, roles, and authentication; application configuration to control application specific key-value pairs, SMTP settings, and debug configurations; and provider configuration to control the way the user administration data is stored for the site.

Security

The security section of the tool provides you with a summary of the users and roles defined in the site, and the authentication mode. You can change individual settings from this summary page by clicking on their associated link, or use the Security Setup Wizard to step through each section of the security settings in turn.

The authentication mode is controlled by the access method page (shown in the wizard in Figure 41-24). If you choose From the Internet, the tool sets the authentication mode to Forms, while the From a Local Area Network option results in an authentication mode of Windows.

The most useful part of this tool is the capability to add and edit roles. In the wizard you'll first need to enable role management by checking the Enable Roles for this Web Site option. Once roles are active, you can define them either through the wizard or from the summary page. Each role is defined by a single string value, and it's up to you to control how that role will be used in your web application (with the exception of access rules, which are discussed in a moment).

The next step of the wizard is to create user accounts. The information on this page is a replication of the `CreateUserAccount` component, and enables you to create an initial user who can serve as administrator for your web site.

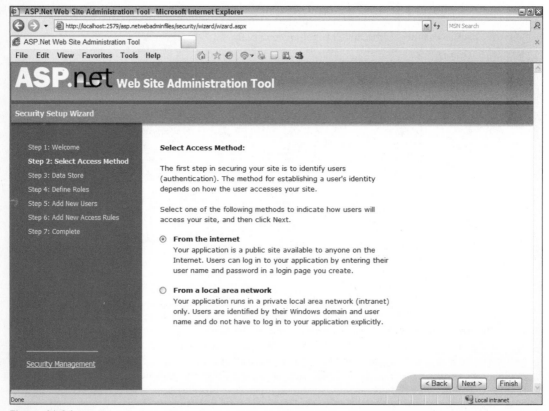

Figure 41-24

The access rules page (shown in Figure 41-25) enables you to restrict access to certain parts of your site to a specific role, a specific user, or only when any user is logged in. As Figure 41-25 shows, by default there is a single rule (which is actually implicitly defined and inherited from the server) that defines full access to the entire site for all users.

Web site processing will look at the rules in the order they are defined, stopping at the first rule that applies to the particular context. For example, if you defined first a rule that allowed access to the App_Data folder for anyone belonging to the Administrator role and then a subsequent rule that denied access to the same folder for all users, it would effectively block access to the App_Data folder to all users who do not belong to the Administrator role.

Once you've got users, roles, and rules defined in your site, you can then start applying the access by clicking the Manage Users link from the summary security page. This will present you with a list of all users defined in the system. Click on the Edit User or Edit Roles links to specify the roles to which each user belongs.

This information can be used to customize the content in your web pages with the `LoginView` component discussed earlier in this chapter.

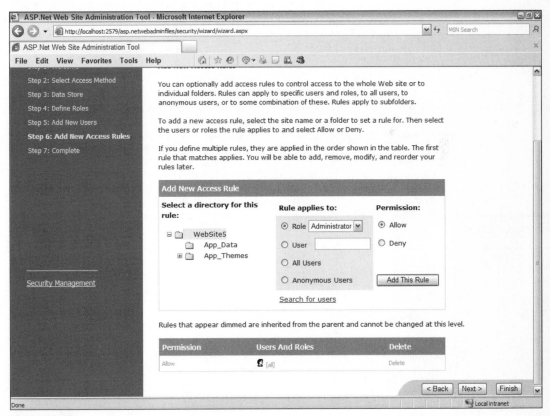

Figure 41-25

Application Settings

The application section of the Web Site Administration Tool enables you to define and edit application-specific settings in the form of key-value pairs, as well as configure the SMTP e-mail settings, including the default SMTP mail server and sender e-mail address.

You can also specify what level of debugging you want to perform on the application, and customize the tracing information being kept as you run the application.

ASP.NET 2.0 Configuration Settings

An alternative to using the Web Site Administration Tool is to edit the configuration settings directly within Internet Information Services, located in the Administrative Tools section of the Control Panel. When ASP.NET 2.0 is installed on your machine, you'll find that each web site (including virtual directories) will have a new ASP.NET tab in the site's Properties pages.

If the site is defined as using ASP.NET 2.0, you can then edit the configuration settings directly without having to get into the `Web.config` file of the application. The Configuration Settings dialog displayed in Figure 41-26 reveals the default SQL Server Express database that is used for user authentication settings that were discussed earlier. You can easily add individual application setting key-value pairs as well as other configuration options, such as authentication type and error page redirections, that used to be available only if you edited `Web.config` directly.

To be fair, the Web Site Administration Tool and the Configuration Settings dialog in IIS serve slightly different purposes, so judicious use of both will help maintain your web application without you having to resort to editing XML-based configuration files.

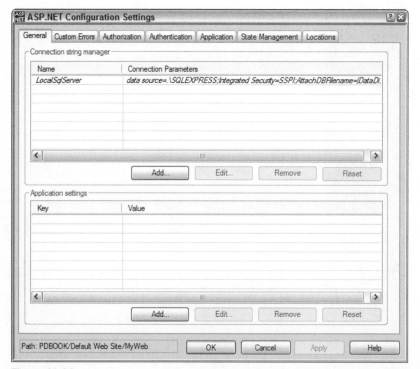

Figure 41-26

Summary

In this chapter you learned how to create web applications of various types, including web services. The discussion included the following highlights:

❑ How Visual Studio 2005 works in the absence of IIS through the use of temporary virtual web servers

❑ Tools to make administration of the site straightforward

❑ Details on some of the new web controls and components

❑ How to theme and style components

❑ Deploying your solution to the production site

❑ Using master pages to apply common components across your site

Of course, there's more to web development than this introduction. In the next chapter you'll see some of the advanced techniques you can use to maintain efficiency on your development projects without sacrificing power. Specifically, you'll look at web parts and templates that help you compartmentalize your web-based development components. In addition, the chapter offers a brief introduction to how you can create custom controls for the web.

Additional Web Techniques

Chapter 41 introduced the basic concepts for web projects, highlighting some of the new controls introduced with .NET 2.0 and Visual Studio 2005. Actually, those were just the tip of the iceberg, with many other features being made available to you while creating web applications. This chapter describes some of the more useful additions that require a little more forethought when implementing, including the `Sitemap` control and how to use the new Web Parts functionality.

In addition, this chapter contains a discussion on building custom controls, and examines the templatization of individual controls for use elsewhere in your web site.

Web Development Revisited

As the previous chapter showed you, while ASP.NET 1.0 revolutionized the way you can build solutions for the Internet, the new features available in ASP.NET 2.0 and Visual Studio 2005 have matured to the point where their use becomes, without question, commercially viable. You are now able to create and maintain development projects at almost any location, including remote FTP servers, enabling you to easily deploy and manage web solutions.

The introduction of an array of user-based controls means that building web sites that incorporate login/logout functionality, and viewing customization based on user roles, is now straightforward, while the new dialogs for choosing colors, styles, and formats are more easily identified with the way web sites are traditionally created.

In addition to these extra controls and design-time enhancements, developing web solutions is made even simpler with a built-in temporary server for easily testing your pages, and additional support is provided with other easy to use features, such as being able to run and debug from any page in the site.

However, you can take advantage of additional features, both in the IDE and with web development in general, to make the creation of web projects even easier. One such feature is the View menu, which is expanded with extra commands when designing a web site.

The modifications made to the View menu of the IDE are a great example of what Visual Studio does to contextually provide you with useful features depending on what you're doing. When you're editing a web page in Design view, additional menu commands become available for adjusting how the design surface appears (see Figure 42-1).

Figure 42-1

For example, when Visible Borders is toggled on via the View menu, it will draw gray borders around all container controls and HTML tags such as <table> and <div> so you can easily see where each component resides on the form.

When creating Windows applications, if you add a nonvisual control such as a Timer to a form's design surface, a tray area below the form is displayed with an icon for the control so you can easily get to it. With web applications, because the tray area is already in use to show what editing mode you're in as well as a breadcrumb trail of where you are in the HTML, nonvisual controls are hidden from view by default. Activating the Non Visual Controls option shows a large placeholder icon in the space where the nonvisual control is situated in the HTML markup, so you can find where they've been added and easily access their property list.

The third option that configures the way your design-time view appears shows the details about every tag present in the HTML markup. To show these additional markers, use the View⇨Details menu command. However, as illustrated in Figure 42-2, showing these visual indicators can affect the way the layout appears in the designer, rendering an accurate representation of how the web page will look next to impossible.

Figure 42-2

The view details option is best suited for finding a rogue tag that isn't in the right place, so using the keyboard shortcut of Ctrl+Shift+Q to quickly toggle the indicators on and off is the most efficient way to use it.

The Sitemap

The sitemap is a method to provide sitewide navigation to your web applications. Unfortunately, to implement sitemap functionality into your projects, you first have to manually create the site data and keep it up-to-date as you add or remove web pages from the site. Once you have created the sitemap file, you can then use it as a Data Source for a number of web controls, including the `SiteMapPath`, which automatically keeps of where you are in the site hierarchy, as well as the `Menu` and `TreeView` controls, which can present a custom subset of the sitemap information.

web.sitemap

The first task you must perform when implementing sitewide navigation is to create an XML representation of your site's structure. Using XML to store the structure is a logical way of keeping the data because it can store information of a hierarchical nature. This default name for this file is `web.sitemap` but you can change it in the `Web.config` file if you need to follow another naming convention.

The `Web.config` file should have a subnode within the `<system.web>` node called `<siteMap>` that defines the kind of provider to be used for the site information. A typical `<siteMap>` node structure looks like this:

```
<system.web>
    <siteMap defaultProvider="XmlSiteMapProvider" enabled="true">
        <providers>
            <add name="XmlSiteMapProvider"
                description="SiteMap provider which reads in .sitemap XML files."
                type="System.Web.XmlSiteMapProvider, System.Web,
Version=2.0.3600.0, Culture=neutral, PublicKeyToken=b03f5f7f11d50a3a"
                siteMapFile="web.sitemap"
                securityTrimmingEnabled="true"/>
        </providers>
    </siteMap>
</system.web>
```

Change the value of the `siteMapFile` attribute to the desired filename, and save the `Web.config` file to update the project.

The sitemap XML file follows a simple syntax. You first create a root node of `<siteMap>` that contains a single node of type `<siteMapNode>`. Within this top-level `<siteMapNode>`, you then add a `<siteMapNode>` for each page you want to map in whatever hierarchical form you want. This means you can create a hierarchical structure to your site that has no resemblance to the real directory and page structure of your projects (which is a good thing because you can keep the user experience separate from the design-time experience).

You should set the following attributes for each `<siteMapNode>`:

❑   `title`: Used to display a readable string in the `SiteMapPath` control and any other controls that use the `web.sitemap` file.

❑   `url`: The page URL relative to the root space of the web, so if your page were located at `http://www.wrox.com/pages/ThisPage.aspx`, then the `url` attribute value would be `pages/ThisPage.aspx`. Omitting the `url` attribute produces a node in the visual controls that cannot be clicked, but can still be used for formatting and logical division of the site.

❑   `description`: A longer description of what the page contains. Not used in most cases, it can be handy for automatically producing sitewide documentation.

The following example illustrates the relationship between physical location, desired virtual location in the site hierarchy, and the corresponding `web.sitemap` file. You have the following pages in your web project:

❑   `Default.aspx`: The main home page of the web site

❑   `ContactUs.aspx`: The contact details of the company

❑   `Products/ProductView.aspx`: A view page of an individual page

❑   `Products/ProductList.aspx`: A full list of products

❑   `CustomerLogin.aspx`: The page where the customer registers and logs in to the site

❑   `CustomerProfile.aspx`: A page where the customer can modify his or her details

You want to present the site information so that the navigational structure appears as shown in Figure 42-3.

Figure 42-3

To implement such a hierarchy, you would need to create a `web.sitemap` file similar to the following listing:

```xml
<?xml version="1.0" encoding="utf-8" ?>
<siteMap>
  <siteMapNode title="Home Page" url="Default.aspx">
    <siteMapNode title="Contact Us" url="ContactUs.aspx" />
    <siteMapNode title="Product List" url="Products/ProductList.aspx" >
      <siteMapNode title="Product View" url="Products/ProductView.aspx" />
    </siteMapNode>
    <siteMapNode title="Customers" >
      <siteMapNode title="Login/Register" url="CustomerLogin.aspx" />
      <siteMapNode title="Your Profile" url="CustomerProfile.aspx" />
    </siteMapNode>
  </siteMapNode>
</siteMap>
```

When creating the `web.sitemap` file you must remember to keep it up-to-date. Unfortunately, Visual Studio 2005 doesn't have any automated way of doing this, so if you rename or remove a page, you have to also remove its entry from the sitemap file. Similarly, if you add new pages to your site, they won't be included in any sitemap-based user interface controls until you also add them to the sitemap layout.

The SiteMapPath Control

Once you have your site hierarchy defined, the easiest way to use it is to drag and drop a `SiteMapPath` control onto your web page design surface (see Figure 42-4). This control automatically binds to the default sitemap provider, as specified in the `Web.config` file, to generate the nodes for display.

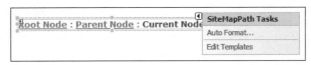

Figure 42-4

The SiteMapPath control works as a breadcrumb trail of the site, meaning it only displays the current page the user is on, tracking back up the hierarchy to display the parent nodes, right up to the root node. Figure 42-5 shows how this control might look when a user is viewing the Product View page.

Figure 42-5

As you can see, the only links visible are the root node tracking directly down to the page being viewed. In this case, the only other page is the Product List page, which was defined in the web.sitemap file as being the parent of the Product View page.

The SiteMapResolve Event

Sometimes you might want to modify the URLs that are generated from the sitemap to include additional details. This is usually the case when you need to specify a parameter on the URL that will redirect users to a specific view of the page. For example, if the sample site divides the product list into Product Groups, it may include an optional parameter containing the product group, such as www.myproductsite.com/Products/ProductList.aspc?ProductGroupID=3.

The basic view presented by the SiteMapPath control (and any other controls that use the sitemap as their Data Source) does not include these additional parameters, as they are not specified in the web.sitemap configuration file. However, you can customize the properties of each siteMapNode as it is rendered by handling the SiteMapResolve event.

To handle the SiteMapResolve event, you must first create a subroutine that will be executed when the event is raised. This event has the following syntax:

```
Private Function MySiteMapResolveEventHandler(ByVal sender As Object, _
    ByVal e As SiteMapResolveEventArgs) As SiteMapNode
End Function
```

You then need to connect this function to the event by using an AddHandler event in the Load event of the page. You use AddHandler in the same way you would when adding handlers in Windows applications.

To customize the appearance of the nodes as they display on the page, you need to clone the current node to a new SiteMapNode object. This enables you to modify the contents of the node and its parents (which you cannot do to the permanent SiteMapNode). After you modify the properties of the node and its parents, you then return this cloned version of the SiteMapNode from the event handler function so that the new details are used.

The following listing is a more complete code sample that could be used to customize the Product List node when viewing an individual product:

```
Protected Sub Page_Load(ByVal sender As Object, ByVal e As System.EventArgs) _
    Handles Me.Load
    AddHandler SiteMap.SiteMapResolve, AddressOf Me.TweakUrls
End Sub

Private Function TweakUrls(ByVal sender As Object, _
    ByVal e As SiteMapResolveEventArgs) As SiteMapNode
    Dim myCurrentNode As SiteMapNode = SiteMap.CurrentNode.Clone(True)
    Dim MyTraversingNode As SiteMapNode = myCurrentNode

    Dim ProductGroupID As Integer = DetermineProductGroup()

    MyTraversingNode = MyTraversingNode.ParentNode
    If Not (MyTraversingNode Is Nothing) Then
        MyTraversingNode.Url = MyTraversingNode.Url & "?ProductGroupID=" & _
            ProductGroupID.ToString()
        MyTraversingNode.Title = "Product List (Group " & ProductGroupID.ToString _
            & ")"
    End If

    Return myCurrentNode

End Function
```

The function `TweakUrls` is created with the same signature as the event it will handle. The `Page_Load` routine is then modified so that this function is hooked up to the event when the page loads. When the event is raised, the `TweaKUrls` function is called, which in turn calls the `DetermineProductGroup` function to retrieve the corresponding Product Group ID for the currently displayed product.

The `DetermineProductGroup` *function is not shown in this example, but could access a database to determine the correct value, or simply extract it from the currently displayed product's key value.*

Once the ID value is determined, the code gets the parent node of the current node. As you've seen previously, the parent node in this structure equates to the `ProductList.aspx` page. It then modifies the `Url` and `Title` properties of this node to contain information about the ID, and then finally returns the temporary `SiteMapNode` object. The result is shown in Figure 42-6.

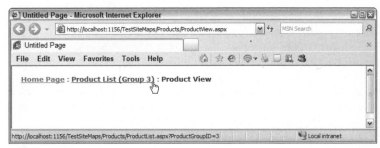

Figure 42-6

The Product List title has been changed to include the product group to which the product belongs. Notice that the status bar text indicating the URL has also been updated, indicating that when this link is clicked, the user will navigate to a specific group of products.

The Web Menu Control

While the `SiteMapPath` control displays only the breadcrumb trail leading directly to the currently viewed page, at times you will want to display a list of pages in your site. The `Menu` ASP.NET control can be used to achieve this, and has modes for both horizontal and vertical viewing of the information.

`Menu` controls work slightly differently than `SiteMapPath` controls in that you need to associate them with a Data Source, and they can control how much of the data is displayed. To add menu functionality to your site, first add a `SiteMapDataSource` control to the page. As you might expect, this control is found in the Data category in the Toolbox.

> This is a nonvisual control, so you might need to toggle invisible controls on with View➪Non Visual Controls to see it on the design surface.

By default, the `SiteMapDataSource` uses the `web.sitemap` configuration file in its entirety, starting from the top-level root node and using all children nodes. However, you have two options to fine-tune this behavior so that the Data Source is only populated with a subset of the hierarchy: `StartingNode Url` and `StartingNodeOffset`.

`StartingNodeUrl` enables you to set a specific starting point within the sitemap information. The Data Source will only contain nodes that represent that starting page and any of its children (and their children, and so on). Use the tilde (~) character to specify the root of the website — for example, specifying `~/Products/ProductList.aspx` would result in a Data Source that only contains the Product List node and its children (which in this sample site is the Product View page only).

This enables you to define a comprehensive sitemap for your entire web application, and then provide custom views of the site depending on where the user is.

The other way to filter the node information is to use `StartingNodeOffset`. Rather than specify a specific page to start from, this property tells the Data Source component to only include nodes for a certain level and down, excluding any nodes that are further up the chain. The value is zero-based, so a value of 1 will ignore the top-level node but include everything else. For the sample site, this would mean all pages but the home page are included.

When you have configured the `SiteMapDataSource` component to return the site information you want to use, place a `Menu` control on the design surface and position and format it to suit the rest of your site. To connect the `Menu` to the Data Source, set the `DataSourceID` property to the name of your `SiteMap DataSource` control from the drop-down list shown in the Properties window.

As soon as you change this value, the appearance of the `Menu` control is updated to reflect the contents of the Data Source, so you can preview how it will look at design time. The default view of the `Menu` control shows the root node only and orients the menu vertically.

To change the amount of the sitemap that is displayed in the menu's static area, set the `StaticDisplay Levels` property to the depth you require. If you want the static portion of the menu to appear horizontally, change the `Orientation` property. Figure 42-7 shows the original Product View page with the `SiteMapPath` control, along with two new `Menu` controls.

The horizontal menu had its `StaticDisplaylevels` property set to 2 so it would display the Home Page link, along with any pages that were on the second level of the sitemap, while the vertical map used a `StaticDisplayLevels` value of 3 to show all pages.

The menu automatically generates the client-side script required for menus to pop out like the Customers submenu shown in Figure 42-7.

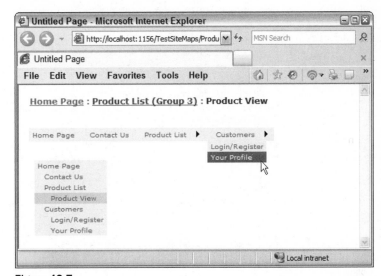

Figure 42-7

A great place to use the `SiteMapPath` and `Menu` controls is in a master page, which can then be used to pass the controls around for all your details pages, with the nodes displayed to users automatically updating based on which page they're on.

Web Parts

Another excellent feature added to Visual Studio 2005 is the capability to create Web Parts controls and pages so that your site can be divided into chunks that either you or your users can move around, and show and hide, to create a unique viewing experience. Web Parts for Visual Studio are loosely based on custom web controls but owe their inclusion in Visual Studio to the huge popularity of Web Parts in SharePoint Portals.

With a Web Parts page, you first create a `WebPartManager` component that sits on the page to look after any areas of the page design that are defined as parts. You then use `WebPartZone` containers to set where you want customizable content on the page, and then finally place the actual content into the `WebPartZone` container.

While these two components are the core of implementing Web Parts, you need only look at the WebParts group in the Toolbox to discover a whole array of additional components that can be used as well (see Figure 42-8). You use these additional components to enable your users to customize their experience of your web site. They will be discussed in a moment.

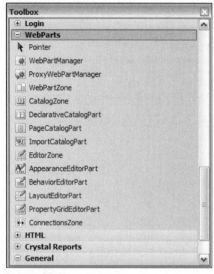

Figure 42-8

WebPartManager

The `WebPartManager` component represents a class that controls a set of `WebPart` objects. This is basically the engine for the entire Web Parts experience, providing methods to add, move, and remove individual `WebPart` components and add the personalization aspects to the page for the user. It also manages connections between `WebPart` controls.

The `DisplayMode` property is used to specify what state the Web Parts are being shown in, out of the five possible states that the `WebPartManager` allows. You can programmatically change the `DisplayMode` to whichever state you require, thus making it easy to turn the user customization of the page layout on and off. The five states are as follows:

❑ **Browse:** The default view, which presents users with a normal view of the page, with the Web Parts displayed as static entities on the page

❑ **Design:** Enables users to move or delete individual Web Part controls to change their page's layout

❑ **Edit:** Enables any `EditorZone` controls to be shown, which users can then use to customize the appearance of each of the Web Parts

❏ **Catalog:** Includes any `CatalogZone` components you have defined on the page, from which users can select individual Web Parts to add to their existing page layout for additional content

❏ **Connect:** Enables users to control how different Web Parts connect to each other. This requires Web Parts to have compatible communications paths set up so they can talk to each other.

`WebPartZones` define sections of your page that contain the customizable sections. In other words, a `Web PartZone` contains a Web Part. Each `WebPartZone` component can be themed individually, and is used to contain any kind of control. It does this by enclosing the content that makes up the static part of the Web Part with `ZoneTemplate` tags.

The best way to explain how this works is to show the source view of a page that has Web Parts. The following listing is from the sample site used previously. It uses two `WebPartZone` components to store a `Menu` (which uses the sitemap information discussed previously in this chapter) and a main content area with some static text. Here's the page in its entirety:

```
<%@ Page Language="VB" AutoEventWireup="false" CodeFile="Default.aspx.vb"
Inherits="_Default" %>

<!DOCTYPE html PUBLIC "-//W3C//DTD XHTML 1.0 Transitional//EN"
"http://www.w3.org/TR/xhtml1/DTD/xhtml1-transitional.dtd">

<html xmlns="http://www.w3.org/1999/xhtml" >
<head runat="server">
    <title>Untitled Page</title>
</head>
<body>
    <form id="form1" runat="server">
        <asp:WebPartManager ID="WebPartManager1" runat="server">
        </asp:WebPartManager>
        <asp:SiteMapDataSource ID="SiteMapDataSource1" runat="server" />
    <div>
        <table style="width: 100%">
            <tr>
                <td style="width: 21px" valign="top">
            <asp:WebPartZone ID="WebPartZone1" runat="server" HeaderText="Navigation">
                    <ZoneTemplate>
            <asp:Menu ID="Menu1" runat="server" DataSourceID="SiteMapDataSource1">
                        </asp:Menu>
                    </ZoneTemplate>
                </asp:WebPartZone>
                </td>
                <td style="width: 100px" valign="top">
    <asp:WebPartZone ID="WebPartZone2" runat="server" HeaderText="Main" Width="408px">
                    <ZoneTemplate>
                      <asp:Label ID="Label1" runat="server" title="MainContent">
                        <h1>Home Page For My Products</h1>
                        <p>Welcome to my main page!</p>
                        </asp:Label>
                    </ZoneTemplate>
                </asp:WebPartZone>
                </td>
```

```
            </tr>
         </table>
      </div>
      </form>
   </body>
   </html>
```

Notice that each `WebPartZone` component contains a set of `ZoneTemplate` tags, which in turn encapsulate the code that is to be treated as the actual contents of the Web Part. Within the `ZoneTemplate` tags, you can insert any web or custom control.

The Design view of this page, with the `WebPartZone` controls formatted with some of the built-in themes, is shown in Figure 42-9. Notice how the controls within the `WebPartZone` components are also formatted with the theme.

Figure 42-9

Using just these two classes, you can build a web site that is fully customizable in your program code. You first define all the variable parts of your site into `WebPartZone` components, and then use the `WebPartManager` component's methods to add or remove the Web Parts as needed. However, you can also use other controls to enable users to personalize their own unique experience of your site.

EditorZone

The `EditorZone` control is used to position and house the different types of editing of your design you want to allow. It works much like a `WebPartZone`, but instead of containing normal web controls, the `EditorZone` can only contain the `EditorPart` controls that define access to different settings.

You can place multiple `EditorPart` components in the one `EditorZone` by adding them one after the other in the container zone. If you apply a theme to the `EditorZone`, it is applied across all contained `EditorPart` components. When the `WebPartManager` component's `DisplayMode` is set to `Edit`, any `EditorZone` components defined on the page are displayed to the user.

The EditorPart components are contextually relative to whichever Web Part component is selected, enabling users to customize each part of your site defined in a WebPartZone to suit their own requirements. You can add four EditorPart components to the EditorZone, each controlling a different set of properties for the selected Web Part.

AppearanceEditorPart

The AppearanceEditorPart enables users to change several aspects of the user interface for the Web Part, including the title and how big it is. They can also use this EditorPart to turn off the title completely, or turn off the borders around the Web Part. Figure 42-10 shows an AppearanceEditorPart in design mode, inheriting the theme from the containing EditorZone.

Users can use the Chrome Type setting to specify whether the title or borders should be shown, while the Hidden checkbox will remove the Web Part from view completely.

Figure 42-10

BehaviorEditorPart

The BehaviorEditorPart provides direct access to a number of system-level properties for the selected Web Part, and is usually not used for general user access. The properties that can be adjusted with BehaviorEditorPart include a number of flags that dictate what actions can be performed on the Web Part, such as AllowClose and AllowEdit. Because an end-user could accidentally disable editing on a Web Part, you should consider carefully whether this part will be included in your exposure of customization settings.

In addition to these flags, users can also set the description and a URL associated with the title, among other items.

LayoutEditorPart

The LayoutEditorPart (shown in Figure 42-11) provides some simple settings that users can change to affect how and where the Web Part will be shown. The first property shown in Figure 42-11 is the Chrome State, which enables users to minimize the Web Part to an icon, while the Zone property gives them the capability to move the chosen Web Part to another WebPartZone elsewhere on the page.

The Zone Index reflects where the Web Part is within the WebPartZone to which it belongs. A value of 0 indicates that it is the first part in the zone, with the others appearing in sequential order down the page.

Figure 42-11

PropertyGridEditorPart

The PropertyGridEditorPart enables you to define custom properties on your Web Parts and then expose those properties to the users of your site. You could use PropertyGridEditorPart to enable your users to specify parameters to specific Web Parts. For example, you might have a Web Part that contains a weather forecast based on a custom property that stores the associated zip code. Exposing the zip code property to the end users would enable them to choose their own location for the weather forecast data.

CatalogZone

The CatalogZone (see Figure 42-12) is used to keep track of all the Web Parts known to the WebPartManager. You can use the CatalogZone to store Web Parts that are not active by default, as well as save Web Parts that are removed from the user's current configuration so they can be restored if the user chooses.

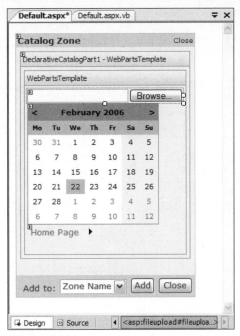

Figure 42-12

A `CatalogZone` can contain `CatalogPart` components, of which there are three types. The `Import CatalogPart` is used to import new Web Part definition files, and is beyond the scope of this discussion.

DeclarativeCatalogPart

The `DeclarativeCatalogPart` is where you define all Web Parts that are not visible by default. Once you add the `DeclarativeCatalogPart`, you need to then enter Template Editing mode to gain access to the container area. In Template Editing mode, you add the Web Parts you want to the `DeclarativeCatalogPart` by dragging components from the Toolbox, or dragging custom controls from the Solution Explorer.

As you add each component to the `DeclarativeCatalogPart`, you should switch to Source view and add the `title` attribute so users have meaningful names to view. For example, you could modify the source definition for a `FileUpload` control so users see the text File Upload like so:

```
<asp:FileUpload ID="FileUpload1" title="File Upload" runat="server" />
```

Without setting the `title` attribute all your Web Parts will display as Untitled, so make sure you follow this step.

When you've finished adding your controls that will serve as additional Web Parts for users to choose from, quit Template Editing mode and verify that you're happy with the way the catalog list appears.

Figure 42-13 shows the same `DeclarativeCatalogPart` after quitting Template Editing mode. When users see this list, they can simply check the boxes next to the Web Parts they want, select which `WebPartZone` to add them to, and then the click Add button to insert the extra functionality to the page layout.

Figure 42-13

PageCatalogPart

Conversely, the `PageCatalogPart` is used to store a list of all Web Parts that were originally on the page but have since been closed by a user. This enables the `WebPartManager`, in conjunction with the `CatalogZone`, to keep track of every Web Part available to users, regardless of their state.

If you are going to implement a `CatalogZone`, you should always include the `PageCatalogPart` so users can restore Web Parts they have previously hidden from view.

This discussion of Web Parts offers only a basic introduction to how the different components work together to build a customizable web site that can be controlled either programmatically or by your end users depending on your individual requirements. If you would like to know more, Peter Vogel's *Professional Web Parts and Custom Controls with ASP.NET 2.0* is a fantastic resource that deals with Web Parts.

Summary

This chapter expanded on the web techniques discussed in Chapter 41 to include more advanced features found in Visual Studio 2005. Notably, the sitemap functionality enables you to automate your navigation controls with a custom-built hierarchical representation of your web site, while Web Parts introduces a comprehensive solution to building customizable web sites.

Building Device Applications

In the past, building applications for mobile phones or PDAs was not for the fainthearted. It required not only a special set of tools, but also a great deal of patience to get everything to work properly. The .NET Compact Framework — a smaller, limited feature subset of the full .NET Framework available for Windows Mobile devices, and the associated designer support within Visual Studio — opened up the world of mobile application development to the general developer community. Now developers could build, test, and deploy applications in the same way that they built Windows applications.

Visual Studio 2005 and the .NET Compact Framework 2.0 improve this experience with much richer designer support and a complete set of controls for building applications. This chapter shows you how easy it is to build and test device applications within Visual Studio 2005. (In this chapter you'll notice references to the .NET Framework; in the absence of any clarification (such as the full .NET Framework), this chapter refers to the .NET Compact Framework.)

Getting Started

The first thing you need to do to get started building a device application is to create a smart device project. You can either create this in a new solution or, if you are adding a device component to a larger application, add it to an existing solution. Creating a smart device project is done in the same way as you would create any other project type. Select the File⇨New⇨Project menu command, or you can select the Add⇨New Project solution right-click context menu in the Solution Explorer window. Figure 43-1 shows the New Project dialog with the Smart Device node expanded. Notice that the most common types of projects are all present, such as Device (Windows) Application, Control and Class libraries, and Console Application.

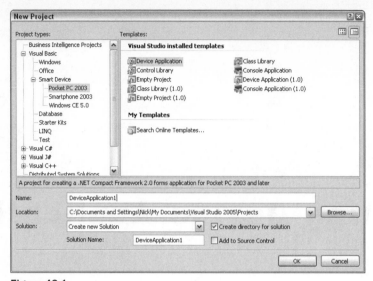

Figure 43-1

After selecting the project type (in this case, a Device Application), and providing a name and location for the project, click OK to generate the device application.

.NET Compact Framework Versions

The other thing you will notice in Figure 43-1 is that the project types are all repeated with the (1.0) suffix. These projects types enable you to build applications based on version 1.0 of the .NET Compact Framework. Visual Studio 2005 supports building device applications for both versions of the .NET Compact Framework, which is not possible for the full .NET Framework. However, you must specify when you create the project that you want it to be a version 1.0 project. If you are in doubt, select the version 1.0 projects, as this project can be upgraded to a version 2.0 project at a later stage. The remainder of this chapter focuses on version 2.0 of the .NET Compact Framework.

Choosing a Version

Building applications using the full .NET Framework within Visual Studio 2005, you don't have any choice regarding which version of the .NET Framework to use. For the most part, you don't need to worry about whether the target market will have version 2.0 of the .NET Framework installed because it is easy for them to download and install it as required. However, when building device applications, one of the limitations that you commonly face is storage space. With this limitation in mind, it might be best to target the version of the framework that comes within the ROM of the device. As such, you need to consider which framework version you're targeting when building your application.

To make an educated decision about which framework version to target, you need to know a bit more about which versions of the framework are packaged with which devices. Just to complicate matters further, there are multiple service packs for version 1.0 of the .NET Framework, and Microsoft has recently released Windows Mobile 5.0, which supports additional functionality. The following table shows which versions of the .NET Framework are packaged with the different versions of the PocketPC and Smartphone operating systems.

Device	Operating System	Version
Pocket PC	Pocket PC 2002	None
	Windows Mobile 2003	.NET Compact Framework 1.0
	Windows Mobile 2003 Second Edition	.NET Compact Framework 1.0, Service Pack 2
	Windows Mobile 5.0	.NET Compact Framework 1.0, Service Pack 3
Smartphone	Smartphone	None
	Windows Mobile 5.0	.NET Compact Framework 1.0, Service Pack 3

You will notice from this table that due to the relative timing of the release of Windows Mobile 5.0 and the .NET Compact Framework 2.0, currently no devices with version 2.0 of the .NET Framework are installed by default. This version of the framework will need to be installed on any device that you are planning to deploy to.

The other consideration when deciding which version of the .NET Framework to use is which devices support version 2.0. While version 1.0 of the .NET Framework is supported on devices back to Pocket PC 2002, version 2.0 can only be installed on Windows Mobile 2003 Second Edition and later. This is an important consideration because it means that older devices will not be able to run applications built with version 2.0 of the .NET Framework.

Framework Compatibility

One of the main design goals of the .NET Compact Framework team was to ensure (as much as possible) that there was 100% backward compatibility between the framework versions. The goal was that any application compiled using version 1.0 of the framework should be able to run on version 2.0 of the .NET Framework. The results from this team have been quite staggering, as they have for the most part achieved this goal, and existing applications can get massive performance benefits without even needing to be recompiled.

Solution Explorer

When the device project is created, it will appear in the Solution Explorer window with the same layout as a full .NET Framework project. The only difference is that the device project is distinguished from other projects by the icon used. Figure 43-2 shows a single VB.NET device project in the Solution Explorer window.

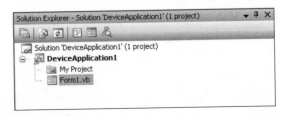

Figure 43-2

Selecting the DeviceApplication1 node brings up additional information about the project in the properties grid. This includes the version of the .NET Framework and platform for which this project is being written.

Design Skin

One of the significant improvements in Visual Studio 2005 is the inclusion of design skins for device applications. In the past, developers building forms for devices used the standard form designer to lay out controls, which approximated what the form would look like when it was run on the device. In most cases this layout had to be tweaked, and in some cases redesigned, to fit the target device. Figure 43-3 shows two forms: Form1 with the design skin turned on, and Form2 with the design skin turned off.

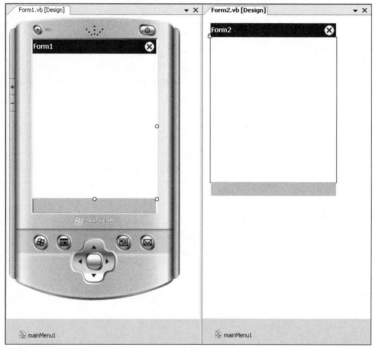

Figure 43-3

The design skin can be toggled on and off using the right-click context menu off the form design surface. You might be wondering why you would want to turn off the design skin. Other than giving you a better illustration of what the form is going to look like, the design skin does not add very much functionality. It also adds overhead every time the form is rendered in the designer. As such, Visual Studio 2005 is more responsive with the design skin disabled. Although the examples in this chapter show the design skin, there is no reason why you can't work with the design skin disabled.

Orientation

Windows Mobile 2003 Second Edition added the capability to change the orientation on a Pocket PC from portrait to landscape. Support has been added to Visual Studio 2005 to switch the orientation of the design surface. This automatically resizes the form to the appropriate dimensions, enabling you to validate that all of your controls are correctly positioned for both orientations.

To alter the orientation of the design surface you can select Rotate Left or Rotate Right from the right-click context menu off the design surface. If you have the design skin enabled, it will be rotated in the direction specified, while the form you are working on will remain upright. Without the design skin, the form will be resized as if the skin were present so you can still see the effect on your visual layout.

Buttons

The one bit of functionality that the design skin does add is the capability to automatically generate a code stub for handling hardware button events. As you move your mouse over the hardware buttons on the design skin, a tooltip appears, letting you know which button it is (such as Soft Key 1). Clicking on a button takes you to an event handler for the KeyDown event of the Form shown in the following code snippet:

```
Public Class Form1
    Private Sub Form1_KeyDown(ByVal sender As Object, ByVal e As KeyEventArgs)_
                                                    Handles MyBase.KeyDown
        If (e.KeyCode = System.Windows.Forms.Keys.Up) Then
            'Rocker Up
            'Up
        End If
        If (e.KeyCode = System.Windows.Forms.Keys.Down) Then
            'Rocker Down
            'Down
        End If
        If (e.KeyCode = System.Windows.Forms.Keys.Left) Then
            'Left
        End If
        If (e.KeyCode = System.Windows.Forms.Keys.Right) Then
            'Right
        End If
        If (e.KeyCode = System.Windows.Forms.Keys.Enter) Then
            'Enter
        End If
    End Sub
End Class
```

Note a few important points in this code snippet. First, the event handler actually handles the KeyDown event of the form. Because the keys may have different functionality depending on which form of your application is open, it makes sense for them to map to the form. Second, note that this event handler only handles the directional keys, the rocker, and the Enter key.

Most devices have a number of additional hardware buttons, referred to as *application keys*. These keys do not have a set function and can appear anywhere (if at all) on the device. Unfortunately, there is no automatic mapping to the form events for any of the application keys, although use of the Hardware Button control (which provides this functionality) is covered later in this chapter.

The last point to take away from this snippet is that it is generated code, and you should probably replace the entire contents of the event handler with your own code that uses a more efficient syntax, such as a SELECT statement.

Toolbox

Device applications have their own set of tabs within the Toolbox window. These are essentially the same as the tabs shown for building normal applications except that they are prefixed with the word "Device." Any developer who has worked with controls for a Windows application will feel at home using the device controls. Some controls are specific to device applications and enable you to take advantage of some of the device-specific functionality.

Common Controls

The standard controls such as textboxes, checkboxes, labels, and buttons are all available from the Common Device Controls tab. Figure 43-4 illustrates a simple form with a number of controls visible. Note that device developers benefit from the same set of designer features as Windows developers. These include the alignment guides, as shown in Figure 43-4.

Figure 43-4

The first version of the .NET Compact Framework was missing not only several of the standard controls, such as a DateTimePicker, but also basic layout functionality such as anchoring and docking. Version 2.0 of the .NET Compact Framework supports a wide range of controls, including splitters and status bars, as well as anchoring, docking, and auto-scrolling for panels and forms.

Mobile Controls

When building device applications, it is important to design them with the user interface in mind. Simply taking an existing Windows application and rebuilding it for the device is unlikely to work. The best device applications not only have intuitive form designs, they also make use of the available device-specific functionality, including the hardware buttons, the input panel, and the notification bubble.

Hardware Button

The discussion of the design skin noted that although the form KeyDown event handler could be used to trap some of the hardware buttons, it doesn't trap application key events. To handle one or more application keys, you need to add a HardwareButton control to the form. This control does not have a visual component, so it appears in the nonvisual area of the designer.

Figure 43-5 shows the associated properties for a HardwareButton control that has been added to Form1. The HardwareButton redirects the hardware button events to an AssociatedControl. The AssociatedControl must be a Form, Panel, or CustomControl; otherwise, a NotSupportedException will be raised when the application is run. Any of the six application keys can be selected as the Hardware Key. Unfortunately, these are not flags, so they cannot be concatenated to allow a single HardwareButton to wire up all of the application keys.

Figure 43-5

Once the HardwareButton control has been added to the form and the appropriate properties set, you still need to handle the click events. This can be done using an event handler for either the KeyPress or KeyUp event for the AssociatedControl. For example, if you were to use Form1 as the Associated Control, the event handler might look like the following:

```
Private Sub Form1_KeyUp(ByVal sender As Object, ByVal e As KeyEventArgs) _
                                            Handles MyBase.KeyUp
    If e.KeyCode = Microsoft.WindowsCE.Forms.HardwareKeys.ApplicationKey1 Then
        MsgBox("Hardware Key event")
    End If
End Sub
```

Input Panel

Most device applications require some form of text input, and this is usually done through the Soft Input Panel, or SIP, as it is more commonly known. The SIP is a visual keyboard that can be used to tap out words. Alternative input methods such as the Letter Recognizer use the same input panel for text entry. Figure 43-6 shows an emulator for a Pocket PC 2003 Second Edition device with the SIP showing. In this case, the SIP is displaying the keyboard.

Figure 43-6

The SIP takes up valuable screen real estate when it is both open (as in Figure 43-6) and closed (only the bottom bar is visible). As such, it should only be added to a form when required. However, the default behavior when a menu is added to the form is for the SIP to become visible, allowing it to be opened and closed at will. Hence, it is important to be able to control what happens when the SIP changes status.

The first step in working with the SIP is to add an `InputPanel` control to the form. Again, this control appears in the nonvisual area of the form designer and has a single property, `Enabled`, which determines whether the SIP is open or closed. This control also exposes an `EnabledChanged` event, which is raised when the status of the SIP changes.

Double-clicking on the newly created `InputPanel` generates an event handler for the `EnabledChanged` event. This handler needs to reposition the controls to optimize the layout for the reduced real estate.

Because the `InputPanel` appears as if it were a control that sits on top of the form, when it changes state it does not resize the form. This means that there is no resize event on the form, so any repositioning of controls needs to be done via the `EnabledChanged` event handler.

At this stage, it is worth noting that the standard controls all support anchoring and docking. On applications designed for a desktop computer, these layout options make sense. However, on a mobile device, where screen real estate is already limited, allowing the controls to automatically resize often results in a clunky and difficult to use interface. For example, take a simple screen layout that contains a client list and two buttons. If the device is in portrait mode the list should be positioned above the two buttons so the maximum number of items can be displayed. However, in landscape mode, instead of repositioning the controls so the list takes the full width of the device, the list should be repositioned alongside the two buttons.

This could be achieved by defining multiple screen layouts based on the size and orientation of the screen. The following code snippet shows how a number of screen layouts can be toggled between depending on the screen orientation:

```
Public Class Form1

    <Flags()> _
    Private Enum FormLayout
        SIP_Open
        SIP_Closed
        Portrait
        Landscape
    End Enum

    Private Sub Form1_Resize(ByVal sender As Object, ByVal e As System.EventArgs)
Handles MyBase.Resize
        Layout()
    End Sub

    Private Sub InputPanel1_EnabledChanged(ByVal sender As System.Object, ByVal e
As System.EventArgs) Handles InputPanel1.EnabledChanged
        Layout()
    End Sub

    Private Function DetermineCurrentLayout() As FormLayout
        Dim currentLayout As FormLayout
        'Determine whether it is landscape or portrait
        If Me.Width > Me.Height Then
            currentLayout = FormLayout.Landscape
        Else
            currentLayout = FormLayout.Portrait
        End If

        'Determine whether the SIP is Open or Closed
        If Me.InputPanel1.Enabled Then
            currentLayout = currentLayout Or FormLayout.SIP_Open
        Else
            currentLayout = currentLayout Or FormLayout.SIP_Closed
        End If
        Return currentLayout
```

```
        End Function

        Private Sub Layout()
            Dim newLayout As FormLayout = DetermineCurrentLayout()

            Select Case newLayout
                Case FormLayout.Portrait Or FormLayout.SIP_Open
                    Layout_PortraitWithInput()
                Case FormLayout.Portrait Or FormLayout.SIP_Closed
                    Layout_PortraitWithOutInput()
                Case FormLayout.Landscape Or FormLayout.SIP_Open
                    Layout_LandscapeWithInput()
                Case FormLayout.Landscape Or FormLayout.SIP_Closed
                    Layout_LandscapeWithOutInput()
            End Select

        End Sub

        Private Sub Layout_PortraitWithOutInput()
            'Position list control above the two buttons
        End Sub

        Private Sub Layout_PortraitWithInput()
            'Position list control above the two buttons
            'Reduce the height of the list and move the buttons up
            '   so that they are both visible above the SIP
        End Sub

        Private Sub Layout_LandscapeWithOutInput()
            'Position list control along side the two buttons
        End Sub

        Private Sub Layout_LandscapeWithInput()
            'Position list control along side the two buttons
            'Reduce the height of the list control so that all
            '   items are visible above the SIP
        End Sub

    End Class
```

This code snippet defines an enumeration that can be used to specify the current screen orientation. Two factors warrant consideration: the orientation of the screen and whether the SIP is visible. It may be that other form factors, such as a square screen, could be added to this list.

When an event is triggered that alters the orientation of the screen (such as the form resize event) or the status of the SIP (such as the InputPanel EnabledChanged event), the new screen configuration is detected using the DetermineCurrentLayout method, and the contents of the form are rearranged.

Notification

There are times when a background application might want to notify a user about a particular event, or get user feedback without bringing the application to the foreground. This can be done with a Notification bubble. The contents of the bubble are essentially an HTML document that can use form input controls such as textboxes and buttons to retrieve user input.

Similar to both the `HardwareButton` and the `InputPanel`, when a `Notification` control is added to the form it appears in the nonvisual section of the designer. A number of properties can be set on a `Notification` control that determine the caption, icon, and text of the notification. There is also a `Critical` property, which can be set to heighten the importance of the notification, and an `Initial Duration` property, which controls how long the notification is shown. The `Text` property is where the HTML content is added to the notification bubble. While it is possible to use the property grid to enter this property, you will likely need to dynamically build the HTML content based on the status of your application. The following code snippet creates and displays the notification bubble illustrated in Figure 43-7:

```
Private Sub NotifyUser()
    'Build the HTML content for the Notification Bubble
    Dim htmlContent As System.Text.StringBuilder

    htmlContent = New System.Text.StringBuilder("<html><body>")
    htmlContent.Append("<a href=""Reference.htm"">Test Link</a>")
    htmlContent.Append("<p><form method=""GET"" action=mybubble>")
    htmlContent.Append("<p>This is an <font color=""#0000FF""><b>HTML</b></font>")
    htmlContent.Append("notification stored in a  <font color=""#FF0000"">")
    htmlContent.Append("<i>string</i></font> table!</p>")
    htmlContent.Append("<p><input type=text name=textinput ")
    htmlContent.Append("value=""Input Sample""><input type='submit'></p>")
    htmlContent.Append("<p align=right><input type=button name=OK value='Ok'>")
    htmlContent.Append("<input type=button name='cmd:2' value='Cancel'></p>")
    htmlContent.Append("</body></html>")

    'Set the Notification content
    Notification1.Text = htmlContent.ToString

    'Set the title and make this a critical bubble (red border)
    Notification1.Caption = "Title"
    Notification1.Critical = True

    'Display the Notification bubble
    Notification1.Visible = True
End Sub
```

In addition to building the HTML content for the notification bubble, this code also sets the `Caption`, or title, for the bubble, makes it `Critical`, which will make the border appear red, and finally displays the bubble. Instead of the more common `Show` method that is used for forms, to display the notification bubble, set the `Visible` property to `True`. In Figure 43-7 you can see that the notification bubble is made up of three distinct parts. The icon is placed in the main menu bar at the top of the screen, and this icon remains visible until the user dismisses the bubble. Below the icon, the bubble expands to include a title bar and the main notification window, where the HTML controls are displayed.

Double-clicking the `Notification` control attaches an event handler to the `ResponseSubmitted` event. This is one of two key events raised by the `Notification` control, and is raised whenever a user dismisses the notification bubble. To dismiss a notification bubble, there must be at least one control, such as a hyperlink or a button, that can submit information. Failing to include one of these controls results in users being unable to get rid of the notification bubble.

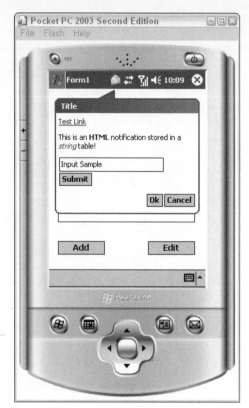

Figure 43-7

The event handler for the `ResponseSubmitted` event has a `ResponseSubmittedEventArgs` type as a parameter. This class has a single `String` property, which is the `Response`. The contents of this string will vary depending on the type of response given. In this example, three types of responses might be received from the user:

❑ Clicking Test Link would have set the response string equal to the URL specified for the link. In this case, the URL was `Reference.htm`. It is up to the application how this is processed, as it does not automatically navigate to this URL.

❑ The Submit button is actually a form `Input` control of type `Submit`, and as such submits the data collected by the form. In this case, you have a text box, so the response would appear as follows:

```
mybubble?textinput=Input+Sample
```

Notice that the name of the form being submitted is at the beginning of the string, and then all input controls are appended after the question mark in a `name=value` pattern. This pattern is useful when parsing the response string for form data.

❑ The last form of response is the value of any form button. In this case, clicking OK would generate a response equal to the `value` property of the button, which would be `Ok`.

One other action can be performed on the form, which is to click the Cancel button. Clicking this button does not raise the `ResponseSubmitted` event, but instead minimizes the notification bubble so only the icon appears in the menu bar. What makes this button special is the use of cmd:2 as the name of the button. This is actually a non-documented feature, but you can use cmd:0–4 as identifiers for buttons for which you want to simply close the bubble and not send a response.

The other event is the `BubbleChanged` event, which is triggered when the visibility of the notification bubble changes. In most cases the application will have displayed the bubble and will receive notification when the bubble is dismissed, via the `ResponseSubmitted` event. On some occasions, however, a user is not quick enough to interact with the notification, or perhaps chooses to ignore it. Once the `InitialDuration` has expired, the notification bubble automatically hides itself. In this case, it is important for the application to be notified when the visibility of the bubble changes, because a timer may need to be started to re-prompt the user.

Debugging

In the past, writing applications for mobile devices was a time-consuming process. The release of the Compact Framework brought with it a new wave of interactive debugger support for building device applications. Now developers wanting to build mobile applications have the same support for debugging applications as they do for desktop or web applications. Subsequent chapters in this book cover the new debugging features within Visual Studio 2005. Most of these apply equally to debugging device applications. This section examines how you can use either an emulator or a real device to debug your application.

Emulator

Although mobile devices have decreased in price considerably over the last year or so, they are still an expensive investment for a developer to make. This is especially true given the speed at which devices change and become obsolete. As such, it became evident that if there were to be more mobile developers, they would need to be able to build and test their applications without having to purchase real devices. Device emulators are important because they provide a low-cost alternative for developers.

While emulators are a good alternative, they are not a complete substitute for the real thing. It is always preferable to know and have access to the device that will be used to run the application. However, this is not always an option, and definitely not a requirement for building mobile applications.

Visual Studio 2005 ships with a number of emulators, varying in size and resolution, for the Windows Mobile 2003 Second Edition (Pocket PC and Smartphone) and Windows CE 5.0. This enables developers to test their application on a variety of different form factor devices. The emulators also come with built-in virtual radio antennas so that phone and SMS activity can be simulated.

The first time you run your mobile application, Visual Studio 2005 prompts you to specify a device to deploy to. This list will display both physical devices and emulators that are compatible with your current project type. Figure 43-8 illustrates this dialog for a Pocket PC application. You can use the checkbox to suppress this dialog to improve the rate at which you can build and test your application. The dialog can be re-enabled via the Device Tools node on the Options window, accessible from the Tools menu.

Figure 43-8

Selecting one of the Pocket PC 2003 emulators either launches the emulator in a separate window, or, if an instance of that emulator is already running, simply connects to that one. The first time you run your application, you can expect to wait up to 10 minutes for the .NET Compact Framework to be deployed and installed on the device. Don't be put off, as this only happens once, and the next time you run your application it will be much faster. Between developer sessions you can preserve the state of the emulator by electing to Save State and Exit.

When the emulator loads up, it will appear similar to what is shown in Figure 43-9. The emulators are very similar to the design skins that have been incorporated into Visual Studio 2005. They have a series of functioning buttons and can be rotated to test portrait-to-landscape application resizing. In addition, various options can be configured, such as the size of the RAM and which serial ports are available. It is also possible to share a folder from the host computer so files can easily be transferred between the emulator and the host. These options are all available from the Configure item on the File menu, although some options cannot be configured when the emulator is running.

Device

As mentioned previously, although emulators are a good alternative for a large portion of mobile application development, they are not a complete substitute. In addition to being a more realistic test of how the application will behave, debugging using a real device is much quicker than debugging via the emulator.

Prior to deploying a mobile application, it is essential that you test your application on one or more devices. Ideally you would test your application on every device on the market. This is clearly not a feasible option due to the time and expense involved. A minimum alternative is to identify a single device for each operating system you are planning to support. For example, if you are targeting devices running Windows Mobile 2003 SE and later, then you should test on devices that are running both this operating system and Windows Mobile 5.

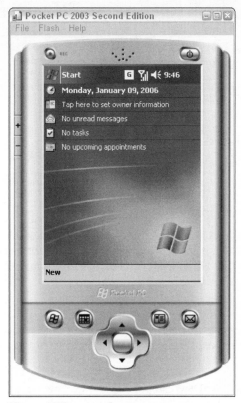

Figure 43-9

Device Emulator Manager

In the previous version of Visual Studio, building device applications was still quite painful. If you didn't have your computer set up exactly right, Visual Studio would refuse to talk to the emulator. Unlike debugging on a real device, which made use of ActiveSync, debugging on an emulator used its own communication layer, which was very unreliable. This has been addressed in Visual Studio 2005 with the inclusion of the Device Emulator Manager.

The Device Emulator Manager gives you much better control over the state of emulators installed on your computer. Figure 43-10 shows the Device Emulator Manager with the Pocket PC 2003 SE Emulator running, which is evident from the green play symbol next to the emulator (although the green isn't visible in the book, of course).

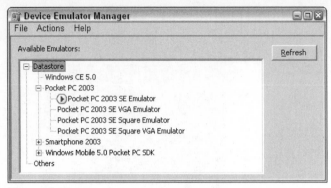

Figure 43-10

When you run your application from Visual Studio and select to use an emulator, the Device Emulator Manager (DEM) is also started. If you try to close the DEM using the close button it will actually minimize itself into the system tray, as it is useful to have open while you work with the emulators.

Connecting

If an emulator is not currently active (i.e., it appears without an icon beside it), you can start it by selecting Connect from the right-click context menu for that item in the tree. Once the emulator has been started using the emulator, Visual Studio 2005 will use that emulator when you begin to debug your application.

After connecting to a device, the DEM can be used to shut down, reset, or even clear the saved state of the device. Clearing the saved state restores the device to the default state and requires Visual Studio to reinstall the .NET Compact Framework prior to you debugging your application again. However, this might be necessary if you get your device into an invalid state.

Cradling

The only remaining difference between running your application on a real device versus on the emulator is the communication layer involved. As mentioned previously, real devices use ActiveSync to connect to the desktop. The communication layer provided by ActiveSync is not only used by Visual Studio 2005 to debug your application, it can also be the primary channel through which you synchronize data.

The ideal scenario is to have Visual Studio 2005 debug the emulator via the ActiveSync layer. This has been achieved in the latest version of ActiveSync combined with the DEM. From the right-click context menu for a running emulator, you can elect to cradle the device. This launches ActiveSync, which may prompt you to set up a partnership between the device and the host computer. You can either set this up (if you are going to be doing a lot of debugging using the emulator) or just select the guest partnership. Once the partnership has been established, ActiveSync will appear as shown in Figure 43-11, indicating that the device is connected.

Remember that once you have cradled the emulator, it is as if it were a real device at the end of the ActiveSync communication layer. The host cannot tell the difference. As such, when you select which device you want to debug on, you need to select the Pocket PC 2003 device, rather than any of the emulators.

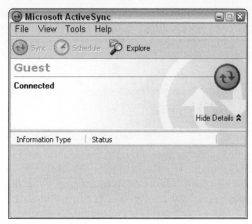

Figure 43-11

Project Settings

As you would imagine, there are additional project settings that pertain specifically to device projects. There are only a few, and they mainly pertain to setting additional debugging settings required for device applications. Figure 43-12 shows the Devices tab of the Project Settings window for a device project.

The Target Device field is used to specify the default device when your application is run from within Visual Studio 2005. You can also nominate the output file folder and whether the latest version of the .NET Compact Framework should be installed as part of the debugging process.

DeviceApplication1		▾ ✕
Application	Configuration: N/A	Platform: N/A
Compile		
Debug	Deployment Options	
References	Target device:	
Resources	Pocket PC 2003 SE Emulator	▾
Signing	Output file folder:	
Devices	%CSIDL_PROGRAM_FILES%\DeviceApplication2	...
Code Analysis	☑ Deploy the latest version of the .NET Compact Framework (including Service Packs)	
	Authenticode Signing	
	☐ Sign the project output with this certificate	
		Select Certificate...
	Provision certificate to device:	
	Do not provision the device	▾

Figure 43-12

The last part of this tab enables you to sign your application so it can be installed on a provisioned device. Essentially, the provisioning of a device entails installing digital certificates onto the device. This can be used to limit which applications can be installed or run, or even which resources an application can use. Applications that have been signed with one of these certificates will be permitted to run on a provisioned device.

Device Options

It was mentioned earlier in this chapter that some device options can be configured via the Options window, accessible from the Tools menu. There are three nodes under the Device Tools node in the Options window, as shown in Figure 43-13. The General tab controls whether the design skins are applied to forms by default in the designer, and whether you're prompted with the device selector dialog when debugging an application.

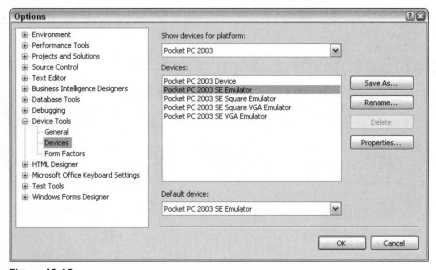

Figure 43-13

Figure 43-13 shows the list of devices available for debugging. To extend this list you need to install either new emulators or an SDK, such as the Windows Mobile 5.0 SDK, which is discussed in the next chapter.

Clicking the Properties button brings up the dialog shown in Figure 43-14, which enables you to fine-tune the debugging process. For example, you can elect to use either the default DMA Transport layer or the TCP Connect Transport layer that was used previously. In most cases you will not have to modify these settings, as the DMA Transport layer is much quicker to use while debugging your application. However, sometimes you have to connect to an older device that may not support the DMA Transport layer. In these cases you will need to select the TCP Connect Transport option. Alternatively, you may want to provision the emulator to simulate the target devices more closely by providing an XML provisioning file for the Device Emulation Startup Provider to use.

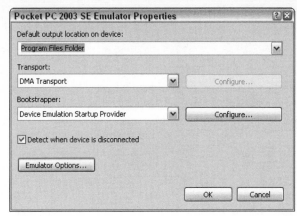

Figure 43-14

Summary

This chapter introduced you to building device applications using Visual Studio 2005. Desktop developers will feel right at home with a familiar environment and all the tools at hand to rapidly build, test, and deploy a mobile application.

The next chapter extends this discussion by looking at some of the new functionality introduced with Windows Mobile 5.0 and describing how you can deploy your application using CAB files and MSI installers.

44

Advanced Device Application Programming

Programming for mobile applications is all about optimizing the small form factor, the mobility, and the unique functionality offered by these devices. The previous chapter examined the support available within Visual Studio 2005 for building device applications. This chapter looks at some more advanced techniques for building and deploying mobile applications, including rich support for building data applications, new functionality offered by Windows Mobile 5.0, and deploying your application using CAB files and installers.

Data Source

Support for building data-bound applications in Visual Studio 2005 has been improved across the board. This includes building mobile applications where it is useful to have a portable database that resides on the device. As with other project types, to add a Data Source to your application, select Add New Data Source from the Data Sources window. Select Database as the Data Source Type and you will be prompted to select the database connection to use.

Mobile applications can connect directly to a SQL Server database using the same classes as desktop or web applications. However, this can limit the mobility of such a device, as it will require connectivity to the database to function. A better solution is to right-click on the New Connection button and change the database connection type to point to a SQL Mobile database. By default, this displays the Add Connection dialog for a SQL Server connection. Selecting Change next to the Data Source label enables you to change the connection type to use SQL Server Mobile Edition, as shown in Figure 44-1.

Figure 44-1

Accepting this change prompts you to select the parameters for the SQL Mobile database to connect to. Here you can select either an existing database, as shown in Figure 44-2 (where the Northwind database that ships with Visual Studio 2005 has been selected), or create a new database. If you have an existing database on your mobile device, that can also be selected.

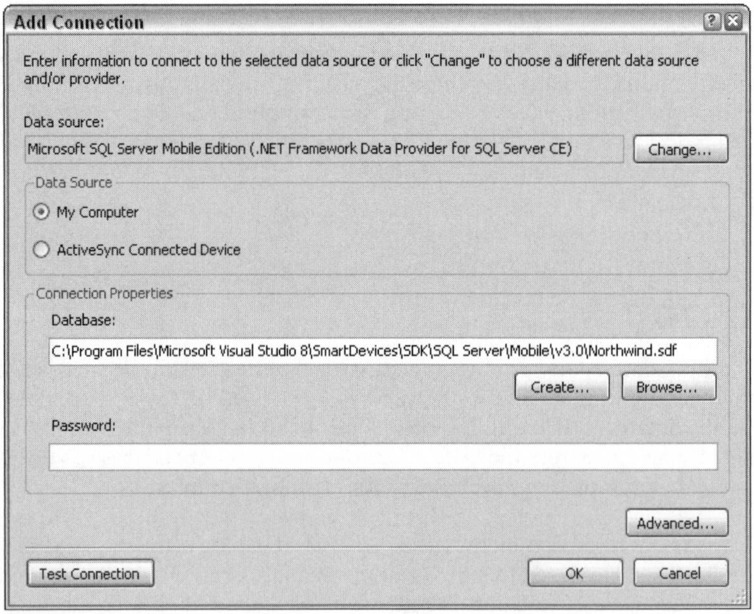

Figure 44-2

If you select a database that is not in the project folder, upon accepting the connection properties you are asked if you want a copy to be made and included in your solution. This is a good idea, as it ensures that you can easily deploy your application without verifying whether the database already exists on the device. For debugging purposes, you can define when the database is deployed with your application. Select the database file that has been added to your solution and use the Copy to Output Directory property to specify whether the database is always copied, never copied, or copied if newer than what is on the device.

When the Data Source is added to the solution, it is added both to the Data Sources window and the Solution Explorer as an XSD file. Other files are also added to the project to support strongly typed access to the data via a DataSet. These are created by the custom tool, MSDataSetGenerator, which is specified in the property grid for the XSD file. Later in this chapter you will look at an alternative tool that generates a SQLCeResultSet instead of a DataSet.

DataSet

Once the Data Source has been added to the project, the Data Sources window can be used to add data-bound controls to the design surface for the device. This is the same process described earlier in the book when you were working with DataSets for a desktop application. This section shows you how easily you can build a user interface to not only view the data, but also add and edit records. For this purpose, consider a limited scenario that works with the Northwind sample database that ships with Visual Studio 2005. This database is located in the SmartDevices SDK folder (C:\Program Files\Microsoft Visual Studio 8\SmartDevices\SDK\SQL Server\Mobile\v3.0\Northwind.sdf), and can be added to the project as outlined in the previous section.

The scenario is to provide an interface for managing Customers and Orders. When adding the Northwind Data Source, you need to include these two tables, plus the Employees table for selecting the employee who took the order. This adds them to the Northwind DataSet and ensures that you have appropriate table adapters for retrieving and updating information in the database. The Northwind Data Source appears in the Data Sources window and has nodes for Customers, Orders, and Employees. Because there is a relationship between these tables when you expand the Customers node, you will see a subnode for Orders.

For this scenario, add a new form to the project to lay out Customer information. From the Data Sources window, select the Customers node and ensure that the drop-down field is set to DataGrid. You also want to prevent the Customer ID from being added to the DataGrid, so select None from the Display Type drop-down for this field. Now drag the Customers node onto the form. This adds a DataGrid to the form, along with a NorthwindDataSet, a CustomersBindingSource, and a CustomersTableAdapter to the nonvisual area of the designer, as shown in Figure 44-3.

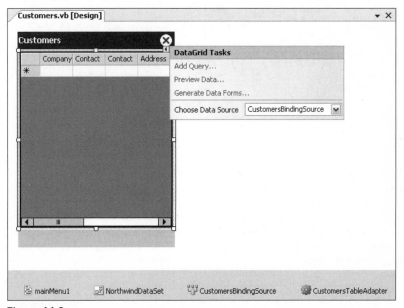

Figure 44-3

In Figure 44-3 you can see that the Company column is relatively narrow, and it is unlikely that many company names are going to be that short. To change the width of this column, you need to edit the column styling information. When building applications using the full .NET Framework, use the property called `Columns` for the `DataGridView` to control how the columns are arranged. This is also accessible from the smart tag associated with this control. The `DataGrid` for mobile applications does not have this property; the column layout information is buried in the `TableStyles` property. Selecting this property from the Property grid opens the Table Style Collection Editor, shown in Figure 44-4.

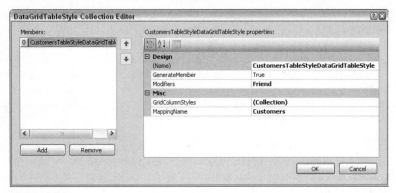

Figure 44-4

To adjust the column layout information, select the `GridColumnStyles` property, which in turn opens another Collection Editor window, this time for editing column styles, as shown in Figure 44-5.

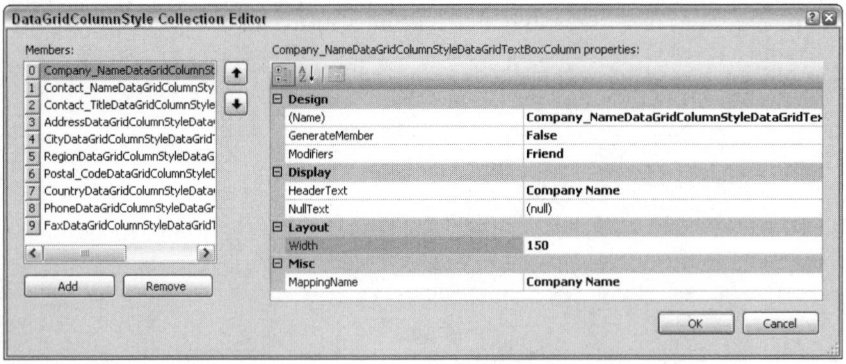

Figure 44-5

Selecting the Company entry in the Members list, adjust the width to 150, as shown in Figure 44-5, which is a more reasonable width for this field. The `MappingName` property is also important, as it is used to associate a field in the Data Source with this column. In this case, the `MappingName` property is linked to the Company Name field. The editor has some built-in smarts that determine what fields are available from the associated Data Source. Selecting the `MappingName` property reveals a drop-down list of the available fields. While on this screen, you can remove several of the Customer fields, as they don't need to be visible on this opening screen.

Going back to Figure 44-3, you can see a couple of smart tag tasks for the `DataGrid`. Of importance here is the capability to Generate Data Forms. Selecting this option automatically generates forms for viewing and editing information for Customers selected from the `DataGrid`. Before generating the forms, you need to configure the Data Sources window so you get only the fields you want available for editing. In this case, you don't want the Company Name to be changed, so select Label from the display type drop-down for that item. Now you can generate the data forms using the smart tag on the `DataGrid`. Depending on the number of fields in the table, this process might take a few minutes, but eventually it will not only generate the forms, with appropriate controls rendered to display and edit data fields, but also wire up appropriate event handlers. Figure 44-6 illustrates the three customer forms you now have. On the left is the customer list, in the middle is the summary information form for the customer, and on the right is the customer edit form. You will notice that for the Company Name field, a label was generated instead of a textbox, thereby preventing editing of this field.

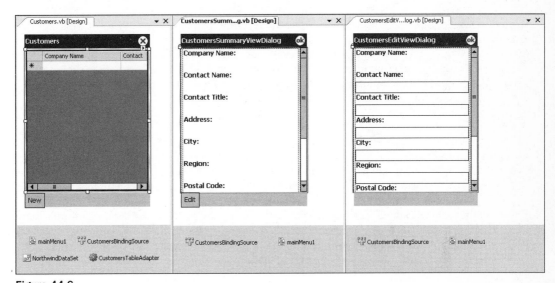

Figure 44-6

The one problem introduced in making the Company Name field read-only for editing is that the same form is used for creating a new record. As such, you need to provide a mechanism for assigning a company name to a new record. This can be done in the `Click` event handler for the New menu item. Double-clicking this menu item takes you to the generated event handler, where you can call an `InputBox` to get the company name for the new record. Notice in the following code snippet that you also need to provide the Customer ID field for this new record. Here you make a call to a method that ensures the ID will be unique. Pass in the company name as a seed for the unique ID:

```
Private Sub NewMenuItemMenuItem_Click(ByVal sender As Object, _
                             ByVal e As EventArgs) _
                                        Handles NewMenuItemMenuItem.Click
    Dim newCompanyName As String = InputBox("Please enter the new company name:")
    If newCompanyName = "" Then Return

    Dim customer As NorthwindDataSet.CustomersRow = _
          CType(CType(CustomersBindingSource.AddNew, Data.DataRowView).Row, _
```

```
                                                    NorthwindDataSet.CustomersRow)
        customer.Company_Name = newCompanyName
        customer.Customer_ID = GenerateUniqueCustomerID(newCompanyName)
        Dim customerEditDialog As CustomersEditViewDialog = _
                    CustomersEditViewDialog.Instance(Me.CustomersBindingSource)
        customerEditDialog.ShowDialog()
    End Sub
```

So far you have an application that enables you to browse the summary list of customers using a `DataGrid`, view the full information about a customer using the summary form, and add or edit a customer using the edit form. The next part in this scenario involves linking Order information so orders for a particular customer appear on the customer summary page. This information could also be added to the edit page using this process, but for brevity, only add it to the summary page.

From the Data Sources window, drag the Orders node to the customer summary form. This requires some fiddling, as the existing controls are docked, but eventually you should be able to get it laid out with the `DataGrid` at the bottom of the list of customer attributes. Notice that it has again added a `NorthwindDataSet`, a table adapter, and a binding source to the nonvisual area of the design surface. Unfortunately, the generated bindings will not link the orders with the customer you're viewing, because it is referencing a new instance of the `NorthwindDataSet`.

Before correcting the issue with the data binding, you need to inject a step here to create the summary and edit forms for the Order information. Unfortunately, when you correct the data binding, you lose the ability to generate these forms. In the same way you created the customer summary and edit forms, select the Generate Data Forms smart tag task from the Orders `DataGrid`. As before, this adds a New item to the existing menu, which can be renamed New Order to prevent confusion with the Edit menu item.

To correct the issue with the data binding, you need to select the `OrdersBindingSource` and change the `DataBinding` property to be the `CustomerBindingSource`. In the `DataMember` property, select Orders_FK00 to set up the relationship between the two binding sources. You should also remove the additional `NorthwindDataSet` and `TableAdapter`, leaving the form looking like the one shown in Figure 44-7.

The last thing you need to do to display the list of orders for a customer is to retrieve the orders from the database by creating a second `TableAdapter` for the `NorthwindDataSet` that will be used to fill the Orders table. Return to the Customers form and you can easily add an `OrdersTableAdapter` by dragging it onto the form from the Toolbox. When you added the `NorthwindDataSet`, these strongly typed adapters were added to the solution, and were subsequently added to the Components tab of the Toolbox. To activate the `TableAdapter`, call the `Fill` method as part of the `Load` event for the form:

```
Private Sub CustomersSummaryViewDialog_Load(ByVal sender As System.Object, _
                    ByVal e As System.EventArgs) Handles MyBase.Load
        If NorthwindDataSetUtil.DesignerUtil.IsRunTime Then
            Me.CustomersTableAdapter.Fill(Me.NorthwindDataSet.Customers)
            Me.OrdersTableAdapter1.Fill(Me.NorthwindDataSet.Orders)
            me.EmployeesTableAdapter1.Fill(me.NorthwindDataSet.Employees)
        End If
    End Sub
```

In this code snippet, notice that the `TableAdapter` *for* Employees *has been filled. This adapter also needs to be added to the* `CustomersSummaryViewDialog` *form, just as you did for Orders.*

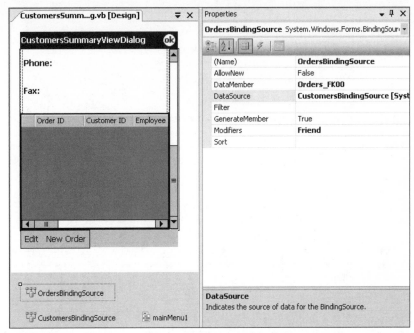

Figure 44-7

The order summary and order edit forms currently list all the attributes of the Order, including the Customer ID and Employee ID. Because you have arrived at this order via the Customer summary page, you don't need that field displayed. The Employee ID field is not really that useful unless you have committed all these IDs to memory. This would be more useful if it displayed a name instead of an ID. To do this, you can combine the information from the Employees table.

You already have the information from the Employees table loaded into the NorthwindDataSet, so all you need to do is select the correct record from that table based on the Employee ID of the Order and display the name of the employee. Unfortunately, the Employees table currently returns First and Last Name fields, which makes it difficult to display, as you need to bind to a single field. To correct this, edit the Employee information via the NorthwindDataSet by double-clicking the NorthWind.XSD in the Solution Explorer. This opens the DataSet designer. Right-click on the Employees entity and select Configure to open the TableAdapter Configuration Wizard. Here you can change the information retrieved from the database to include a concatenated Name field, for displaying information, and the Employee ID field, for data binding. You can remove all the other fields, resulting in a SQL statement that should appear as shown in Figure 44-8.

In Figure 44-8, the return values are ordered by last name so they are easier to identify. Clicking Finish regenerates the NorthwindDataSet with only these two fields in the Employees table.

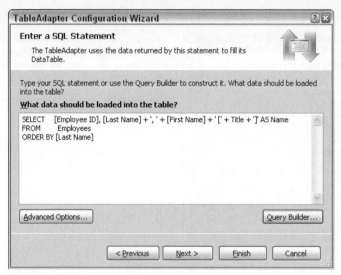

Figure 44-8

The next step in the process is to add a data-bound field to both the summary and edit dialogs for Order information. Ideally, you want a label on the summary dialog and a drop-down list for the edit dialog. Begin with the edit dialog because it is the easier of the two to implement. This dialog, as it was automatically generated, contains text fields for Order ID, Customer ID, and Employee ID. Because the first two of these are not editable, remove both the Order ID and Customer ID fields and their associated labels from the dialog. In addition, remove the text field under the Employee ID label, rename the label to read Employee, and finally add a Combobox to the form. The final result, after a bit of rearranging, should look similar to what is shown in Figure 44-9.

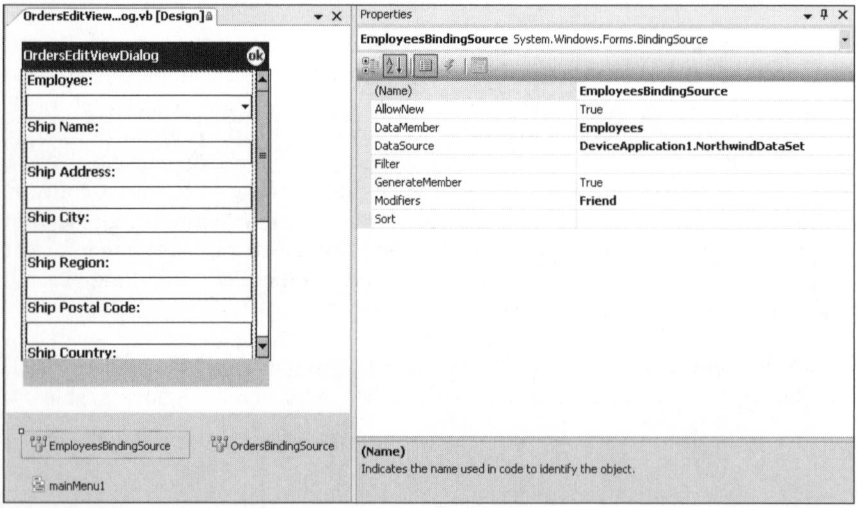

Figure 44-9

Figure 44-9 also shows a new `EmployeeBindingSource`, which will be used to populate the Employees drop-down list. This is created by dragging a new `BindingSource` component from the Toolbox onto the form and renaming it `EmployeeBindingSource`. The `DataSource` for this `BindingSource` has been set to `NorthwindDataSet`, but you will notice that unlike previous examples there is no `NorthwindDataSet` on this form. The following generated code snippet shows that it specifies a type to bind to, rather than an actual object:

```
'
'EmployeesBindingSource
'
Me.EmployeesBindingSource.DataMember = "Employees"
Me.EmployeesBindingSource.DataSource = GetType(DeviceApplication1.NorthwindDataSet)
```

Setting the `DataSource` to a type is useful for design-time manipulation. However, at runtime you must change this `DataSource` to point to an actual Data Source so there is data to bind to. As such, you need to set the `DataSource` property equal to the `NorthwindDataSet` that is populated on the Customers form by modifying the auto-generated `Instance` method, highlighted below. Although this method appears in the `OrdersEditViewDialog.Designer.vb` file, which you should normally avoid modifying, this particular method will not be overwritten by subsequent changes to the layout of the form:

```
Public Shared Function Instance(ByVal bindingSource As BindingSource) _
                                                    As OrdersEditViewDialog
    System.Windows.Forms.Cursor.Current = Cursors.WaitCursor
    If (defaultInstance Is Nothing) Then
        defaultInstance = New DeviceApplication1.OrdersEditViewDialog
        defaultInstance.OrdersBindingSource.DataSource = bindingSource
        defaultInstance.EmployeesBindingSource.DataSource = _
                        My.Forms.CustomersSummaryViewDialog.NorthwindDataSet
    End If
    defaultInstance.CboEmployee.Focus()
    defaultInstance.AutoScrollPosition = New System.Drawing.Point(0, 0)
    defaultInstance.OrdersBindingSource.Position = bindingSource.Position
    System.Windows.Forms.Cursor.Current = System.Windows.Forms.Cursors.Default
    Return defaultInstance
End Function
```

The last thing you need to do to wire up the Employees drop-down list is to both set the `DataSource` property, to populate the drop-down, and bind the `SelectedValue` property, to provide two-way binding for the Order. Select the drop-down list and configure the `Data` properties so they match Figure 44-10.

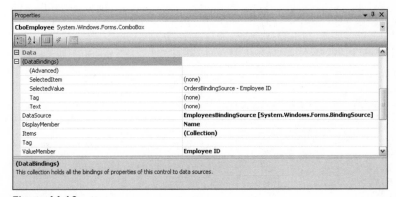

Figure 44-10

In Figure 44-10 the drop-down list is populated using the `EmployeesBindindSource` as the `DataSource`, displaying the `Name` attribute in the list and using the Employee ID attribute for the value of the items in the list. The drop-down list is also data-bound to the Employee ID attribute on the `OrdersBindingSource`.

This completes the edit dialog for Order information. The Orders summary dialog is done in a similar manner, so begin by copying both the `EmployeeBindingSource` and the Employees drop-down from the edit dialog and pasting them onto the summary dialog. Again, the summary dialog presents the Order ID and Customer ID, which are not really required and can be removed. After tidying up, the summary dialog should look similar to Figure 44-11.

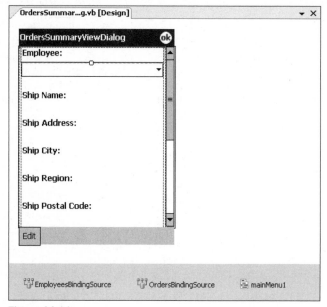

Figure 44-11

Because this is a summary dialog, you don't really want the Employee information to be presented in a drop-down list. A simple option here is to disable the drop-down list. However, this makes the interface look a little untidy. To fix this issue, bind the current value of the drop-down list to the Employee label. Again, this can be done in the `Instance` method for this form, along with binding the `DataSource` property of the `EmployeesBindingSource` to the `NorthwindDataSet`, as you did previously:

```
Public Shared Function Instance(ByVal bindingSource As BindingSource) _
                                                As OrdersSummaryViewDialog
    System.Windows.Forms.Cursor.Current = Cursors.WaitCursor
    If (defaultInstance Is Nothing) Then
        defaultInstance = New DeviceApplication1.OrdersSummaryViewDialog
        defaultInstance.OrdersBindingSource.DataSource = bindingSource
        defaultInstance.EmployeesBindingSource.DataSource = _
                My.Forms.CustomersSummaryViewDialog.NorthwindDataSet.Employees
        defaultInstance.Employee_IDLabel.DataBindings.Add _
                            ("Text", defaultInstance.CboEmployee, "Text")
```

```
        End If
        defaultInstance.AutoScrollPosition = New System.Drawing.Point(0, 0)
        defaultInstance.OrdersBindingSource.Position = bindingSource.Position
        System.Windows.Forms.Cursor.Current = System.Windows.Forms.Cursors.Default
        Return defaultInstance
    End Function
```

From this code snippet, you can see that the `Text` property of the Employee drop-down, `CboEmployee`, is bound to the `Text` property of the Employee label, `Employee_IDLabel`. You can now set the `Visible` property of the drop-down list to `False` so only the label is visible at runtime.

This completes the scenario for working with Customers and Orders. Clearly, this example could be extended to work with OrderDetails, which requires a Product list lookup, using the same process you just walked through.

ResultSet

So far this chapter has focused on using automatically generated DataSets to work with data from a SQL Mobile database. This was generated by MSDataSetGenerator, which was the custom tool assigned to the `NorthwindDataSet.xsd` file. A much lighter weight alternative is available using a SQLCeResultSet. A little documented fact is that you can again get Visual Studio 2005 to do the heavy lifting by using the MSResultSetGenerator to automatically generate strongly typed result sets.

To create a ResultSet, begin as you would for creating a DataSet — by adding a new DataSource. This will in fact add a DataSet to your solution, but this is a result of the MSDataSetGenerator being used instead of the MSResultSetGenerator. Once you have created the Data Source, select the XSD file in the Solution Explorer and bring up the Properties window. Change the custom tool property to be MSResultSetGenerator in order to update your solution to include a strongly typed ResultSet. Once generated, the ResultSet can be used in a similar fashion to the DataSet.

Windows Mobile 5.0

Microsoft's much anticipated release of Windows Mobile 5.0 last year gave mobile developers access to the next generation of APIs. The improvements included managed APIs for existing functionality, as well as a Notification Broker that enables developers to tap into system events. This section tackles how you can get started developing for Windows Mobile 5.0 devices.

SDK Download

The first thing you need to do before you get started building applications for Windows Mobile 5.0 devices is to download the Windows Mobile 5.0 SDK, available from the Windows Mobile Developer Center at `http://msdn.microsoft.com/mobility/windowsmobile/default.aspx`, where you can follow the links to downloads of SDKs and emulators. Due to space limitations on the disks that ship with Visual Studio 2005, the SDKs and emulators for Windows Mobile 5.0 were not included, and unfortunately they are quite a large download.

There are two SDKs, one for Pocket PC and one for Smartphone, so if you are doing development for both types of devices, you need to download both of them. After you install the SDK, you will notice that additional project types appear under the Smart Device node in the New Project dialog. Alternatively, if you have a Pocket PC 2003 project, you can upgrade the project by selecting Change Target Platform from the right-click context menu for that project in the Solution Explorer. This opens the Change Platform Dialog shown in Figure 44-12.

Figure 44-12

Managed APIs

To access the Windows Mobile 5.0 managed APIs, you need to add references to the WindowsMobile assemblies. This can be done using the Add Reference item from the project's right-click context menu off the Solution Explorer. Six assemblies are listed with the prefix `Microsoft.WindowsMobile` in the .NET tab of the Add Reference dialog. The functionality can be broken down according to the namespaces that are included.

Configuration

The configuration namespace includes a single class, the `ConfigurationManager`, which is used to test and process an XML configuration file that can be used to configure a device. For example, the following code adds the Microsoft web site to the list of favorites:

```
Imports Microsoft.WindowsMobile
Imports System.Xml
Public Class Form1
    Private Sub configurationExample(ByVal sender As System.Object, _
                                ByVal e As System.EventArgs) _
                                            Handles SampleButton.Click
        Dim configDoc As XmlDocument = New XmlDocument()
        configDoc.LoadXml( _
            "<wap-provisioningdoc>" + _
            "<characteristic type=""BrowserFavorite"">" + _
            "<characteristic type=""Microsoft"">" + _
            "<parm name=""URL"" value=""http://www.microsoft.com""/>" + _
            "</characteristic>" + _
            "</characteristic>" + _
            "</wap-provisioningdoc>" _
            )
        Configuration.ConfigurationManager.ProcessConfiguration(configDoc, False)

    End Sub
End Class
```

In addition to the `ProcessConfiguration` method, which applies changes on the device, there is also a `TestConfiguration` method that can be used to validate a particular configuration file without any impact on the device on which the code is being run.

Forms

The `Forms` namespace has managed wrappers for three forms that can be used to collect an image from a camera (`CameraCaptureDialog`), select a contact (`ChooseContactDialog`), and select an image (`SelectPictureDialog`). The following code snippet makes use of each of the dialogs:

```
Imports Microsoft.WindowsMobile
Public Class Form1
    Private Sub Example(ByVal sender As System.Object, _
                        ByVal e As System.EventArgs) Handles SampleButton.Click

        Dim camera As New Forms.CameraCaptureDialog
        camera.Mode = Forms.CameraCaptureMode.Still
        camera.StillQuality = Forms.CameraCaptureStillQuality.High
        camera.Title = "Get me a picture!!!"
        If camera.ShowDialog() = Windows.Forms.DialogResult.OK Then
            MsgBox("Photo taken.....stored as" & camera.FileName)
        End If

        Dim picture As New Forms.SelectPictureDialog
        picture.CameraAccess = True
        picture.SortOrder = Forms.SortOrder.DateDescending
        If picture.ShowDialog() = Windows.Forms.DialogResult.OK Then
            MsgBox("Found that picture - " & picture.FileName)
        End If

        Dim contact As New Forms.ChooseContactDialog
        contact.RequiredProperties = New PocketOutlook.ContactProperty() _
                            {PocketOutlook.ContactProperty.Email1Address}
        contact.ChooseContactOnly = True
        If contact.ShowDialog Then
            MsgBox("Contact selected - " & contact.SelectedContactName)
        End If
    End Sub
End Class
```

PocketOutlook

The `PocketOutlook` namespace includes a series of classes that make sending and receiving e-mail and SMS messages straightforward. As the following sample shows, writing an e-mail is as easy as starting an Outlook session, putting the e-mail together, and sending it:

```
Imports Microsoft.WindowsMobile
Public Class Form1
    Private Sub POOMExample(ByVal sender As System.Object, _
                            ByVal e As System.EventArgs) Handles
SampleButton.Click
        Using poom As New PocketOutlook.OutlookSession
            Dim email As New PocketOutlook.EmailMessage
            email.To.Add(New
PocketOutlook.Recipient("destination@randomaccount.com"))
```

```
            email.Subject = "Sample Email"
            email.BodyText = "This email contains sample text to show how easy
email is..."
            poom.EmailAccounts(0).Send(email)
        End Using
    End Sub
End Class
```

Status

The `Status` namespace contains a wealth of information about the status of the device, including static attributes, such as whether there is a camera on the device, and dynamic attributes, such as the ActiveSync status. The following example shows how these two attributes can be queried:

```
Imports Microsoft.WindowsMobile
Public Class Form1
    Private Sub StatusExample(ByVal sender As System.Object, _
                              ByVal e As System.EventArgs) Handles
SampleButton.Click
        If Status.SystemState.ActiveSyncStatus = _
            Status.ActiveSyncStatus.Synchronizing Then _
                MsgBox("Active sync is synchronising now, don't go away!")
        If Status.SystemState.CameraPresent = True Then _
                MsgBox("There is a camera, why not take a photo")
    End Sub
End Class
```

Registry entries can also be queried using the `RegistryState` class in this namespace.

Telephony

The `Telephony` namespace contains a single class, `Phone`, which has a single static method called `Talk`, which can be used to initiate a phone call. An optional parameter, `showPrompt`, determines whether the user is prompted to proceed with the call or not. In the following code, the user is not prompted before the call is initiated:

```
Imports Microsoft.WindowsMobile
Public Class Form1
    Private Sub TelephonyExample(ByVal sender As System.Object, _
                                 ByVal e As System.EventArgs) _
                                        Handles SampleButton.Click
        Dim t As New Telephony.Phone
        t.Talk("0412413425", False)
    End Sub
End Class
```

Notification Broker

One of the significant improvements in Windows Mobile 5.0 is the Notification Broker, which can be used to notify an application of a particular system event. This may be a change in any of the status states or it may be an incoming SMS or e-mail. The following example shows how you can register your application to intercept an SMS containing a particular string (in this case, " : : "). If an incoming SMS is found to contain this string, then the application is notified via the appropriate event handler and given an opportunity to process the SMS, after which the SMS is deleted. The other `InterceptionAction` is to just notify the application, without deleting the SMS after processing:

```
Imports Microsoft.WindowsMobile.PocketOutlook
Imports Microsoft.WindowsMobile.PocketOutlook.MessageInterception

Public Class Form1
    'Create the Interceptor
    Dim SMSProcessor As New MessageInterceptor( _
                                    InterceptionAction.NotifyAndDelete, True)
    Private Sub NotificationExample(ByVal sender As System.Object, _
                            ByVal e As System.EventArgs) _
                                            Handles SampleButton.Click


        'Define the search condition, in this case must contain ::
        Dim msgCondition As New MessageCondition()
        msgCondition.Property = MessageProperty.Body
        msgCondition.ComparisonType = MessagePropertyComparisonType.Contains
        msgCondition.ComparisonValue = "::"
        SMSProcessor.MessageCondition = msgCondition

        'Attach an event handler
        AddHandler SMSProcessor.MessageReceived, _
                                    AddressOf SMSProcessor_MessageReceived
    End Sub

    'Event handler for when a matching SMS is received
    Private Sub SMSProcessor_MessageReceived _
                (ByVal sender As Object, ByVal e As MessageInterceptorEventArgs)
        Dim theSMS As SmsMessage = CType(e.Message, SmsMessage)
        MsgBox("Message: " & theSMS.Body)
        Me.BringToFront()
    End Sub

End Class
```

Note that there is a trick to writing these types of SMS-intercepting applications using the emulators. As mentioned in Chapter 43, some of the emulators have built-in radio stacks, which means that they can simulate sending and receiving SMS. If you want to test the SMS interceptor, you can send an SMS, using Pocket Outlook or another application on the emulator, to the emulator's built-in test number, which is +1 425 001 0001. The SMS is delayed so that it doesn't appear immediately, enabling you to navigate back to your application if needed.

Deployment

Deployment of device applications has been a much-debated topic, and numerous white papers have been written about how to package an application for installation. In the past, packaging an application required considerable fiddling within Visual Studio to generate an installer for a mobile application. Although Visual Studio 2005 provides much better support, several steps are still required to deliver an easy-to-install application. This section looks at how you can use CAB files to install your application, and describes how a desktop MSI installer can really make your application look professional.

CAB Files

The easiest way to deploy your application is via a *CAB file*, which is essentially a compressed file that contains all the assemblies and resources that your application requires to run. It can also contain registry settings that may need to be applied during installation. To install an application, the CAB file needs to be downloaded to the device before being executed. Executing the CAB file decompresses the contents, installs the application, and performs any installation activities. The final stage is to remove the CAB file from the device. If you use a storage card to deploy a CAB file to multiple devices, it is a good idea to make the card read-only so the CAB file does not get removed.

Visual Studio 2005 has a new project type called a Smart Device CAB Project, which is listed under Setup and Deployment projects in the Add New Project window, shown in Figure 44-13.

Selecting this project type adds a CAB project to your solution. Unlike an installer for the desktop, which has a number of views, the Smart Device CAB Project only has two views, which present a view of the file system and the registry settings. This is shown in the left-hand pane of Figure 44-14, where the primary output for the project DeviceApplication1 has been added to the CAB project, which is achieved by right-clicking on the CAB project and selecting Add⇨Project Output from the context menu.

The File System view can be used to add files and shortcuts on the device itself. Right-clicking on the Target Machine node in the File System view enables you to select Add Special Folder. This includes directories such as Programs, Start menu, and Startup. Right-clicking on one of the folders prompts you to add subfolders, project output, or files. These will be installed on the target machine when the CAB file is installed.

In the Properties window are several properties that can be configured for the CAB file itself. It is, of course, good practice to ensure that the Manufacturer and ProductName reflect the application being deployed.

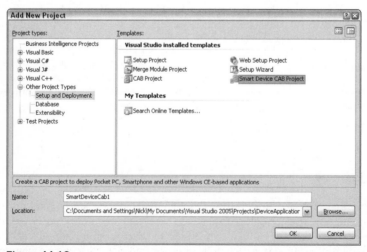

Figure 44-13

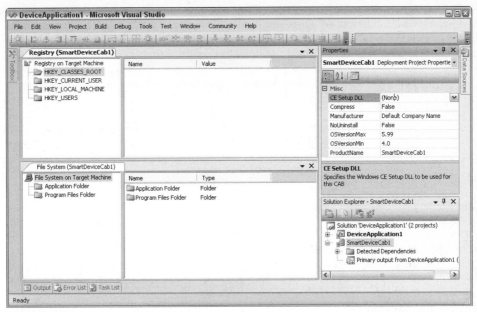

Figure 44-14

MSI Installer

The CAB project enables developers to create a CAB file that can be installed on a mobile device. The difficulty lies in getting the CAB file onto the device in the first place. Although as a developer you can easily copy the file to the device via ActiveSync, or even download the CAB file from a web site, unless your application is designed for fellow developers or IT professionals, it is necessary to have an easier mechanism by which the application can be installed.

This can be done using a desktop installer with a custom action to install the CAB using the ActiveSync CEAppMgr application (which can be run from `C:\Program Files\Microsoft ActiveSync\ CEAppMgr.exe`). The installer works as follows:

1. The end user double-clicks the MSI installer (e.g., MyApplication.msi).

2. The MSI installer copies files to the installation directory.

3. The MSI installer launches a custom installer action.

4. The custom installer action copies the installed files to an application directory used by CEAppMgr.

5. The custom installer action launches CEAppMgr to install CAB files on the device.

6. The Uninstaller: Custom installer action cleans up installed files in the application directory used by CEAppMgr.

The first step in creating this installer is to add a Setup project, which is done the same way as you would create an installer for a desktop application. Select Add⇨New Project from the right-click context menu in Solution Explorer and then select Setup Project from the Setup and Deployment node. This installer needs to do two things: copy the CAB file onto the desktop and initiate the custom installer action, which will install the CAB file on the device. The easiest way to add the CAB file to the installer is to right-click on the Installer node in the Solution Explorer window and select Add⇨Project Output. In the Add Project Output Group dialog, you then select Build Outputs from the CAB project to add to your installer project. This automatically adds the Build Outputs to the application folder; and because you will be copying the CAB file into the appropriate location with the custom installer action, it doesn't matter where the files are initially placed.

The next step is to add custom installer actions to copy the installed files to the CEAppMgr application folder and then to run the CEAppMgr, which installs the CAB on the device. To create the custom installer actions, perform the following steps:

1. Create a Class Library project within the existing solution.

2. Remove the default Class1 that is in the solution.

3. Add a new item based on the Installer Class item template.

4. Add event handlers for the `BeforeInstall` and `BeforeUninstall`.

5. Add an INI file to Class Library project (for example, DeviceApplication1.ini) and set the Build Action property to `Content`.

6. Add Class Library primary output and content files to the installer. This can be done by selecting Add⇨Project Outputs from the right-click context menu from the Installer node in Solution Explorer.

7. Wire up custom installer actions to the Setup Project. Select View⇨Custom Actions from the right-click context menu from the Setup Project node in Solution Explorer. Right-click the Custom Actions node and select Add Custom Action. Select the custom installer actions' class library from within the application folder. This attaches the necessary event handlers to the Windows installer to ensure that the custom installer actions are executed as part of the installation process.

These steps set up the template for the file structure and the custom installer actions. What remains is to fill in the contents for the INI file, which is used by CEAppMgr to install the correct CAB files, and to fill in the event handlers. The INI file needs to define the CAB files that are to be installed on the device for a particular application. The CEAppManager section is required, as it indicates that this is a configuration file for the CEAppMgr application and lists the component to be installed. The component section describes the application and provides a comma-delimited list of CAB files, without spaces, that are to be installed for this application:

```
[CEAppManager]
Version = 1.0
Component = DeviceApp

[DeviceApp]
Description = Sample Device Application
CabFiles = SmartDeviceCab1.cab
```

The `BeforeInstall` event handler needs to copy the application files from where they are installed by the desktop installer to an application folder that sits within the ActiveSync folder. It then needs to run the CEAppMgr process, passing it the INI file just created. The `BeforeUninstall` event handler has to clean up the application folder under ActiveSync to ensure that the application is entirely removed. The following code provides a template with which you can include your own installer activities:

```
Imports System.ComponentModel
Imports System.Configuration.Install
Imports System.IO
Imports Microsoft.Win32

Public Class Actions

    Public Sub New()
        MyBase.New()

        'This call is required by the Component Designer.
        InitializeComponent()

        'Add initialization code after the call to InitializeComponent

    End Sub

    Private Shared Function CEAppMgrApplicationDirectory() As String
        Dim activeSyncKey As RegistryKey = _
            Registry.LocalMachine.OpenSubKey(My.Resources.ActiveSync_Registry_Key)
        Dim activeSyncPath As String = _
        CStr(activeSyncKey.GetValue(My.Resources.CEAppMgr_Install_Dir_Registry_Key))
        Dim installPath As String = activeSyncPath + _
                                                My.Resources.Application_Directory
        activeSyncKey.Close()
        Return installPath
    End Function

    Private Shared Function CEAppMgrExecutable() As String
        Dim appMgrKey As RegistryKey = _
                    Registry.LocalMachine.OpenSubKey(My.Resources.CEApp_Mgr_Path)
        Dim appMgrPath As String = CStr(appMgrKey.GetValue(Nothing))
        appMgrKey.Close()
        Return appMgrPath
    End Function

    Private Sub ActionBeforeInstall(ByVal sender As Object, _
                        ByVal e As InstallEventArgs) _
                                            Handles Me.BeforeInstall

        Debugger.Break()

        'Copy installation files to the CEAppMgr application directory
        Dim installPath As String = CEAppMgrApplicationDirectory()
        Dim tmpPath As String = (New FileInfo(Me.Context.Parameters.Item _
                (My.Resources.Installation_Context_Assembly_Key))).DirectoryName
        My.Computer.FileSystem.CopyDirectory(tmpPath, installPath, True)

        'Run CEAppMgr to install the application on the device
        System.Diagnostics.Process.Start(CEAppMgrExecutable, _
                        """" + Path.Combine(installPath, _
                    My.Resources.Application_Cab_INI_File) + " "" ")
```

```
        End Sub

        Public Sub ActionBeforeUninstall(ByVal sender As Object, _
                                    ByVal e As InstallEventArgs) _
                                                    Handles Me.BeforeUninstall
            'Remove the installation files we manually copied
            My.Computer.FileSystem.DeleteDirectory(CEAppMgrApplicationDirectory, _
                                    FileIO.DeleteDirectoryOption.DeleteAllContents)
        End Sub
    End Class
```

This code makes use of a number of resources that are embedded in the Custom Installer Action class library. These constants are provided as shown in Figure 44-15, which illustrates the `String` resource editor tab of the project properties window.

Name	Value	Comment
ActiveSync_Registry_Key	SOFTWARE\Microsoft\Windows CE Services	
Application_Cab_INI_File	DeviceInstallation.ini	
Application_Directory	\DeviceApplication1	
CEApp_Mgr_Path	SOFTWARE\Microsoft\Windows\CurrentVersion\App Paths\CEAPPMGR.EXE	
CEAppMgr_Install_Dir_Registry_Key	InstalledDir	
Installation_Context_Assembly_Key	assemblypath	

Figure 44-15

The installer is now ready to be built and deployed to your clients. You can be sure that not only will the application be easy to install, it can also be successfully uninstalled without leaving any traces on the desktop computer. Clearly, in order for the application to be installed on the device, the device needs to be connected to the desktop computer through ActiveSync. However, CEAppMgr can be run at a later stage to install the application on any device attached to the computer via ActiveSync.

OpenNetCF Smart Devices Framework

Over the past couple of years, a number of Microsoft Most Valuable Professionals (MVPs) have been hard at work writing the OpenNETCF Smart Devices Framework (SDF). Unfortunately, working with version 1.0 of the .NET Compact Framework was a painful process because it lacked so much functionality. The SDF filled most, if not all, of the gaps that mobile developers came up against. It can be downloaded from the OpenNETCF web site at www.opennetcf.org.

Version 2.0 of the .NET Compact Framework has a much richer control library and exposes much of the functionality that was included in the SDF. The team at OpenNETCF will be releasing version 2.0 of the SDF, which again adds functionality that didn't quite make it into the current version of the .NET Compact Framework.

One of the other frameworks that the team at OpenNETCF has released is a part of some of the most common application blocks. These blocks include the Caching, Exception Management, and Smart Client. Using these blocks can greatly improve the design of the application and reduce the amount of code you have to write to implement similar features. The application blocks can also be downloaded from www.opennetcf.org.

Summary

As you have seen in this chapter, you can build quite complex mobile applications using Visual Studio 2005. The data-binding capabilities, combined with the rich functionality provided in Windows Mobile 5.0, enable you to harness the power of these devices.

Over the next several years, you are going to see a massive growth in mobile technologies as the lines dividing mobile phones, cameras, PDAs, laptops, and tablets begin to fade. Soon you will be writing applications that can reside on a device of any form factor, that will have the capability to record and display data, and can access an arbitrary set of device-specific features, such as taking a photo or making a phone call. With Visual Studio 2005, you are able to start the journey and begin developing for what will become the devices of the future.

Part VIII

Build and Deployment

45

Upgrading to Visual Studio 2005

Moving to a new development environment can sometimes be daunting. Visual Basic 6 users came head to head with a significant learning curve when Visual Basic .NET was first released in 2002. In fact, the transition to the new language was so overwhelming that some high-profile gurus in the language refused to move over and started campaigns to bring back the original language constructs.

Many corporations faced with the effort required in converting to .NET also decided to hold off, and as a result the current Visual Basic programming world is divided into two sizable camps, Visual Basic 6 programmers and Visual Basic .NET developers, with the rare few using both tools. The crux of the problem in transitioning to the new language was that the core Visual Basic language evolved to more closely suit object-oriented principles and to synchronize with the .NET Framework.

Therefore, instead of a language that had its origins in an interpretive compiler, Visual Basic .NET utilized the paradigm of everything being an object and therefore being treated as such; even forms and their controls were transformed into "just another" object that inherited from a class in the .NET Framework. As a result of these functional changes to the language, it was difficult to automatically upgrade Visual Basic 6 code to the new .NET environment, even with the Upgrade Wizard.

Besides the significant language changes, there were new concepts to consider, including proper inheritance and features such as method overloading. Coupled with these language-side issues, the environment itself also changed. Mostly the changes were improvements over the old way of doing things, but in the process of creating a new development environment, Microsoft left out some major features on which Visual Basic 6 developers depended. The most prominent feature that got left behind was the edit-and-continue process that enabled programmers to edit their code while the program was running in debug mode and then allow the program to continue running, taking advantage of the new altered code without having to restart the program.

When Microsoft began work on Visual Studio 2005, they told the programming world that their intention was to make this version of Visual Studio full of features that developers wanted, as opposed to those features that Microsoft itself thought they needed. Two such features that were on the lips of every Visual Basic programmer were the return of the edit-and-continue feature and a more convenient way of upgrading Visual Basic 6 code. Edit-and-continue is dealt with in Section IX, where the debugging features of Visual Studio 2005 are discussed, but this chapter is all about upgrading Visual Basic 6 code to Visual Basic 2005.

The Upgrade Process

You should approach the upgrading process carefully. In fact, the first serious decision you have to make is whether to upgrade at all. Visual Studio 2005 applications can interact with Visual Basic 6 applications through the COM Interop layer, so if you have an existing application that just needs to talk to new programs, then your best option may actually be to leave the VB6 project as is. However, if you need to do a major rewrite of an existing project, then it might be a great time to convert it up to Visual Basic 2005 to take advantage of the many benefits of producing applications in .NET 2.0.

Either way, besides the most basic program, it is most likely that the upgrade process will include a list of tasks as well as compilation errors and warnings, all of which need to be addressed before the converted program will run as expected. In addition, you'll need to check every conversion point in the application code to ensure that it still acts as you expect.

If you're going through a total rewrite of an existing application, you may even want to start a new project in Visual Studio 2005 and use the Upgrade Visual Basic 6 Code tool to migrate the old program code a section at a time to make it more manageable.

Getting Ready to Upgrade

To give the upgrade process the best chance of success, there are some guidelines to follow in preparing the Visual Basic 6 code for the conversion. These optional tasks minimize the impact of some common issues that the Upgrade Wizard faces, such as default properties.

Things That Just Won't Work

Some features of Visual Basic 6 are so incompatible with Visual Basic 2005's new language model that the Upgrade Wizard can't handle them at all. For instance, code that uses the graphic methods on forms (or even the `Line` and various `Shape` controls) cannot be converted at all and needs to be completely rewritten.

Similarly, applications that take advantage of the drag-and-drop commands in Visual Basic 6 need to have those sections recreated using the new techniques within .NET 2.0.

A large number of Windows API definitions cannot be converted over to Visual Basic 2005 because they rely on `Variant` and `Any`. Variants will be converted to Objects, which means in some cases the behavior of the application will change, while the Upgrade Wizard can't replicate the behavior of `Any`. However, the .NET Framework contains many functions that eliminate the need for calling the Windows API directly. Therefore, while you'll need to rewrite those sections of code that call Windows APIs, you can take advantage of the managed code functionality found in the framework instead.

One last issue worth mentioning is that if the Visual Basic 6 application uses DAO for its data access (such as to a Microsoft Access database), then it will require a reworking of the data access layer because Visual Studio 2005 doesn't support data-binding to DAO.

Changing the Original Code

The many issues that can occur during the upgrade can be loosely grouped into two sets. The first set of problems is items that work fine in Visual Basic 6 but don't work at all in Visual Basic 2005; however, changing them in the original code doesn't necessarily make sense. For instance, the graphics methods for a form such as Cls and PSet are not available in Visual Basic 2005. However, you can't easily change the code in Visual Basic 6 before you perform the upgrade to the new graphics methods, because the .NET Framework–based methods aren't available from the Visual Basic 6 code. Control examples include the Line and Shape controls mentioned previously; these don't have a corresponding component in .NET and are converted to empty Label controls at best.

In both of these situations, you're forced to accept your fate and perform development on the converted code to regain your original application's behavior.

However, other features of Visual Basic 6 that do not convert well in the Upgrade Wizard have alternatives in Visual Basic 6 itself. If you're more comfortable with working in Visual Basic 6, a little bit of work in the original code base can help immensely with the upgrade process.

For example, the Timer control in Visual Basic 6 has an Enabled property, but many programmers chose to simply set the Interval property to 0, which effectively paused the Timer. However, whenever you set the Interval value to 0 in Visual Basic 2005, it implicitly converts the setting to 1, which means the Timer continues to run and fire. To avoid this issue cropping up when you upgrade your application code, make sure you use the Enabled property instead of setting Interval to 0.

> *This problem is a great example of code that will be converted without error but have unexpected results. If you leave the code with the improperly coded* Interval = 0 *statement, your* Timer *may fire a little more frequently than you ever intended it to!*

Upgrading other Visual Basic 6 code features may produce warning messages that can be easily avoided by changing the code before the upgrade process. The most common issue of this type is the capability to use default properties in Visual Basic 6. This is the practice of simply referring to the object or control and letting Visual Basic determine what property should be used. For example, a TextBox has a default property of Text, so instead of assigning a string to the Text property explicitly like this

```
TextBox1.Text = myString
```

you can simply specify the TextBox1 control and Visual Basic implicitly assumes the Text property; the following line is the equivalent of the previous line of code in Visual Basic 6:

```
TextBox1 = myString
```

Visual Basic 2005 does not support default properties at all, requiring you to explicitly specify the property to which you're referring. The Upgrade Wizard does a great job of trying to determine what property it should use when converting the code, but sometimes it just doesn't know what to do. Figure 45-1 shows an example of this kind of problem — the Upgrade Wizard couldn't determine the default property of the ListView control's Item object.

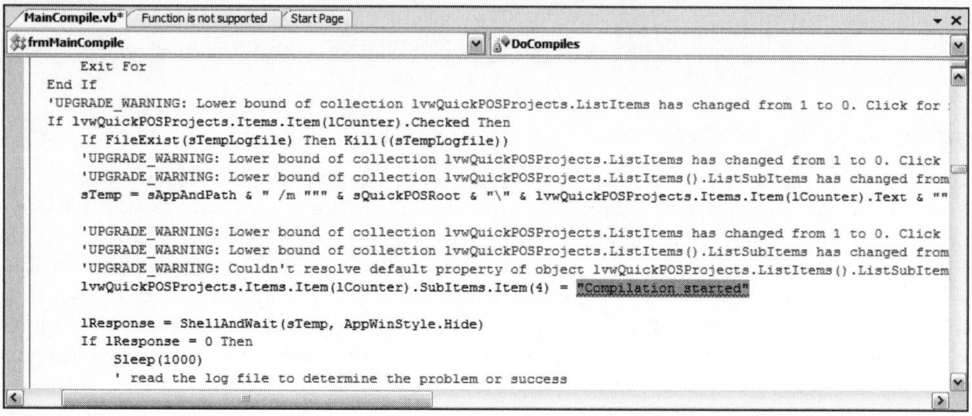

Figure 45-1

Explicitly coding the property names in the original Visual Basic 6 code in the first place avoids this problem entirely. The MSDN Library documentation that comes with Visual Studio has many other recommendations (look for the topics entitled *Preparing a Visual Basic 6.0 Application for Upgrading* and *Language Recommendations for Upgrading*).

Using the Upgrade Project Wizard

When you are ready to convert a Visual Basic 6 application project to Visual Basic 2005, you can do so by simply opening the project file (with a .vbj extension) in Visual Studio 2005. The Visual Studio IDE determines that the project is from an older version of Visual Basic and automatically starts the Visual Basic Upgrade Wizard.

After reviewing the goals of the Upgrade Wizard, click the Next button to progress to the first step. The first choice you have is whether the application should be converted to a Windows application (.exe) or a binary library such as a DLL or custom control. Normally this choice is taken out of your hands, as the wizard attempts to determine the project type by reading the original project information.

The next step is to select the destination for the Visual Basic 2005 version of the project (see Figure 45-2). Note that the Upgrade Wizard will not convert the project in place. In fact, it won't allow you to convert the application into anything but an empty folder. If you specify a location that doesn't exist, the wizard will ask you if you want it to create the folder automatically for you.

> *The default location for the wizard is a subfolder underneath the original project file's location, but you can set it to anywhere within your local file system.*

Your work is now done. Click Next to get to the confirmation page, and then click Next one more time to start the actual Upgrade Wizard. As the wizard progresses through the conversion, the dialog updates the status message with the current module and member being upgraded (see Figure 45-3). The status bar of the main Visual Studio IDE also dynamically updates, showing the percentage of completion for the upgrade process.

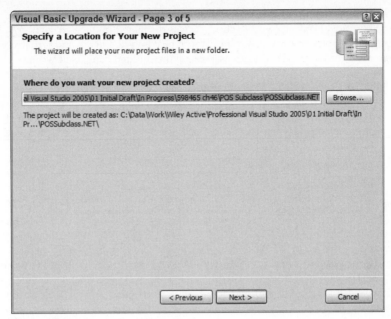

Figure 45-2

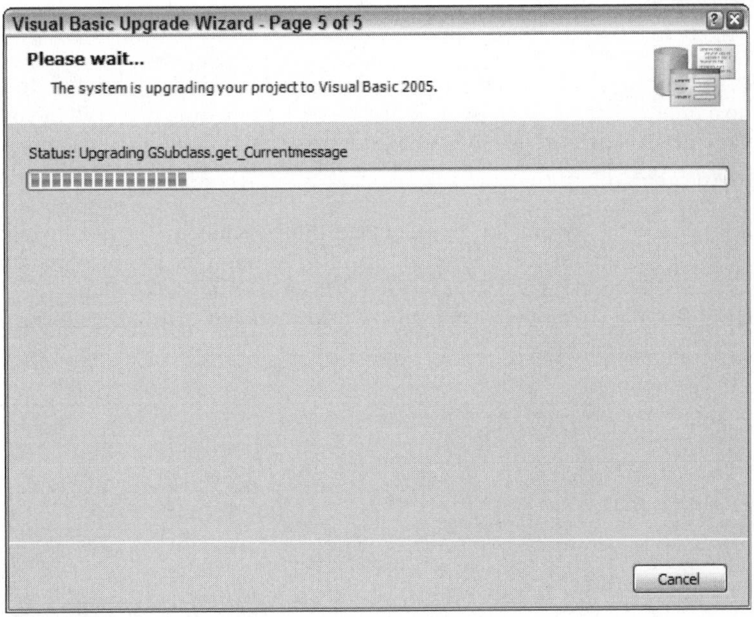

Figure 45-3

Most of the time, the Upgrade Wizard will complete the process and present you with a list of errors, warnings, and additional tasks for you to check (this is discussed in the next section "Checking the Upgrade Output"). However, some programs cannot be converted at all, and will present you with an error message. Usually, when this occurs it is because the original code itself wouldn't compile.

Figure 45-4 shows an example of the kind of message that can be produced. This example application didn't convert because the referenced DLLs in the project were not registered on the machine doing the conversion. As noted at the bottom of the message text, if this kind of error occurs, your first step should be to make sure the program compiles and runs in Visual Basic 6 before trying the Upgrade Wizard again.

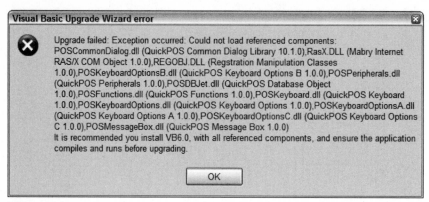

Visual Basic Upgrade Wizard error

Upgrade failed: Exception occurred: Could not load referenced components: POSCommonDialog.dll (QuickPOS Common Dialog Library 10.1.0),RasX.DLL (Mabry Internet RAS/X COM Object 1.0.0),REGOBJ.DLL (Regstration Manipulation Classes 1.0.0),POSKeyboardOptionsB.dll (QuickPOS Keyboard Options B 1.0.0),POSPeripherals.dll (QuickPOS Peripherals 1.0.0),POSDBJet.dll (QuickPOS Database Object 1.0.0),POSFunctions.dll (QuickPOS Functions 1.0.0),POSKeyboard.dll (QuickPOS Keyboard 1.0.0),POSKeyboardOptions.dll (QuickPOS Keyboard Options 1.0.0),POSKeyboardOptionsA.dll (QuickPOS Keyboard Options A 1.0.0),POSKeyboardOptionsC.dll (QuickPOS Keyboard Options C 1.0.0),POSMessageBox.dll (QuickPOS Message Box 1.0.0)
It is recommended you install VB6.0, with all referenced components, and ensure the application compiles and runs before upgrading.

OK

Figure 45-4

Unfortunately, sometimes you'll get a blank error message. This kind of error is extremely rare, and normally points to a project that is somehow incomplete, such as missing files. When you encounter this kind of error, you can still determine where the error occurred by viewing the log file that is produced as the Upgrade Wizard does its work.

This log file is located in the destination project folder you specified in the wizard, and is made up of XML nodes detailing each file as it is upgraded. Scrolling through the log you can identify the point at which the upgrade failed, and then look at that specific file's contents (see Figure 45-5). In this sample case, it turned out that the attempted conversion of the source file failed because the file didn't exist where the project file expected it to.

```
POSOptions.log   Function is not supported   Start Page                              ▾ ✕
            Upgraded = "True"
        />
        <File
            OldPath = "C:\Data\Work\Wiley Active\Professional Visual Studio 2005\(
            NewPath = "C:\Data\Work\Wiley Active\Professional Visual Studio 2005\(
            FileType = "Module"
            Upgraded = "True"
        />
        <File
            OldPath = "C:\Data\Work\Wiley Active\Professional Visual Studio 2005\(
            NewPath = "C:\Data\Work\Wiley Active\Professional Visual Studio 2005\(
            FileType = "Module"
            Upgraded = "False"
        />
        <Issue
            Type = "Global Error"
            Number = "83BD8814-6D52-4F59-B392-A7837C4DC5F2"
        />
    </UpgradeLog>
```

Figure 45-5

Checking the Upgrade Output

When the Upgrade Wizard is complete, it opens the new Visual Basic 2005 project in the IDE. If there are any issues to address, they are added to the Task List and the Error List with all the associated IntelliSense formatting that comes with warnings and errors applied to the code listings themselves. In addition, an Upgrade Report is generated and added to the project's file list in the Solution Explorer. Examining each of these upgrade output elements is the best way to make sure your application was converted successfully.

Task List

The first port of call when reviewing the upgrade output is the Task List. Visual Studio 2005 should display this automatically, but if it's not shown, use the View⇨Other Windows⇨Task List menu command to display it. The result of a typical conversion will appear similar to what is shown in Figure 45-6.

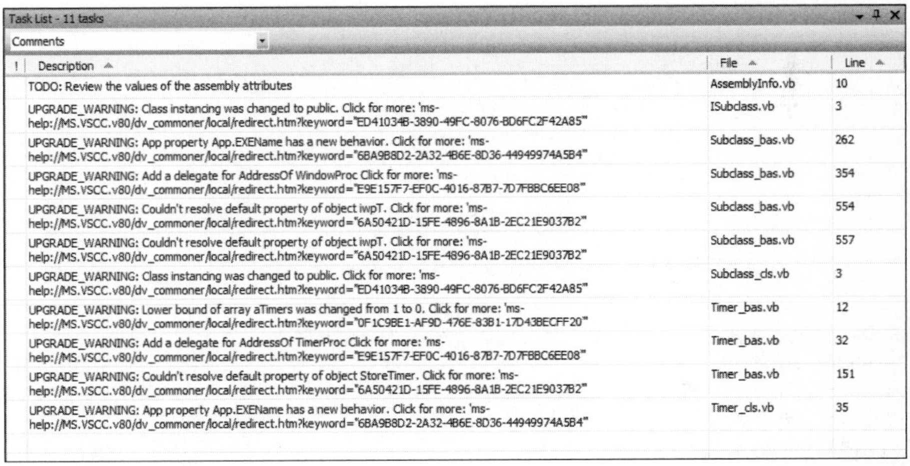

Figure 45-6

Generally, the warnings and TODO tasks are added to the code where actual compilation warnings or errors will not occur. This is because while the Upgrade Wizard was able to successfully convert the code to what it expects is the correct Visual Basic 2005 code, you are encouraged to review its changes.

The majority of messages in this list will be of the variety that you can simply acknowledge and delete. For instance, Figure 45-6 shows a warning about the lower bound of an array being changed from 1 to 0. This is because arrays in Visual Basic 6 are 1-based, skipping over the 0th element, while Visual Basic 2005 follows the more common mechanism of including a 0th element in the array. While most of the time you can simply ignore the extra element in the array, some particular code constructs may exhibit different behavior.

The other warnings in the list may require more interaction. Again, looking at the sample list in Figure 45-6, there are some warnings about default properties for certain objects not being resolved. This situation causes a compilation error and needs to be addressed before the converted project can be built successfully.

Each entry in the Task List links to the associated line of code containing the problem. Double-clicking the entry in the list takes you directly to the line in question and the full warning message (see Figure 45-7).

Every warning message also contains a link to a documentation entry in the MSDN Library explaining why there could be an issue with the particular statement. For example, the warning shown in Figure 45-7 indicates that the `App.EXEName` was converted to `My.Application.Info.Assembly Name`, but that there are differences between the two objects. Clicking the link ultimately takes you to a help topic that explains in great detail any differences between the old Visual Basic 6 `App` object and its equivalent in Visual Basic 2005.

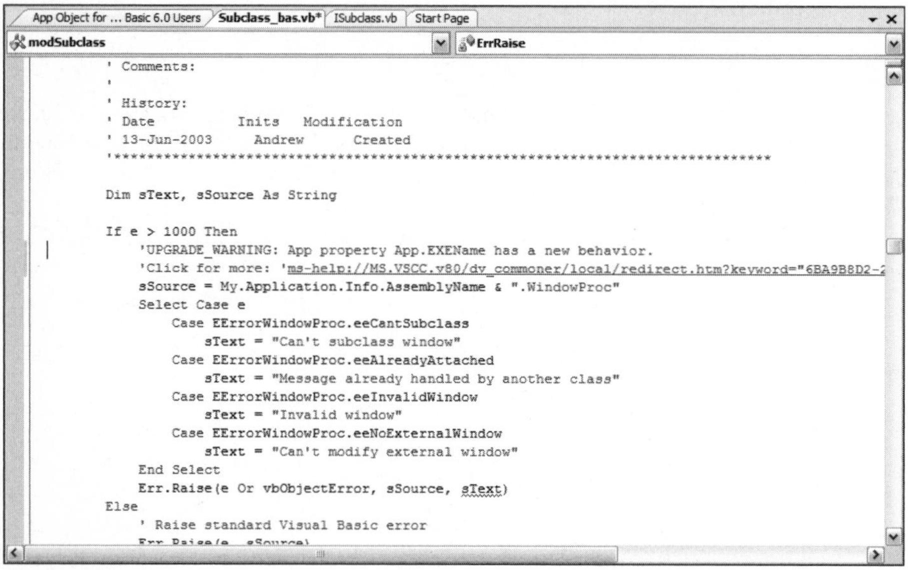

Figure 45-7

Errors and Warnings

Once you've reviewed the Task List, you should next turn to the Error List tool window (accessible via the View⇨Error List menu command). Because Visual Basic 2005 performs background compilation of code, any compilation errors that have been produced in the process of creating the new project are automatically flagged, added to the Error List, and marked in the code through the IntelliSense engine.

Figure 45-8 shows a sample Error List after the upgrade of a Visual Basic DLL project. This project was very small but contained a sizeable number of errors due to the purpose of the code. As mentioned previously, the `As Any` construct is not supported in Visual Basic and cannot be upgraded (you would need to define individual declarations for each variable type you were going to pass to the function). In addition, the code is using the unsupported `ObjPtr` function.

Some errors will be easier to fix. While the Upgrade Wizard may not be able to determine the default property of the `Item` object in a `ListView`, a human programmer can easily determine that the `Text` property was intended to be used, and correct it in just a few moments.

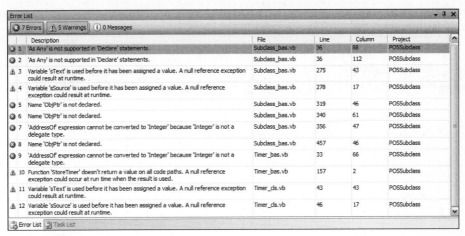

Figure 45-8

While compilation warnings don't stop your application from running, you should seriously consider and investigate each warning after an upgrade process to ensure that the expected behavior will occur. In the sample shown in Figure 45-8, errors 3 and 4 occur because String variables are accessed without first being assigned a value (you could leave these, or correct them by setting them to vbNullString in the declaration of each variable).

However, error 10 may be more serious depending on how the Upgrade Wizard handled the function. In some cases the wizard would be able to convert the appropriate statements to Return values, but if the return type is an unusual type it may not even be able to do that. Either way, you should definitely investigate the code that has produced the warning.

Upgrade Report

If you prefer a more visually pleasing view of the upgrade output, you can view the Upgrade Report. This report is generated after the Upgrade Wizard has completed and is placed in the project's folder with a name of _UpgradeReport.htm. It is then added to the Files list in the Solution Explorer.

Opening the page in a browser shows a nicely formatted report, as shown in Figure 45-9. At the top of the report is a summary showing how many errors and warnings were found during the upgrade process and of what type.

Underneath this summary section is a details table containing the errors per physical file contained in the project. This details view is handy for determining which parts of the project require the most work. Each of the tables can be collapsed and expanded to manage the detail.

Printing the report will only include the visible information; if you need to print the report in its entirety, make sure you first expand all nodes in both tables.

Chapter 45

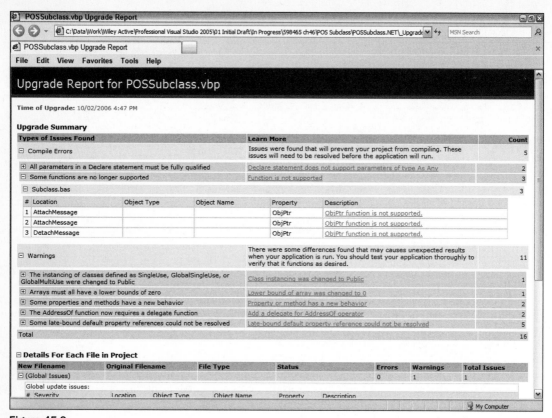

Figure 45-9

Unflagged Issues

Some issues can crop up in your conversion that are not flagged at all. These are usually related to situations that the Upgrade Wizard cannot determine, such as differences in literal value meanings.

A great example of this is the kinds of errors that can occur at runtime. When trapping errors using the `On Error` statement, often code is hard-coded with specific error numbers. Because the behavior may be different in Visual Basic 2005, different errors may be produced, which can cause unexpected results. The MSDN documentation has the following sample listing that illustrates this issue:

```
On Local Error GoTo Result
Dim x() As Boolean
Dim y As Variant

y = x(10)

Result:
If Err.Number = 9 Then
    ' Do something.
Else
    ' Do something else.
End If
```

When this code is run in Visual Basic 6 it will generate an `Err` object with a value of 9, which means "Subscript out of range." However, because Visual Basic 2005 requires you to initialize any object (which includes arrays) before using it, you will get a different error number.

Because this kind of unseen issue can occur, it is always highly recommended to do a complete code review of upgraded projects.

The Upgrade Visual Basic 6 Tool

If you need only to convert a block of code instead of an entire project, whether it's a single code statement or a full module, you will find the Upgrade Visual Basic 6 Code tool extremely useful. New to Visual Studio 2005, this utility is available from the Tool menu when you are editing a class or module in Code view.

When you start the utility, it displays a small dialog window containing a blank text area in which you can enter the Visual Basic 6 code to be converted (as shown in Figure 45-10). If the code uses COM objects, you can add the references to each COM object you require in the References tab.

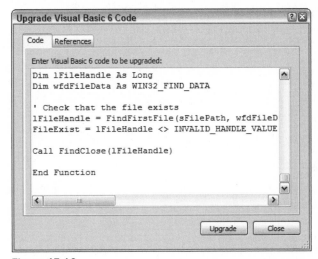

Figure 45-10

When the code and references are ready for conversion, click the Upgrade button to start the conversion process. This uses the same internal engine as the Upgrade Wizard, and automatically inserts the newly converted Visual Basic 2005 code into the module at the current insertion point. Any necessary COM references are automatically added to the project's reference list.

Some additional errors may occur when converting a small block of Visual Basic code, such as converting a statement that includes an undefined variable. To avoid these, try to include everything that the particular code will need prior to clicking the Upgrade button.

Summary

Visual Studio 2005 comes with two utilities to migrate your Visual Basic 6 code over to the new language constructs — an Upgrade Wizard to convert complete projects to Visual Basic 2005, and a code snippet converter utility for converting individual functions or single modules of code. The two tools in conjunction enable you to upgrade Visual Basic 6 code more easily than ever, and along with the new features of Visual Studio 2005 (such as edit-and-continue), pave the way for Visual Basic 6 programmers to transition to .NET.

Build Customization

While you can build most of your projects using the default compilation options set up by Visual Studio 2005, occasionally you'll need to modify some aspect of the build process to achieve what you want. This chapter looks at the various build options available to you in both Visual Basic and C#, outlining what the different settings do so you can customize them to suit your own requirements.

In addition, you'll learn how Visual Studio 2005 uses the new MSBuild engine to perform its compilations and how you can get under the hood of the configuration files that control the compilation of your projects.

General Build Options

Before you even get started on a project, you can modify some settings in the Options pages for Visual Studio 2005. These options apply to every project and solution that you open in the IDE, and as such can be used to customize your general experience when it comes to compiling your projects.

The first port of call for professional Visual Basic developers should be the General page of the Projects and Solutions group. By default, the Visual Basic setup of the IDE hides some of the build options from view, so the only way to show them is to activate the Show Advanced Build Configurations option.

When this is active, the IDE displays the Build Configuration options in the My Project pages, and the Build➪Configuration Manager menu command is also accessible. Other language environments don't need to do this as these options are activated on startup (although you could certainly turn them off if you didn't want them cluttering your menus and pages).

The other option on this page relating to building your projects is whether or not to automatically show the Error List if compilation errors are encountered during the build process. In this case, all language configurations have the option turned on.

The Build and Run options page (shown in Figure 46-1) in the Projects and Solutions group has many more options available to you to customize the way your builds take place.

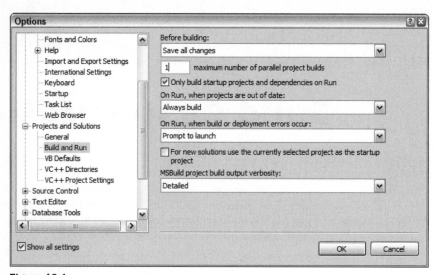

Figure 46-1

Under some environment setups, the Show All Settings option will not be visible. It's only there to simplify Options access for Visual Basic developers.

It's unclear from this page, but some of these options affect only C++ projects, so it's worth running through each option, what it does, and what languages it affects:

❑ **Before building:** This tells Visual Studio how to handle changes that have been made to any part of your project prior to the build process. You have three options:

    ❑ **Save all changes** automatically saves any changes without prompting you. This is perhaps the best option, as you don't have to remember to save your work. This is the default setting.

    ❑ **Save changes to open documents only** also automatically saves changes, but only to open documents. Previous versions of Visual Studio would not allow you to close an edited file without either saving it or canceling the changes. However, Visual Studio 2005 allows you to do so.

    ❑ **Prompt to save changes to open documents** gives you the chance to save any changes before the build commences. When the build process is started it displays a dialog prompting you to save the changes or not. If you decline to save the changes, the build still continues but uses the last saved version of the file. This option can be good to use when you want to know when you've made changes (perhaps inadvertently) to the source code.

❑ **Maximum number of parallel project builds:** This controls how many simultaneous build processes can be active at any one time (assuming the solution being compiled has multiple projects). This option only affects how C++ solutions are built and has no effect on Visual Basic or C# projects.

❑ **Only build startup projects and dependencies on Run:** This option only builds the part of the solution directly connected to the startup projects. This means that any projects that are not dependencies for the startup projects are excluded from the default build process. This option is active by default, so if you've got a solution that has multiple projects called by the startup projects through late-bound calls or other similar means, they will not be built automatically. You can either deactivate this option or manually build those projects separately.

❑ **On Run, when projects are out of date:** This option is used for C++ projects only and gives you three options for out-of-date projects (projects that have changed since the last build). The default is Prompt to Build, which gives you an option to build for each out-of-date project. The Always Build option forces the build process to occur whenever you run the application, while the Never Build option always uses the previous build of out-of-date projects. Note that this only applies to the Run command, and if you force a build through the Build menu, projects are rebuilt according to the other settings in the build configuration and on this Options page.

❑ **On Run, when build or deployment errors occur:** This controls the action to take when errors occur during the build process. Despite official documentation to the contrary, this option does indeed affect the behavior of builds in Visual Basic and C#. Your options here are the default Prompt to Launch, which displays a dialog prompting you for which action to take; Do Not Launch, which does not start the solution and returns to design time; and Launch Old Version, which ignores compilation errors and runs the last successful build of the project.

The option to launch an old version enables you to ignore errors in subordinate projects and still run your application; but because it doesn't warn you that errors occurred, you run the risk of getting confused about what version of the project is active.

Note that when you use the Prompt to Launch option, if you subsequently check the "Do not show this dialog again" option in the prompt dialog, this setting will be updated to either Do Not Launch or Launch Old Version depending on whether you to choose to continue or not.

❑ **For new solutions use the currently selected project as the startup project:** This option is useful when you're building a solution with multiple projects. When the solution is being built, the Visual Studio build process assumes that the currently selected project is the startup project and determines all dependencies and the starting point for execution from there.

❑ **MSBuild project build output verbosity:** Visual Studio 2005 uses the new MSBuild engine for its compilation. MSBuild produces its own set of compilation output, reporting on the state of each project as it's built. You have the option to control how much of this output is reported to you:

    ❑ By default, the MSBuild verbosity is set to Minimal, which produces only a very small amount of information about each project, but you can turn it off completely by setting this option to Quiet, or expand on the information you get by choosing one of the more detailed verbosity settings.

❑ MSBuild output is sent to the Output window, which is accessible via View➪Other Windows➪Output (under some environmental setups this will be View➪Output). If you can't see your build output, make sure you have set the Show Output From option to Build (see Figure 46-2).

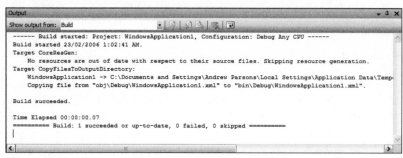

Figure 46-2

It's also worth taking a look at the other Options pages in the Projects and Solutions category, as they control the way Visual Basic deals with its compilation options by default (Option Explicit, Option Strict, and Option Compare), and other C++-specific options relating to build.

Of note for C++ developers is the capability to specify PATH variables for the different component types of their projects, such as executables and include files, for different platform builds; and whether or not to log the build output.

Batch Building

You can perform batch builds of multiple project configurations. If your project has multiple configurations defined, an additional command is displayed on the Build menu to perform a Batch Build. The Batch Build dialog enables you to select which configurations should be built from those defined in the solution (see Figure 46-3). For instance, you can build a debug version of the application, complete with debugging symbols, at the same time as a full release version of the solution, without any debugging and trace information.

Manual Dependencies

You can also set manual project dependencies to indicate how projects are related to each other. This is useful if you're using the "Only build startup projects and dependencies on Run" setting to enforce the compilation of your late-bound projects. You can access the dialog shown in Figure 46-4 by selecting either the Project➪Project Dependencies or Project➪Build Order menu commands.

Note that these menu commands are only available when you have a solution with multiple projects in the IDE.

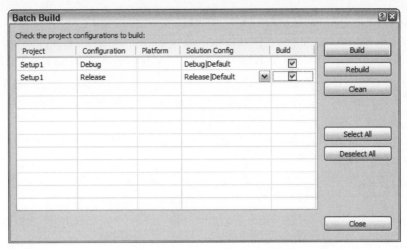

Figure 46-3

Figure 46-4

You first select the project that is dependent on others from the drop-down, and then check the projects it depends on in the bottom list. Any dependencies that are automatically detected by Visual Studio 2005 will already be marked in this list. The Build Order tab can be used to confirm the order in which the projects will be built.

Visual Basic Compile Page

Visual Basic projects have an additional set of options that control how the build process will occur. To access the compile options for a specific project, open My Project by double-clicking its entry in the Solution Explorer. When the project Options page is shown, navigate to the Compile page from the list on the left side (see Figure 46-5).

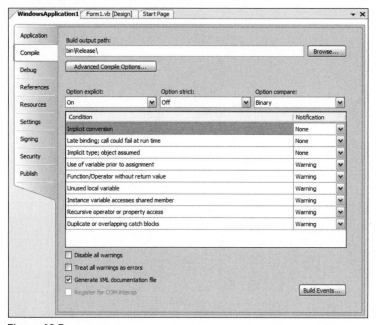

Figure 46-5

The Build Output Path option controls where the executable version (application or DLL) of your project is stored. For Visual Basic, the default setting is the `bin\Release\` directory, but you can change this by browsing to the desired location. The majority of the other settings on this page are dealt with in other chapters. Particularly, the conditions and warning-related options are discussed in Chapter 29.

You should be aware of two additional sets of hidden options. The Build Events button in the lower-right corner is available to Visual Basic developers who want to run actions or scripts before or after the build has been performed. They are discussed in a moment.

Advanced Compiler Settings

Clicking the Advanced Compile Options button displays the Advanced Compiler Settings dialog (see Figure 46-6) in which you can fine-tune the build process for the selected project, with settings divided into two broad groups: Optimizations and Compilation Constants.

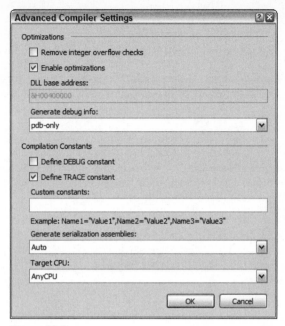

Figure 46-6

Optimizations

The settings in the Optimizations group control how the compilation is performed to make the built output or the build process itself faster or to minimize the output size. Normally, you can leave these options alone, but if you do require tweaks to your compilation, here's a summary of what each option does:

- ❑ **Remove integer overflow checks:** By default, your code is checked for any instance of a possible integer overflow, which can be a potential cause for memory leaks. Deactivating this option removes those checks, resulting in a faster-running executable at the expense of safety.

- ❑ **Enable optimizations:** The default behavior for Visual Basic projects is to disable all compiler optimizations to ensure an accurate execution, but you can enable the optimizations, which results in a faster-running executable that may not have an exact behavior due to the differences in the optimization code.

- ❑ **DLL base address:** Used for, you guessed it, DLLs, this option enables you to specify the base address of the DLL in hexadecimal format. This option is disabled when the project type will not produce a DLL.

- ❑ **Generate debug info:** This controls when debug information will be generated into your application output. By default, the option is set to pdb-only, which will only produce PDB debugging information, but you can either turn debugging information off completely or set the option to Full to include additional debugging sources.

Compilation Constants

Compilation constants can be used to control what information is included in the build output and even what code is compiled. The Compilation Constants options control the following:

❑ **Define DEBUG constant and Define TRACE constant:** Enable debug and trace information to be included in the compiled application based on the DEBUG and TRACE flags, respectively.

❑ **Custom constants:** If your application build process requires custom constants you can specify them here in the form ConstantName="Value". If you have multiple constants, they should be delimited by commas.

❑ **Generate serialization assemblies:** By default this option is set to Auto, which enables the build process to determine whether serialization assemblies are needed or not, but you can change it to On or Off if you want to hard-code the behavior.

❑ **Target CPU:** Depending on what CPU types are known to your system, this option enables you to optimize the build output to a specific platform. The default option of AnyCPU provides output that can be run on any CPU capable of running .NET 2.0 software.

Build Events

You can perform additional actions before or after the build process by adding them to an events list. Click the Build Events button on the My Project Compile page to display the Build Events dialog (shown in Figure 46-7).

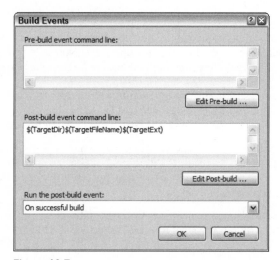

Figure 46-7

Each action you want to perform should be on a separate line, and can be added directly into either the "Pre-build event command line" text area or the "Post-build event command line" text area, or you can use the Edit Pre-build and Edit Post-build buttons to access the known predefined aliases that you can use in the actions.

Shown in Figure 46-8, the Event Command Line dialog includes a list of macros you can use in the creation of your actions. A value is displayed for each macro so you know exactly what text will be included if you use it.

In this sample, the developer has created a command line of $(TargetDir)$(TargetFileName)$(TargetExt), assuming that it would execute the built application when finished. However, analyzing the values of each of the macros, it's easy to see that the extension will be included twice, which can be amended quickly by either simply removing the $(TargetExt) macro or replacing the $(TargetFileName) macro with $(TargetFile).

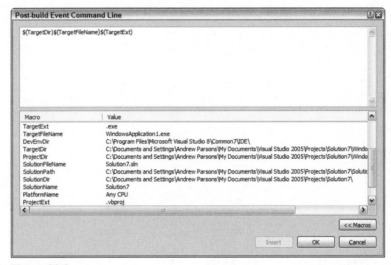

Figure 46-8

C# Build Pages

C# provides its own set of build options. In general, the options are the same as those available to a Visual Basic project, but in a different location because it's more likely that C# programmers will want to tweak the output than Visual Basic developers, who are typically more interested in rapid development than fine-tuning performance.

Instead of a single Compile page in the project property pages, C# has a Build page and a Build Events page. The Build Events page acts in exactly the same way as the Build Events dialog in Visual Basic, so refer to the previous discussion for information on that page.

As you can see in Figure 46-9, many of the options on the Build page have direct correlations to settings found in the Compile page or in the Advanced Compiler Settings area of Visual Basic. Some settings, such as the Define DEBUG constant and the Define TRACE constant, are identical to their Visual Basic counterparts.

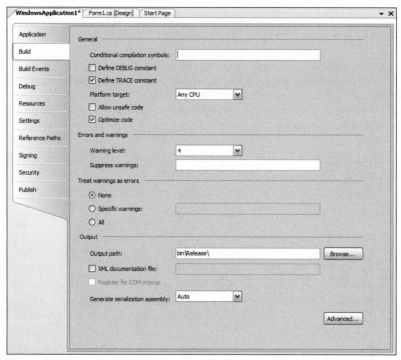

Figure 46-9

However, some are renamed to fit in with a C-based vocabulary, so Allow Unsafe Code is effectively the same as the Visual Basic "Remove integer overflow checks," "Optimize code is equivalent to Enable optimizations," and so on.

The Errors and Warnings section of the C# Build page, covered in Chapter 29, is the same as the Visual Basic Conditions and Warnings settings, as they deal with conditional and pre-emptive messages warning you of potential errors in your code.

Advanced

Clicking the Advanced button on the Build page invokes the Advanced Build Settings dialog, shown in Figure 46-10, which includes settings that are not accessible to Visual Basic developers. These settings give you tight control over how the build will be performed, including information on the internal errors that occur during the compilation process and what debug information is to be generated.

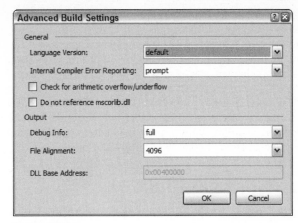

Figure 46-10

These settings are mostly self-explanatory, so the following list is a quick summary of what effect each one has on the build:

❏ **Language Version:** Specifies which version of the C# language to use. The default is to use the current version. In Visual Studio 2005, the only other option is ISO-1, which restricts the available language features to the ISO standard.

❏ **Internal Compiler Error Reporting:** If errors occur during the compilation (not compilation errors, but errors with the compilation process itself), you can have information sent to Microsoft so they can add it to their revision of the compiler code. The default setting is prompt, which asks you whether you want to send the information to Microsoft.

Other values include none, which won't send the information; send, to automatically send the error information; and queue, which adds the details to a queue to be sent later.

❏ **Check for arithmetic overflow/underflow:** Checks for overflow errors that can cause unsafe execution. Underflow errors occur when the precision of the number is too fine for the system.

❏ **Do not reference mscorlib.dll:** By default, the mscorlib.dll, which defines the System namespace, is automatically referenced in your project, but you can check this option to build your own System namespace and associated objects.

❏ **Debug Info:** Identical to the Visual Basic Generate debug info setting

❏ **File Alignment:** Used to set the section boundaries in the output file, and enables you to control the internal layout of the compiled output. The values are measured in bytes.

❏ **DLL Base Address:** Identical to the Visual Basic setting of the same name

Using these settings for your projects enables you to closely control how the build process will perform. However, you have another option with Visual Studio 2005, which is to edit the build scripts directly. This is made possible because Visual Studio 2005 uses MSBuild for its compilations.

MSBuild

MSBuild is the new compilation engine Microsoft has released simultaneously with Visual Studio 2005. It uses XML-based configuration files to identify the layout of a build project, including all of the settings discussed earlier in this chapter, as well as what files should be included in the actual compilation.

In fact, Visual Studio 2005 uses MSBuild configuration files as its project definition files, in place of the old project file formats used by previous versions of Visual Studio. This enables the MSBuild engine to be used automatically when compiling your applications within the IDE because the same settings file is used for both your project definition in the IDE and the build process.

How Visual Studio Uses MSBuild

As already mentioned, the contents of Visual Studio 2005 project files are based on the MSBuild XML Schema and can be edited directly in Visual Studio so you can customize how the project is loaded and compiled.

However, to edit the project file you need to effectively remove the project's active status from the Solution Explorer. Right-click the project you want to edit in the Solution Explorer and choose the Unload Project command from the bottom of the context menu that is displayed.

The project will be collapsed in the Solution Explorer and marked as unavailable. In addition, any open files that belong to the project will be closed while it is unloaded from the solution. Right-click the project entry again and an additional menu command will be available to edit the project file (see Figure 46-11).

Figure 46-11

The XML-based project file will be correspondingly opened in the XML editor of Visual Studio 2005, enabling you to collapse and expand nodes. The following listing is a sample MSBuild project file for an empty Visual Basic project:

```xml
<?xml version="1.0" encoding="utf-8"?>
<Project DefaultTargets="Build"
xmlns="http://schemas.microsoft.com/developer/msbuild/2003">
  <PropertyGroup>
    <Configuration Condition=" '$(Configuration)' == '' ">Debug</Configuration>
    <Platform Condition=" '$(Platform)' == '' ">AnyCPU</Platform>
    <ProductVersion>8.0.50727</ProductVersion>
    <SchemaVersion>2.0</SchemaVersion>
    <ProjectGuid>{7ED1BE7E-502C-4AF2-83FD-F441848A567B}</ProjectGuid>
    <OutputType>WinExe</OutputType>
    <RootNamespace>Project1</RootNamespace>
    <AssemblyName>Project1</AssemblyName>
    <MyType>Empty</MyType>
  </PropertyGroup>
  <PropertyGroup Condition=" '$(Configuration)|$(Platform)' == 'Debug|AnyCPU' ">
    <DebugSymbols>true</DebugSymbols>
    <DebugType>full</DebugType>
    <DefineDebug>true</DefineDebug>
    <DefineTrace>true</DefineTrace>
    <OutputPath>bin\Debug\</OutputPath>
    <DocumentationFile>
    </DocumentationFile>
  </PropertyGroup>
  <PropertyGroup Condition=" '$(Configuration)|$(Platform)' == 'Release|AnyCPU' ">
    <DebugType>pdbonly</DebugType>
    <DefineDebug>false</DefineDebug>
    <DefineTrace>true</DefineTrace>
    <Optimize>true</Optimize>
    <OutputPath>bin\Release\</OutputPath>
    <DocumentationFile>
    </DocumentationFile>
  </PropertyGroup>
  <ItemGroup>
    <Import Include="Microsoft.VisualBasic" />
    <Import Include="System" />
  </ItemGroup>
  <ItemGroup>
    <Folder Include="My Project\" />
  </ItemGroup>
  <Import Project="$(MSBuildBinPath)\Microsoft.VisualBasic.targets" />
  <!-- To modify your build process, add your task inside one of the targets below
and uncomment it.
      Other similar extension points exist, see Microsoft.Common.targets.
  <Target Name="BeforeBuild">
  </Target>
  <Target Name="AfterBuild">
  </Target>
  -->
</Project>
```

The XML contains the information about the build. In fact, most of these nodes directly relate to settings you saw earlier in the Compile and Build pages, but also include any Framework namespaces that are required.

When the project includes additional files, such as forms and user controls, each one is defined in the project file with its own set of nodes. For example, the following listing shows the additional XML that is included in a standard WindowsApplication project, identifying the Form, its designer code file, and the additional system files required for a Windows-based application:

```
<ItemGroup>
  <Compile Include="Form1.vb">
    <SubType>Form</SubType>
  </Compile>
  <Compile Include="Form1.Designer.vb">
    <DependentUpon>Form1.vb</DependentUpon>
    <SubType>Form</SubType>
  </Compile>
  <Compile Include="My Project\AssemblyInfo.vb" />
  <Compile Include="My Project\Application.Designer.vb">
    <AutoGen>True</AutoGen>
    <DependentUpon>Application.myapp</DependentUpon>
  </Compile>
  <Compile Include="My Project\Resources.Designer.vb">
    <AutoGen>True</AutoGen>
    <DesignTime>True</DesignTime>
    <DependentUpon>Resources.resx</DependentUpon>
  </Compile>
  <Compile Include="My Project\Settings.Designer.vb">
    <AutoGen>True</AutoGen>
    <DependentUpon>Settings.settings</DependentUpon>
    <DesignTimeSharedInput>True</DesignTimeSharedInput>
  </Compile>
</ItemGroup>
```

You can also include additional tasks in the build process in the included Target nodes for BeforeBuild and AfterBuild, but if you use a new PropertyGroup node that includes PreBuildEvent and PostBuildEvent entries, you can then view the included actions in the Build Events window discussed earlier in this chapter.

For instance, if you wanted to execute the application after it was successfully built, you could include the following XML block immediately before the closing </Project> tag:

```
<PropertyGroup>
  <PostBuildEvent>$(TargetDir)$(TargetFileName)</PostBuildEvent>
</PropertyGroup>
```

Once you've finished editing the project file's XML, you need to re-enable it in the solution by right-clicking the project's entry in the Solution Explorer and selecting the Reload Project command. If you still have the project file open, Visual Studio will close it automatically.

MSBuild Schema

An extended discussion on the MSBuild engine is beyond the scope of this book. However, it's useful to understand the different components that make up the MSBuild project file so you can look at and update your own projects.

Four major elements form the basis of the project file: *items*, *properties*, *targets*, and *tasks*. Brought together, you can use these four node types to create a configuration file that describes a project in full, as shown in the previous sample Visual Basic project file.

Items

Items are those elements that define inputs to the build system and project. They are defined as children of an `ItemGroup` node, and the most common item is the `Compile` node used to identify to MSBuild that the specified file is to be included in the compilation. The following snippet from a project file shows an `Item` element defined for the `Form1.Designer.vb` file of a WindowsApplication project:

```
<ItemGroup>
  <Compile Include="Form1.Designer.vb">
    <DependentUpon>Form1.vb</DependentUpon>
    <SubType>Form</SubType>
  </Compile>
</ItemGroup>
```

Properties

`PropertyGroup` nodes are used to contain any properties defined to the project. Properties are typically key/value pairings. They can only contain a single value and are used to store the project settings you can access in the Build and Compile pages in the IDE.

`PropertyGroup` nodes can be optionally included by specifying a `Condition` attribute, as shown in the following sample listing:

```
<PropertyGroup Condition=" '$(Configuration)|$(Platform)' == 'Release|AnyCPU' ">
    <DebugType>pdbonly</DebugType>
    <DefineDebug>false</DefineDebug>
    <DefineTrace>true</DefineTrace>
    <Optimize>true</Optimize>
    <OutputPath>bin\Release\</OutputPath>
</PropertyGroup>
```

This XML defines a `PropertyGroup` that will only be included in the build if the project is being built as a `Release` for the `AnyCPU` platform. Each of the five property nodes within the `PropertyGroup` uses the name of the property as the name of the node.

Targets

`Target` elements enable you to arrange tasks (discussed in the next section) into a sequence. Each `Target` element should have a `Name` attribute to identify it, and it can be called directly, thus enabling you to provide multiple entry points into the build process. The following snippet defines a `Target` with a name of `BeforeBuild`:

```
<Target Name="BeforeBuild">
</Target>
```

Tasks

Tasks define actions that MSBuild will execute under certain conditions. You can define your own tasks or take advantage of the many built-in tasks such as `Copy`. Shown in the following snippet, `Copy` can copy one or more files from one location to another:

```
<Target Name="CopyFiles">
    <Copy
        SourceFiles="@(MySourceFiles)"
        DestinationFolder="\\PDSERVER01\SourceBackup\"
    />
</Target>
```

Summary

The default build behavior can be customized with an enormous range of options in Visual Studio 2005, particularly for Visual Basic and C# projects because they're based on the MSBuild engine. Within the project file you can include additional actions to perform both before and after the build has taken place, as well as include additional files in the compilation.

With the information in this chapter, you can now set up your projects to build in a way that makes sense for your own requirements.

Deployment: ClickOnce and Other Methods

One area of software development that is often overlooked is how to deploy the application. Building an installer is a simple process and can transform your application from being an amateur utility to a professional tool. This chapter looks at how you can build a Windows installer for any type of .NET application. Visual Studio 2005 also includes support for a ClickOnce deployment, which can be used to build applications that can be dynamically updated. To round off this discussion, this chapter also examines other techniques you can use to deploy your application.

Installers

The traditional way to deploy applications is to use an installer, which can typically be used to install and, in most cases, uninstall an application. Visual Studio 2005 comes with a rich user interface for building an installer for any type of .NET application. That said, there are a number of tricks to building installers for services and mobile applications. Building an installer for a mobile application is covered in Chapter 44.

Building an Installer

To build an installer with Visual Studio 2005 you need to add an additional project to the application that you want to deploy. Figure 47-1 shows the available setup and deployment project types. The Setup project should be used for Windows forms or service applications, while the Web Setup project should be used for ASP.NET web sites or web services. If you want to build an installer that will be integrated into a larger installer, you may want to build a merge module. Alternatively, a CAB project can be used to create an alternative package that can be deployed via a web browser. The Setup Wizard steps you through the process of creating the correct project for the type of application you're deploying.

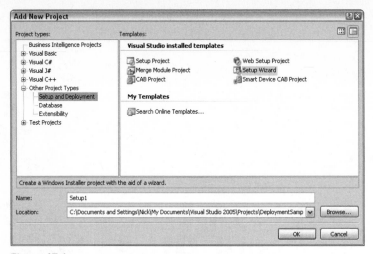

Figure 47-1

After acknowledging the Setup Wizard splash screen, the first decision is specifying whether you want to create an installer or a redistributable package. For an installer, it is important to select either a Windows application or a web application installer. The basic difference is that the Windows application installer places the application in the appropriate folder within Program Files, whereas the web application installer creates a virtual directory under the root folder for the specified web site. In the case of a redistributable package, the choice is between a merge module, which can be integrated into a larger installer, or a CAB file.

Regardless of the type of deployment project you are creating, the next step in the Setup Wizard is the most important because it determines the set of files to be deployed. Figure 47-2 shows the third screen in the Setup Wizard, which prompts you to select which files or project outputs will be included in the deployment project. In this case, the primary output for our DeploymentSample application has been selected, as you want to include the main executable and any assemblies on which this executable depends. In the remaining step in the Setup Wizard, you can choose to add files that were not part of any existing project. This might include release notes or README files.

Once the deployment project has been created, it is added to the Solution Explorer, as shown in Figure 47-3. Although you didn't explicitly add any files or output from the MainClassLibrary to the deployment project, it has been added as a calculated dependency. If the dependencies are guaranteed to exist on the target computer, they can be manually excluded from the deployment project by selecting the Exclude item from the right-click context menu. For example, if this were an add-in for another application that already has a copy of the MainClassLibrary, you could exclude that from the dependency list. The resulting installer would be smaller, and thus easier to deploy.

When a deployment project (DeploymentInstaller) is selected, a number of new icons appear across the top of the Solution Explorer window. Clicking the first icon (Properties) opens the Property Pages dialog, as shown in Figure 47-4, which can be used to customize how the deployment module is built. This dialog can also be accessed via the Properties item on the right-click context menu for the deployment project in the Solution Explorer.

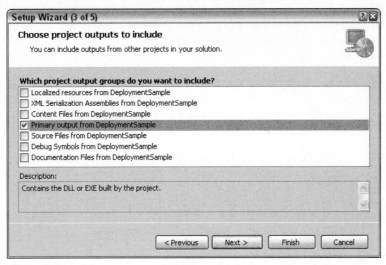

Figure 47-2

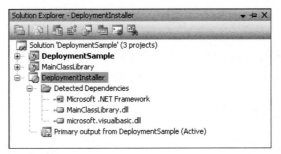

Figure 47-3

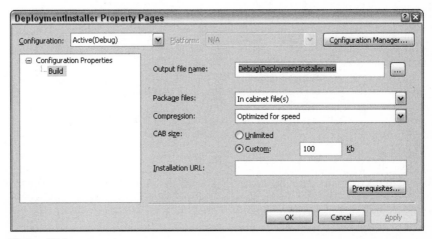

Figure 47-4

By default, the Package Files property is set to In Setup File, so all executables and associated dependencies are placed into the .msi file that is created. The deployment project also creates a Setup.exe file that checks for minimum requirements, such as the presence of the .NET Framework, prior to calling the .msi file to install the application. Although the compression can be adjusted to optimize for file size, including everything into a single distributable might be an issue for large projects. An alternative, as shown in Figure 47-4, is to package the application into a series of CAB files. In this scenario, the size of the CAB file is limited to 100Kb, as this will aid deployment over a slow network. Another scenario where this would be useful is if you were planning to deploy your application via CD and your application exceeded the capacity of a single CD.

The final property on this page is the Installation URL. If you are planning to deploy your application via a web site, you can select to package everything into a single file, in which case you do not need to specify the Installation URL because you can simply add a reference to the Setup.exe file to the appropriate web site and a user can install the application simply by clicking on the link. Alternatively, you can package your application into smaller units that can be incrementally downloaded. To do this you must specify the Installation URL from which they will be installed.

As just discussed, the default deployment project creates a Setup.exe file. The Prerequisites button opens a dialog like the one shown in Figure 47-5, where you can configure the behavior of this file. You can indicate that a setup file should not be created, in which case the application can be installed by double-clicking the .msi file. This, of course, removes the initial check to ensure that the .NET Framework has been installed.

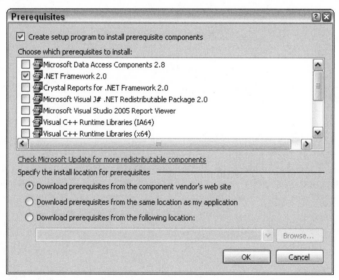

Figure 47-5

In addition to the .NET Framework, you can also specify that other components, such as MDAC, need to be installed. These checks will be carried out, and the user prompted to install any missing components prior to the main installer file being invoked.

Just to confuse matters, there is an additional Properties window for deployment projects that can be opened by selecting the appropriate project and pressing F4. This opens the standard Properties window, shown in Figure 47-6, which can be used to tailor the deployment for the application it is installing.

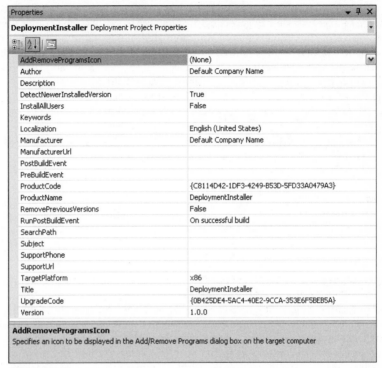

Figure 47-6

The properties for the deployment project shown on this screen configure the appearance, icons, and behavior of the installation wizard. It is highly recommended that you adjust these properties so your application is easily identifiable in the Add/Remove Programs dialog and the installation looks professional, rather than half finished.

Customizing the Installer

The remaining icons at the top of the Solution Explorer are used to customize what is included in the deployment package. In addition to the shortcut icons, these views of the deployment project can be accessed via the View item on the right-click context menu. Start with the File System view, which indicates where files will be installed on the target machine. By default, the primary output for a Windows application is added to the Application Folder, as shown in Figure 47-7. Selecting this node and looking at the Properties window shows that this folder has a default location of [ProgramFilesFolder] [Manufacturer]\[ProductName]. This location is made up of three predefined installation variables: ProgramFilesFolder, Manufacturer, and ProductName, which will be evaluated and combined during installation. As you will see later, the installation wizard allows users to change this location when they install the application.

Earlier you saw that the DeploymentSample application had a dependency on the MainClassLibrary assembly. Here this assembly has been removed from the Application Folder and placed instead in the Global Assembly Cache Folder. When this application is installed, the main executable will be installed in the relevant directory under Program Files, but the MainClassLibrary will be installed in the Global Assembly Cache so it is available to any .NET application. To achieve this, you first need to create the new folder in the File System view by selecting the Global Assembly Cache Folder from the Add Special Folder item on the right-click context menu. You can install files to a number of other special folders as part of the installer. The next step is to move the MainClassLibrary assembly to the Global Assembly Cache by selecting the assembly in the right pane of the File System view and changing the `Folder` property from Application Folder to Global Assembly Cache Folder.

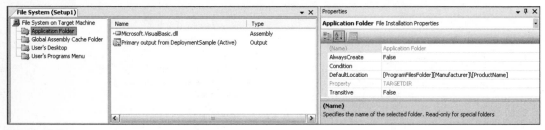

Figure 47-7

In addition to installing files on the target machine, you can also add keys to the registry. Some developers argue for and other developers argue against the use of the registry. Although it can provide a convenient store for per-user configuration information, the new application settings with user scope are an alternative that makes them easier to manage. The Registry view, as shown in Figure 47-8, can be used to add registry keys and values. To add a new key, right-click the appropriate node in the Registry tree and select Add Key from the context menu. To add a new value, right-click the appropriate key in the Registry tree and select the type of value from the New item on the context menu anywhere on the pane on the right of Figure 47-8. The Name and Value can then be set using the Properties window.

Figure 47-8

Figure 47-9 shows the File Types view of the deployment project. This view is used to add file extensions that should be installed. For example, in this case you are installing the extension .nic. You can specify an icon for this type of file as well as specify the executable that should be called for this file type. In most cases this will be the primary output for your application. To add a new file type, right-click the root node of the File Types tree and select Add File Types from the context menu. This creates a node for the new file type and for the default action (in bold) for that file type. For the .nic extension, the default action is Open, and it can be executed by double-clicking a file of the appropriate file type. The Open action also appears, again in bold, in the right-click context menu for a file with the .nic extension.

Other actions can be added for this file type by selecting Add Action from the right-click context menu for the file type. An alternative action can be made the default by selecting Set as Default from that action's context menu. You can change the order in which the actions appear in the context menu by moving the action up or down in the tree.

Figure 47-9

.NET applications can be autonomous so that their list of dependencies only contains the .NET Framework. However, web applications require IIS, and more complex applications may require SQL Server to be installed. Checking for these dependencies can be done using a *launch condition* via the view shown in Figure 47-10. By default, the .NET Framework is added to this launch condition. Previously you saw that Setup.exe also did a check for the .NET Framework and would install it if it was not found. Launch conditions are embedded in the .msi file and, unlike conditions in the Setup.exe file, are validated even if the .msi file is installed directly. The only limitation is that the launch conditions only provide a warning message and a URL reference for more information.

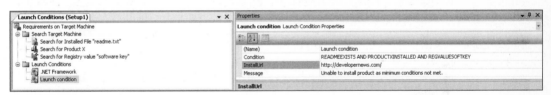

Figure 47-10

Figure 47-10 shows the Launch Conditions view of the deployment project. This view is actually split into two sections. The top half of the tree is used to specify searches to be performed on the target machine. Searches can be carried out for files, for installed components or applications, and for registry values. Properties for a file search include the search folder, version and modification dates, and file size. To search for an installed component, you need to know the Component ID, which is embedded in the .msi file used to install the product. This information can be retrieved using a product such as MSI Spy, which is included in the Windows Installer SDK that can be downloaded from the Microsoft web site (www.microsoft.com/downloads/). A registry search requires properties indicating the key, name, and value to search for. In each of these cases the search needs to be assigned a Property identifier. If the search is successful, the installer property with that identifier is True.

The Property identifiers assigned to searches on the target machine can be used by a launch condition in the lower half of the tree. As you can see in Figure 47-10, there is a condition that checks for the .NET Framework, as well as another launch condition. The Condition property is set to a logical AND operation across the three search results. If any of the searches fail, the associated property identifier is replaced with False, making the whole logical expression false. This results in the application failing to install, and a warning message will be displayed.

Note that some other views have a `Condition` property for some of the tree nodes. For example, in the File System view, each file or output has a `Condition` property that can be specified. If this condition fails, the file is not installed on the target machine. In each of these cases the syntax of the `Condition` property must be valid for the `MsiEvaluateCondition` function that is called as part of the installation process. This function accepts standard comparison operators, such as equals (=), not equals (<>), less than (>), and greater than (<), as well as Boolean operators NOT, AND, OR, and XOR. There are also some predefined Windows installer properties that can be included in the condition property. The following is a subset of the full list, which can be found in the documentation for the Windows Installer SDK:

- ❑ `ComputerName`: Target computer name
- ❑ `VersionNT`: Version of Windows NT/2000 on the target computer
- ❑ `ServicePackLevel`: The service pack that has been installed
- ❑ `LogonUser`: The username of the current user
- ❑ `AdminUser`: Whether the current user has administrative privileges
- ❑ `COMPANYNAME`: The company name, as specified in the installation wizard
- ❑ `USERNAME`: The username, as specified in the installation wizard

One of the main reasons for creating an installer is to make the process of deploying an application much smoother. To do this you need to create a simple user interface into which an end user can specify values. This might be the installation directory or other parameters that are required to configure the application. Clearly, the fewer steps in the installer the easier the application will be to install. However, it can be better to prompt for information during the installation than for the user to later sit wondering why the application is not working. The User Interface view, shown in Figure 47-11, enables you to customize the screens that the user sees as part of the installation process.

Figure 47-11

Two user interfaces are defined in this view: the standard installation and an Administrative install (not visible). Both processes follow the same structure: Start, where you typically collect information from the user prior to installing the product; Progress, used for providing a visual cue as to the installation's progress; and End, at which point the user is presented with a summary of the installation. The Administrative install is typically used when a network setup is required, and can be invoked by calling `msiexec` with the /a flag.

You can customize either of the installation processes by adding and/or removing dialogs from the user interface tree. To add a new dialog, right-click any of the three stages in the installation process and select Add Dialog from the context menu. This displays a list of the predefined dialogs from which you can choose. Each of the dialogs has a different layout; some are used for accepting user input while others are used to display information to the user. Input controls are allocated a property identifier so that the value entered during the installation process can be used later in the process. For example, a checkbox might be used to indicate whether the tools for a product should be installed. A condition could be placed on an output in the File System view so the tools are only installed if the checkbox is enabled.

Adding Custom Actions

It is often necessary to perform some actions either prior to or after the application is installed. To do this, you can create a custom action to be executed as part of the install or uninstall process. Adding a custom action entails creating the code to be executed and linking the appropriate installer event so that the code is executed. Custom actions use an event model similar to what Windows components use to link the code that you write to the appropriate installer event. To add a custom action to an installer event, you need to create a class that inherits from the `Installer` base class. This base class exposes a number of events for which you can write event handlers. Because writing custom installer actions is quite a common task, the Add New Item dialog includes an Installer Class template item. The new class opens using the component designer, as shown in Figure 47-12.

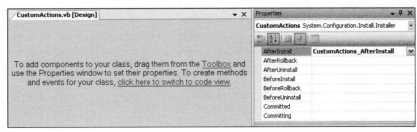

Figure 47-12

From the Events tab of the Properties window, select the installer event for which you want to add an event handler. If no event handler exists, a new event handler will be created and opened in the code window. The following code is automatically generated when an event handler is created. A simple message box is inserted to notify the user that the `AfterInstall` event handler has completed:

```
Imports System.ComponentModel
Imports System.Configuration.Install

Public Class CustomActions

    Public Sub New()
        MyBase.New()

        InitializeComponent()
    End Sub

    Private Sub CustomActions_AfterInstall(ByVal sender As Object, _
                                ByVal e As InstallEventArgs) _
                                            Handles Me.AfterInstall

        MsgBox("Installation process completed!")
    End Sub
End Class
```

As with forms and other components, the rest of this class is stored in a designer class file. The rest of the class definition is as follows:

```
<System.ComponentModel.RunInstaller(True)> _
Partial Class CustomActions
    Inherits System.Configuration.Install.Installer

    ' The Dispose and InitializeComponent methods have been omitted as they do
    ' not add anything to the code sample

End Class
```

Here you can see that the partial `CustomActions` class inherits from the `Installer` class and is attributed with the `RunInstaller` attribute. This combination ensures that this class is given the opportunity to handle events raised by the installer.

The `CustomActions` class you have just created was added to the `MainClassLibrary` assembly. For the events to be wired up to the `CustomActions` class, the installer needs to know that there is a class that contains custom actions. To make this association, add the `MainClassLibrary` assembly to the Custom Actions view for the deployment project by right-clicking any of the nodes shown in Figure 47-13 and selecting Add Custom Action from the context menu. In this case, you want to wire up the `MainClassLibrary`. In Figure 47-13, this association has only been made for the `Install` action. If you want to wire up the custom action class for all of the actions, you need to add the custom action to the root Custom Actions node.

Figure 47-13

To complete this discussion, understand that it is important to be able to pass information collected from the user during the Start phase of the installation process to the custom action. Unfortunately, because the custom action is invoked after the installer has finished, you have to use a special channel to pass installer properties to the custom action event handler. In the Custom Actions view (refer to Figure 47-13), select Properties Window from the right-click context menu for the Primary output node. The `CustomActionData` property is used to define name/value pairs that will be sent through to the custom installer. For example, you might have `/PhoneNumber= "+1 425 001 0001"`, in which case you can access this value in the event handler as follows:

```
Private Sub CustomActions_AfterInstall(ByVal sender As Object, _
                                       ByVal e As InstallEventArgs) _
                                                            Handles Me.AfterInstall
    MsgBox("Phone number: " & Me.Context.Parameters("PhoneNumber").ToString)
End Sub
```

Of course, hard-coded values are not a good idea and it would be better if this were a user-specified value. To use a property defined in the installer user interface, replace the specified string with the property identifier in square brackets. For example, `/PhoneNumber=[TxtPhoneNumber]` would include the text in the `TxtPhoneNumber` text box.

Web Project Installers

As mentioned earlier in this chapter, there are some slight differences when it comes to creating installers for web projects. In earlier versions of Visual Studio, the typical installer was limited to installing the application into a virtual directory on the default web site. Unfortunately, a large number of organizations support multiple web sites for applications such as SharePoint, Team Foundation Server, and other sites. A significant improvement in the template installer that comes with Visual Studio 2005 enables users to select which web site to install the web application onto, as shown in Figure 47-14.

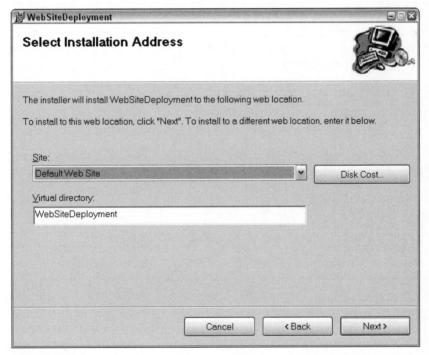

Figure 47-14

In the past, the web site installation wizard would prompt the user to specify the name of the virtual directory into which the application was to be installed, and this directory would then be created in the default web site. If multiple web sites were hosted on the same server (often the case with products such as SharePoint installed), then this could result in the application being installed on the wrong web site. Being able to specify the web site during installation reduces any post-installation administration that would have been required in the past.

Service Installer

Also requiring some discussion is writing an installer for a Windows Service application. You create an installer the same way you would create an installer for a Windows application. However, a Windows Service installer not only needs to install the files into the appropriate location, it also needs to register the service so it appears in the services list. This is easily done using the `ServiceInstaller` and `ServiceProcessInstaller` components (you'll probably need to add these to the Toolbox, as they are not visible by default). An instance of each of these components needs to be dragged onto the designer surface of the installer.

The `ServiceInstaller` class is used to specify the display name (the name of the service as it will appear in the Windows services list), the service name (the name of the service class that will be executed when the service is run), and the startup type (whether it is manually started or automatically started when Windows starts up). For each service you want to install you need to create a separate instance of the `ServiceInstaller` class, specifying a different display and service name. Only a single instance of the `ServiceProcessInstaller` class is required, which is used to specify the account information that the service(s) will run as. In the following example, the `InstallerforService` constructor specifies that the class `Service1` should be installed as a service, and that it should automatically start using the `NetworkService` account:

```
Imports System.ComponentModel
Imports System.Configuration.Install

Public Class InstallerForService

    Private Const cServiceDisplayName As String = "My Generic Service"
    Private Const cStartAfterInstall As String = "STARTAFTERINSTALL"
    Private Const cNETProcessName As String = "Net"
    Private Const cNETStart As String = "Start ""{0}"""
    Private Const cNETWaitTimeout As Integer = 5000
    Private Const cNETWaitError As String = "WARNING: Process took longer than
expected to start, it may need to be restarted manually"

    Public Sub New()
        MyBase.New()

        'This call is required by the Component Designer.
        InitializeComponent()

        'Add initialization code after the call to InitializeComponent
        Me.ServiceInstaller1.DisplayName = cServiceDisplayName
        Me.ServiceInstaller1.ServiceName = GetType(Service1).ToString
        Me.ServiceInstaller1.StartType = ServiceProcess.ServiceStartMode.Automatic
        Me.ServiceProcessInstaller1.Account = _
                                    ServiceProcess.ServiceAccount.NetworkService
    End Sub


    Private Sub InstallerForService_AfterInstall(ByVal sender As Object, _
                                        ByVal e As InstallEventArgs) _
                                        Handles Me.AfterInstall
        'Retrieve the user input (unchecked box can return empty string,
```

```
        'whereas a checked box will return "1")
        Dim startString As String = Me.Context.Parameters(cStartAfterInstall)
        If startString = "" Then Return
        Dim shouldStart As Boolean = CBool(startString)
        If Not shouldStart Then Return

        'Service should be started, so create a process and wait for completion
        Dim proc As Process = Process.Start(CreateNetStartProcessInfo)
        If Not proc.WaitForExit(cNETWaitTimeout) Then MsgBox(cNETWaitError)

    End Sub

    Private Function CreateNetStartProcessInfo() As ProcessStartInfo
        Dim x As New ProcessStartInfo(cNETProcessName, _
                            String.Format(cNETStart, cServiceDisplayName))
        x.WindowStyle = ProcessWindowStyle.Hidden
        Return x
    End Function
End Class
```

Also included in this listing is an event handler for the `AfterInstall` event that is used to start the service on completion of the installation process. By default, even when the startup is set to automatic, the service will not be started by the installer. However, when uninstalling the service, the installer does attempt to stop the service.

The user interface for this deployment project includes a Checkboxes (A) dialog using the User Interface view for the project. Refer to Figure 47-11 for a view of the default user interface. Right-click the Start node and select Add Dialog from the context menu. Highlight the dialog titled Checkboxes (A) from the Add Dialog window and click OK. This will insert the new dialog at the end of the installation process. The order of the dialogs can be adjusted using the Move Up/Down items from the right-click context menu on the nodes in the User Interface window.

Selecting Properties Window from the right-click context menu on the new dialog will bring up the Properties window. Set the property identifier for `Checkbox1` to STARTAFTERINSTALL and the set the `Visible` property for the remaining checkboxes to `false`. As discussed earlier in the chapter, you also needed to add `/STARTAFTERINSTALL=[STARTAFTERINSTALL]` to the `CustomActionData` property for the assembly in the Custom Actions view of the deployment project. With this user input you can decide whether to start the service when the installer completes.

ClickOnce

Using a Windows installer is a sensible approach for any application development. However, deploying an installer to thousands of machines, and then potentially having to update them, is a daunting task. Although management products help reduce the burden associated with application deployment, web applications often replace rich Windows applications because they can be dynamically updated, affecting all users of the system. *ClickOnce* is a new technology — included in version 2.0 of the .NET Framework — that enables you to build self-updating Windows applications. This section shows you how to use Visual Studio 2005 to build applications that can be deployed and updated using ClickOnce.

Click to Deploy

To demonstrate the functionality of ClickOnce deployment, this section uses a simple application, DeploymentSample, which initially displays an empty form. Begin with a freshly created WindowsApplication, which of course has a single blank form. This can be created by clicking File⇨New Project⇨Windows Application. Without making any changes, you can run this from within Visual Studio 2005 and the form is displayed. To deploy this application, "click once" on the Publish Now button in the Publish tab of the project settings window, as shown in Figure 47-15.

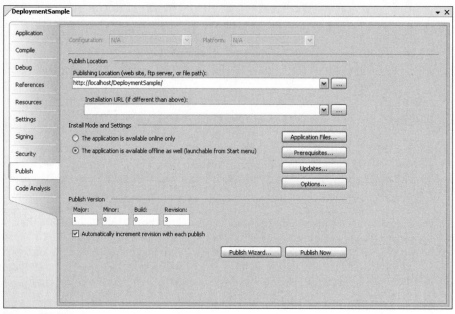

Figure 47-15

Publishing the application deploys the current version of the application to the location defined in the Publishing Location path (in this case, `http://localhost/DeploymentSample/`) along with a deployment manifest that details the application components and security. Although the publish location appears as a drop-down list, it is only populated with previous locations to which you have published the application, so initially it will be empty. Clicking the ellipses button displays the Open Web Site dialog, which assists you in specifying the publishing location. After this process has completed, the installation URL is launched, as shown in Figure 47-16.

Clicking the Install button at this location displays the Launching Application dialog, shown in Figure 47-17, while the requirements for the application are being retrieved from the server. This step is similar to the role of the `Setup.exe` for the traditional Windows Installer.

After information about the DeploymentSample application has been downloaded, a security warning is launched, as shown in Figure 47-18. In this case, the security warning is raised because although the deployment manifest has been signed, it has been signed with a certificate that is not known on the machine on which it is being installed.

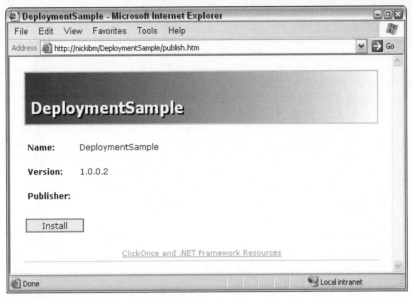

Figure 47-16

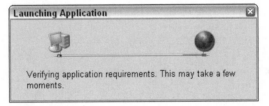

Figure 47-17

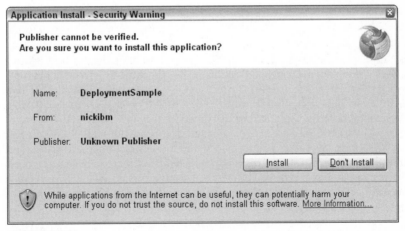

Figure 47-18

Three options are available when it comes to signing the deployment manifest. By default, Visual Studio 2005 creates a test certificate to sign the manifest, which has the format `application name_TemporaryKey.pfx` and is automatically added to the solution (this happens when the application is first published using the Publish Now button, as shown on Figure 47-15). While this certificate can be used during development, it is not recommended for deployment. The other alternatives are to purchase a third-party certificate, from a company such as VeriSign, or to use the certificate server within Windows Server 2003 to create an internal certificate.

The advantage of getting a certificate from a well-known certificate authority is that it can automatically be verified by any machine. Using either the test certificate or an internal certificate requires installation of that certificate in the appropriate certificate store. Figure 47-19 shows the Signing tab of the project properties window, where you can see that the ClickOnce manifest is being signed with a certificate that has been generated on the local computer. An existing certificate can be used by selecting it from the store or from a file. Alternatively, another test certificate can be created.

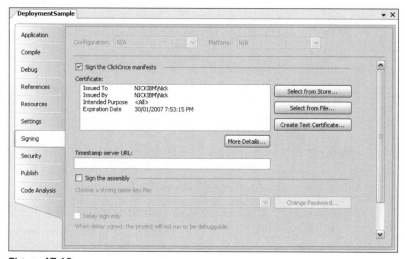

Figure 47-19

If you want your application to install with a known publisher, you need to add the test certificate into the root certificate store on the machine on which you're installing the product. Because this also happens to be the deployment machine, you can do this by clicking More Details. This opens a dialog that outlines the certificate details, including the fact that it can't be authenticated. (If you are using the certificate created by default by Visual Studio 2005, you will need to use the Select from File button to re-select the generated certificate, and then use the More Details button. There seems to be an issue here in that the details window does not show the Install Certificate button without this additional step.) Clicking Install Certificate enables you to specify that the certificate should be installed into the Trusted Root Certification Authorities store. This is not the default certificate store, so you need to browse for it. Because this is a test certificate you can ignore the warning that is given, but remember that you should not use this certificate in production. Now when you publish your application and try to install it, you will see that the dialog has changed, looking similar to the one shown in Figure 47-20.

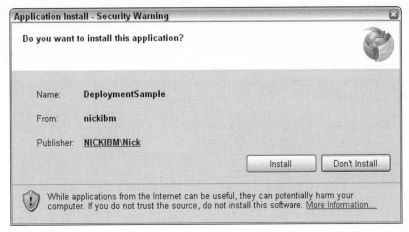

Figure 47-20

Although you have a known publisher, you are still being warned that additional security permissions need to be granted to this application in order for it to execute. Clicking the rather minimalist More Information hyperlink opens a more informative dialog, shown in Figure 47-21. As with the security coding within Windows XP SP2, there are three icons: green for positive security, red for potential security weaknesses, and yellow for informative or best practice guidance.

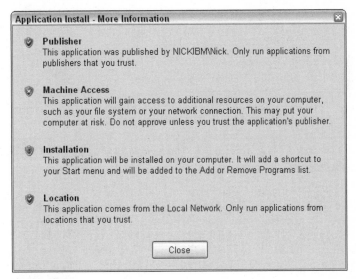

Figure 47-21

ClickOnce deployment manifests are rated on four security dimensions. You've just seen how you can specify a well-known publisher, critical for safe installation of an application. By default, ClickOnce publishes applications as full trust applications, giving them maximum control over the local computer.

This is unusual, as in most other cases Microsoft has adopted a security-first approach. To run with full trust, the application requires additional security permissions, which might be exploited. The DeploymentSample application will be available online and offline; and while this isn't a major security risk, it does modify the local file system. Lastly, the location from which the application is being installed is almost as important as the publisher in determining how dangerous the application might be. In this case, the application was published within the local network so it is unlikely to be a security threat.

Because this application doesn't really do anything, you can decrease the trust level that the application requires. As shown in Figure 47-22, this application is made a partial trust application based on the Local Intranet zone. This changes the Machine Access icon to green, leaving only the Installation icon yellow. Unfortunately, the only way you can get this to be green would be to not install the application, which means that it would not be available offline.

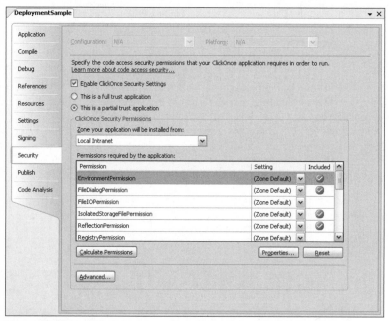

Figure 47-22

Ideally, you would like to be able to bypass the Application Install dialog and have the application automatically be granted appropriate permissions. You can do this by adding the certificate to the Trusted Publishers store. Even for well-known certificate authorities, in order for the application to install automatically, the certificate needs to be added to this store. With this completed, you are presented with the dialog shown in Figure 47-23 as the application downloads. Once the application has completed downloading, it is installed onto the local computer, shortcuts are added to the Start menu, and the application is launched.

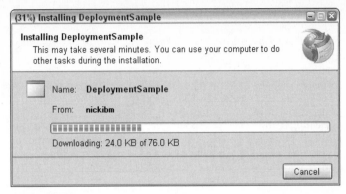

Figure 47-23

Click to Update

At some point in the future you might make a change to your application — for example, you might add a button to the simple form you created previously. ClickOnce supports a powerful update process that enables you to publish the new version of your application in the same way you did previously, and all existing versions will be upgraded the next time they are online. In Figure 47-15 you saw that the deployment manifest was assigned a version number, and at least in this case it automatically increments each time you publish the application. When you publish the new version of your application, any existing users will be prompted to update their application to the most recent version, as shown in Figure 47-24.

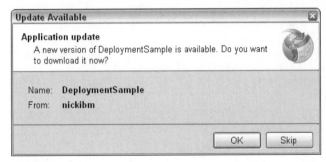

Figure 47-24

One of the most powerful features of ClickOnce deployment is that it tracks a previous version of the application that was installed. This means that at any stage, not only can it do a clean uninstall, it can also roll back to the earlier version. The application can be rolled back or uninstalled from the Add/Remove Programs list on the Control Panel.

Other Techniques

To round off the discussion on application deployment, this section covers some other manual techniques you can use.

XCopy

One of the most appealing features of .NET assemblies is that they do not require any sort of registering in order to function. This means that a .NET application can be copied from one directory to another, between machines, or even e-mailed to a colleague. As long as the destination computer has a compatible version of the .NET Framework installed, the application will run.

Clearly, some care needs to be taken to ensure that any configuration files are updated accordingly. Some .NET applications do install shared assemblies into the GAC, so unless it is your application and you know what dependencies it has, it is always worthwhile to use the installer that shipped with it.

Publish Website

An alternative for distributing web applications is to publish them via the Publish Website item on the Build menu. Figure 47-25 displays the options that are available, including the capability to pre-compile and sign the assemblies for a web site.

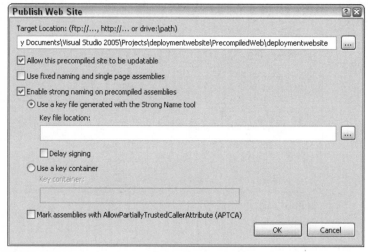

Figure 47-25

Copy Web Project

Once a web site has been published, it is important that you have some way of updating it. Instead of just repeatedly publishing the web site, you can use the Copy Web Site tool, shown in Figure 47-26, to synchronize files between your development project and the web site. This tool can be accessed from the right-click context menu in the Solution Explorer.

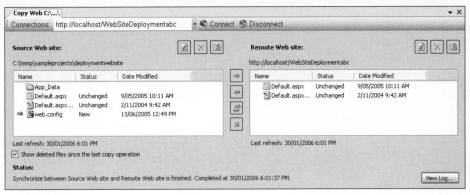

Figure 47-26

Summary

This chapter walked you through the details of building installers for various types of applications. Building a good-quality installer can make a significant difference in how professional your application appears. ClickOnce also offers an important alternative for those who want to deploy their application to a large audience. Lastly, there are tools (including XCopy, Publish Website, and Copy Web Project) for those who just need to copy an application or update a web site.

Part IX

Debugging and Testing

48

Using the Debugging Windows

This chapter examines the numerous windows available in Visual Studio 2005 to support you in building and debugging applications. Debugging applications is one of the hardest tasks developers have to tackle, but correct use of the Visual Studio 2005 debugging windows will help you analyze the state of the application and determine the cause of any bugs.

Code Window

The most important window for debugging purposes is, of course, the code window. With the capability to set breakpoints and step through code, this window becomes the basis for nearly all debugging. Figure 48-1 shows a simple snippet of code with both a breakpoint and the current execution point visible.

Breakpoints

The first stage in debugging an application is usually to identify the area that is causing the error by setting a breakpoint and gradually stepping through the code. Setting breakpoints and working with the current execution point is covered in more detail in the next chapter. Although you can't see the color in Figure 48-1, breakpoints are marked in the code window with a red dot in the margin of the page and red highlighting of the code itself.

When a breakpoint is encountered, the current execution point is marked with a yellow arrow in the margin and the actual code is also highlighted in yellow. As discussed in the next chapter, this marker can be dragged forward and backward to control the order of execution. However, this should be done sparingly because it modifies the behavior of the application.

Figure 48-1

DataTips

After hitting a breakpoint, the application is paused, or is in *Break* mode. In this mode, you can retrieve information about current variables simply by hovering your mouse over the variable name. Figure 48-1 shows that the value of the m_Name variable is currently Nothing. This debugging tooltip is commonly referred to as a *DataTip*, and can be used not only to view the data stored by a variable, but also to modify this information. In Chapter 50 you will learn how the layout of this DataTip can be customized using Type Proxies and Type Visualizers.

Breakpoint Window

When debugging a complex issue, it is possible to set numerous breakpoints to isolate the problem. Unfortunately, this has two side effects. One, the execution of the application is hampered, as you have to continually press F5 to resume execution. More significantly, the execution of the application is slowed considerably by the presence of breakpoints; the more complex the breakpoint conditions, the slower the application will run. Because these breakpoints can be scattered through multiple source files, it becomes difficult to locate and remove breakpoints that are no longer required.

The breakpoint window, accessible via Debug⇨Windows⇨Breakpoints, is a useful summary of all the breakpoints currently set within the application. Using this window, breakpoints can easily be navigated to, disabled, and removed.

Figure 48-2

Figure 48-2 shows two currently active breakpoints in the Customer.vb file. The first is a regular breakpoint with no conditions. The second has a condition whereby the application will only break if the m_Name variable has the value Fred. This condition is also in bold, as the application is currently in Break mode at that breakpoint.

The Breakpoints window, like most other debugging windows, is made up of two regions: the toolbar and the breakpoint list. From left to right, the breakpoint toolbar icons are as follows: create, delete, delete all, and disable all breakpoints, go to source and go to disassembler, and finally column selection.

Each item in the breakpoint list is represented by a checkbox that indicates whether the breakpoint is enabled, an icon and breakpoint descriptor, and any number of columns that show properties of the breakpoint. The columns can be adjusted using the Columns drop-down from the toolbar. You can set additional breakpoint properties by right-clicking on the appropriate breakpoint.

Output Window

One of the first debugging windows you will encounter when you run your application for the first time is the Output window. By default, this window appears when you build your application and show the build progress. Figure 48-3 shows the successful build of a sample solution. The final line of the Output window indicates a summary of the build, which in this case indicates four successfully built projects. Earlier in the output there was a summary of the errors encountered during the build. In this case there were no errors, but there were four warnings. Although the Output window can be useful if for some reason the build fails unexpectedly, most of the time the errors and warnings are reported in the Error List.

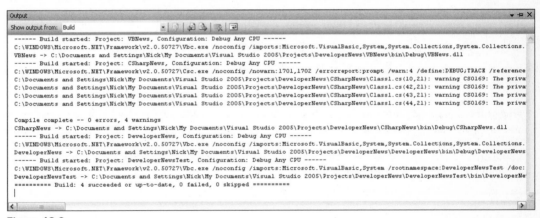

Figure 48-3

The Output window has a secondary role as the standard output while the application is running. The drop-down on the left of the toolbar can be used to toggle between output sources. Figure 48-3 shows the output of the build, but this can be changed to show the debug output. The debug output shows any messages that either the runtime or your code has emitted using `Debug.Write` or `Debug.Writeline`.

The other icons on the toolbar, in order from left to right, enable you to navigate to the source of a build message, go to the previous message, go to the next message, clear the window contents, and toggle word wrapping for the Output window.

Immediate Window

Quite often when you are writing code or debugging your application, you will want to evaluate a simple expression either to test a bit of functionality or to remind yourself of how something works. This is where the Immediate Window comes in handy. This window enables you to run expressions as you type them. Figure 48-4 shows a number of statements — from basic assignment and print operations through to more advanced object creation and manipulation.

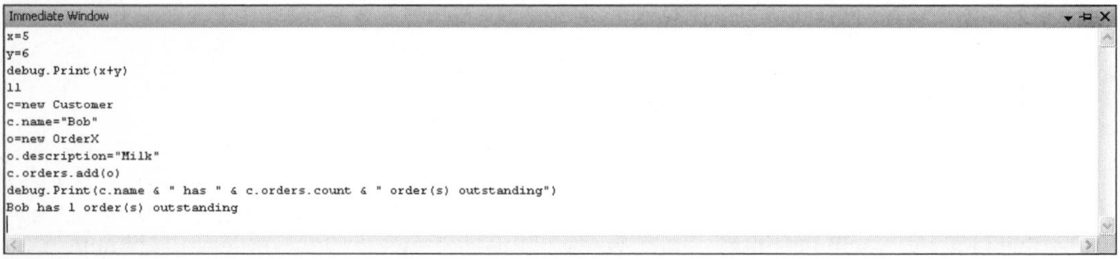

```
Immediate Window                                                          ▾ ┱ X
x=5
y=6
debug.Print(x+y)
11
c=new Customer
c.name="Bob"
o=new OrderX
o.description="Milk"
c.orders.add(o)
debug.Print(c.name & " has " & c.orders.count & " order(s) outstanding")
Bob has 1 order(s) outstanding
```

Figure 48-4

Although you can't do explicit variable declaration (for example, Dim x as Integer), it is done implicitly using the assignment operator. The example shown in Figure 48-4 shows a new Customer being created, assigned to a variable c, and then used in a series of operations.

The Immediate Window supports a limited form of IntelliSense, and you can use the arrow keys to track back through the history of previous commands executed. Variable values can be displayed using the Debug.Print statement.

One of the significant improvements in Visual Studio 2005 is that the Immediate Window can now be used while you are writing code. Previously your application had to be in Break mode for the expressions to be evaluated. In fact, if you execute code that has an active breakpoint, the command will break at the breakpoint. This can be useful if you are working on a particular method that you want to test without running the entire application.

Script Explorer

The Script Explorer is designed to bridge the gap between the rich debugging experience of managed languages, such as C# and VB.NET, and other scripting languages such as VBScript and JavaScript. Most web sites would not be complete without at least some script providing some client-side functionality, rather than repeated postbacks to the server. The Script Explorer shows a list of current web pages that can be opened so that the scripts can be debugged.

Note, however, a gotcha that needs to be explained before going any further with the Script Explorer. By default, Internet Explorer disables script debugging because it is a potential security hazard. To work with the Script Explorer you must first uncheck the Disable Script Debugging (Internet Explorer) item on the Advanced tab of the Options dialog, accessible from the Tools menu within Internet Explorer.

When you run your web application after enabling script debugging, notice that the current page being viewed appears in the Script Explorer (see Figure 48-5). Double-clicking on this item opens the page in the main code window. As with managed code, you can set breakpoints and move the current execution point around. Unlike managed code debugging, in which the debugging is carried out on the source code file, script debugging is done using a copy of the web page as it would appear if you selected View Source within Internet Explorer.

Figure 48-5

Watch Windows

Earlier in this chapter you saw how DataTips can be used in the code window to examine the content of a variable by hovering the mouse over a variable name. When the structure of the object is more complex it becomes difficult to navigate the values using just the DataTip. Visual Studio 2005 has a series of watch windows that can be used to display variables, providing an easy-to-use interface for drilling down into the structure.

QuickWatch

The QuickWatch window is a modal dialog that can be launched by right-clicking on the code window. Whatever you have selected in the code window is inserted into the Expression field of the dialog, as shown in Figure 48-6 where a `Customer` object is visible. Previous expressions you have evaluated appear in the drop-down associated with the Expression field.

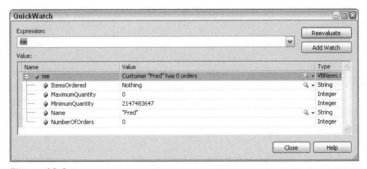

Figure 48-6

The layout of the Value tree in the QuickWatch window is similar to the DataTip, without the annoyance of it disappearing. Each row shows the variable name, the current value, and the type of object. The value of the variable can be adjusted by typing in the Value column.

Use the Add Watch button to add the current expression to one of the watch windows. These are variables to be continuously watched.

Watch Windows 1–4

Unlike the QuickWatch window, which is modal and shows a variable value at a particular execution point, the watch windows can be used to monitor a variable value as you step through your code. Although there are four watch windows, a single window is sufficient in most cases. Having four separate windows means that you can have different sets of variables in the different windows, which might be useful if you are working through a more complex issue that involves multiple classes.

Figure 48-7 shows the `Orders` property of the current `Customer` object. Similar to both the QuickWatch window and the DataTips discussed previously, the user interface can be used to drill down into more complex data types.

Figure 48-7

Additional variables to be watched can be added either by typing into the Name column on an empty line or by right-clicking the variable in the code window and selecting Add Watch from the context menu.

Autos and Locals

The Autos and Locals windows are two special watch windows in which the variables are automatically added by the debugger. The Autos window contains variables that are used in the current, preceding, and future lines of code. Similarly, the Locals window shows all variables used in the current method. Other than being automatically generated, these windows behave the same as the watch windows.

Call Stack

As applications grow in complexity, it is quite common for the execution path to become difficult to follow. The use of deep inheritance trees and interfaces can often obscure the execution path. This is where the call stack is useful. Each path of execution must have a finite number of entries on the stack (unless a cyclic pattern emerges, in which case a stack overflow is inevitable). The stack can be viewed using the Call Stack window, shown in Figure 48-8.

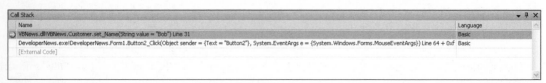

Figure 48-8

Using the Call Stack window, it is easy to navigate up the execution path to determine from where the current executing method is being called. This can be done by clicking on any of the rows in the call stack, known as a *stack frame*. Other options available from the call stack, using the right-click context menu, enable viewing the disassembler for a particular stack frame, setting breakpoints, and varying what information is displayed. In Figure 48-8 the Show External Code option has been unchecked so that only code that you have written is visible.

Threads

Most applications make use of multiple threads at some point. In particular for Windows applications, in order for the user interface to always appear responsive, it is important to run time-consuming tasks on a separate thread from the main application. Of course, concurrent execution of threads makes debugging more difficult, especially when the threads are accessing the same classes and methods.

Figure 48-9 shows the Threads window, which lists all the active threads for a particular application. Notice that in addition to the threads created in the code, there are additional background threads created by the debugger. For simplicity, the threads used by this application, including the main user interface thread, have been given a name so they can easily be distinguished.

ID	Name	Location	Priority	Suspend
5128	<No Name>		Normal	0
6032	.NET SystemEvents		Normal	0
4980	Main Application Thread	VBNews.Customer.set_Name	Normal	0
5836	Thread 0	VBNews.Customer.threadRun	Normal	0
4788	Thread 1	VBNews.Customer.threadRun	Normal	0
5584	Thread 2	VBNews.Customer.threadRun	Normal	0
1908	Thread 3	VBNews.Customer.threadRun	Normal	0
2872	Thread 4	VBNews.Customer.threadRun	Normal	0
3128	Thread 5		Normal	0

Figure 48-9

The Threads window shows a yellow arrow next to the thread that is currently being viewed in the code window. To navigate to another thread, simply double-click on that thread to bring the current location of that thread into view in the code window and update the call stack to reflect the new thread.

In Break mode, all threads of an application are paused. However, when you are stepping through your code with the debugger, the next statement to be executed may or may not be on the same thread you are interested in. If you are only interested in the execution path of a single thread, and the execution of other threads can be suspended, right-click the thread in the Threads window and select Freeze from the context menu. To resume the suspended thread, select Thaw from the same menu.

Modules

The Modules window (see Figure 48-10) shows a list of assemblies that are referenced by the running application. Those assemblies that make up the application will also have debugging symbols loaded, which means that they can be debugged without dropping into the disassembler. This window also provides useful assembly version information and indicates whether the assembly is optimized.

In Figure 48-10 the symbols have been loaded for the DeveloperNews application as well as the VBNews assembly. All the other assemblies have been skipped, as they contain no user code and are optimized. If an appropriate symbol file is available, it is possible to load it for an assembly via the Load Symbols option from the right-click context menu.

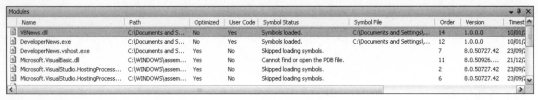

Figure 48-10

Processes

Building multi-tier applications can be quite complex, and it is often necessary to have all the tiers running. To do this, Visual Studio 2005 can start multiple projects at the same stage, enabling true end-to-end debugging. Alternatively, you can attach to other processes to debug running applications. Each time Visual Studio attaches to a process, that process is added to the list of attached processes. Figure 48-11 shows a solution containing two Windows applications and a web application. To debug the web application, Internet Explorer is started and Visual Studio 2005 attaches to that process in addition to the ASP.NET process.

Figure 48-11

The toolbar at the top of the Processes window enables you to detach or terminate a process that is currently attached, or attach to another process.

Memory Windows

The next series of windows are typically used for low-level debugging when all other alternatives have been exhausted. Stepping into memory locations, using a disassembler, or looking at registry values erodes any potential benefits of a managed environment, so the following windows should be used sparingly.

Memory Windows 1–4

Similar to the watch windows, four memory windows can be used to view the contents of memory at a particular address. Each window can examine different memory addresses to simplify debugging your application. Figure 48-12 shows an example of the information that can be seen using this window. The scrollbar on the right of the window can be used to navigate forward or backward through the memory addresses to view information contained in neighboring addresses.

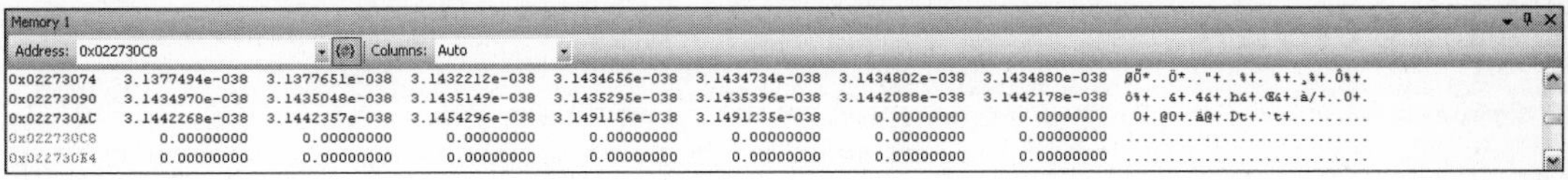

Figure 48-12

Disassembly

Interesting debates arise periodically over the relative performance of two different code blocks. Occasionally this discussion degrades to talking about which MSIL instructions are used, and why one code block is faster because it generates one fewer instruction. Clearly, if you are calling that code block millions of times, disassembly might give your application a significant benefit. However, more often than not, a bit of high-level refactoring saves much more time and with much less arguing. Figure 48-13 shows the Disassembly window for a button click — the runtime is about to make a call to the method `testMethod`. You can see the memory address and the MSIL instruction.

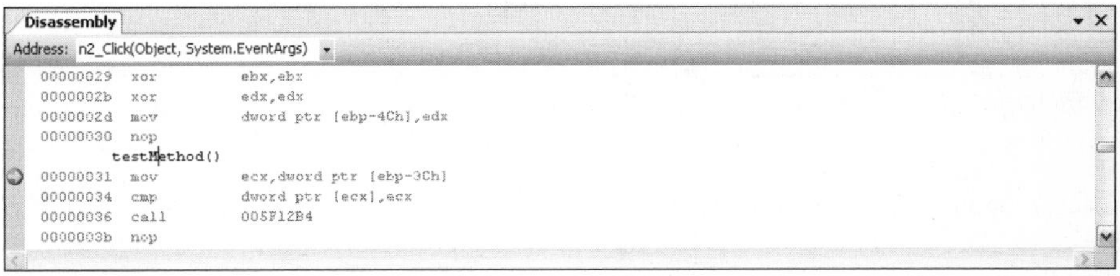

Figure 48-13

You can see from Figure 48-13 that a breakpoint has been set on the call to `testMethod` and that the execution point is at this breakpoint. While still in this window you can step through the lines of MSIL and review what instructions are being executed.

Registers

Using the Disassembly window to step through MSIL instructions can become very difficult to follow as different information is loaded, moved, and compared using a series of registers. The Registers window, shown in Figure 48-14, enables the contents of the various registers to be monitored. Changes in a register value are highlighted in red, making it easy to see what happens as each line is stepped through in the Disassembly window.

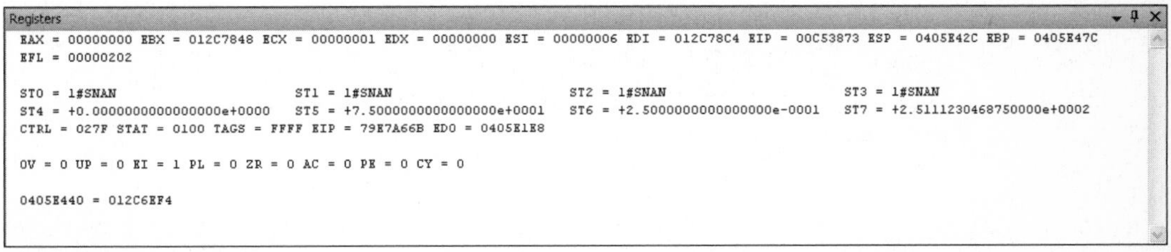

Figure 48-14

Exceptions

Visual Studio 2005 has a brand-new exception handler that provides you with more useful information. Figure 48-15 shows the exception assistant dialog that is shown when an exception is raised. In addition to providing more information, it also displays a series of actions. The Actions list varies depending on the type of exception being thrown. In this case, the two options are to view details of the exception or copy it to the clipboard.

Figure 48-15

If you select the View Detail action item from the exception, you are presented with a modal dialog that provides a breakdown of the exception that was raised. Figure 48-16 shows the attributes of the exception, including the `StackTrace`, which can be viewed in full by clicking the down arrow to the right of the screen.

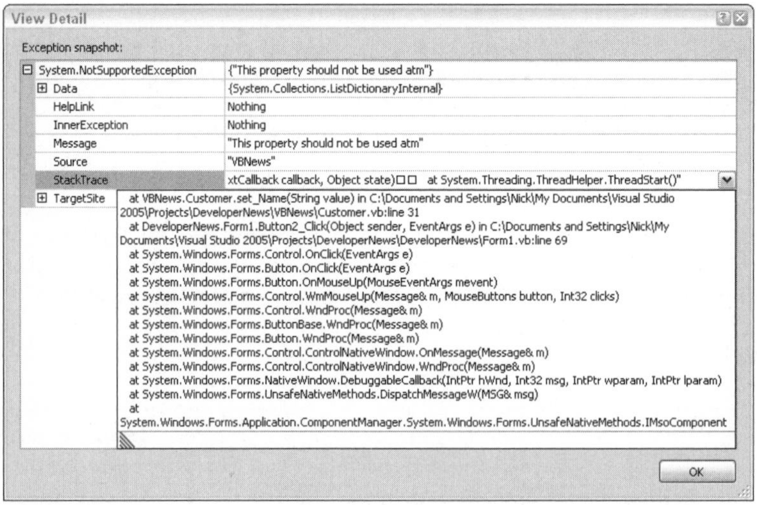

Figure 48-16

Of course, there are times when exceptions are used to control the execution path in an application. For example, some user input may not adhere to a particular formatting constraint, and instead of using a regular expression to determine whether it matches, a parse operation has been attempted on the string. When this fails, it raises an exception, which can easily be trapped without stopping the entire application.

By default, all exceptions are trapped by the debugger, as they are assumed to be exceptions to the norm that shouldn't have happened. In special cases, such as invalid user input, it may be important to ignore specific types of exceptions. This can be done via the Exceptions window, accessible from the Debug menu.

Figure 48-17 shows the Exceptions window, which lists all the exception types that exist in the .NET Framework. For each exception there are two debugging options. The debugger can be set to break when an exception is thrown regardless of whether it is handled. If the Just My Code option has been enabled, checking the User-unhandled box causes the debugger to break for any exception that is not handled within a user code region. More information on Just My Code is provided in Chapter 50, which examines debugging attributes.

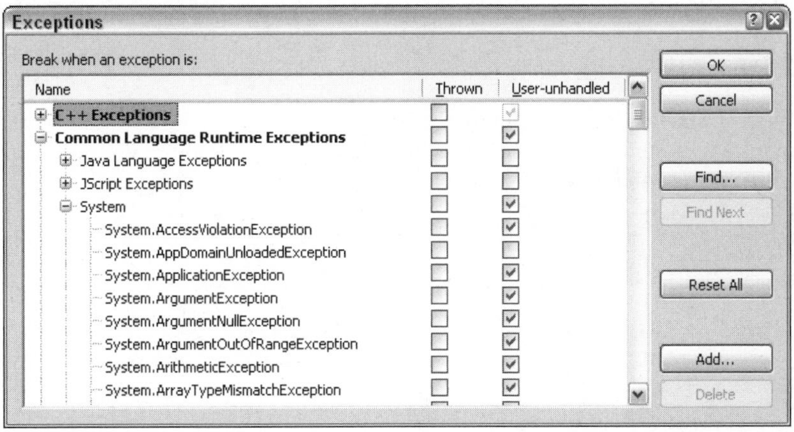

Figure 48-17

Unfortunately, the Exceptions window doesn't pick up any exception types that you may have created, but you can add them manually using the Add button in the lower-right corner of the window. You need to ensure that you provide the full class name, including the namespace; otherwise, the debugger will not break on handled exceptions. Clearly, unhandled exceptions will still cause the application to crash.

Customizing the Exception Assistant

As with a lot of the configurable parts within Visual Studio 2005, the information displayed by the Exception Assistant is stored in an XML file (`C:\Program Files\Microsoft Visual Studio 8\ Common7\IDE\ExceptionAssistantContent\1033\DefaultContent.xml`). This file can be modified either to alter the assistant information for existing exception types or to add your own custom exception types. If you have your own exception types, it is better practice to create your own XML document. Simply placing it in the same directory as the `DefaultContent.xml` is sufficient to register it with Visual Studio for the next time your application is debugged. An example XML file is provided in the following code snippet:

```
<?xml version="1.0" encoding="utf-8" ?>
<AssistantContent Version="1.0" xmlns="urn:schemas-microsoft-com:xml-
msdata:exception-assistant-content">
```

```
    <ContentInfo>
        <ContentName>Additional Content</ContentName>
        <ContentID>urn:exception-content-microsoft-com:visual-studio-7-default-
content</ContentID>
        <ContentFileVersion>1.0</ContentFileVersion>
        <ContentAuthor>DeveloperNews</ContentAuthor>
        <ContentComment>Additional Exception Assistant Content for Visual Studio
8.0.</ContentComment>
    </ContentInfo>
    <Exception>
        <Type>DeveloperNews.MyException</Type>
        <Tip HelpID="http://www.developernews.com/MyExceptionHelp.htm">
            <Description>Silly error, you should know better......</Description>
        </Tip>
    </Exception>
</AssistantContent>
```

This example registers help information for the exception type MyException. The HelpID attribute is used to provide a hyperlink for more information about the exception. When this exception is raised, the debugger displays the window (see Figure 48-18).

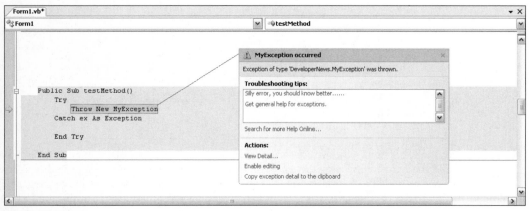

Figure 48-18

Unwinding an Exception

In Figure 48-18 there is an additional item in the Actions list, which is to enable editing. This is effectively the capability to unwind the execution of the application to just before the exception was raised. In other words, you can effectively debug your application without having to restart your debugging session.

An alternative way to unwind the exception is to select the Unwind to This Frame item from the right-click context menu off the Call Stack window after an exception has been raised.

As with many of the debugging features, both the Exception Assistant and the capability to unwind exceptions can be disabled via the Debugging tab of the Options window.

Summary

This chapter has described each of the debugging windows in detail so you can optimize your debugging experience. Although the number of windows can seem somewhat overwhelming at first, they each perform an isolated task or provide access to a specific piece of information about the running application. As such, you will easily learn to navigate between them, returning to those that provide the most relevant information for you.

The following chapter provides more detail about how you can customize the debugging information. This includes changing the information displayed in the DataTip and visualizing more complex variable information.

Debugging Breakpoints

Long gone are the days where debugging an application involved adding superfluous output statements to track down where an application was failing. Visual Studio 2005 provides a rich debugging experience that includes breakpoints and the Edit and Continue feature. This chapter covers how you can use these features to debug your application.

Breakpoints

A *breakpoint* is used to pause, or break, an application at a particular point of execution. An application that has been paused is said to be in Break mode, causing a number of the Visual Studio 2005 windows to become active. For example, the Watch window can be used to view variable values. Figure 49-1 shows a breakpoint that has been added to the constructor of the Customer class. The application will break on this line if the Customer class constructor is called.

Figure 49-1

Setting a Breakpoint

Breakpoints can be set either through the Debug menu, using the Breakpoint item from right-click context menu or by using the keyboard shortcut, F9. The Visual Studio 2005 code editor also provides a shortcut for setting breakpoint using a single mouse click.

An application can only be paused on a line of executing code. This means that a breakpoint set on either a comment or a variable declaration will be repositioned to the next line of executable code when the application is run.

Simple Breakpoints

A breakpoint can be set on a line of code by placing the cursor on that line and enabling a breakpoint using any of the following:

❑ Selecting Toggle Breakpoint from the Debug menu

❑ Selecting Insert Breakpoint from the Breakpoint item on the right-click context menu

❑ Pressing F9

❑ Clicking once in the margin of the code window with the mouse. Figure 49-1 shows the location of the mouse immediately after a breakpoint has been set using the mouse.

Selecting Location from the Breakpoint item on the right-click context menu for the line of code with the breakpoint set displays the File Breakpoint dialog, shown in Figure 49-2. Here you can see that the break point is set at line 4 of the Customer.vb file. There is also a character number, which provides for special cases in which multiple statements appear on a single line.

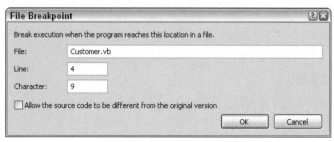

Figure 49-2

Function Breakpoints

Another type of breakpoint that can be set is a *function breakpoint*. The usual way to set a breakpoint on a function is to select the function signature and either press F9 or use the mouse to create a breakpoint. This will create a file breakpoint as you did previously. In the case of multiple overloads, this would require you to locate all the overloads and add the appropriate breakpoints. Setting a function break-point enables you to set a breakpoint on one or more functions by specifying the function name.

To set a function breakpoint, select Break at Function from the Breakpoint item on the Debug menu. This loads the New Breakpoint dialog shown in Figure 49-3, in which you can specify the name of the function on which to break. There is a toggle to enable IntelliSense checking for the function name. The recommendation is to leave this checked, as it becomes almost impossible to set a valid breakpoint without this support.

Unfortunately, the IntelliSense option doesn't give you true IntelliSense as you type, unlike other debugging windows. However, if you select the name of the function in the code window before creating the breakpoint, the name of the function is automatically inserted into the dialog.

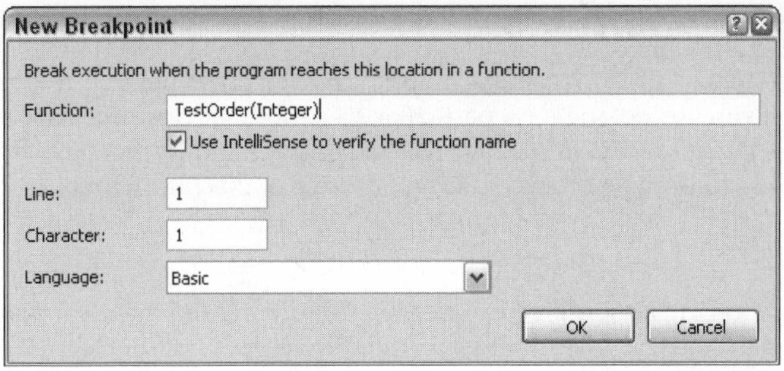

New Breakpoint

Break execution when the program reaches this location in a function.

Function: TestOrder(Integer)|

☑ Use IntelliSense to verify the function name

Line: 1

Character: 1

Language: Basic

OK   Cancel

Figure 49-3

When setting a function breakpoint, you can specify either the exact overload you wish to set the breakpoint on or just the function name. In Figure 49-3, the overload with a single Integer parameter has been selected. Notice that unlike a full method signature, which requires a parameter name, to select a particular function overload, you should only provide the parameter type. If you omit the parameter information, and there are multiple overloads, you will be prompted to select the overloads on which to place the breakpoint, as illustrated in Figure 49-4.

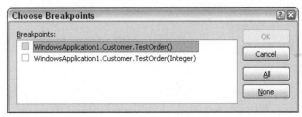

Choose Breakpoints

Breakpoints:

☐ WindowsApplication1.Customer.TestOrder()
☐ WindowsApplication1.Customer.TestOrder(Integer)

OK
Cancel
All
None

Figure 49-4

Address Breakpoints

Another way to set a breakpoint is via the Call Stack window. When the application is in Break mode, the call stack shows the current list of function calls. After selecting any line in the call stack, a breakpoint can be set in the same way as a file breakpoint, as described earlier (toggle Breakpoint from the Debug menu, use the F9 keyboard shortcut, or use Insert Breakpoint from the context menu). Figure 49-5 shows a short call stack with a new breakpoint set within the constructor for the Customer class.

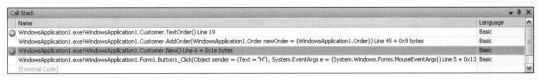

Figure 49-5

The call stack is generated using function addresses. As such, the breakpoint that is set is an address breakpoint. This type of breakpoint is only useful within a single debugging session, as function addresses are likely to change when an application is modified and rebuilt.

Adding Break Conditions

While breakpoints are useful for pausing an application at a given point to review variables and watch application flow, if you are looking for a particular scenario it may be necessary to break only when certain conditions are valid. Breakpoints can be tailored to search for particular conditions, to break after a number of iterations, or even be filtered based on process or machine name.

Condition

A breakpoint condition can be specified by selecting Condition from the Breakpoint item on the right-click context menu for the breakpoint. This brings up the Breakpoint Condition dialog shown in Figure 49-6, which accepts a Boolean condition that determines whether the breakpoint will be hit. If the condition evaluates to `false`, the application continues past the breakpoint without breaking.

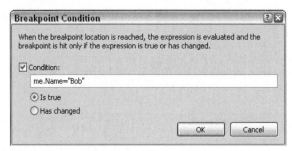

Figure 49-6

In the case of Figure 49-6, which is for a breakpoint set within the `Customer` class, the condition specifies that the customer's name must be Bob. As with most debugging windows, the Condition field provides rich IntelliSense support to aid writing valid conditions. If an invalid condition is specified, the debugger throws an appropriate error message and the application will break the first time the breakpoint is reached.

When a condition, or a Hit Count, as shown in the next section, is placed on a breakpoint, the breakpoint changes appearance. The solid red dot is replaced with a red dot with a white cross. When you move your mouse across this dot, the tooltip provides useful information about the breakpoint condition, as illustrated in Figure 49-7.

```
Customer.vb                                                                    ▾ ✕
⛐ Customer                                              ▾   (Declarations)      ▾
                                                                                ▲
  ⬤ ⊟      Public Sub TestOrder()
  ⚠ Customer.vb, line 24 character 5 ('TestOrder'), when 'me.Name="Bob"' is true
     ⊢        End Sub                                                           ▾
  ◄                            ▥                                      ►
```

Figure 49-7

Sometimes it is more relevant to know when this condition changes status, rather than when it is true. The Has Changed option will break the application when the status of the condition changes. If this option is selected, then the application will not break the first time the breakpoint is hit, as there is no previous status to compare against.

Using multiple breakpoints with complex conditions can significantly slow down the execution of your application, so it is recommended that you remove breakpoints that are no longer relevant in order to speed up the running of your application.

Hit Count

Perhaps not as useful as breakpoint conditions, it is also possible to break after a particular number of iterations through a breakpoint. To do this, select Hit Count from the Breakpoint item on the right-click context menu. Figure 49-8 shows the Breakpoint Hit Count dialog, which can be used to specify when the breakpoint should be hit.

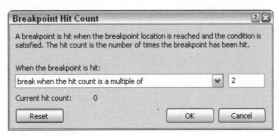

Figure 49-8

Every time the application is run, the hit counter is reset to zero, and it can be manually reset using the Reset button. The hit counter is also unique to each breakpoint. The hit count condition is one of four options:

- ❏ **Always:** Disregard the hit counter.

- ❏ **Is equal to:** Break if the hit counter is equal to the value specified.

- ❏ **Multiple of:** Break if the hit counter is a multiple of the value specified (as shown in Figure 49-7).

- ❏ **Is greater than or equal to:** Break if the hit counter is greater than or equal to the value specified.

Figure 49-9 shows the Breakpoints window, which provides additional information about the status of each of the breakpoints. In this case, the breakpoint is set to break every second time. The current hit counter is 4.

Figure 49-9

Filter

A single solution may contain multiple applications that need to be run at the same time. This is a common scenario when building a multi-tier application. When the application is run, the debugger can attach to all of these processes, enabling them to be debugged. By default, when a breakpoint is reached all the processes will break. This behavior can be controlled from the Debugging (General) node in the Options window, accessible from the Options item on the Tools menu. Unchecking the "Break all processes when one process breaks" checkbox enables processes to be debugged individually.

If a breakpoint is set in a class library that is used by more than one process, each process will break when it reaches that breakpoint. Because you might only be interested in debugging one of these processes, you can place a filter on the breakpoint that limits it to the process you are interested in. If you are debugging applications on multiple machines, then it is also possible to specify a machine name filter.

In fact, filtering can be useful for a multi-threaded application for which you want to limit the breakpoints to a particular thread. However, in this case, when the breakpoint is hit (such as when the current thread being executed meets the filter criteria), all threads are paused regardless of whether they meet the filter criteria. Figure 49-10 shows the Breakpoint Filter dialog and the possible filter conditions.

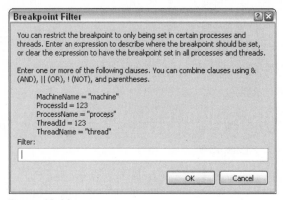

Figure 49-10

Working with Breakpoints

It's often necessary to adjust a breakpoint, as it might be in the wrong location or no longer relevant. In most cases it is easiest to remove the breakpoint, but in some cases — for example, when you have a complex breakpoint condition — it might be necessary to adjust the existing breakpoint.

Deleting

To remove a breakpoint that is no longer required, select it, either in the code editor or in the Breakpoints window, and remove it using the Toggle Breakpoint item from the Debug menu. Alternatively, the Delete Breakpoint item from the right-click context menu or the Delete Breakpoint icon from the Breakpoints window toolbar will remove the breakpoint.

Disable

Instead of deleting a breakpoint, simply disabling the breakpoint can be useful when you have a breakpoint condition set or you are tracking a hit count. To disable a breakpoint, select it either in the code editor or in the Breakpoints window, and disable it using the Disable Breakpoint item from the right-click context menu. Alternatively, you can uncheck the checkbox against the breakpoint in the Breakpoints window. Figure 49-11 shows how a disabled breakpoint would appear in the code window.

Changing Location

The location of a breakpoint can be modified by selecting Location from the Breakpoint item on the right-click context menu. Depending on what type of breakpoint has been set, the dialog shows the location of the breakpoint as either a line and character position in a file or function, or as an address within an assembly. If the location is either a file or function position, the breakpoint can be adjusted so it is in the correct location. Address breakpoints are harder to relocate, as you need to ensure that the new address is a valid location for a breakpoint.

Figure 49-11

Tracepoints

A *tracepoint* differs from a breakpoint in that it triggers an additional action when it is hit. In fact, for purposes such as applying filters, conditions, and hit counts, a tracepoint can be thought of as a breakpoint.

Tracepoints can be compared to using either `Debug` or `Trace` statements in your code, but tracepoints can be dynamically set as the application is being debugged and do not affect your code.

Creating a Tracepoint

Tracepoints can be created from either an existing breakpoint or the Breakpoint right-click context menu. To create a tracepoint from an existing breakpoint, select When Hit from the Breakpoint right-click context menu. The resulting dialog, shown in Figure 49-12, gives you the option of printing a message to the console window or running a macro. Alternatively, to create a tracepoint at a new location, select Insert Tracepoint from the Breakpoint item on the right-click context menu. This again loads the dialog shown in Figure 49-12 so you can customize the tracepoint action.

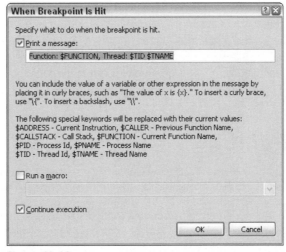

Figure 49-12

Once you set a tracepoint, the code window changes the appearance of that line of code to indicate that a tracepoint has been set. This is shown in Figure 49-13, where the tracepoint appears with a diamond in the margin. (The diamond is red, although this can't be seen in the figure.)

Figure 49-13

Tracepoint Actions

Two types of actions can be performed when a tracepoint is hit: either print a message to the console window or run a macro. In the dialog shown in Figure 49-12, you can indicate which action should be run when the tracepoint is hit. If both actions are unchecked, the tracepoint will fall back to being a breakpoint.

By default, once a tracepoint action has been indicated, the Continue Execution checkbox will be checked so the application will not break at this point. Unchecking this option causes the application to break at the tracepoint as if it were a breakpoint. The action defined will be performed prior to the application breaking. The appearance of this tracepoint will be the same as that of a breakpoint, as the visual cue indicates that the debugger will not stop at the tracepoint, rather than indicate that there are actions associated with the tracepoint.

Output Messages

As the dialog in Figure 49-12 suggests, a number of keywords can be used in conjunction with your trace message. However, a couple of keywords are not listed by the dialog: $FILEPOS, which gives the location of the current file, and $TICKS, which can be used as a relative time indicator.

Macros

Tracepoints can execute any Visual Studio macro, which includes macros you may have created. Because macros can be used to modify source code, be careful which macros you execute within a tracepoint. Modifying code while debugging an application may result in the source code being out of sync with the running application.

Execution Point

After reaching a breakpoint, it is often useful to be able to step through code and review both variable values and program execution. Visual Studio 2005 not only enables you to step through your code, it also permits you to adjust the execution point to backtrack or even repeat operations. The line of code that is about to be executed is highlighted, as shown in Figure 49-14. (The highlighting is yellow, which can't be seen in the figure, of course.)

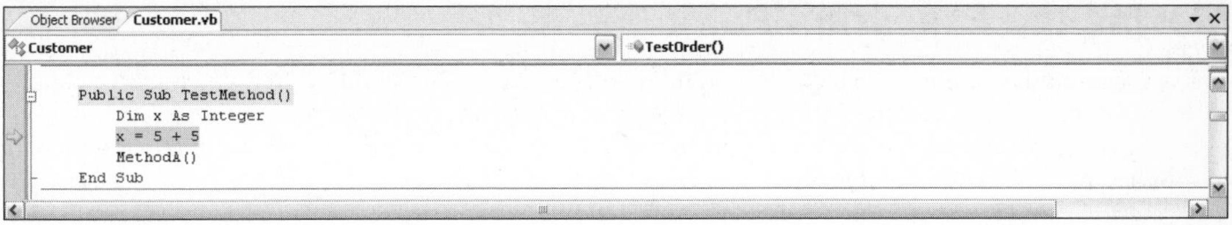

Figure 49-14

Stepping Through Code

The first step in manipulating the execution point is simply to step through code in the expected order of execution. Three size increments can be used to step the debugger forward. It is important to remember that when stepping through code it is actually being run, so variable values may change as you progress through the application.

Stepping Over (F10)

Stepping Over is fully executing the line that currently has focus and progressing to the next line in the current code block. If the end of the code block has been reached, stepping returns to the calling code block.

Stepping In (F11)

Stepping In behaves the same as Stepping Over when the line is a simple operator, such as a numeric operation or a cast. When the line is more complex, Stepping In steps through all user code. For example, in the following code snippet, pressing F10 through the TestMethod only steps through the lines of code within TestMethod. Pressing F11 steps through TestMethod until the MethodA call is made, and then the debugger steps through MethodA before returning to TestMethod:

```vb
Public Sub TestMethod()
    Dim x As Integer
    x = 5 + 5
    MethodA()
End Sub

Public Sub MethodA()
    Console.WriteLine("Method A being executed")
End Sub
```

Stepping Out (Shift+F11)

If you step into a long method by accident, it is quite often convenient to be able to step back out of that method without having to either step over every line in that method or setting a breakpoint at the end of the method. Stepping Out moves the cursor out of the current method to where it was being called. Considering the previous snippet, if you entered MethodA, pressing Shift+F11 would immediately return the cursor to the end of TestMethod.

Moving the Execution Point

As you become familiar with stepping in and out of functions, you will find that you are occasionally overzealous and accidentally step over the method call you are interested in. In this case, what you really want to do is rewind the last action. While you can't do that entirely, you can move the execution point so the method is reevaluated.

To move the current execution point, select and drag the yellow arrow next to the current line of execution (refer to Figure 49-12) forward or backward in the current method. Use this functionality with care, as it can result in unintended behavior and variable values.

Edit and Continue

One of the features of Visual Studio 2005 that a lot of developers have been waiting for is Edit and Continue. The good news is that both C# and VB.NET have support for Edit and Continue, enabling you to make changes to your application on-the-fly. Whenever your application is paused, you can make changes to your code and then resume execution. The new or modified code is dynamically added to your application, with the changes taking immediate effect.

Rude Edits

At this point, you are likely wondering whether there are any limitations on the changes that you can make. The answer is yes, and there are quite a few types of *rude edits*, which refer to any code change that requires the application to be stopped and rebuilt. A full list of rude edits is available from the Visual Studio 2005 help resource, but they include the following:

- ❑ Making changes to the current, or active, statement
- ❑ Changes to the list of global symbols — such as new types or methods — or changing the signatures of methods, events, or properties
- ❑ Changes to attributes

Stop Applying Changes

When changes are made to the source code while the application is paused, Visual Studio has to integrate, or apply, the changes into the running application. Depending on the type or complexity of the changes made, this might take some time. If you wish to cancel this action, you can select Stop Applying Code Changes from the Debug menu.

Summary

Most developers who use Visual Studio 2005 will use breakpoints to track down issues with their application. In this chapter you learned how to optimize the use of breakpoints to reduce the amount of time spent locating the issue.

The following chapter examines the various debugging windows that become active when the application is in Break mode. These enable you to probe variable values, identify and manage threads, as well as work with the Call Stack window.

Debugging Proxies and Visualizers

Other than writing code, debugging is likely the most time-consuming activity when writing an application. If you think about all the time you spend stepping through code, looking at the watch window to see the value of a variable, or even just running the application looking for any exceptions being raised, you will realize that this is one of the most complex and time-consuming parts of writing software.

Previous chapters have focused on how you can use the various debugging windows to retrieve information about the current status of your application, and how you can set breakpoints and tracepoints to generate debugging information. This chapter goes beyond what is provided out of the box, and looks at how you can customize the debugging experience to reduce the time spent wading through unnecessary lines of code.

Attributes

This section begins by outlining a number of debugging attributes that can be applied to code to affect the way the debugger steps through it. In addition, some attributes can be used to customize the appearance of your types when you hover over them in Break mode.

DebuggerBrowsable

The first attribute you can apply to fields and properties that belong to a C# class is the DebuggerBrowsable attribute. Although this attribute can be applied to both C# and VB.NET code, it is only interpreted by the C# debugger. This attribute takes a single parameter that determines how the member is displayed in the variable tree. In the following code snippet, the field Orders is set to Collapsed:

```
Public Class Customer
    <DebuggerBrowsable(DebuggerBrowsableState.Collapsed)> _
    Private Orders as List(Of Order)

End Class
```

Figure 50-1 shows the same snippet of code with the `DebuggerBrowsable` initially set to `Collapsed` (or not specified). The middle snippet shows the `RootHidden` value, where the actual `Orders` item does not appear, just the contents of the collection. Finally, the `Never` value is used, in which case the `Orders` member does not appear at all.

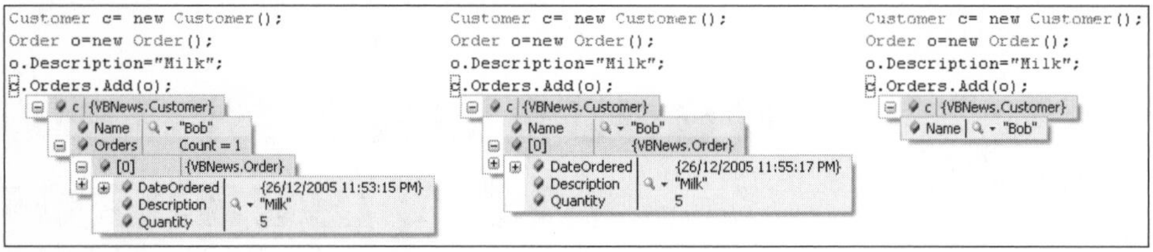

Figure 50-1

DebuggerDisplay

When you hover your mouse over a variable while you are in Break mode, the first thing you will see in the tooltip is the type of object you are hovering over. In Figure 50-1, a mouse was initially hovering over the `Customer` class, followed by the `Order` class. This information is not particularly useful, as most of the time you have a fairly good idea about the type of object you are dealing with. It would be better for this single line to contain more useful information about the object. This is the case for well-known types such as strings and integers where the actual value is displayed.

The `DebuggerDisplay` attribute can be used to change the single line representation of the object from the default full class name. This attribute takes a single parameter, which is a `String`. The format of this `String` can accept member injections using the `String.Format` breakout syntax. For example, the attributes applied to the `Customer` and `Order` classes might be as follows:

```
<DebuggerDisplay("Customer {Name} has {Orders.Count} orders")> _
Public Class Customer

<DebuggerDisplay("Order for {Quantity} of {Description} made on {DateOrdered}")> _
Public Class Order
```

This would give you the debugger output shown in Figure 50-2, which indicates that customer Bob has one order, which, as you can see from the description, was made on December 27 for five cartons of milk.

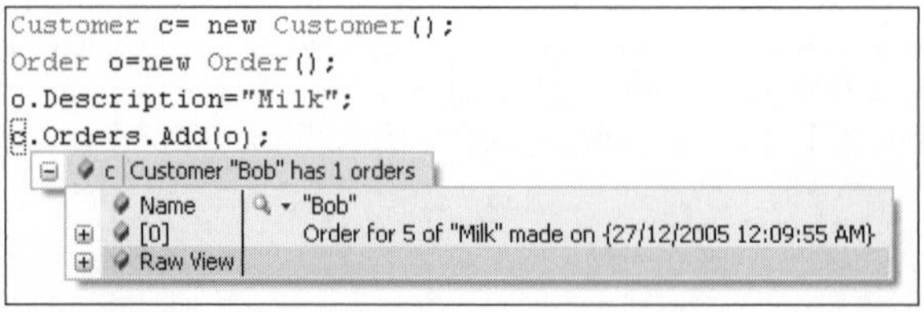

Figure 50-2

Looking back at the syntax for the DebuggerDisplay attribute, you can see that the output string consists of both static text and field and property information from the object. For example, the Name property for the Customer object is referenced using the {Name} syntax within the static text.

DebuggerHidden

The DebuggerHidden attribute can be added to code that you don't want to step through when debugging. Code marked with this attribute is stepped over and does not support breakpoints. If this code makes a call to another method, the debugger steps into that method. Taking the following code snippet, a breakpoint can be set in both ClickHandler and NotSoHiddenMethod:

```
Private Sub ClickHandler(ByVal sender As System.Object, _
                  ByVal e As System.EventArgs) Handles BtnTest.Click
    HiddenMethod()
End Sub

<DebuggerHidden()> _
Public Sub HiddenMethod()
    Console.WriteLine("Can't set a breakpoint here")
    NotSoHiddenMethod()
End Sub

Public Sub NotSoHiddenMethod()
    Console.WriteLine("Can set a breakpoint here!")
End Sub
```

If you step through this code, the debugger goes from the call to HiddenMethod in the ClickHandler method straight to the NotSoHiddenMethod. The call stack at this point is shown in Figure 50-3, and you can see that HiddenMethod does not appear in the stack.

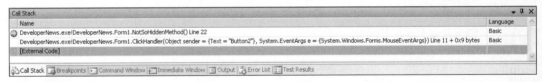

Figure 50-3

DebuggerStepThrough

Like the DebuggerHidden attribute, when the DebuggerStepThrough attribute is applied to a piece of code, that code is stepped over when debugging regardless of whether this code calls other methods.

Similar to the DebuggerHidden attribute, breakpoints cannot be set within a block of code marked with the DebuggerStepThrough attribute. However, if a breakpoint is set within a section of code that is called by that code, the attributed code will be marked as *external code* in the call stack. This is illustrated in Figures 50-4 and 50-5.

Figure 50-4

Figure 50-5

Visual Studio 2005 introduces the Just My Code option, configurable from the Debugging node in the Options dialog (select Tools⇨Options). Unchecking this option makes all code contained within your application appear in the call stack. This includes designer and other generated code that you might not want to debug. Once this option is unchecked, breakpoints can also be set in blocks of code marked with this attribute.

DebuggerNonUserCode

The `DebuggerNonUserCode` attribute combines the `DebuggerHidden` and `DebuggerStepThrough` attributes. When the Just My Code option is selected, breakpoints cannot be set in blocks of code marked with this attribute, and the code will appear as external code in the call stack. However, stepping through code will step into any code called by that block of code in the same way it does for the `DebuggerHidden` attribute.

Type Proxies

So far, you have seen how you can modify the tooltip to show information that is more relevant to debugging your application. However, the attributes discussed so far have been limited in how they control what information is presented in the expanded tree. The `DebuggerBrowsable` attribute enables you to hide particular members, but there is no way to add more fields. This is where the `DebuggerTypeProxy` attribute can be used to provide you with complete control over the layout of the tooltip.

The other scenario where a type proxy is useful is where a property of a class changes values within the class. For example, the following snippet from the `Customer` class tracks the number of times the `OrderCount` property has been accessed. Whenever the tooltip is accessed, the `CountAccessed` property is incremented by one:

```
Public Class Customer
    ...

    Private m_CountAccessed As Integer
    Public ReadOnly Property OrderCount() As Integer
        Get
            m_CountAccessed += 1
```

```
            Return Me.Orders.Count
        End Get
    End Property

    Public ReadOnly Property CountAccessed() As Integer
        Get
            Return Me.m_CountAccessed
        End Get
    End Property

End Class
```

Figure 50-6 illustrates the tooltip you want to be shown for the `Customer` class. Instead of showing the full list of orders to navigate through, it provides a summary about the number of orders, the maximum and minimum order quantities, and a list of the items on order.

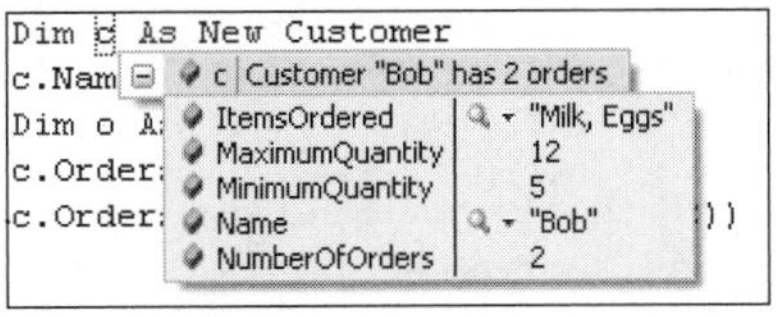

Figure 50-6

The first line in the tooltip is the same as what you created using the `DebuggerDisplay` attribute. To generate the rest of the tooltip, you need to create an additional class that will act as a substitute when it comes to presenting this information. You then need to attribute the `Customer` class with the `DebuggerTypeProxy` attribute so the debugger knows to use that class instead of the `Customer` class when displaying the tooltip. The following code snippet shows the `CustomerProxy` class that has been nested within the `Customer` class:

```
<DebuggerDisplay("Customer {Name} has {Orders.Count} orders")> _
<DebuggerTypeProxy(GetType(Customer.CustomerProxy))> _
Public Class Customer
    ...

    Private m_CountAccessed As Integer
    Public ReadOnly Property OrderCount() As Integer
        Get
            m_CountAccessed += 1
            Return Me.Orders.Count
        End Get
    End Property

    Public ReadOnly Property CountAccessed() As Integer
        Get
            Return Me.m_CountAccessed
        End Get
    End Property

    Public Class CustomerProxy

        Public Name As String
```

```
        Public NumberOfOrders As Integer
        Public MaximumQuantity As Integer = 0
        Public MinimumQuantity As Integer = Integer.MaxValue
        Public ItemsOrdered As String

        Public Sub New(ByVal c As Customer)
            Me.Name = c.m_Name
            Me.NumberOfOrders = c.m_orders.Count
            For Each o As Order In c.m_orders
                Me.MaximumQuantity = Math.Max(o.Quantity, Me.MaximumQuantity)
                Me.MinimumQuantity = Math.Min(o.Quantity, Me.MinimumQuantity)
                If Not Me.ItemsOrdered = "" Then Me.ItemsOrdered &= ", "
                Me.ItemsOrdered &= o.Description
            Next
        End Sub

    End Class

End Class
```

There are very few reasons why you should create public nested classes, but a type proxy is a good example because it needs to be public so it can be specified in the `DebuggerTypeProxy` attribute, and it should be nested so it can access private members from the `Customer` class without using the public accessors.

In fact, the `CustomerProxy` class breaks another good coding practice, which states you should have private fields with public accessors. When the debugger tooltips are generated, both private and public fields and properties are displayed. As such, if you were to follow good coding practice here, you would end up with 10 elements being displayed, which only adds confusion.

The Full Picture

On occasion, you might want to ignore the proxy type. For example, this might be true if you are consuming a third-party component that has a proxy type defined for it that disguises the underlying data structure. If something is going wrong with the way the component is behaving, you might need to review the internal contents of the component to trace the source of the issue.

In the Options dialog, accessible from the Tools menu, there is a node that covers Debugging. This includes nodes for controlling both the Edit and Continue feature and just-in-time debugging. To ignore the proxy type and see the original structure of a third-party component, check the box on the General tab that says "Show raw structure of objects in variables window."

Visualizers

The last part of this chapter looks at a new concept added to Visual Studio 2005 to assist with debugging more complex data structures. Two of the most common data types programmers work with are *strings* and *datatables*. Strings are often much larger than the area that can be displayed within a tooltip, and the structure of the Datatable object is not suitable for displaying in a tooltip, even using a type proxy. In both of these cases, a visualizer has been created that enables the data to be viewed in a sensible format.

Once a visualizer has been created for a particular type, a magnifying glass icon appears in the first line of the debugger tooltip. Clicking this icon displays the visualizer. Figure 50-7 shows the Text Visualizer dialog that appears.

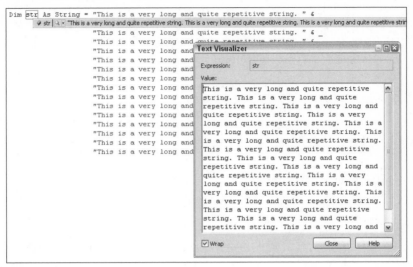

Figure 50-7

Before you can start writing a visualizer, you need to add a reference to the `Microsoft.VisualStudio` `.DebuggerVisualizers` namespace. To do this, right-click in the Solution Explorer and select Add Reference from the context menu.

A visualizer is typically made up of two parts: the class that acts as a host for the visualizer and is referenced by the `DebuggerVisualizer` attribute applied to the class being visualized, and the form that is then used to display, or visualize, the class. Figure 50-8 shows a simple form, CustomerForm, that can be used to represent the customer information. This is a standard Windows form with a `BindingSource` used to link the `TextBox` and `DataGrid` to the `Customer` object.

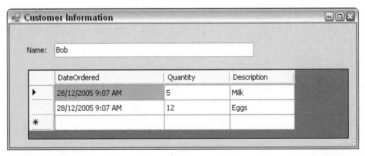

Figure 50-8

The next stage is to wire this form up to be used as the visualizer for the `Customer` class. This is done by creating the nested `CustomerVisualizer` class, which inherits from the `DialogDebuggerVisualizer` abstract class, as shown in the following code:

```
<Serializable()> _
<DebuggerDisplay("Customer {Name} has {Orders.Count} orders")> _
<DebuggerTypeProxy(GetType(Customer.CustomerProxy))> _
<DebuggerVisualizer(GetType(Customer.CustomerVisualizer))> _
Public Class Customer
    ...

    Public Class CustomerVisualizer
        Inherits DialogDebuggerVisualizer

        Protected Overrides Sub Show _
                (ByVal windowService As IDialogVisualizerService, _
                ByVal objectProvider As IVisualizerObjectProvider)

            Dim c As Customer = CType(objectProvider.GetObject, Customer)

            Dim cf As New CustomerForm
            cf.CustomerBindingSource.DataSource = c

            windowService.ShowDialog(cf)
        End Sub
    End Class

End Class
```

Unlike the type proxy, which interacts with the actual `Customer` object being debugged, visualizers need to be able to serialize the class being debugged so the class can be moved from the debuggee process (the process being debugged) to the debugger process (the process that is doing the debugging and will show the visualizer). As such, both the `Customer` and `Order` classes need to be marked with the `Serializable` attribute.

The `Show` method of the `CustomerVisualizer` class does three things. To display the `Customer` object being debugged, first you need to get a reference to this object. This is done via the `GetObject` method on the `ObjectProvider` object. Because the communication between the two processes is done via a stream, this method does the heavy lifting associated with deserializing the object so you can work with it.

Next you need to create and bind the `Customer` object to an instance of the `CustomerForm`. Finally, use the `ShowDialog` method on the `WindowSerivce` object to display the form. It is important that you display the form using this object because it will ensure that the form is displayed on the appropriate UI thread.

Lastly, note that the `CustomerVisualizer` class is referenced in the `DebuggerVisualizer` attribute, ensuring that the debugger uses this class to load the visualizer for `Customer` objects.

As a side note, if you write components and want to ship visualizers separately from the components themselves, visualizers can be installed by placing the appropriate assembly into either the `C:\Program Files\Microsoft Visual Studio 8\Common7\Packages\Debugger\Visualizers` directory, or the `My Documents\Visual Studio 2005\Visualizers` directory.

Advanced Techniques

Thus far, this chapter has covered how to display and visualize objects you are debugging. In earlier chapters you learned how to modify field and property values on the object being debugged via the DataTip. The missing link is being able to edit more complex data objects. The final section in this chapter looks at how to extend your visualizer so you can save changes to the Customer object.

Saving Changes to Your Object

When you created the CustomerVisualizer, you had to retrieve the Customer object from the communication stream using the GetObject method. This essentially gave you a clone of the Customer object being debugged to use with the visualizer. To save any changes you make in the CustomerVisualizer, you need to send the new Customer object back to the debuggee process. This can be done using the ReplaceObject method on the ObjectProvider, which gives you a CustomerVisualizer as follows:

```
Public Class CustomerVisualizer
    Inherits DialogDebuggerVisualizer

    Protected Overrides Sub Show _
            (ByVal windowService As IDialogVisualizerService, _
            ByVal objectProvider As IVisualizerObjectProvider)

        Dim c As Customer = CType(objectProvider.GetObject, Customer)

        Dim cf As New CustomerForm
        cf.CustomerBindingSource.DataSource = c

        If windowService.ShowDialog(cf) = Windows.Forms.DialogResult.OK Then
            objectProvider.ReplaceObject(c)
        End If
    End Sub
End Class
```

Summary

Debugging applications is one of the most time-consuming and frustrating activities in the development cycle. In this chapter you learned how you can take charge of Visual Studio 2005 by customizing the debugging experience.

Using debugging proxy types and visualizers, you can control how information is presented to you while you are debugging your application. This means that you can easily determine when your application is not functioning correctly and be able to trace the source of the issue.

Maintaining Web Applications

With Visual Studio 2005, debugging solutions for the web is just as straightforward as doing the same for Windows-based applications. You can use many of the same debugging windows already discussed in previous chapters, as well as deal with errors through the Exception Assistant. However, there are some minor differences and additional features specific to web applications that you can use to target your debugging practices more closely to the web paradigm.

In addition to the available debugging techniques, ASP.NET 2.0 also provides you with a comprehensive tracing capability, and even the capability to perform health monitoring on your system to ensure it is running in the manner you expect, and exposing problematic scenarios when it doesn't.

Debugging

Before you can perform any level of debugging in a web application, you first need to ensure that ASP.NET debugging is enabled in your web site. To make sure it's active, right-click the project entry in the Solution Explorer and select Property Pages from the context menu.

When the Property Pages dialog is displayed, navigate to the Start Options page, and ensure that the ASP.NET debugger option is checked, as illustrated in Figure 51-1. While you've got this page open, you can also customize how the web site is to be started, including not opening any specific page, but running the server so it listens for a request from another application.

In addition, if you want to be able to include unmanaged code or even stored procedures in your debugging of the web applications, you can activate the Native code and SQL Server debuggers here (take a look at Chapter 52 for more information on debugging stored procedures).

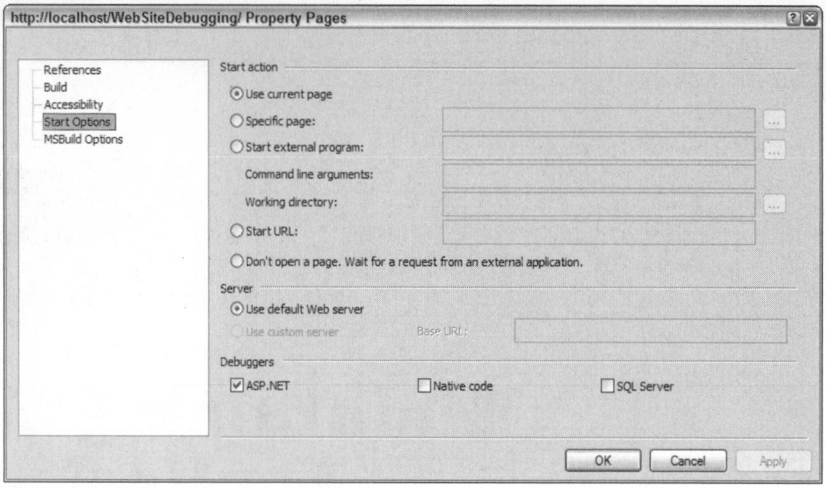

Figure 51-1

An alternative method of implementing web debugging is to use the `Web.config` file. Locate the `compilation` node within `system.web` and set the `debug` attribute to `true`. The following listing shows a minimal `Web.config` file with the `debug` option set, ready for hooking the debugger to the application:

```
<configuration>
    <appSettings/>
    <connectionStrings/>
    <system.web>
        <compilation debug="true" strict="false" explicit="true" />
    </system.web>
</configuration>
```

Note that even when you activate the ASP.NET debugger in the Start Options, without setting the `debug` attribute to `true` you will be unable to debug the application. However, Visual Studio will detect this discrepancy and present you with a dialog informing you that in order to debug you will need to change `Web.config`. It also provides an option for Visual Studio to automatically change this attribute for you.

While you're editing the `Web.config` file, you may also want to configure redirections for any normal HTTP error codes. While this doesn't help you with debugging, it enables you to specify a nicely formatted page for your end users, explaining the problem instead of displaying a generic page potentially filled with information you don't want the user to know. Modifying the previous `Web.config` file to include these redirection options for 403 (access denied) and 404 (page not found) can result in a configuration similar to the following:

```
<configuration>
    <appSettings/>
    <connectionStrings/>
    <system.web>
        <compilation debug="true" strict="false" explicit="true" />
        <customErrors mode="RemoteOnly" defaultRedirect="GenericErrorPage.htm">
            <error statusCode="403" redirect="AccessDenied.html" />
            <error statusCode="404" redirect="PageNotFound.html" />
```

```
        </customErrors>
    </system.web>
</configuration>
```

Breaking on Errors Automatically

When your web application encounters an error, Visual Studio 2005 drops back into the IDE and positions the workspace so the statement at issue is visible. Just like Windows-based applications, Visual Studio can aid you when errors occur by displaying the Exception Assistant. As shown in Figure 51-2, web errors are fully detailed and include information about which part of the statement is in error.

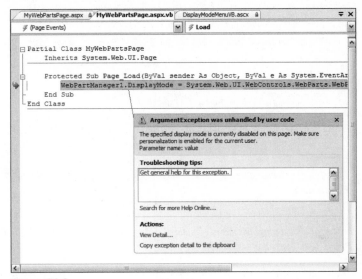

Figure 51-2

You can gather additional information on the error by clicking the View Detail link, which provides you with a comprehensive exception object visualizer that you can navigate to determine the content of the error at hand.

Debugging an Executing Web Application

Sometimes you'll need to debug an application after it has already been deployed onto IIS and is executing. If the application was started with debugging enabled, this is not really a problem, as you can simply break it in the IDE, or even just insert breakpoints on the page you want to debug and wait until that page is used.

However, if the web application was started without debugging enabled, you can still debug the application by attaching to the process that's handling the web site. The process you'll need to attach to is the ASP.NET worker process, and it will either be the native process within IIS (normally named aspnet_wp .exe) or the Visual Studio 2005 test server application WebDev.WebServer.exe, which is used for local testing and debugging.

Either way, the method to attach to the running web application is the same. From the Debug menu in Visual Studio 2005, use the Attach to Process command. This displays the Attach to Process dialog window (see Figure 51-3) from which you can browse all active processes. Locate the ASP.NET worker process from the Available Processes list and click the Attach button.

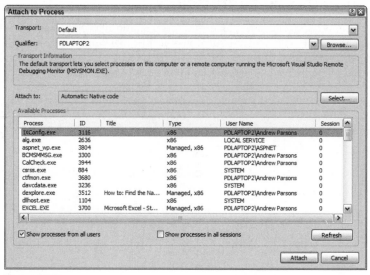

Figure 51-3

You need to check the "Show processes from all users" option because the IIS process is usually running under the ASPNET user instead of your own.

Once you've finished debugging in this manner, you should always cleanly detach from the process by selecting Debug➪Detach All.

Error Handling

While debugging your applications is indeed easy with the tools Visual Studio 2005 provides, it is always best to try to avoid error situations proactively. You can do this in web applications with standard `Try-Catch` blocks, but you will also want to make your solutions more solid by including code to handle any errors that fall outside any `Catch` conditions.

You can debug on two levels — on an individual page you can intercept unexpected errors and produce a custom-built error, or you can debug on an applicationwide level through the implementation of a routine to handle errors in the `global.asax` file.

Page-Level Errors

To handle an error on an individual page, you need to implement an event handler routine that intercepts the `MyBase.Error` event. When this event is raised, you can then perform whatever actions you need to take place when unexpected errors occur. A typical routine might look like this:

```
Private Sub Page_Error(ByVal sender As Object, ByVal e As System.EventArgs) _
    Handles MyBase.Error
    Response.Write("An unexpected error has occurred.")
    Server.ClearError()
End Sub
```

Remember that you can also set custom redirections for standard HTTP error codes in the `Web.config` file, so you should only use this method for errors that are not already handled and are specific to the individual page.

Application-Level Errors

At the web application level, you can also trap a series of errors through the `global.asax` file. By default, Visual Studio 2005 web projects do not include this file, so you'll first need to add it to the project through the Website⇨Add New Item menu command. Select the Global Application Class item, leave the name as `Global.asax`, and click Add to add the file to your project.

When this class is added to the project, the template includes stubs for the commonly encountered application events, including the error event. To handle any errors that are not catered to elsewhere in the project, add your processing code to this `Application_Error` routine, like so:

```
Sub Application_Error(ByVal sender As Object, ByVal e As EventArgs)
    Server.Transfer("UnexpectedError.aspx")
End Sub
```

This sample routine simply transfers the user to an errors page that determines what to do by interrogating the `Server.GetLastError` property.

Tracing

In addition to actively debugging your web applications when things go wrong, you can also implement ASP.NET tracing functionality to look at the information produced in an individual page request. Using tracing enables you to add debug statements to your code that are only viewable when viewing locally; when the web application is deployed to the remote server, users see only the proper page.

Trace information can include variables and simple objects to help you determine the state of the specific request and how it was executed. Note that ASP.NET tracing is different from using the `Trace` class in normal Windows applications in that its output is produced on the actual ASP.NET web page or in a standalone trace viewer, rather than the output windows that `Trace` commands use.

Tracing has been available since the first release of ASP.NET but with Visual Studio 2005 and ASP.NET 2.0 you can now redirect the `Trace` commands to the ASP.NET tracing output destination as well, enabling a more comprehensive capability to follow the diagnostic information in your web site page requests. In addition, you can now perform application-level tracing much more easily than before.

Page-Level Tracing

To implement page-level tracing, you simply need to include a `trace` attribute in the `@Page` directive at the top of the page you wish to trace. A simple Visual Basic page with tracing activated might look like the following:

```
<%@ Page Language="VB" Trace="true" AutoEventWireup="false"
CodeFile="Default.aspx.vb" Inherits="_Default" %>

<!DOCTYPE html PUBLIC "-//W3C//DTD XHTML 1.0 Transitional//EN"
"http://www.w3.org/TR/xhtml1/DTD/xhtml1-transitional.dtd">

<html xmlns="http://www.w3.org/1999/xhtml" >
<head runat="server">
    <title>Untitled Page</title>
</head>
<body>
    <form id="form1" runat="server">
    <div>
        Hello!</div>
    </form>
</body>
</html>
```

In addition, you can specify how the tracing messages associated with the page request should appear by using the `TraceMode` attribute. Set this to `SortByTime` to output the tracing messages in the order that they were produced, or `SortByCategory` to categorize them into different message types. Figure 51-4 shows the trace output for the sample page defined in the previous listing when sorted by category.

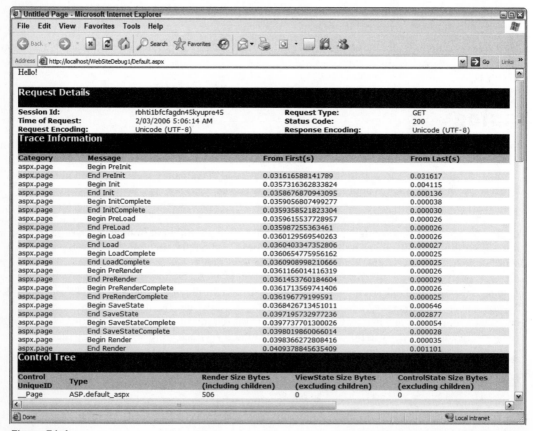

Figure 51-4

Application-Level Tracing

Application-level tracing can be enabled through the `Web.config` file. Within the `system.web` node you need to include a `trace` node that contains the attribute `enabled` with a value of `true`. When using application-level tracing, you can control how the tracing is produced through the `pageOutput` attribute. When set to `true`, you receive the tracing information at the bottom of every page (similar to how it appears in Figure 51-4), while a value of `false` ensures that the tracing information never appears on the page, and is instead only accessible through the Trace Viewer (covered later in this chapter). You can also restrict the amount of information to trace with the `requestLimit` attribute. Including a `trace` node for the `Web.config` file you saw earlier in this chapter results in a configuration like the following:

```
<configuration>
    <appSettings/>
    <connectionStrings/>
    <system.web>
        <compilation debug="true" strict="false" explicit="true" />
        <customErrors mode="RemoteOnly" defaultRedirect="GenericErrorPage.htm">
            <error statusCode="403" redirect="AccessDenied.html" />
            <error statusCode="404" redirect="PageNotFound.html" />
        </customErrors>
        <trace enabled="true" pageOutput="false" traceMode="SortByCategory"/>
    </system.web>
</configuration>
```

Trace Output

Tracing output is voluminous. The simple Hello page defined earlier produces almost three full printed pages of information, including the following categories of data:

❑ **Request Details:** The specific details of the current session, time of the request, what type of request it was, and the HTTP code that is returned to the browser

❑ **Trace Information:** A full listing of each event as it begins and then ends, including the amount of time taken to process each event

❑ **Control Tree:** A listing of all controls defined on the page, including the page object itself as well as HTML elements. Each object also has a size listed, so you can determine whether there are any abnormal object sizes affecting your application's performance.

❑ **Session State and Application State:** These two lists show the keys and their values for the individual session and the application overall.

❑ **Request Cookies Collection and Response Cookies Collection:** A list of any known ASP.NET request and response cookies on the system that your application may be able to access

❑ **Headers Collection:** A list of the HTTP headers included in the page

❑ **Response Headers Collection:** The HTTP headers associated with the response, indicating what type of object is being returned

❑ **Form Collection:** A list of any forms defined in the page

❑ **Querystring Collection:** A list of any query strings used in the page request

❑ **Server Variables:** A list of all server variables known to the ASP.NET server and application you're currently executing

As you can see, when tracing is implemented for a web page or application, you gain access to an enormous amount of information that you can then use to determine how your application is performing. You can see whether there are problems in the various collections in the way of missing or extraneous data, as well as analyze the Trace Information list to determine whether there are any abnormally long processing times for any specific events.

Trace Viewer

The Trace Viewer is a custom page included in your web application when you have application tracing activated. When tracing is being reported at the application level, you can navigate to this page and view all page tracing output as it occurs. To view the Trace Viewer, browse to the `trace.axd` page in the root directory of your web site.

The Trace Viewer provides a summary table of all requests made in the application, along with the time the request was made and the HTTP status code returned in the response. It also provides a link to detailed information for each request (which is the same information that you can see on a page trace discussed earlier), as shown in Figure 51-5.

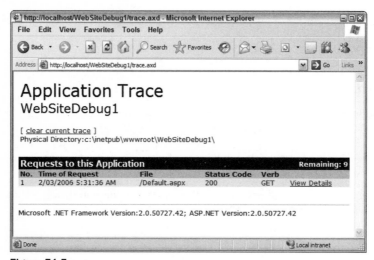

Figure 51-5

Custom Trace Output

You can supplement the default trace information with your own custom-built trace messages, using the `Trace.Warn` and `Trace.Write` methods. Both have the same set of syntactical overloads, and the only real difference is that messages outputted using the `Warn` method are displayed in red text.

The simplest form for these commands is to include a message string like so:

```
Trace.Warn("Encountered a potential issue")
```

However, you can categorize your warnings and messages by using the second and third forms of the methods, including a category and optionally an error object as well:

```
Trace.Warn("MyApp Error Category", "Encountered a potential issue", myAppException)
```

Summary

With the combination of Visual Studio 2005 and ASP.NET 2.0 server-side capabilities, you have a wide array of tools to help you look after your web solutions. These features enhance the already impressive feature set available with normal Windows application debugging, with web-specific features such as page- and application-level error handling, and the capability to keep track of your application as it runs on the server.

In addition, by adding tracing code, which you can view through the Trace Viewer, you can monitor the way issues are produced in your web applications without stopping the execution for your end-users.

Other Debugging Techniques

As you've seen throughout the last several chapters, Visual Studio 2005 comes with a great variety of ways to debug and run through your applications, including catching errors and displaying them to you for action before the code executes too far, a number of tool windows specifically dealing with the area of testing, and other features such as breakpoints and visualizing errors.

However, there is still more functionality to be found in the Visual Studio IDE that you can use to customize your experience with debugging projects, databases, and even macros, and that's what this chapter is all about. In it you'll find a summary of the additional options you have at your disposal for testing and debugging your projects regardless of language or technology.

Debugging Options Pages

There is a whole group of options pages dedicated to the area of debugging. You can use these pages to customize the way debugging occurs in the application, controlling when and how debug messages are displayed, as well as implementing specific features that cater to different workflow methodologies, such as Edit and Continue.

To access these options, use the Tools⇨Options menu command and then navigate to the Debugging group, expanding it to show the individual pages if necessary. Selecting the root node of Debugging displays the General debugging options page automatically, so you may not need to expand the node if your customization will take place in that page alone.

General Options

The General options page contains more than twenty settings that tweak the way you can experience debugging projects (see Figure 52-1). Be aware that Visual Studio will choose a different set of default properties depending on the environment setup you selected, with the Visual Basic programmer environment having the most marked difference from the other language options sets. Because of this variance in setup, you should review these options carefully to ensure that each option you require has been activated. To aid you in getting this right, the following list explains what each option does when activated.

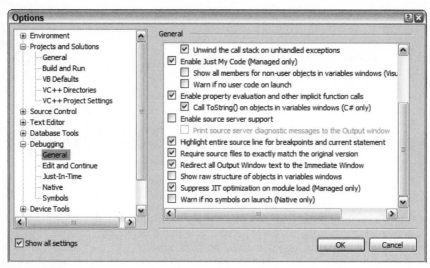

Figure 52-1

❑ **Ask before deleting all breakpoints:** You can clear all breakpoints appearing in a particular document or window through the Edit⇨Breakpoints submenu. Because the action cannot be undone, you can activate this option to ask for confirmation before performing it. Interestingly, for Visual Basic programmers this option is not on by default, meaning all breakpoints will be cleared without confirmation.

❑ **Break all processes when one process breaks:** This option is active by default in all situations and causes all processes in a multi-process project to halt whenever a breakpoint or error is encountered. This enables all processes to be kept in sync, but in some rare situations you may want to allow background or second-tier processes to continue to execute while you debug the module that was paused.

❑ **Break when exceptions cross AppDomain or managed/native boundaries:** Inactive by default, this option enables you to break when processing exceptions that cross managed code and unmanaged code such as COM applications. You can usually ignore this setting, but it can be handy when debugging applications that use the COM Interop to interface between the two types of programming language.

❑ **Enable address-level debugging:** Many of the debugging windows, such as Registers and Disassembly, are only appropriate for address-level debugging. While this is useful, in some rare situations it can affect the way your code is executed, particularly in real-time sensitive processing.

 ❑ **Show disassembly if source is not available:** When using address-level debugging, you can also include a disassembly of any portion of the application that does not have source code associated with it. By default, this option is turned off, as it can affect performance slightly.

❑ **Enable breakpoint filters:** Breakpoint filters can control when breakpoints are activated by setting them for specific threads or processes. This option, active by default, can control whether these filters are active or not.

❑ **Enable the exception assistant:** Another useful feature discussed previously, the Exception Assistant can be turned off when debugging managed code. When deactivated, the exception dialog window used in previous versions of Visual Studio is used instead when an exception is encountered.

  ❑ **Unwind the call stack on unhandled exceptions:** This option enables you to examine the detail found in the call stack even if the current error was not caught by an exception handler.

❑ **Enable Just My Code:** Any code that is specifically part of your project and not part of the underlying system framework or external to the current application is termed by Visual Studio as My Code. Activating this option enables you to restrict the step-through process of the debugger only to that code considered part of the My Code block. Note that this option only affects debugging of managed code.

  ❑ **Show all members for non-user objects in variables windows:** Non-public members of objects in the non-My Code sections can be included in the variables windows. This option is only appropriate for Visual Basic code.

  ❑ **Warn if no user code on launch:** On by default for all environmental setups except for Visual Basic, this option displays a dialog warning when no code is found in the My Code section of your application.

❑ **Enable property evaluation and other implicit function calls:** This option enables you to access properties and function calls in both the QuickWatch dialog window and the variables windows. Without this option active you will need to explicitly call functions.

  ❑ **Call ToString() on objects in variables windows:** C# code normally requires explicit `ToString()` function calls for any object type to display the string representation of the object. Without this option active, displaying an object in a variable window only displays the type name instead of the actual data contents. You can change this behavior with this option.

❑ **Enable source server support:** The source server is a way of retrieving otherwise unavailable source code. It requires a special DLL called `srcsrv.dll` and reads the application's PDB file to determine the exact version of source files.

  ❑ **Print source server diagnostic messages to the Output window:** When using source server support, you can output any diagnostic messages to the Output window by activating this option.

❑ **Highlight entire source line for breakpoints and current statement:** For statements that break over multiple lines, this option controls how the breakpoints are displayed. With the option on, which is true for Visual Basic environment setups only, the entire source line is highlighted.

❑ **Require source files to exactly match the original version:** Activating this option forces the debugger to first verify the source code that is to be used to debug against the original source. If they do not match, you will be prompted to locate the original source before the debugging can continue.

❑ **Redirect all Output Window text to the Immediate Window:** This controls where the debugging output that normally goes to the Output tool window will end up. Activating this option forces the content to be directed to the Immediate window instead. This can be useful when you want to see all of your output in one location, with functions you perform in the Immediate window being displayed in the context of any debugging output that is also displayed.

❑ **Show raw structure of objects in variables windows:** As discussed in the previous chapters, Visual Studio goes a long way in visualizing the data found in objects into a readable form. However, if you want to view the information as it appears in the original object definition without any view customizing, you can activate this option.

❑ **Suppress JIT optimization on module load:** By default, when running an application in debug mode, the JIT optimization options are disabled so you can more easily determine the exact source of a particular issue. Deactivating this option enables the JIT compiler to also optimize the code when a module is loaded, in the same way as it does in a non-debug build. You will see the same performance increase as if you were running the project outside the debugging environment, but you may find it more difficult to track down problems. Obviously, this option has no effect on native code.

❑ **Warn if no symbols on launch:** When debugging native code, you normally use debugging symbols to track down issues. If no symbols are defined, then this option will produce a warning dialog window to let you know that you will not be able to successfully debug the code.

Debug Page in My Project

In addition to the global options you have available to you in Visual Studio 2005, you can also customize the debugging experience further for an individual project. The Debug page (see Figure 52-2) is accessible for managed code languages such as Visual Basic and C# and can be used to control how the project should be started.

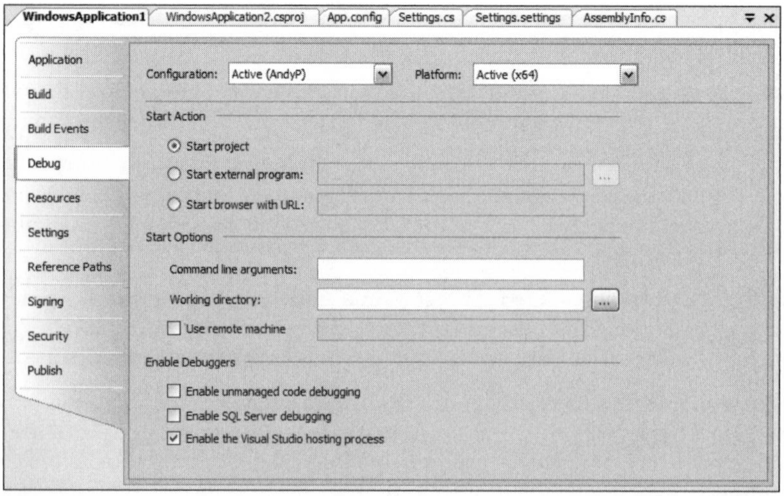

Figure 52-2

By default, Visual Studio assumes that you want to start the project directly, but you can also choose to start an external program that presumably will subsequently call your project into the execution process. Alternatively, you can choose to launch the default web browser on your system with a specific URL, again with the assumption that the URL will ultimately invoke your project.

Often, applications are built with the capability to exhibit different behavior depending on command-line arguments. If your project is of this variety and you need to test the different configurations, the Command Line Arguments textbox can be used to specify which set of arguments are to be included in the execution of the project. You should enter the command-line arguments in exactly the same way you expect the end user to when invoking your application once it has been deployed.

You can override the default directory from which the application should be executed by setting the Working Directory option. This equates to the same setting when you edit a Windows shortcut. In addition, you can also specify a different machine to control the debugging process of the application by activating the Use Remote Machine option. Note that you will need to explicitly specify the remote computer path, as it does not have an associated browse option.

The final section of the Debug page pertains to the different kinds of debugging that will be performed during the execution of your application. By default, the only debugging process active is the debugging of managed code inside the Visual Studio environment, but you can optionally include unmanaged COM code or other native code that falls outside the managed code arena in the debugging process by selecting the Enable Unmanaged Code Debugging option.

Finally, if your application includes SQL Server 2005 databases, then you can debug right into the stored procedures associated with the database by activating the Enable SQL Server Debugging option.

> *The configuration and platform settings are available only when you have the Show Advanced Build Configurations setting activated. This can be found in the Projects and Solutions⇨General options page and is on by default for all environment configurations except for Visual Basic programmers.*

Exception Assistant

The basic usage of the Exception Assistant was discussed in previous chapters, along with some information about how to create your own visualization options to customize its appearance. However, it's worth recapping the usefulness of this window when debugging, and how to retrieve further information via the Exception Assistant dialog window when it is displayed.

The first thing to note is that the Exception Assistant is available to you in all managed code projects regardless of project type. This means you get the benefit of this feature for web debugging as well as Windows-based application programming. However, if you would prefer the older style exception dialog window that was used in previous versions of Visual Studio, you can deactivate the feature through Visual Studio options (see the "General Options" section earlier in this chapter).

Every exception intercepted by the Exception Assistant has an associated section in the documentation to further explain the issue and what action you can take to fix any problems. This includes more detail about the associated tips that are displayed in the dialog so you can understand what each suggestion means, and additional links to other parts of the documentation if you want to investigate a particular solution further. Figure 52-3 shows a typical documentation page for one of the more commonly encountered errors, NullReferenceException.

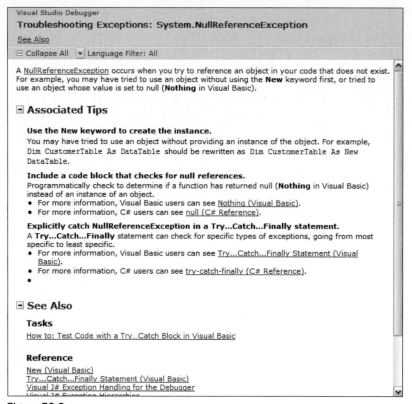

Figure 52-3

When dealing with a particular issue reported by the Exception Assistant, sometimes it is difficult to determine which particular action you should take to rectify the problem without additional information. To help you with this, the View Detail link, available for every exception, can be used to access full details for the error.

The View Detail dialog uses a default object visualizer to display the information found in the exception object structure in a readable format (see Figure 52-4).

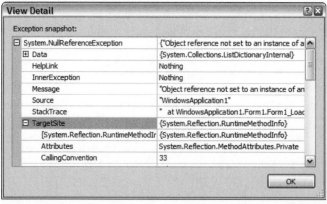

Figure 52-4

As you can see, you can navigate right down to the individual property level within the exception object, which enables you to accurately determine what data is included in the issue so you can establish what corrective action you should take.

Debugging Macros

In Chapter 26 you learned how to use macros to automate series of tasks within the Visual Studio IDE. These macros are written in Visual Basic and have an extensive programming model associated with them, including their own IDE for development.

Included with the IDE is a standalone debugging process. As a result, unlike other development tools that simply halt when an error is encountered in macro code, Visual Studio 2005 macros can be fully debugged using an interface very similar to that found in the main IDE.

As Figure 52-5 shows, you have access to a wide array of debugging windows and features, just like in the main Visual Studio 2005 IDE. You can also add manual breakpoints to the macro code, which forces the Visual Studio Macros IDE to open and display the code at the breakpoint when you execute the command from within the main IDE.

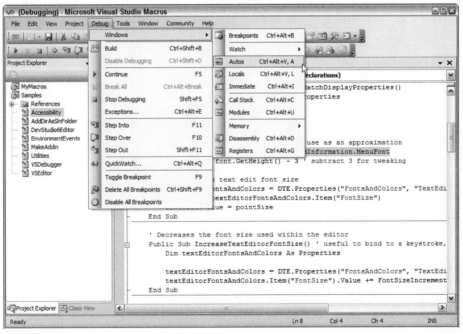

Figure 52-5

There are some limitations to macros, unfortunately, and one in particular can impact your understanding of the underlying objects that allow the macro code to act on the Visual Studio environment. Debugging macros only acts on the managed code of the macros themselves, so all native code is excluded from the debugging session. This includes the COM objects related to the IDE itself, such as the DTE object, which means you cannot look at certain properties of these objects during a debugging session. Instead, you need to use the Immediate window to determine the values.

Debugging Database Stored Procedures

Another incredibly useful feature of the debugging model found in Visual Studio 2005 is the capability to debug stored procedures in SQL Server 2005 databases. You'll need to first check the Enable SQL Server debugging setting in the Debug page of your project. Once activated, whenever your code encounters a stored procedure, you can debug the procedure code inline with your own code.

You can even include breakpoints within a stored procedure so you can trace through the SQL Server code without halting the application code execution (see Figure 52-6).

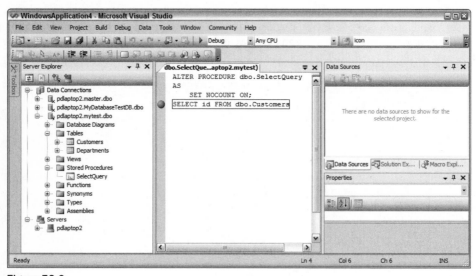

Figure 52-6

Summary

This chapter completes the discussion on debugging your projects and applications, offering details about how you can customize the general experience of your debugging sessions. In addition, Visual Studio 2005 is capable of debugging other areas of your code that previously were excluded from the debugging process, such as stored procedures and macro code, so you have a more cohesive testing experience that includes familiar debugging options regardless of what issue you're facing.

Armed with the information in this chapter, along with the coverage of unit testing in the next chapter, Visual Studio 2005 will help you address almost every situation you encounter as you create your applications, regardless of the technology you're using.

53

Unit Testing

Application testing is one of the most time-consuming parts of writing software. The statistics available from research into development teams and how they operate has revealed quite staggering results. Some teams employ a tester for every developer they have. Others maintain that the testing process can be longer than the initial development. This indicates that contrary to the way development tools are oriented, testing is a significant portion of the software development life cycle. This chapter looks at a specific type of automated testing that focuses on testing individual components, or units, of a system.

Visual Studio Team System is the first version of Visual Studio that has a built-in framework for authoring, executing, and reporting on test cases. This chapter focuses on unit tests and adding support to drive the tests from a set of data. Chapter 56 covers the other types of tests that can be created, along with the various testing windows that can be used to manage the test cases and results.

Your First Test Case

Writing test cases is not easily automated, as the test cases have to mirror the functionality of the software being developed. However, at several steps in the process code stubs can be generated by a tool. To illustrate this, start with a relatively straightforward snippet of code to learn how you can go about writing test cases that fully exercise the code. Setting the scene is a `Subscription` class that has a private property called `CurrentStatus`, which returns the status of the current subscription as an enumeration value:

```
Public Class Subscription
    Public Enum Status
        Temporary
        Financial
        Unfinancial
        Suspended
```

```
        End Enum

    Private _PaidUpTo As Nullable(Of Date)

    Public Property PaidUpTo() As Nullable(Of Date)
        Get
            Return _PaidUpTo
        End Get
        Set(ByVal value As Nullable(Of Date))
            _PaidUpTo = value
        End Set
    End Property

    Public ReadOnly Property CurrentStatus() As Status
        Get
            If Not Me.PaidUpTo.HasValue Then Return Status.Temporary
            If Me.PaidUpTo.Value > Now Then
                Return Status.Financial
            Else
                If Me.PaidUpTo >= Now.AddMonths(-3) Then
                    Return Status.Unfinancial
                Else
                    Return Status.Suspended
                End If
            End If
        End Get
    End Property
End Class
```

As you can see from the code snippet, four code paths need to be tested for this property. In the past you would have to manually create a separate SubscriptionTest class, either in the same project or in a new project, into which you would manually write code to instantiate a Subscription object, set initial values, and test the property. The last part would have to be repeated for each of the code paths through this property.

Visual Studio Team System automates the process of creating a new test project, creating the appropriate SubscriptionTest class and writing the code to create the Subscription object. All you have to do is complete the test method. It also provides a runtime engine that is used to run the test case, monitor its progress, and report on any outcome from the test. As such, the only part that remains for you to do is write the code to test the property in question. In fact, Team System generates a code stub that executes the property being tested. However, it does not generate code to ensure that the Subscription object is in the correct initial state; this you must do yourself.

Test cases can be created from the Test menu by selecting the New Test item. This prompts you to select the type of test to create, after which it creates a blank test in which you need to manually write the appropriate test cases. To automate the mundane work of writing the stub code, you need to create the unit test by selecting the Create Unit Tests menu item from the right-click context menu off the main code window. For example, right-clicking within the CurrentStatus property and selecting this menu item brings up the Create Unit Tests dialog displayed in Figure 53-1. This dialog shows all the members of all the classes within the current solution and enables you to select the items for which you want to generate a test stub.

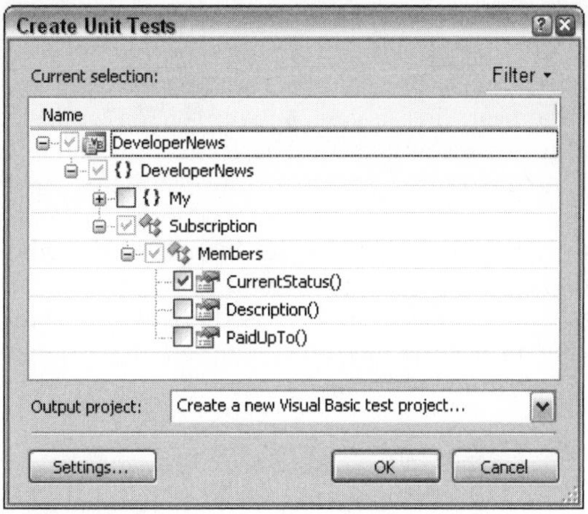

Figure 53-1

If this is the first time you have created a unit test, you will be prompted to create a new test project. Unlike alternatives such as NUnit that allow test classes to reside in the same project as the source code, the testing framework within Visual Studio Team System requires that all test cases reside in a test project. When test cases are created from the dialog shown in Figure 53-1, they are named according to the name of the member and the name of the class to which they belong. For example, the following code is generated when the OK button is selected:

```
<TestClass()> _
Public Class SubscriptionTest


    Private testContextInstance As TestContext
    Public Property TestContext() As TestContext
        Get
            Return testContextInstance
        End Get
        Set(ByVal value As TestContext)
            testContextInstance = Value
        End Set
    End Property

    <TestMethod()> _
    Public Sub CurrentStatusTest()
        Dim target As Subscription = New Subscription

        'TODO: Assign to an appropriate value for the property
        Dim val As Subscription.Status

        Assert.AreEqual(val, target.CurrentStatus, _
                "DeveloperNews.Subscription.CurrentStatus was not set correctly.")
        Assert.Inconclusive("Verify the correctness of this test method.")
    End Sub
End Class
```

The test case generated for the CurrentStatus property appears in the lower half of this code snippet. The top half of this class is discussed later in this chapter. As you can see, the test case was created with a name that reflects the property it is testing (in this case, CurrentStatusTest) in a class that reflects the class in which the property appears (in this case, SubscriptionTest). One of the difficulties with test cases is that they can quickly become unmanageable. This simple naming convention ensures that test cases can be easily found and identified.

If you look at the test case in more detail, you can see that the generated code stub actually contains most of the code required to test at least one path through the property being tested. A Subscription object is created, and a test Status variable is then used to test against the CurrentStatus property of that object. Before going any further, run this test case to see what happens by opening the Test View window, shown in Figure 53-2, from the Test menu.

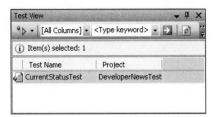

Figure 53-2

Selecting the CurrentStatusTest item and clicking the Run Selection button, the first on the left, invokes the test. This also opens the Test Results window, which initially shows the test as being either Pending or In Progress. Once the test has completed, the Test Results window will look like the one shown in Figure 53-3.

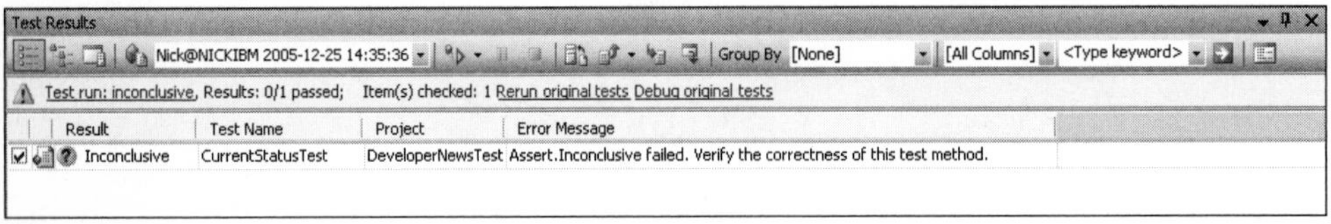

	Result	Test Name	Project	Error Message
☑	Inconclusive	CurrentStatusTest	DeveloperNewsTest	Assert.Inconclusive failed. Verify the correctness of this test method.

Test run: inconclusive, Results: 0/1 passed;   Item(s) checked: 1 Rerun original tests Debug original tests

Figure 53-3

You can see from Figure 53-3 that the test case has returned an inconclusive result. Essentially, this indicates that a test is either not complete or the results should not be relied upon, as changes may have been made to make this test invalid. When test cases are generated by Visual Studio they are all initially marked as inconclusive using the Assert.Inconclusive statement. In addition, depending on the test stub that was created, there may be additional TODO statements that will prompt you to complete the test case.

Returning to the code snippet generated for the CurrentStatusTest method, you can see both an Assert.Inconclusive statement and a TODO item. To complete this test case, remove the TODO statement, assign an appropriate value to the Status variable, and remove the Assert.Inconclusive statement:

```
<TestMethod()> _
Public Sub CurrentStatusTest()
    Dim target As Subscription = New Subscription

    Dim val As Subscription.Status = Subscription.Status.Temporary

    Assert.AreEqual(val, target.CurrentStatus, _
            "DeveloperNews.Subscription.CurrentStatus was not set correctly.")
End Sub
```

Rerunning this test case will now indicate that the test case has passed successfully, as shown in Figure 53-4.

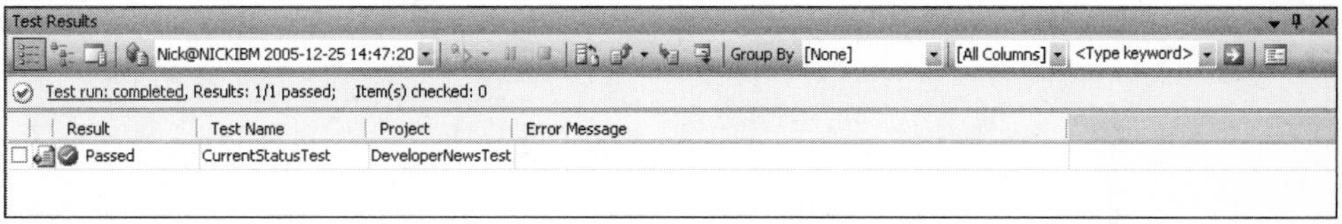

Figure 53-4

By removing the inconclusive warning from the test case, you are indicating that it is complete. Be a little careful in doing this, as you have only tested one path through the code. From the Test Results window, click the code coverage button on the far right of the toolbar. This opens the code coverage window, which by default will state that code coverage is not enabled for this test run. To enable code coverage, select Edit Test Run Configurations from the Test menu, which brings up the dialog shown in Figure 53-5.

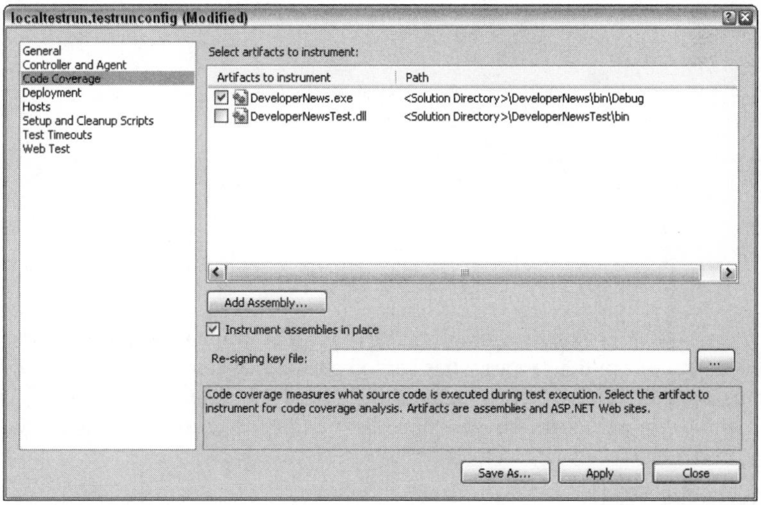

Figure 53-5

The settings for this test configuration are partitioned into a number of sections, indicated by the list on the left of the dialog. Selecting Code Coverage, for example, allows you to enable code coverage for specific assemblies. Other aspects of the test configuration can also be modified here, such as scripts to be run before and after test cases, and the default test timeouts. This window can also be used to manage external test agents, which are used to run test cases remotely for load and concurrency testing.

To see the code coverage results, after enabling code coverage for the assembly in question, you need to rerun the test case. This time when you select the code coverage button you will see the code coverage results illustrated in Figure 53-6.

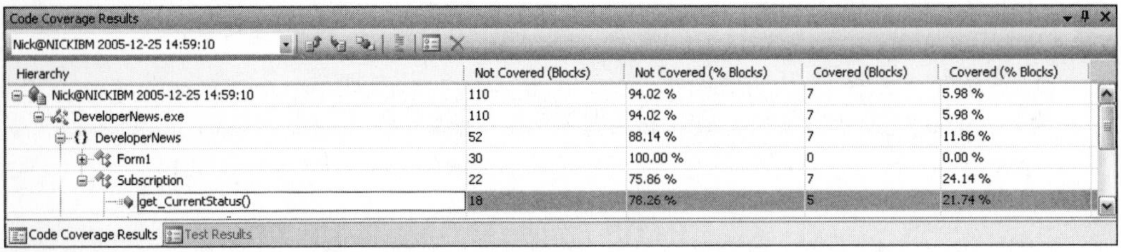

Figure 53-6

As you can see, approximately 21 percent of the property has been covered by this test case. Although a percentage is useful when trying to evaluate how thoroughly a project has been tested, it is not really helpful for determining what code still needs to be tested. Double-clicking this method not only takes you to the code for this method, it also highlights the code so you can see the proportion that has been covered, as shown in Figure 53-7.

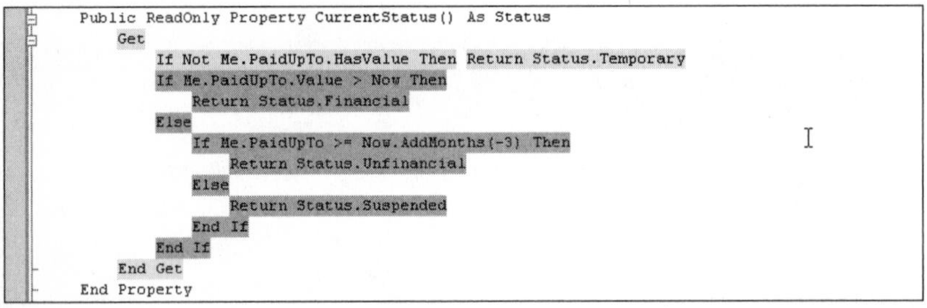

Figure 53-7

Although you can't see the colors in the figure, the first code path has been executed, as it is highlighted in blue. However, the rest of the property has yet to be tested, as it is highlighted in red. Your test case needs to be augmented to include cases for each of these paths. Later in this chapter, you will examine a data-driven approach to reduce the amount of code you have to write to test all of these permutations.

Test Attributes

Before going any further with this scenario, take a step back and consider how testing is carried out within Visual Studio Team System. As mentioned earlier, all test cases have to exist within test classes that themselves reside in a test project, but what really distinguishes a method, class, or project as containing test cases? Starting with the test project, if you look at the underlying XML project file, you will see that there is virtually no difference between a test project file and a normal class library project file. In fact, the only difference appears to be the project type, and as such, when this project is built it simply outputs a standard .NET class library assembly. The key difference is that Visual Studio recognizes this as a test project and automatically analyzes it for any test cases in order to populate the various test windows.

Classes and methods used in the testing process are marked with an appropriate attribute. The attributes are used by the testing engine to enumerate all the test cases within a particular assembly.

TestClass

All test cases must reside within a test class that is appropriately marked with the `TestClass` attribute. Although it would appear that there is no reason for this attribute, other than aligning test cases with the class and member that they are testing, you will later see some benefits associated with grouping test cases using a test class. In the case of testing the `Subscription` class, a test class called `SubscriptionTest` was created and marked with the `TestClass` attribute. Because Team System uses attributes, the name of this class is irrelevant, although a suitable naming convention makes it easier to manage a large number of test cases.

TestMethod

Individual test cases are marked with the `TestMethod` attribute, which is used by Visual Studio to enumerate the list of tests that can be executed. The `CurrentStatusTest` method in the `SubscriptionTest` class is marked with the `TestMethod` attribute. Again, the actual name of this method is irrelevant, as Team System only uses the attributes. However, the method name is used in the various test windows when presenting a list of the test cases, so it is useful for test methods to have appropriate names.

Test Attributes

As you have seen, the unit testing subsystem within Team System uses attributes to identify test cases. A number of additional properties can be set to provide additional information about a test case. This information is then accessible either via the Properties window associated with a test case or within the other test windows (a complete description of these is contained in Chapter 56). This section goes through the descriptive attributes that can be applied to a test method.

Description

Because test cases are listed using the test method name, a number of tests may have similar names, or names that are not descriptive enough to indicate what functionality they test. The `description` attribute, which takes a `String` as its sole argument, can be applied to a test method to provide additional information about a test case.

Owner

The `Owner` attribute, which also takes a `String` argument, is useful for indicating who owns, wrote, or is currently working on a particular test case.

Priority

The `Priority` attribute, which takes an integer argument, can be applied to a test case to indicate the relative importance of a test case. While the testing framework does not use this attribute, it is useful for prioritizing test cases when determining the order in which failing, or incomplete, test cases are resolved.

Work Items

An important artifact of working with Team System is that all activities can be associated with a work item. Applying one or more `WorkItem` attributes to a test case means that the test case can be reviewed when making changes to existing functionality.

Timeout

A test case can fail for any number of reasons, one of which might be a performance test that requires a particular functionality to complete within a particular time frame. Instead of the tester having to write complex multi-threading tests that stop the test case once a particular timeout has been reached, the `Timeout` attribute can be applied to a test case, as shown in the following shaded code, which ensures that the test case fails when that timeout has been reached:

```
<TestMethod()> _
<Description("Tests the functionality of the CurrentStatus method")> _
<Priority(3)> _
<WorkItem(52), WorkItem(67)> _
<Timeout(10000)> _
Public Sub CurrentStatusTest()
    Dim target As Subscription = New Subscription

    Dim val As Subscription.Status = Subscription.Status.Temporary

    Assert.AreEqual(val, target.CurrentStatus, _
            "DeveloperNews.Subscription.CurrentStatus was not set correctly.")

End Sub
```

This snippet augments the original `CurrentStatusTest` method with these attributes to illustrate their usage. In addition to providing additional information about what the test case does and who wrote it, it is assigned a priority of 3 and is associated with work items 52 and 67. Lastly, the code indicates that this test case should fail if it takes more than 10 seconds (10,000 milliseconds) to execute.

Asserting the Facts

So far, this chapter has examined the structure of the test environment and how test cases are nested within test classes in a test project. What remains is to look at the body of the test case and review how test cases either pass or fail. When a test case is generated, you saw that an `Assert.Inconclusive` statement is added to the end of the test to indicate that the test is incomplete. Another `Assert` statement is also generated that tests the outcome of the test case.

The idea behind unit testing is that you start with the system, component, or object in a known state, and then run a method, modify a property, or trigger an event. The testing phase comes at the end, when you need to validate that the system, component, or object is in the correct state. Alternatively, you may need to validate that the correct output was returned from a method or property. This is done by attempting to assert a particular condition. If this condition is not true, then the testing system reports this result and ends the test case. Asserting a condition, not surprisingly, is done using the `Assert` class. There is also a `StringAssert` class and a `CollectionAssert` class, which provide additional assertions for dealing with `String` objects and collections of objects.

Assert

The `Assert` class in the `UnitTesting` namespace, not to be confused with the `Assert` class in the `Diagnostics` namespace, is the primary class used to make assertions about a test case. The basic assertion is of the following format:

```
Assert.IsTrue(variableToTest,"Output message if this fails")
```

As you can imagine, the first argument is the condition to be tested. If this is true, the test case continues operation. However, if this condition fails, the output message is emitted and the test case exists with a failed result.

There are multiple overloads to this statement whereby the output message can be omitted or `String` formatting parameters supplied. Because quite often you won't be testing a single positive condition, several additional methods simplify making assertions within a test case:

- ❑ `IsFalse`: Tests for a negative, or false, condition
- ❑ `AreEqual`: Tests whether two arguments have the same value
- ❑ `AreSame`: Tests whether two arguments refer to the same object
- ❑ `IsInstanceOfType`: Tests whether an argument is an instance of a particular type
- ❑ `IsNull`: Tests whether an argument is nothing

This list is not exhaustive, as most of these methods have both a number of overloads as well as appropriate negative equivalents.

StringAssert

The `StringAssert` class does not provide any additional functionality that cannot be achieved with one or more assertions using the `Assert` class. However, it not only simplifies the test case code by making it clear that `String` assertions are being made; it also reduces the mundane task associated with testing for particular conditions. The additional assertions are as follows:

- ❑ `Contains`: Tests whether a `String` contains another `String`
- ❑ `DoesNotMatch`: Tests whether a `String` does not match a regular expression
- ❑ `EndsWith`: Tests whether a `String` ends with a particular `String`
- ❑ `Matches`: Tests whether a `String` matches a regular expression
- ❑ `StartsWith`: Tests whether a `String` starts with a particular `String`

CollectionAssert

Similar to the StringAssert class, the CollectionAssert class is a helper class that is used to make assertions about a collection of items. For example, two of the assertions are as follows:

❑   Contains: Tests whether a collection contains a particular object

❑   IsSubsetOf: Tests whether a collection is a subset of another collection

ExpectedException Attribute

Sometimes test cases have to execute paths of code that can cause exceptions to be raised. While exception coding should be avoided, there are conditions where this might be appropriate. Instead of writing a test case that includes a Try-Catch block with an appropriate assertion to test that an exception was raised, this can be achieved by marking the test case with an ExpectedException attribute. For example, change the CurrentStatus property to throw an exception if the PaidUp date is prior to the date the subscription opened, which in this case is a constant:

```
Public Const SubscriptionOpenedOn As Date = #1/1/2000#
Public ReadOnly Property CurrentStatus() As Status
    Get
        If Not Me.PaidUpTo.HasValue Then Return Status.Temporary
        If Me.PaidUpTo.Value > Now Then
            Return Status.Financial
        Else
            If Me.PaidUpTo >= Now.AddMonths(-3) Then
                Return Status.Unfinancial
            ElseIf Me.PaidUpTo >= SubscriptionOpenedOn Then
                Return Status.Suspended
            Else
                Throw New ArgumentOutOfRangeException("Paid up date is not
valid as it is before the subscription opened")
            End If
        End If
    End Get
End Property
```

Using the same procedure as before, you can create a separate test case for testing this code path, as shown in the following example:

```
<TestMethod()> _
<ExpectedException(GetType(ArgumentOutOfRangeException), _
    "Argument exception not raised for invalid PaidUp date")> _
Public Sub CurrentStatusExceptionTest()
    Dim target As Subscription = New Subscription

    target.PaidUpTo = Subscription.SubscriptionOpenedOn.AddMonths(-1)
    Dim val As Subscription.Status = Subscription.Status.Temporary

    Assert.AreEqual(val, target.CurrentStatus, _
        "This assertion should never actually be evaluated")
End Sub
```

The `ExpectedException` attribute not only catches any exception raised by the test case; it also ensures that the type of exception matches the type expected. If no exception is raised by the test case, then it will fail the test case.

Initializing and Cleaning Up

Despite Visual Studio generating the stub code for test cases you are to write, typically you have to write a lot of setup code whenever you run a test case. Where an application uses a database, to ensure the test cases are completely repeatable, after each test the database should be returned to its initial state. This is also true for applications that modify other resources such as the file system. Team System provides rich support for writing methods that can be used to initialize and clean up around test cases. Again, attributes are used to mark the appropriate methods that should be used to initialize and clean up the test cases.

More Attributes

The attributes for initializing and cleaning up around test cases are broken down into three levels: those that apply to individual tests, those that apply to an entire test class, and those that apply to an entire test project.

TestInitialize and TestCleanup

As their names suggest, the `TestInitialize` and `TestCleanup` attributes indicate methods that should be run prior to and after each test case within a particular test class.

ClassInitialize and ClassCleanup

Sometimes, instead of setting up and cleaning up between each test, it can be easier to ensure that the environment is in the correct state at the beginning and end of running an entire test class. Previously you saw that test classes were a useful mechanism for grouping test cases; this is where you put that knowledge to use. Test cases can be grouped into test classes that contain a single `Initialize` and `Cleanup` method, marked with the appropriate class-level attribute.

AssemblyInitialize and AssemblyCleanup

The final level of initialization and cleanup attributes is at the assembly, or project, level. Methods for initializing prior to running an entire test project, and cleaning up after, can be marked using the `AssemblyInitialize` and `AssemblyCleanup` attributes, respectively. Because these methods apply to any test case within the test project, only a single method can be marked with each of these attributes.

For both the assembly-level and class-level attributes, it is important to remember that even if only one test case is run, the methods marked with these attributes will be run.

Testing Context

When you are writing test cases, the testing engine can assist you in a number of ways, including managing sets of data so you can run a test case with a range of data, and allowing you to output additional information for the test case to aid in debugging. This functionality is available through the `TestContext` object that is generated within a test class.

Data

The `CurrentStatusTest` method generated in the first section of this chapter tested only a single path through the `CurrentStatus` property. To fully test this method, you could have written additional statements and assertions to set up and test the `Subscription` object. However, this process is fairly repetitive and would need to be updated if you ever changed the structure of the `CurrentStatus` property. An alternative is to provide a `DataSource` for the `CurrentStatusTest` method whereby each row of data tests a different path through the property. To add appropriate data to this method, use the following process:

1. Create an appropriate database and database table to store the various test data. In this case, create a database called LoadTest with a table called Subscription_CurrentStatus. The table has an Identity ID column, a nullable DateTime column (`PaidUp` value), and an `nvarchar(20)` column (expected Status).

2. Add appropriate data values to the table to cover all paths through the code. Test values for the `CurrentStatus` property are shown in Figure 53-8.

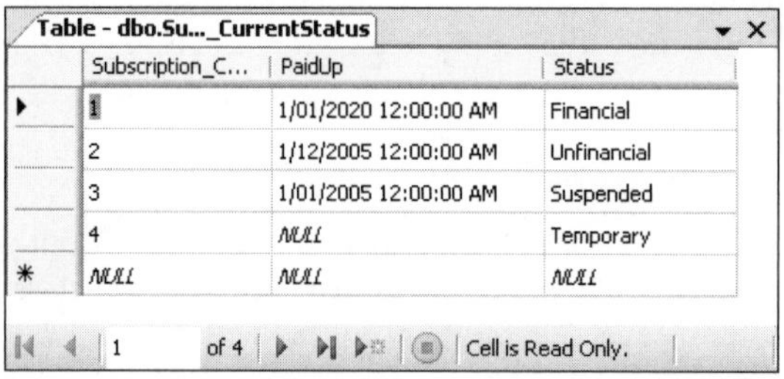

Subscription_C...	PaidUp	Status
1	1/01/2020 12:00:00 AM	Financial
2	1/12/2005 12:00:00 AM	Unfinancial
3	1/01/2005 12:00:00 AM	Suspended
4	NULL	Temporary
* NULL	NULL	NULL

Figure 53-8

3. Select the appropriate test case in the Test View window and open the Properties window. Select the Data Connection String property, and click the ellipses button to open the Connection Properties dialog.

4. Use the Connection Properties dialog to attach to the database created in step 1. You should see a connection string similar to the following:

```
Data Source=localhost;Initial Catalog=LoadTest;Integrated Security=True
```

5. A drop-down box appears if the connection string is valid when you select in the Data Table Name property, enabling you to select the `DataTable` you created in step 1.

6. Return to the Test View window and select Open Test from the right-click context menu for the test case to open the test case in the main window. Notice that a `DataSource` attribute has been added to the test case. This attribute is used by the testing engine to load the appropriate data from the specified table. This data is then exposed to the test case through the `TestContext` object.

7. Modify the test case to access data from the `TestContext` object and use this to drive the test case, which gives you the following `CurrentStatusTest` method:

```
<DataSource("System.Data.SqlClient", "Data Source=localhost;Initial
Catalog=LoadTest;Integrated Security=True", "Subscription_CurrentStatus",
DataAccessMethod.Sequential)> _
```

```
    <TestMethod()> _
    Public Sub CurrentStatusTest()
        Dim target As Subscription = New Subscription

        If Not IsDBNull(Me.TestContext.DataRow.Item("PaidUp")) Then
            target.PaidUpTo = CType(Me.TestContext.DataRow.Item("PaidUp"), Date)
        End If
        Dim val As Status = CType([Enum].Parse(GetType(Subscription.Status),
CStr(Me.TestContext.DataRow.Item("Status"))), Subscription.Status)

        Assert.AreEqual(val, target.CurrentStatus, _
               "DeveloperNews.Subscription.CurrentStatus was not set correctly.")

    End Sub
```

When this test case is executed the `CurrentStatusTest` method is executed four times (once for each row of data in the `DataTable`). Each time it is executed, the appropriate `DataRow` is retrieved from the `DataTable` and exposed to the test method via the `TestContext.DataRow` property. Executing this test case you now achieve 100 percent code coverage for the `CurrentStatus` property. You can also add cases to the `DataTable` to allow for additional code paths that may be introduced later.

Before moving on, take one last look at the `DataSource` attribute that was applied to the `CurrentStatusTest`. This attribute takes four arguments, the first three of which are used to determine which `DataTable` needs to be extracted. The remaining argument is a `DataAccessMethod` enumeration, which determines the order in which rows are returned from the `DataTable`. By default, this is `Sequential`, but it can be changed to `Random` so the order is varied every time the test is run. This is particularly important when the data is representative of end user data but does not have any dependency on the order in which data is processed.

Writing Test Output

Writing unit tests is all about automating the process of testing an application. As such, these test cases can be executed as part of a build process, perhaps even on a remote computer. This means that the normal output windows, such as the console, are not a suitable place for outputting test-related information. Clearly, you also don't want test-related information interspersed within the debug or trace information being generated by the application. For this reason, there is a separate channel for writing test-related information so it can be viewed alongside the test results.

The `TestContext` object exposes a `WriteLine` method that takes a `String` and a series of `String .Format` arguments that can be used to output information to the results for a particular test. For example, adding the following line to the `CurrentStatusTest` method generates the test results shown in Figure 53-9:

```
TestContext.WriteLine("No exceptions thrown for test number {0}", _
                   CInt(Me.TestContext.DataRow.Item(0)))
```

In Figure 53-9 you can see in the Additional Information section the output from the `WriteLine` method you added to the test method. Although you only added one line to the test method, the `WriteLine` method was executed for each row in the `DataTable`. The Data Driven Test Results section of Figure 53-9 provides more information about each of the test passes, with a row for each row in the `DataTable`. Your results may differ from those shown in Figure 53-9 depending on the code you have in your `Subscription` class.

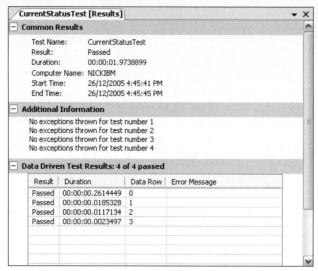

Figure 53-9

Advanced

Up until now, you have seen how to write and execute unit tests. This section goes on to examine how you can add custom properties to a test case and how you can use the same framework to test private methods and properties.

Custom Properties

The testing framework provides a number of test attributes that can be applied to a method to record additional information about a test case. This information can be edited via the Properties window and updates the appropriate attributes on the test method. There are times when you want to drive your test methods by specifying your own properties, which can also be set using the Properties window. To do this, add TestProperty attributes to the test method. For example, the following code adds two attributes to the test method to enable you to specify an arbitrary date and an expected status. This might be convenient for ad hoc testing using the Test View and properties window:

```
<TestMethod()> _
<TestProperty("SpecialDate", "1/1/2005")> _
<TestProperty("SpecialStatus", "Suspended")> _
Public Sub SpecialCurrentStatusTest()
    Dim target As Subscription = New Subscription

    target.PaidUpTo = CDate(Me.TestContext.Properties.Item("SpecialDate"))
    Dim val As Subscription.Status =
CType([Enum].Parse(GetType(Subscription.Status), _
```

```
                    CStr(Me.TestContext.Properties.Item("SpecialStatus"))),
    Subscription.Status)

        Assert.AreEqual(val, target.CurrentStatus, _
                    "Correct status not set for Paid up date {0}", target.PaidUpTo)
    End Sub
```

Using the Test View to navigate to this test case and accessing the Properties window, you can see that this generates two additional properties: `SpecialDate` and `SpecialStatus`, as shown in Figure 53-10.

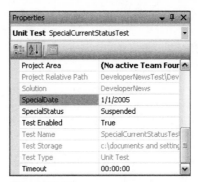

Figure 53-10

The Properties window can be used to adjust the `SpecialDate` and `SpecialStatus` values. Unfortunately, the limitation here is that there is no way to specify the data type for the values. As such, the property grid only displays and allows edits as if they were `String` data types.

Note one other limitation to using custom properties as defined for the `SpecialCurrentStatusTest` method. Looking at the code, you can see that you are able to access the property values using the Properties dictionary provided by the `TestContext`. Unfortunately, although custom properties automatically appear in the Properties window, they are *not* automatically added to this Properties dictionary. As such, a bit of heavy lifting has to be done to extract these properties from the custom attributes list and place them into the Properties dictionary. Luckily, this can be done in the `TestInitialize` method, as illustrated in the following code. Note that although this method will be executed for each test case in the class, and as such will load all custom properties, it is not bound to any particular test case, as it uses the `TestContext.Name` property to look up the test method being executed:

```
    <TestInitialize()> _
    Public Sub Setup()
        Dim t As Type = Me.GetType
        Dim mi As Reflection.MethodInfo = t.GetMethod(Me.TestContext.TestName)
        Dim MyType As Type = GetType(TestPropertyAttribute)
        Dim attributes As Object() = mi.GetCustomAttributes(MyType, False)

        For Each attrib As TestPropertyAttribute In attributes
            Me.TestContext.Properties.Add(attrib.Name, attrib.Value)
        Next
    End Sub
```

Testing Private Members

One of the selling features of unit testing is that it is particularly effective for testing the internals of your class to ensure that they function correctly. The assumption here is that if each of your classes works in isolation, then there is a better chance that they will work together correctly; and in fact, unit testing can be used to test classes working together. However, you might be wondering how well the unit testing framework handles testing private methods.

One of the features of the .NET Framework is the capability to reflect over any type that has been loaded into memory and execute any member regardless of its accessibility. This functionality does come at a performance cost, however, as the reflection calls obviously include an additional level of redirection, which can prove costly if done frequently. Nonetheless, for testing, reflection enables you to call into the inner workings of a class and not worry about the potential performance penalties for making those calls.

The other more significant issue with using reflection to access non-public members of a class is that the code to do so is somewhat messy. Luckily, Visual Studio 2005 does a very good job of generating a wrapper class that makes testing even private methods easy. To show this, return to the CurrentStatus property and change its access from public to private. If you follow the same process you did previously to generate the test method for this property, you will see that an additional class is generated to support the test method. The first snippet of the following code is the new test method that is generated (there may be naming differences if your Subscription class is in a different namespace from DeveloperNews):

```
<TestMethod()> _
Public Sub PrivateCurrentStatusTest()
    Dim target As Subscription = New Subscription

    Dim val As Subscription.Status = Subscription.Status.Temporary

    Dim accessor As DeveloperNews_SubscriptionAccessor = _
                            New DeveloperNews_SubscriptionAccessor(target)

    Assert.AreEqual(val, accessor.CurrentStatus, _
              "DeveloperNews.Subscription.CurrentStatus was not set correctly.")
End Sub
```

As you can see, the preceding example uses an instance of the DeveloperNews_SubscriptionAccessor class to access the CurrentStatus property. In the test project is a new file, VSCodeGenAccessors.vb, which contains this class definition:

```
<System.Diagnostics.DebuggerStepThrough(), _
System.CodeDom.Compiler.GeneratedCodeAttribute _
          ("Microsoft.VisualStudio.TestTools.UnitTestGeneration", "1.0.0.0")> _
Friend Class DeveloperNews_SubscriptionAccessor
    Inherits BaseAccessor

    Protected Shared m_privateType As PrivateType = _
```

```
                    New PrivateType(GetType(Global.DeveloperNews.Subscription))

        Friend Sub New(ByVal target As Global.DeveloperNews.Subscription)
            MyBase.New(target, m_privateType)
        End Sub

        Friend Property m_Description() As String
            Get
                Dim ret As String = _
                        CType(m_privateObject.GetFieldOrProperty("m_Description"),String)
                Return ret
            End Get
            Set
                m_privateObject.SetFieldOrProperty("m_Description", value)
            End Set
        End Property

        Friend Property m_PaidUpTo() As System.Nullable(Of Date)
            Get
                Dim ret As System.Nullable(Of Date) = _
                        CType(m_privateObject.GetFieldOrProperty("m_PaidUpTo"), _
                            System.Nullable(Of Date))
                Return ret
            End Get
            Set
                m_privateObject.SetFieldOrProperty("m_PaidUpTo", value)
            End Set
        End Property

        Friend Property SubscriptionOpenedOn() As Date
            Get
                Dim ret As Date = _
                  CType(m_privateObject.GetFieldOrProperty("SubscriptionOpenedOn"),Date)
                Return ret
            End Get
            Set
                m_privateObject.SetFieldOrProperty("SubscriptionOpenedOn", value)
            End Set
        End Property

        Friend ReadOnly Property CurrentStatus() As Subscription.Status
            Get
                Dim ret As Subscription.Status = _
                CType(m_privateObject.GetProperty("CurrentStatus"), Subscription.Status)
                Return ret
            End Get
        End Property
    End Class
```

It's clear from this code snippet that another base class is used to provide the underlying reflection methods. The DeveloperNews_SubscriptionAccessor class inherits from the BaseAccessor object to provide access to specific members, instead of having to use a string-based lookup, which would make the test code very untidy.

Summary

This chapter described how unit testing can be used to ensure the correct functionality of your code using proper testing. The unit testing framework within Visual Studio Team System is quite comprehensive, enabling you to both document and manage test cases.

The testing framework can be fully exercised using an appropriate Data Source to minimize the repetitive code that has to be written to test your code. It can also be extended to test all the inner workings of your application.

Chapter 56 provides more detail on the various test windows available to testers, and the other types of testing you can perform using Visual Studio Team System.

Part X

Extensions for Visual Studio 2005

54

InfoPath 2003 Toolkit

When Microsoft first released InfoPath, it was seen as an excellent option for enabling corporations to build forms easily without having to resort to writing code. While it was indeed the answer for many, providing the capability to create complex form designs with a robust graphical user interface and easy connection to data sources, all bound up in XML, it was problematic when a developer wanted to create a form that was backed by code.

One of the reasons for this is that the code behind an InfoPath form is written in JavaScript rather than a full programming language, and it is interpretive instead of being a properly compiled application. As a result, form design with code was more suited to web designers, given their familiarity with JavaScript and XML formatting, than application developers.

With the release of Visual Studio 2005, Microsoft also released the *InfoPath 2003 Toolkit for Visual Studio 2005*. The Toolkit integrates with InfoPath 2003 SP1 to provide a managed code solution for creating and managing InfoPath forms that rely on program code to perform part of their functionality. This chapter discusses some of the new features in the object model of InfoPath 2003 with the release of SP1, and how they can be harnessed with the Toolkit for Visual Studio 2005.

Creating Managed InfoPath Solutions

When you install the Toolkit, it merges a number of files into the Visual Studio 2005 environment. The first addition to notice is the additional project templates created for Visual Basic and C# languages. These are added to the Office group (see Figure 54-1).

If the Office groups don't already exist (for example, if you haven't installed Visual Studio Tools for Office 2005), then the installation of the InfoPath 2003 Toolkit creates them for you.

When you create an InfoPath Form Template project, you are given the option to create an associated solution as shown in Figure 54-1. This option is not available if you are adding the project to an existing solution.

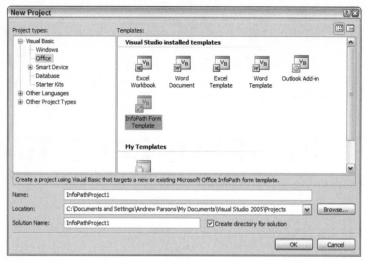

Figure 54-1

After specifying the name of your InfoPath-based project and clicking OK to tell Visual Studio to create the project, the Microsoft Office Project Wizard opens with a single page of options (see Figure 54-2).

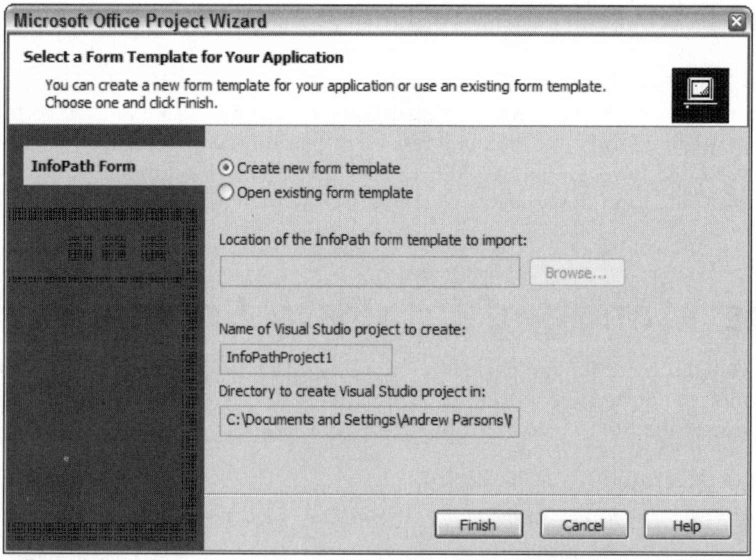

Figure 54-2

If you're creating the project from scratch, you should use the Create New Form Template option. Unfortunately, the wizard does not allow you to name the InfoPath form, so it inherits the name from the project name.

When using an existing form template, it doesn't have to have the same name. When you select an existing template, the wizard makes a copy of it in the project folder along with any associated files. To confirm that the action has taken place, Visual Studio displays a dialog explaining what happened.

When you convert an existing form template that contains code, the code is saved as associated JavaScript (.js) files in the project folder and added to the Solution Explorer. These files may contain code supporting one or more objects. Therefore, be careful when you're creating solutions that use older templates.

For example, if a template had a JavaScript OnClick event for a button on the form design, then when you wrap the InfoPath with the new .NET-based project the JavaScript function will still be present; but when you click on the Edit Form Code from InfoPath, the wizard will add the new managed code OnClick event handler in your Visual Basic or C# code.

The Generated Solution

An InfoPath project is slightly more complex than a typical Windows Forms application because the different components of the InfoPath template are separated into individual files. Figure 54-3 shows how a basic InfoPath project first appears.

Figure 54-3

The code associated with the form is split into an AssemblyInfo.vb or AssemblyInfo.cs file that can be used to sign the assembly (which you'll need to do if you want to deploy your form outside the semi-trust security zone of InfoPath), and a FormCode module that is used to perform the initialization and cleanup code for the InfoPath form. This module also connects your .NET project to the InfoPath namespace.

The _Startup and _Shutdown functions should be present in every InfoPath managed solution in order for it to work correctly. In addition, the project template automatically generates managed code objects for the InfoPath application and form objects for use in your own code. The following listing shows the initial code that is generated for a typical C# InfoPath project. The generated class in Visual Basic is identical in functionality:

```
public class InfoPathProject4
    {
        private XDocument thisXDocument;
        private Application thisApplication;

        public void _Startup(Application app, XDocument doc)
        {
            thisXDocument = doc;
            thisApplication = app;

            // You can add additional initialization code here.
        }

        public void _Shutdown()
        {
        }
    }
```

In addition to these two code files, XML-based files are generated from the InfoPath template itself. At a minimum, you'll have the following files:

Filename	Purpose
manifest.xsf	Contains the custom buttons and menus for the form's user interface along with any validation rules that have been assigned to the nodes of the internal XML document.
	In addition, the manifest.xsf file contains a list of all the files that make up the InfoPath form.
myschema.xsd	Contains information about the data elements in the form's design, and mirrors the contents of the Data Source Tasks pane
sampledata.xml	Contains a sample data file that can be associated with the data layout found in myschema.xsd
template.xml	Used in conjunction with myschema.xsd to pre-populate the fields on the InfoPath form
view1.xsl	Contains the actual user interface layout design for the form. It is a mix of XML, to define various attributes and data nodes, and HTML, for the user interface formatting.

As you continue to edit the form in InfoPath, additional files will be automatically added to the solution in Visual Studio, including additional view.xsl files for extra views of the form, and an upgrade.xsl file for upgrading an InfoPath document from a previous version.

Switching Between Visual Studio and InfoPath

Unlike regular projects, to edit the user interface of an InfoPath project you have to go through a different process. This is because the actual user interface design is performed in InfoPath itself, rather than being housed inside the Visual Studio 2005 IDE.

Initially, when you first create or open the InfoPath project, Visual Studio automatically starts InfoPath and opens the form template, ready for user interface design. However, once you've closed it, there's no immediately easy way to open the designer again. Instead you need to either use the Tools⇨Open InfoPath menu command (see Figure 54-4) or right-click on the project's entry in the Solution Explorer and choose Open InfoPath. This command not only opens InfoPath as it suggests, but also opens the form in Design view, ready for any customizing you need to perform.

Figure 54-4

All user interface design takes place inside InfoPath instead of Visual Studio 2005 (see Figure 54-5). This includes adding any data fields and binding them to a Data Source (although you can add a secondary Data Source with code later), as well as all aspects of the form's layout, including additional views, controls such as buttons and text boxes, and the InfoPath-specific features such as repeating and optional sections.

Once the user interface is laid out the way you want, you can access any of the document's components in your code, including views and data fields.

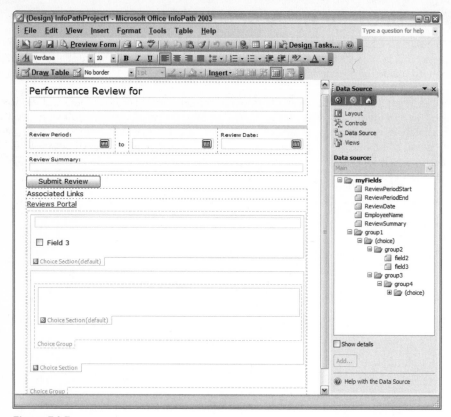

Figure 54-5

Adding Code to InfoPath Forms

Adding code to respond to your InfoPath forms is convoluted because you hook the event handlers in via the InfoPath designer, and the events for different components are in a variety of locations in the application.

To help you find the different events you can use in your project code, the following discussion walks through the location of each type of event and describes each event's purpose.

Form-Related Events

Form-related events are based on the whole document and are accessed through the Tools⇨ Programming submenu in InfoPath 2003 (see Figure 54-6).

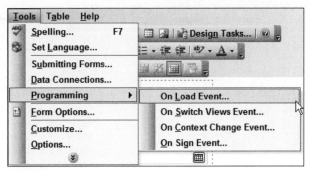

Figure 54-6

The four events listed here are associated with the document directly, and selecting any of them will switch to Visual Studio 2005 and generate a stub event handler. For example, the following code is generated when you choose the On Load Event option:

```
<InfoPathEventHandler(EventType:=InfoPathEventType.OnLoad)> _
Public Sub OnLoad(ByVal e As DocReturnEvent)
    ' Write your code here.

End Sub
```

This routine shows how the event handlers are hooked in Visual Basic code; an attribute of `InfoPathEventHandler` is prefixed to the subroutine definition, with the `EventType` value specifying which event should be connected to the managed code subroutine. Each of the four events has a particular argument object associated with it, as shown in the following table:

InfoPath Event	EventArg Object	Accessible Information
On Load	DocReturnEvent	The `DocReturnEvent` object type contains the `XmlDocument` associated with the form, along with a `ReturnStatus` flag that you can set to control whether the load should succeed or not. In this event handler you can do your own initialization and if something fails, set `ReturnStatus` to `False` so the load will not continue.
On Switch Views	DocEvent	This event object only includes the `XmlDocument` associated with the form.

Table continued on following page

InfoPath Event	EventArg Object	Accessible Information
On Context Change	DocContextChangeEvent	This event object contains the XmlDocument, the node that is associated with the changed context, and a flag to indicate whether the context changed in response to an Undo or Redo command. The object also contains a Type property, which is always ContextNode in InfoPath 2003 SP1. Microsoft recommends that because this may change in the future, always check the Type value so the generated code automatically adds this check.
On Sign	SignEvent	Contains a ReturnStatus flag to control whether or not to digitally sign the document's data block, the actual data block, and the XmlDocument associated with the form

You can also add code to control how the data associated with an InfoPath form is submitted. By default, submitting of forms is disabled, so you first need to enable it using the Tools⇨Submitting Forms menu command in the InfoPath designer, which will display the Submitting Forms dialog (shown in Figure 54-7).

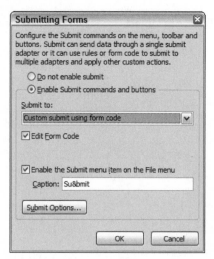

Figure 54-7

To bind the Submit Request event to a managed code event handler, first select the "Enable Submit commands and buttons" radio button and then change the Submit To drop-down list to "Custom submit using form code." Normally, like all the other events discussed here, this would generate a JavaScript routine to handle the event, but with the Toolkit it switches to Visual Studio 2005 and creates the event handler there, instead using the language you've chosen.

If you uncheck the Edit Form Code option, the event handler is added to your FormCode.vb file in the project, but the InfoPath designer remains active. As the generated code in the following listing illustrates, the OnSubmitRequest event is associated with submitting a form and contains a DocReturnEvent argument (the same object type used in the OnLoad event):

```
<InfoPathEventHandler(EventType:=InfoPathEventType.OnSubmitRequest)> _
Public Sub OnSubmitRequest(ByVal e As DocReturnEvent)
    ' If the submit operation is successful, set
    ' e.ReturnStatus = true
    ' Write your code here.

End Sub
```

When you handle the OnSubmitRequest event, saving the data contained in the InfoPath form is left up to your code. However, because the InfoPath designer can display messages indicating whether the submission was successful or not (accessed through the Submit Options button shown in Figure 54-7), you should set the ReturnStatus property appropriately.

Rather than submit the form, what happens if the user edits and then saves the form? The answer is that there is yet another form-wide event called OnSaveRequest that you can intercept, and then perform your own functionality (including rejecting their changes).

To generate the event handler for this event, open the Form Options dialog and switch to the Open and Save tab (shown in Figure 54-8). Check the Save Using Custom Code option to generate the event handler routine and click the Edit button alongside it to switch to the Visual Studio IDE and locate the routine in the FormCode.vb module.

The automatically generated code for the OnSaveRequest event appears similar to the following listing:

```
<InfoPathEventHandler(EventType:=InfoPathEventType.OnSaveRequest)> _
Public Sub OnSaveRequest(ByVal e As SaveEvent)
    ' Write the code to be run before saving here.

    e.IsCancelled = e.PerformSaveOperation

    ' Write the code to be run after saving here.

    e.ReturnStatus = true
End Sub
```

The SaveEvent argument contains a number of useful properties when saving the form. Because intercepting the event means that InfoPath won't perform its own default Save (or Save As) functionality, you need to set the ReturnStatus property to indicate whether your own save process worked. If you do not set this property to True, InfoPath displays an error message to the end user indicating that the save was unsuccessful.

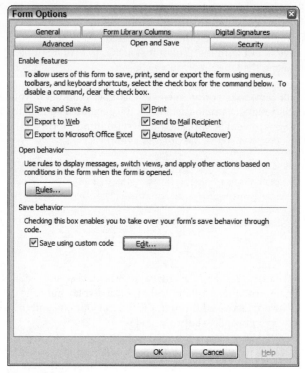

Figure 54-8

The IsSaveAs flag indicates whether the user chose Save or Save As. The flag is set to True if the function is Save As, allowing you to perform different functionality, including showing a dialog box to specify the new document name. The IsCancelled flag is used to indicate whether the save function was cancelled by the user, so you should set this to True if they cancel the Save As functionality you implement.

The PerformSaveOperation method performs the intrinsic InfoPath save functionality based on whichever option (Save or Save As) is chosen by the user. As the generated code shows, this function returns a Boolean value indicating success or failure.

A few other form events are used when upgrading the InfoPath form layout from a previous version, and when data is imported or merged. These are not likely to be used often, but they can still be useful in certain situations.

To add a routine to handle the OnVersionUpgrade event, open the Advanced tab of the Form Options dialog in InfoPath and select Use Custom Event from the drop-down list labeled On Version Upgrade. You can switch to the generated event handler by subsequently clicking the Edit button.

If you need to intercept the OnAfterImport or OnMergeRequest events, you need to hook them up manually in the FormCode.vb module. The syntax for the OnAfterImport event handler routine (which will be fired when an import or merge action in InfoPath is successfully performed) is as follows:

```
<InfoPathEventHandler(EventType:=InfoPathEventType.OnAfterImport)> _
Public Sub OnSubmitRequest(ByVal e As DocEvent)
    ' Write your code here.

End Sub
```

The `OnMergeRequest` is fired when a request is made to merge InfoPath forms and data. The syntax for a routine that handles this event appears like this:

```
<InfoPathEventHandler(EventType:=InfoPathEventType.OnMergeRequest)> _
Public Sub OnSubmitRequest(ByVal e As MergeEvent)
    ' Write your code here.

End Sub
```

You should set the `ReturnStatus` flag to `True` upon successful merging of the data.

Field Events

Fields such as textboxes, checkboxes, option buttons, and lists can fire three different events that you can intercept in your managed code project:

❑ `OnBeforeChange`: This is fired when changes have been made to the underlying `XmlDocument` for an InfoPath form but before they've been accepted.

❑ `OnValidate`: Raised after the changes have been accepted. However, the `XmlDocument` is in a read-only form and you normally only use this event to handle any errors that may have occurred when the data was changed

❑ `OnAfterChange`: Raised last, this is used to change the data in the form in response to the underlying `XmlDocument` changes.

All three have their event handler routines generated in the same way. Select the field you need to handle and then select the Format➪*fieldname* Properties menu command. You can also use the keyboard shortcut Alt+Enter to display the Properties dialog, or right-click the field in question and select the Properties command from the context menu that is displayed.

On the Data tab, click the Data Validation button. The location of this button varies depending on which control type you're editing but it will be present somewhere. When clicked, this button displays the Data Validation dialog (see Figure 54-9).

From the Events drop-down list in the Script section of the dialog window, you can choose from the three events. Select the event you need to handle and then click the Edit button to have Visual Studio generate the event handler routine (shown in the following listing) and switch to the IDE so you can add your own code:

```
<InfoPathEventHandler(MatchPath:="/my:myFields/my:ReviewPeriodStart",
EventType:=InfoPathEventType.OnBeforeChange)> _
Public Sub ReviewPeriodStart_OnBeforeChange(ByVal e As DataDOMEvent)
    ' Write your code here. Warning: ensure that the constraint you are enforcing is
    ' compatible with the default value you set for this XML node.

End Sub
```

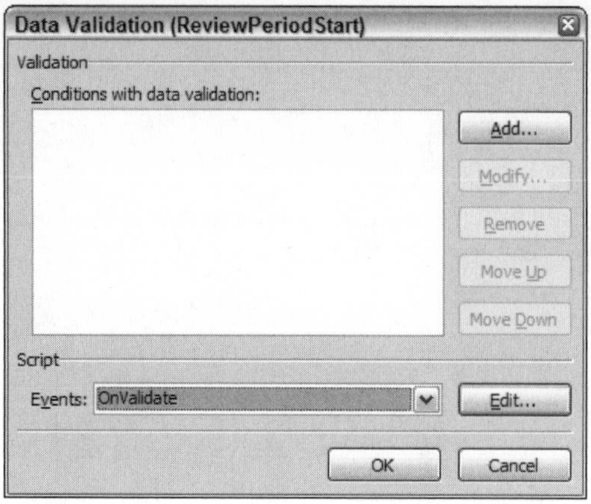

Figure 54-9

The values found in the `InfoPathEventHandler` attribute prefixed to the subroutine definition are slightly different from the events you've looked at previously. In addition to the `EventType`, which is set to whichever event you chose in InfoPath, there is a `MatchPath` value that contains the unique XPath string to identify the field.

In the preceding sample routine, the `MatchPath` value tells Visual Studio to hook the routine to the `OnBeforeChange` event for the `ReviewPeriodStart` field in the `myFields` data collection. The corresponding field can be seen in Figure 54-10 in both the form's user interface design and the Data Source pane on the right.

The Button Click Event

Buttons are a special case, having their own event. To generate a subroutine to handle the `OnClick` event of a button, bring up the Button Properties dialog (see Figure 54-11). This dialog is accessed by first selecting the `Button` and then choosing the Format➪Button Properties menu command or right-clicking the `Button` and selecting Button Properties from the context menu.

The ID field specifies the name of the button and can be changed to suit your own naming conventions. To create the event handler routine, click the Edit Form Code button. It will be automatically generated in the `FormCode.vb` file and you will be switched to the Visual Studio IDE, positioned in the routine and able to write your own program logic.

The event handler attributes are similar in structure to the field events just discussed. The following code shows a sample `OnClick` event handler for the button being edited in Figure 54-11:

```
<InfoPathEventHandler(MatchPath:="SubmitReview",
EventType:=InfoPathEventType.OnClick)> _
Public Sub SubmitReview_OnClick(ByVal e As DocActionEvent)
    ' Write your code here.

End Sub
```

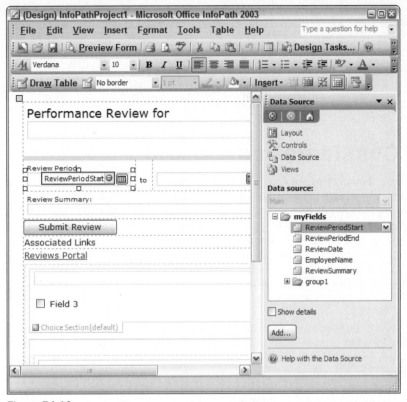

Figure 54-10

Figure 54-11

The `InfoPathEventHandler` attribute has two properties. `EventType` should be set to the `OnClick` event so it will be hooked up with the proper event, while `MatchPath` should contain the name (the ID value) of the button control.

The `DocActionEvent` argument contains the `XmlDocument` associated with the InfoPath form, a `ReturnStatus` flag you can use to indicate the success or failure of your subroutine's functionality, and a `Source XmlNode` object that contains the inner XML associated with the form.

Other Considerations

Keep a couple of other things in mind when developing InfoPath solutions with the Toolkit for Visual Studio. First, even though the documentation is installed, it is neither merged into the Office Solutions Development group nor displayed if you filter the Document Explorer by Office Development. It is found under its own category filter, Microsoft Office InfoPath 2003, or in its own root node in the full table of contents, InfoPath 2003 Toolkit for Visual Studio 2005.

Second, make sure you don't obfuscate any code that will be required by InfoPath. InfoPath requires the code to have the member names it expects, rather than obfuscated terms, and doesn't understand obfuscation at all.

When deploying your managed code solutions, you can choose from one of two options. If neither the code nor the InfoPath form template requires full trust, you can publish the form directly by using the Tools⇨Publish Form menu command in Visual Studio 2005. This will switch over to InfoPath and kick off the normal Publishing Wizard.

However, if you need full trust, you'll need to take some additional steps because by default the managed code InfoPath projects belong to the semi-trust zone of InfoPath and do not have full access to the computer system.

For full-trust solutions, you'll need to either digitally sign the form template or use the RegForm utility that comes with the InfoPath SDK. The digital certification process can be done within InfoPath as long as you have an existing certificate. In the Security tab of the Form Options dialog, select Full Trust as the security level and then select the certificate that should be attached to the form.

Summary

Building InfoPath solutions with extensive code processing is now available from within the managed code environment of Visual Studio 2005. Using the Toolkit, you can create solutions in either Visual Basic or C#, and as this chapter demonstrated, have direct access to form and field events so that you can easily affect the solution in a way that meets your requirements, rather than write JavaScript to perform this functionality.

55

Visual Studio Tools for Office

Microsoft Office applications have always been extensible via add-ins and various automation techniques. Even languages such as Visual Basic 6, which are widely known for various limitations in accessing system files, had the capability to create add-ins for Office applications such as Microsoft Word, Microsoft Excel, and Microsoft Outlook. Developers could also write applications that used an instance of an Office application to achieve certain tasks (one such example is the prevalence of applications that take advantage of Word's spell checking feature), but it was often difficult to get the solution just right.

Microsoft then released a technology called *smart tags* that enabled developers to build applications that hooked into Microsoft Word and Microsoft Excel, tracking the user's input and providing the opportunity to give feedback, and even actions that the user could take in response to certain recognized terms.

When Visual Studio .NET (2002) was released, Microsoft soon followed with the first release of Visual Studio Tools for Office (known by the abbreviation VSTO, pronounced *visto*). This initial version of VSTO didn't really produce anything new except for an easier way of creating application projects that would use Microsoft Word or Microsoft Excel. However, VSTO 2003, which works with Microsoft Office 2003 and Visual Studio .NET (2003), introduced a whole new concept known as *smart documents*.

Smart documents are special kinds of documents based on an XML schema. The schema's contents control the information that can be entered into the document or worksheet, and provide some limited actions that the user could perform. Although Microsoft demonstrated some advanced solutions combining smart documents with smart tags that went a long way toward solving particular problems, the reality was that smart documents were incredibly difficult to get right beyond a simple document with one or two actions.

That has all changed with the release of Visual Studio 2005 and Visual Studio Tools for Office 2005. Now, developing applications with Microsoft Word and Microsoft Excel is straightforward, and the integration of Windows Forms development and Office development has come a long way since the first versions. This chapter begins with a look at each of the new features for Office developers in VSTO 2005 in turn, showing how it can make your life easier, and ends with a walk-through for creating a sample Word document application, complete with smart tags, Actions pane commands, and interaction among user, document contents, and code.

The New Visual Studio Tools for Office

When you install Visual Studio Tools for Office 2005, the setup includes a number of items that fully integrate Office development into Visual Studio. This includes new project types, an array of code snippets to ease your way into creating Office solutions, documentation integrated into the main MSDN library, and menu and option additions.

After a successful installation of VSTO, the first things you'll notice in Visual Studio 2005 are the new project types now available to you when creating a new project. In the Visual Basic and C# language groups, a new group named Office is added containing a number of project templates for Office solutions (see Figure 55-1). VSTO solutions are only available in these two languages, so if you normally code in some other language and want to do VSTO development, you'll have to switch.

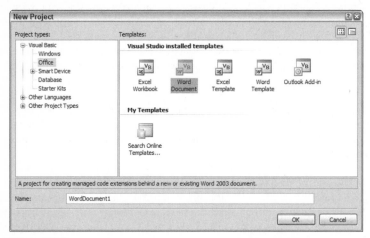

Figure 55-1

The project templates cover the three Office applications capable of VSTO development; with Microsoft Excel and Microsoft Word, the templates include both Document (or Workbook) projects and Template projects. The difference in development is minimal — template projects are used to create documents or workbooks from a template, whereas the others create an individual document or workbook.

Because of the prevalence of macro viruses in Windows, Microsoft has restricted programmatic access to the macro system and VBA project model in Office by default. To ease development, VSTO insists on having direct access to the VBA project system. When you create a new VSTO project, Visual Studio checks the access level it has for VBA in Office. When it detects that the access level is not high enough, it prompts you to allow it access (see Figure 55-2).

Figure 55-2

If you don't allow access, Visual Studio cancels the creation of the project, so this kind of message is really just warning you that if you proceed, the security access level in Office will be lowered.

You only have one question to answer when creating a VSTO project for either Word or Excel: whether to copy an existing document or create a new one (see Figure 55-3). Using an existing document can be useful if you have first created the document in Word or Excel and now want to attach the programmatic elements to the solution to the document, but with VSTO 2005's integrated designer directly utilizing the Word and Excel applications for editing documents, you can just as easily create a new document and work with that.

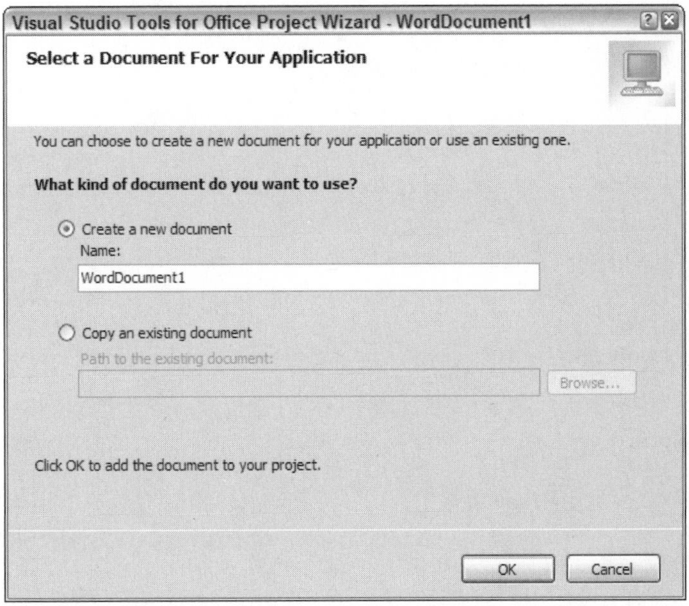

Figure 55-3

The majority of the discussion in this chapter uses Microsoft Word for illustrative purposes. The differences in most functionality between Microsoft Word and Microsoft Excel are minimal, and you can usually apply what is discussed here directly to an Excel solution in the same way.

The Visual Designer

When you created applications that used Word and Excel in previous versions of VSTO, everything was achieved by writing code and designing XML files and schemas. Because this included positioning controls in the Actions pane and setting other visual properties, it was sometimes difficult to get it right, resulting in a design process that relied heavily on trial and error.

With VSTO 2005 that's all changed, and you can now design your Word and Excel solutions directly within the Visual Studio 2005 IDE. The document or workbook that is used as the basis for the project is part of the project files list in the Solution Explorer and can be opened in the main workspace area of the IDE.

As Figure 55-4 illustrates, the editor for a Word document project includes the toolbars from Word and the same visual presentation as Word. You can type directly into the document as if you were editing it in Word (and the same applies for Excel workbooks). All the same formatting functions are available to you so you can work in a familiar environment.

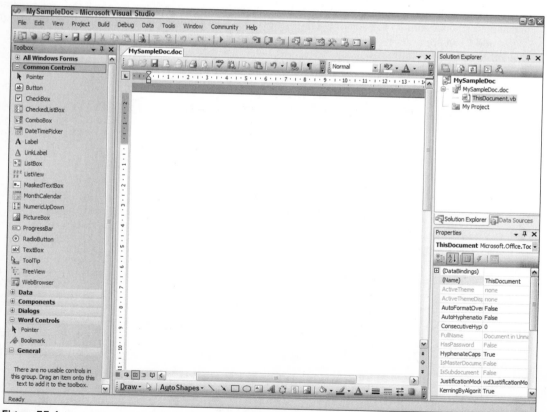

Figure 55-4

In fact, the in-place editor exactly replicates the settings you have in Word itself, so any customizations you've made to the different views, such as showing paragraph marks and the style area in Normal view, are applied to the Visual Studio IDE.

Word and Excel are so well integrated into the development environment that you'll find an additional submenu under the Tools menu of the IDE containing specific tools for the particular application you're developing. Figure 55-5 shows the Tools menu that is added for Word Document and Word Template projects. You can even change the main Word application options from within Visual Studio, avoiding the need to start Word to change the application environment configuration.

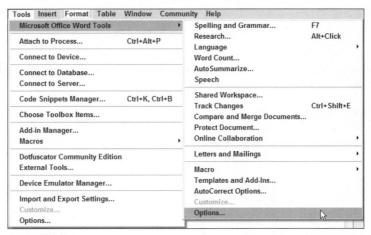

Figure 55-5

As you've probably guessed, the reason for such an integrated replication of Word and Excel is because Visual Studio implements an instance of the appropriate application object and uses it to get the various settings, much like you might do if you were creating your own application that housed an instance of a Word document or Excel spreadsheet.

Control Design

When designing the visual interface of the document you can use most of the Windows Forms components in the layout. You can achieve this the same way you would if you were designing a Windows form or web application in flow mode, whereby each control is added after the next. The controls will flow around the text in the document as well, so you can create richly formatted documents that include controls that the user can interact with. An example of using Windows Forms controls in this way is when you want the majority of the document locked from edits but still want the user to be able to enter limited information, such as on a form.

Because the VSTO project is fully integrated into Word and Excel, you can use these controls in the same way you would if they were on a Windows form, including trapping their events and invoking their methods.

In addition to the standard Windows Forms components, VSTO projects have an additional group of custom controls associated with the particular application. Known as *host controls,* these controls extend objects found within Word or Excel by wrapping them with a .NET layer, thus enabling them to be used at both design time (for layout) and runtime (to trap their events and interact with them like any other control).

In Word-based projects, there is a single host control called the `Bookmark` control, which enables you to mark a selection in the document or template with a named bookmark, which can be used later programmatically in your application. Excel-based projects have two host controls: `ListObject` components replicate the behavior of sorted and filtered list columns in Excel, and `NamedRange` controls enable you to specify a section of a worksheet with a unique name to identify it in your program code.

Figure 55-6 shows a portion of an Excel worksheet in the Visual Studio designer. The spreadsheet contains both Windows Forms controls (the `Button1` and `TextBox1` components) and a `ListObject` host control with its filtering menu displayed. Each of these three controls can be customized in the Properties window just as you would for a normal Windows application.

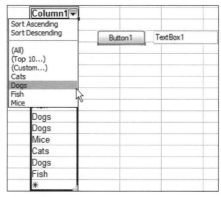

Figure 55-6

Writing Code

VSTO enables you to write code for your Office-based applications in the same way as you would for a Windows application. You have full access to the application (Word or Excel) object, the current document's object representation, and the events, methods, and properties exposed by them and their constituent controls.

When you create a VSTO project, in addition to the .doc or .xls file that contains the actual document contents, a code-behind file is also created and added to the Solution Explorer. Figure 55-7 illustrates this with an Excel-based project, showing four additional code files associated with the .xls file: one code-behind file for each of the default worksheet objects in the workbook and one workbook module. If you've ever used Visual Basic for Applications, you will see how this mirrors the same internal setup when editing the VBA code in Excel for a particular workbook.

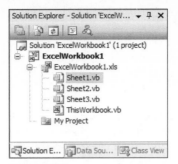

Figure 55-7

Every code-behind file has two subroutine stubs added to account for the interface into the Office applica-tion. These two subroutines, Startup and Shutdown, are used to initialize your application ready for execution, and can be used to integrate documents and their associated Actions panes, add VSTO-specific smart tags, and customize the user interface of Word or Excel with additional menus or toolbar items.

One problem that developers new to Office programming face is how to achieve common tasks. The pro-gram code required is not necessarily difficult, but because the object models of both Word and Excel are extensive, it is easy to become overwhelmed with the sheer number of members available.

Fortunately, VSTO 2005 ships with its own set of code snippets, which are automatically integrated into the main Code Snippet library. The code snippet collection has a sizable number of Word- and Excel-specific functions, such as programmatically filtering a ListObject control and adding tables in Word, but it also has more general snippets grouped into an Office category (see Figure 55-8). The snippets in this category provide you with the code to customize the environment with your own toolbars and menu commands.

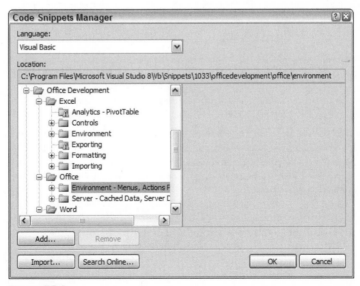

Figure 55-8

The Actions Pane

One of the more difficult aspects of smart documents in the previous version of VSTO was customizing the Actions pane to do what you wanted. It involved editing XML schemas and using code to control how each component was added and how it interacted with the application, whether it was Word or Excel.

VSTO 2005 solves all this by providing you with a new control known as an *Actions Pane control*, which comes with its own visual designer and programming model. Adding an Actions Pane component to your project is done in the same way as you would add any other type of item. Use the Project⇨Add New Item menu command, or right-click the project file in the Solution Explorer and select Add⇨New Item. Either of these actions displays the regular Add New Item dialog (shown in Figure 55-9), but besides the normal Windows Forms components there will be an Actions Pane Control template. Select that template, name the file to suit the purpose of your Actions Pane, and click Add.

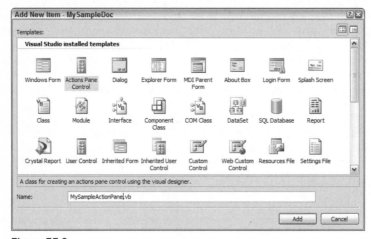

Figure 55-9

You can actually use all of the item templates shown in Figure 55-9 in your VSTO application, so if you need to present a dialog box or want to separate your code into separate classes and modules, then you can do so by adding whatever items you need.

The visual designer for the Actions Pane component works much like a User Control. The design area is borderless, as it is housed in the main Actions pane in Word or Excel, and unlike the design for the document itself, you can precisely place and size your Windows Forms controls just as you would in a typical User Control. Figure 55-10 shows a simple Actions Pane component with `Button`, `Label`, and `TextBox` controls sited on its design surface.

Figure 55-10

You can write code to handle the events for the child controls or even for the Actions Pane itself, calling their methods and setting and retrieving properties as needed. However, once your code for the Actions Pane is complete, you still need to hook the Actions Pane component to your document in order for it to be displayed properly.

The Actions Pane components are not added automatically to the document because you may want to show different Actions panes, depending on the context users find themselves in when editing the document. However, if you have a single Actions Pane component and simply want to add it immediately when the document is opened, add the component to the `ActionsPane.Controls` collection of the document at startup, as demonstrated in the following code:

```
Private Sub ThisDocument_Startup(ByVal sender As Object, _
    ByVal e As System.EventArgs) Handles Me.Startup
    Me.ActionsPane.Controls.Add(NameOfActionsPaneComponent)
End Sub
```

Figure 55-11 shows a Word document project. The Document Actions pane has been populated with the sample Actions Pane component, and the document text displays visual indicators where Bookmark host controls are sited.

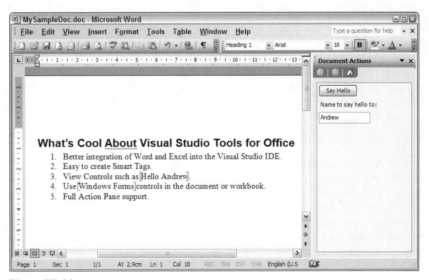

Figure 55-11

Smart Tags

Smart Tag technology has been around since Microsoft Office XP, but the initial implementation was difficult to code against. Smart Tags 2.0 introduced some necessary functionality to make the feature workable in anything beyond a demonstration environment, by giving the smart tag developer the capability to create extensive nested dynamic menus of actions when a term was found by the recognizer, and providing more information internally about recognized terms.

How Smart Tags Work

The functionality of a smart tag is divided into two distinct phases: recognition and action. The *recognition* phase is the background process that searches through your document looking for strings that match its search criteria.

The most basic smart tag doesn't even need code, just a specially formatted list containing an array of strings, each one being equivalent to an individual term that should be recognized by the tag code. Code-based smart tags can use complex search criteria to determine what parts of a document should be recognized by the tag, including regular expressions and sourcing the term list from a Data Source.

Once the recognizer side of the smart tag determines that a section of the document should be recognized, it returns information to Word or Excel, which visually marks the range with a smart tag indicator (in Word this is a small purple, dotted line, whereas in Excel it's a small purple triangle in one corner of the cell). When you hover your mouse pointer over the smart tag, an icon appears, enabling you to open a special smart tag menu.

This is where the second main phase of the smart tag code comes into play. The *actions* phase controls how this smart tag menu should look, specifying the menu commands (and a hierarchy of submenus if needed), and what action should be taken based on a user's selection. Word and Excel pass information about the document to the smart tag DLL, which in turn performs whatever function is selected.

An example might be a customer smart tag that recognizes customer names. When you open the smart tag menu for a particular recognized customer, you could insert additional information about that customer into the document, such as their address or financial data.

Smart tag development required you to create a standalone DLL containing classes that implemented a series of interfaces for both the recognition phase and the action phase of a smart tag (if you're not sure how smart tags work, take a look at the sidebar, "How Smart Tags Work").

One problem with this implementation of smart tags was that once installed, smart tags were either active for all documents or inactive for the entire application. This resulted in unexpected behavior in Word and Excel, such as people's initials being recognized by a financial stock smart tag, or ill-defined search terms of small words being located within a bigger word (an example of this might be having the word *step* marked as a recognized term when it was part of the full word *footstep*).

VSTO 2005 introduces a special type of smart tag that only exists for the specific document or template in which it's created. This enables you to create search criteria that are much more general without worrying about false positives in other documents.

They are also integrated right into the programming mode of the VSTO applications, resulting in a much easier implementation. In fact, once a VSTO smart tag has been defined in the code, you need to write one statement to add it to the document's smart tag collection:

```
Me.VstoSmartTags.Add(TheSmartTagObject)
```

The `SmartTag` object is straightforward to use. First, you need to declare the `SmartTag` object and then populate the `Terms` or `Expressions` collection to specify the search criteria. Next, you need to create an `Action` object and assign it to the `Actions` collection. That's all that is necessary, so the simplest code to achieve this would look like the following:

```
Dim TheSmartTagObject As New Microsoft.Office.Tools.Word.SmartTag( _
    "www.parsonsdesigns.com/VSTO#MySmartTag", "The VSTO Smart Tag")

TheSmartTagObject.Terms.Add("myTerm")
Dim MyAction As Microsoft.Office.Tools.Word.Action = _
    New Microsoft.Office.Tools.Word.Action("My Action")
TheSmartTagObject.Actions = New Microsoft.Office.Tools.Word.Action() { _
    MyAction }
```

```
Me.VstoSmartTags.Add(TheSmartTagObject)
```

While this is technically correct, it does not achieve anything, because you need to be able to intercept the events of the `Action` object so you can act when a user selects the smart tag menu. The definition of the `Action` object needs to be moved to the module level, and a `WithEvents` keyword must be added so Visual Studio knows you need to intercept its events. Changing the code accordingly, the following listing is all you need to have a properly functioning and implemented smart tag:

```
WithEvents MyAction As Microsoft.Office.Tools.Word.Action
...
Dim TheSmartTagObject As New Microsoft.Office.Tools.Word.SmartTag( _
    "www.parsonsdesigns.com/VSTO#MySmartTag", "The VSTO Smart Tag")

TheSmartTagObject.Terms.Add("myTerm")
MyAction = New Microsoft.Office.Tools.Word.Action("My Action")
TheSmartTagObject.Actions = New Microsoft.Office.Tools.Word.Action() { _
    MyAction }
```

```
Me.VstoSmartTags.Add(TheSmartTagObject)
```

Microsoft Outlook Add-Ins

New to VSTO in 2005 is Outlook add-in support. Traditionally, Outlook add-ins used the `IDTExtensibility2` interface when connecting to Outlook, but with VSTO 2005 the project template includes an implementation of the `IStartup` interface instead. This is a much simpler interface, requiring only that you handle the `Startup` and `Shutdown` events, similar to those for the Word and Excel project types.

VSTO 2005 has managed this difficult feat by wrapping the add-in with a preloader, which loads the .NET CLR and then the VSTO runtime before finally running the assembly containing the add-in code. This ensures that Outlook can run the managed code routines within the add-in itself and enables your code to intercept events raised by Outlook and to write code that will automate Outlook through the object model. The events belong to the VSTO supplied classes in the `Microsoft.Office.Tools.Outlook` namespace.

The VSTO 2005 Sample Project

The best way to understand the power of the new features of Visual Studio Tools for Office is to walk through the creation of an application that takes advantage of them. The following pages take you through the process of creating a Word document project, designing the document layout, marking it up with Bookmark host controls, and adding some Windows Forms controls to the document as well. Then, multiple Actions Pane components are added to demonstrate how you can contextually change the Document Actions pane dynamically, and some smart tag processing is added to recognize and act on particular terms.

1. Before you begin this walk-through, first ensure that you have installed Visual Studio Tools for Office 2005 and have Microsoft Word 2003 set up with the *Primary Interop Assemblies (PIAs)*. The PIAs are necessary for the integration of Word and .NET. To confirm that the PIAs are installed, run the setup for Microsoft Office, choose advanced customization, and ensure that the .NET Programmability Support component is installed.

2. Once you're ready to create the project, start Visual Studio 2005 and use the File⇨New Project command to display the New Project dialog. Select the Office templates group and locate and select the Word Document project template. Change the name of the project to "CoolVSTOFeatures" and click OK to create the project.

    When Visual Studio 2005 prompts you to pick a document, accept the default selection of Create a New Document and leave the name as is (it will default to CoolVSTOFeatures to match the project name).

    You may also be prompted to enable access to the Visual Basic for Applications engine (see Figure 55-2). If you don't do this, you won't be able to continue to create the project, so accept this change to Word's options.

3. It's time to create the skeleton Word document that will be used to show off the new features of Visual Studio Tools for Office. When Visual Studio creates the project, the document will be opened in the main workspace of the IDE in Design view. Type the text **The Report Heading** and assign it the Heading 1 style. Remember that you have access to all of the Word toolbars for editing the document, so if you can't see the Styles drop-down list, locate the toolbar command just as you would in Word.

4. Press Enter to go to a new line, and type the following(because you're using Word, it automatically sets this new line's style to Normal, as it is following the Word rules about styles):

```
The summary information for the report will go here.
```

5. Again, press Enter to go to a new line, this time adding a Word table. The table should be one row high and two columns wide. In the first cell of the table add the words **Company Name**, and in the second add the word **Information**. This table is automatically populated with company names based on the summary content.

    So far, you've created a straightforward document with no VSTO features, so you'll now add the VSTO controls to the document that will be used to interact with the user of the document.

6. Add a `Bookmark` host control to the document by double-clicking its entry in the Word Controls group in the Toolbox. This displays a dialog box asking you to mark the section of the document for inclusion in the bookmarked region. Highlight the three words in the heading line and click OK (see Figure 55-12). Name the Bookmark `DocumentHeading`.

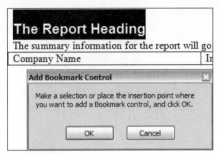

Figure 55-12

7. Repeat this process to add a second `Bookmark` host control that contains the entire summary paragraph line, this time including the paragraph mark. Name this second `Bookmark` control `DocumentSummary`. Add a final `Bookmark` host control that encloses the table and set its `Name` property to `TableArea`. These three `Bookmark` controls are referred to in the code you'll write in subsequent steps.

8. To illustrate how Windows Forms controls can be used in Office document solutions as well, add a `TextBox` and `Button` below the table. Notice how the controls follow the Word flow pattern of layout, appearing in a separate paragraph. Because the controls are set tightly against each other the design looks a little awkward, so add a couple of spaces between them. Set the following properties on the `TextBox`:

   - ❑ Name: DocAuthorName
   - ❑ Text: (null)
   - ❑ Width: 200

9. Set the following properties on the `Button`:

   - ❑ Name: SaveAuthorName
   - ❑ Text: Save Author Name
   - ❑ Width: 80

The document user interface design is now complete, so you can start adding code behind the document. The first task is to add a smart tag that recognizes a list of company names that can be used in other functionality in the document:

1. Open the `ThisDocument.vb` file that contains the code for the document by right-clicking its entry in the Solution Explorer and selecting the View Code menu command. At the top of the class definition and just before the `ThisDocument_Startup` method definition, add a subroutine that creates the smart tag, defines its recognizers, and hooks in two action objects. First, define the subroutine with a name of `AddCompanySmartTag` and add a statement to define and instantiate a new VSTO Word smart tag object named `CompanyDetails`:

```
Private Sub AddCompanySmartTag()
    Dim CompanyDetails As New Microsoft.Office.Tools.Word.SmartTag( _
        "www.wrox.com/CompanyDetails#CompanyDetailsSample", "Company Details")
End Sub
```

The first parameter in the instantiation of the `SmartTag` object should be unique to your project, so feel free to change the URI to something you'll recognize. The second parameter, `CompanyDetails`, will be the name of the smart tag displayed to the end user of the document.

2. Define a set of company names to look for. For this sample walk-through, you'll just use a list of simple one-word names by adding to the `Terms` collection in the smart tag, but you could just as easily create search criteria using the `Expressions` collection and build a series of regular expressions. Use the `Terms.Add` method to add a number of company names. This sample adds five terms as follows:

```
Private Sub AddCompanySmartTag()
    Dim CompanyDetails As New Microsoft.Office.Tools.Word.SmartTag( _
        "www.test.com/CompanyDetails#CompanyDetailsSample", "Company Details")

    CompanyDetails.Terms.Add("Microsoft")
    CompanyDetails.Terms.Add("ParsonsDesigns")
    CompanyDetails.Terms.Add("AutumnCare")
    CompanyDetails.Terms.Add("Wrox")
    CompanyDetails.Terms.Add("Wiley")
End Sub
```

3. The only thing left to do to prepare the smart tag in the document is to connect the smart tag action and recognizer. At the end of the subroutine, add the statement `Me.VstoSmartTags` `.Add(CompanyDetails)`. The `VstoSmartTags` collection object is used to store the `SmartTag` objects that are bound to a specific document or template solution.

4. The smart tag will now recognize the terms and mark them up in the Word document, but there are no `Actions` associated with the smart tag, so it's pretty useless. The sample solution enables users to save company names to a list for later use and displays a small bit of information about the company. Define two smart tag `Action` objects at the top of the `ThisDocument` class. Because you want to be able to intercept some of the `Action` objects' events, you need to define them `WithEvents`:

```
Private WithEvents SaveCompanyName As Microsoft.Office.Tools.Word.Action
Private WithEvents DisplayCompanyValue As Microsoft.Office.Tools.Word.Action
```

5. Now you can return to the `AddCompanySmartTag` subroutine and create new instances of the `Action` class for these objects. After you add the search criteria to the `Terms` collection, create the two new `Actions` like this:

```
SaveCompanyName = New Microsoft.Office.Tools.Word.Action("Save Name")
DisplayCompanyValue = New Microsoft.Office.Tools.Word.Action("Show Details")
```

The `Action` objects are now ready to be hooked up to the `CompanyDetails` `SmartTag` object. To do this, assign a new collection of `Action` objects to the `Actions` collection:

```
CompanyDetails.Actions = New Microsoft.Office.Tools.Word.Action() _
    {SaveCompanyName, DisplayCompanyValue}
```

Make sure your final subroutine matches the following listing:

```
Private Sub AddCompanySmartTag()
    Dim CompanyDetails As New Microsoft.Office.Tools.Word.SmartTag( _
        "www.test.com/CompanyDetails#CompanyDetailsSample", "Company Details")

    CompanyDetails.Terms.Add("Microsoft")
```

```
        CompanyDetails.Terms.Add("ParsonsDesigns")
        CompanyDetails.Terms.Add("AutumnCare")
        CompanyDetails.Terms.Add("Wrox")
        CompanyDetails.Terms.Add("Wiley")

        SaveCompanyName = New Microsoft.Office.Tools.Word.Action("Save Name")
        DisplayCompanyValue = New Microsoft.Office.Tools.Word.Action("Show Details")

        CompanyDetails.Actions = New Microsoft.Office.Tools.Word.Action() _
            {SaveCompanyName, DisplayCompanyValue}

        Me.VstoSmartTags.Add(CompanyDetails)
    End Sub
```

6. Because they're based on the Smart Tags 2.0 library, VSTO smart tag captions can be modified dynamically through the `BeforeCaptionShow` event. To demonstrate this in action, add the following two simple subroutines. Each one handles the `BeforeCaptionShow` and sets the `Caption` property to a value that includes the string recognized by the `SmartTag` object's recognizer:

```
Sub SaveCompanyName_BeforeCaptionShow(ByVal sender As Object, _
    ByVal e As Microsoft.Office.Tools.Word.ActionEventArgs) Handles _
    SaveCompanyName.BeforeCaptionShow

    SaveCompanyName.Caption = "Save " & e.Text & " to name list"
End Sub

Sub DisplayCompanyValue_BeforeCaptionShow(ByVal sender As Object, _
    ByVal e As Microsoft.Office.Tools.Word.ActionEventArgs) Handles _
    DisplayCompanyValue.BeforeCaptionShow

    DisplayCompanyValue.Caption = "Display information about " & e.Text
End Sub
```

7. You'll use the `SaveCompanyName` action in a later step, so for now create an event handler routine for the `Click` event of the `DisplayCompanyValue` action (see Figure 55-13). You can easily create event handler routines for both the `Click` and `BeforeCaptionShow` events by first selecting the specific object you want (for example, `DisplayCompanyValue`) in the Class Name drop-down list, and then selecting the event you need to handle from the Method drop-down list.

Figure 55-13

In a real-life situation, you might use the `DisplayCompanyValue` action to access the Internet or an internal company web site and download some useful financial information about the recognized company. However, for this example, simply display a message that contains the company name and a temporary value string to demonstrate how you can perform normal code. A sample `Click` event handler routine appears in the following listing:

```
Sub DisplayCompanyValue_Click(ByVal sender As Object, _
    ByVal e As Microsoft.Office.Tools.Word.ActionEventArgs) Handles _
    DisplayCompanyValue.Click

    Dim TempValue As String = vbNullString
    Select Case e.Text
        Case "Microsoft"
            TempValue = "NO COMPLAINTS"
        Case "ParsonsDesigns"
            TempValue = "UH OH"
        Case "AutumnCare"
            TempValue = "COULD BE BETTER"
        Case "Wrox"
            TempValue = "SOLID GOLD"
        Case "Wiley"
            TempValue = "SKY HIGH"
    End Select

    MessageBox.Show("The current value of " & e.Text & " is " & TempValue)
End Sub
```

8. You'll need to call the `AddCompanySmartTag` subroutine in the `Startup` routine of the document. At the same time, call the `Select` method on the `DocumentSummary` `Bookmark` object so that when the document is first opened, the summary section is always selected, ready for users to begin adding their own entries:

```
Private Sub ThisDocument_Startup(ByVal sender As Object, _
    ByVal e As System.EventArgs) Handles Me.Startup

    AddCompanySmartTag()
    DocumentSummary.Select()
End Sub
```

9. Before testing the document solution, you should also add some functionality to the Windows Forms `Button` control you added to the design. The simplest way to add the event handler is to return to the Design view of the document and double-click the `SaveAuthorName` button. Visual Studio 2005 automatically creates the event handler stub for you. In this subroutine, add the following two statements:

```
Private Sub SaveAuthorName_Click(ByVal sender As System.Object, _
    ByVal e As System.EventArgs) Handles SaveAuthorName.Click

    Me.BuiltInDocumentProperties("Author").value = DocAuthorName.Text
    MessageBox.Show("The Author Name property has been set to " & _
        DocAuthorName.Text & ". You can check by looking at File->Properties.")
End Sub
```

The first statement uses the `BuiltInDocumentProperties` key-value pair collection of the Word `Document` object. This is just one of hundreds of properties exposed by Word through either the `Application` object or the `Document` object. This particular collection maintains the list of pre-defined properties pertaining to a particular document, including the `Title`, `Author`, and `Subject`, as well as other information.

The code overwrites the `Author` value with whatever text is in the `DocAuthorName TextBox` situated in the document. The second statement simply shows a dialog informing the user of what action took place.

10. Run the document solution by pressing F5. This enables you to debug the code if anything goes wrong. After the project is compiled, Microsoft Word automatically starts and loads your document. Figure 55-14 shows the document after an end user types some information in the summary area, replacing the placeholder text. Note how several words have been recognized as smart tag terms, and how the user has selected one to perform an action.

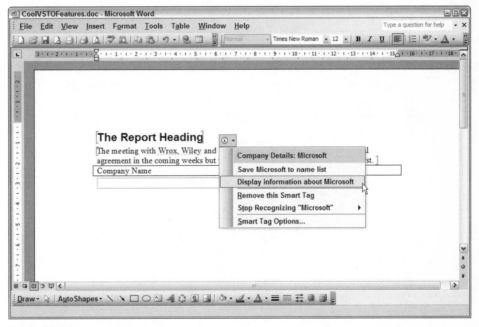

Figure 55-14

Test the features you've added to the document so far by selecting the DisplayCompanyValue smart tag action for different recognized company names. In addition, try typing text in the textbox and clicking the Save Author Name button to save it to the built-in properties list of the document.

When you're satisfied that the functionality is working as expected so far, close the document (without saving) and return to the Visual Studio 2005 IDE. The next stage of development is to add two Actions Pane controls to the project. One will be visible at all times and will provide some limited information, while the second component should only be shown when the end user is in the table area of the document. While this situation is forced, it demonstrates how to use both multiple and optional Actions Pane controls in a document solution.

1. Add the first Actions Pane control by right-clicking the project entry in the Solution Explorer and choosing the Add New Item from the context menu. Select the Actions Pane item template, name the control `MainActions.vb`, and click OK to add it to the project.

2. The design surface for an Actions Pane control is similar to a regular custom control, presenting a borderless form to work with. Add two `Button` controls, a `Label` control, and a `TextBox` control to the design with the following properties:

- ❑   `Button1.Name: FormatDocument`
- ❑   `Button1.Text: Format Document`
- ❑   `Button2.Name: SaveProperties`
- ❑   `Button2.Text: Save Properties`
- ❑   `Label1.Text: Author Name:`
- ❑   `TextBox1.Name: PaneAuthorName`
- ❑   `TextBox1.Text: (null)`

3. To distinguish the areas of the two Actions Pane controls when they are displayed, change the `BackColor` property of the `MainActions` component to the web color `SkyBlue`. The final design should look like what is shown in Figure 55-15 (without color, of course).

Figure 55-15

4. To demonstrate how the objects of the main document can be passed around in code, take a reference to the `DocumentHeading` `Bookmark` control to this Actions Pane control. Open `MainActions.vb` in Code view and define a public variable at the top of the class to contain the object reference (you could define a property to properly interface the Actions Pane to the document, but it's simpler this way for the example):

```
Public HeadingAreaRef As Microsoft.Office.Tools.Word.Bookmark
```

You'll connect this object to the `Bookmark` *object in the document in a later step.*

5. Add an event handler routine for the `Click` event of the FormatDocument button and write some code to format sections of the document based on different aspects of the information contained in the heading area. The following subroutine first formats the contents of the `DocumentHeading` bookmark itself with a built-in Word style. If the text contains the word Wrox, it will be styled using Heading 1; otherwise, it will be styled with Heading 2.

The other part of the listing sets a set of font properties in the table area of the document. Note how you can write code that references the objects in the Word document just like any other .NET class. These properties vary depending on whether the length of the `DocumentHeading` bookmarked text is more or less than 10. Here's the listing:

```
Private Sub FormatDocument_Click(ByVal sender As System.Object, _
    ByVal e As System.EventArgs) Handles FormatDocument.Click

    If InStr(HeadingAreaRef.Range.Text, "Wrox") > 0 Then
        HeadingAreaRef.Style = "Heading 1"
    Else
        HeadingAreaRef.Style = "Heading 2"
    End If

    With Globals.ThisDocument.Tables(1).Rows(1)
        If (HeadingAreaRef.End - HeadingAreaRef.Start) > 10 Then
            .Range.Font.Bold = True
            .Range.Font.Color = Word.WdColor.wdColorBlue
            .Range.Font.Size = 16
        Else
            .Range.Font.Bold = False
            .Range.Font.Color = Word.WdColor.wdColorDarkGreen
            .Range.Font.Size = 24
        End If
    End With
End Sub
```

6. Add an event handler subroutine for the `Click` event of the SaveProperties button. The code for this subroutine is similar to the code you wrote for the `Button` control sited on the Word document itself, but this time you need to refer to the document using the `Globals.ThisDocument` object:

```
Private Sub SaveProperties_Click(ByVal sender As System.Object, _
    ByVal e As System.EventArgs) Handles SaveProperties.Click

    Globals.ThisDocument.BuiltInDocumentProperties("Author").Value = _
        PaneAuthorName.Text
    MessageBox.Show("The Author Name property has been set to " & _
        PaneAuthorName.Text & ". You can check by looking at File->Properties.")
End Sub
```

7. You can now hook up the first Actions Pane control to the document itself. Return to the `ThisDocument.vb` code module for the document and define an instance of the `MainActions` component at the top of the class. Because the pane doesn't have any events, you can just define it normally, even including the instantiation at declaration time:

```
Private MainPane As New MainActions
```

8. Locate the document's `Startup` event handler. Earlier you added code to this module to connect the `SmartTag` object and to select the contents of the `DocumentSummary` bookmark control. Below these statements, insert a statement to add the `MainPane` object you just defined to the `ActionsPane.Controls` collection of the document itself.

In addition, connect the `DocumentHeading` component to the `MainPane HeadingAreaRef` object so that the Actions Pane control will be able to use the contents of `DocumentHeading`. The `Startup` subroutine should now look like this:

```
Private Sub ThisDocument_Startup(ByVal sender As Object, _
    ByVal e As System.EventArgs) Handles Me.Startup

AddCompanySmartTag()
DocumentSummary.Select()

Me.ActionsPane.Controls.Add(MainPane)
MainPane.HeadingAreaRef = DocumentHeading
End Sub
```

9.   It's now time to add the conditional Actions Pane control. Add it to the project just as you did for the `MainActions` component, this time naming it `CompanyNameActions.vb`. Add a `Button` and a `ListView` to the design surface of the new Actions Pane component and set the `BackColor` of the component to `SteelBlue` to differentiate it from the other Actions Pane contents. Set the following properties for the objects:

   ❑   `Button1.Name: InsertNames`

   ❑   `Button1.Text: Insert Name(s)`

   ❑   `ListView1.Name: NameList`

   ❑   `ListView1.MultiSelect: True`

   The final design layout for the `CompanyNameActions` component should look like what is shown in Figure 55-16.

Figure 55-16

10.   You're going to enable the user to select names from the `ListView` (once it's populated with data) and then click the `InsertNames` button. Add an event handler for the `Click` event of the `InsertNames` button and ensure that the user has first selected some items from the list. If they haven't, display a message letting them know that the function cannot work unless they first select items from the list, and then set the focus of Microsoft Word to the `NameList` `ListView` control. You can do this in exactly the same way you would if you were building a Windows Forms application:

```
Private Sub InsertNames_Click(ByVal sender As System.Object, _
    ByVal e As System.EventArgs) Handles InsertNames.Click
    If NameList.SelectedItems.Count > 0 Then
        ' code to add information to the table will go here
    Else
        MessageBox.Show("You must first select an entry in the list")
        NameList.Focus()
    End If
End Sub
```

Once you have determined that items have been selected, iterate through the SelectedItems collection of the NameList object and add a row to the table for each item, setting the first cell in the row to the name of the company, and putting some placeholder text in the second cell. Your final subroutine should look like the following listing:

```
Private Sub InsertNames_Click(ByVal sender As System.Object, _
    ByVal e As System.EventArgs) Handles InsertNames.Click
    If NameList.SelectedItems.Count > 0 Then
        For Each NameToInsert As ListViewItem In NameList.SelectedItems
            With Globals.ThisDocument.Tables(1)
                .Rows.Add()
                .Rows(.Rows.Count).Cells(1).Range.Text = NameToInsert.Text
                .Rows(.Rows.Count).Cells(2).Range.Text = "Put information here"
            End With
        Next
    Else
        MessageBox.Show("You must first select an entry in the list")
        NameList.Focus()
    End If
End Sub
```

11. You're almost done. The only tasks left are to connect the CompanyNameActions component to the document and write some code to populate the ListView control. Open the ThisDocument.vb code module and define the CompanyNameActions object at the top of the class. Again, because you don't need to intercept any events, just define it as a regular object:

```
Private TableAreaPane As New CompanyNameActions
```

12. Rather than being visible at all times, the TableAreaPane object will only be shown when the user is currently editing the table in the document. To determine when the user is within a bookmarked area, you can use the Selected and Deselected events. Add event handler routines for both events to add and remove the TableAreaPane to the ActionsPane.Controls collection as appropriate. The following code shows you how this can be achieved:

```
Private Sub TableArea_Selected(ByVal sender As Object, _
    ByVal e As Microsoft.Office.Tools.Word.SelectionEventArgs) Handles _
    TableArea.Selected

    Me.ActionsPane.Controls.Add(TableAreaPane)

End Sub
Private Sub TableArea_Deselected(ByVal sender As Object, _
    ByVal e As Microsoft.Office.Tools.Word.SelectionEventArgs) Handles _
    TableArea.Deselected

    Me.ActionsPane.Controls.Remove(TableAreaPane)

End Sub
```

13. This will display the TableAreaPane object when the user places the cursor inside the bookmarked table of the document, so the only task left is to populate the ListView. You'll do this by directly accessing the NameList control within the TableAreaPane object from the document, which demonstrates how you can access properties and controls in the Actions Pane components attached to a document.

The information you'll add to the `ListView` will come from the smart tag action you left earlier, `SaveCompanyName`. Add an event handler for the `Click` event of `SaveCompanyName` and add the contents of `e.Text` (which contains the text that was recognized) to the `NameList` control's `Items` collection. When completed, this subroutine appears as follows:

```
Sub SaveCompanyName_Click(ByVal sender As Object, _
    ByVal e As Microsoft.Office.Tools.Word.ActionEventArgs) Handles _
    SaveCompanyName.Click

    TableAreaPane.NameList.Items.Add(e.Text)
End Sub
```

14. Run the project by pressing F5. This time, when Microsoft Word first starts, you'll be presented with a rich interface containing not only the bookmarked areas and Windows Forms controls in the document itself, but also an Actions Pane area populated with the main Actions Pane control you defined (see Figure 55-17).

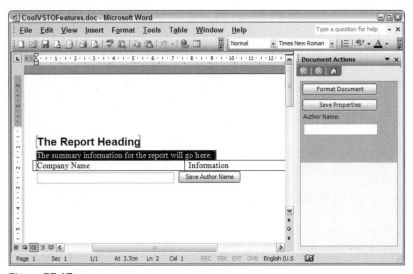

Figure 55-17

15. Perform the following actions:

❑ Type information into the summary area, making sure you include the company names that were included in the `Terms` collection of the recognizer.

❑ Open the smart tag menu for a recognized term and select the Display information about [*companyname*] action to see how smart tags can interact with the user.

❑ Open the smart tag menu for a recognized term and select the Save [*companyname*] to name list action to save the string to the `ListView` (which is initially invisible).

❑ Change the heading to different length text strings, and click the Format Document button in the main Actions pane to see how it affects the table area formatting.

❑ Change the heading to include the word Wrox, and again click the Format Document button to see how it affects the heading's style.

❑ Enter information in the TextBox control on the document and click the associated Save Author Name button. Use the File⇨Properties menu to confirm that the built-in property of the document was indeed set (see Figure 55-18).

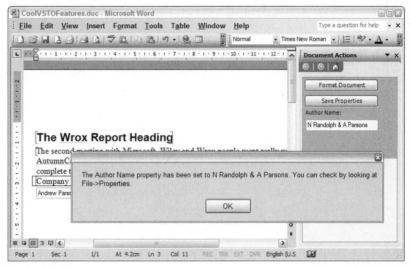

Figure 55-18

❑ Enter information in the TextBox control in the main Actions pane and click its associated Save Properties button and again check the File⇨Properties menu to check the property's value.

❑ Place the cursor anywhere in the table area of the document. The secondary Actions Pane component should be added to the Document Actions pane of Microsoft Word, underneath the other Actions pane. You can see which one is which by the different background colors you set.

❑ Select several names from the ListView. These were added when you used the Save [companyname] to name list action earlier.

❑ Click the Insert Name(s) button to automatically add additional rows to the table and populate them with data sourced from the list.

Figure 55-19 shows the document with formatting applied, multiple smart tag terms recognized and their actions performed, and the Insert Name(s) function used to add rows to the table. Note how users can select multiple companies in the ListView and how the Document Actions pane can accommodate multiple Actions pane controls concurrently.

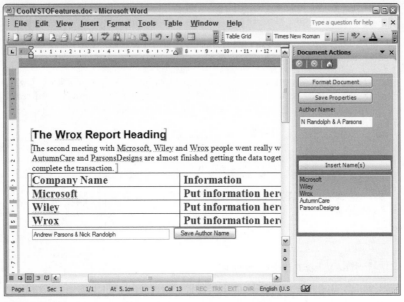

Figure 55-19

Summary

This chapter introduced you to the major new features in Visual Studio Tools for Office 2005. It is no longer difficult to build feature-rich applications using Word and Excel because now they are fully integrated into the Visual Studio 2005 development environment, enabling you to create .NET solutions that can customize the appearance of the user interface with your own components in both the application and the document. This enables you to have unprecedented control over how end users interact with Word and Excel.

In addition, Outlook is now also supported, with a project template providing the initial code that is required to hook into its complex object model. In conclusion, VSTO 2005 is an excellent resource for Office developers.

Visual Studio Team System

In the past, one of the limitations of Visual Studio was that it did not provide support for enterprise-level development. For example, there was no way to track requirements or bugs, no built-in test engine, and no support for code or performance analysis. Visual Studio Team System gives organizations a single tool that can be used to support the entire software life cycle. This chapter examines the additional features only available in the Team System versions of Visual Studio 2005. In addition, you'll also learn how the Team Foundation Server provides an essential tool for managing software projects.

Team System Editions

There are three editions of Team System that enable the functionality of Visual Studio Team System to be tailored for the role that an individual plays in the software development team. The three editions target architects, developers, and testers. Visual Studio Team Suite is the fourth edition, which incorporates all of the functionality found within the other editions. The following sections cover the functionality specific to those editions.

For Everyone

Much of the functionality provided by Team System makes use of the Team Foundation Server — a server-based product that combines the document management functions of SharePoint with the data storage capability of SQL Server 2005, and one that is central to the capability of Team System to track work items and act as a source code repository.

Team Explorer

To access information from the Team Foundation Server, you have to establish a connection by clicking Tools⇨Connect to Team Foundation Server. This prompts you through the process of entering information about the location of the server to which you will be connecting. It is possible to add multiple servers to this list, although Team System can only be connected to a single server at any given time.

After connecting to a server, you can elect to open one or more existing projects. These projects appear in the Team Explorer, as shown in Figure 56-1. Each project is initially divided into five sections: Source Control, Work Items, Documents, Reports, and Team Builds. If you do not select an existing project, or no projects exist, the Team Explorer will be empty. You can add a new project from the toolbar at the top of the Team Explorer window.

Figure 56-1

Creating a new project requires information such as a name and description for the project. Visual Studio 2005 also prompts you to specify whether you want to create a source control branch for the project and to elect which process template to use; the latter is shown in Figure 56-2.

Team Foundation ships with two process templates called MSF Agile and MSF CMMI; however, other process templates are being built by third parties. The process template you select determines the structure of the project that is created for you. This includes the information contained on a work item, the roles within the team, and a base set of work items to kick off your project.

Figure 56-2

Project Guidance

Both process templates that ship with Visual Studio 2005 include a reference web site that provides project guidance. The project guidance defines roles, work items, processes, and iterations for the development process. Figure 56-3 illustrates the project guidance site for the MSF Agile process template.

The project guidance pages are initially shown immediately after a new Team Project has been created, and can also be opened from the Process Guidance node under Documents in the Team Explorer window.

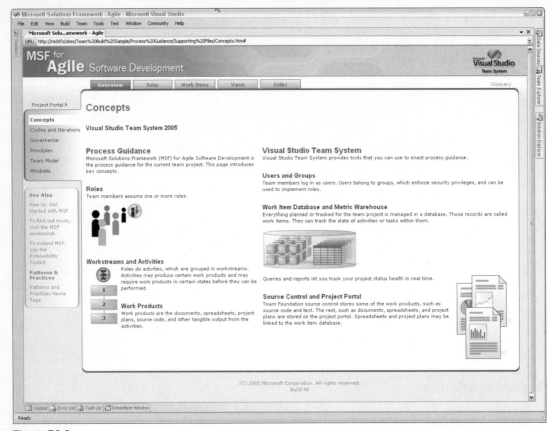

Figure 56-3

Work Item Tracking

Team Foundation makes extensive use of SQL Server 2005 Reporting Services to provide status information about the project you are working on. A series of predefined Reporting Service queries can be run directly from the Team Explorer window by double-clicking any of the nodes under the Team Queries (refer to Figure 56-1). It is also possible to define your own query that can filter and present data about your project. Examples of this might be the number of tasks completed in the last 24 hours, or the number of tasks currently in progress. Figure 56-4 shows the All Work Items query being run across a new MSF Agile project.

The top portion of the window shows the list of work items that meet the criteria of the query — in this case, all work items. In the lower window the full details of the selected work item are shown and can be edited in place. As work is carried out on a work item, it should be updated so that the status of the project is up-to-date.

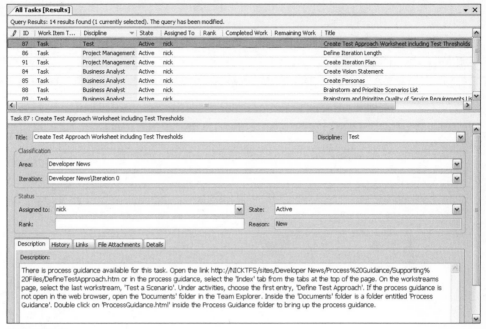

Figure 56-4

SharePoint Portal

Although most architects, developers, and testers feel at home using Visual Studio to access information about the project, there are a number of other stakeholders in a project that would not be able to use Visual Studio. When a new project is created in Team Foundation, a SharePoint portal is also created for that project. Included in this portal are all the Reporting Service queries, as well as any documentation that might have been added to the project. This enables project managers, clients, and anyone else with an interest in the project to access the status of the project at any given time. As the reports are dynamically run across the information within Team Foundation, the information is guaranteed to be current. The project portal can be viewed by right-clicking on the project in the Team Explorer and selecting Show Project Portal. Figure 56-5 illustrates the main page of the portal for a new project. From this page various reports can be run to report on the status of the project.

The project portal controls access to all the documents related to the project other than code files tracked in the source control repository. These can be accessed via the Documents and Lists menu. Information on process guidance, as well as additional predefined reports, can be accessed from the quick launch bar on the left of the screen.

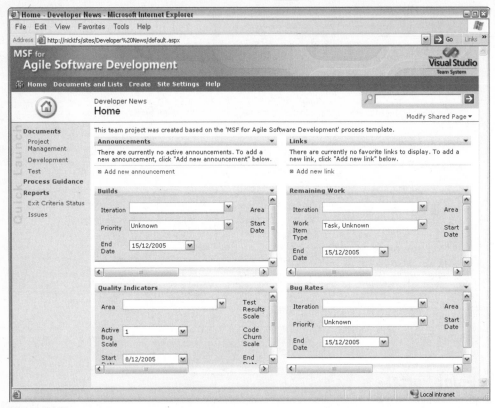

Figure 56-5

Office Integration

Being able to view the status of work items using SharePoint is sufficient for stakeholders that do not play an active role in the project. However, for project managers who need to be able to update work items and lodge and/or update bug and requirements information, this interface is not sufficient. Although these updates can be performed from within Visual Studio, quite often these stakeholders will either not have access to Visual Studio or not be familiar with the product. For this reason Team System provides a rich extension to Office that enables Excel and Project to be used to add and edit work items.

To view a set of work items in Excel or Project, select the query from the Team Explorer. The results of this query appear in the main window. Above this window is a toolbar, as shown in Figure 56-6. The middle icons can be used to export the current query results to either Excel or Project.

Figure 56-6

A couple of nice artifacts result from using these Office applications to manipulate work items. First, because most people are familiar with these products, working with them is second nature, meaning users can generate the information they are interested in quickly and effectively. Second, information can be worked on even when no connection to the server is available.

Unlike the Visual Studio interface, which relies heavily on a link to the server to execute queries and open and close work items, once the Office document has been built, it can be worked on without any interaction with the server. In order for the changes to be made available to other project team members, the document needs to be synchronized with the server. This can be done using the Team Foundation toolbar that appears within the Office application. Figure 56-7 shows the same query results shown in Figure 56-4 within Excel. Here the work items can be edited and then published back to the server.

	A	B	C	D	E	F
1	Project: Developer News		Server: nicktfs	Query: [None]		
2	ID	Work Item Type	Discipline	State	Assigned To	Title
3	86	Task	Project Management	Active	nick	Define Iteration Length
4	78	Task		Active	nick	Setup: Set Permissions
5	79	Task		Active	nick	Setup: Migration of Source Code
6	80	Task		Active	nick	Setup: Migration of Work Items
7	81	Task		Active	nick	Setup: Set Check-in Policies
8	82	Task		Active	nick	Setup: Configure Build
9	83	Task		Active	nick	Setup: Send Mail to Users for Installation and Getting started
10	84	Task	Business Analyst	Active	nick	Create Vision Statement
11	85	Task	Business Analyst	Active	nick	Create Personas
12	87	Task	Test	Active	nick	Create Test Approach Worksheet including Test Thresholds
13	88	Task	Business Analyst	Active	nick	Brainstorm and Prioritize Scenarios List
14	89	Task	Business Analyst	Active	nick	Brainstorm and Prioritize Quality of Service Requirements List
15	90	Task		Active	nick	Setup: Create Project Structure
16	91	Task	Project Management	Active	nick	Create Iteration Plan
17						

Figure 56-7

Source Control Explorer

Although Source Control appears as a node under each project in the Team Explorer, it is only there as a shortcut for bringing up the Source Control Explorer. This explorer can also be found in the Other Windows list on the View menu.

As discussed in Chapter 8, Team Foundation Server exposes a completely reengineered source code repository that is available to developers using Team System. Although the interface has been changed to incorporate new functionality such as workspaces, branching, and shelving, it should still be familiar enough to anyone who has worked with source control in Visual Studio in the past.

For Software Architects

One of the weaknesses of Visual Studio in the past was that it didn't provide support for software architects. Team System provides a rich user interface for architects to design the system architecture. These are not just static diagrams that have to be manually updated to keep them in sync with the project. As with the Class Designer discussed in Chapter 25, the distributed system diagrams are a visualization of the actual application architecture.

Application Diagram

During the design of an application, an important decision that must be made early on is the architecture of the application. An *application diagram* is the first of four distributed system diagrams that can be created using Team System. Figure 56-8 illustrates a windows application that accesses data from a database via an ASP.NET web service.

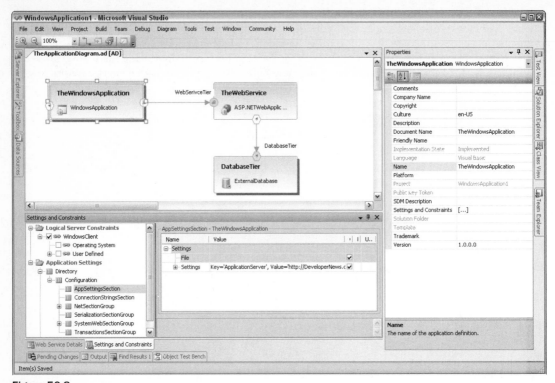

Figure 56-8

Application components can be added to the design surface by selecting them from the toolbar. Once added to the diagram, the component can be arranged on the diagram and connected to existing components using connectors. Properties, such as the name of the component, can be adjusted using the Properties window. More specific settings for a component can be set using the Settings and Constraints pane in the lower half of the window.

Once the architecture has been mapped out on the application diagram, the various components can be automatically generated directly from the diagram. When the application diagram does not align with the solution structure, the missing projects can be implemented by selecting the Implement All Applications from the Implementation option from the Diagram menu. This prompts you to confirm the creation of the new project, as shown in Figure 56-9. A word of caution: Once the project has been created, some properties, such as the default namespace, will be difficult to modify.

Logical Datacenter Diagram

While the application diagram is useful for architecting an application, to deploy an application successfully it is important to make sure the application can be mapped to the target infrastructure. The first step in this process is to define the target infrastructure. In the past this has again been the role of third-party tools. With Team System you can create a *logical datacenter diagram* to map out the proposed infrastructure. Although the intent of this diagram is for application deployment, it can also be useful for the documentation of an organization's infrastructure. Figure 56-10 shows the proposed infrastructure for a small organization proposing to deploy the three-tier application discussed earlier.

Figure 56-9

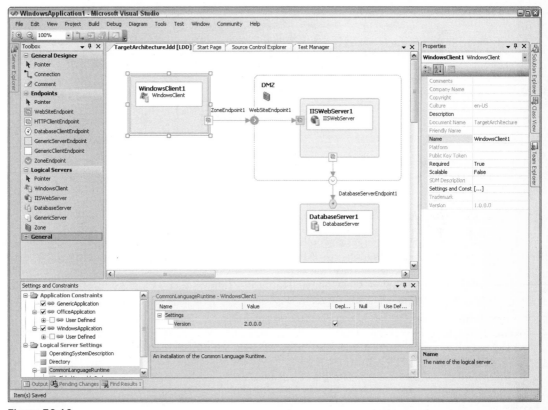

Figure 56-10

Figure 56-10 contains three main entities: the Windows client, the IIS web server, and the database server. It also shows that the web server is contained within a DMZ. All communications between the Windows client, which might be across the Internet, and the database server, which will be internal to the organization, must be transferred via the DMZ.

Similar to the application diagram, the logical datacenter diagram includes the Toolbox, the Settings and Constraints window, and the Properties window, which can be used to fine-tune the datacenter diagram to match the infrastructure.

System Diagram

The set of applications defined in the application diagram typically have a number of settings that need to be configured based on how the system is to be deployed. Using a systems diagram, an instance of the application can be preconfigured and saved. An example of this is shown in Figure 56-11, which again shows our three-tier application, this time with settings preconfigured ready for deployment.

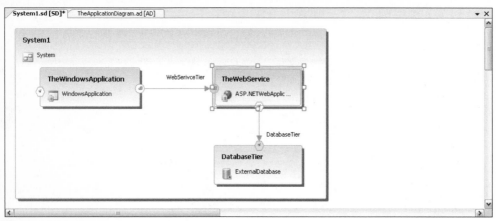

Figure 56-11

Deployment Diagram

The final distributed systems diagram combines the previous three diagrams to evaluate how the system will map to the proposed infrastructure. When this diagram is created, the contents of the datacenter diagram appear on the design surface. Each entity has placeholders for locations to which you can drag an application from the System View toolbar. Figure 56-12 shows such a diagram whereby the database tier has been bound to the database server.

At any point, a report can be generated about the proposed deployment on the target infrastructure. This can be used to review the changes needed to successfully deploy the application. Once the diagram has been successfully validated, the deployment team can use the deployment report to ensure that the infrastructure and applications are configured appropriately.

Figure 56-13 shows the top portion of a deployment report indicating several errors were generated because the diagram could not be validated.

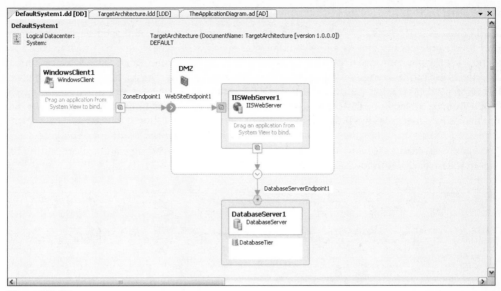

Figure 56-12

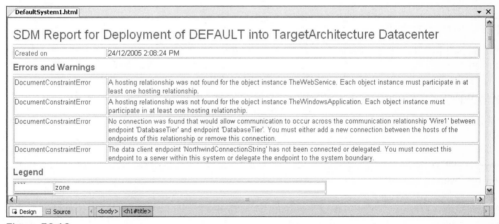

Figure 56-13

For Software Developers

In addition to writing lines of code, developers also have to make sure that they adhere to coding standards, perform reviews and refactor code for performance, write test cases to ensure their code meets the requirements, and finally build the application so it can be deployed. In the past, each of these tasks has involved a third-party product, as the functionality was not built into Visual Studio.

Code Analysis

Most development teams have a set of documented or agreed upon coding standards. Unfortunately, very few teams actually enforce these standards, as even a stringent reviewing process would fail to identify all the nonconformances. The only true way to enforce coding standards is to use a tool that automates the process of reviewing code and reports any cases in which a standard has not been met. In Chapter 7 you saw that you can enable code analysis from the Project properties window so it is run every time the project is built. Unfortunately, this can be a time-consuming task, so it is often better to run this as required from the Build menu.

Code analysis searches for any code that does not conform to the coding standards, reporting its findings in the Error List window, as shown in Figure 56-14.

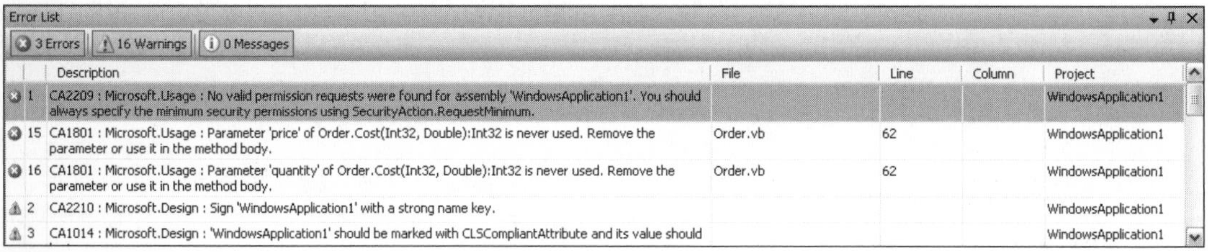

	Description	File	Line	Column	Project	
🔴 1	CA2209 : Microsoft.Usage : No valid permission requests were found for assembly 'WindowsApplication1'. You should always specify the minimum security permissions using SecurityAction.RequestMinimum.				WindowsApplication1	
🔴 15	CA1801 : Microsoft.Usage : Parameter 'price' of Order.Cost(Int32, Double):Int32 is never used. Remove the parameter or use it in the method body.	Order.vb	62		WindowsApplication1	
🔴 16	CA1801 : Microsoft.Usage : Parameter 'quantity' of Order.Cost(Int32, Double):Int32 is never used. Remove the parameter or use it in the method body.	Order.vb	62		WindowsApplication1	
⚠ 2	CA2210 : Microsoft.Design : Sign 'WindowsApplication1' with a strong name key.				WindowsApplication1	
⚠ 3	CA1014 : Microsoft.Design : 'WindowsApplication1' should be marked with CLSCompliantAttribute and its value should				WindowsApplication1	

Figure 56-14

Performance Analysis

While static code analysis is a good way to pick up on a lot of potential issues in code, it will not pick up runtime performance issues. Applications can perform poorly for a number of reasons, but they can usually be tracked back to issues that can be easily identified by reviewing memory consumption. These reviews can include looking at the number and frequency of object allocation, the duration and size of objects in memory, and the location and class stack from which objects were created. The best way to review this information is using a profiling tool to monitor an application as it is running.

Profiling an application with Visual Studio Team System begins with the Performance Wizard, which creates a new performance session. To illustrate this, analyze a small section of code that handles the `Click` event of a button:

```
Public Class Form1
Private Sub Button1_Click _
                    (ByVal sender As System.Object, _
                        ByVal e As System.EventArgs) Handles Button1.Click
        Windows.Forms.Cursor.Current = Cursors.WaitCursor
        For i As Integer = 0 To 100000
            Dim str As New String("a"c, i)
        Next
    End Sub
End Class
```

Start by clicking Tools⇨Performance Tools⇨Performance Wizard. Stepping through the wizard generates a new performance session that appears within the Performance Explorer window, as shown in Figure 56-15.

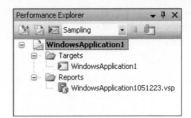

Figure 56-15

Prior to running the analysis, two options should be considered, as they affect the report that is generated. Properties for the Performance Session node can be opened from the right-click context menu in the Performance Explorer. For the most detailed profiling information, both options in the .NET Memory Profiling Collection (on the General tab) should be checked. This ensures that object allocation and lifetime information will be tracked.

To analyze the application, it needs to be run from within the Performance Explorer. This is done by clicking the play button from the toolbar within the Performance Explorer. Each time the performance analysis is run, a new report is generated and added to the performance session. An example report is shown in Figure 56-16.

Performance Report Summary

Functions Allocating Most Memory

Name	Bytes	%
System.String.CtorCharCount	10001900342	708.021
System.String.CtorCharArrayStartLength	91378	0.006
...em.Xml.XmlTextReaderImpl.InitStreamInput	67084	0.005

Types With Most Memory Allocated

Name	Bytes	%
System.String	10002107600	99.995
System.Char[]	75390	0.001
System.Byte[]	67391	0.001

Types With Most Instances

Name	Instances
System.String	102029
System.Reflection.CustomAttributeRecord[]	571
System.Version	564

Summary   Functions   Caller/Callee   Call Tree   Allocation   Objects Lifetime

Figure 56-16

Each performance report is divided into a number of tabs that present the analysis information. The initial page summarizes memory allocation by function and by type. On the other tabs this information is presented in a different format to show the most frequently used functions, where functions were being called from, the allocation of objects, and a breakdown of the object lifetimes.

The performance summary in Figure 56-16 indicates that there are significantly more String instances than any other types and that they consume several orders of magnitude more memory than any other type. This, coupled with the String constructor being the function that allocates most memory, is a sure indicator that something is wrong with the way the application is behaving. If you drill down into the Objects Lifetime tab, you can see from Figure 56-17 that again the String object dominates the list of objects. More significant, a large number of `String` objects were collected from Generation 1, Generation 2, and the Large Object Heap (the third, fourth, and fifth columns from the left, respectively). This is a good indicator that these objects are not being collected as frequently as they should be.

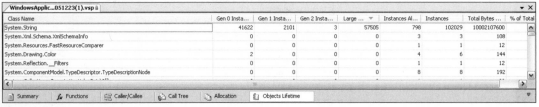

Class Name	Gen 0 Insta...	Gen 1 Insta...	Gen 2 Insta...	Large ... ▼	Instances Al...	Instances	Total Bytes ...	% of Total
System.String	41622	2101	3	57505	798	102029	10002107600	
System.Xml.Schema.XmlSchemaInfo	0	0	0	0	3	3	108	
System.Resources.FastResourceComparer	0	0	0	0	1	1	12	
System.Drawing.Color	2	0	0	0	4	6	144	
System.Reflection.__Filters	0	0	0	0	1	1	12	
System.ComponentModel.TypeDescriptor.TypeDescriptionNode	0	0	0	0	8	8	192	

Summary   Functions   Caller/Callee   Call Tree   Allocation   Objects Lifetime

Figure 56-17

From the snippet of code for which you were running the performance analysis, you can see that in each iteration of the loop, a new `String` was being created. The performance analysis indicates that not only are some very large `String` objects being allocated, the Garbage Collector is not collecting them in a timely manner. Examining the code a little more closely, you can see why: The length of the `String` is dependent on the loop index, which grows considerably. Most likely, this was supposed to be some other variable. Using the performance analysis, you have located the performance issue.

Build Automation

Although Visual Studio has always provided a rich environment in which developers can write and build applications, it has lacked the capability to automate building and testing applications. Building applications could be done manually by calling Visual Studio from the command line, or in a batch file, but this was tedious to set up. Team System includes a feature called *Team Build,* which provides a rich user interface to the new build engine, *MSBuild,* that has been released in conjunction with Visual Studio. As discussed in Chapter 7, project files are now build configuration files because they determine what MSBuild should do when an application is built. However, Team Build also enables development teams to define build types, which may include a number of projects, tests, and activities, and to schedule these to be run on remote computers.

In Figure 56-1 you saw the project structure within the Team Explorer window. At the bottom of this structure is a node entitled Team Builds, which contains all the build types for a project. To take advantage of being able to run builds on a remote computer and track build progress and status, you need to define a build type by selecting New Team Build Type from the right-click context menu for the Team Builds node.

The process of creating a build type requires a number of parameters, such as a name and description for the build, which solutions are to be built (any that are in the source control branch for the Team Project), and which configuration to use when building the selected solutions. The last two pages of the wizard are used to define which machine should be used to build the solutions, where any outputs are to be dropped, and whether to run any test cases or code analysis as part of the build. Figure 56-18 shows the Creation Wizard dialog, where the build machine and drop location are defined.

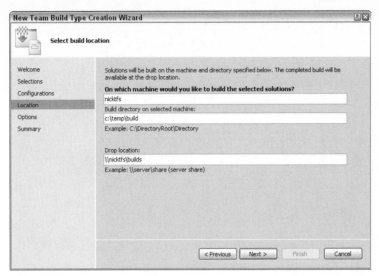

Figure 56-18

The machine used for the build process does not need to be the same machine as the Team Foundation server or a development machine. It does, however, need to have the Team Build Service running, which can be installed from the BB directory on the Team Foundation media. Before installing this server, create a separate account, such as TFSBuild, that the service can run as. This account needs to be added to the Build Service security group for each Team Project. It also has to have write access to the drop folder.

The build directory defined is where any temporary files are copied during the build process. To support analysis of a failed build process, this folder is not removed after the build has completed. However, subsequent builds will overwrite the contents of this folder. Conversely, within the drop location each build is assigned a unique directory, such as Incremental Build_20060114.2. This can easily be broken down into the build name, the date of the build, and the build number for that date.

Once the build server has been set up and a build type has been defined, the build type can be either opened, as shown in Figure 56-19, or run, by selecting Build Team Project from the right-click context menu.

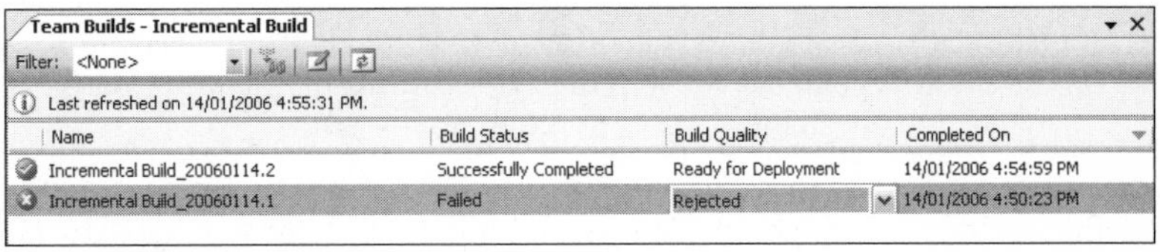

Figure 56-19

Figure 56-19 shows two builds that have been run using the Incremental Build; the first failed and the second passed. This build type can be built by clicking the Build toolbar button (third from the right). This opens the Build dialog, which enables you to specify the build location, as shown in Figure 56-20.

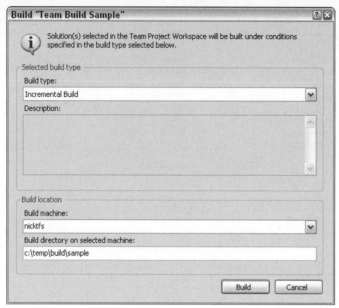

Figure 56-20

As the number of builds increases, the list of builds in the Team Builds window can be filtered based on a time interval, such as this week or last week. The only thing that can be changed in this window is the build quality. This can be used to indicate which builds are suitable for deployment, need testing, have failed, or need investigating. Of course, this list can be customized to suit the development team.

More information can be retrieved for a particular build by double-clicking on it in the Team Builds window. Figure 56-21 shows an example of the build output for a successful build. It is divided into five sections, which include a summary of the build; the steps involved in the build process; test, code coverage and code analysis results; associated changesets; and associated work items. Essentially, the information contained in the build report indicates what has changed since the last time that build type was run. Clicking on the links provided in the build report opens the associated changeset or work item for review. This is particularly useful for tracking down any errors that may have arisen between builds.

After a build type has been created using the wizard, any modifications need to be made directly to the MSBuild file. Unfortunately, you can't make modifications directly from the Team Explorer window. Right-clicking on the Build Type node and selecting View brings up the MSBuild file for you to view. This is a temporary file and any changes made to it will not be saved.

Figure 56-22 shows the source control branch for a sample Team Project called Team Build Sample. Alongside the solution folder is an automatically generated folder, TeamBuildTypes, under which the two build types for this project are defined. Within the Incremental Build folder, the name of the build type, four files determine the build process. The main one is `TFSBuild.proj`, which is the MSBuild file used by the Team Build. To make changes to the build process, this file should be checked out. Because Team Build uses the version that is currently in Source Control, this file must be checked back in, even if you are going to run the build process on the same machine on which you are editing it.

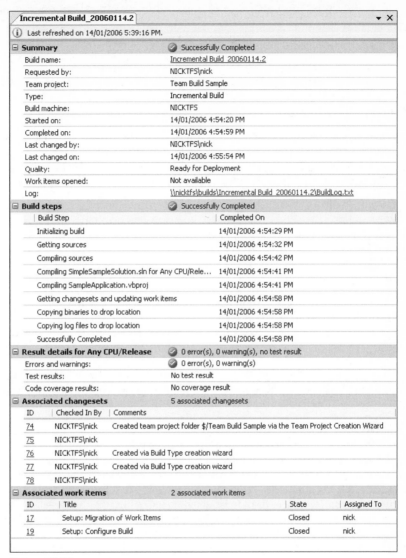

Figure 56-21

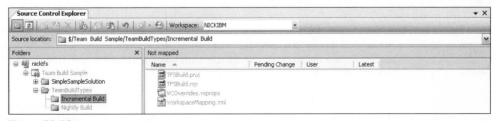

Figure 56-22

The other option currently missing from Team Explorer is the capability to delete a build type after it has been created. Because the build type is just a folder within the source code repository, it can be removed by deleting the appropriate folder using the Source Control Explorer. As with all changes made in the Source Control Explorer, this change can be rolled back at a later stage if you realize you still require that build type.

For Software Testers

Testers, like architects, have always felt that they are the poor (or expensive in the case of some of the testing tools on the market) cousins to software developers. They have never had support within Visual Studio for creating, executing, or reporting on test cases. Team System now includes the capability to create test cases, as well as strong support for managing them.

Unit Testing

Chapter 53 covers creating unit test cases for existing classes. These can be run individually or attached to a database to provide data to drive the test cases.

Web Testing

Testing web applications can also be automated from within Team System using the web recorder, which records actions on a web site and enables them to be replayed. In isolation this is not very useful because it just ensures that the functionality of the site does not vary. However, it is possible to add parameters to the script to vary the test cases.

The default output from the web recorder is a script file that documents interaction with the web site. This can be converted into code that can be tailored to provide extensive control over how the script is run.

Manual Testing

Team System does not provide an equivalent to the web recorder for Windows applications. To test functionality in a Windows application, it is important first to separate as much functionality as possible from the user interface. This way, the core functionality of the system can be tested using unit test cases, which can be fully automated. For the remaining functionality and to ensure that the user interface behaves correctly, manual test cases have to be documented. Although this doesn't automate testing of the application, it does help to document the list of test cases that need to be run prior to releasing the application.

Manual tests can be generated in two formats: plain text or Word. Essentially, the format doesn't matter, because it is not how the test looks, but rather the content, that is important. Creating a new manual test generates a stub test case that contains various placeholders for things such as the title, details, test steps, and revision history. Although it makes sense to follow this structure, the manual test case can contain whatever activities or process the tester needs to follow to carry out the test. Figure 56-23 illustrates running a simple test case that is being used to test the launch functionality of an application. As the manual test case is to be run manually, the only information that needs to be recorded is whether the test passed or not, and any associated comments.

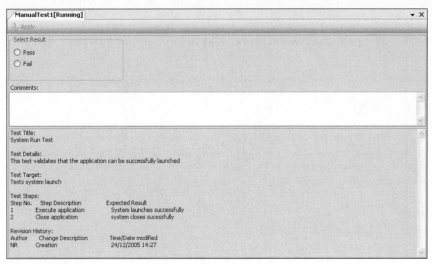

Figure 56-23

As an aside to running manual test cases, if code coverage is enabled for an application, then it will track which lines of code are executed as part of that test case. This can be useful if you want to assess how much of the system functionality has been tested from the set of user scenario tests.

Load Testing

Automating test cases means that the tests are repeatable. This is important because a failure can easily be reproduced and traced back to the cause. Rerunning tests, known as *regression testing,* is a simple mechanism to test whether an application is going to behave the same way every time.

Having a set of test cases that can be run repeatedly also has the implicit benefit that they can be used to load test a system. For example, if you have a simple web site, you might want to load test it to see how many concurrent users can access the site before significant performance issues, or even system failures, are experienced. Using load agents, these test cases can be distributed onto multiple computers to simulate thousands of concurrent users. The response time is recorded and can be graphed for easy interpretation.

Click Test⇔New Test to create a load test. Unlike other tests, the load test actually consists of a number of existing tests run as a particular scenario to load the application. The Load Test Wizard can be used to control the number of simulated users. Figure 56-24 shows that an application will be progressively loaded, from 10 users through to 200 users in ten-user increments every 10 seconds.

As testing is carried out to ensure the application will perform under expected loads, it is necessary to be able to specify not only which tests are to be carried out, but also what mix to use. Figure 56-25 shows how multiple tests can be distributed according to a user's selection. If you need to return to an even distribution, you can click the Distribute button.

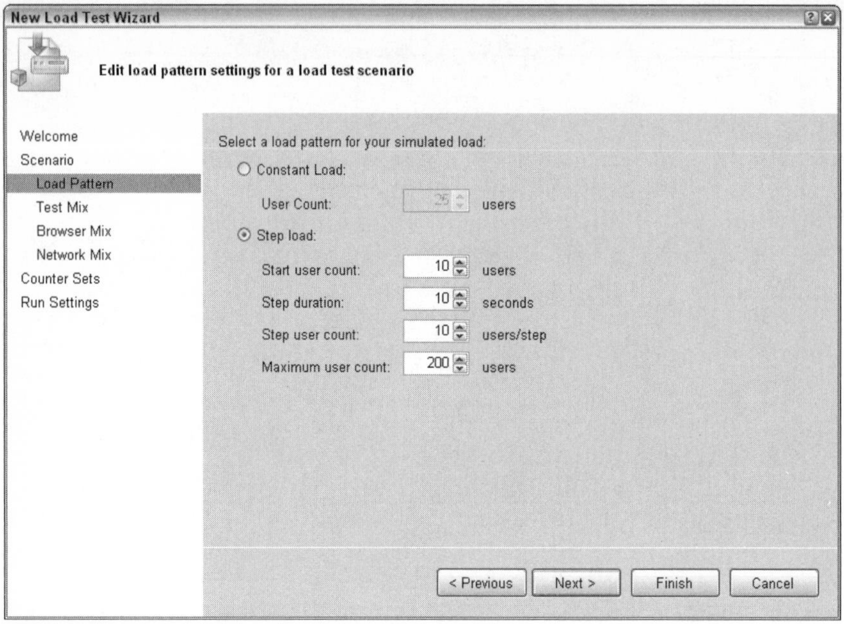

Figure 56-24

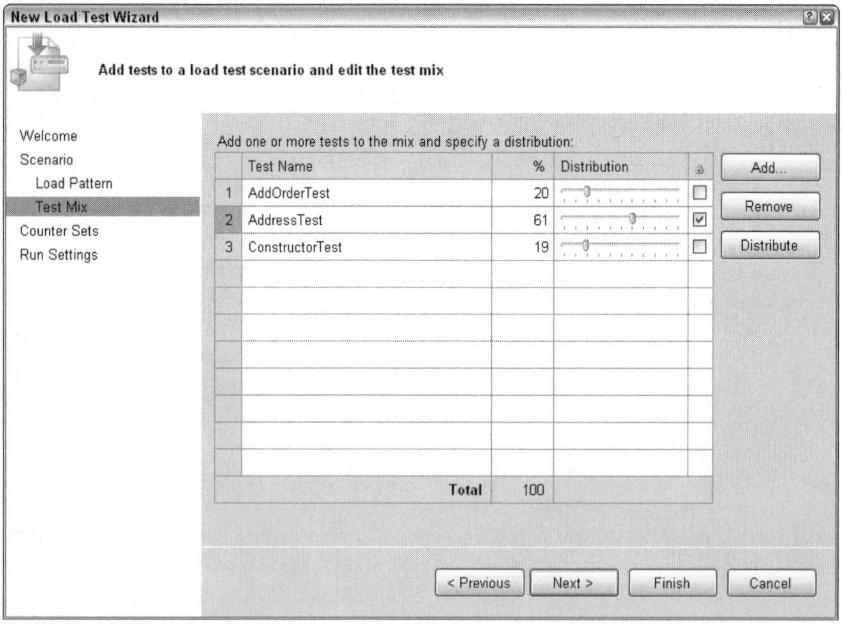

Figure 56-25

Once the load test has been created, you can modify any of the properties set by the wizard by opening the load test in the main window (see Figure 56-26).

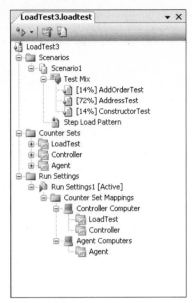

Figure 56-26

The test mix is clearly visible in Figure 56-26, as are the counters that are to be used while the test is running. These counters are used to provide metrics that are graphed in real time as the load test progresses. Figure 56-27 shows an aborted load test. In the center is a graph showing the user load, the tests per second, the average test time, and the percentage of processor time.

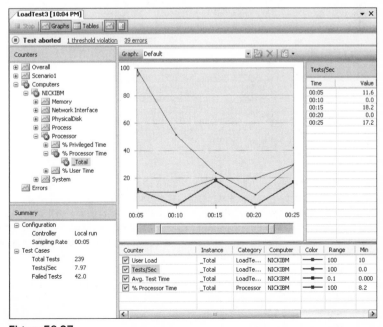

Figure 56-27

On the right of Figure 56-27 is a grid showing the actual values for the selected data line. For a closer look at a particular section of the graph, the scrollbar at the bottom of the center window can be reduced from either end. In this case, the bars on the time frame between 5 and 25 seconds are in focus.

One of the features of Team Test is that the load tests can be distributed over a number of load agents. The test information is recorded on the agents and stored against the load test so that information for specific agents can be monitored and analyzed. This is an important part of identifying weaknesses in high-throughput applications.

Testing Windows

To test all the functionality of an application, it is necessary to create a lot of test cases. Some estimates suggest that the number of lines of test code should be approximately the same as the lines of code within the system. For a typical application this might result in hundreds, if not thousands, of test cases. Clearly, this requires an effective way to manage test cases and test results. Team System includes five new windows that enable testers to navigate test cases, manage which test cases are to be run, and report on test results.

Test View

The Test View window, shown in Figure 56-28, is the simplest window for viewing and executing test cases. By default it shows all test cases that are contained within a solution. This can be filtered using the keyword search, and grouped so test cases can be easily identified. The list of columns visible can be adjusted using the Add/Remove Columns item from the right-click context menu on the Test View window.

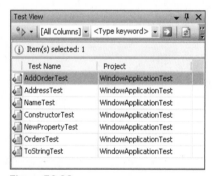

Figure 56-28

You can run the test in two ways: either select the test in the list and press the play button in the toolbar, or right-click the test you want to run and select Run Selection from the context menu. By default, clicking the play button runs the test without attaching the debugger. This is the most reliable in terms of testing true system behavior. However, it can be difficult to analyze what might be going wrong in the case of a test case that fails. For this reason, test cases can also be run with the debugger attached. In this case, breakpoints and exceptions are included, which enables you to fix any issues that may be encountered. To run test cases with the debugger attached, use the Debug Selection menu item either from the right-click context menu or from the toolbar drop-down next to the play button.

Test Manager

Although the Test View window is useful for selecting and running individual, or selected, test cases it cannot be used to run a specific set of test cases. For better control over test cases, use the Test Manager (see Figure 56-29), which enables you to create lists of test cases that can all be run. The test list can then be run as part of the build process or made a requirement to execute before checking in code.

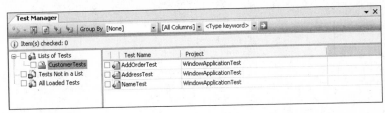

Figure 56-29

The Test Manager loads in the main window, which simplifies organizing a large number of test cases. It behaves similarly to the Test View window, allowing the list of test cases to be filtered and grouped. On the right of the window is a tree of test lists available for the current project. At the bottom of the tree are two project lists that show all the test cases (All Loaded Tests) and those test cases that haven't been put in a list (Tests Not in a List). Under the Lists of Tests node are all the test lists created for the project.

To create a new test list click Test⇨Create New Test List. Test cases can be dragged from any existing list into the new list. Initially this can be a little confusing because the tests will be moved to the new list, and therefore removed from their original list, instead of just being added to the new list. To add a test case to multiple lists, either hold the Ctrl button while dragging the test case or copy and paste the test case from the original list to the new list.

After creating a test list, you can run the whole list by checking the box next to the list in the Test Manager. The run button executes all lists that are checked. Alternatively, the lists can be run with the debugger attached using the Debug Checked Tests menu item.

Test Results

Once a test case or a test list has been executed, the results of the test are displayed in the Test Results window, which provides a useful summary of all the test cases that were run and the status of the output. Where more information is required, the specific test case result can be opened in the main window.

In Figure 56-30 three test cases were executed, each returning a different result. The AddressTest passed without exception, the NameTest failed one of the assertions being made in the test case, and the AddOrderTest returned inconclusive. The inconclusive result is useful for marking test cases that have not been completely written and as such may be unreliable. Additional states such as Pending and In Progress indicate that a test case is either waiting to be run or currently being executed.

Double-clicking the NameTest brings up the detail of the test case in the main window, as shown in Figure 56-31. This shows a summary of the test case, such as when and on which computer it was run, the duration, and the error message. It also returns the stack trace so the test case can be reviewed. While this is a simple test case, more complex test cases — for example, those that are data driven — return more information about which of the data cases failed or passed.

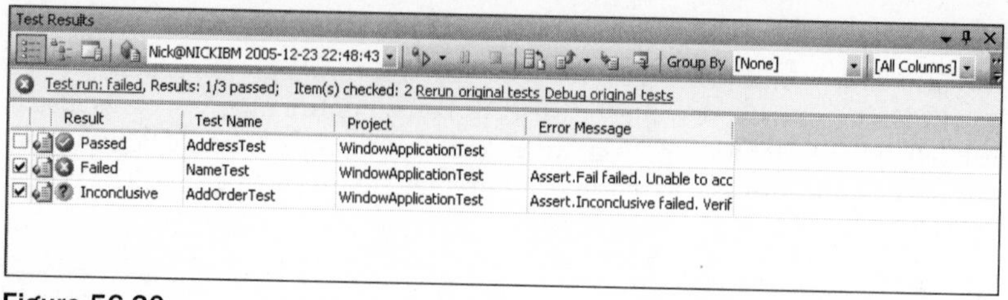

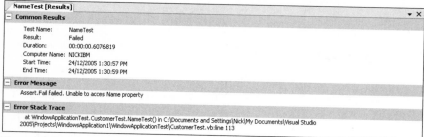

Figure 56-30

Figure 56-31

Code Coverage Results

One of the challenges of writing test cases is knowing how many or how few test cases to write. Clearly, the more test cases you have, the better the application is tested, or so you would hope. However, this also adds administrative burden, particularly when functionality in the application changes. *Code coverage* is a metric that can be used to measure how much of an application has been tested. Code coverage reports on which lines of code have been executed during the run of a test case, as shown in Figure 56-32, and can be used to determine which test cases still need to be written. Although ideally 100 percent of the application code would be covered by the test cases, this can be an unrealistic objective, especially when there is a large proportion of designer generated code.

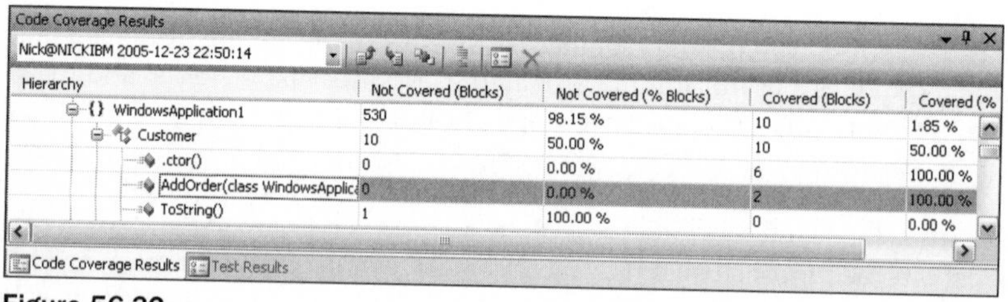

Figure 56-32

Double-clicking on a method in the Code Coverage Results window brings up the code for that method, as shown in Figure 56-33. Although the color doesn't show in the figure, color-coding is used to indicate the level of coverage. (In Figure 56-33, most of the method is colored blue to indicate that code was executed as part of the test run.) If the Code Coverage Results window is not already visible, it can be opened by clicking Test⇨Windows⇨Code Coverage Results. The remaining portion that is colored red indicates unexecuted code. In a few cases, such as a SELECT statement, code is marked in pink to indicate that it has been partially executed.

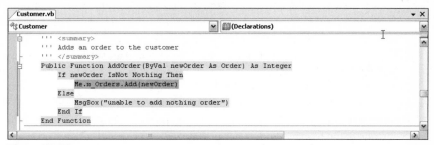

Figure 56-33

Test Runs

The final test window is the Test Runs window, shown in Figure 56-34. This window is accessible via Test⇨Windows⇨Test Runs. Test lists can be scheduled for execution on remote machines. Using this window, these test runs can be monitored and reviewed. This is an important step in load testing an application.

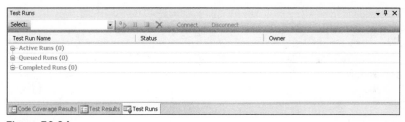

Figure 56-34

Advanced

Microsoft put a significant amount of work into the way Team System works. However, a development team may always have additional requirements. For this reason, Team System has been designed so it can be adapted or extended to suit your individual needs. Two examples examined in this section are the capability to add code analysis rules and the capability to customize the process templates.

Writing Custom Code Analysis Rules

The Code Analysis engine built in to Visual Studio 2005 is the same engine used by FXCop, so the extensibility model is essentially the same. In order to write your own code analysis rules, you have to do a couple of things to ensure that the rules appear within the IDE. This section describes how you can build your code analysis rules and integrate them into Visual Studio 2005.

1. Start by creating a new Class Library project. The name of the project is not important, as it is not displayed when the rules are integrated into the IDE.

2. To access the code analysis information in your code, you need to add references to both the FXCop SDK library (FxCopSdk.dll) and the Microsoft.CCI library (Microsoft.Cci.dll). These are both found at C:\Program Files\Microsoft Visual Studio 8\Team Tools\Static Analysis Tools\FxCop.

3. For each code analysis rule you want to create, you need to add a class to your project. For example, you might want to have a rule that issues a warning when a method has more than 100 instructions, which would make it a good candidate for refactoring, so you might call the class LongMethod. Again, the name of this class is not important, as it is not displayed in the IDE.

4. The code analysis rule class needs to inherit from the BaseIntrospectionRule class and override one of the base methods — for example, the Check method, which is used to check a particular aspect of the library being analyzed.

5. The code analysis rule class also needs to implement a zero parameter constructor that calls the base class constructor, passing in the name of the rule class, the name of an XML resource descriptor file, and the assembly in which the rule class and XML resource file reside. The following example uses runtime information about the rule class, instead of strings, to make sure that any future changes to the assembly don't break the functionality:

```
Imports Microsoft.Cci
Imports Microsoft.FxCop.Sdk
Imports Microsoft.FxCop.Sdk.Introspection
Imports System
Imports System.Globalization

Public Class LongMethods
    Inherits BaseIntrospectionRule

    Private Const cMaximumInstructions As Integer = 100

    Public Sub New()
        MyBase.New(GetType(LongMethods).Name, _
                                "NicksRules", GetType(LongMethods).Assembly)
    End Sub

    Public Overrides Function Check(ByVal m As Member) As ProblemCollection
        'Check to ensure that this is a method Check
        Dim mthd As Method = TryCast(m, Method)
        If (mthd Is Nothing) Then
            Return Nothing
        End If
        'Check how many instructions this method has
        If mthd.Instructions.Length > cMaximumInstructions Then
            'Add issue to the problems collection
            Dim outputArray As String() = New String() _
                        {RuleUtilities.Format(m), _
                        mthd.Instructions.Length.ToString _
                                                (CultureInfo.CurrentCulture), _
                        cMaximumInstructions.ToString(CultureInfo.CurrentCulture)}
            MyBase.Problems.Add(New Problem(MyBase.GetResolution(outputArray)))
        End If
```

```
        Return MyBase.Problems
    End Function
End Class
```

6. In this example, we have made reference to an XML resource file called `NicksRules.xml` (the .xml is omitted in the base constructor because it is inferred by the runtime engine). To ensure that your rule appears in Visual Studio 2005, you need to include `NicksRules.xml` as an embedded resource file in your project. The easiest way to do this is to include a file called `NicksRules.xml` in the project and set its Build Action to Embedded Resource.

    Two words of caution here: First, if you have a default namespace specified in your project settings (such as `SampleApplication`), then the embedded resource will be `SampleApplication.NicksRules.xml`. String matching is used to retrieve the XML resource file based on the resource name in the constructor, so in this case an error will be thrown, as the resource could not be located. Two solutions are possible: Either remove the default namespace or add the default namespace to the resource name in the constructor. Second, the XML file *must* end with `Rules.xml`, and this is case sensitive. If the XML file does not end with this string, the rules assembly will not be loaded correctly into Visual Studio 2005.

7. The XML resource file is made up of a list of the rules defined within the rules assembly. The first element in the XML block is the `Rules` tag. This denotes the category in which the rules will appear on the code analysis page within Visual Studio 2005. In the following example only a single code analysis rule is declared within the `"Nicks Rules"` category. Additional rules can be added by repeating the `Rule` XML block:

```xml
<?xml version="1.0" encoding="utf-8" ?>
<Rules FriendlyName="Nicks Rules">
  <Rule TypeName="LongMethods" Category="RefactorAlerts" CheckId="RA1000">
    <Name>Long methods are bad</Name>
    <Description>Methods that are longer than 100 lines should most likely be
refactored</Description>
    <Owner>Nick Randolph</Owner>
    <Url></Url>
    <Resolution>'{0}' has {1} instructions. Refactor '{0}' so that it calls fewer
than {2} instructions.</Resolution>
    <Email>nick@randomemail.com</Email>
    <MessageLevel Certainty="95">Warning</MessageLevel>
    <FixCategories>NonBreaking</FixCategories>
  </Rule>
</Rules>
```

Each rule needs to reference a `Rule` class using the `TypeName` attribute. The name of the `Rule` class specified in the XML file must match the class name exactly, including case. All the other attributes and elements of the rule are used to determine how the rule appears in Visual Studio. The `CheckId` and the `Name` appear in the code analysis window, while the `Category`, `Description`, and other attributes are used in the Error List window, as shown in Figure 56-35.

Figure 56-35

8. The last thing to do is build the project and copy the Class Library assembly to the code analysis rules folder at `C:\Program Files\Microsoft Visual Studio 8\Team Tools\Static Analysis Tools\FxCop\Rules`. This automatically registers your code analysis rules within Visual Studio 2005 the next time it is loaded.

Customizing the Process Templates

Visual Studio Team System supports two models of extensibility. The first is geared toward third-party tools that integrate with and provide additional services to the development process. These make use of the core services provided by Team Foundation. The second model is the capability to customize the process to suit the way that a particular development team is organized. Although Microsoft has tried to provide a one-size-fits-all set of process templates, a development team will likely want to tweak the process, even if it is to change the terminology that is used. In this section, you'll see how easy it is to take the process templates that ship with Visual Studio 2005 and export them, make changes, and then import them as a new process template.

The first step in customizing an existing process template is to export the process to a working folder by clicking Team⇨Team Foundation Server Settings⇨Process Template Manager. This opens a dialog similar to the one shown in Figure 56-36.

Figure 56-36

In earlier versions of the product, the buttons were labeled Import and Export, rather than the less obvious Upload and Download. This terminology reflects the process by which an existing process template can be downloaded from the server to a working folder. After changes have been made, the template can be uploaded to the server as a new process template. To make changes, select the MSF for Agile Development option and click Download. This prompts you to select a folder to which you can download the process template.

Figure 56-37 shows the folder structure of the process template after it has been exported. Each folder contains either XML documents or other template documents, such as reports, that will be included in a new project based on this template.

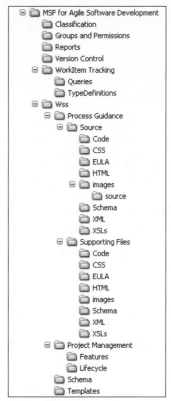

Figure 56-37

For example, in the Reports folder is the list of Reporting Services reports that will be included in the new project, such as All Work Items or Remaining Items. Another example is the `VersionControl.xml` file, which resides in the Version Control folder, and is shown in the following example code:

```xml
<?xml version="1.0" encoding="utf-8" ?>
<tasks>
    <task id="VersionControlTask"
        name="Create Version Control area"
        plugin="Microsoft.ProjectCreationWizard.VersionControl"
        completionMessage="Version control Task completed.">
        <dependencies/>
        <taskXml>
            <permission allow="Read, PendChange, Checkin, Label, Lock, ReviseOther,
UnlockOther, UndoOther, LabelOther, AdminProjectRights, CheckinOther"
identity="[$$PROJECTNAME$$]\Project Administrators"/>
            <permission allow="Read, PendChange, Checkin, Label, Lock"
identity="[$$PROJECTNAME$$]\Contributors"/>
            <permission allow="Read" identity="[$$PROJECTNAME$$]\Readers"/>
            <permission allow="Read, PendChange, Checkin, Label, Lock"
identity="[$$PROJECTNAME$$]\Build Services"/>

            <checkin_note label="Code Reviewer" required="false" order="1"/>
```

```
            <checkin_note label="Security Reviewer" required="false" order="2"/>
            <checkin_note label="Performance Reviewer" required="false" order="3"/>

            <exclusive_checkout required="false"/>
        </taskXml>
    </task>
</tasks>
```

This document outlines a number of things related to the version control requirements for the project, such as the permissions for various groups of users, what notes are required when checking in, and whether checkouts are exclusive. To make changes to the process, you can simply change this XML document. For example, you might want to ensure that all check-ins have notes from the Code, Security, and Performance reviewers. To do this you would change the `required` flag to `true`.

Once the required changes have been made, the new process template can be uploaded to the Team Foundation server via the Process Template Manager.

Summary

This chapter presented a very brief overview of Visual Studio Team System. Team System extends Visual Studio beyond the individual developer, making it suitable for large-scale application development. Development teams ranging from one or two developers through to a team of hundreds of developers can use Team System to design, build, and deploy applications. More important, Team System can be used to manage, monitor, and report on the status of a project in real time.

Although organizations have their own development processes that may not align with any of the default process templates that ship with the product, Team System has been designed from the ground up to be extensible and customizable.

Index

N

O

Q

R